Short
Stories
for Students

Short Stories
for Students

Presenting Analysis, Context and Criticism on Commonly Studied Short Stories

Volume 5

Tim Akers and Jerry Moore, Editors

Foreword by Nancy Rosenberger, Conestoga High School, Berwyn, Pennsylvania

The Gale Group
DETROIT • SAN FRANCISCO • LONDON • BOSTON • WOODBRIDGE, CT

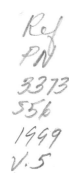

Short Stories for Students

Staff

Editorial: Tim Akers, Jerry Moore, *Editors*. Tim Akers, Joseph Alvarez, James Aren, Christine G. Berg, Thomas Bertonneau, Cynthia Bily, Yoonmee Chang, Carol Dell'Amico, Catherine Dominic, Catherine V. Donaldson, Tom Faulkner, Angela Frattarola, Tanya Gardiner-Scott, Terry Girard, Diane Andrews Henningfeld, Richard Henry, Erik Huber, Kendall Johnson, Dustie Kellet, David Kippen, Rena Korb, Ondine Le Blanc, Jean Leverich, Sarah Madsen Hardy, Thomas March, Jerry Moore, Carl Mowery, Robert Peltier, Jane Phillips, Elisabeth Piedmont-Marton, Shaun Strohmer, *Sketchwriters*. Jeffrey W. Hunter, Daniel Jones, John D. Jorgenson, Deborah A. Schmitt, Polly Vedder, Timothy J. White, Kathleen Wilson, *Contributing Editors*. James P. Draper, *Managing Editor*.

Research: Victoria B. Cariappa, *Research Team Manager*. Andrew Malonis, *Research Specialist*.

Permissions: Susan M. Trosky, *Permissions Manager*. Kimberly Smilay, *Permissions Specialist*. Kelly Quin, *Permissions Associate*.

Production: Mary Beth Trimper, *Production Director*. Evi Seoud, *Assistant Production Manager*. Shanna Heilveil, *Production Assistant*.

Graphic Services: Randy Bassett, *Image Database Supervisor*. Mikal Ansari, Robert Duncan, *Imaging Specialists*. Pamela A. Reed, *Photography Coordinator*.

Table of Contents

An Adventure in Reading

Sitting on top of my desk is a Pueblo storytelling doll. Her legs stick straight out before her and around her neck and flowing down into her lap are wide-eyed children. Her mouth is open as though she were telling the Zuni tale of the young husband who followed his wife to the Land of the Dead, a story strangely like the Greek myth of Orpheus and Euridice, as both teach the dangers of youthful impatience.

Although the Pueblo doll was created in New Mexico, she symbolizes a universal human activity. The pharaohs listened intently to tales of the goddess Isis, who traveled to foreign lands to rescue the dismembered body of her husband Osiris. Biblical narratives thrill the reader with stories like that of mortal combat between David and the giant Goliath. Greek and Roman myths immortalize the struggles of the wandering warriors Odysseus and Aeneas. In the Middle Ages, kings, queens and courtiers sat spellbound in drafty halls as troubadours sang of tragic lovers and pious pilgrims.

Around the world and down through the ages, myths, folktales, and legends have spoken to us about the human condition and our place in the world of nature and of spirit. Despite its ancient beginnings, however, there is no rigid criteria to which a story must adhere. It is one of the most protean literary forms. Though many scholars credit the nineteenth-century Romantic writers Edgar Allan Poe and Nathaniel Hawthorne with creating the modern short story, the form refuses to be frozen by a list of essential characteristics. Perhaps this is one of the reasons William Faulkner called it the "most demanding form after poetry." Jack London felt it should be "concrete, to the point, with snap and go and life, crisp and crackling and interesting." Eudora Welty wrote that each story should reveal something new yet also contain something "as old as time."

Below are some of the qualities you may observe as you explore the works discussed in *Short Stories for Students*. These characteristics also demonstrate some of the ways the short story differs from the novel:

1. Because time is compressed or accelerated, **unity** in plot, character development, tone, or mood is essential.

2. The author has chosen to **focus** on one character, event, or conflict within a limited time.

3. Poe wrote that **careful craftsmanship** serves unity by ensuring that every word must contribute to the story's design.

4. Poe also believed that reading should take place in **one sitting** so that the story's unity is not lost.

5. A character is **revealed** through a series of incidents or a conflict. The short story generally stops when it has achieved this purpose. A novel **develops** a character throughout its many chapters.

Now that we have briefly explored the history of the short story and heard from a few of its creators, let us consider the role of the reader. Readers are not empty vessels that wait, lids raised, to receive a teacher's or a critic's interpretation. They bring their unique life experiences to the story. With these associations, the best readers also bring their attention (a word that means ''leaning towards''), their reading skills, and, most importantly, their imagination to a reading of a story.

My students always challenged me to discuss, analyze, interpret, and evaluate the stories we read without destroying the thrill of being beamed up into another world. For years I grappled with one response after the other to this challenge. Then one day I read an article by a botanist who had explored the beauty of flowers by x-raying them. His illustrations showed the rose and the lily in their external beauty, and his x-rays presented the wonders of their construction. I brought the article to class, where we discussed the benefits of examining the internal design of flowers, relationships, current events, and short stories.

A short story, however, is not a fossil to admire. Readers must ask questions, guess at the answers, predict what will happen next, then read to discover. They and the author form a partnership that brings the story to life. Awareness of this partnership keeps the original excitement alive through discussion, analysis, interpretation, and evaluation. Literary explorations allow the reader to admire the authors' craftsmanship as well as their artistry. In fact, original appreciation may be enhanced by this x-ray vision. The final step is to appreciate once again the story in its entirety—to put the pieces back together.

Now it is your turn. Form a partnership with your author. During or following your adventure in reading, enter into a dialogue with the published scholars featured in *Short Stories for Students*. Through this dialogue with experts you will revise, enrich, and/or confirm your original observations and interpretations.

During this adventure, I hope you will feel the same awe that illuminates the faces of the listeners that surround the neck of my Pueblo storyteller.

Nancy Rosenberger
Conestoga High School
Berwyn, Pennsylvania

Introduction

Purpose of the Book

The purpose of *Short Stories for Students* (*SSfS*) is to provide readers with a guide to understanding, enjoying, and studying short stories by giving them easy access to information about the work. Part of Gale's "For Students" Literature line, *SSfS* is specifically designed to meet the curricular needs of high school and undergraduate college students and their teachers, as well as the interests of general readers and researchers considering specific short fiction. While each volume contains entries on classic stories frequently studied in classrooms, there are also entries containing hard-to-find information on contemporary stories, including works by multicultural, international, and women writers.

The information covered in each entry includes an introduction to the story and the story's author; a plot summary, to help readers unravel and understand the events in the work; descriptions of important characters, including explanation of a given character's role in the narrative as well as discussion about that character's relationship to other characters in the story; analysis of important themes in the story; and an explanation of important literary techniques and movements as they are demonstrated in the work.

In addition to this material, which helps the readers analyze the story itself, students are also provided with important information on the literary and historical background informing each work.

This includes a historical context essay, a box comparing the time or place the story was written to modern Western culture, a critical overview essay, and excerpts from critical essays on the story or author. A unique feature of *SSfS* is a specially commissioned overview essay on each story by an academic expert, targeted toward the student reader.

To further aid the student in studying and enjoying each story, information on media adaptations is provided, as well as reading suggestions for works of fiction and nonfiction on similar themes and topics. Classroom aids include ideas for research papers and lists of critical sources that provide additional material on the work.

Selection Criteria

The titles for each volume of *SSfS* were selected by surveying numerous sources on teaching literature and analyzing course curricula for various school districts. Some of the sources surveyed include: literature anthologies, *Reading Lists for College-Bound Students: The Books Most Recommended by America's Top Colleges; Teaching the Short Story: A Guide to Using Stories from Around the World,* by the National Council of Teachers of English (NTCE); and ''A Study of High School Literature Anthologies,'' conducted by Arthur Applebee at the Center for the Learning and Teaching of Literature and sponsored by the National Endowment for the Arts and the Office of Educational Research and Improvement.

Input was also solicited from our expert advisory board, as well as educators from various areas. From these discussions, it was determined that each volume should have a mix of "classic" stories (those works commonly taught in literature classes) and contemporary stories for which information is often hard to find. Because of the interest in expanding the canon of literature, an emphasis was also placed on including works by international, multicultural, and women authors. Our advisory board members—current high-school teachers—helped pare down the list for each volume. Works not selected for the present volume were noted as possibilities for future volumes. As always, the editor welcomes suggestions for titles to be included in future volumes.

How Each Entry Is Organized

Each entry, or chapter, in *SSfS* focuses on one story. Each entry heading lists the title of the story, the author's name, and the date of the story's publication. The following elements are contained in each entry:

- **Introduction:** a brief overview of the story which provides information about its first appearance, its literary standing, any controversies surrounding the work, and major conflicts or themes within the work.

- **Author Biography:** this section includes basic facts about the author's life, and focuses on events and times in the author's life that may have inspired the story in question.

- **Plot Summary:** a description of the events in the story, with interpretation of how these events help articulate the story's themes.

- **Characters:** an alphabetical listing of the characters who appear in the story. Each character name is followed by a brief to an extensive description of the character's role in the story, as well as discussion of the character's actions, relationships, and possible motivation.

  Characters are listed alphabetically by last name. If a character is unnamed—for instance, the narrator in "The Eatonville Anthology"—the character is listed as "The Narrator" and alphabetized as "Narrator." If a character's first name is the only one given, the name will appear alphabetically by that name.

- **Themes:** a thorough overview of how the topics, themes, and issues are addressed within the story. Each theme discussed appears in a sepa-

rate subhead, and is easily accessed through the boldface entries in the Subject/Theme Index.

- **Style:** this section addresses important style elements of the story, such as setting, point of view, and narration; important literary devices used, such as imagery, foreshadowing, symbolism; and, if applicable, genres to which the work might have belonged, such as Gothicism or Romanticism. Literary terms are explained within the entry, but can also be found in the Glossary of Literary Terms.

- **Historical and Cultural Context:** This section outlines the social, political, and cultural climate *in which the author lived and the work was created.* This section may include descriptions of related historical events, pertinent aspects of daily life in the culture, and the artistic and literary sensibilities of the time in which the work was written. If the story is historical in nature, information regarding the time in which the story is set is also included. Long sections are broken down with helpful subheads.

- **Critical Overview:** this section provides background on the critical reputation of the author and the story, including bannings or any other public controversies surrounding the work. For older works, this section may include a history of how story was first received and how perceptions of it may have changed over the years; for more recent works, direct quotes from early reviews may also be included.

- **Sources:** an alphabetical list of critical material quoted in the entry, with bibliographical information.

- **For Further Study:** an alphabetical list of other critical sources which may prove useful for the student. Includes full bibliographical information and a brief annotation.

- **Criticism:** an essay commissioned by *SSfS* which specifically deals with the story and is written specifically for the student audience, as well as excerpts from previously published criticism on the work.

In addition, each entry contains the following highlighted sections, if applicable, set separate from the main text:

- **Media Adaptations:** where applicable, a list of film and television adaptations of the story, including source information. The list also includes stage adaptations, audio recordings, musical adaptations, etc.

- **Compare and Contrast Box:** an ''at-a-glance'' comparison of the cultural and historical differences between the author's time and culture and late twentieth-century Western culture. This box includes pertinent parallels between the major scientific, political, and cultural movements of the time or place the story was written, the time or place the story was set (if a historical work), and modern Western culture. Works written after the mid-1970s may not have this box.

- **What Do I Read Next?:** a list of works that might complement the featured story or serve as a contrast to it. This includes works by the same author and others, works of fiction and nonfiction, and works from various genres, cultures, and eras.

- **Study Questions:** a list of potential study questions or research topics dealing with the story. This section includes questions related to other disciplines the student may be studying, such as American history, world history, science, math, government, business, geography, economics, psychology, etc.

Other Features

SSfS includes ''An Adventure in Reading,'' a foreword by Nancy Rosenberger, chair of the English department at Conestoga High School in Berwyn, Pennsylvania. This essay provides an enlightening look at how readers interact with literature and how *Short Stories for Students* can help students enrich their own reading experiences.

A Cumulative Author/Title Index lists the authors and titles covered in each volume of the *SSfS* series.

A Cumulative Nationality/Ethnicity Index breaks down the authors and titles covered in each volume of the *SSfS* series by nationality and ethnicity.

A Subject/Theme Index, specific to each volume, provides easy reference for users who may be studying a particular subject or theme rather than a single work. Significant subjects from events to broad themes are included, and the entries pointing to the specific theme discussions in each entry are indicated in **boldface.**

Entries may include illustrations, including an author portrait, stills from film adaptations (when

available), maps, and/or photos of key historical events.

Citing Short Stories for Students

When writing papers, students who quote directly from any volume of *SSfS* may use the following general forms to document their source. These examples are based on MLA style; teachers may request that students adhere to a different style, thus, the following examples may be adapted as needed.

When citing text from *SSfS* that is not attributed to a particular author (for example, the Themes, Style, Historical Context sections, etc.) the following format may be used:

''The Celebrated Jumping Frog of Calaveras County.'' *Short Stories for Students.* Ed. Kathleen Wilson. Vol. 1. Detroit: Gale, 1997. 19-20.

When quoting the specially commissioned essay from *SSfS* (usually the first essay under the Criticism subhead), the following format may be used:

Korb, Rena. Essay on ''Children of the Sea.'' *Short Stories for Students.* Ed. Kathleen Wilson. Vol. 1. Detroit: Gale, 1997. 42.

When quoting a journal essay that is reprinted in a volume of *Short Stories for Students,* the following form may be used:

Schmidt, Paul. ''The Deadpan on Simon Wheeler.'' *The Southwest Review* XLI, No. 3 (Summer, 1956), 270-77; excerpted and reprinted in *Short Stories for Students,* Vol. 1, ed. Kathleen Wilson (Detroit: Gale, 1997), pp. 29-31.

When quoting material from a book that is reprinted in a volume of *SSfS,* the following form may be used:

Bell-Villada, Gene H. ''The Master of Short Forms,'' in *Garcia Marquez: The Man and His Work* (University of North Carolina Press, 1990); excerpted and reprinted in *Short Stories for Students,* Vol. 1, ed. Kathleen Wilson (Detroit: Gale, 1997), pp. 90-1.

We Welcome Your Suggestions

The editor of *Short Stories for Students* welcomes your comments and ideas. Readers who wish to suggest short stories to appear in future volumes, or who have other suggestions, are cordially invited to contact the editor. You may write to the editor at:

Editor, *Short Stories for Students*
The Gale Group
27500 Drake Rd.
Farmington Hills, MI 48331-3535

Literary Chronology

1828: Leo Tolstoy is born in Russia on September 9.

1860: Anton Chekhov is born in Taganrog, Russia, on January 16.

1861: The U.S. Civil War begins when Confederate forces capture Fort Sumter in South Carolina.

1865: The U.S. Civil War ends; Abraham Lincoln is assassinated.

1874: Gertrude Stein is born in Alleghany, Pennsylvania, on February 3.

1883: Shiga Naoya is born in Japan on February 20.

1886: "The Death of Ivan Ilych" by Leo Tolstoy is published.

1886: English translations of Leo Tolstoy's *War and Peace* and *Anna Karenina* are published.

1893: Dorothy Parker is born in West End, New Jersey, on August 22.

1894: Jean Toomer is born in Washington, D.C., on December 26.

1896: Liam O'Flaherty born on Innishmore, Aran Islands, Ireland, on August 28.

1897: William Faulkner is born in New Albany, Mississippi, on September 25.

1899: Elizabeth Bowen is born in Dublin, Ireland, on June 7.

1899: *Uncle Vanya* by Anton Chekhov is first produced at the Moscow Art Theater.

1899: "The Lady with the Pet Dog" by Anton Chekhov is published.

1903: Frank O'Connor is born in County Cork, Ireland.

1904: Anton Chekhov dies in Badenweiler, Germany, on July 2.

1906: R. K. Narayan is born in Madras, India, on October 10.

1909: "Melanctha" by Gertrude Stein is published.

1910: Leo Tolstoy dies in Russia on November 10.

1912: The *U.S.S. Titanic* sinks on her maiden voyage.

1913: "Han's Crime" by Shiga Naoya is published.

1914: With the assassination of Archduke Ferdinand of Austria, long-festering tensions in Europe erupt into what becomes known as the Great War.

1916: "The Easter Rising," in which Irish nationalists take control of the Dublin post office and declare a provisional government apart from British rule, takes place on April 24.

1917: Carson McCullers is born in Columbus, Georgia, on February 19.

1917: Russian Revolution takes place. Czar Nicholas II abdicates the throne and a provisional government is established.

1918: World War I, the most deadly war in history, ends with the signing of the Treaty of Versailles.

1920: The 18th Amendment, outlawing the sale, manufacture, and transportation of alcohol—known as Prohibition—goes into effect. This law led to the creation of ''speakeasies''—illegal bars—and an increase in organized crime. The law is repealed in 1933.

1920: The efforts of the Women's Suffrage movement, directed by women such as Susan B. Anthony and Elizabeth Cady Stanton, finally succeeds. The 19th Amendment, which granted the right to vote to women, is adopted.

1922: Kurt Vonnegut is born in Indianapolis, Indiana, on November 11.

1923: ''Blood-Burning Moon'' by Jean Toomer is published in his collection, *Cane.*

1924: ''The Wave'' by Liam O'Flaherty is published in his collection, *Spring Sowing.*

1925: Yukio Mishima is born in Tokyo, Japan, on January 14.

1929: ''Big Blonde'' by Dorothy Parker is published and earns an O. Henry award for short fiction.

1929: The stock market crash in October signals the beginning of a worldwide economic depression.

1929: *The Sound and the Fury* by William Faulkner is published.

1931: Toni Morrison is born in Loraine, Ohio, on February 18.

1931: ''Guests of the Nation'' by Frank O'Connor is published.

1933: *Autobiography of Alice B. Toklas* by Gertrude Stein is published.

1933: Ernest J. Gaines is born in Oscar, Louisiana, on January 15.

1936: ''Wunderkind'' by Carson McCullers is published.

1937: Bessie Head is born in Pietermaritzburg, South Africa, on July 6.

1939: ''Barn Burning'' by William Faulkner is published.

1939: World War II begins when Nazi Germany, led by Adolf Hitler, invades Poland; England and France declare war in response.

1940: *The Heart is a Lonely Hunter* by Carson McCullers is published.

1945: World War II ends in August with the atomic bombing of Hiroshima and Nagasaki, Japan.

1945: ''The Demon Lover'' by Elizabeth Bowen is published.

1946: Gertrude Stein dies in France on July 27.

1946: Tim O'Brien is born in Austin, Minnesota, on October 1.

1947: India achieves independence from British rule.

1949: Jamaica Kincaid is born in St. Johns, Antigua, on May 25.

1949: William Faulkner wins Nobel Prize for literature.

1950: Senator Joseph McCarthy of Wisconsin sets off the ''Red Scare'' that leads to government hearings and blacklisting of suspected communists.

1954: United States Supreme Court, in *Brown vs. Board of Education of Topeka,* rules unanimously that public school segregation is unconstitutional under the 14th amendment.

1955: ''Swaddling Clothes'' by Yukio Mishima is published in *Bungei.*

1960: ''A Horse and Two Goats'' by R. K. Narayan is published in *The Hindu.*

1961: ''Harrison Bergeron'' by Kurt Vonnegut is published in *The Magazine of Fantasy and Science Fiction.*

1962: William Faulkner dies in Byhalia, Mississippi, on July 6.

1963: President John F. Kennedy is assassinated in Dallas, Texas, on November 22.

1963: ''The Sky Is Gray'' by Ernest J. Gaines is published.

1966: Frank O'Connor dies in Dublin, Ireland, on March 10.

1967: Jean Toomer dies in Doylestown, Pennsylvania, on March 30.

1967: Dorothy Parker dies on June 7.

1967: Carson McCullers dies in Nyack, New York, on September 29.

1968: ''Boys and Girls'' by Alice Munro is published in *The Montrealer.*

1969: *Slaughterhouse Five* by Kurt Vonnegut is published.

1970: Yukio Mishima dies in Tokyo, Japan, on November 25.

1971: Shiga Naoya dies in Tokyo, Japan, on October 21.

1971: *The Autobiography of Miss Jane Pittman* by Ernest J. Gaines is published.

1972: President Richard Nixon resigns following the Watergate scandal.

1973: Elizabeth Bowen dies in London on February 22.

1975: Saigon, the South Vietnamese capital, falls to the North Vietnamese army, bringing an end to the Vietnam War.

1977: ''Snapshots of a Wedding'' by Bessie Head is published in *The Collector of Treasures and Other Botswana Village Tales.*

1979: Tim O'Brien wins National Book Award for *Going After Cacciato.*

1981: ''What I Have Been Doing Lately'' by Jamaica Kincaid in published in *Paris Review.*

1983: ''Recitatif'' by Toni Morrison is published in *Confirmation: An Anthology of African-American Women,* edited by Amiri and Amina Baraka.

1984: Liam O'Flaherty dies in Dublin, Ireland, on September 7.

1986: Bessie Head dies in Botswana on April 17.

1986: ''The Things They Carried'' by Tim O'Brien is published in *Esquire.*

1987: *Beloved* by Toni Morrison is published.

1989: The Berlin Wall, a symbol of the 28 years of division between East and West Germany, is torn down.

1990: Soviet leader Mikhail Gorbachev's policy of *glasnost* results in the fracturing of the Iron Curtain. By December the Soviet flag is lowered from the Kremlin.

1993: Toni Morrison wins Nobel Prize for literature.

Acknowledgments

The editors wish to thank the copyright holders of the excerpted criticism included in this volume and the permissions managers of many book and magazine publishing companies for assisting us in securing reproduction rights. We are also grateful to the staffs of the Detroit Public Library, the Library of Congress, the University of Detroit Mercy Library, Wayne State University Purdy/Kresge Library Complex, and the University of Michigan Libraries for making their resources available to us. Following is a list of the copyright holders who have granted us permission to reproduce material in this volume of *SSFS*. Every effort has been made to trace copyright, but if omissions have been made, please let us know.

COPYRIGHTED EXCERPTS IN *SSFS*, VOLUME 5, WERE REPRODUCED FROM THE FOLLOWING PERIODICALS:

The American Scholar, v. 45, Winter, 1975-76. Copyright © 1975-76 by the United Chapters of the Phi Beta Kappa Society. Reproduced by permission of the publishers.—*Black American Literature Forum,* currently *African American Review,* v. 18, Fall, 1984 for "Black Brutes and Mulatto Saints: The Racial Hierarchy of Stein's 'Melanctha'" by Milton A. Cohen; v. 18, Fall, 1984 for "The Individual and the Community in Two Short Stories by Ernest J. Gaines" by John W. Roberts. Copyright © 1984 Indiana State University. Both reproduced by permission of Indiana State University

and the respective authors.—*CLA Journal,* v. XIV, March, 1971; v. XXXIV, June, 1991. Copyright © 1971, 1991 by The College Language Association. Both used by permission of The College Language Association.—*College Literature,* v. XVI, 1989; v. 23, October, 1996. Copyright © 1989, 1996 by West Chester University. Both reproduced by permission.—*Critical Inquiry,* v. 19, Spring, 1993 for "Black Writing, White Reading: Race and the Politics of Feminist Interpretation" by Elizabeth Abel. Copyright © 1993 by The University of Chicago. Reproduced by permission of the publisher and the author.—*Critique,* v. XXXVI, Fall, 1994. Copyright © 1994 Helen Dwight Reid Educational Foundation. Reproduced with permission of the Helen Dwight Reid Educational Foundation, published by Heldref Publications, 1319 18th Street, NW, Washington, DC 20036-1802.—*The Faulkner Journal,* v. VI, n. 2, Spring, 1991. Copyright © 1991 by the University of Akron. Reproduced by permission of the University of Central Florida and the author.—*The Journal of Commonwealth Literature,* v. XXIV, 1989 for "Myth, Exile, and the Female Condition: Bessie Head's 'The Collector of Treasures'" by Sara Chetin. Copyright by the author. Reproduced with the kind permission of Bowker-Saur, a part of Reed Business Information Ltd.—*Short Story,* v. 5, Spring, 1997. Reproduced by permission.—*Slavic and East-European Journal,* v. 5, Winter, 1961. © 1977 by AATSEEL of the U.S., Inc. Reproduced by permission.—*The South-*

ern Literary Journal, v. 19, Fall, 1986. Copyright 1986 by the Department of English, University of North Carolina at Chapel Hill. Reproduced by permission.—*The Southern Quarterly,* v. 26, Spring, 1988. Copyright © 1988 by the University of Southern Mississippi. Reproduced by permission.—*Studies in Canadian Literature,* v. 15, 1990 for ''Penning in the Bodies: The Construction of Gendered Subjects in Alice Munro's 'Boys and Girls''' by Marlene Goldman. Copyright by the author. Reproduced by permission of the editors.—*Studies in Short Fiction,* v. V, Winter, 1968; v. X, Fall, 1973; v. 17, Fall, 1980; v. 27, Spring, 1990; v. 31, Winter, 1994. Copyright 1968, 1973, 1980, 1990, 1994 by Newberry College. All reproduced by permission.—*Studies in the Novel,* v. III, Summer, 1971. Copyright 1971 by North Texas State University. Reproduced by permission.

COPYRIGHTED EXCERPTS IN *SSFS*, VOLUME 5, WERE REPRODUCED FROM THE FOLLOWING BOOKS:

Blackwell, Louise. From ''Jean Toomer's 'Cane' and Biblical Myth'' in *Jean Toomer: A Critical Evaluation.* Edited by Therman B. O'Daniel. Howard University Press, 1988. Copyright © 1988 by the College Language Association. All rights reserved. Reproduced by permission of The College Language Association.—Cook, Richard M. From *Carson McCullers.* Frederick Ungar Publishing Co., 1975. Copyright © 1975 by Frederick Ungar Publishing Co., Inc. Reproduced by permission.—Eldridge, Richard. From ''The Unifying Images in Part One of Jean Toomer's 'Cane''' in *Jean Toomer: A Critical Evaluation.* Edited by Therman B. O'Daniel. Howard University Press, 1988. Copyright © 1988 by the College Language Association. All rights reserved. Reproduced by permission of The College Language Association.—Ferguson, Moira. From *Jamaica Kincaid: Where the Land Meets the Body.* University Press of Virginia, 1994. Copyright © 1994 by the Rector and Visitors of the University of Virginia. Reproduced by permission of the University Press of Virginia.—Festa, Conrad. From *Vonnegut in America: An Introduction to the Life and Work of Kurt Vonnegut.* Edited by Jerome Klinkowitz and Donald L. Lawler. Delacorte Press/Seymour Lawrence, 1977. Copyright © 1977 by Jerome Klinkowitz and Donald L. Lawler. Reprinted by permission of Delacorte Press/Seymour Lawrence, a division of Bantam Double Dell Publishing Group, Inc.—Mangum, Bryant. From ''Jamaica Kincaid'' in *Fifty Caribbean Writers: A Bio-Bibliographical Critical Sourcebook.* Edited by Daryl Cumber Dance. Greenwood Press, 1986. Copyright © 1986 by Daaryl Cumber Dance. All rights reserved. Reproduced by permission of Greenwood Publishing Group, Inc., Westport, CT.—Mathy, Francis. From *Shiga Naoya.* Twayne, 1974. Copyright © 1974 by Twayne Publishers, Inc. All rights reserved. Reproduced with the permission of the author.—Rao, V. Panduranga. From ''The Craftmanship of R. K. Narayan'' in *Indian Writing in English.* Edited by Ramesh Mohan. Orient Longman, 1978. © 1978 Central Institute of English and Foreign Languages, Hyderabad. Reproduced by permission.—Smith, Virginia Llewellyn. From *Anton Chekhov and the Lady with the Dog.* Oxford University Press, London, 1973. © Oxford University Press 1973. All rights reserved. Reproduced by permission.—Sutherland, Donald. From *Gertrude Stein: A Biography of Her Work.* Yale University Press, 1951. Copyright, 1951, by Yale University Press. Renewed 1979 by Donald Sutherland. All rights reserved. Reproduced by permission.—Wasiolek, Edward. From *Tolstoy's Major Fiction.* University of Chicago Press, 1978. Reproduced by permission of The University of Chicago Press and the author.—Wood, Karen and Charles. From *The Vonnegut Statement.* Edited by Jerome Klinkowitz and John Somer. Dell Publishing Co., 1973. Copyright © 1973 by Jerome Klinkowitz and John Somer. Reprinted by permission of Dell Publishing Co., a division of Bantam Doubleday Dell Publishing Group, Inc.

PHOTOGRAPHS AND ILLUSTRATIONS APPEARING IN *SSFS*, VOLUME 5, WERE RECEIVED FROM THE FOLLOWING SOURCES:

by permission.—Fox cubs in cage at Fox Farm, Sireniki, Chukotka Peninsula, Russia, July, 1993, photograph by Pat O'Hara. Pat O'Hara/Corbis. Reproduced by permission.—Gafni, Miklos, Carnegie Hall, 1950-51, New York, photograph. Archive Photos, Inc. Reproduced by permission.—Gaines, Ernest, photograph. AP/Wide World Photos. Reproduced with permission.—''Gertrude Stein,'' painting by Pablo Picasso. © 1998 Estate of Pablo Picasso/Artist Rights Society (ARS), New York and The Metropolitan Museum of Art, Bequest of Gertrude Stein, 1946. Reproduced by permission.—Glamourous woman in circus knife throwing act, photograph. Archive Photos, Inc. Reproduced by permission.—Head, Bessie, photograph. Reproduced by the kind permission of the Estate of Bessie Head.—Kinkaid, Jamaica, photograph. © Jerry Bauer. Reproduced by permission.—Linden, Natchez, Mississippi, photograph. AP/Wide World Photos, Inc. Reproduced by permission.—McCullers, Carson, photograph. AP/Wide World Photos. Reproduced by permission.—Mishima, Yukio, photograph. AP/Wide World Photos. Reproduced by permission.—Morrison, Toni, photograph. AP/Wide World Photos. Reproduced by permission.—Munro, Alice, photograph. © Jerry Bauer. Reproduced by permission.—Narayan, R.K., photograph. The Library of Congress.—O'Brien, Tim, photograph. © Jerry Bauer. Reproduced by permission.—O'Connor, Frank, photograph. Bord Failte Eireann (The Irish Tourist Board). Reproduced by permission.—O'Flaherty, Liam, photograph. UPI/Bettmann Newsphotos. Reproduced by permission.—Parker, Dorothy, c. 1939, photograph. The Library of Congress.—Police Watch as Black children bused from Roxbury section of Boston arrive at South Boston High School, January 8, 1975, Boston, MA, photograph. Corbis/Bettmann. Reproduced by permission.—Policeman prodding sleeping homeless man, Grand Central Station, 1987, New York, photograph by Angel Franco. New York Times Co./ Archive Photos, Inc. Reproduced by permission.— Rural Indian village (huts and mosque), 1848, Sheebpore, India, lithograph by Philip DeBay. Historical Picture Archive/Corbis. Reproduced by permission.—Shiga Naoya, photograph by Setsuzo Katayama.—St. Paul's Cathederal surrounded by smoke, photograph. UPI/ Corbis-Bettmann. Reproduced by permission.—Stein, Gertrude, photograph by Carl Van Vechten. The Library of Congress.— Tolstoy, Leo, 1897, photograph. The Library of Congress.—Toomer, Jean with Margery Latimer, photograph. The Bettmann Archive/Newsphotos, Inc. Reproduced by permission.—U.S. Marine patrol embassy grounds perimeter, 1996, Liberia, photograph. Reuters/Corinne Dufka/Archive Photos, Inc. Reproduced by permission.—Unidentified African American students at Woolworth's Lunch Counter in Greensboro, North Carolina, February, 1960, photograph by Jack Moe. Corbis/Jack Moe. Reproduced by permission.—View of Antigua, photograph by Max Hunn. Archive Photos, Inc. Reproduced by permission.—View of Moscow, Summer, 1912, photograph by Thomas H. Hartshorne. Archive Photos, Inc. Reproduced by permission.— Vonnegut, Kurt, photograph. AP/Wide World Photos. Reproduced by permission.

Contributors

ALVAREZ, Joseph. Instructor in the English and Foreign Languages department at Central Piedmont Community College in North Carolina. Entry: "Harrison Bergeron."

AREN, James. Freelance writer. Entries: Compare and contrast sections for many entries.

BERG, Christine G. Has taught English at Lehigh University, Raritan Valley Community College, and Allentown College of Saint Francis de Sales. Entry: "Snapshots of a Wedding."

BERTONNEAU, Thomas. Temporary Assistant Professor of English and the Humanities at Central Michigan University, and Senior Policy Analyst at the Mackinac Center for Public Policy. Entry: "Barn Burning."

BILY, Cynthia. Instructor at Adrian College in Michigan. Contributor to reference publications including *Feminist Writers, Gay and Lesbian Biography,* and *Chronology of Women Worldwide.* Entry: "A Horse and Two Goats."

CHANG, Yoonmee. Ph.D. candidate in English and American literature at the University of Pennsylvania. Entry: "Swaddling Clothes," "Han's Crime."

DELL'AMICO, Carol. Ph.D. candidate in the Program of Literatures in English at Rutgers, The State University of New Jersey. Entry: "Boys and Girls."

DOMINIC, Catherine. Editor of *Shakespeare's Characters for Students* and freelance writer. Entries: Compare and contrast sections for many entries.

FAULKNER, Tom. Freelance writer and copyeditor. Entry: "Wunderkind."

FRATTAROLA, Angela. Freelance writer and scholar. Entry: "The Death of Ivan Ilych."

GARDINER-SCOTT, Tanya. Associate Professor of English at Mount Ida College in Newton, Massachusetts. Entry: "The Demon Lover."

GIRARD, Terry. Professor of English at Wayne State University in Detroit, Michigan. Entry: "Swaddling Clothes."

HENNINGFELD, Diane Andrews. Assistant professor of English at Adrian College in Michigan and contributor to reference works for Salem Press. Entry: "The Wave."

HENRY, Richard. Ph.D. in literature. Associate Professor of English at Adrian College in Michigan. Entry: "The Wave."

HUBER, Erik. Master of Fine Arts degree in Fiction Writing, currently teaches at the New York School of Continuing Education. Entry: "The Lady with the Pet Dog."

JOHNSON, Kendall. Ph.D. candidate in literature at the University of Pennsylvania. Entry: ''Swaddling Clothes.''

KELLET, Dustie. Has taught Developmental Writing and tutored at the Fullerton Writing Center at California State University. Entry: ''What I Have Been Doing Lately.''

KIPPEN, David. Ph.D. in English from State University of New York at Stony Brook and a specialist in British colonial literature and twentieth-century South African literature. Entry: ''The Sky is Gray.''

KORB, Rena. Freelance writer and editor with a master's degree in English literature and creative writing. Entries: ''Boys and Girls,'' ''The Things They Carried,'' and ''The Wave.''

LE BLANC, Ondine. Editor and writer who has taught at the University of Michigan. Entry: ''Melanctha.''

LEVERICH, Jean. Ph.D. in literature from the University of Michigan. Has taught English at the University of Michigan, New York University, and Georgetown University. Entry: ''Han's Crime.''

MADSEN HARDY, Sarah. Ph.D. in English literature at the University of Michigan. Entries: ''Big Blonde'' and ''Recitatif.''

MARCH, Thomas. Ph.D. candidate in English at New York University. Entry: ''Snapshots of a Wedding.''

MOWERY, Carl. Ph.D. in Rhetoric, Composition and Literature from Southern Illinois University. Entries: ''Guests of the Nation'' and ''Harrison Bergeron.''

PELTIER, Robert. Instructor of English at Trinity College in East Hartford, Connecticut. Entry: ''The Wave.''

PHILLIPS, Jane. Has taught in the English Department at University of California-Riverside and at several other schools. Entry: ''Blood Burning Moon.''

PIEDMONT-MARTON, Elisabeth. Ph.D. in American literature. Entry: ''The Things They Carried.''

STROHMER, Shaun. Freelance writer; has taught at the University of Michigan. Entry: ''What I Have Been Doing Lately.''

Barn Burning

William Faulkner

1939

William Faulkner's "Barn Burning" (1939) comes from the mid-point of its author's career and finds its creator in consummate control of the modernist devices that he, more than any other, had brought to American prose: stream-of-consciousness narration, decadent and even culturally degenerate settings, extended sentences—interrupted by qualifying clauses—that give the effect of continuously suspended or deferred resolution of the action, and images of extreme violence. These modernist gestures disturbed Faulkner's early readers, and critics reacted harshly to his works of the late 1920s and early 1930s, such as the novels *The Sound and the Fury* (1929) and *Light in August* (1932). Faulkner stood accused of excessive mannerism and obscurity, and of a morbid interest in unhealthy types. Northerners found his depiction of the unassimilated South too regional and Southerners found it too harsh and scandalous to be acceptable.

Before he developed his signature style, however, Faulkner had proven himself a powerful writer of ordinary, perfectly accessible prose. A good example of this is the early story "Turnabout" (1925), in which an American aviator in World War I befriends a British torpedo-boat pilot and comes to see the conflict from a perspective less remote and abstract than that provided by aerial bombing. To some extent, "Barn Burning" represents a compromise between the brutal themes of Faulkner's high modernist style and the accessibility of his early prose. The result is still a powerful, more-straight-

forward-than-usual, glimpse into the author's fictional world.

Author Biography

William Faulkner—store-clerk, carpenter, general construction-worker, coal shoveler, deck-hand, cadet-aviator, and ultimately a prime incarnation of the Great American Novelist—was a product of the Deep South. Born in New Albany, Mississippi, the son of a railroad worker, he joined Britain's Royal Air Force in 1918, attended the University of Mississippi, Oxford, and then seemed to lurch through life, changing jobs and travelling. With the appearance of *Soldiers' Pay* (1926), a novel published with the assistance of his friend Sherwood Anderson, he launched himself on the career for which he would become famous.

Many a paradox clings to Faulkner, a traditionalist and even a reactionary who struck out into the realms of extreme literary innovation. Focusing on simple, or sometimes even simpleminded, characters, he employed complex syntax, interior monologue, disrupted chronology, and multiple perspectives to create what might be called realistic allegories. Often, at the core of the most complicated narrative, one finds a Biblical or folkloric motif; and, despite his frequent defense of peculiarly Southern values, Faulkner was often a penetrating critic of America's perennial race conflict. Then again, this extraordinary artist turned out to be an ordinary man, afflicted by his own peccadillos (a taste for strong drink, for example); and at moments, though in complete control of his formidable literary powers, he allowed himself to be drawn into situations that compromised his gifts, as when he worked briefly as a studio writer in Hollywood.

Soldiers' Pay was followed, in rather rapid succession, by *Mosquitoes* (1927), *Sartoris* (1929), *The Sound and the Fury* (1929), *As I Lay Dying* (1929), *Sanctuary* (1931), *Light in August* (1932), and *Absalom, Absalom!* (1936), a sequence which established Faulkner's reputation as a major presence in American letters and a leading figure in experimental prose. Considering the density of these novels, the achievement which they represent can only be considered as one of the most remarkable in the twentieth century. Unlike James Joyce, who labored for forty years over two immense and experimental novels, Faulkner turned out one book after another, as if possessed. Much of Faulkner's

work is unified through being integrated into the fictional—or rather mythical—Yoknapatawpha County in northern Mississippi, the imaginary setting of his best-known stories and novels, including "Barn-Burning" and "The Bear." Like Thomas Hardy's Wessex, Yoknapatawpha County represents an immense act of creative imagination. Faulkner's synthesis of place, history, character, and atmosphere easily leads the reader into believing that Yoknapatawpha is a real place. Of course, real elements go into its making, drawn from the actual South that Faulkner knew so well.

Because the novels that he wanted to write—the difficult ones—sold poorly, Faulkner sometimes produced potboilers (works deliberately and entirely designed to make money for the author), of which *Sanctuary,* a story of abduction, rape, and murder, is a good example. It was probably on the strength of *Sanctuary* that Faulkner found himself summoned to Hollywood. His best-known screenwriting effort is his film adaptation of the 1939 Raymond Chandler novel *The Big Sleep* (1939). After a short while, Faulkner returned to novel-writing, which he practiced until his death in 1962. He was awarded the Nobel Prize for Literature in 1949 as well as two Pulitzer Prizes for his novels *A Fable* (in 1955) and *The Reivers* (posthumously, in 1963). Faulkner's later work (including, ironically, *A Fable*) sometimes seems to be a parody of the earlier writing, but there are enough exceptions to the trend to justify the claim that Faulkner was a great artist from the beginning of his career until the end.

Plot Summary

The opening scene of "Barn Burning" finds the story's protagonist, a ten-year-old named Colonel Sartoris or "Sarty," waiting with his father, Abner Snopes, in a Southern small-town general store being used as a courtroom; the time is ten or fifteen years after the Civil War. As we learn from the interior monologue through which Faulkner conveys all of the story's events, Ab Snopes has been called into court on a charge of arson by his landlord-employer. (Ab is a sharecropper, someone who "rents" farmland by promising to remit part of his harvest to the property owner). Sarty is acutely aware of the physical aspects of the place, the aroma of the goods, the appearance of cans and jars on the shelves. His overwhelming thought is of an enemy, "ourn! mine and hisn both!" The reference is to the plaintiff. Faulkner underscores Sarty's sense of family loyalty to his father.

Mr. Harris, who charges Ab with the crime of burning his barn, explains how Ab's hog ruined his corn, how he took the hog as payment for the damage, and how Ab sent a go-between to him with the message that "wood and hay kin burn," which he interpreted as a threat against his life and property. Sarty knows that Ab did set the fire (Ab is, in fact, in the habit of setting fires) and knows also that his father expects him to lie in court. Sarty never testifies. The justice of the peace finds insufficient evidence and dismisses the case, but he tells Ab to his face that he believes him guilty and orders him to leave town. As they step from the store into the street, a boy hisses "barn-burner" at Ab and his son. Sarty launches himself in a fury at the insulter, only to be struck down by a blow to the face from the larger boy. He feels nothing; it is all a blur. A mule-drawn wagon, with the Snopes's pathetic belongings, is meanwhile already loaded, and Ab apparently has another lodging already lined up, on the plantation of Major de Spain.

The Snopeses camp that night. Ab builds a fire, which Sarty finds curiously meager given that it burns on rails plundered from a nearby fence and might be as big as the plunderer wanted to make it. Abruptly, Ab accuses Sarty of having been on the verge of telling the truth to the judge, or, as Ab sees it, of betraying him, the father. Although he doesn't answer, Sarty senses this to be true, and in any case Ab is convinced that it is true and slaps Sarty across his face.

The next day, they arrive at the de Spain plantation. Ordering his wife and their two daughters to make their shack livable, Ab decides to visit the manor house and make himself known to his new employer. The visit involves a deliberate provocation, however, as Ab deliberately steps in horse manure, refuses to wipe his feet before entering, and soils the rug in the parlor. Major de Spain is not home, but his frightened wife finally gets the gloomy apparition to leave. Later in the day, de Spain brings the rug to the shack to be cleaned by the Snopes women, who, watched over by Ab, promptly ruin it

William Faulkner

with the crude lye soap that they use. Ab then returns it to the manor. De Spain soon arrives at the shack to complain that the rug—an expensive one— has been ruined; he also says that he is going to charge Ab an additional twenty bushels of corn as payment. Beknownst to no one, Ab sues Major de Spain in the local court, claiming that twenty bushels of corn represents too high a price for the damaged rug. Surprisingly the judge agrees, though he is nevertheless adamant that Ab is responsible for the damage. Feeling insufficiently vindicated, Ab decides to burn down de Spain's barn.

Sarty rebels at this plan and determines to thwart his father. But Ab, suspecting as much, tells his wife and two daughters to keep Sarty in the shack. But Sarty escapes, thinking all the time about the long succession of burnt barns, the endless lies, and the ceaseless movement from one humiliating domicile to another that the cycle entails. He runs to the manor and shouts to de Spain. At that moment, de Spain sees someone entering his barn. Sarty runs.

From a hilltop that night, Sarty looks at the sky and sees the stars and constellations wheeling overhead. He feels a strange peace which he is too young to understand. In the last line, he is walking— away—and he does not look back.

Characters

de Spain

Major de Spain hires Abner Snopes to tenant his land as a sharecropper. De Spain is a property owner of some stature and thus the social opposite of Ab, who owns nothing and has virtually no social standing. De Spain bears the title Major as an ex-officer of the Confederate Army; here again, he is Ab's social opposite, for Ab was a private soldier (and not a very good one). The Major presumably owned slaves before the war; he still keeps black servants, some of them in livery in the house, others no doubt bound for a pittance in the yards and fields. He is a member of the Southern aristocracy, but with a qualification: his name, which connects him with neither the Protestant upper class nor the Bourbons or other French-descended grandees of the Old South; the name de Spain suggests the nearly-submerged Spanish presence in Louisiana and Florida, or even the creole, or ''light-skinned free blacks'' of New Orleans. If de Spain were a creole, an individual with some African ancestors, then his lording his stature over Ab would presumably be even more stinging for Ab than usual in such confrontations. But this is speculative.

De Spain rides a sorrel horse; Ab drives mules. Again the contrast is emphatic. But it is important not to deprive Major de Spain of his humanity by characterizing him as a stereotypical oppressor. Ab Snopes, after all, is the real villain of the tale. In fact, compared to Ab, the Major strikes one as a reasonable man. His reaction to Ab's deliberate provocation of soiling the expensive rug is simply to order Ab, his employee, to clean the damaged item. When Ab deliberately does further damage to the rug, de Spain is technically within his rights to demand payment in kind (the twenty bushels of corn). To his great surprise, the tenant sues him and asks for a lower punitive remission, which the judge grants. De Spain is a man subjected to uninvited exasperation, and one could even say that he restrains himself. He is also within his customary rights when he shoots the arsonist (Ab) dead when he catches him in the act.

De Spain keeps a fine house, which impresses Sarty with its order. In the context of ''Barn Burning'' de Spain might be said to stand for social and aesthetic order, two things which Sarty has been deprived of all his life.

Mr. Harris

Mr. Harris is Abner Snopes's current landlord-employer when the story ''Barn Burning'' opens. Snopes has burnt down Harris's barn and Harris has brought Snopes up on charges; the case is being heard by the local justice of the peace in the general store. Mr. Harris is a man affronted. He tells the story of his grievance himself. In paraphrase: Ab's hog got loose in Harris's corn and trampled it; Harris instructed his tenant to tie up the pig and even gave him sufficient wire to mend the pigpen. Abner simply left the wire laying around, with the pigpen ramshackle and no restriction on the hog. When the hog escaped again, Harris confined it to his own barn—keeping it in lieu of the damages it had caused. Abner then sent a man to Harris to deliver the message ''wood and hay kin burn,'' which Harris properly took as a threat. Shortly thereafter, his barn took fire and burned.

During the course of the hearing, Harris points to Sarty and tells the judge to let the boy testify because ''he knows,'' meaning that Sarty knows the truth—that his father is an incendiary. Harris thus functions as a catalyst in the awakening of Sarty's moral sense. Harris then declines to put Sarty to the test—to Sarty's relief—since the boy was in fact bursting with the truth and would have spoken it, to his father's chagrin. Sarty is thus morally in debt to Mr. Harris.

Mother

See Lennie Snopes

Sarty

Sarty—short for Colonel Sartoris Snopes—bears the name of a famous Rebel commander from the Civil War under whom, perhaps, his father, Abner Snopes, served; Ab appears to have bestowed the name on his son for its public-relations value in the post-Civil War South, where the story ''Barn Burning'' takes place. The ten-year-old male child (he has two older sisters) of an itinerant sharecropper, Sarty has the intellectual development that one would expect—he does not analyze events and brings no book-learning to bear on his experience of the world; however, he does display evidence of natural, if undeveloped, brightness, of which his intense consciousness of physical aspects of the world serves as one sign. (See, for example, his intense perception of the interior of the general store in the opening scene of the story.) Sarty's emerging sense of morality—a characteristic not shared by his father—is also a sign of his brightness.

Sarty's father has raised the boy to be fiercely devoted to his family. Thus, during the hearing in the general store, when Ab faces Mr. Harris's charge of arson, Sarty sees Harris as his father's and his own enemy. ("Enemy" is the term that Faulkner places in Sarty's mind in the interior monologue which constitutes much of the narrative.) When an older boy hisses "barn-burner" at Sarty and Ab as they leave the general store-cum-courthouse, Sarty springs at him like a wild animal—and is immediately beaten back and bloodied by the stronger contender. Later, Sarty allows Ab to slap him, and he acquiesces to the tyranny that Ab exercises over the family, until the end of the story.

Somewhere in Sarty a spark burns, however, that will not be extinguished by Ab's dark tyranny. In particular, Sarty rebels, at long last, over the wrongness of Ab's habitual acts of arson. The notion of an abstract right and wrong, separable from persons but applicable universally to any and every individual despite the context, takes hold of Sarty and compels him to warn Major de Spain of Ab's intended fire-setting, even though he knows that this act will separate him from his father forever. The forced lying and the lack of love from his father have helped to turn Sarty in the direction of a new moral conception that transcends the demands of his father for family loyalty. At the story's end, Major de Spain catches Ab in the act of setting his barn afire and shoots him dead. Sarty's reaction is curious: He finds a strange serenity in his nighttime isolation on a hilltop as the constellations wheel eternally overhead.

Abner Snopes

Ab Snopes enlisted as a soldier in the Confederate Army during the Civil War, but his choice of sides signified convenience and nothing more, for, as the reader is told, Ab had gone to war as a "private" in the "fine old European sense"—for purely mercenary reasons, to get what booty he could. "It meant nothing and less than nothing to him if it were enemy booty or his own." Snopes took a musket-ball in his heel and limped afterwards because of it, but he does not deserve, as Faulkner makes plain, the usual respect due to wounded veterans (of either side). Snopes bears another, more important wound, of unknown origin, perhaps as old as original sin: He suffers from an inflamed ego and a thin skin, and he takes offense with the swiftness of a cobra striking. His life, indeed, seems to be a continuing hell comprised of offense, retribution, and flight. The barn-burning of the story's

Media Adaptations

• "Barn Burning" was adapted as a film in 1980, starring Tommy Lee Jones and Diane Kagan. It runs forty-one minutes and can be purchased from Monterey Home Video, Karol Video.

title refers to Snopes's habit of setting fire to the property of those who (in his eyes) slight him.

Like Captain Sutpen in *Absalom, Absalom!* who tries to build his own world separate from the larger world, Ab has something like a God-complex, but he has none of Sutpen's creativity, and his madness expresses itself through dominance, destruction, and wrath. Ab's wife and daughters, for example, live entirely in his shadow, serving him in their apathetic way, showing little initiative or imagination as he bullies them and others. (Only Sarty, Ab's son, has a self equal to his father's.) But the God-complex is really only the surface manifestation of a complete lack of confidence. It is the insecurity of a man who sees himself as rejected by society and dejected under a sinister fate that makes him seethe with the sense of injury on every hand.

Although he never lays plans that might extract him from the cycle of itinerant land-tenancy—thus condemning himself to it—Ab nevertheless hates those who employ him. When he deliberately tracks dung into Major de Spain's manor house, for example, he is expressing his contempt for all those who, in his eyes and because of his own doing, hold some kind of sway over him; it is almost as if he invites conflict so as to find an excuse for his stealthy acts of retributive arson.

There is, finally, something paltry and brutal about Ab, whose thievery of fence-posts to make a fire merely results in a pathetic little blaze insufficient to warm his encamped family. He slaps Sarty and pushes his wife and daughter with a heavy hand; meanwhile, he harps on the sacredness of family bonds. Ab is a living failure and a living provocation, and the hell that he constructs for himself by

The Linden plantation house in Natchez, Mississippi.

maintaining a constant state of war with all other human beings becomes a hell for others—most significantly for Sarty and Sarty's mother and sisters, all of whom are fated to endure an endless amount of humiliation until Ab's death.

Colonel Sartoris Snopes
See Sarty

Lennie Snopes
When we first meet Sarty's mother, Mrs. Snopes (who at one point her husband calls Lennie), she is wearing her Sunday dress, sitting in a wagon (loaded down with the Snopes's pathetic belongings), and crying. She has cause to cry: Her husband has been called to legal account on a charge of arson, the latest of such acts which have led, once again, to the uprooting of the Snopes family. Mrs. Snopes is sobbing because of the wretchedness of her life and the cruelty of her husband. On the wagon with the other household goods is a clock, described as her dowry, which has long been uselessly stopped at fourteen minutes past two o'clock. The broken piece of furniture serves as a metaphor for Mrs. Snopes's life, which came to a stop, spiritually,

when she bound her fortune, for whatever reason, to Ab Snopes.

Mrs. Snopes has two daughters and a son, in addition to her ten-year-old son Sarty. On seeing Sarty and his father approaching, she moves to climb down from the wagon, but Ab orders her to stay where she is. This, too, is a figure of her life: Ab dominates her and their children totally and (on occasion) brutally; when Sarty appears with his father after the hearing, his nose is bloodied, courtesy of a blow from Ab. His bloody nose inspires her to maternal concern and affection; she wants to wipe Sarty's face clean, though he refuses her comfort.

When the family arrives at their shack on the de Spain plantation, it is Mrs. Snopes who unloads the wagon, like a beast of burden, and it is she, significantly, who utters a single word to her husband when he instructs Sarty to come with him to the de Spain manor. "Abner," she says, the implication being that her husband should control himself, which she probably knows that he will not do. Ab silences her with a grim look, but with this one word she demonstrates that she has a moral sense and a grasp, however crude, of her husband's psychology. If one asks where Sarty gains *his* moral insight, then—since it cannot be from Ab—it could perhaps have come from his mother. She also evidences love and a sense of tradition, in her own way, as Faulkner reveals that she somehow saved enough money to present Sarty with a Christmas present, a chopping ax.

Mrs. Snopes's moral test comes at the same time as Sarty's, when Ab orders her to keep hold of Sarty while Ab sneaks off to the de Spain barn to set it afire. The dialogue that follows suggests that Mrs. Snopes does not struggle very hard to keep Sarty from escaping to warn Major de Spain. Yet, as he escapes her, she cries, "I can't," meaning that she feels that she should not let him go—but she makes no great effort to stop him. Her limits of self-assertion are smaller than Sarty's, but they model and anticipate his.

Mrs. Snopes
See Lennie Snopes

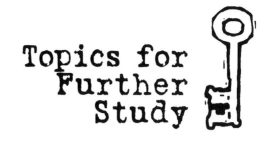

Topics for Further Study

- Read another Faulkner story, "Turnabout," in which an American aviator in World War I meets a British torpedo-boat pilot and experiences the war from the sailor's perspective. Compare the "conversion experience" of the aviator at the end of the story, when he wishes that the German target he is bombing were in fact the Allied Headquarters, with Sarty Snopes's "conversion experience" in "Barn Burning."

- "Barn Burning" relies on Sarty's point of view, and to a lesser extent on Abner's and the narrator's, to convey its events; but Sarty's older brother, his mother, an aunt, and two sisters are also present. Read the story carefully and try to construct an account of events as one of these others might see them.

- Explore the symbolic expressions of fire in "Barn Burning." What are the properties of fire in general that make it an apt symbol for certain human traits? What particular manifestations of fire does Faulkner deploy in his story to give his readers insight into the character of Ab Snopes?

Themes

Alienation and Loneliness
In "Barn Burning," Faulkner depicts a child, on the verge of moral awareness, who finds himself cut off from the larger social world of which he is growing conscious; this sense of alienation takes root, moreover, in Sarty's relation with his father, who should be the moral model and means of entry of the child into the larger world. Because of his father's criminal recklessness, Sarty finds himself, in the first part of the story, the object of an insult, and he attacks a boy who, in more ordinary circumstances, might be a school-companion or a friend. His father has taught him to regard others as the "enemy." Mr. Harris, the bringer of the arson charge, is thus "our enemy . . . hisn and ourn." In fact, Mr. Harris is simply a man who has been mistreated by an egomaniacal provocateur. The story concludes with Sarty alone on a hilltop at night, watching the stars. This, too, reflects the boy's loneliness, and lack of social ties, but it also suggests his liberation from his family on the basis

of a moral insight which just possibly signifies a bridge to link him with the greater social world.

Anger and Hatred

Abner Snopes is anger embodied, ready to take offense over any interaction with other people, but especially with those whom he sees as his social superiors (which means most of them, since he lives at the lowest rung of the socioeconomic ladder). Ab is locked into a hell of personal revenge, and his viciousness appears to have played a large part in the misery of his family. Readers witness the anger of others, too, but often this is anger with a cause, as in the case of the exasperated Mr. Harris, or even the haughty Major de Spain. Sarty also experiences anger—at his father—precisely on account of the father's maniacal anger at the world.

Loyalty and Betrayal

Abner's crude psychological stratagem for gaining the complicity of his family in his bizarre way of life is to press his claim of family ties, of loyalty. This surfaces in Sarty's interior monologue, in the first court scene, concerning enemies, ''mine and hisn both.'' But this represents only a degraded view of loyalty, since there is no moral requirement to be loyal to particular persons without qualification, not even to parents. Abner's criminality absolves Sarty morally from maintaining loyalty, a view to which Sarty himself eventually comes. In a technical sense, Sarty betrays his father to Major de Spain, but in a larger moral sense, Sarty expresses his real loyalty to normative ethics, in which revenge is an aberration and aggressive violence a sin.

Morals and Morality

Morality has to do with reciprocity among individuals and is encapsulated in ''The Golden Rule,'' that you should do unto others what you would have others do unto you. Ab Snopes persistently and willfully flouts morality so conceived. He beats his son, tyrannizes his wife, picks fights with people who have done him no harm, and is an arsonist. He was equally rabid and self-serving as a soldier, for he enlisted solely to make the best of the opportunity for looting. Morality is expressed ethically in the form of law, which requires an objective sorting-out of truth. ''Barn Burning'' traces Sarty's passage from immersion in the egocentric Hell of his father's life to his espousal of morality and law. This is also a passage from the natural state of animal solidarity to the cultural state of concession to institutions.

Order and Disorder

Abner Snopes's life, symbolized by his constant removal to new quarters on account of his quarrels with everyone and by the random wretchedness of the family's meager belongings, is a life of violent disorder. Ab cannot integrate himself into any aspect of the social matrix, and even as a soldier he was out for himself. Ab's tendency toward barn-burning sums up his warlike attitude toward social structure. Sarty trades this disorder for order, symbolized most powerfully during the first courtroom scene, when Mr. Harris points to him with the enunciation that this boy knows the truth. The objective truth, the account of what really happened between Abner and Mr. Harris, is the first revelation to Sarty of an order obtained by the individual's subordinating himself to abstract concepts of existence and proper behavior. In this sense, Sarty's denunciation of his father to Major de Spain is a cry for order, for the liberation of his family from the infernal disorder of Ab's criminal tyranny.

Style

Syntax

The most noticeable feature of Faulkner's style, in ''Barn Burning'' and elsewhere, is his syntax or sentence structure. Faulkner's sentences tend to be long, full of interruptions, but work basically by stringing out seemingly meandering sequences of clauses. The second sentence of ''Barn Burning'' offers a case in point: It is 116 words long and contains between twelve and sixteen clauses, depending on how one parses it out; its content is heterogeneous, moving from Sarty's awareness of the smell of cheese in the general store through the visual impression made by canned goods on the shelves to the boy's sense of blood loyalty with his accused father. It is the subjectivity of the content—sense impressions, random emotions and convictions—which reveals the purpose of the syntax, which is to convey experience in the form of an intense stream-of-consciousness as recorded by the protagonist. The reiterated ''and . . . and . . . and . . .'' of these sequences creates a type of organic flow, as of a raw, unanalyzed encounter with the world and its variety of people and things.

Point of View

Faulkner was a perspectivist: That is to say he liked to tell a story from some particular point of view—or sometimes, as in the novels, from many divergent points of view, each with its own insistent emphasis. "Barn Burning" offers a fairly controlled example of the application of perspectivism. Faulkner tells his story primarily from the point of view of young Sarty, a ten-year-old boy. This requires that Faulkner gives us the raw reportage of scene and event that an illiterate ten-year-old would give us, if he could. Thus, Sarty sees the pictures on the labels of the goods in the general store but cannot understand the lettering; adults loom over him, so that he feels dwarfed by them; and he struggles with moral and intellectual categories, as when he can only see Mr. Harris as an "enemy." There are few departures from this strict perspectivism, but they are telling, as when, in the penultimate paragraph of the tale, an omniscient narrator divulges the truth about Ab's behavior as a soldier during the Civil War. But even this is a calculated feature of Faulkner's style: the breaking-in of the omniscient narrator is another way of fracturing the continuity of the narrative, of reminding readers that there are many perspectives, including a transcendental one in which all facts are known to the author. One further note about the story's confined perspective: Sharing Sarty's immediate impressions and judgments forges a strong bond between the boy and the reader.

Setting

The setting of "Barn Burning" is extremely important to the story: It is the post-Civil War South, the South of Reconstruction, in which a defeated and in many ways humiliated society is trying to hold its own against the Northern victor. This South has retreated into plantation life and small-town existence, and it maintains in private the social hierarchy that characterized the region in its pre-war phase. Slavery has been abolished, but a vast distance still separates the land-owning Southern aristocracy from the tenant-farmers and bonded workers who do the trench-labor required by the plantation economy, itself in a state of disruption and decadence. The Snopeses belong to the lowest echelon of white postwar Southern society. They are itinerant sharecroppers, who move from one locale to another, paying for their habitation in this or that shack by remitting part of the crop to the landlord. This is a setting of intense vulnerability and therefore of intense resentment. But "setting" is a word which needs to be qualified in reference to "Barn Burning" because, as Sarty notes, he has lived in at least a dozen ramshackle buildings on at least a dozen plantations in his ten short years. In a way, then, the story's "setting" is the road, or rather the Snopes' constant removal from one place to another due to Ab's quarreling and violence. The wagon, heaped with miserable chattel, is the setting, as is Abner's egomaniacal personality and Sarty's miserable yet rebellious heart.

Historical Context

Any discussion of William Faulkner in a historical context necessarily involves a discussion of modernism, the philosophical and artistic movement to which Faulkner, perhaps reluctantly, belonged. Modernism is generally considered *the* peculiarly twentieth-century school of artistic expression, and it is associated in literature with, for example, the poetry of T. S. Eliot and Ezra Pound, the painting of Georges Braque and Pablo Picasso, the music of Igor Stravinsky and Arnold Schoenberg, and the prose fiction of James Joyce, Marcel Proust, John Dos Passos, and Faulkner. In each of these cases, one observes a conscious breaking with traditional ideas about style, content, and purpose. In the poetry of Pound, as for example in his *Cantos,* experience is broken in pieces, and the reader is faced with a collage of fragments, allusions, declarations, and epiphanies; so, too, in the poems of Eliot, who also typifies the moral atmosphere of modernism, which could be summed up as despair over the condition of humanity in the aftermath of the soul-wrenching and materially devastating First World War (1914-18). Eliot's *The Waste Land* (1922) offers the paradigm of the modernist consciousness. It is often said that modernism expresses the alienation of the twentieth-century soul, its dislocation, its detachment from traditional sources of moral and intellectual authority, its search for new values to replace those rendered obsolete (as the modernists typically saw it) by massive human violence in the trenches. Artist Pablo Picasso (1881-1973) rejected unitary perspective, rejected the naturalistic or representational style, and concocted his "cubism," with its fractured planes and combinations of broken perspectives; Georges Braque (1882-1963) went even further, into the abstraction of shapes and colors, so that the painting no longer depicted recognizable objects of the real world. Igor Stravinsky (1882-1971) introduced new and violent rhythms, intense dissonances, and dry, unsentimental melodies into shocking orchestral works like his *Rite of Spring* (1914); and Arnold Schoenberg (1874-1951) did away entirely with traditional harmony,

Compare & Contrast

- **1941:** Fire damage to personal property in the United States is estimated at $286,000.

  1997: Arson is the second leading cause of residential deaths in the United States, claiming 740 lives. Personal property losses from arson total nearly $28 million.

- **Early 1900s:** Although the United States is shifting from an agrarian to an industrial society, a large portion of the country's gross national product results from agricultural production. Due to the abolishment of slavery, many landowners turn to tenant farming for their workforce. There are an estimated 250,000 sharecroppers in the United States.

  1990s: Many farmers begin to sell off large parcels of their land to real estate speculators because of high land values. Most food production is left to large corporations.

- **1930s:** William Faulkner's regionalist Southern subject matter, featuring the fictional Yoknapatawpha County, meets with criticism on two fronts: Northern critics find Faulkner's work too narrow, while Southern critics feel his work casts the South in an unfavorable light.

  1990s: Regionalist Southern writers including Faulkner, Flannery O'Connor, and Cormac McCarthy, are praised for the detail with which they portray their subject matter.

substituting his "twelve-tone" method, with the result of constant unresolved dissonance.

Modernism is complex, and while some of these formal experimenters rejected received values (Pound), others wanted to uphold old values by new means (Eliot). Thus Pound's work includes a sustained attack on Judeo-Christian values and embraces the radical relativism of philosopher Friedrich Nietzsche (1844-1900), a German precursor of twentieth-century modernism who called for a "revaluation of all values," while Eliot uses his experimentations to plead for the continued validity of traditional morals in a morally degenerate world. Faulkner is closer to Eliot than to Pound, which means that he is formally a modernist while being morally and philosophically a type of traditionalist. Faulkner could even be called a reactionary—and in truth he was reacting, negatively, to much of the transformation taking place in the world of his time.

In the aftermath of World War I the Western nations, including the United States, saw an unprecedented abandonment of small towns for the economic benefits, some real and some illusory, of big cities; the war had also stimulated the growth of industry and had provoked massive technical innovation. With Europe in debt, and with America in possession of thousands of new factories, the United States enjoyed an economic boom. This coincided with a new, devil-may-care moral attitude best summed up in the ideas of the "Jazz Age" or "the Roaring Twenties." The winked-at consumption of illegal alcoholic beverages outlawed by Prohibition, relaxed sexual attitudes, the unprecedented freedom of the private automobile, mass entertainments in the cinema and radio, gangster wars—all of these things suggested that the sedate world of pre-World War I agricultural and small-town America had yielded to something else. Smokestack America was burgeoning, and this entailed vast changes not only in the habits and interests of the average American, but in the very landscape.

Faulkner, a son of the traditional South, with its agricultural values and intense devotion to Protestant Christianity, understood all of this with an artist's acuity. He had prepared to fight in the war as an aviator with the British and though he did not see combat, he was close enough to it to understand it. His response to modernity in all of its social and technical manifestations was conditioned by his closeness to the war and to its dehumanizing effects. The new age seemed to represent a breakdown of the human spirit itself, seduced by the gewgaws of technology and the ease of undisciplined living. Faulkner would also have been aware, in the 1930s, of the tide of dictatorship rising in Europe, for this decade was the decade of fascism and militarism in Germany, Italy, the Soviet Union, Romania, and Japan.

Faulkner's reaction to the twentieth century runs in parallel with Oswald Spengler's and Jose Ortega y Gassett's. In *The Decline of the West* (1919) Spengler expressed in vast detail his contention that Western Civilization had entered a decadent phase in which the mass of people and their leaders lived off the stored-up cultural and economic capital of previous ages while contributing nothing by themselves. Ortega y Gassett wrote about *The Revolt of the Masses* (1932). The modern age, he claimed, was the age in which mass man replaced aristocratic man and in which the moral laxity of the masses had become the social norm. Ortega y Gassett's thesis was very close to Spengler's, and both of them together suggest in an explicitly philosophical way much of what Faulkner thought, though Faulkner chose to express himself primarily in fiction.

Critical Overview

In one sense, criticism of "Barn Burning" has displayed a remarkable unanimity, for this story throws into sharp relief a young boy's existential choice involving the two notions of "blood relation" and "morality." Whatever conclusion individual critics draw about the tale, their arguments necessarily center on the meaning of that choice. In preparing to read the story and again in considering it afterwards, readers must ask themselves a key question: If family ties constitute a moral obligation on the individual, is there any higher morality which might require the individual to act against a family member? This is the question that ten-year-old Sarty confronts—and answers.

Early reactions to Faulkner's modernistic work in general reflected the uneasiness that modernism itself inspired in the older generation of traditional critics. As late as 1941, Warren Beck could write that Faulkner had been "severely criticized for his style" but was nevertheless a "versatile stylist." Even so, Beck judged that Faulkner "remained guilty of carelessness, especially in sentence con-

struction" and had "persisted in mannerisms." Beck commented on a "profuseness of language . . . elaborate lyrical descriptions [and] persistent lyrical embroidery." The whole aim in Faulkner's writing, Beck wrote, was "perspective." Around the same time, Alfred Kazin referred negatively to Faulkner's "mountainous rhetoric" and his "discursive fog." In 1954, reviewing *The Hamlet,* in which "Barn Burning" appears, Peter Lisca noted "the complex symbolism and character evaluation" inherent in Faulkner's style. But Lisca assumes the validity of Faulkner's style and does not express the reservations still present in Beck's assessment of a decade or so earlier.

Percy H. Boynton, writing at the same time as Beck, directed his attention not to style but to content, and called attention to *The Hamlet* as an instance of Faulkner's representation "of a defeated and outdated gentry, victims of the northern enemy, of their own natures." Boynton noted that, in the stories of the Snopeses in particular, "degeneracy in itself" has become Faulkner's theme, so that he "has come to fill several other volumes with pimps, prostitutes, and perverts in ultimate forms of decadence."

In respect to "Barn Burning" particularly, critics have recognized it as an especially clear statement of Faulkner's central, existential issue: The interior struggle of the individual to discern right from wrong and to act on the discernment. As James B. Carruthers has written, in *William Faulkner's Short Stories* (1985), Sarty becomes "aware of alternatives to his own and his father's choice of action." Carruthers's essay also points up a trend in criticism of this particular tale from *The Hamlet,* that of seeking to justify Abner's violence. Carruthers characterizes Ab as stern but not violent towards his family, as the victim, in some sense, of his social caste.

M. E. Bradford states that "Barn Burning" is "a very important story" in the Faulknerian oeuvre; but Bradford, unlike Carruthers, upholds the intuitive notion that Ab Snopes is a very bad man indeed: "The very real justice of Harris and the rural magistrate in the first trial scene, when taken in conjunction with the moderation of de Spain and the Peace Justice of his county . . . marks how little is required of Ab" and by contrast how truly monstrous is Ab's sense of absolute self-justification. In other words, one could say that the division among critics of this story lies between those who wish, for whatever reason, to excuse Abner and those who side with Sarty in his decision to embrace an external measure of morality rather than sustain blind (or blood) loyalty.

Karl Zender's essay, "Character and Symbol in 'Barn Burning'" (1989), shows some elements of the apology for Abner. Understanding the story, this critic argues, requires our "overcoming our distaste for Ab to the point where we understand anew the 'mainspring' of his character." Zender readily admits that Ab is "vengeful" and "tyrannous," but claims that he is nevertheless motivated by "a desire for his son's affection." Zender believes that there is "partial justification" for Ab's fiery rage. By contrast, Susan Yunis (1991) complains that Faulkner himself is "intent on explaining and justifying Abner's barn-burning." Yunis represents a typical development in contemporary criticism: the putative discovery that canonical works of literature embody "oppressive" values and legitimate so-called patriarchal oppression. Yunis refers to "the silencing of personal pain" effected by Faulkner's supposed refusal to give voice to Sarty's mother and sisters.

Yunis thus operates within a variant of the class-conflict school of socially oriented criticism. Edmund Volpe (1980) says, however, that "Barn Burning" "is not really concerned with class conflict. The story is centered upon Sarty's emotional dilemma. His conflict would not have been altered in any way if the person whose barn Ab burns had been a simple poor farmer, rather than an aristocratic plantation owner."

John E. Bassett's "Faulkner in the Eighties: Crosscurrents in Criticism," examines recent trends in Faulknerian scholarship. Bassett summarizes the many contemporary techniques that have been applied to Faulkner, including semiotics, deconstruction, Marxist and Feminist hermeneutics, and reader-response criticism. Among critics, Faulkner remains one of the most-discussed American writers of the twentieth century.

Criticism

Thomas Bertonneau

Bertonneau is a Temporary Assistant Professor of English and the humanities at Central Michigan University, and Senior Policy Analyst at the Mackinac Center for Public Policy. In the following essay, he examines the tormented character of Ab Snopes and the high price for self-knowledge that Sarty must pay.

Abner Snopes, in William Faulkner's "Barn Burning," is everyone's double, and that is the source of the misery in which he immerses his family and all of those with whom he comes into contact. Snopes feels challenged, it seems, by the pure existence of others and succumbs on each occasion to the demon of incendiary rivalry. At the conclusion of the first courtroom scene, for example, when the justice of the peace, failing to find Snopes guilty of arson against Mr. Harris, nevertheless orders him to "leave this county," Faulkner reports the following as Snopes' reply:

> [Abner] spoke for the first time, his voice cold and harsh, level, without emphasis: "I aim to. I don't figure to stay in a country among people who . . . " he said something unprintable and vile, addressed to no one.

The utterance performs two rhetorical tricks revelatory of Abner's essential character. First, it wrests an order, directed at him by an authority figure, from the authority figure, and presents it as Abner's own prior determination, as if to say, "You can't order me to leave since I've already decided to leave of my own volition." Second, it attempts to reverse the moral judgment that the justice of the peace has ascribed to Abner by vilifying ("he said something unprintable and vile") those who would condemn him; if you call me a barn-burner, Abner implicitly says, then I'll call you something even worse. A third observation might be added. Abner's vilification is addressed, Faulkner writes, "to no one." Abner does not look his accusers in the eye when he insults them, he simply mutters the insult as if to himself. His rivalry is also, then, a cowardly rivalry.

The phenomena of doubles and rivals is extremely important to "Barn Burning," as to Faulkner's work in general. Faulkner appears to have understood what philosophical anthropologists like Rene Girard and Eric Gans have understood: That human beings are mimetic (or imitative) creatures and that the problem of violence is directly related to mimesis (or imitation). Perhaps the most common type of problematic imitation in which people engage is acquisitive imitation. When Smith possesses something and makes a show of it, then Jones wants it, too, and to the extent that there is only one object of ownership, it is easy for Smith and Jones to come to blows in a struggle over possession (Smith defensively, Jones aggressively). But there are subtler forms of acquisitive imitation, as when Smith thinks

What Do I Read Next?

- The stories in Faulkner's *The Hamlet* form a cycle of tales dealing with the Sartoris and Snopes families, tracing their intertwinings and degenerations from the time of Abner Snopes to the early twentieth century.

- Faulkner's *Sanctuary* (1931) is a novel of irrationality and violence that has been criticized for exploiting the violence that "Barn Burning" seems to condemn. Written as a potboiler, *Sanctuary* will also give a sense of Faulkner's more commercial side.

- Like Faulkner, H. P. Lovecraft was an agrarian anti-modernist who took a keen and almost obsessive interest in the phenomenon of degeneration. Lovecraft's "Shadow over Innsmouth" (1936) is a story of inbreeding, isolation, and violence in a small New England town. Lovecraft's "Whisperer in Darkness" and "The Dunwich Horror" make use of a fictional American region, Arkham County, in Massachusetts, which has many points in common with Faulkner's Yoknapatawpha. These stories appear in Lovecraft's *The Dunwich Horror and Others.*

- Harper Lee's *To Kill a Mockingbird* (1960) deals with the moral and emotional growth of a young girl in Alabama. Winner of the Pulitzer Prize in 1961, *To Kill a Mockingbird* is regarded as an excellent example of Southern regionalism.

- The California poet Robinson Jeffers wrote narrative verse which explores nineteenth-century California in much the same manner as Faulkner explores the nineteenth and early twentieth-century South. Jeffers's "The Roan Stallion," in *Selected Poems of Robinson Jeffers,* is a strong example of regionalism used to convey a universal vision.

---

that Jones enjoys a richer life, gets more attention, commands more prerogatives, or wields more authority than he. In such a case, what Smith ends up desiring is Jones's very existence; Smith becomes an unwitting double of Jones and challenges Jones for his very existence. If Smith then fails to become Jones by appropriating Jones's richer life, and so on, then Smith might instead seek a kind of revenge against Jones for being—as Smith sees it—unjustly and unbearably superior, a model whose greater amplitude seems to mock Smith's perpetually wounded dignity. Social order, with its roots in religion, is based on channeling the imitative impulse in human nature; the net gain when people follow the laws that inhibit uncontrolled imitation is a lessening of conflict and a corresponding increase in peace and happiness.

Abner Snopes is not only at odds with other people, in this sense, but he is also at odds with the very notion of social order. Abner's son Sarty thinks, as they leave town for the de Spain planta-tion (their next domicile), that "maybe he's done satisfied now; now that he has...." But Abner, wounded by the perceived superiority of everyone to himself, cannot be satisfied; he remains trapped in a cycle of rivalry of which his fire-setting is the perfect symbol. Abner's injunction to Sarty "to stick to your own blood" is really a demand, by Abner to his family, that they actively endorse his "ferocious conviction in this rightness of his own actions." Faulkner's diction is important. The word "ferocious" is related to the word "feral," or "wild." Abner is literally a wild-man, someone unassimilated and perhaps inassimilable to society, which requires a suppression of ego and individual appetite for the net good of the community. Morality is reciprocity, and Abner's only notion of reciprocity is revenge for imagined or grossly magnified slights.

Take Abner's behavior on arriving at the de Spain plantation. "I reckon I'll have a word with the man that aims to begin to-morrow owning me body

---

"Faulkner appears to have understood what philosophical anthropologists like Rene Girard and Eric Gans have understood: That human beings are mimetic (or imitative) creatures and that the problem of violence is directly related to mimesis (or imitation)."

and soul for the next eight months." Approaching the impressive manor, Sarty sees Abner bring his stiff left foot "squarely down in a pile of fresh droppings where a horse had stood in the drive and which his father could have avoided by a simple change of his stride." Abner now barges into the de Spain house, tracking manure on the rug; he frightens Mrs. de Spain and humiliates the servant. Everything in this chain of actions suggests deliberate provocation by Abner spurred by his own prior assumption that the de Spains have insulted him. But in Abner's "ferocious" psychology, the mere existence of the de Spains, with their fine house in contrast with the Snopeses' "battered stove" and "broken bed and chairs," constitutes an insult; it strikes at Abner's haunting sense of his own diminution before others. Abner has thus immediately picked a fight with Major de Spain, a conflict which he exacerbates by ruining the rug further when de Spain bids him (reasonably) to clean it up. Abner's resentment, pumped up by his own provocative misbehavior, now incites him to the usual climax, setting fire to his rival's barn.

Another kind of imitation is at work in "Barn Burning," however. This is the type of constructive imitation by which the child becomes assimilated to society. Sarty, from whose viewpoint Faulkner largely tells the story, has up until now had only his father as a primary model. In the first trial scene, however, something happens which undoubtedly affects Sarty. Mr. Harris, who has brought the charge of incendiarism against Abner, designates Sarty as one who "knows," that is to say, knows the truth about his father's

guilt. Harris wants the boy to testify. Sarty knows that his father *"aims for me to lie."* In the end, Harris will not make the boy choose between lying for his father and betraying the paternal bond by telling the truth. Sarty feels reprieved from the "abyss" that such a choice would have constituted for him. Harris has thus provided a model of concession and decency not available to Sarty in Abner. Again, at the de Spain plantation, Sarty sees the manor as an image of order, *"as big as a courthouse"* exuding a *"spell of peace."* The metaphor of the courthouse links the manor to Harris; the notion of "peace" contrasts with Abner's imposition of eternal dislocation and terror on his family. Sarty then witnesses his father's willful disruption of the manorial serenity.

When Major de Spain appears with the rug, he assumes an image which can only arouse Abner to further rancor. Sarty sees "a linen-clad man on a fine sorrel mare" with a "suffused, angry face." Considering the provocation, de Spain maintains remarkable control; but Abner, despite his wife's pleas, insists on amplifying the insult by burning the rug with lye in a sham attempt to acquiesce in the employer's direction. When de Spain lays an indemnity of twenty bushels of corn against Abner, Abner surprisingly sues de Spain to get the indemnity dismissed. The justice of the peace upholds the charge, but he does reduce the indemnity, to ten bushels. This fails to mollify Abner, of course, who now determines to execute his usual retribution. He will burn down de Spain's barn.

Sarty is acutely aware of the probable course of events and for the first time articulates his own dilemma: "corn, rug, fire; the terror and the grief, the being pulled two ways like between two teams of horses." On the one hand, there is the blood-bond between father and son. "You got to learn to stick to your own blood or you ain't going to have any blood to stick to," Abner has told Sarty. On the other hand, there is an abstract morality, the foundation of community, modeled by Harris and by the life of the de Spain plantation. But Sarty now understands that the blood-bond entails his acquiescence in his father's violence and his own submission to an authority whose demonic character he begins to recognize. The nature of that authority is suggested by his mother's pathetic cries when she divines that Abner is about to go incendiary again: "Abner! No! No! Oh, God, Oh, God. Abner!" By invoking God, Mrs. Snopes invokes the morality, the transcendental model of ideal human relations, which Abner's egomaniacal rivalry with all and sundry repeatedly and terrifically violates. Mrs. Snopes's cries also implicitly ask for deliverance from the cycle of violence.

Sarty's actions—escaping from his mother, whom Abner has charged to keep him confined to the house, running to the de Spain manor to warn the Major about his father's likely plans—do not form a perfectly calculated or transparent whole; Sarty, a ten-year-old illiterate, responds to partly assimilated intuitions about right and wrong. It seems to be the case that he has no clear intention except to thwart an act of violence, and to thwart thereby the continuous dislocation and meaninglessness of his family's wretched life. De Spain, of course, takes heed quickly and decisively, shooting Abner dead in the very moment when he sneaks into the barn with his pail of oil. This occurs "offstage." Sarty is running away from the manor, in aimless flight, and is aware only of two gunshots, at the sound of which, recognizing (one guesses) what they mean, he yells "Pap! Pap!" and then again "Father! Father!"

Exhausted on a hilltop as morning approaches, Sarty thinks with pity that his father, who had been a soldier during the Civil War, "was brave!" Faulkner obtrudes as narrator to contradict the lad: "His father had [in fact] gone to that war a private in the fine old European sense, wearing no uniform, admitting the authority of and giving fidelity to no man or army or flag, going to war as Malbrouck himself did: for booty—it meant nothing and less than nothing to him if it were enemy booty or his own." The phrase "that war" might casually be read as, simply, the Civil War, but it must be treated carefully and credited with the ambiguity that it deserves, for "that war" was only chronologically the Civil War. Faulkner's comments make it clear that Abner fought his own war, against everyone, for his own purposes; his entire life was "war," and war, as they say, is Hell. Is it coincidence that Abner's war-wound is a minie-ball lodged in his left foot? The Devil, in folklore, limps in his left (cleft) foot, and given his connection with fire there is something truly devilish about Abner Snopes.

Sarty's situation at the end of "Barn Burning" is still unenviable; but some progress has occurred which must be recognized as such. Sarty has, by an act of his own will, turned from a primitive bond (the supposed blood-bond) toward an abstract morality which, because it is not a person, tends to minimize the resentment of those who espouse it. The "slow constellations" which rotate in the sky

as Sarty watches from his hilltop symbolize the raising (however meager) of the pitiable boy's consciousness. The price of wisdom is suffering, but the price of freedom, of whatever kind, is wisdom, and this, painfully, in some tiny measure, Sarty has gained.

Source: Thomas Bertonneau, "An Overview of 'Barn Burning'," in *Short Stories for Students,* The Gale Group, 1999.

Susan S. Yunis

Yunis is professor of Languages and Literature at The College of St. Scholastica. In the following essay, she discusses Faulkner's narrative technique in "Barn Burning."

Faulkner's short story "Barn Burning" poses a problem for me as a reader in that the narrator seems in several instances more intent upon explaining and justifying Abner's barn-burning than in registering the pain his family suffers in the context of these fires. The often quoted fire-building passage provides a good illustration:

> The nights were still cool and they had a fire against it, of a rail lifted from a nearby fence and cut into lengths—a small fire, neat, niggard almost, a shrewd fire; such fires were his father's habit and custom always, even in freezing weather. Older, the boy might have remarked this and wondered why not a big one; why should not a man who had not only seen the waste and extravagance of war, but who had in his blood an inherent voracious prodigality with material not his own, have burned everything in sight? Then he might have gone a step farther and thought that that was the reason: that niggard blaze was the living fruit of nights passed during those four years in the woods hiding from all men, blue or gray, with his strings of horses (captured horses, he called them). And older still he might have divined the true reason: that the element of fire spoke to some deep mainspring of his father's being, as the element of steel or of powder spoke to other men, as the one weapon for the preservation of integrity, else breath were not worth the breathing, and hence to be regarded with respect and used with discretion.

Though this voice seems in part to articulate Sarty's viewpoint, it speaks with a peculiar degree of detachment from Sarty's sensations. That is, if I try to imagine Sarty in this scene, I see a boy whose family has been forced to leave their home, huddled by a small fire in the cool night, and who has huddled by such a small fire even on freezing nights to evade the retaliation of angry landlords. I see discomfort, anger, even despair at the repetition of this situation and at the powerlessness of the family to change it. And yet this discomfort is never spoken by the narrator. "Barn Burning" seems so clearly to

> **"**Reading the narrator's voice as the model for our response to the characters, exposes the narrator's failure to attend to many of the physical and emotional needs of the characters: the narrator is as defensive, as capable of neglect and abuse as the Snopes men are.**"**

be Sarty's story, that a narrator who focuses less on the child than on the motivation of his violent, even abusive parent seems incongruous.

Karl F. Zender explains [in *College Literature*] this incongruity as the author's effort to get us beyond Sarty's limited perspective: the narrator is modeling for the child how he should learn to regard his father. Zender writes that ''the story invites us not . . . to limit ourselves [to Sarty's perspective on his father] for it provides . . . a model not only for Sarty's development but for our performance as readers of Faulkner's fiction . . . [The story] invites us to move by stages to a condition of active, intuitive, passionately engaged reading . . . [which] means overcoming our distaste for Ab to the point where we understand anew the 'mainspring' of his character.'' Similarly, Richard C. Moreland argues [in *Faulkner and Modernism*] that the narrator urges us to read Ab's own history and potential humor better than Sarty does, adding that what Ab himself is instructing Sarty to understand is what is excluded by the structures of Southern oppositions of master, slave, white, black. Likewise, Zender reads Abner's coercion of Sarty, his insistence that Sarty participate in his vendettas against his landlords, as attempts to instruct Sarty on the ''injustice of (the) family's subjection to the quasi-slavery of turn-of-the-century tenant farming.'' Though Abner's lesson may be lost on Sarty, Zender argues that it should not be lost on us: the ''peace and dignity'' of the plantation is purchased with the sweat of blacks and tenant farmers like Abner.

I would agree with both critics that the narrator is trying to model, even control our response to Abner—to mitigate our dislike of the man, just as Abner is trying to control Sarty's response to himself. But for me, reading the narrator's voice as the model for our response to the characters, exposes the narrator's failure to attend to many of the physical and emotional needs of the characters: the narrator is as defensive, as capable of neglect and abuse as the Snopes men are. If we examine closely the context of the voice—that the narrative arises in an abusive situation as a defense—a strategy for controlling abuse, we can appreciate the similarity of the narrative voice to the abuse it defends against. If we heed too carefully the narrator's instructions on how to read Abner, we fail to hear the voices that the narrator and the men he speaks for abruptly silence.

For instance, consider the scene in which Abner deposits Sarty in his mother's grip for fear Sarty will warn de Spain of Abner's intention to burn the barn. Zender reads this action as the desperate attempt ''at personal risk, to confine his son inside an infancy in which doubts about his father's courage and fairness could not occur,'' as ''enclosing Sarty inside the embrace [as a] last urgent expression of a fatherly need, even a love, never spoken in its own form.'' Clearly Zender is following what he sees as the narrator's lead in understanding the mainspring of Abner's behavior. And the narrator, if he's not quite so sympathetic to Abner in his telling of the incident, at least allows such a reading by detaching from the pain and humiliation Sarty must feel as he is dragged by the collar across the floor of two rooms:

> Then the boy was moving, his bunched shirt and the hard, bony hand between his shoulder-blades, his toes just touching the floor, across the room and into the other one, past the sisters sitting with spread heavy thighs in the two chairs over the cold hearth, and to where his mother and aunt sat side by side on the bed. . . .
>
> ''Hold him,'' the father said.

In this instance, the narrator's silencing of Sarty's pain would correspond to a strategy frequently used by victims of abuse: a refusal to feel pain or anger or the impulse to resist, or any other response which might incur further abuse. And furthermore, Zender's reading of the incident from Abner's viewpoint corresponds to a strategy used by victims to help them predict and control abuse. For instance, if Sarty were to try to understand and control his father's behavior, he might well rationalize Abner's behavior as love (as Zender does) and figure that the one way to keep Abner's love, to control his anger, is to stay small and dependent: to do what Abner expects before he demands it. It is a strategy we see throughout the earlier parts of the story, used by Sarty and voiced by the narrator. But what is lost in the narrator's and Zender's readings of Abner, in Sarty's early attempts to read Abner, and in all of their refusals to feel Sarty's pain is the violence done to Sarty.

Most readers, I think, feel Sarty's abuse anyway, resisting the narrator's efforts to control their response to Abner. And Moreland himself acknowledges Abner's brutality in a footnote, admitting that "Ab's violence toward blacks, toward women, and toward his son Sarty is obvious throughout the story. It is not in defense of this violence but in an effort *to understand it*— the 'savage blows . . . but without heat' that I might add that Ab seems here to be passing on, in a more explicitly despotic, violent form, the naturalized, axiomatic social and economic violence he feels directed against himself" (emphasis added). But the very footnoting of their emotional experience reveals the marginalization of Abner's family's pain which the narrator's focus upon Abner entails.

This silencing of personal pain and the intentional focusing upon the experience and motivation of another are for me what the narrator speaks. It is a strategy used by all of the Snopes men in their dealings with abusive, powerful others. Looked at in this way, the narrator's voice is not discordant but articulates the strategies, if not the pain and anger, of the powerless in their attempts to control abuse.

The narrative begins in a "courtroom," as Sarty agonizes over his inability to please both groups of men who demand compliance: the Snopes men, who demand loyalty; and the Justice and his likes, who demand honesty. As he sits hungry among cheeses and tinned cans of meat whose labels he cannot read, Sarty seems sealed in his body and its fierce pull, unable to label his experience, his conflict, unable to understand its dynamics or to begin to resolve it.

Sarty feels potential relief from the weight of his body when he is asked to testify about his father: "it was as if he had swung outward at the end of a grape vine . . . and at the top of the swing had been caught in a prolonged instant of mesmerized gravity, weightless in time." Telling about his father, he senses, would give him relief. But he lacks the literary and rhetorical skills to be able to satisfy both of the audiences in the courtroom. He cannot tell "the truth" and exonerate his father at the same

time. Yet the need to control the anger of both audiences is crucial to Sarty. For a judgment against Abner means the family must move again, which provokes Abner's retaliation and his abusive treatment of his family. In addition, Sarty must control his own anger against his abusive father which, though it is not explored, we feel must exist, and probably impels him at some level to testify against this man who sacrifices the needs of his family to satisfy his own vendettas. The enormous job of using words to understand and control two sets of powerful and angry men and their demand for justice is overwhelming to the small, illiterate child. This job of using language to control anger is left to the narrator.

The narrator can do for Sarty what the young Sarty cannot: he can understand Abner's anti-social behavior, his anger, in a way Sarty as yet cannot; he can read, and therefore he can tell the truth about Abner's fires while placing him in the context of heroes respected by his audience. The narrator uses language and literature to speak in a way that appeases powerful men—but still at the expense of the abused body and its hungers. For Sarty's experience is eclipsed by narrative attention to Abner not only in the fire-building passage, but in the story as a whole. "Barn Burning" is told twenty years after the events described, and though we can infer from a brief reference to Sarty's thoughts as a thirty-year-old man that the narrator apparently knows what has happened to Sarty in this intervening period ("Later, twenty years later, he was to tell himself, 'If I had said they wanted only truth, justice, he would have hit me again'."), we get no glimpse into Sarty's life story. The mature Sarty has no present, only a past the narrative voice circles endlessly around—Sarty's telling the truth about his father.

The narrator's voice of literate understanding, this voice without a body or a life, this penetration into the feelings, motives, behaviors of powerful others, is a total erasure of self, the weightless liberation which Sarty dreams of in anticipation of telling about his father. "Barn Burning" lays bare that stories about powerful others may be an attempt both to placate the powerful and to escape personal pain. Here, both reading and writing—the construction of the meaning of an event—take place in a context of power relationships so threatening that the meaning constructed inevitably reflects the image of the powerful abusive audience. And the price of these strategies for identifying with the powerful in order to control them is emotional death—a numbing of the self to personal injuries which is symbolized in Abner's frozen leg. The narrator's storytelling is so focused upon intuiting its audience and controlling its response that the self and its injuries are momentarily forgotten.

The narrator expresses Sarty's defensive rhetorical impulse: he is able to placate both powerful audiences, remaining loyal to Abner and still telling ''the truth'' about Abner's fires. For he needn't answer right away—he has the space of the text to use as he chooses; he can withhold revealing Abner's guilt until an opportune moment. He can choose the time and method for telling about Abner's fires. When the narrator finally does admit to Abner's habitual fire building, in the fire building passage quoted above, he couches the admission in abstract language which resonates with heroic adjectives, with implicit reference to the most famous and heroic builder of fires, Prometheus. Storytelling, based as it is upon the carefully timed disclosure of events in order to manipulate audience response, is a strategy well suited to characters who feel the need to control the emotions of those around them. And Prometheus is an apt image here since, in his stealing the secrets of the control of fire, he is an archetypal symbol for the control of libidinal impulse.

We can see Abner using similar strategies to control anger, his own and that of his most powerful audience, his landlords. Abner is generally able to tolerate his landlords' insults and injuries without obvious anger because, we assume, he holds out to himself the promise of a burning barn, the promise of retribution at the time and place of his choosing, after he has secured another tenancy for himself. Not only does the promise of the fire enable Abner to control his own anger, the fires themselves enable him to control his landlord's angry response to him. The fires, set as Abner flees to a new location, control the landlord's behavior in a way other acts of vandalism might not: because of the value he places on his property, the landlord will extinguish the fire rather than pursue Abner. Abner understands his oppressors well enough to know that they won't fly off half-cocked and shoot him; they will safeguard their property first. The careful timing of Abner's fires to control his audience is voiced in the narrator's careful timing of the disclosure of those fires.

Abner's fires are both a mechanism for and a numinous symbol of his control over rage—his own and his landlords': the ''niggardly'' fires he builds for his fleeing family remind Abner to control his rage. The well controlled fire is symbolic of the passion, the energy, he must control and use to his best advantage in his war with his landlords: it is ''the one weapon for the preservation of integrity, else breath were not worth the breathing, and hence to be regarded with respect and used with discretion.'' As he understands the careful use of fire, the conservation of it, the insulation of it so that it does not spread, so his fires remind him to understand and predict anger, his own and his landlords', to keep it contained, to insulate against its spread, and to indulge it only occasionally, and at a safe distance, when he has secured another tenancy.

Sarty has strategies as well for controlling anger, his own and his father's. In fact, so skilled is Sarty at avoiding his own anger we seldom, if ever, see it; and we may suspect that he himself is unaware of it. Immediately before Abner stains the de Spains' rug, Sarty has been hoping that the peace and dignity of the house will change Abner. Abner's failure to clean his boot deflates Sarty's romantic notions about the ability of the house to change the direction of Abner's life, and yet Sarty never registers anger at Abner over the stained rug or over Abner's vengeful scraping it clean; Sarty evades his own response by worrying about Abner's anger— by trying to anticipate his father's response:

> ''Pap,'' he said. His father looked at him—the inscrutable face, the shaggy brows beneath which the gray eyes glinted coldly. . . . ''You did the best you could!'' . . . ''If he wanted it done different why didn't he wait and tell you how? He won't git no twenty bushels!'' . . . [Sarty] whisper[ed] up at the harsh, calm face beneath the weathered hat: ''He wont git no ten bushels neither. He wont get one. We'll . . .'' until his father glanced for an instant down on him, the face absolutely calm, the grizzled eyebrows tangled above the cold eyes, the voice almost pleasant, almost gentle:

> ''You think so? Well, we'll wait till October anyway.''

Sarty's job of anticipating his father's anger is complicated by Abner's self-control. Sarty is often unable to predict his father's responses because Abner is so controlled that his rage seldom shows; his face is ''absolutely calm,'' ''inscrutable.'' But Sarty's survival depends upon his ability to see beneath his father's calm exterior, to intuit what his father wants him to do: to read him. In the opening scene, in the courtroom, Sarty's attention is focused on his father: ''His father, stiff in his black Sunday coat donned not for the trial but for the moving, did not even look at him. He aims for me to lie, he thought, again with that frantic grief and despair. And I will have to do hit.'' When Sarty finally risks telling the truth about his father's fires he tells de Spain when Abner is out of earshot. The careful reading of one's audiences and the careful timing of disclosures are strategies that both Sarty and the narrator use to control angry responses.

Just as Sarty and Abner struggle to control their own emotional responses and those of their enemies, so they control any expression of feeling by the females. When Sarty is tackled by another boy outside the courtroom, his mother cries, "Does hit hurt?" yet Sarty silences her cry of pain just as he silences his own: "'Naw,' he said. 'Hit dont hurt. Lemme be'." Likewise the women express disgust with their living conditions, and for this instinctive anger they are humiliated by Abner: "'Likely hit [their house] ain't fitten for hawgs,' one of the sisters said. 'Nevertheless, fit it will and you'll hog it and like it,' his father said." Only the women express anger at having to clean the shit from de Spain's rug. And at least initially only the women express fear or guilt at Abner's fires: "the mother tugged at [Abner's] arm until he shifted the lamp to the other hand and flung her back, not savagely or viciously, just hard, into the wall, her hands flung out against the wall for balance, her mouth open and in her face the same quality of hopeless despair as had been in her voice."

In his wife and daughters and children, Abner and Sarty silence the anger, fear, despair and human sympathy which they fear would overwhelm them. The women's voices are reminders of vulnerability; the Snopes men deny these feelings in themselves, punish them in the females, and ritually display their understanding of and control over these dangerous impulses in their fires.

The narrative voice silences the emotional women just as Sarty and Abner do. Abner and Sarty let them cry, and then silence or humiliate them. So, too, the narrator describes the women as crying, their voices having the quality of "hopeless despair," but he splits off from their emotionality in a refusal to translate their grief into words ("the hysteric and indistinguishable woman-wail"). The narrator refuses to speak pain and labels that voice in others as hysterical and not worth attending to. The narrator, like Sarty, uses his telling to separate from despair, to silence it.

In the same way the narrator refuses to tell Sarty's pain: "he leaping in the red haze toward the face, feeling no blow, feeling no shock when his head struck the earth . . . feeling no blow this time either and tasting no blood." And when Abner hits

Sarty, the narrator focuses upon Abner and the way he hits, not on the way it feels to Sarty:

> His father struck him with the flat of his hand on the side of the head, hard but without heat, exactly as he had struck the two mules at the store, exactly as he would strike either of them with any stick in order to kill a horse fly, his voice still without heat or anger.

The narration is a deliberate focusing upon the abuser, not the feelings of the abused. The narrator is the voice of Sarty's evasion of pain through identification with the oppressor instead of the oppressed as a technique of survival, but also as a means of detaching from pain. The narrator is also the voice of Sarty's effort to control the response of his audiences to Abner, to soften their judgment of him: Abner's brutality is less liable to outrage an audience that is not focused upon the pain that his brutality inflicts.

There are moments when Abner loses control of his anger: around his family of course, he is less controlled, since they are powerless: they do not threaten him with retaliation. But the staining of the rug with horse shit is one moment when Abner spontaneously vents his rage at his landlord rather than at his family. Abner's momentary loss of control when he stains the rug and his vengeful scraping it clean, connect him with both the narrator and Faulkner as writer. Abner, "stiff," "black," "flat," like "something cut ruthlessly from tin" whose stiff foot "strike[s]" with "machinelike deliberation" the pale rug of the de Spains, leaving indelible "prints," suggests a typewriter whose stiff, tin-type leaves its print on a pale sheet of paper. He then "erases" the prints at the insistence of de Spain: he agrees to wash the shit from the rug. Though his act begins in angry protest against the conventions of aristocratic culture, a sort of written protest, Abner adapts, amends his message: he erases the heel mark, though he damages the rug in the process. Residual marks remain. The narrator has done the same thing. In the story itself he has erased Abner's passionate outburst against his landlord, "'I dont figure to stay in a country among people who . . .' he said something unprintable and vile." Similarly, in a letter dated July 8, 1939, six months before his completion of "Barn Burning," Faulkner, apparently at his publisher's suggestion (another type of landlord who skims a percentage from his tenant's labor?), agrees to what he calls the "whitewashing" of his just completed novel, *The Wild Palms*, by which he means the deletion of "objectionable words." One of those words is ''shit.'' In his letter Faulkner agrees to the ellipses, but demurs that ''there are a few people whom I hope will read the book, among whom the preservation of my integrity as a faithful . . . portrayer of living men and women is dear enough for me to wish not to betray it.'' Faulkner's demurrer about the ''preservation of my integrity,'' which he will later use in reference to Abner's fires (''the one weapon for the preservation of his integrity''), and the possible similarity of the look of the ellipsis (. . .) in *The Wild Palms* which replaces the word ''shit,'' to the abrasions in the rug left by Abner's rock as he scrapes off the actual shit may suggest Faulkner's identification with Abner, and the insistence of both men to leave the traces of their censored outrage. Perhaps at some level Faulkner sees himself and Abner as truth-tellers who betray their own integrity when they bend to the niceties of those upon whom they are economically dependent, when they erase the humiliating traces of their own instinctive humanity to placate their more powerful audiences. The personal cost of a voice which agrees to cauterize its feelings to control the anger of its audience is a betrayal of one's own integrity—of one's self.

Source: Susan S. Yunis, ''The Narrator of Faulkner's 'Barn Burning','' in *The Faulkner Journal,* Vol. VI, No. 2, Spring, 1991, pp. 23–31.

Karl F. Zender

Zender is a professor of English at the University of California—Davis. In the following excerpt, he provides a thematic and stylistic analysis of ''Barn Burning,'' relating the story to Faulkner's other works and to American literature in general.

Allowing us to inhabit Ab's point of view is an act of artistic courage on Faulkner's part. It is a striking example of how much of the human condition lies inside the pale of his imaginative sympathy. But allowing identification with Ab also places almost intolerable pressure on the conclusion of the story, by forcing a single signifier to serve incommensurate artistic purposes. Once we have attained to intimate knowledge of Ab's true motives, the father that Sarty ''forgets'' can never again be only an interior, imaginary, symbolic figure. He must also be Adam, flesh and blood, Ab as social and physical reality. An uneasy sense of the explosiveness of this combination of symbolism and realism, and of the need to defuse it somewhat, reveals itself in various ways in the conclusion of the story—in the off-stage

location of Ab's apparent demise, in the irresolution of the question of whether he actually dies, and (regrettably) in the narrator's censorious reminder, after Sarty affirms the truth of his father's bravery, that Ab went to war ''a private in the fine old European sense . . . giving fidelity to no man or army or flag.'' These moderating touches have an air of existing independently of the story and of intruding into it. They gloss over the story's explosive tensions to some degree, but they do not greatly alleviate our sense that the action of the story pulls against itself in a troubling way.

Faulkner's failure—or inability—to accommodate the demands of psychic growth to the realities of social existence is by no means limited to ''Barn Burning.'' It characterizes relations between parents and children in much of his fiction. One thinks, for example, of the destructiveness of the encounters between Mr. Compson and Quentin Compson, Simon McEachern and Joe Christmas, and the Old General and the Corporal—to mention only relations between fathers (or father-figures) and sons. The accuracy of these depictions as descriptions of an aspect of human experience cannot be denied. But the exclusivity of Faulkner's emphasis may trouble us. One need not be a Pollyanna to insist that the symbolic father can be, and usually is, slain without irremediable damage being done to the social relation between father and son. The widespread absence of this optimistic view from Faulkner's fiction has implications that merit attention.

If we cast our minds back over American literature in search of a precursor for Sarty Snopes, one figure comes immediately to mind—Huckleberry Finn. The resemblances are obvious: a tyrannical father who dies, an initiation—extended in the one case, brief in the other—into an awareness of American social and economic injustice, a final journey into freedom. But the differences are equally obvious. *Huckleberry Finn* is gentler and more optimistic than ''Barn Burning'' not merely because Huck, unlike Sarty, escapes responsibility for his father's death but because the final condition of freedom into which he moves has a geographical and temporal plausibility Sarty's lacks. It is true that in important ways Huck Finn remains always a child. As James Cox argues [in *Mark Twain: The Fate of Humor,* 1966], the subversive power of the novel lies in its enactment of the dream of a timeless condition of innocent, prepubescent, polymorphous pleasure. But it is also true that the ''territory'' toward which Huck ''light[s] out'' had a real existence when the novel was being written, one capable of sustaining an opposed dream of human growth and maturation. "Turn your face to the great West," Horace Greeley counseled, "and there build up a home and fortune"—or, in Greeley's more familiar phrasing, "Go west, young man, and grow up with the country."

By comparison, what space and time does Sarty move toward at the end of "Barn Burning?" The only space mentioned is the "dark woods" toward which he walks at the end of the story; the only time, the period "twenty years later" when he tells himself, "If I had said they wanted only truth, justice, he [Ab] would have hit me again." This space and time are symbolic, not real. The space, unlocatable on any map, is the dark terrain of the self through which Sarty must journey if he is to become a mature adult. The time is a moment somewhere beyond the completion of this journey. But this moment, like the space itself, connects only tenuously to any realistically construed understanding of Sarty's post-adolescent life. The truth and justice Sarty mentions can best be understood privatively, as terms without positive content, for we have no reason to believe that a truth and a justice so casually alluded to can encompass the after-trauma of inadvertent father-slaughter or the *in* justice of Sarty's family's subjection to the quasi-slavery of turn-of-the-century tenant farming. This truth, this justice, this vision of Sarty's future resembles Sarty's own naive hope that the de Spain mansion might embody a peace and dignity exempt from social and economic inequalities and from the rage that accompanies them. It intimates a successful completion for Sarty's journey into moral adulthood, but at the expense of diminishing that journey's complexity.

We risk breaking the butterfly on the wheel if we load large cultural implications onto a single short story. Nevertheless, behind "Barn Burning" looms the cultural transformation symbolized by the contrast between the story and *Huckleberry Finn*, and this transformation also looms behind literary modernism generally. The relation of modernist writers to their American heritage is, of course, ambivalent. They certainly exhibit an eagerness, in Ezra Pound's phrase, to "make it new," to break free of stultifying conventions and outworn ideologies. But they also exhibit a pervasive melancholy over the passing of an earlier, more spacious, more optimistic America. Out of this melancholy arises (to cite three examples from among many) the

> " The truth and justice Sarty mentions can best be understood privatively, as terms without positive content, for we have no reason to believe that a truth and a justice so casually alluded to can encompass the after-trauma of inadvertent father-slaughter or the <u>in</u> justice of Sarty's family's subjection to the quasi-slavery of turn-of-the-century tenant farming."

urgent depiction, in Willa Cather's *My Antonia,* of a frontier arrested in a condition of pastoral timelessness; the equally urgent account, in Ernest Hemingway's *The Sun Also Rises,* of a quest for regenerative contact with an agrarian culture; and the elegiac description, at the end of F. Scott Fitzgerald's *The Great Gatsby,* of Gatsby's dream as "already behind him, somewhere back in that vast obscurity . . . where the dark fields of the republic rolled on under the night."

Faulkner fully participates in this work of mourning and remembrance. To a far greater extent than is commonly acknowledged, he descends from Emerson and Whitman, and his fictional avatars—Quentin Compson, Isaac McCaslin, Gavin Stevens—fight desperate, even if usually unsuccessful, rear-guard actions in the service of a nineteenth-century vision of America's promise. In the second half of his career, Faulkner's allegiance to this vision manifested itself in attempts to become, as he said in a letter written in 1942, "articulate in the national voice." In a variety of willingly assumed roles— State Department Cultural Representative, university lecturer, writer of public letters—he sought to remind both his fellow citizens and a world audience of their great heritage—of what he called, in the Nobel Prize Speech, "the courage and honor and hope and pride and compassion and pity and sacrifice which have been the glory of [mankind's] past.'' And he sought as well to remind his readers and listeners of the social and ethical obligations these values entail.

This effort at recollection and reaffirmation was generous and courageous—more so, given the political tensions of the times, than is sometimes now understood. But it was also relatively ineffectual, and it is now not very convincing. This is so because the abstractions and ethical imperatives Faulkner invokes in the Nobel Prize Speech and elsewhere are as void of contact with lived experience as are the truth and justice of his comment about Sarty's future. As Richard H. King has argued [in *Southern Literary Journal*], Faulkner had a strong political impulse, but no very coherent political program or ideology, nor even any very strong belief in the usefulness of collective action. Hence his affirmations of traditional values do not arise out of a political commitment but out of the absence of one. They entail, in King's words, ''a violent wrenching away *from* necessity . . . which is only momentarily an intervention *in* history.'' They inhabit, that is, a transcendental vacancy, a timeless space outside and above, but only tenuously in contact with, the realities of mid-century American life.

As I have argued elsewhere [chapter 5 in *The Crossing of the Ways,* 1989], the emergence of Faulkner's desire to be articulate in the national voice was accompanied by a change in his attitude toward teaching. In the first half of his career—in *The Sound and the Fury* and ''Light in August'' especially—his scenes of instruction tend to be strongly colored with negative emotions. These scenes, which focus almost exclusively on parents and children (especially on fathers and sons), depict teaching as an act of violence, an imposition by force of a parental identity on the mind of a vainly resisting child. As Faulkner's career advanced, and his desire to inculcate moral and ethical values grew, he moderated this negative image of teaching, replacing it with scenes in which instruction is more-or-less freely given and received. But this shift never fully completes itself. Although in *Go Down, Moses, Intruder in the Dust,* and elsewhere Faulkner depicts positive and successful scenes of instruction, these always involve father-surrogates, never fathers. Only by moving outside the patrilineal line of descent, it seems, could Faulkner affirm the possibility of a life-sustaining transmission of values from one generation to the next. But this is a formal equivalent of the vacancy of his

transcendentalizing rhetoric. It affirms the possibility of the transmission of values from one generation to the next, but at the expense of avoiding one of the more important questions about family life in our time: how fathers may legitimately and successfully teach their sons.

''Barn Burning'' occupies a pivotal position in the career-long transformation just described. What might be termed the first half of Faulkner's contemplation of the theme of instruction reaches its culmination in the closing chapters of *Absalom, Absalom!,* with the depiction of a life-and-death struggle between brother-brother and father-son modes of teaching and learning. ''Barn Burning'' inaugurates the second half of Faulkner's contemplation of the theme. Written in 1938, it is the first of his works of fiction to admit of the possibility of identification with an adult teacher as well as with a child pupil. In depicting this possibility in a father-son relation, in fact, the story comes closer than *Go Down, Moses* or *Intruder in the Dust* to exposing some of the more important psychic issues at stake in inter-generational acts of instruction. But the story also foreshadows the problematics, and the incompleteness, of Faulkner's presentation of scenes of instruction in his later fiction. Where is narrator sympathy invested in ''Barn Burning?'' Everywhere and nowhere. It is invested in Sarty, and in Ab, but never, sadly, in the two of them together.

Source: Karl F. Zender, ''Character and Symbol in 'Barn Burning','' in *College Literature,* Vol. XVI, No. 1, 1989, pp. 48–59.

Sources

Bassett, John E. ''Faulkner in the Eighties: Crosscurrents in Criticism,'' in *College Literature,* Vol. XVI, No. 1, 1989, pp. 1-27.

Beck, Warren. ''Faulkner and the South,'' in *The Antioch Review,* No. 1, 1941, pp. 82-94.

———. ''Faulkner's Style,'' in *American Prefaces,* Vol. VI, No. 3, Spring, 1941, pp. 195-211.

Boynton, Percy H. ''Retrospective South,'' in *America in Contemporary Fiction,* Chicago: University of Chicago Press, 1940, pp. 103-12.

Carruthers, James B. *William Faulkner's Short Stories,* Ann Arbor, MI: UMI Research Press, 1985, pp. 61-7.

Kazin, Alfred. ''Faulkner: The Rhetoric and the Agony,'' in *The Virginia Quarterly Review,* Vol. 18, Summer, 1942, pp. 389-402.

Lisca, Peter. "The Hamlet: Genesis and Revisions," in *Faulkner Studies,* Vol. 3, No. 4, 1954, pp. 5-13.

Volpe, Edmund. "'Barn Burning': A Definition of Evil," in *Faulkner: The Unappeased Imagination: A Collection of Critical Essays,* edited by Glenn O. Carey, New York: Whiston Publishing Company, 1980, pp. 75-82.

Further Reading

Beach, Joseph Warren. "William Faulkner, Virtuoso," in *American Fiction, 1920-1940,* New York: Macmillan, 1941, pp. 147-69.

    Beach devotes his attention to Faulkner's style; this chapter is a perceptive early attempt to deal with Faulkner's prose innovations.

Brooks, Cleanth. *William Faulkner, First Encounters,* New Haven, Conn.: Yale University Press, 1983, pp. 16-19, 97-101.

    From the perspective of decades of familiarity with his subject, Brooks undertakes a reasoned and objective assessment of Faulkner; in the sections on "Barn Burning," Brooks is especially sensitive to the moral nuances of the tale.

Geismar, Maxwell. "William Faulkner: The Negro and the Female," in *Writers in Crisis (The American Novel: 1925-1940),* London: Secker and Warburg, 1947, pp. 123-83.

    Geismar offers a full discussion of the roles played by blacks and women in Faulkner's fiction; the critic deals with the importance of outsiders and pariahs in Faulkner's vision of things.

O'Donnell, George Marion. "Faulkner's Mythology," in *The Kenyon Review,* Vol. I, No. 3, Summer, 1939, pp. 285-99.

    O'Donnell addresses the mythic structure of Faulkner's fiction, his building-up of a purely fictitious world complete with its own distinctive geography and traditions; the critic also examines the archetypal nature of this world and its relation to myth in the tragic sense.

Big Blonde

Dorothy Parker

1929

Author, critic, and celebrated wit Dorothy Parker first published ''Big Blonde'' in a popular magazine in 1929, at the end of the decade with which she is closely associated. The story presents a sad and biting view of a woman's life in the 1920s, an era often considered both fun and liberating for women. ''Big Blonde'' received a warm critical and popular reception and was honored as the best short story of the year in the prestigious O. Henry competition for 1929. A year later it appeared in a collection of stories by Parker entitled *Laments for the Living,* and has since been reprinted in many anthologies and readers. ''Big Blonde'' is considered Parker's most significant literary accomplishment and also her most autobiographical piece of writing. For this reason, it has continued to command the fascination and respect of readers. The story is admired for its unconventional narrative structure and its controlled tone.

In Mrs. Morse, the passive, aging ''big blonde'' to whom the title refers, Parker offers readers a protagonist who is both tragic and pathetic. There are several interesting links between the events in the story and those of Parker's life. Both Parker and her fictional counterpart had brief, disillusioning marriages and a string of unsatisfying love affairs, and both attempted suicide. Parker does not depict Mrs. Morse sentimentally or even completely sympathetically, however; rather, she uses her character to make a cutting critique of gender dynamics and the subtle psychological forms that oppression can take in a supposedly modern and liberated environment. Mrs. Morse's lack of insight and general ineffectuality may also reflect Parker's famous self-deprecation.

Author Biography

Parker was born Dorothy Rothschild on August 22, 1893, in West End, New Jersey, to a Jewish garment manufacturer and his Baptist wife. Though she was privileged with material comforts, she was shown little affection as a child. Her mother died when she was an infant and her father was strict and remote. She received an excellent high school education at a prestigious "finishing school," but at the time it was not considered proper for a girl to go to college. Her father died shortly after her graduation and she moved to a boarding house in Manhattan—a decidedly improper decision. Here she made her first friendships in literary circles. Within five years she had published her first poem and was writing fashion items for *Vogue* magazine. Soon afterward she moved up to the post of theater critic at *Vanity Fair.*

In the 1920s Parker was closely associated with a clique of New York writers and journalists, famous for their biting wits, known as the Algonquin Round Table for the fashionable Manhattan hotel where they regularly ate lunch. Parker was the only woman in the inner circle of the Round Table, which she shared with Robert Benchley, Franklin P. Adams, Robert Sherwood, Harold Ross, and others. She was reportedly quiet and demure in demeanor, but with a rapier-like wit that was second to none. She is famous for quips such as "You can lead a horticulture but you can't make her think" and "Men seldom make passes at girls who wear glasses," but she also often made jokes at her own expense.

She was married briefly during this period to a bland if charming alcoholic named Eddie Parker and was referred to as Mrs. Parker from her early twenties. They married shortly before Eddie went off to fight in World War I, and the marriage ended for practical purposes in 1922, though they did not divorce legally until 1928. Parker had a string of affairs, most notable that with Charles McArthur. He was a philanderer who broke her heart and left her pregnant. Parker had an illegal abortion and, not long after, made her first attempt at suicide; she was to make two more attempts, both unsuccessful. Despite her emotional vulnerability, Parker main-

tained a facade of toughness through verbal cleverness and black humor.

Parker struggled with alcoholism for much of her life. She dressed stylishly and spent lavishly, despite a meager income. In the late 1920s she enjoyed literary success with *Enough Rope,* a book of poetry, and "Big Blonde." Much of Parker's writing concerns unhappy relationships between modern men and women. By the end of the decade the Algonquin group was falling apart, and Parker left for Europe. She went on to a successful career as a Hollywood screenwriter, and also continued to write stories, poetry, and reviews. Parker married two more times, both to the same man, Alan Campbell, and expended much energy supporting the Civil Rights Movement before dying in 1967.

Plot Summary

The story opens with a description of the main character, Hazel Morse. She is defined in terms of her appearance, men's desire for her, and her vanity. A brief and vague description of her early adulthood follows: Her mother had died when she was in her twenties and she had taken a job as a model. During this period she worked to be popular, especially with men. This entailed going out, being fun, and being a "good sport."

She meets Herbie Morse when she is nearly thirty and marries him six weeks later. Herbie is a dapper man and a heavy drinker. During the first months of the marriage she is happy. She begins to realize how tired she had grown of being the sort of woman who was popular with men. She is relieved that she no longer has to be so much fun, and she takes to crying frequently. At first her husband is solicitous of her when she is in her frequent melancholy moods, but before long he objects to her "crabbing" and begins to go out without her.

Mrs. Morse decides to start going out again, and soon she begins to drink, something she had never done in her single days. While sometimes this helps temporarily, the couple fights more and more. Herbie often threatens to leave her and on one occasion resorts to abuse, giving her a black eye. Mrs. Morse continues to hope that things will work out in their marriage and starts to drink alone at home. In Herbie's frequent absence, Mrs. Morse takes up a friendship with a woman across the hall, Mrs. Martin, who drinks with her during the day. At

Dorothy Parker

night Mrs. Martin entertains an admirer, Joe, and several of his friends. Mrs. Morse enjoys the attention of these men. One of them, a married man named Ed, pays Mrs. Morse particular attention. Ed starts to assert his ''proprietorship,'' kissing her on the mouth in greeting.

One day after a long drinking bout, Herbie comes home and tells his wife that he is leaving her. They have a drink together and he makes a toast—''Here's mud in your eye''—before he leaves. Mrs. Morse drinks heavily at Mrs. Martin's that night and tells Ed that Herbie has left her. That night Ed takes Mrs. Morse back to her apartment and stays the night. She becomes Ed's mistress, and he gives her an allowance. Ed soon suggests that she move near the train station, to make it more convenient for him to see her when he is in town. Mrs. Morse drinks steadily. When she doesn't drink enough, she feels melancholy.

Ed takes Mrs. Morse to a bar called Jimmy's and she becomes friendly with a group of women there. These women are married but either do not live with their spouses, or are divorced. When they run out of money, ''a new donor'' appears among the men who frequent the bar. Mrs. Morse doesn't worry about money because Ed is doing well financially. She still feels melancholy, however. Ed and her new acquaintances encourage her to drink in order to act happy.

After three years together, Ed moves to Florida, leaving Mrs. Morse with some money for living expenses. She becomes the mistress of a series of men, all about whom she feels fairly neutral. Mrs. Morse is tired and depressed much of the time. She drinks heavily, but drinking no longer offers the solace it once had. She begins to think about killing herself. One night, at Jimmy's, Mrs. Morse has a conversation with a woman there, who tells her about a sleeping pill called veronal. Mrs. Morse finds out that veronal is powerful and easy to buy in New Jersey. The next morning she goes to two different drug stores there, buying a vial of sleeping pills at each. She puts them in her drawer and they make her feel happy.

At this time Mrs. Morse is seeing a man named Art. She makes an effort to be gay around him and he considers her ''the best sport in the world.'' But one night she becomes very depressed on her way to meet him. She drinks heavily to try to get in a better mood, but cannot. Art is angry with her and tells her to cheer up by their next date. She returns home and takes both vials of veronal, washing them down with the toast, ''Here's mud in your eye.''

The next day Mrs. Morse's maid, Nettie, comes to clean the house and discovers her unconscious body. She is frightened and elicits the help of the elevator attendant. Together they find a doctor who lives in the building. He is drinking with a ''dark girl'' and is unhappy to be disturbed. He comes to examine Mrs. Morse and asks Nettie what she had been drinking. Nettie discovers the veronal vials in the bathroom and the doctor declares that Mrs. Morse is cowardly and that they will have to pump her stomach, but that she will not die.

Two days later Mrs. Morse awakens and starts to cry. Nettie, who has been caring for her, asks her why she had taken the pills and tells her how much trouble she has been. Mrs. Morse asks Nettie if she has ever felt like committing suicide. Nettie declares that she never has and tells Mrs. Morse to cheer up. She gives Mrs. Morse a postcard from Art, which also says to cheer up. Mrs. Morse feels miserable and asks Nettie for a drink. Nettie hesitates until Mrs. Morse tells her that she can have one too. Mrs. Morse toasts, ''Here's mud in your eye,'' and Nettie encourages her for acting cheerful. ''Sure,'' Mrs. Morse responds.

Characters

Art

Art is the last in the string of boyfriends that Mrs. Morse has over the course of the story. He is "short and fat and exacting and hard on her patience when he was drunk." Other than this, there is little to distinguish him from Charley, Sydney, Billy, and Fred—other men Mrs. Morse has had sexual relationships with and accepts money from but cares for little. She becomes involved with Art about the time she starts to think about suicide. Like all of the others, Art enjoys Mrs. Morse's company only when she is cheerful. She finds it restful when he is out of town on business. After her suicide attempt, Nettie, her maid, gives her a "pretty postcard" from Art that again implores her to "cheer up." This has the opposite effect of filling Mrs. Morse with crushing despair. He represents the repressive and monotonous future of trying to act happy in order to please her interchangeable male companions.

Doctor

The young doctor who lives in Mrs. Morse's apartment building is summoned when Nettie finds Mrs. Morse unconscious in her room. He is angry at being interrupted because he is in the midst of a vaguely sexual encounter with a "dark girl," trying to unwind after a "hard day." Like the other men in the story, he uses women for pleasure and entertainment while remaining oblivious to their pain. He examines Mrs. Morse impatiently and roughly. When he finds out that Mrs. Morse has taken sedatives to attempt suicide he is unsympathetic, regarding it as a nuisance. "Rotten yellow trick, that's what a thing like that is. Now we'll have to pump her out, and all that stuff," he says.

Ed

Mrs. Morse meets Ed playing poker at her neighbor Mrs. Martin's apartment during the period when her marriage to Herbie is dissolving. He is one of "The Boys" with whom Mrs. Martin socializes. He is a married man with a business in Utica, but he comes to New York frequently on business. He soon adopts a proprietary attitude toward Mrs. Morse, sitting next to her and lending her money during poker games, and eventually squeezing her knee and kissing her on the mouth. When Herbie leaves her, Ed immediately steps in, supporting her financially in exchange for her sexual compliance. As Ed's mistress, Mrs. Morse gives up the facade of

Media Adaptations

- In 1995 "Big Blonde" was performed by Elaine Stritch on a Penguin audiocassette entitled *Dorothy Parker: Selected Stories.*

domestic married life and moves into a flat near the train station for his convenience. Like all of the other men in her life, Ed gets angry with her when she is not cheerful and lighthearted. However, Ed stands out from Mrs. Morse's other boyfriends because he appears to be genuinely attached to her, despite the fact that she feels little for him.

Elevator attendant

The elevator attendant comes to Nettie's aid when she discovers Mrs. Morse's unconscious body after her suicide attempt. He pokes at her "so lustily that he left marks in the soft flesh," and initiates in Nettie a feeling of excitement about the drama of the event. Like other men in the story he approaches Mrs. Morse as an object, but in this case there is a different power dynamic.

Joe

Joe is one of "The Boys" who Mrs. Martin entertains at her poker games. He is euphemistically referred to as Mrs. Martin's "admirer," but the clear implication is that he is her lover. Ed is one of his friends and Joe's relationship with Mrs. Martin foreshadows that between Ed and Mrs. Morse.

Mrs. Martin

Mrs. Martin moves into the apartment across the hall from Mrs. Morse during the time when Mrs. Morse's marriage is suffering and she is beginning to drink a great deal. Mrs. Martin and Mrs. Morse drink together during the day, and at night she holds poker games, which Mrs. Morse attends. Mrs. Martin initiates Mrs. Morse into the way of life she will

A flapper defying prohibition at a speakeasy in the 1920s.

take up after Herbie leaves her and serves as a model for the type of woman Mrs. Morse is becoming. Mrs. Martin is "a great blonde woman of forty, a promise in looks of what Mrs. Morse was to be." She is apparently married, but the only visible man in her life is her lover Joe. "Husbands, as such, played but shadowy parts in Mrs. Martin's circle."

Mrs. Florence Miller

Mrs. Florence Miller is one of the women who Mrs. Morse meets at Jimmy's, the speakeasy that she and Ed frequent. Like all of the people Mrs. Morse associates with there, she is not characterized as an individual, but a type. She, like Mrs. Vera Riley and Mrs. Lilian Block, and like Mrs. Morse herself, is a middle-aged woman who survives by taking long-term lovers, yet maintains the facade of respectability through using her married name. Mrs. Florence Miller is distinguished from the others because she tells Mrs. Morse about veronal, the sleeping pill she later uses to try to commit suicide. Another parallel between Mrs. Morse and Mrs. Florence Miller exists because Mrs. Morse notices that when Mrs. Florence Miller cries, men try to comfort her. Both women live a similar lifestyle and find that it brings then despair, but they are only able to form the most superficial social connection with one another.

Hazel Morse

Hazel Morse is the protagonist of the story, which narrates several decades of her life. Though she is not married at the story's opening and divorces before its halfway point, she is referred to throughout as Mrs. Morse. This suggests not so much that she is defined by her husband, who exerts no more particular influence on her than any other man, but that she is defined by the social roles available to her as a woman. She relies on the status of a married woman to superficially mask her position as a "kept woman" or mistress, and this role occupies all of her energy and imagination.

The events of Mrs. Morse's life are described with little sense of forward momentum, even as she experiences tumultuous events such as marriage, divorce, and a suicide attempt. Most of the events that take place are described in vague and general terms, suggesting that this is how Mrs. Morse experiences them and reinforcing her characterization as passive. There is a deep rift between Mrs. Morse's external appearance and her internal experience. She is relentlessly defined and rewarded by men for being fun, easygoing, and cheerful, but she finds life deeply sad. She struggles throughout the story to contain her despair until the point when she attempts to commit suicide. Mrs. Morse is pathetic in her ineffectuality. Even the gesture of suicide is not enough to allow her to escape from the oppressive expectations of others. When she recovers from the attempt she is barraged with still more demands that she cheer up, ending the story on a bleak and tragic note.

Herbie Morse

Herbie Morse is Hazel Morse's husband. He is a hard drinker and a charmer. Mrs. Morse had had "a couple thousand evenings of being a good sport" when she met him and she was nearly thirty, so she was eager to get married and make a change. For Mrs. Morse marriage is a welcomed alternative to the life she had known. But Herbie's expectations of married life are different. He apparently was attracted to her for the same reasons other men were—because she was fun and indulgent of his drinking and passive in the face of his desires. When Mrs. Morse—at last "wedded and relaxed"—begins to cry and wants to stay home, Herbie soon becomes impatient with her. In an attempt to save their relationship she begins to drink with him, but to no avail. Despite the fact that the institution of marriage appears superficially to have little in common with the more informal social, sexual, and financial relationships Mrs. Morse has later, Herbie sees her and treats her in a way that is strikingly similar to the way her later lovers do.

Nettie

Nettie is the black maid whom Ed hires to clean for Mrs. Morse when she gives up her former domestic life and moves to an apartment near the train station. She is not named until the final section of the story when she becomes pivotal to the plot. Nettie comes in to clean and discovers Mrs. Morse's unconscious body. It is Nettie who summons help and she who tends to Mrs. Morse in her recovery. While Nettie saves Mrs. Morse on a literal level, her role is more ambiguous when considered symbolically. Mrs. Morse looks to Nettie as someone who might understand her suffering, and reaches out to her by asking if she ever thinks of committing suicide. Nettie declines and echoes the words of so many of Mrs. Morse's male companions, telling her to cheer up. The story ends with Mrs. Morse toasting Nettie, whom she has bribed with a drink in order to get her to pour her one, with the false cheer of the refrain "Here's mud in your eye."

Themes

Beauty

The title of the story identifies Mrs. Morse in terms of her physical appearance and highlights the significance of this issue. The narrator in no place describes her as beautiful. To the contrary, many descriptions of her body, such as her "flabby white arms splattered with pale tan spots," are negative. However, she does meet a certain standard of attractiveness. When she was in her twenties she worked as a model. "It was still the day of the big woman, and she was then prettily colored and erect and high-breasted." This suggests that she once conformed to a certain ideal of feminine beauty, an ideal that changed as she grew older.

Mrs. Morse's physical attractiveness defines her as a type as opposed to an individual. People, especially men, see her and form expectations of her personality based on her appearance, especially her blonde hair. In the first paragraph she is described as "a large, fair woman of the type that incites some men when they use the word 'blonde' to click their tongues and wag their heads roguishly." Later in the story it is mentioned that she uses peroxide (in "inexpert dabbings") to lighten her hair. Though men view her as attractive, and thus valuable, because she is a "blonde," and though she is emotionally and financially dependent on being seen this way, it does not accurately reflect her true identity.

Sex and Sex Roles

Mrs. Morse's blondeness represents a specific idea of femininity and also has an implication of sexuality. She seems to understand implicitly that her worth as a person and her economic well-being are dependent on fulfilling men's ideas of what a woman is or should be. While she seems to do very little with her time, her life is occupied with the attempt to meet expectations about the female sex role and, relatedly, of feminine sexuality. She exhausts herself trying to live out men's unrealistic ideas of her as a blonde, a popular girl, and a "good sport."

When she works as a model she is relatively independent, though she still reflects social ideals of womanly beauty through her job and behaves in ways that make her popular with men. Being a "good sport" has sexual connotations, suggesting that she will go along with what men want to do, sexually and otherwise. After she marries, she becomes absorbed in living out a preconceived notion of domestic life, but her husband still wants her to go out, something that she finds harder and harder to

Topics for Further Study

- None of the characters in the story seems to understand why Mrs. Morse is so sad. Contemporary psychology and medicine might explain her sadness as related to the diseases of alcoholism and depression. Learn as much as you can about the causes and symptoms of alcoholism or depression and then try to apply this knowledge to the story. Does thinking of her as having an illness help you to understand Mrs. Morse better?

- Another approach to the question of why Mrs. Morse is so sad is to consider the relationships between men and women in the story. List some ways that Mrs. Morse is powerful and some ways that the different men in the story are powerful. What can you conclude about the power dynamic between the sexes as Parker describes it? Does this help you better understand Mrs. Morse's despair?

- As the story's title makes clear, Mrs. Morse is defined in terms of her physical appearance. What are some of the personal and social qualities attributed to a "big blonde" in the story? Does this role or type still exist today? If not, what are some other labels used to define people in terms of their appearance? Can you draw some general conclusions about how ideas of physical attractiveness are used to categorize people?

- Research the social roles of women in the 1920s. How are they similar to those for today's women? How are they different? Do you think that women like Mrs. Morse still exist today? How much of Mrs. Morse's plight do you think should be attributed to her personal weaknesses and how much should be attributed to social conditions?

---

do. When he leaves her, she is not only emotionally but also financially vulnerable. Ed steps in to assume the masculine role and protect her in exchange for her cheerful company and her sexual compliance. After Ed, she fulfills the same role for a series of different men, all of whom enjoy her company only when she acts the part of a woman who exists only for their pleasure and recreation.

Passivity

One of the most significant aspects of the feminine sex role that destroys Mrs. Morse is her passivity. The repeated term "good sport" implies giving in to the wishes of others and effacing her own will. She is driven to drink because it helps her feel numb, allowing her to more easily live out the role expected of her. She is financially dependent on a string of men but, after Herbie, she feels very little affection for any of them. She has no desire for any of the men she sees, despite the fact that she survives by means of their desire for her. As she gets older, her only desires are passive ones—sleep,

drunken oblivion and, eventually, death. Nevertheless, she attempts to the end to comply with the demands of those around her that she act happy and cheerful, despite her deep sadness. Her suicide attempt is her only active effort to assert who she is over and against the wishes of those around her.

Identity and Alienation

Mrs. Morse is a woman whose identity is determined almost completely by the expectations of those around her and, more significantly, by the cultural codes of femininity that shape such expectations. It is through her sadness that her alienation is most apparent. The role that she is expected and attempts to fulfill is incompatible with the feelings of exhaustion and despair she persistently experiences. She cannot act or assert her identity in any way other than acting blue, which inevitably evokes negative and even punitive responses from those who want to see her as a fun, easygoing, passive "blonde." No one seems able to recognize the division between her public persona, created in order to secure approval and economic security from men, and her inner self.

Style

Setting

"Big Blonde" is set in New York City during the 1920s. The story reflects certain conflicts in this moment in cultural history, particularly those concerning sex roles and sexual mores. The 1920s were an era of growing legal rights for women and loosening strictures against sexuality. The story examines, however, how these changes may not benefit a woman who thinks of her identity and her self-worth in terms of fulfilling men's desires. Relaxed social strictures against divorce, drinking, socializing, and sex lead to Mrs. Morse's entrapment and despair rather than her liberation. The story does not include very much concrete or detailed description of physical settings, contributing to an atmosphere of haziness, malaise, and passivity that stands in contrast to the idea of 1920s New York as vital and stimulating. Though the world in which she lives is the dynamic one of the "roaring twenties," composed of poker games and nights out on the town, Mrs. Morse remains inert.

Narration

The story is told through omniscient third person narration. This means that a narrator who is not a character in the story describes Mrs. Morse's life, and that this narrator has access to her inner thoughts and feelings. This form of narration is critical to the story, since how Mrs. Morse appears to those around her is so very different from how the omniscient narrator shows her to be internally. Through this gap or difference, the third person omniscient narration creates the effect of alienation, which is a crucial part of Mrs. Morse's characterization.

While a view of Mrs. Morse's inner thoughts helps to create empathy for the character, the narration also allows for some distance from her through the use of irony. Irony is created through the difference between what readers know and what characters know. In this case, the narration reveals Mrs. Morse's associates to lack insight about her troubles

and despair, while readers see them clearly. But the narration also allows readers more knowledge about Mrs. Morse's predicament than she has herself. The narrator characterizes Mrs. Morse as limited and blind: "She never pondered if she might not be better occupied doing something else. Her ideas, or better, her acceptances, ran right along with those of the other substantially built blondes in whom she had found her friends." While she is completely absorbed in her role, and sees it as inevitable that she live out the fate of a "big blonde," the narration allows readers to see Mrs. Morse as a socially constructed type who is entrapped in the way of thinking that defines her. Thus the reader sympathizes with Mrs. Morse, but pities her more than identifying with her.

Symbolism

Several subtle kinds of symbolism are at work in "Big Blonde." Naming is one form of symbolism. Hazel Morse is entrapped in social codes of gender and sexuality, and her last name, Morse, suggests codes. It is significant that she gets her name from her husband, because it is men in the story who enforce the codes that define what a "big blonde" is. Her maiden name is never mentioned, and she is referred to throughout as Mrs. Morse, despite the fact that her marriage is brief. Mrs. Morse's first name, Hazel, is also symbolic: her actions, impressions, and memories are all "hazy." Alcohol makes her life bearable and also imposes a kind of blurring associated with her given name. The two parts of her name suggest a divide in Hazel Morse between roles and codes, which are definite, and experiences and feelings, which are hazy.

The use of slang and colloquial language also creates a form of symbolism. Several slang terms and phrases are repeated throughout the story. Mrs. Morse tries continually to be a "good sport"; she is caught up in a game, with certain rules of behavior. Much of her despair is brought on by the unspoken rules of this game. The term "good sport," used casually in Mrs. Morse's milieu, has several implications, including loose morality, sexual permissiveness, and compliance to the wishes of others. Whenever she doesn't fulfill her role of cheerful feminine passivity, she is afraid of being a bad sport. The fact that the term is casual and playful suggests just how subtle Mrs. Morse's entrapment is. More poignant still is the repetition of the toast, ''Here's mud in your eye.'' The toast is ironic on several levels. A toast by nature implies celebration and good cheer, while wishing mud in one's eye is, on a literal level, suggestive of humiliation and blindness. Mrs. Morse makes this toast three times, each in a situation of despair covered over with the facade of good cheer.

Historical Context

Women's Rights

In 1920 the 19th Amendment to the Constitution passed, giving women the right to vote for the first time. This legal change for the most part ended the first wave of American feminism, which was based on the long, politically organized struggle for Suffrage. It ushered in a decade that brought about many more subtle changes in cultural attitudes relating to sex and gender. Having gained the legal landmark of the right to vote, women became less politically oriented and made more changes in the social arena. They demanded that the Victorian strictures of dress and behavior of their mothers' generation be loosened. Men and women mixed freely socially, and sexual banter and premarital sex became far more tolerated. Women drank, smoked, and drove. They entered the workforce in greater numbers than ever before, with a smaller proportion of these working in traditional domestic jobs. The 1920s are sometimes considered an era dominated by women, as men returned from World War I bitter and disillusioned, while the image of women was young, flamboyant, energetic, and hopeful.

Beauty and Femininity in the 1920s

An indication of these changes in women's status was the new standard of beauty and fashion of the 1920s. In the 1910s the ''Gibson Girl'' represented the feminine ideal. She had long hair and a voluptuous hourglass figure. She wore floor length skirts and had the demure, wholesome, modest manner appropriate to a wife and mother. In the 1920s, the model of style and beauty was the ''flapper.'' She bobbed her hair to her chin, bound her breasts, and wore straight dresses to conceal her waistline for a childish or boyish effect. But she also wore make-up, flaunting her feminine artifice. In the 1920s women everywhere started wearing much simpler, scantier underwear and skirts to the knee, a length that would have been considered outrageous or even obscene only a decade earlier. Along with these changes in fashion came changes in conduct. The looser, simpler clothes allowed women to participate in athletic activities and to be more comfortable and at ease when out in public. The young American woman of the 1920s was celebrated for her youthful flamboyance, her daring, and her knowing demeanor. These idealized qualities represented a precipitous change in standards of femininity.

Prohibition

The ''roaring twenties'' were famous for after-hours jazz clubs and indiscriminate drinking. This was also a period, however, when the sale of alcohol was legally prohibited nationwide. Prohibition began in 1920 after ratification of the 18th Amendment. Some of the same women's political organizations that were behind the 19th Amendment helped pass Prohibition. Prohibition was controversial and difficult to enforce. Despite the fact that alcohol consumption was reduced nationwide, the permissive social climate of the decade made it easy and fashionable for many to keep on drinking. Bootlegging, or the illegal trade of alcohol, was common all over the country, and speakeasies, where one could buy hard liquor illegally, replaced neighborhood bars and saloons. Women, who had been a political force behind Prohibition a decade earlier, began to go out and drink alongside their husbands. Because hard alcohol was more profitable, it became much more popular than before, in most cases replacing wine and beer. Prohibition was not repealed until 1933.

Critical Overview

From the time she was a struggling young writer and a member of the high-profile Algonquin literary clique, Dorothy Parker's reputation as a serious author has been overshadowed by her fame as a public figure and a wit. ''Big Blonde'' is the achievement that earned Parker her greatest literary respect and it remains a staple of anthologies and readers. Even this most famous of Parker's stories, however, is less well-known than some of her frequently cited witticisms, such as ''Men seldom make passes at women in glasses.'' Since ''Big Blonde'' is the

Compare & Contrast

- **1920s:** Forty-seven percent of American college students are female, signaling gender parity in higher education for the first time. Eight million American women are employed, a far higher number than ever before. Of these, 1.9 million are married. Architects design middle-class houses for families who use modern appliances instead of servants. Thirty percent of bread is baked at home, down from 70% at the turn of the century.

  1990s: Most working- and middle-class families need two incomes to meet their costs, and the majority of women are employed. Women are prominent in most professions. In 1990, however, women make only 67 cents for every dollar earned by a man in an equivalent position, up from 59 cents in the 1970s. Studies show that even women who work full-time spend significantly more time on housework and childcare than do their husbands.

- **1920s:** Sigmund Freud's psychological theories—drawing heavily upon early childhood sex roles and sexual desire—are in vogue among sophisticated urbanites, and his method of therapy, called psychoanalysis or the "talking cure," is the preferred treatment for depression. Depression is far more common among women than men.

  1990s: Freud's theories have been largely discredited. Psycho-pharmaceuticals, based on brain chemistry, are the new wave in the treatment of depression and other psychological disorders. Far more people than ever before are diagnosed and treated. Approximately twice as many women as men suffer from clinical depression.

- **1920s:** Silent film stars Clara Bow, a saucy flapper, and Theda Bara, a femme fatale, are icons of female desirability. In 1927 hemlines rise to just below the knee.

  1990s: Rail thin supermodel Kate Moss ushers in the "waif" look, ending an era of athletic, muscularly sculpted female ideals. Women wear skirts anywhere from ankle-length to mid-thigh mini.

- **1920s:** Reproductive rights activist Margaret Sanger organizes the first conference on birth control in the United States. Contraceptive diaphragms are manufactured in the United States for the first time. Abortion is illegal.

  1990s: Forty-nine percent of all American women between 18 and 24 use the birth control pill, and almost as high a proportion of women in the 25-29 and 30-34 age brackets take the pill as well. Surgical abortion is legal but hotly debated. The manufacture of RU-486, an abortifacient medication, is blocked in the United States.

---

most autobiographical of Parker's stories, criticism has tended to focus on parallels to Parker's life, rather than the story's craft.

Parker has been credited with breaking the boundaries that circumscribed earlier generations of women writers in terms of both style and subject matter. Biographer Marion Meade, in *Dorothy Parker: What Fresh Hell is This?*, identified the beginning of Parker's literary reputation with the *Vanity Fair* drama criticism column Parker began to write at age 24. "What makes that particular column so interesting is its rejection of the prevailing standards for female writing and thinking," wrote Meade. "She had chosen to present herself not so much as a bad girl but as a bad boy, a firecracker who was aggressively proud of being tough." Parker used a similar approach in her first book of poetry, *Enough Rope* (1927), which flouted the conventions of the gentle lady poet and faced modern love head on, or, in the words of a *New York Herald Tribune* critic quoted by Meade, "whiskey-straight." The collection was a bestseller and a critical success.

Despite her success as a poet, Parker saw fiction as the true benchmark of literary credibility.

She wrote "Big Blonde" in 1928 and published it in *The Bookman* in 1929. Since Parker was friends with many of the arbiters of literary opinion, the story's unanimous praise must be taken with a grain of salt. For example, Meade reported that Parker's good friend Franklin P. Adams described "Big Blonde" as "the best story I have read in so long a time that I cannot say," in *The Conning Tower*. The story cemented Parker's literary reputation, garnering her even more respect when the prestigious O. Henry competition named it the best short story of 1929. In 1930, having failed to fulfill a contract for a novel, Parker published a collection of short stories called *Laments for the Living* in which "Big Blonde" served as the centerpiece. According to Meade, the collection was a popular success, but the stories other than "Big Blonde" were assessed by some critics as "slight." Parker herself considered her literary career a failure, in part due to her inability to complete a novel.

In the following decades, critics often described Parker's writing, including "Big Blonde," as summing up the ethos of the 1920s. "Mrs. Parker strips our society down to its festering bones, rips aside the sheltering curtains of the cruel and respectable. . . . [She] has purity and indignation and a terrible, almost painful warmth, so that tragedy underlies the acid," wrote Ruth McKenny in *The Saturday Review of Literature* in 1939. While some critics used this same line of argument to suggest that Parker's writing did not meet the criteria of timelessness that makes great literature, W. Somerset Maugham came to her defense in his 1944 introduction to her writings, using "Big Blonde" as an example. He complimented the story's formal unity, writing that it "has all the earmarks of a masterpiece." Maugham continued: "Perhaps what gives her writing its particular tang is her gift for seeing something to laugh at in the bitterest tragedies of the human animal. It is a devastating truth that she has discovered, and a salutary one. . . ."

There has been relatively little critical attention paid to Parker's writings more recently, though she continues to hold fascination for biographers as a symbol of the 1920s. Her status as a major writer remains up for grabs. A 1995 *Publisher's Weekly* review of Parker's *Complete Stories* criticizes her work for being too homogeneous and describes her stories as "tend[ing] to float to the shallow end of the literary pool." "Big Blonde," however, is often singled out as surpassing her other achievements.

Criticism

Sarah Madsen Hardy

Madsen Hardy has a doctorate in English literature and is a freelance writer and editor. In the following essay, she discusses the meanings of work, recreation, and freedom in "Big Blonde."

For much of the span of the story's narration, Mrs. Morse is a "kept woman"—the mistress to a series of married men. Her role in the men's lives is to entertain them and to comply with their sexual desires, in exchange for which they offer her financial support. According to this arrangement, she doesn't need to hold a job or even to clean her own apartment. Her only obligation is to have fun and be fun. She goes out at night to drink and socialize with various male companions and appears to do very little else. Yet one of Mrs. Morse's complaints—one serious enough to drive her to attempt suicide—is that she is exhausted. In this essay I would like to consider the causes for Mrs. Morse's exhausted despair by exploring the meanings of work and leisure that Parker creates through her narrative and imagery. Thinking about Mrs. Morse's womanly role as a kind of work brings into focus Parker's critique of gender dynamics in the story.

Mrs. Morse's "job" as a pleasing woman and a good sport reflects the cultural and historical contexts of "Big Blonde." The possibilities for both recreation and labor expanded dramatically for women during the 1920s. In a decade ushered in by women's victory in their struggle to gain the vote, both work and pleasure were associated with female liberation. Social and sexual expectations of the earlier Victorian era were overthrown, changing most women's everyday lives. It became generally acceptable for women to wear much shorter skirts and to socialize much more freely with men. They drank and smoked, and drove if they pleased. Women enjoyed themselves in new ways and they also earned money in new ways. Many women joined the workforce for the first time, and it became more acceptable for even a married woman to hold a job. Women worked in traditional feminine professions like nursing and teaching, in the mills and factories of an increasingly industrialized society, and they also made inroads into the professions such as law and, in the case of Parker, journalism.

Perched between World War I and the Great Depression, the 1920s are mythologized as a time when Americans—especially American women—

What Do I Read Next?

- *The Complete Stories* (1995) edited by Breese, Breese, and Berecca, compiles all of Dorothy Parker's narrative writings, including classics such as "Big Blonde" and many little-known stories.

- *Not Much Fun: The Lost Poems of Dorothy Parker* (1996), a new collection edited by Stuart Silverstein, offers readers access to Parker's previously unpublished poetry, which takes up themes of femininity, sexuality, and depression.

- *Gentlemen Prefer Blondes* (1925), a novel by Anita Loos, is better known in its form as a film adaptation of the same name starring Marilyn Monroe. Loos was a contemporary of Parker's and in this novel takes up similar questions of "the blonde" as an icon of female sexuality, but with a more comic approach.

- *The Company She Keeps* (1942), the first novel by Mary McCarthy, is a frank, loosely autobiographical account of a young, modern woman struggling with love, sex, and politics as she flaunts convention in the New York of the 1920s and 30s.

- *The Beautiful and the Damned* (1922) by F. Scott Fitzgerald, author of *The Great Gatsby,* explores the freedoms and failures of a modern marriage of the 1920s, illustrating how changing social mores and gender relations affect a hard-drinking, upper-class young couple.

- *Portrait of a Lady* (1881), a classic by Henry James, portrays the devastating effects of one headstrong young woman's struggle to find love and freedom in a social climate where economics and social class determine the criteria for marriage.

- *The Bell Jar* (1963), by poet Sylvia Plath, offers a biting and often satiric portrait of the events leading up to the author's first suicide attempt. This autobiographical account addresses questions of gender, sexuality, depression, and the struggle to become an artist in the repressive social climate of 1950s New England.

---

were independent and carefree. However, there is, of course, another side to women's experience during this decade. Parker was certainly among the most socially adventurous and professionally successful women of her era, and she is remembered as spirited and self-possessed—the quintessential woman of the roaring twenties. Thus it is interesting to note that Parker chose to reflect some of her most intimate and traumatic personal experiences through the character of Mrs. Morse, a sad and ineffectual woman whose fading, out-dated style of beauty marks her as a creature of a bygone era. George H. Douglas, in his book *Women of the Twenties,* refers to "the cost, the difficulty and, above all, the *vulnerability* of leaving oneself open to experience" from which women of the 1920s suffered. He identifies psychological exhaustion, alcoholism, and illness as the fate of many. In "Big Blonde" Parker deflates a romanticized idea of the 1920s according to which women enjoyed a new freedom to both enjoy and assert themselves without negative consequences. Mrs. Morse reflects the fact that many women were left behind and consigned to more traditional female roles even as standards for gender-related behavior changed radically. And, furthermore, while Mrs. Morse might be seen as enjoying the freedoms of a less socially and sexually restricted culture, Parker makes it clear that she must also pay a heavy price.

As the story opens, Mrs. Morse's life has the superficial appearance of liberation. Unbeholden to parents or to earlier social customs, she lives on her own, works as a model, goes out frequently, and is popular with men—all of which seems to fit the image of glamorous 1920s youth culture. However, the stresses of this lifestyle are apparent in the fact that when Mrs. Morse marries—and thus gives up

> In 'Big Blonde' Parker deflates a romanticized idea of the 1920s according to which women enjoyed a new freedom to both enjoy and assert themselves without negative consequences. Mrs. Morse reflects the fact that many women were left behind and consigned to more traditional female roles even as standards for gender-related behavior changed radically."

these freedoms for a conventional and respectable feminine role—she feels relieved. And, curiously, she is relieved that she does not have to have fun and that she can finally be sad. "Wedded and relaxed," Parker writes, "she poured her tears freely." Thus Parker makes a striking new definition of a woman's liberation as freedom *from* recreation—freedom *to* be sad. Unfortunately, Mrs. Morse's respite from fun is a very brief one. While liberalized standards for socializing and sexuality are often understood as empowering women, Parker shows that it is the *men* in Mrs. Morse's life who benefit from such "liberation" and, indeed, enforce it. One way of understanding Herbie's abandonment is to say that he left her when she stopped performing her role as a popular girl and a good sport. Another is to say that he stopped supporting her when she stopped doing her job.

This social and economic dynamic becomes clearer in Mrs. Morse's relationships with Ed and the other men who "keep" her. The transactions become simpler and clearer. First Ed gives her poker money and in return she offers her attention and lets him squeeze her knee. After Herbie leaves her, Ed offers her a new status as his mistress, which has greater benefits and also greater demands. When Mrs. Morse is married she cooks and cleans, but

once she becomes Ed's mistress she gives up anything that one might normally describe as work, in the interest of fulfilling the role that Ed desires of her—that she be his source of recreation when he visits the city. A maid came in every day to clean and make coffee for her—she was "through with that housekeeping stuff," she said, and Ed, twenty years married to a passionately domestic woman, admired this romantic uselessness and felt doubly a man of the world for abetting it. Parker is again offering a new definition, this time critiquing gender relations by inverting a commonly held concept of work. In order to do her job as Ed's mistress, Mrs. Morse recognizes that she must give up things she had formerly done—modeling and domestic work. While both of these earlier jobs inscribe extremely conventional femininity, neither was quite as restrictive as the imperative to do *nothing* other than provide a carefree source for Ed's enjoyment.

This restriction is most clear in the repeated demands from Mrs. Morse's lovers that she be cheerful. When Ed has a good year, he treats her to an expensive sealskin coat. "But she had to be careful of her moods with him. He insisted upon gaiety." She understands that "she was instantly undesirable when she was in low spirits." Mrs. Morse's sadness is her only form of freedom from her role—or job—as the amusing and attractive companion of men. But because it jeopardizes her desirability, it jeopardizes her basic material security. So she has no choice but to live out the modern female "liberties" of drinking and sex that are appealing to her male companions at the cost of any real freedom to express herself.

When Mrs. Morse first realizes that she is sad, her sympathy encompasses everything. "All sorrows become her sorrows," Parker writes, and lists things that would make Mrs. Morse cry: "newspaper accounts of kidnapped babies, deserted wives, unemployed men, strayed cats, heroic dogs." But as the story nears its climax, Parker gives particular emphasis to one image—that of a tired workhorse—as a trigger for Mrs. Morse's despair.

> Almost everything could give her the blues. Those old horses she saw on Sixth Avenue—struggling and slipping along the car-tracks, or standing at the curb, their heads dropped level with their worn knees. The tightly stored tears would squeeze from her eyes as she teetered past on her aching feet in the stubby, champagne-colored slippers.

The image of a tired workhorse pulling a heavy load may seem incongruous with that of a woman headed out for a night of drinking, which is nominally a night of leisure and fun. Parker reflects this incongruity through the deliberate contrast of the horse's clunky, bestial hooves, with Mrs. Morse's small and delicately shod feet. However, the description of feet suggests a stronger, underlying parallel between Mrs. Morse and the horse. The fact that Mrs. Morse feels like a workhorse is suggested through the connection between the horse's exertion to pull its load through the streets, ''struggling and slipping,'' and Mrs. Morse's effort as she teeters toward Jimmy's on ''aching feet.'' The horse's exhaustion is physical and literal, while Mrs. Morse's is caused by carrying a load that is less tangible but just as heavy. One of the very first things that readers learn about Mrs. Morse is that she ''prided herself upon her small feet and suffered for her vanity, boxing them in snub-toes, high-heeled slippers of the shortest bearable size.'' By this point in the story readers may understand Mrs. Morse's vanity as a part of the constant demand that she act as an object of desire, a luxury, and a form of amusement—or risk her very livelihood.

The metaphorical connection between Mrs. Morse and a beast of burden is extended in the second description Parker offers of a workhorse. Mrs. Morse again encounters a horse on the way out to Jimmy's, and in this scene it is a direct catalyst to the black mood that leads by the end of the night to Mrs. Morse's suicide attempt. Again, there is a parallel established between Mrs. Morse's struggle to walk and the horse's.

> As she slowly crossed Sixth Avenue, consciously dragging one foot past the other, a big, scarred horse pulling a rickety express-wagon crashed to its knees before her. The driver swore and screamed and lashed the beast insanely, bringing the whip back over his shoulder for every blow, while the horse struggled to get a footing on the slippery asphalt.

On the modern streets of Manhattan, recently overtaken by the new invention of the automobile, the workhorse is a symbol of a bygone era that nevertheless plods on. Mrs. Morse identifies with the horse because, unlike a car, it feels and suffers and yet it is not treated like a sentient being. With her outdated figure and fading beauty, Mrs. Morse does not conform to the image of the modern woman, yet she struggles within the conflicted social codes of liberated modern womanhood to survive in a world that denies her feeling.

Source: Sarah Madsen Hardy, ''Working Woman,'' in *Short Stories for Students,* The Gale Group, 1999.

Amelia Simpson

In the following essay, Simpson explores how Parker renders race in ''Big Blonde,'' and shows it to be an integral part of the story.

The story ''Big Blonde'' (1929) articulates some of the ambivalence with which Dorothy Parker's work approaches feminist inquiry. There is a vicious style to Parker's compassionate portrait of a woman hopelessly trapped in social codes of femininity. Just as intriguing, however, is the way race is inscribed in a text so overtly marked as a reflection on gender. Foregrounding the Africanist presence in the text discloses the real source of the story's power to disturb. Blackness surfaces in Parker's story in a way that provides an unusually clear example of the use of racial difference in white America's contemplation of itself. In concert with the critical project Toni Morrison pursues in *Playing in the Dark: Whiteness and the Literary Imagination* (1992), the present observations represent an effort to ''avert the critical gaze from the racial object to the racial subject; from the described and imagined to the describers and imaginers; from the serving to the served.'' By shifting our sights to consider the function of three seemingly minor black characters in Parker's ''Big Blonde,'' we are given a penetrating view of the divides of American identity, and of one white author's attempt to write that identity. Parker's story compellingly exposes the way gender and race are mutually constitutive, and how blackness constructs and contests the privilege of whiteness.

''Big Blonde'' won Parker the national O'Henry Prize for the best short story published that year. Arguably her strongest work, it is generally viewed as an unusually affecting tale about feminine vulnerability. The story is frequently read as a kind of ''autobiographical fiction,'' and it contains many echoes of the author's own failed relationships with men, her drinking problems, and her loneliness and suicide attempts. But the connection is probably more subtle. Parker's writing and her life reveal a drama of negotiation with the urge to challenge on the one hand, and to surrender on the other. As Nina Miller points out [in *American Literature*], Parker's public persona was ''desirable to the extent that she was . . . modern and reassuring to the extent that she left certain basic femininities intact.'' Parker's biographers suggest she was both liberated and constrained, exploited and self-exploiting. The nasty tongue she cultivated earned her a name as one of the founders of the male-dominated Algonquin

> " Parker produces a narrative about the subjugation of white women in America, using the scaffolding of blacks in America. Three Africanist figures who at first glance appear to serve only the interests of narrative expediency, are in fact the key to Parker's architectural paradox."

Round Table, yet the record shows little room at that table for moods not witty or cynical. Parker's trademark mouth gave her entry to a masculine domain she evidently aspired to join, but much of her work is devoted to complaining relentlessly about the terms by which women are forced to operate in a male-dominated world. Her telephone stories, for example, find women always on the short end of the conversation. Parker invented herself as a bad girl, and she was original in her badness, but often sorry in her girlness. She successfully wisecracked her way to a seat at the table with the boys, but she is frequently remembered more for that status than for her writing.

The 1994 film *Mrs. Parker and the Vicious Circle* does little to disturb the conventional view of Dorothy Parker as a clever but self-aggrandizing and troubled personality. The "vicious circle" seems to refer as much to Parker's drinking habits and penchant for sleeping around as to the sharp-tongued crowd she joined regularly for banter at the Algonquin. Not much is made of her literary talent. The film is sprinkled with poems, but they are delivered in a slurred and mumbled undertone that is difficult to decipher and hints at manic depression and drunkenness more than the idea of serious literary endeavor. An editor of Parker's once complained that her work didn't amount to much more than a series of "asides." But Parker was a gifted writer who struggled seriously alongside others engaged in

mapping the social and moral contours of American culture. She is more than a camp follower, as John Updike implies when he writes [in *New Yorker*]: "[Her] life brushed against most of the strands of American literary life from 1920 to 1950."

Parker survives in the push and shove of contradiction that gives a story like "Big Blonde" a hold on us still. In that text, the author produces a narrative about the subjugation of white women in America, using the scaffolding of blacks in America. Three Africanist figures who at first glance appear to serve only the interests of narrative expediency, are in fact the key to Parker's architectural paradox. Their presence problematizes the text beyond its interrogation of the cultural construction of the "big blonde" as an ideal of femininity. The question of gender resonates in another, more suggestive way in the presence of Africanist figures who reveal that such a construction is also informed by views of race. The proximity of the historically bought black body to the kept white one contaminates and opens the narrative to a wider contemplation of the institutions and practices of slavery.

I

"Big Blonde" is the tale of Hazel Morse. The story's title gives a familiar formula for femininity, a code tapped out by the appropriately named Morse. Her surname reminds us that the dumb blonde, like any stereotype, is human identity reduced to uninflected code. Her given name records the haziness of the view from inside such a construction. The author uses blondeness to eroticize the character and give her a badge of shallowness. Morse is the blonde built for amusement and display, a woman "of the type that incites their heads roguishly." Morse and her women friends, "other substantially built blondes," are supported by such men who call up when they are in town on business.

Morse is a woman whose identity is something others bestow on her. When the story begins, she is a dress model in her twenties. By the end, she is a tired party girl in her mid-thirties, surviving an alcoholic haze, self-destructing before ever building a self. She is dumb blondeness reduced to a blur, to "flabby white" flesh made low by age and alcohol. Morse's body is Parker's subject. The author details its decline in increments of degradation, from the "inexpert dabblings with peroxide," to the feet squeezed each night into undersized "champagne-colored slippers." Morse, like the other blondes in the story, is passed around from man to man, yet "in her haze, she never recalled how men entered her life and left it.''

Parker's protagonist is distinguished from the others by a more radical emptiness. The author has her materialize out of nowhere. Her only relative, a ''hazy widowed mother,'' dies when the story begins. Morse surfaces intact, a big blonde in her mid-twenties, in New York City, in the 1920s, a woman with no history, no future, and only a vague sense of the present. She is no different a decade later: ''At her middle thirties, her old days were a blurred and flickering sequence, an imperfect film, dealing with the actions of strangers.'' Morse is a permanent stranger with a familiar face.

Parker insistently presses her protagonist into the corsetted role of the party girl. A brief marriage is an experiment with emotional liberty: ''To her who had laughed so much, crying was delicious.'' But the experiment fails, Morse is unreadable except as the party girl, the ''good sport.'' She is permitted only one mood, that of gaiety, and her role is rigidly enforced:

> She was instantly undesirable when she was low in spirits. Once, at Jimmy's, when she could not make herself lively, Ed had walked out and left her. ''Why the hell don't you stay home and not go spoiling everybody's evening?'' he had roared.

Morse is quickly and brutally punished for the least deviation. Apart from her role as party girl, she hardly exists, and indeed tries not to: ''She slept, aided by whisky, till deep into the afternoons, then lay abed, a bottle and glass at her hand, until it was time to dress and go out for dinner.'' Eventually Morse longs for escape: ''She dreamed by day of never again putting on tight shoes, of never having to laugh and listen and admire, of never more being a good sport. Never.'' She buys a quantity of sleeping pills and sinks into unconsciousness.

At this juncture, Parker introduces a set of three new characters. It is no coincidence that they are black. These figures bear the heavy body of the sleeping Morse across the narrative bridge back to speech. They rescue her, and they do more. They illuminate Morse's condition, and they complicate the narrative. They engage the story of the blonde in a deeper dialogue with her keepers. Morse's ''colored maid'' Nettie, the ''Negro'' elevator attendant George, and a ''dark girl,'' constitute the Africanist presence in ''Big Blonde'' Nettie keeps house and, after Morse's suicide attempt, carries out the ''ugly, incessant tasks in the nursing of the unconscious.'' It is Nettie, too, who discovers Morse in a coma and goes to George for help. Together, they find a doctor

in the building, interrupting him while he is entertaining a ''dark girl,'' evidently a prostitute, in his apartment. Although the ''dark girl'' is not explicitly identified as black, the adjective and her working status contrast conspicuously with the blondeness and nonprofessional status of Morse and her women friends.

The white figures (Morse, the doctor) and the black figures (Nettie, George, the prostitute) emerge in sharp contrast to each other. Morse herself has become a blank, drooling slab of a body:

> Mrs. Morse lay on her back, one flabby white arm flung up, the wrist against her forehead. Her stiff hair hung untenderly along her face. The bed covers were pushed down, exposing a deep square of soft neck and a pink nightgown, its fabric worn uneven by many launderings; her great breasts freed from their tight container, sagged beneath her arm-pits. Now and then she made knotted, snoring sounds, and from the corner of her opened mouth to the blurred turn of her jaw ran a lane of crusted spittle.

The doctor's approach to the medical emergency is professional, impersonal, and remote. He barely speaks, and regards Morse as nothing but a ''nuisance.'' The black figures, on the other hand, negotiate a range of emotions, from fear, wonder, and excitement, to compassion, irritation, and scorn. Their manner is impulsive, intimate, and indiscreet. The black figures are set apart by their expressiveness, and by other markers as well. They are portrayed as childlike, their speech is different, and they have no names or first names only. Although they are adults, the black characters are referred to as ''boy'' and ''girl,'' where the whites are ''men'' and ''women.'' The black figures are even shunted off to the end of the narrative, positioned away from the body of the text.

From the start, then, the text formally establishes a disjuncture between black and white. That structural and figurative separation exposes white as central commanding, and controlled, while black is shown as peripheral, subordinate, and undisciplined. Parker is clearly implicated in the conventions of representations that place blackness in a sphere inhabited by primitive or childlike others. From that position, the black figures serve to highlight white stature and authority. The segregating structure, however, also allows blackness to inform whiteness in other, unintended ways. As Morrison observes in another context, ''there are unmanageable slips.'' If blackness shows white in control, it is also seen as detached and lifeless. The inhumanity blackness ascribes to whiteness shapes and sharpens the author's vision of femininity, while yielding unanticipated significance as well. Nettie is the most important of the three black figures in "Big Blonde." One wonders why the other two are there at all. The answer lies in their function as surrogates, stand-ins for missing registers of experience. In this case, and in keeping with the well-documented history of blackness as a sexualizing trope in Western discourse, the two characters foreground the theme that is implicit throughout the story, starting with the title itself—that of illicit sexuality. The conspicuous fashion in which two minor black figures raise the subject of sexual commerce and desire contrasts to its muted treatment elsewhere. Morse and her crowd represent a marketplace where men pay and women are kept, but the commercial nature of the transaction is masked by a logic of social alliances. Racial difference undercuts that logic to expose a politics behind Morse's abandonment of her own body. She is depicted as sexually indifferent, neutral to the advances, for example, of boyfriend Ed:

> It became his custom to kiss her on the mouth when he came in, as well as for farewell, and he gave her little quick kisses of approval all through the evening. She liked this rather more than she disliked it. She never thought of his kisses when she was not with him.

The expression of sexual awareness, desire and agency is displaced onto the Africanist figures of the elevator attendant and the prostitute. Called to the bedside of the comatose Morse, George prods her "so lustily that he left marks in the soft flesh [of] the unconscious woman." The prostitute, in turn, cries after the doctor as he reluctantly departs to tend to the emergency: "Snap it up there, big boy . . . Don't be all night." Along with their usefulness to the narrative design, these two, apparently marginal, black characters function discursively to underline the theme of illicit sexuality. The dark girl makes transparent the nature of the transaction that commodifies the big blonde in America. She articulates and links the codes of commerce and sex. By introducing race to the gendered field of sexual commerce, her meaning also spills over into another trade in bodies to connect Morse to the historical text of the black body. George, too, functions through his blackness. The contact between his blackness and Morse's whiteness makes his poking at an unconscious body more than just sexual taboo.

Only a page after the episode in which Parker has George prod Morse's soft flesh, the author describes the doctor's treatment of the same body:

> With one quick movement [the doctor] swept the covers down to the foot of the bed. With another he flung her nightgown back and lifted the thick, white legs, cross-hatched with blocks of tiny, iris-colored veins. He pinched them repeatedly, with long, cruel nips, back of the knees.

The infliction of a series of pinches, which Parker pointedly labels as "long" and "cruel," indicates an impulse to punish. Since the doctor's duty is to police the border Morse has attempted to cross, his reaction to her is necessarily punitive as well—one that is challenged by the sexualized contact between the black male (George) and the white female (Morse), and between the black female (the "dark girl") and the white male (the doctor). It is worth noting, in this regard, that the author calls attention in the passages depicting these episodes to the whiteness of Morse's body. The intervention of the Africanist figures, whose presence serves but also threatens to disrupt racial hierarchy, elaborates on the meaning of Morse's "punishment" by placing her in the context of a disintegrating self that is explicitly white.

Although their roles are brief, George and the prostitute draw attention to the function of the racial Other to serve and also to complicate and disturb. The third of Parker's Africanist figures—Nettie, the "colored maid" has a larger role in "Big Blonde." Nettie is central to the narrative play of accommodation and disruption that the Africanist presence represents. On the one hand she is a serviceable figure. She cooks, cleans, and runs errands for Morse. Yet for all her serviceability and subaltern status, Nettie is pivotal. She is particularly important to the narrative denouement. Nettie foregrounds and inflates the white woman's unfolding drama of isolation, and she can do so because her blackness guarantees her separateness. Parker reminds us explicitly each time Nettie appears that she is the "colored maid," as if to give special emphasis to her difference. Nettie becomes the final enforcer of the social code that imprisons the big blonde. It is Nettie who delivers that last blow. Parker makes the black figure the embodiment of the bonds of slavery.

The maid makes three appearances in "Big Blonde," each linked to a stage of Morse's descent into increasingly bewildering confinement and dependence. Nettie first surfaces when Morse's short-lived marriage fizzles and Ed, the first boyfriend, takes possession. He persuades Morse to move to an apartment more convenient to him, near the train station:

> She took a little flat in the Forties. A colored maid came in every day to clean and to make coffee for her—she was "through with that housekeeping stuff," she said, and Ed, twenty years married to a passionate-

ly domestic woman, admired this romantic uselessness and felt doubly a man of the world in abetting it.

The maid facilitates an arrangement that deepens Morse's isolation and renders increasingly conditional her apparent freedom. Nettie gives coherence to a domain explicitly framed to serve male interests. The maid's function is to keep the narrative house in order. Yet, while Nettie allows the author at this point in the text to foreground a paradigm of gender oppression, the regular reminders of racial difference introduce another element to the developing theme of freedom and enslavement.

When Nettie next appears, she is buying liquor for the suicidal alcoholic. Morse has managed to purchase a quantity of veronal tablets, and she addresses the tablets with religious fervor. Nettie hovers helpfully nearby, an "angel" of deliverance:

> She put the little vials in the drawer of her dressing-table and stood looking at them with a dreamy tenderness.
>
> "There they are, God bless them," she said, and she kissed her finger-tip and touched each bottle.
>
> The colored maid was busy in the living room.
>
> "Hey, Nettie," Mrs. Morse called. "Be an angel, will you? Run around to Jimmy's and get me a quart of Scotch."
>
> She hummed while she awaited the girl's return.

When Morse takes the final step and swallows her pills, the maid will be the net that catches her in her fall. She is Parker's solution to the problem of how to end the story. Without Nettie, Morse dies in a haze, pleasantly knocked out, herself cheated, and cheating us, of the full spectacle of her misery. A rescued Morse, on the other hand, is a woman without the blinds, finally and fully alive and aware. The character who saves Morse assumes the ungenerous, dismissive, inhuman qualities of all of the blonde's keepers. Nettie becomes, in effect, the punishing voice of the social body that creates and destroys Morse. Rather than embrace across the racial divide, the two women mark it. Nettie is the net that catches, but also traps. Although she nurses Morse back to life, no understanding grows between them. The gender identity that Parker explores through the figure of Morse is inscribed in a hegemonic discourse of racial difference.

Nettie's role after Morse regains consciousness is an example of the ironic reversal that Michele A. Birnbaum notes in her analysis of the literary function of the racialized Other in Kate Chopin's *The Awakening*. In "Big Blonde," as in Chopin's text, the racialized Other can serve as a marker of the status quo of social hierarchy. In this context, "the oppressed become the oppressors." When Morse finally comes out of a coma, able to do little more then weep at the "saturating wretchedness" that slowly returns with consciousness, Nettie only looks "coldly at the big, blown woman in the bed." "You can thank you' stars you heah at all," the maid scolds. Nettie irritably prompts Morse to express gratitude for the care: "Here I ain' had no sleep at all for two nights, an' had to give up goin' out to my other ladies!" Parker brings Nettie to witness but not treat, to rescue but not save. When Morse asks "Didn't you ever feel like doing it? When everything looks just lousy to you," Nettie's response is a cool rebuke: "I wouldn't think o' no such thing."

Immediately following this exchange is another which Nettie initiates and which effects a fundamental transformation in Morse. Her voice will split open for the first time and become knowing. She will shed her speechlessness, the vacuum of cliche, and speak for the first time with irony. The shift occurs after Nettie's scolding when she continues, using the same words Morse has heard many times before from her various escorts: "You got to cheer up. That's what you got to do. Everybody's got their troubles." Lying in what she had hoped would be her deathbed, Morse's response, "Yeah, I know," is her first declaration of self, of knowledge of her place in the world. This is the first ironic Morse we have seen.

Parker ends her story by repeating the epiphany. Morse has persuaded Nettie to pour them both a drink and she proposes a toast:

> "Thanks, Nettie," she said. "Here's mud in your eye."
>
> The maid giggled. "Tha's the way, Mis' Morse," she said. "You cheer up, now."
>
> "Yeah," said Mrs. Morse. "Sure."

Morse's "Yeah . . . sure" is, again, a signal of recognition. She has emerged finally from a verbal world of formula—where small talk is all the talk there is—into the grip of powerful, disabused utterance. Enforcement of the code of the party girl has fallen to Nettie, its brutal tyranny displaced onto the black figure, whose giggle marks her difference and her indifference.

It is Nettie who is assigned the racial identity that erects a barrier between the two women. When the maid does not stay to share a drink with Morse, but instead, "deferentially [leaves] hers in the bathroom to be taken in solitude," the social code that is played out is structured by a racialized paradigm. The mistress/servant dichotomy casts the relationship as one of domination and subordination. The white woman's status, gradually eroded in the course of a narrative of gendered subjugation, is nevertheless still marked as a position of privilege in relation to the black servant. Thus if the rhetoric of racial oppression emerges suggestively in relation to Parker's theme of gender oppression, the text continues to operate on another level to reinforce, not interrogate, racial difference. When Morse hits bottom, for example, and survives to feel misery ''crush her as if she were between great smooth stones,'' she compares herself to ''weary horses and shivering beggars and all beaten, driven, stumbling things''— but not to Nettie.

The doctor is the one white figure who participates in Morse's ''rescue.'' He saves her, but without piercing her isolation. Parker's ambivalence about assigning that role to a white character is reflected in the way she taints him making him not quite white. Through his contact with the ''dark'' prostitute, the doctor is distinguished from other white men in the story who prefer blondes. He is linked to blackness through George as well. There is a similar element of violence in the way the two men pinch and poke as they handle Morse's unconscious body. The two men meet across her body, as well as across the racial boundary where each seeks sexual contact. Blackness releases the doctor from the exacting codes of whiteness. His grayness makes possible his indifference to Morse's fate, an attitude that American slang tells us is not ''white.''

II

Parker's black figures divulge a departure from personal to social pathology, from the solitary, pitiable drift Morse embodies to the menacing current in which she is caught. At the heart of ''Big Blonde'' is the commerce of human bodies. The Africanist presence alludes to that commerce, but also conceals it. Parker uses the subordinate, othered, inconsequential Nettie to outline the dilemma of captivity. She and other Africanist figures in ''Big Blonde'' both serve and shield the author. They make it possible for her [as Toni Morrison says in *Playing in the Dark: Whiteness and the Literary Imagination*] ''to say and not say, to inscribe and erase.'' Parker's narrative is thus rhetorically implicated in the perpetuation of racial difference and inequality.

It may be useful to imagine the consequences if Africanism were not available as a discursive device for Parker to employ, if there were no black figures in ''Big Blonde,'' if the maid, the elevator attendant, and the prostitute were white. Certainly, the distance between that group of characters and Morse would be reduced. She would be familiarized, rather than estranged, by the surrounding figures. She would be more like them, one among them. In the absence of blackness, Morse would be less white, less innocent, less alone. She would be less effective in dramatizing her story of estrangement and alienation, and less able to contain and isolate the germ of another idea: That all American freedom is broadly and historically conditional.

Parker's narrative burrows into the vagueness of Morse's flesh in order to express a hard bone of truth about femininity. The racial implications of the big blonde are remarked only indirectly. She is regarded above all as an icon of male desire. But blondeness is liminal, not democratic. Blonde hair on non-white skin is a marker of difference, appropriation, or deviation. Gender displaces race in the consumption of the image of the blonde, yet the ideology that fuels that elision still binds the two together. In the context of Parker's story, blonde is connected to black through the vulnerability of the body. The leaks that allow race to surface in ''Big Blonde'' are a consequence of the author's willingness to expose fully the vulnerability of the female body.

Parker's work suggests she regarded women as crucially expressive of the American identity. Her fiction and poetry are all about them. Most of Parker's women are closely attached to the American landscape. They evoke the stylish abandon and ''modern love'' of the twenties, the slippery pleasure and curse of American money, the rise and fall of one's place on the social ladder. Parker's women are caught up in the space and movement of loosening times. They are not introspective, not grounded or protected. They are placed in a gendered narrative with the view that ease of circulation is attached to a condition that menaces, entraps, and often dooms. Parker's women are not free. The authority they wield is contingent, and so they are rendered vulnerable, easily disabled, replaced. To the degree that Parker compares the status of women like Morse to that of slaves, ''Big Blonde'' represents a radical confrontation with American identity.

But if Parker places women in the same arena of vulnerability and oppression as blacks, at the same time she makes use of the codes of racial separation to create her narrative. That apparent contradiction, or sympathetic break, introduces to Parker's tale a breach that exposes the convergence of race and gender. Through that gap we see that the privilege of the big blonde is granted by racially-constituted desire. Concerning the intersections of the oppressions of gender and race expressed in antebellum feminist-abolitionist texts, Karen Sanchez-Eppler observes [in *Touching Liberty: Abolition, Feminism, and the Politics of the Body*] that "although the identifications of woman and slave . . . occasionally prove mutually empowering, such pairings generally tend toward asymmetry and exploitation." Many decades later, Parker's story reflects the same struggle. The association of the condition of women with that of slaves in "Big Blonde" unfolds virtually exclusively through the story of a white woman.

Parker's use of racial difference is not the same as racism. The author was sensitive to racial prejudice, and denounced it explicitly in two stories from her major collections—"Arrangement in Black and White" (1927) and "Clothe the Naked" (1938). Unlike in those tales, however, the Africanism in "Big Blonde" is not studied. Indeed, it is likely inadvertent. As such, it is revealing of a different register, of blackness not as a theme but as a mechanism of and for the imagination. The blackness in "Big Blonde" brings race into the story of gender oppression, but the oblique approach leaves unexamined their interdependence and the consequent possibilities for negotiating of otherness.

Morrison shows how black characters in American literature by white authors do not have to be mere background detail, simple props for setting up action, but rather that they "ignite critical moments of discovery or change or emphasis." She explores Africanism in literary expression as a device that develops from the need to write a social identity that rests in a fundamental sense on a shudder of recognition. American literature tells again and again the compelling story of "a nation of people who decided that their world view would combine agendas for individual freedom and mechanisms for devastating racial oppression." Literature is one site where the unfree body is put to work to guarantee the free one. Reading the Africanist presence in Parker's story not only illustrates how crucial blackness is to American literary expression, but also helps to explain an elusive author. To ignore the way American Africanism shapes the visions and structure of works by writers like Dorothy Parker depletes us. Morrison warns that "all of us, readers and writers, are bereft when criticism remains too polite or too fearful to notice a disrupting darkness before its eyes." If Hazel Morse is more than a forgettable

floozy, it is because Parker's story charts a passage of cultural conception and deception through the channels of gender and race in America.

Source: Amelia Simpson, "Black on Blonde: The Africanist Presence in Dorothy Parker's 'Big Blonde'," in *College Literature*, October, 1996, pp. 105–116.

Arthur F. Kinney

In the following essay, Kinney covers Parker's background and influences as a writer, before examining her autobiographical character in "Big Blonde," Hazel Morse.

Dorothy Parker first attracted attention as a flippant and bittersweet poet and irreverent and acerbic satirist whose aim at the shallow and superficial social customs and social climbers often turned on a *bon mot*, a turn of phrase or perspective or a pun that was both striking and memorable. Closer attention to her work, however, shows a talented and dedicated artist whose persistent concern with spare, economical, pure language—even when cliched and colloquial, which she often used for effect—drew both on her classical education at Dana's School in Morristown, New Jersey, a private secondary school where she took several years of Latin, and her less formal teachers, especially Ernest Hemingway. Like him, she learned to foreshorten time and place in her short stories, so that the central characters and events were always prominently in focus. She learned to rely more on monologue or dialogue than on description. She sought the typical that was also archetypal. Thus however a "slice-of-life" her fiction might seem, the real emphasis often resembles that of James Joyce, whom she also admired. Whether acts and the people who perceive them are substantial or trivial, her stories deal with epiphanic moments of self-awareness or self-exposure (leading to the reader's new judgment and awareness). She frequently spoke of Hemingway as a model and convinced *The New Yorker* to pay her sea voyage to Paris so that she could interview him there, producing the first profile in that magazine ("The Artist's Reward," November 30, 1929). But she also praised F. Scott Fitzgerald, from whom she learned the value of particular, selected objects as symbols of broader social significance, and Ring Lardner, who taught her how to use colloquial dialogue.

The strategy for her fiction—both the early, obvious satires and the later, more sophisticated ones—is often the same: the energy and significance reside in irony, where one shallow person

❝ . . . 'Big Blonde' is
masterfully rendered, told
with astonishing power and
technique. Parker reduces the
long and despairing years of
a woman's life into short
panels and compresses an
entire autobiography into the
strictly limited range of the
short story. It is both
startlingly panoramic and
severely concentrated.**❞**

condemns another or is in turn exposed. Nearly all her short stories chart the same course: they affect sophistication while nevertheless displaying the manners of an ignorant ''bambosie.'' But if some of their customs and behavior seems obvious or transparent now, such revealing stories in the 1920s and 1930s had significant power. The bohemian style following World War I, affected and derivative, fit awkwardly with the Puritan values that were still prevalent among Parker's readers, and a considerable part of her strength and importance as a writer lies in her awareness that both strains that together constituted American culture had their serious weaknesses. Her fiction thus constantly turns to the disjunction between intention and performance, pretended knowledge and real ignorance, feigned concern and real pride and greed. In her short stories, the barbed and acid criticism of her satirical verse is still central, but it is both more incisive and more subtle. Gilbert Seldes's praise of Lardner fits her equally well: ''the swift, destructive, and tremendously funny turn of phrase, the hard and resistant mind, the gaiety of spirit,'' but compounded, in Parker's case, with great labor and care. ''It takes me six months to do a story. I think it out and then write it sentence by sentence,'' she once told Marion Capron an interview; ''I can't write five words but that I change seven.'' This caution, purchased at such cost, was also necessary to keep guard over Parker's more sentimental, sympathetic side, the

kind of emotion she could show in public but ruthlessly exempted from her writing.

The best example of all her qualities is seen in her most successful, most anthologized, and most enduring story, ''Big Blonde'' (first published in 1929, and collected in 1930 in *Laments for the Living*). It is also her most daring story, for it recounts unflinchingly her own alcoholic depressions and attempts at suicide in the years immediately preceding its composition. Like Parker, the story's protagonist, Hazel Morse, is terrified of loneliness and despair, even when she is thought by her friends to be a party girl, a barrel of laughs, always ready for a carefree time. While the stark and unrelieved tragedy of Hazel was new for Parker, a risk that seriously challenged her popular reputation as a wit, on which her career had relied so completely, the story of ''Big Blonde'' is masterfully rendered, told with astonishing power and technique. Parker reduces the long and despairing years of a woman's life into short panels and compresses an entire autobiography into the strictly limited range of the short story. It is both startlingly panoramic and severely concentrated. In its portrait of the birth and growth of alcoholism and suicidal despair and in its clinical analysis, painfully detailed and piercingly accurate, it is an unrelenting study of the possibility of the brutality of life—the brutality of an uncaring society and of an uncaring self, without self-esteem. The close and steady focus on Hazel Morse's decline and fall is Parker's searing attempt to record society's victimization of its more vulnerable members, and the self-victimization of those who cannot earn even self-respect.

From the start, Hazel Morse finds no advantage in living. She never knew the pleasure of family; her later popularity is artificial. But she has no distorted sense of herself; she is willing to settle for the nearly worthless Herbie Morse to gain some security and stability. Herbie leads Hazel to alcohol, which in turn produces tenderness, self-pity, ''misty melancholies.'' Herbie finally leaves her, despising himself, despising him in her, and she becomes a party girl, seeking favors from anyone willing to give them to her, however temporarily.

Hazel Morse is mirrored in her husband, the speakeasies, her lovers, and finally, the maid, yet all these painful doublings are not nearly so pathetic as the comparison Parker makes between Hazel and a wretched horse nor as tragic as Hazel Morse looking at herself in an actual mirror when taking Veronal.

Here, at the moment of suicide, the best she can manage is a bad joke: "Gee, I'm nearly dead, ... That's a hot one!"

But that is not the end of Hazel Morse. As she survived desertion by her husband and by a string of anonymous lovers, so she survives the deadly poison: her punishment is to remain alive amid the squalor of the poor and unfortunate yearning to breathe free. Yet what survives is at best what we see when Hazel Morse, drugged, is at greatest peace with herself: "Mrs. Morse lay on her back, one flabby, white arm flung up, the wrist against her forehead. Her stiff hair hung tenderly along her face. The bed covers were pushed down, exposing a deep square of soft neck and a pink nightgown, its fabric worn uneven by many launderings; her great breast, freed from their tight confiner, sagged beneath her arm-pits. Now and then she made knotted, snorting sounds, and from the corner of her opened mouth to the blurred turn of her jaw ran a lane of crusted spittle." The spittle doubtless descends from that of her literary prototype, the suicide Emma Bovary of Flaubert, from whose mouth at death trickles black bile. But Emma leaves a respectable husband, a doctor, and their daughter. Hazel lives rather than dies, and she still has no one. She remains, at the close of the story, symbolically limp and weakened in bed, a bottle close to her hand—but no more pills.

From more than 2,000 entries in 1929, the unrelenting story of the "Big Blonde," the good-time girl, was awarded the eleventh annual first prize of $500 in the O. Henry Memorial Prizes for the best short story appearing in an American magazine for that year. It was instantly a classic. From as far away as Cannes, Fitzgerald himself was elated. He urged his agent to take up Parker as a client: "Just now she's at a high point as a producer and as to reputation," he wrote Max Perkins, "I wouldn't lose any time about this if it interests you." For him as for many later critics, this was masterful storytelling. However closely it scraped along the bones of Parker's own life, they were bones with the beauty of artifice stripped bare and a detail clean with truth.

But like Hazel Morse, alone at the end, feeling unwanted and unsuccessful, there is no record that Parker ever knew what her model Fitzgerald thought of the story or what he said of it.

Source: Arthur F. Kinney, "Big Blonde," in *Reference Guide to Short Fiction,* Detroit: St. James Press, 1994, pp. 645-6.

Sources

Douglas, George H. *Women of the Twenties.* Dallas, TX: Saybrook, 1986.

Maugham, W. Somerset. "Variations on a Theme," in *Dorothy Parker,* Viking Press, 1944, pp. 11-18.

McKenney, Ruth. "Satire and Tragedy," in *The Saturday Review of Books,* Vol. 20, No. 1, April 29, 1939, p. 7.

Meade, Marion. *Dorothy Parker: What Fresh Hell is This?,* New York: Villard Books, 1988.

Further Reading

Gaines, James R. *Wit's End: Days and Nights of the Algonquin Round Table,* New York: Harcourt Brace Jovanovich, 1977.
    An approachable glimpse into Parker's immediate social milieu, this well-illustrated history covers biographical information about the various colorful figures in Parker's set, as well as offering some basic cultural and historical context.

Horn, Pamela. *Women in the 1920s,* Stroud, Gloucestershire, England: A. Sutton, 1995.
    A social history of women in the rapidly changing cultural climate of the "roaring twenties," this study fleshes out what life was like for women of different classes, races, and regions during the era with which Parker is most closely associated.

Nolan-Hoeksema, Susan. *Sex Differences in Depression,* Stanford, CA: Stanford University Press, 1990.
    A psychological study presenting evidence that women are twice as likely as men to experience clinical depression, and offering theories to explain this gender-linked phenomenon.

Blood-Burning Moon

Jean Toomer

1923

The short story "Blood-Burning Moon" is part of Jean Toomer's book *Cane,* which was first published in 1923. The book is divided into three parts: the first two contain short stories and poetry, while the third part consists of a loosely-structured play that is sometimes considered a short story. All the stories in this first section take place in the rural South, usually with an African-American woman as the focus. For the most part, they take place at dusk and outdoors, often in the cane fields. "Blood-Burning Moon" is the last story in this part and, interestingly, it is the only one that does not have a woman's name as its title.

"Blood-Burning Moon" is exemplary of Toomer's theme of African-American identity and his setting of rural Southern life during segregation. It tells the story of the conflict between Bob Stone, a white man, and Tom Burwell, an African American, who are rivals for the affection of Louisa, a light-skinned African-American woman. During the course of one evening, each man learns of the other's relationship with Louisa. After Bob challenges Tom to a knife fight in front of Louisa, Tom slashes the throat of the white man. Bob is able to stumble back to the white part of town and tell the townfolk who knifed him. A mob of white men immediately lynch Tom by tying him to a stake and burning him.

Author Biography

Jean Toomer was born in Washington, D.C., where he spent much of his childhood in an affluent white section of the city. He lived in the home of his maternal grandfather, P. B. S. Pinchback, a prominent black Louisiana politician of the Reconstruction era and a former U. S. Senator. His father, a Georgia planter, left his mother shortly after he was born. Toomer's mother died when he was fifteen. Soon afterwards, the Pinchbacks experienced heavy financial losses, requiring the family to move to a modest African-American neighborhood.

Although his ancestry was racially mixed, Toomer's appearance suggested he was white. His experience living in both black and white society offered him an unusual perspective on racial identity. Writing to his publishers in the summer before *Cane* was published, he commented on his racial heritage: "Racially, I seem to have (who knows for sure) seven blood mixtures: French, Dutch, Welsh, Negro, German, Jewish, and Indian. Because of these, my position in America is a curious one."

After graduating from high school in Washington, D.C., Toomer led a transient existence. He attended several colleges and universities, studying subjects from agriculture to history. He tried his hand at various jobs, including selling cars, teaching physical education, and welding. While living in New York City in 1919 and 1920 he was active in the Greenwich Village literary circle, making the acquaintance of writers such as Edwin Arlington Robinson and Waldo Frank. His life underwent a profound change during the fall of 1921, when he ran a small school in Sparta, Georgia. During those months, Toomer developed a new feeling for his African-American roots, especially through his encounters with poor people who worked in the cotton and cane fields. As he listened to their folk songs and spirituals, he was deeply moved. He returned to the South on a tour with Waldo Frank during 1922. His experiences in the South inspired much of his book *Cane*.

Shortly after the publication of *Cane* in 1923, Toomer became a follower of George Gurdjieff, an Armenian mystic whose philosophy aspired toward the achievement of "objective consciousness": awareness of one's status as part of a larger, universal being. Toomer spent the summer of 1924 at the Gurdjieff Institute in Fontainebleau, France. When he returned to the United States he dedicated himself to spreading Gurdjieff's beliefs. He continued

to be involved with Gurdjieff and his movement until 1940, when he renounced Gurdjieff and converted to Quakerism. Although he continued to write during these years, most of his writing concerned his religious beliefs, and little of it was published. Toomer died in 1967, two years before the republication of *Cane* and the subsequent revival of interest in his work.

Plot Summary

The story opens with a description of the full moon rising as the women of the poor, African-American part of town—"factory town"—sing songs against its evil spell. Louisa, a black woman, is walking home from her job as a domestic servant for a white family, the Stones. She, too, sings as she thinks about Bob Stone, the younger son of her employers, with whom she has a clandestine relationship, and about Tom Burwell, a black man who works in the fields and has been showing an interest in her. The thought of the two men cause a "strange stir" within her, and she tries vaguely to determine which of the men is the cause of her agitation. Her song becomes "agitant and restless." Animals sense her agitation, and dogs begin to bark and yowl while chickens cackle and roosters crow. Louisa finally arrives home and sits down on the front step. The moon moves towards a "thick cloud-bank which soon would hide it." This section ends with the refrain of a song that is the source of the story's title and will be repeated twice more:

> Red nigger moon. Sinner! Blood-burning moon. Sinner! Come out that fact'ry door.

At the edge of the forest outside the factory town, a group of African-American men, including Tom, sit around the "glowing stove" boiling cane and listening to Old David Georgia tell tales. Tom becomes irate when someone suggests that Louisa received a gift of silk stockings from Bob. When he tells the group, "She's my gal," Will Manning laughs. Tom starts a fight with him, but several of Will's friends come to his defense. They run into the woods when Tom pulls a knife. Tom returns to town and goes to Louisa's house, where she is sitting on the front step. After telling Louisa how often he thinks of her and how hard he works, he asks her if the rumors are true about her relationship with Bob. When she asks him what he would do if they were true, he replies, "Cut him jes like I cut a nigger." Tom sits beside her and they hold hands while they watch an old woman hang a lantern at the well. As

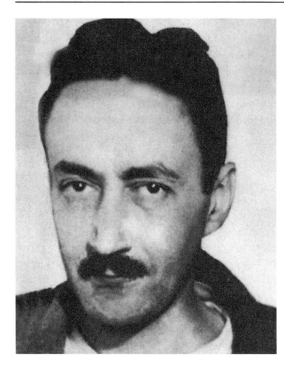

Jean Toomer

the old woman sings, Louisa and Tom join her. Eventually, the whole street is singing the refrain mentioned at the end of Part 1.

The third and final section of the story opens with Bob Stone leaving his home to meet Louisa. He thinks about his family and how they might react if they knew of his relationship with Louisa. He wishes he could just take Louisa whenever he wanted, as would have been the case during the days of slavery. He also reflects vaguely about the source of his attraction to Louisa and what her race means to him, concluding that ''it was because she was nigger that he went to her.'' He has heard of Tom's interest in Louisa, and it makes him angry: ''No nigger had ever been with his girl.''

His path to the canefield leads him to the same group of men that Tom has just left. He overhears them talking about Tom's temper. One man says that ''Tom Burwell's been on th gang three times fo cuttin men.'' The men ponder what Tom will do to Bob when he meets him. Bob stumbles away feverishly and throws himself on the ground. When he finally continues on to his meeting place with Louisa she is not there, and he concludes that she is with Tom Burwell. He sets out for factory town. On his way, he stumbles over a dog. When the dog yelps, animals awaken and begin to yelp, cackle, or

crow. Singers in town become silent. As Tom and Louisa huddle together in the silence, Bob appears. He lunges at Tom twice, and each time Tom easily knocks him to the ground. When Bob persists, Tom begins beating him, and Bob pulls a knife. Tom then pulls his own knife and slashes Bob's throat. As Bob staggers toward the white part of town, those who witnessed the fight go into their houses, except for Louisa and Tom. ''Dazed'' and ''hysterical,'' Louisa slumps down against the well, while Tom ''seem[s] rooted'' next to it.

When Bob reaches Broad Street, he collapses in the arms of the white men. A mob quickly gathers and heads toward the factory town, where they grab Tom, tie his wrists and drag him into the deserted cotton mill. There, they tie him to a stake, pile wood around him, and burn him alive. The mob watches and yells as Tom is tortured and killed. Meanwhile, Louisa is still on her front step, but she is not aware of the noise.

Characters

Tom Burwell

Tom Burwell is the African-American man who loves Louisa, a kitchen maid in the house of the Stone family. Because Tom works all day in the fields, he has little time to spend with her or even to show his feelings for her. Even when he is with her in the evenings, he seems to be somewhat shy in expressing himself: ''Strong as he was with hands upon the ax or plow, he found it difficult to hold her.'' Known in the town by the nickname ''Big Boy,'' he has a reputation for losing his temper and for using his knife as a threat and as a weapon. Although he admits to having ''cut two niggers,'' one of the workmen says that he has ''been on th gang three times fo cuttin men.'' When a man suggests that Bob Stone gave Louisa silk stockings, Tom quickly asserts that she is his ''gal.'' Will Manning laughs at this statement, and Tom knocks him down, pulling a knife on him and the friends who come to Will's defense. When Bob Stone challenges him, Tom easily kills the other man. Tom is burned to death by a white mob immediately after the fight.

Louisa

Louisa is a light-skinned African-American woman who is loved by both Tom Burwell, a black field hand, and Bob Stone, son of the white planter

A cotton mill in the South. The cotton mill in "Blood Burning Moon" is deserted, reflecting the decline of the cotton industry in the South in the decades after the Civil War.

who employs her. As she walks home from her job, she anticipates her usual meeting with Bob in the canefield, even as she imagines that Tom will soon propose marriage to her. She feels a "strange stir" within herself, which she senses is caused by her unresolved relationships with Bob and Tom. She seems to have not been honest with either man regarding her interactions with the two of them. Thus, when Tom shows up at her home and questions her about Bob, she avoids answering him directly. Louisa's indecisiveness and lack of honesty contribute to the violent and fatal confrontation between Tom and Bob. After witnessing the fight and Tom's confrontation with the white mob, Louisa sits alone on the steps of her house, singing and dreaming that Tom may reappear.

Bob Stone

Bob Stone, the youngest son of a white planter, has an affair with Louisa, a black woman who works for his family as a servant. He is killed in a confrontation with her black suitor, Tom Burwell. As a member of a Southern white family that once owned slaves, he feels that he has the right to enjoy a sexual relationship with an African-American woman

who is also a domestic servant in his household. Nonetheless he becomes embarrassed when he thinks about how his mother, sister, or his friends up North would react if they knew about his relationship with her. He thinks nostalgically of "the good old days" when a white slave owner could do as he pleased with his slave women. Bob reveals his jealousy and anger when he learns that Tom has been at Louisa's house shortly before Bob was planning to meet her. Particularly irksome to him is the thought that Louisa may have been intimate with Tom. Bob's possessiveness and jealousy lead him to instigate the scuffle with Tom and then to make the fatal decision to challenge Tom with a knife.

Themes

Racism

White racism within the context of the segregated South is one of the major themes in "Blood-Burning Moon." The town in which Louisa, Tom, and Bob live is rigidly segregated, a hill dividing the "white town" from the shanties of the black "factory town." Although slavery no longer exists, the

Topics for Further Study

- Investigate the resurgence of lynchings in the South during the 1920s and explain why or why not Tom's lynching is representative of what was happening.

- Research the anti-lynching crusade that attempted to get federal legislation passed. In addition to Ida B. Wells, who else was involved? What finally happened to the movement?

- Research the ways in which segregation was practiced in the South during the 1920s and 1930s. In what other ways might Louisa and Tom have experienced segregation during this period?

- Explore symbolic meanings given to the moon in African American folktales and culture. How might various beliefs about the moon suggest different meanings in "Blood-Burning Moon?"

---

pattern of impoverished blacks working for wealthy whites continues: Louisa works as a domestic servant in the Stone family household, while Tom works as a field hand for the same family.

Bob Stone's racism is a significant component of both his attraction to Louisa and his furious jealousy towards Tom. Stone nostalgically recalls the days of slavery, when a white master could have any black woman he chose. He sees the need to hide his sexual relationship with Louisa as a sign that the Stones have "lost ground." The thought that he might have a black rival is intolerable to him: "No sir. No nigger had ever been with his girl. He'd like to see one try. Some position for him to be in. Him, Bob Stone, of the old Stone family, in a scrap with a nigger over a nigger girl. In the good old days . . . Ha! Those were the days." Stone's racism also appears to fuel his foolhardy attack on Tom: "Fight like a man," he tells Tom, "and I'll lick ya."

The story's most drastic example of white racism, of course, is the lynching of Tom. The white men don't question what happened during the fight,

nor do they even consider the possibility of a trial. Instead, they immediately set off to torture, burn, and kill Tom.

Love and Passion

In examining the feelings of both Bob Stone and Tom Burwell toward Louisa, "Blood-Burning Moon" probes the relationship between love, lust, racism, and a need to dominate.

As Bob Stone sets out to meet Louisa in the cane field, his thoughts reflect the confusion of his feelings for her and the blocks that his racism sets up against the possibility of any tender, human emotion towards her. His thoughts of her are continually qualified by her blackness, although he is unable to define the difference that her blackness makes: "She was lovely—in her way. Nigger way. What way was that? Damned if he knew. . . . Beautiful nigger gal. Why nigger? Why not, just gal? No, it was because she was nigger that he went to her." His own thoughts, however, suggest that her blackness is important to him because the racist superiority he feels toward her enhances his feeling of mastery and possession. This is suggested early on in the passage, when he imagines himself back in the days of slavery: "He saw Louisa bent over that hearth. He went in as a master should and took her. . . . [H]is family still owned the niggers, practically." The interrelatedness of racism and possession is emphasized again in Bob's frenzied reaction to the thought of Tom Burwell's rivalry: "No nigger had even been with his girl. . . . Some position for him to be in. Him, Bob Stone, of the old Stone family, in a scrap with a nigger over a nigger girl." While Tom's interest in Louisa is a threat to Bob's sexual possession of her, Tom's blackness is a threat to the feeling of racial superiority that makes that possession so gratifying.

Tom's feeling for Louisa, on the other hand, is presented as more tender and genuine. In contrast with Bob's boldness and directness, Tom is tongue-tied in Louisa's presence. Instead of seeking an assignation in a cane field, he comes to her doorstep, respectfully confesses his love, and sits holding her hand. His feelings, however, like Bob's, are touched by a desire for possession and control. In offering to buy her what she "gets from white folks now" and in threatening to knife any rival, he reveals that he, too, sees Louisa as a possession to be purchased or won rather than as a free agent with the right to choose.

Identity

For both of the main male characters in "Blood-Burning Moon," identity is inextricably mixed up with issues of sexual possession and race. Bob Stone defines himself largely in terms of his ability to dominate black people. Setting out to meet Louisa, his thoughts become "consciously a white man's." The limits on his right to Louisa seem a personal affront, an indication that his family has "lost ground" since slave days. The possibility that Tom may be a rival poses an even greater threat to his identity: "Some position for him to be in. Him, Bob Stone, of the old Stone family, in a scrap with a nigger over a nigger girl." When he overhears black workers discussing their rivalry, he becomes nearly senseless with rage. Ultimately, possession of Louisa and dominance of Tom are so essential to his sense of who he is that he risks and loses his life trying to enforce them.

For Tom, too, dominance and control are essential to his sense of identity. The mere suggestion that the woman he has chosen might prefer another man leads him to pull a knife on Will Manning, and he tells Louisa that he has already knifed two men for making the same sort of suggestion. His need to dominate places him in an impossible dilemma when Bob Stone confronts him. To back down meekly in front of Louisa would be contrary to everything he is, but to fight a white man means certain death.

Style

Setting

Set in an unnamed town in the American South during the early part of the twentieth century, "Blood-Burning Moon" tells the story of an ultimately fatal rivalry between two men, one white and one black, for the love of a black woman. Segregation and Jim Crow laws are still in effect, and white supremacy shapes and threatens the lives of the African-American members of the community. Within this historical and social context, the events and eventual conflict between Tom Burwell and Bob Stone take place during the early evening hours while the full moon—an evil omen in African-American folklore—is rising. This also adds to the sinister and foreboding atmosphere that pervades the story.

Point of View

The story is told in the third person, from the perspective of each of the three main characters in turn. Thus, each section of the story is told from what is called a limited omniscient point of view: the third person narrator sees into the mind of a single character and recounts the events of that part of the story from that character's perspective. In the first section, the narrator tells the reader Louisa's thoughts as she walks home. The narrator in the second section relates Tom Burwell's thoughts and experience beginning with his visit to the cane boiling and ending with his visit to Louisa. The third section begins with Bob Stone's thoughts as he leaves his house before his planned meeting with Louisa in the canebreak and follows them until his confrontation with Tom. At this point the narrator switches to a simple third-person point of view, reporting events from the outside, until the very end of the story, which ends as it began with Louisa's point of view.

Imagery

As the title suggests, the moon is a principal image in "Blood-Burning Moon." The story begins and ends with the image of "the full moon in the great door," and each of the story's three parts ends with a refrain from the song that the women improvise to counter the moon's "evil omen." The description of its movement and its reflecting light helps set the ominous mood of the story and foreshadows the violence to come.

In addition to the belief that the full moon represents an evil omen, several other folkloric beliefs about the moon lend it symbolic significance in the story. The full moon has traditionally been associated with the unleashing of powerful emotions, especially those associated with animal instincts. The story of the transformation of a man into a werewolf during the full moon is an example of this tradition. When the women stop singing against the threat of the full moon, Tom and Bob have their fatal encounter. The moon is also traditionally associated with women. The Greco-Roman goddess of the moon, Artemis or Diana, is a chaste goddess, and the white of the moon is associated with chastity. The redness of the moon in the story might be interpreted as a sign of Louisa's lack of chastity.

The moon also plays a part in the imagery of dark and light that pervades the story and parallels its racial conflict between black and white. Each scene is bathed in an eerie glow, whether from the moon, the glow of the cane fire, the searchlights of the lynch mob, or the fire in which the mob burns and kills Tom. Usually white, but here described as a "red nigger moon," the moon throughout the story is about to be engulfed or is being engulfed in a "deep purple" bank of clouds. The image of white obscured by dark is repeated when Bob Stone first appears: "The clear white of his skin paled, and the flush of his cheek turned purple."

Structure

"Blood-Burning Moon" is divided into three sections. The first section and the end of the third are told from Louisa's point of view. In this way, Toomer frames the story with Louisa's point of view and her aloneness. Each section also ends with the song: "Red nigger moon. Sinner! / Blood-burning moon. Sinner! / Come out that fact'ry door." The first two instances of the song foreshadow the violence and death that will occur, while all three emphasize the central image of the moon and serve to unify the three sections. This division of the story into three parts, each of which ends with the same refrain, is reminiscent of the structure of folksongs and ballads.

Modernism

Modernism is a literary style and movement of the first half of the twentieth century. It was marked by a break with traditional literary forms and a rejection of mainstream Western civilization and culture. "Blood-Burning Moon" can be seen as a modernist text primarily because of its experimental style and its unorthodox treatment of African-American life. The story's lyrical, rhythmic prose, its song-like structure, and its shifting perspectives represent a departure from the style and techniques of conventional pre-twentieth century literary storytelling. Its frank and complex depiction of racial conflict in the segregationist South also contrasts sharply with the images of African-American life typical in earlier American literature, which tended either to sentimentalize or to sensationalize the topic.

Historical Context

The Harlem Renaissance

During the 1920s, Harlem, a section of New York City, became the largest African-American urban area in the country. After World War I, there had been a large migration of rural Southern African

Americans to large Northern cities in search of employment. Many of Harlem's residents were professionals, including doctors, lawyers, judges, and teachers.

Within the Harlem community, a small but influential group of mostly college-educated intellectuals strove to encourage racial pride among African Americans. Writers and artists sought to define and express a specifically African-American identity, experience, and culture. This movement became known as the Harlem Renaissance. One of the most well-known artists was Aaron Douglas. In 1925, Alain Locke, an African-American philosopher who had graduated from Harvard and Oxford, published *The New Negro: Voices of the Harlem Renaissance,* an anthology of African-American poetry, fiction, drama, and art. Toomer's book *Cane,* published in 1923, was one of the first to depict African-American identity in terms of the South, slavery, and the persistence of white racism.

Writers of the Harlem Renaissance include Langston Hughes, Countee Cullen, James Weldon Johnson, Arna Bontemps, Claude McKay, Zora Neale Hurston, Nella Larsen, and Jessie Redmon Fauset, who was literary editor of the African-American magazine *Crisis* from 1919 to 1926.

Harlem also became known as a center for jazz musicians who brought their music from the South. They often played in big bands at nightclubs such as the Cotton Club. White New Yorkers would come to Harlem to hear such famous musicians as Louis Armstrong and Duke Ellington.

Southern Culture and Segregation

In 1896, the Supreme Court decision in Plessy vs. Ferguson upheld the right of states to allow racial segregation. The decision was based upon the idea of "separate but equal." Southern states began to pass segregation laws that separated white people from African Americans in most aspects of daily life. These laws were known as Jim Crow laws. By the early 1920s, the South was segregated with respect to housing, education, medical care, religious institutions, and within public buildings. Not only were there separate schools and hospitals, but there were even separate restrooms and drinking fountains. Federal rulings and laws against legal segregation did not occur until the 1950s.

Besides legal segregation, African Americans in the South were also victims of violent activity by the Ku Klux Klan. This organization was dedicated to a belief in white supremacy. Throughout the

Compare
&
Contrast

- **1922:** *Abie's Irish Rose,* a play about a racially mixed marriage is performed 2,532 times on Broadway—a record at the time.

  1993: *The Crying Game,* a movie exploring themes of racial, sexual, and national identity, becomes a mainstream hit after initially being considered ''artistically risky'' and playing to small audiences.

- **1924:** The Ku Klux Klan threatens black actor Paul Robeson's life for his portrayal of a white man married to a black woman in Eugene O'Neill's *All God's Chillun Got Wings.*

  1996: There are more than one million racially mixed marriages in the United States.

- **1923:** There are 33 reported lynchings in the United States; 29 of the victims are black men. In response to an increase in lynchings, activist Mary B. Talbert begins an anti-lynching crusade. By 1925 the number of lynchings drops to ten.

  1998: Three white men in Jasper, Texas, face the death penalty after a racial hate crime in which they chain a black man to the back of a pickup truck and drag him for two miles.

South, members of the Klan would attack and sometimes kill African Americans and destroy their property. They also victimized whites who sympathized openly with African Americans and supported equal rights. By 1923, the Klan also had begun to gain political power in the United States.

Violence against African-Americans, however, was not committed solely by members of the Ku Klux Klan. Other white supremacists also participated in lynching hundreds of African-American men during the 1920s. Often, the excuse for a lynching was an unproven accusation that the man had raped a white woman. An anti-lynching crusade also began during this time, under the strong influence of Ida B. Wells, a former slave. An attempt to pass a federal anti-lynching law, however, failed.

Critical Overview

''Blood-Burning Moon'' is often praised for its musical prose, reminiscent of the rhythms of jazz, and for its depiction of the effects of racism on African-American men and women in the American South. The collection of which it is a part, *Cane,* is generally considered to be one of the finest as well as one of the earliest works of the Harlem Renais-

sance of the 1920s—a period of outstanding literary achievement and innovation by such African-American writers as Langston Hughes, Countee Cullen, and Zora Neale Hurston. Recently, some critics have also considered ''Blood-Burning Moon'' to be a modernist work. Modernism is a literary movement of the first part of the twentieth century that rejected traditional writing styles and tended to be critical of social conventions. Although its original publication was limited, *Cane* was well received by many writers and critics, including W. E. B. Du Bois and Sherwood Anderson; it has often been compared with *Winesburg, Ohio,* Anderson's collection of interrelated short stories. Since its republication in 1969, *Cane* has received increasing critical attention for its experimental style and its portrayal of African-American life in the rural South. Toomer called the book a ''swan song'' for a dying culture.

Criticism

Jane Phillips

Phillips has taught in the English Department at the University of California-Riverside and at several other schools. In the following essay, she

What Do I Read Next?

- *Cane* by Jean Toomer (1923) is the book that includes "Blood-Burning Moon." In addition to short stories, the collection includes poetry and a short drama piece.

- *Invisible Darkness: Jean Toomer and Nella Larsen* (1993), by Charles R. Larson, presents a revision of what has been traditionally written about Jean Toomer's personal life. Larson writes about Toomer's question of his own racial identity, as well as his struggle with spirituality.

- *The Sleeper Wakes: Harlem Renaissance Stories by Women,* edited by Marcy Knopf (1993), includes a selection of short stories by the women writers who were Toomer's contemporaries. Like Toomer, these women write about African-American identity and experience.

- *Their Eyes Were Watching God,* by Zora Neale Hurston (1937), is a novel about African Americans living in the rural South about the same time as the characters in Toomer's book. Hurston was also a writer of the Harlem Renaissance.

- *Winesburg, Ohio,* by Sherwood Anderson, is a novel comprised of short stories about the people living in a small town. *Cane* is often compared with it in terms of style and the theme of rural America.

---

discusses the elements of Cane, *the collection "Blood-Burning Moon" originally appeared in, that connect it to Modernism and to the Harlem Renaissance. She also discusses Toomer's depiction of racism in the South in the 1920s.*

With its unconventional style and experimental form, Jean Toomer's *Cane,* which includes the story "Blood-Burning Moon," continues to puzzle those who wish to classify it as either an early Modernist text or a work of the Harlem Renaissance. Traditionally Toomer has been viewed primarily as a member of the Harlem Renaissance, a movement involving African-American writers and artists in the 1920s that emphasized black culture and identity. During this period, black authors such as Toomer, Langston Hughes, and Zora Neale Hurston received their first widespread recognition and serious critical appraisal. More recently, however, critics have sought to identify *Cane* with the Modernist movement, which began shortly after World War I when writers and artists began to create works that broke away from traditional literary forms and that rejected Western civilization and culture, often in response to the disillusionment caused by the destruction and devastation of the World War. Critic Linda Wagner-Martin asserts that with its "fragmentary

structure and mixed genre base," *Cane* should be considered "a modernist tour de force."

Indeed, Toomer's work is experimental in form and unprecedented in the range and depth of its realistic representations of African-American experience. As Houston Baker explains, most writing about African Americans in the 1920s fell into one of two categories. Either it followed the "Plantation Tradition" (depicting black mammies and Uncle Toms), or it resorted to contemporary images designed to interest a white audience "in search for the bizarre and the exotic," those "who caught the A-train to Harlem," wearing their raccoon coats and drinking bathtub gin. Toomer, instead, writes about the complexity of African-American culture and experience without avoiding its violent heritage. Further, he distinguishes between the experiences of living in the rural South and the urban North. The six short stories in Part I of *Cane* are set in rural locations, often in the cane fields; the seven prose sketches in Part II are set in Washington D.C. and Chicago, in the urban landscape of industrialization.

"Blood-Burning Moon," the final story in Part I, is a distillation of Toomer's condemnation of white racism and the violence and enmity that pervaded rural Southern culture. During the 1920s, not only did segregation affect most aspects of daily life in the South, but the lynching of African-American men was increasing. Having lived in a rural part of Georgia for a short period of time, Toomer was acutely aware of the threatening circumstances under which African Americans lived in the South. Thus as Baker states, "['Blood-Burning Moon'] is a work that protests, in unequivocal terms, the senseless, brutal and sadistic violence perpetrated against the black man by white America."

In order to achieve his depiction of racial hatred, Toomer creates a romantic conflict between Bob Stone and Tom Burwell for possession of Louisa. While Tom loves Louisa and wants to marry her, Bob's interest in Louisa is based upon sexual passion. The centrality of a female character is crucial in several ways for the development of Toomer's themes of both racism and African-American culture. Richard Eldridge suggests that through Louisa, Toomer brings together "with dramatic intensity the love and hate, beauty and ugliness that live side by side in the twilight zone of the interracial South." One way Toomer brings together love and hate is by Louisa's passivity. She likes being desired by both men, so she does not actively choose one or the other. Even though she anticipates Tom's marriage proposal, she thinks it can "be indefinitely put off." Furthermore, when she thinks of Tom and Bob separately, there is "no unusual significance to either one." Thus, through Louisa's passive response and indecisiveness the space is created for romantic love and racial hatred to collide and explode into violence.

Although Bob's racial hatred is revealed through his violent conflict with Tom, his racist beliefs are also embedded in his relationship with Louisa. Bob neither loves Louisa nor considers marrying her. Rather, he enjoys their regular meetings in the canebrake where he can satisfy his sexual desire for her. Bob still lives in the "twilight zone" of the Southern white culture that owned slaves. In fact, he thinks that "his family still owned the niggers, practically." Because Louisa works as a servant in the Stone family kitchen, Bob goes even further and imagines "the good old days": "He saw Louisa bent over the hearth. He went in as a master should and took her." Bob's fantasy clearly reveals the white man's continued belief in his right to the sexual ownership of African-American women, in addition to their labor. Yet, Bob also knows that his seduction and sexual possession of Louisa is not absolute and indisputable as it was under slavery, nor is it now socially acceptable. He blushes when

> " Toomer graphically describes Tom's tortured death under the gaze of the disorderly mob. In this way, Toomer clearly implicates white supremacy and its threatened dissolution by an increasingly vital community of African Americans as the reason for the violence in the South."

he thinks about his mother or sister learning of his liaison with Louisa. He also becomes both embarrassed and indignant when he thinks about the possibility of trying to explain the relationship to his Northern friends. More importantly, Bob's fantasy is impossible because Louisa is a free woman who can choose whether or not to meet in the canebrake and with whom she will do so. When Bob repeats several times that "his family has lost ground," he is acknowledging the white man's loss of absolute power over the sexual possession of African-American women.

Bob's racism as exemplified in his continuing master/slave mentality culminates in his conflict with Tom. Because he maintains the belief in his right to possess Louisa sexually, he is outraged at the possibility that Tom has been with her. "No nigger had ever been with his girl." Because he believes in his racial superiority to Tom, Bob is further astounded that he might have to fight him for Louisa. Bob thinks to himself, "Bob Stone, of the old Stone family, in a scrap with a nigger over a nigger girl." In "the good old days," this situation would never have occurred, since an African-American man was deprived of his power and, in many ways, his manhood. Yet slavery had ended, and as William Fischer states, "Tom's success in representing himself as a man worthy of Louisa's love is a direct affront to Bob Stone's white manhood." Indeed, Bob's manhood seems bound to his belief in his racial superiority and his power over others.

The final and fatal conflict between Tom and Bob brings into the open the racial supremacy that has been seething under the skin of Bob and lurking in the hearts of the other white men. When he doesn't find Louisa at their meeting spot, Bob becomes enraged. He has lost his power to either control or seduce her; and, furthermore, he has been replaced by Tom. In other words, the power of the white man over the African-American woman has been rendered impotent both by her own volition and by the presence of the African-American man. Hence, Stone's assurance of his racial superiority has been destabilized.

This is particularly evident when Bob first begins to fight. His initial challenge is to lunge at Tom. When that is unsuccessful, Bob tries a verbal challenge: "Fight like a man, Tom Burwell, an I'll lick y." Again, Tom remains rational and calm while he easily "fl[ings] him to the ground" for the second time. It is only when Bob resorts to using a racial slur, "you godam nigger you," that Tom is provoked to fight in earnest. When it becomes apparent that Tom is winning, Bob pulls out his knife. Neither his own physical strength nor the power of his words are adequate to weaken or destroy Tom. Instead, at the same time his white supremacy fails him, Tom slashes his throat with one "blue flash" of the "steel blade."

If Stone's notion of his racial superiority has failed him as an individual, the entire white male community will compensate by uniting as a lynch mob. The effective power of racism is to be found in numbers, not in the perception and attitude of one individual. Only as a group do the individual white men gain sufficient power to lynch Tom. Drawing strength from their communal racial hatred, the mob acts to deprive Tom of his power and his manhood, thereby eliminating the possibility of racial equality. As Fischer explains, "should a young boy grow into manhood with his body and heart basically intact, as Tom Burwell does, then this living black embodiment of the white folks' envy and fear . . . can still be exorcised, as Toomer shows us, by means of a sanctioned social ritual." Toomer graphically describes Tom's tortured death under the gaze of the disorderly mob. In this way, Toomer clearly implicates white supremacy and its threatened dissolution by an increasingly vital community of African-Americans as the reason for the violence in the South. Although slavery had ended, the power relations based upon white dominance of African Americans persisted. When threatened, the use of violence was a prevention against any shift in the prevailing power structure.

After witnessing the bloody fight and the subsequent confrontation between Tom and the white mob, Louisa is on the verge of insanity. She does not need to witness Tom's lynching to know what is happening. "She lives," as Patricia Chase describes, "like many of Toomer's women, in the here and now." Since she concerns herself only with the present moment, she hasn't given much thought to her past or to the possible consequences of her actions. "Thus," Chase continues, "how can she comprehend when the past crashes together with the present before her?" In order to make sense of what happened, Louisa would have to understand her own actions as well as the history of her African-American community.

To understand the racism that structures "Blood-Burning Moon" is, however, to grasp only one significant aspect of Toomer's story. Interwoven with the issues of racism are issues of class and gender, especially as they relate to the African-American struggle for survival in the aftermath of slavery. For example, the association of the full moon with women, as well as other aspects of African-American culture, is another worthy topic of consideration. "Blood-Burning Moon" is a story that can be read and reread with increasing satisfaction. With each reading, previously unseen facets of the story and its style reflect more aspects of the African-American identity and history that Toomer wished to convey.

Source: Jane Phillips, "An Overview of 'Blood-Burning Moon'," in *Short Stories for Students,* The Gale Group, 1999.

Louise Blackwell

Blackwell teaches English at Florida A & M University. In the following excerpt, first published in 1974, she presents her view of how Toomer uses moon imagery in "Blood-Burning Moon."

In "Blood-Burning Moon," we find these lines: "Up from the dusk the full moon came. Glowing like a fired pine-knot, it illumined the great door and soft showered the Negro shanties aligned along the single street of factory town. The full moon in the great door was an omen." The story involves Louisa, a black woman, who works for a white family. Bob Stone, the young son of that family, is in love with her. Tom Burwell, a young and powerfully built black man, is also in love with her. After Tom is chided by his friends about Louisa and Bob Stone, he decides that he has had enough and leaves to find Bob Stone. He then "shuddered when he saw the full moon rising toward the cloud-bank." Before going to Bob Stone, however, he stopped to talk to Louisa on her front steps. At that point "the full moon sank upward into the deep purple of the cloud-bank." And various people on the street began to sing:

> Red nigger moon. Sinner! Blood-burning moon.
> Sinner! Come out that fact'ry door.

Finally, after Bob came to look for Louisa, finding her with Tom Burwell, it is the white man who attacks first. Tom cuts him so badly that he barely made it back to Broad Street before collapsing. That same night white men lynch Tom by tying him to a stake inside the abandoned factory and burning it down. From where she sits, Louisa cannot hear the yelling of the lynchers, but she opens her eyes and sees "the full moon glowing in the great door. The full moon, an evil thing, an omen, soft showering the homes of folks she knew." She wonders where these people are, and decides to sing, hoping "they'd come out and join her." Anyway, she had to sing to the moon, for "the full moon in the great door was an omen."

While this tale is a realistic account of the lynching of a black man, there is constantly present the mysticism that has surrounded the moon forever. There is also what most people today would call "superstition," which is made explicit when Tom, after watching the moon move "towards the cloud-bank," thinks to himself that he "didnt give a godam for the fears of old women." And . . . the moon symbolizes the eye of God as it sinks "upward into the deep purple of the cloud-bank." Clouds symbolize the presence of God, while "purple" is symbolically the color of sorrow and penitence. The blood-red moon is frequently used, as in some of the works of Flannery O'Connor, to symbolize the Host drenched in blood. According to the Old Testament, sacrifices, both human and animal, were made under certain forms of the moon, which are frequently explained in the Bible. In this story, the moon is rising toward a dark cloud. Thus God is symbolically trying to hide his face from the evil that is about to take place. When she begins to sing after the lynching, Louisa hopes that her people will come out to join her, and she thinks that perhaps Tom Burwell might come, too. This suggests a Christ-like sacrifice with the possibility of resurrection.

Source: Louise Blackwell, "Jean Toomer's *Cane* and Biblical Myth," in *Jean Toomer: A Critical Evaluation,* edited by

> " While this tale is a realistic account of the lynching of a black man, there is constantly present the mysticism that has surrounded the moon forever."

Therman B. O'Daniel, Howard University Press, 1988, pp. 437-44.

Richard Eldridge

Eldridge teaches in the English Department at the Community College of Baltimore. In the following excerpt from an article originally published in 1979, he discusses Toomer's use of imagery to develop his characters and themes.

"Blood-Burning Moon," the final piece in Part 1 [of *Cane*], is the story that typifies most dramatically the conflict and the union of black and white. A black and a white male, inseparable enemies, destroy each other over a woman who wants them both. Louisa, the focus of both men's love, stands as yet one more woman in Toomer's tales whose passivity, indecision, and self-directed concerns wreak destruction. The fulcrum of a seesaw courtship, she equally desires, and is equally desired by, her black and her white lover. The white Bob Stone and the black Tom Burwell are but reflections of each other; their significance is their togetherness. Louisa feels their complementary pull as she is returning home from work: Tom's "black balanced, and pulled against, the white of Stone, when she thought of them." Her "strange stir," the foreboding of evil to come, is caused by both: "she tried to fix upon Bob or Tom as the cause of it." Trying to separate Bob's courting her in the canebrake from Tom's marriage proposal makes each lover that much more important: together they shrouded her confidence like the clouds about to cover the moon and sent her to sing and the dogs to howl.

The dogs and chickens, like other beasts of intuition, anticipate imminent danger and form a constant link among the fates of Bob, Tom, and Louisa. The animals hoot and cackle as they pick up the significance of Louisa's worrying "tremor."

> In Louisa Toomer fuses with dramatic intensity the love and hate, beauty and ugliness that live side by side in the twilight zone of the interracial South. 'Blood-Burning Moon' embodies the very elements that so attracted, and so repelled, Jean Toomer in his sojourn to find lasting roots in the soil of the South."

When Tom Burwell becomes filled with rage because his friends laugh about Bob and Louisa's liaison, the dogs again start barking, and the roosters crow. Bob, himself burning with jealousy, stumbles over a dog, sending yelps, cackles, and crows reverberating across the countryside. When the threesome are about to converge, however, all noise has stopped, as though the animals are waiting for the final battle.

The link between Bob and Tom is not only through Louisa's thoughts and the animals' alarm. Tom and Bob are mirrors of each other even in their actions. Much as their background and social expectations differ, they are bound together because they love the same woman. Bob Stone claims racial superiority, yet he is an emotional mixture which reflects the white and the black of the Southern society: "The clear white of his skin paled, and the flush of his cheeks turned purple." Toomer's color-image of the black peasant's experience, I have noted, is dusk, and fruit-purple. Bob Stone pales and purples simultaneously; the whiter he gets the darker he gets. Having arrived at his meeting place but not finding Louisa, Bob is enraged that Tom "had her." Bob bites his lips so hard that he tastes blood: "not his own blood; Tom Burwell's blood." Bob is too overwhelmed with jealousy to think about the incongruity of tasting his enemy's blood in his own veins. Rage has formed a union closer than brotherhood; Bob *is* Tom through the bond of hate.

Though both love Louisa, neither accepts the truth that she has an alternate lover. Both Tom and Bob hear the news from the same source, the men boiling cane at the canebrake. Both flee from the men uncontrollably angry, refusing to believe the truth about her disloyalty and immediately attempting to seek her out. Tom tells Louisa, "I dont believe what some folks been whisperin. . . . Bob Stone likes y. Course he does. But not th way folks is awhisperin." Tacitly he knows differently, for Louisa must get her frilly gifts from some lover's source. Bob, too, has been plagued with hints of her unfaithfulness, for "Cartwell had told him that Tom went with Louisa after she reached home." Protesting too much he immediately thinks, "No Sir. No nigger had never been with his girl. He'd like to see one try." In a similar way Tom has overreacted to Louisa's innocent claim that she has no connection with Bob: "Course y dont. Ise already cut two niggers. Had t hon, t tell em so." Jealousy, then, has reduced both men to the same human condition, irrespective of race or caste. Bob is ready to defend his woman in the same way that the antebellum white gentry would defend the purity of a belle. Likewise, Tom Burwell is ready to kill his "master's" son "jes like I cut a nigger." Charged to action by irrational forces, they can no longer delay the inevitable clash, hard as Louisa may try to put it off. Tom's shyness and Bob's secretiveness vanish in preparation for aggressive claims of ownership. The fight is unavoidable, for both have as their "game" the ability to fight with their knives. And, just as inevitably, the killing of one equates the killing of the other. It is not surprising that Bob Stone's last words are "Tom Burwell," or that the last view of Tom is one with "stony" eyes and a head like a "blackened stone."

Except for the stilted, utterly unbelievable speech that Tom Burwell delivers to Louisa, and for the implausible fragment of folk song which is chanted twice to foreshadow the final scene, "Blood-Burning Moon" is among the more effectively constructed short stories in the collection. In Louisa [Toomer] fuses with dramatic intensity the love and hate, beauty and ugliness that live side by side in the twilight zone of the interracial South. "Blood-Burning Moon" embodies the very elements that so attracted, and so repelled, Jean Toomer in his sojourn to find lasting roots in the soil of the South.

Source: Richard Eldridge, "The Unifying Images in Part One of Jean Toomer's *Cane*," in *Jean Toomer: A Critical Evaluation,* edited by Therman B. O'Daniel, Howard University Press, 1988, pp. 213-36.

William C. Fischer

Fischer teaches at the State University of New York, Buffalo. In the following excerpt from an article on Cane, *the collection of prose and poetry in which "Blood-Burning Moon" appears, he analyzes the characters of Tom Burwell and Bob Stone and discusses the importance of music in Toomer's work.*

A palpable man ... does briefly cross Toomer's pages in the last rural piece [of *Cane*], "Blood-Burning Moon." I say briefly, because Tom Burwell, his manly strengths triumphant for a fleeting interval in which he successfully courts his woman and kills a challenging white suitor, is abruptly incinerated on a lynching pyre. Unlike his practice in the previous sketches, Toomer has not assigned a woman's name to the title, even though Louisa is one of the three principal figures in the story, because the experience described is essentially Tom Burwell's, and the force of his living—and dying—is the main focus. But it is his death that stands out finally, not his life, and so the blood-burning madness of the lynching is given to the title, not the name of the man. All the brutalizing influences of white domination that are tacit in the selfishness, frustration, and violence variously associated with Toomer's other men, and manifest in the subsequent anguish of their women, coalesce in the final death ceremony of the lynching. Should all else fail—all the repressive customs and laws of the dominating culture—and should a young boy grow into manhood with his body and heart basically intact, as Tom Burwell does, then this living black embodiment of the white folks' envy and fear (the uncertain supremacy represented by Bob Stone in the story) can still be exorcised, as Toomer shows us, by means of a sanctioned social ritual.

Burwell is not an idealized innocent, nor is he a legend like Barlo [a character in "Esther," another story in *Cane*]. On the one hand his friends characterize him as "one bad nigger when he gets started. . . . been on th gang three times fo cuttin men," proud and virile praise from those men who know him; and on the other he "come near beatin Barlo," as he tells Louisa, a sign of his considerable strength without the dubious aggrandizement of folk legendry. He too has suffered . . . from malevolent pressures, but he is also capable of touching Louisa profoundly with his love. . . . Tom woos Louisa directly and poetically with his emotional talk, making her abandon all thoughts of the insistent white lover, Bob Stone, who feels passion for her, but only as an

> "Louisa's song becomes the direct articulation of the fear and gruesome finality that looms over all the described events in 'Blood-Burning Moon', and she sings in chorus with all black women at the end of each section of the story in the ultimate communal voicing of the loss of their men."

object of sexual possession. Stone, consciously thinking in the tradition of the white Southern male, wants to take her "as a master should," and does not otherwise have any legitimate emotional or humanizing claim: "She was lovely—in her way. Nigger way. What way was that? Damned if he knew." Tom Burwell knows Louisa as a black woman, though, and embodies the very style that will win her. He courts her in a lilting lovemaking dialect that draws from the "common well" of their feelings. But the song Louisa sings in return, although meant to imply her positive response to Tom, is also the portent of his death:

> Red nigger moon. Sinner! Blood-burning moon.
> Sinner! Come out that fact'ry door.

An old factory building is where the lynching takes place. Tom's very success in representing himself as a man worthy of Louisa's love is a direct affront to Bob Stone's white manhood, based as the latter is upon a racial supremacy that he tries to assert by means of sexual exploitation. Tom's superior natural appeal to Louisa triggers the racially induced emotional affliction in Bob Stone's mind that makes him challenge Tom in a physical encounter. Tom beats him easily, then fatally slashes him with a razor when Bob pulls a knife, securing the ultimate victory that in turn seals his own fate.

Black and white alike are affected by the psychosexual strife rippling just below the surface of the story. Tom has cut up several black men for "tryin t make somethin out a nothin" regarding Bob Stone's relationship with Louisa. But he knows that Bob is in fact a real threat, a reality certified by Toomer's brief representation of the initial conflict in Louisa's mind over the two lovers. She momentarily rationalizes in favor of the white man because her own experience has taught her that she has less of a social obligation to Tom: "To meet Bob in the canebrake, as she was going to do an hour or so later, was nothing new. And Tom's proposal which she felt on its way to her could be indefinitely put off." Although she yields to Tom shortly thereafter, her mental willingness to put him off is both symptomatic of the added strain placed on Tom's natural self-assertion and an ironic foretelling of his permanent elimination at white hands. His manhood, however temporarily ascendant, must be destroyed; and Louisa's womanhood, brought closest to fulfillment of any of Toomer's women, must finally be deprived. Tom represents the ultimate development of the aggregate man Toomer gradually draws out through the fictional rendering of the women, a man at once triumphantly emergent and ruthlessly obliterated in the act of expressing his full potential.

The impressionistic effect of Toomer's writing, both in its imagery and rhythms, is accomplished mainly by simple declarative sentences in uncomplicated and sometimes Spartan language. The work is enigmatic and esoteric, say most readers. This is true in the sense that the style and structure of the book [*Cane*] do not so much invite a meditative literary analysis as an immediate and more emotional response, something like the way one would respond to music. Toomer recognized, as almost every major black American writer has, that music is a primary mode of expression in Afro-American culture, the most direct and accurate expression of Afro-American experience. Song, not surprisingly then, is central to Toomer's conception of the way his writing must speak to the reader. In the instances where it is used in the prose sketches, song is an authenticating medium that communicates subjective qualities about people's experiences that literary prose is less able to convey. The effect of the warring elements in Louisa's mind representing her conflicting responses to the demands of Tom and Bob, black man and white, are most strongly expressed in song. The ambivalence of attraction and fear manifest in her singing corresponds intimately to the underlying durability and terror that conditions the collective black heart in that story. For Tom her song expresses the natural forces of love, while for herself and the other women, as well as for Toomer and the reader, it also stands for the brood-

ing presence of racial bloodlust, the vying of black and white manhood that can only be ominous for them all. Her song becomes the direct articulation of the fear and gruesome finality that looms over all the described events, and she sings in chorus with all black women at the end of each section of the story in the ultimate communal voicing of the loss of their men.

Source: William C. Fischer, "The Aggregate Man in Jean Toomer's *Cane*," in *Studies in the Novel*, Vol. III, No. 2, Summer, 1971, pp. 190-215.

Patricia Chase

Chase teaches at Ohio University. In the following excerpt from an essay that discusses female characters in Toomer's collection Cane, *in which "Blood-Burning Moon" appears, she presents her view of the character Louisa.*

If the fabric of *Cane* [the collection in which "Blood-Burning Moon" first appeared] is the life essence and its meaning behind absurdity, then Toomer's women characters are the threads which weave *Cane* together. Like the form in which Toomer chose to express himself, his women characters are no less rare and sensual. Perhaps they are all the same woman, archetypal woman, all wearing different faces, but each possessing an identifiable aspect of womanhood. Each is strange, yet real; each wears a protective mask of indifference; each is as capable of love as well as lust; and each is guilty of or victimized by betrayal—of herself or of a man. There is no aspect of woman that Toomer does not weave inextricably into his archetypal woman, and in the end, through Carrie K., he has fashioned out of flesh and also failure, his vision of woman-kind. . . .

Louisa . . . as well as Tom Burwell and Bob Stone [pays] the price of pride. In describing Louisa, Toomer begins . . . with beauty—soft, sensual, warm. His description of Louisa is lyrical and sweet with the scent of the cane:

> Her skin was the color of oak leaves on young trees in fall. Her breasts firm and up-pointed like ripe acorns. And her singing had the low murmur of winds in the fig trees.

Enjoying woman's rare advantage, Louisa has two men in love with her—and does not care to choose between them. But as the "blood-burning" moon symbolizes, all is not calm. One man is black, like Louisa, and the other is white. There is a price to pay that Louisa hasn't considered. Louisa becomes caught in a web of events over which she no longer has control. Lulled by the heat, the heavy, sweet scent of the sugar cane, which carries the aura of death and violence, as well as love, and drugged by the "blood-burning" moon, Louisa has not considered the effects of her actions in the light of her environment and the ways of men. She lives, like many of Toomer's women, in the here and now. In Factory town, only here and now. She is young and reckless, which is youth's gift. Thus how can she comprehend when the past crashes together with the present before her? Not wishing to choose between Tom and Bob, and in her glory, she has forgotten the pride of men.

> Separately, there was no unusual significance to either one. But for some reason they jumbled when her eyes gazed vacantly at the rising moon.

Quickly, over before it is begun, violence and death snap Louisa from her dreamy indecision to stark reality.

> Blue flash, a steel blade slashed across Bob Stone's throat. Blood began to flow.... Negroes who had seen the fight slunk into their homes and blew the lamps out. Louisa, dazed, hysterical, refused to go indoors. She slipped, crumbled, her body loosely propped against the woodwork of the well.

With gruesome finality, Tom Burwell is murdered by a white mob for killing a white man, refusing in their fear and hate to investigate the circumstances. They are driven, "blood-burning" with mindless hate, to evil and insane acts of violence. They are the hint of violence that fills the air, always waiting behind the sweet smell of the cane, for the scent of blood and the chance to destroy what they cannot understand.

> Stench of burning flesh soaked the air. Tom's eyes popped. His head settled downward. The mob yelled. Its yell echoed against the skeleton stone walls and sounded like a hundred yells. Like a hundred mobs yelling.... It fluttered like a dying thing, down the single street of factory town. Louisa, upon the step before her home, did not hear it, but her eyes opened slowly. They saw the full moon glowing in the great door. The full moon, an evil thing, an omen, soft showering the homes of folks she knew. Where were they, these people? She'd sing and perhaps they'd come out and join her. Perhaps Tom Burwell would come.

The horror is more than Louisa can bear. The fear, the injustice, the evil and the finality are more than she can comprehend, and she loses her mind. Her powerlessness and the consequences of her naivete become for a moment clear to her and exact a price—her sanity.... Louisa withdraws to a world

> " Lulled by the heat, the heavy, sweet scent of the sugar cane, which carries the aura of death and violence, as well as love, and drugged by the 'blood-burning' moon, Louisa has not considered the effects of her actions in the light of her environment and the ways of men."

beyond the real, where she can no longer be wounded. She has cost a man his life.

Source: Patricia Chase, ''The Women in *Cane*,'' in *CLA Journal,* Vol. XIV, No. 3, March, 1971, pp. 259-73.

Sources

Baker, Houston A., Jr. ''Journey Toward Black Art: Jean Toomer's *Cane*,'' in his *Singers of Daybreak: Studies in Black American Literature,* Washington D.C.: Howard University Press, 1983, pp. 53-80.

Blackwell, Louise. ''Jean Toomer's *Cane* and Biblical Myth,'' in *Jean Toomer: A Critical Evaluation,* edited by Therman B. O'Daniel, Washington D.C.: Howard University Press, 1988, pp. 437–44.

Chase, Patricia. ''The Women in *Cane,* '' in *CLA Journal* Vol. 14, March, 1971, pp. 259–73.

Eldridge, Richard. ''The Unifying Images in Part One of Jean Toomer's *Cane*,'' in *Jean Toomer: A Critical Evaluation,* edited by Therman B. O'Daniel, Washington D.C.: Howard University Press, 1988, pp. 213-36.

Fischer, William C. ''The Aggregate Man in Jean Toomer's *Cane*,'' in *Studies in the Novel,* Vol. III, No. 2, Summer, 1971, pp. 190-215.

Wagner-Martin, Linda. ''Toomer's *Cane* as Narrative Sequence'' in *Modern American Short Story Sequences: Composite Fictions and Fictive Communities,* edited by J. Gerald Kennedy, Cambridge: Cambridge University Press, 1995, pp. 19-34.

Further Reading

Benson, Brian Joseph and Mabel Mayle Dillard. ''Lifting the Veil: *Cane*,'' in *Jean Toomer,* Boston: Twayne, 1980, pp. 49–89.

Benson and Dillard discuss their view of the structure and imagery of ''Blood-Burning Moon.''

Lewis, David Levering. *When Harlem Was in Vogue,* New York: Oxford UP, 1981.

A social and cultural analysis of the Harlem Renaissance, including a discussion of Toomer and his participation in the movement.

Boys and Girls

Alice Munro

1968

"Boys and Girls" was first published in 1968 in *The Montrealer*, before it was collected with fourteen other stories and published in Alice Munro's first edition of short stories, *Dance of the Happy Shades* (1968). The story, narrated by a young girl, details the time in her life when she leaves childhood and its freedoms behind and realizes that to be a "girl" is to be, eventually, a woman. The child begins to understand that being socially typed entails a host of serious implications. Thus becoming a "girl" on the way to womanhood is a time fraught with difficulties for the young protagonist because she senses that women are considered the social inferiors of men. Initially, she tries to prevent this from occurring by resisting her parents' and grandparents' attempts to train her in the likes, habits, behavior, and work of women. This resistance, however, proves to be useless. The girl ends the story clearly socially positioned as a girl, something which she apprehends with some trepidation. The story is thus a feminist parable of sorts, where a girl bucks against a future that will prevent her from doing, socially, whatever she might please. Although most of Munro's work does not have such clear and cogent feminist interest, this story eloquently attests to how women worked during this century to change their social position substantially.

Munro's fiction writing evinces subtle but definite changes throughout her career, and one of the pleasures of reading her fiction is noticing these developments. Nevertheless, *"Boys and Girls"* is

also representative of Munro's work as a whole, as the story's formal strategies can be linked to general trends in her writing. For example, Munro is known for her use of irony, and this story contains numerous ironic flourishes. As the girl protagonist is being groomed to curb her wild behavior and pay attention to her manner of dress and her looks in general, Munro lavishly fleshes out the appearance of the mother, whose labor intensive housework makes it necessary for her to ignore such things entirely. Thus, as the young girl is trained to be vain, an adult woman is presented whose lifestyle in fact precludes such vanity. The girl's mother ties up her hair and wraps it in a scarf, and favors simple clothing that suits her workaday habits.

Author Biography

Alice Munro was born Alice Laidlaw in 1931, in Wingham, Ontario, Canada. She grew up near the Great Lakes that border the United States and Canada, in rural environs such as are featured in much of her early fiction. She attended public schools and was considered such a good student that she advanced a grade early on. She began writing fiction while in high school, and even wrote a novel during this time which she has said was derivative of Emily Bronte's famous *Wuthering Heights*. She won a scholarship to attend the University of Western Ontario and spent two years there as an English major. It was there that she first published short stories, in a university publication. She left the university upon her marriage to James Munro, when the couple moved to British Columbia.

During the 1950s, Munro continued to write while raising her first two daughters. She sold some of her stories to the Canadian Broadcasting Corporation for dramatization and radio shows. Munro had a third daughter in 1966, and then in 1968 her first collection of short stories, *The Dance of the Happy Shades*, was published. "Boys and Girls" is from this first collection of stories. Munro's only novel was published in 1971. In 1974 a second collection of stories was published. With this third publication Munro established herself as a contemporary writer of note.

Munro has seven published books to her credit, six of which are collections of short stories, making her a specialist in the short story genre. Most national literatures have writers who specialize in this way, another notable author being Anton Chekhov, an early twentieth-century Russian writer famous for his short stories. It has often been said, therefore, that Munro is Canada's Chekhov.

Munro's fiction is consistently favorably received by critics and the reading public alike, and she has won numerous awards for her writing. She has been invited to be Writer-in-Residence at various universities, including her alma mater, the University of Western Ontario (which conferred her an Honorary D.Litt. in 1976).

Plot Summary

"Boys and Girls" opens with the unnamed narrator describing her father and his work. He is a fox farmer who raises silver foxes which are skinned so that their fur can be sold to fur traders. The narrator, a girl at the time the story takes place, and her smaller brother Laird, enjoy watching their father doing skinning work, which he does in the cellar of their house each fall or early winter when the foxes' coats are prime. The girl also describes her father's farm hand, Henry Bailey.

She tells how in bed at the end of the day she can still smell foxes, and that this makes her comfortable. She describes the room she and her brother share, and the elaborate rules they have so that they feel safe within the surrounding darkness of night. At first, with the bedside light still on, they are "safe" as long they do not stray beyond the carpet surrounding their beds. This is to keep them suitably removed from the terrifying area beyond their beds that serves as a sort of attic storage space, and which seems very menacing when it is dark. Once the light is off only the beds themselves are safe, and the two children sing songs until Laird falls asleep. Once Laird is asleep, the narrator settles down to imagine adventurous stories in which she is in the role of the grand hero.

The narrator then goes on to detail how the foxes are penned and cared for, and what the specific chores are that she performs to help her father. For example, she feeds and waters the foxes, rakes the ground around the pens. Laird is too young to be of much help. The narrator describes how when she helps her mother in the house (something she does not like to do), her mother tells her "all sorts of things." Her father is more reserved and she feels shy around him.

The narrator overhears a conversation in which her mother laments how she (the narrator) always runs off when she can, to avoid more work in the house, and her mother goes on to say that she is looking forward to the day when her daughter will be older and more able and willing to help in the house. The narrator is not pleased to overhear conversations such as these, and although she thinks her mother is "kinder" than her father, she also thinks of her mother as her "enemy," as someone who is plotting to curtail her freedoms.

Next we learn what the foxes are fed. They are fed horsemeat which her father procures by buying old or lame horses which he then shoots. Sometimes he buys perfectly healthy horses due to the fact that farm machinery is replacing the need for workhorses, and farmers sometimes simply have no more use for a horse and so sell it. Time moves on for the narrator and the theme of her becoming more girl-like is increasingly frequently sounded, whether in terms of her needing to do more housework, or in terms of how she behaves (sitting properly, walking nicely, etc.).

As she becomes more "girl-like," the narrator becomes more self-conscious and starts to wonder if she "would be pretty when [she] grew up." At this time the narrator's father brings Flora, a horse, who is healthy, but whose work has been taken over by machines, to feed the foxes. She has managed to escape her bonds, and is off running through a field that will lead her through a gate and thus beyond the precincts of the farm. The narrator's father perceives that his daughter can more quickly reach the gate out of which the horse will undoubtedly run, and he yells for her to try and get there before the horse. The girl runs off, closely trailed by her little brother.

The narrator reaches the gate, sees the horse running, and without actually making a conscious decision to do so, nevertheless finds herself opening the gate wide for the horse instead of closing it. Only her brother sees this act, because she is out of view of her parent. Her father, Henry Bailey, and her little brother go off in a truck in search of the horse. The girl goes back to the house disconsolately. She does not tell her mother what happened. But over dinner, when the men and boy have returned (and the horse has been caught and shot), Laird tells what happened. The narrator is overcome and begins to cry. She thinks she will be sent away from the table. But instead, the whole incident is dismissed: "'Never mind,' my father said. He spoke

Alice Munro

with resignation, even good humor, the words which absolved me and dismissed me for good. 'She's only a girl,' he said."

Characters

Henry Bailey

Henry Bailey is a farmhand. He is like a part of the narrator's family, sharing meals and his life with them. He is mainly a source of entertainment for the children, probably since he does not appear as an authority figure, as the children's parents clearly do. Thus, they can enjoy his teasing of them a great deal, and he, for his part, seems to enjoy thrilling them with his more spectacular accomplishments (like spitting very well).

Father

Like the narrator's mother, the father figure in the story seems a likable, decent and hardworking man. He humors his children, finding ways to praise them that pleases them a great deal. Like his wife, he seems to view a future in which his daughter will eventually leave off helping him to become, exclusively, a help to the mother.

Fox cubs in a cage on a fox farm, similar to the setting in "Boys and Girls."

Female Narrator

The character who narrates this story does so with the hindsight of maturity, although she describes events from her childhood and manages to provide the reader with a youthful point of view. She describes the period in her life when her carefree childhood ended, and she began to feel as if she must conform to various expectations. The traditional socialization undergone by middle-class girls at this time was something she resisted, as she perceived that the roles and choices allotted to women were less attractive and various than those allotted to men. However, regardless of this resistance, she describes how she gradually capitulated to accept this socialization. The narrator is like the lively, frisky horse Flora in the story, a living thing with energy and will that is finally entrapped and used by forces greater than herself.

Laird

Laird is the narrator's younger brother, a seemingly sweet little boy whose helplessness is, at first, contrasted to the narrator's greater ability to be of help to her mother and father in the house and on the fox farm. However, as the story progresses, this image of babyishness falls away as it becomes clear that Laird will be the one to take the narrator's place

at their father's side, a position the young narrator hoped would always belong to her. By the end of the story Laird has been taken into the company of men, and his sister, the narrator, has been relegated to the ranks of being "only a girl."

Mother

The narrator's mother seems to be an exemplary woman, one who fulfills the duties of a homemaker with energy and verve. The portion of the story that describes what goes on inside the farm house shows her putting in a day's work that matches the energies of the men working outside. She looks forward to the day when her daughter will be older and so able to relieve more of her labor's burden. She seems to enjoy the company of her daughter; the narrator tells us that she talks freely about her past and things in general when they are working together.

Themes

Coming of Age

In some respects, "Boys and Girls" is a classic coming of age tale. Most societies have either cultural narratives or cultural rituals that bespeak the

Topics for Further Study

- The narrator's father is in the fur trade in this story, as were many Canadians. Research the history of the Canadian fur trade. Which ''peltries'' (pelts/furs) were its primary exports? Does Canada still specialize in fur? Where are the markets for these goods?

- Then Canadian Prime Minister Pierre Trudeau and his wife were international figures during the 1970s. What made this couple such interesting and vital figures?

- ''Boys and Girls'' uses an old popular saying, ''only a girl,'' to neat effect. Currently, popular culture is evincing a plethora of ''girl'' associations or buzzwords: Girl Power, ''bad grrrls or riot grrrls,'' and so on. This activity is interesting in light of earlier feminist efforts to isolate the word ''girl'' and indicate that it was commonly used to refer to adult females, and not just (female) children or teenagers. The push to insist on the use of the word ''woman'' for an adult female seems to have been largely successful. Do these ''girl'' movements represent something of a retreat even if they are largely in reference to teenaged girls or younger women? Or do they represent something different and new? Discuss.

- Gloria Steinem was a major United States feminist activist around the time Munro wrote ''Boys and Girls.'' Research Canadian feminist history and find out who the major feminists in Canada at this time were.

- Which Native American tribes are indigenous to Canada? What is the history of their reservation or land rights activism in the last twenty years?

---

end of childhood and the entry into adulthood. The way that this shift in a boy or girl's life is depicted will tell a great deal about the values of a particular culture. If the tale is about a boy who goes on his first hunting expedition, then the reader surmises that bravery is paramount to what makes a boy a man in that society. What, then, marks the transition from girlhood to young womanhood? It is this problem that Munro takes on in ''Boys and Girls.'' Interestingly, Munro first depicts the young girl narrator defining herself like a boy seemingly would do. She thinks up stories at night in which she is a hero who is brave and saves other people from peril. However, when this girl begins to think of herself as a gendered person, she no longer thinks in terms of heroic qualities that will have some larger social effect, but instead begins to focus on her person itself (her relative beauty or plainness). Will she be ''pretty,'' she wonders? Will a certain ''fancy'' material for a dress enhance her looks? Coming of age for a young girl at the historical time of this story, then, seems to rest on the future potential of this girl's ability to attract men, and thus her marriageability. Bravery and independence, those qualities that will lead persons to successfully make their public and professional way in the world can be contrasted to this more private and personal mode of self-valuation. Thus, when a woman writer takes on the problem of female coming-of-age as it might have occurred during the first half of this century, what ensues is a parable about how the girl retreats from the public and enwraps herself in the space of private worries.

Style

Allusion

When a writer makes an ''allusion'' within a story, he or she refers to a well-known event or thing that is supposed to conjure up associations that are relevant to what is going on in the story. In saying that her father's favorite book is *Robinson Crusoe*,

Munro, via the narrator, has made an important allusion in her story. This novel by Daniel Defoe is about a man who, on a colonial venture from England to South America, is shipwrecked and becomes the only survivor washed up on an island off the South American coast. Finding he cannot build a seaworthy vessel to contend with the surrounding coast and sea with the implements he has at his disposal (which he either saves from the sunken ship or makes himself), Crusoe goes about building himself a home and a farm and taming and grooming his environment to his purposes. He spends many years alone. Eventually, he witnesses a group of South American Indians land on his island and prepare to kill a hostage from another tribe they have taken in war. Crusoe saves this unfortunate Indian and then the book goes on to depict an idealized relation between the two men in which the Indian, in profound gratitude, willingly and happily submits to Crusoe and becomes his slave. Crusoe dubs the Indian "Friday" to commemorate the day he saved him, and the day he received a companion, for he has been very lonely. Contemporary critics, not surprisingly, have read this last portion of Defoe's book as the dreamy wishes of a European man who imagined that the natives of colonized lands greeted their demise or bondage with little dismay or resentment. Like the fur company's calendar, Defoe's book idealizes the history of colonialism, to the clear benefit of those who had the upper hand. By linking this book to her father within a story that contests women's secondary status to men, Munro aligns Crusoe to her father and herself to Friday. Like Crusoe, she suggests, her father does not recognize that she does not accept her inferior social status.

Foreshadowing

In a story about a young girl's feelings about being trapped into a position she is not looking forward to, the subplot concerning the two horses bought to be used for fodder is an instance of foreshadowing. Although any reader will understand that the success of the fox farm depends upon the sacrifice of these two animals, Munro's attention to Flora's attempt to run away nevertheless provokes feelings of pity for the animal whose life will end while it is in its prime. The inevitability and unpleasantness of this animal's fate foreshadows the fate of the girl protagonist. No matter how hard she tries to resist her future, she is destined to lose to forces greater than herself.

Subplot

The story of the two horses comprises a subplot within the larger story that is "Boys and Girls." Subplots usually serve a specific function in a story. They may provide a counterpoint to the larger plot, outlining a sub-story that contradicts or parodies the main goings-on, or, as in the case of this subplot, they may serve to underscore the main events. The horses' fate is determined and dismal, and so is the fate and future of the girl narrator. Munro's clever interweaving of the larger plot and this subplot makes for a tightly constructed and powerful ending to the story.

Historical Context

Feminism and Social Change

The year the short story collection *Dance of the Happy Shades,* which includes "Boys and Girls" was published, 1968, was also the year that Pierre Elliot Trudeau became Prime Minister of Canada. Eloquent, forward-looking, and energetic, this prime minister's entry into office represented the forces and collective will of a decade of major social change. His winning of this highest office represented the solidification of substantial changes in mores and beliefs that so clearly distinguishes the latter half of the twentieth-century from the earlier half. Before becoming Prime Minister, Trudeau was the Minister of Justice, in which office he liberalized laws on abortion, birth control, divorce, and homosexuality. The late 1950s, but especially the 1960s, was a time in Canada (as it was in the United States and Europe as well) when various social movements changed the face of western society. Many of these social movements pertained directly to the status and freedoms of women within society, and thus "Boys and Girls" is very much a story of its time, as it represents the creative work of a woman writer who sympathizes with those changes in belief that served to expand women's social choices.

Critical Overview

Dance of the Happy Shades, the collection of short stories in which "Boys and Girls" appeared, was published in 1968. The novel *Lives of Girls and Women* (1971) soon followed, and a second collection of stories entitled *Something I've Been Mean-*

Compare & Contrast

- **1960s and 1970s:** In Canada (as in the United States and other locales), the Women's Movement flourishes and establishes itself. Along with other groups of people demanding equal rights, women activists gain significant social advances.

   1990s: In the United States, the Men's Movement, including organizations like the Promise-keepers, begins. Organized by a few charismatic leaders, men begin to get together to renew a sense of their masculinity, or, in the case of one movement, to push for a return to societal arrangements before feminism.

- **1960s:** Native Americans (whether hailing from Canada or the United States), begin to contest

their status within these countries. The Canadians, whose French-English colonial history had long given them a sense of the "multicultural," begin to expand this sense of diversity to accomodate recognition of the persons who were native to that geographical locale. The United States enacts Civil Rights legislation to guarantee equal treatment of racial minorities.

   1990s: The terms "melting pot" and "multicultural" now vie with terms like "diversity," "difference," and "hybridization." All these words attempt to describe the ethnic and cultural scene in highly diverse nations, or, more recently, these notions are being used to refer to the new global space of meeting cultures and groups.

---

ing To Tell You was published in 1974. In an essay written in 1978 in which these three books were discussed, critic Hallward Dahlie said Munro is "a writer who has quietly and firmly established herself over the past decade." To say that Munro gained this reputation "quietly and firmly" seems an apt estimation. From the start, Munro's critics approached her writing as that which deserved careful and serious consideration, whether their praise was highly favorable or more measured in its admiration. Her fiction has inspired a large and highly respectable body of scholarly criticism. By the time *Dance of the Happy Shades* was published, Munro had spent many years honing her talent. Thus, when this collection appeared, it was the work of a writer skilled and confident in her talents, talents that well justified the admiration they inspired. So, even if critic Frederick Busch found Munro's art in her first collection somewhat lacking in "the thrilling economy, the poetry that makes the form [the short story] so valuable," he nevertheless acknowledged that they are stories "you have to call well-made." Most critics, however, greeted *Dance of the Happy Shades* like Martin Levin did. In Levin's review in the *New York Times Book Review*, he said the "short story is alive and well in

Canada"; the "15 tales ... originate like fresh winds from the north."

That Munro deserves this solid place among writers is underscored in an essay written by Rae McCarthy MacDonald in which the critic asserted that "Munro's work bears the marks of a distinctive, vital, and unifying vision." According to MacDonald, this vision is quite somber. Noting that so many of Munro's stories feature minor characters who are "eccentrics, criminals, and the fatally ill," MacDonald suggested that these marginal characters "work as a symbol or externalization of the suffering and deformity of the apparently healthy and adjusted characters." However, other critics differ as to the bleakness of Munro's vision. For instance, while Hallvard Dahlie also noted a pervasiveness of "existential terror or desperation" in her fiction, this "desperation" is, Dahlie suggested, finally offset by a concurrent development of a sense of "existential possibility within a total vision that is much closer to faith rather than despair." Or, from the point of view of the famous novelist and short story writer Joyce Carol Oates, Munro's fiction is described as being so true to its subjects that it somehow "celebrate[s]" them; in Munro's fiction, said Oates, there is a ''wonderful variety of people . . . [whom] we always want to know more about.'' That more critics tend to this latter view is perhaps because, as Kildare Dobbs recorded, so many of her stories ''move quietly to their modest epiphanies or moral insights.'' Certainly, stories like ''Walker Brothers Cowboy'' or ''Dance of the Happy Shades'' (both from *Dance of the Happy Shades*) do work toward these deeply touching resolutions of sudden profound insight and emotional purgation (''epiphanies''), and they do also seem to capture what is most impressive about Munro's art. Munro's solid position within the contemporary canon of English language fiction is shown by the many essays and books that have been written about her fiction, such as Robert Thacker's bibliography of Munro criticism, *Alice Munro: An Annotated Bibliography,* and E. D. Blodgett's book, *Alice Munro,* which explores the complexity of Munro's ''subtly self-aware manner of narration.''

Criticism

Carol Dell'Amico

Dell'Amico is a doctoral candidate in the program of Literatures in English at Rutgers, The State University of New Jersey. She specializes in the twentieth-century novel. The essay ''Literature and Social History'' discusses the connection between fiction and history, generally, and the historical interest of Alice Munro's ''Boys and Girls'' in particular.

The word ''literature'' means different things to different people. Lately, the word is used to mean any type of written material, from government and business reports, to fiction and poetry, to histories and letters. Then, within the category of literature, it is possible to make a distinction between fictive literatures (novels, short stories, poetry) versus factual types of writing, like histories. Yet, the distinction between fact and fiction is not as definite as the opposing words suggest. For example, a book of history is a compilation of facts, but these facts must be interpreted and interwoven into a continuous story by the writer. There is a bit of the ''story'' in ''hi-story,'' as these facts appear within a form of literature that is a narrative (about the past). Or, in terms of fiction like Munro's which places the reader within a recognizable time and place, while it is clearly imaginative work, it is also a historical document of sorts, a place to find out how people

lived and what they thought and wished or dreamed. It may not be history in a strictly technical sense, but it can be consulted for historical information. Of course, it is this imaginative aspect of art that creates the possibility for fiction to be more than, or different than, history. Comments such as the following (found on a jacket of one edition of *Dance of the Happy Shades*), points to this expectation; the writer asserts: ''Alice Munro's short stories probe the interior life of ordinary people in the small towns and farms of southwestern Ontario. The setting may be Canadian—the themes are universal: the joys and cruelties of love, the self-discovery of adolescence, [and so on]. . . .''

What this critic's words suggest is that Munro's work is as good as it is precisely because it is more than history, more than just a document of rural Canadian lifestyles. It is more because it tells us something about ourselves as human beings (''interior life''), and so it transcends time and history and thus achieves the status of the ''universal.'' Yet, despite this, some stories that are widely appreciated by readers and critics are valued not simply for their universality, or their humanity, but also because they seem to capture and document a particularly significant moment in social or historical time. ''Boys and Girls'' is one of these stories, a story that is important not only for its being ''good art,'' but also for its social or historical significance. History and fiction, two sub-types in the larger category of Literature, cannot be wholly distinguished or disassociated from each other. Some stories are important because they record major moments in a culture's social history, and ''Boys and Girls'' is one of these stories.

The title of this story points to the specific social issue which it is concerned with: the difference between boys and girls, or women and men, and the way that many women during this century are concerned with women's rights. The later twentieth-century is distinguished for its women's movement, an on-going event that has shaped the century and the people who have lived it. Most twentieth-century writers take up this issue somewhere in their work, whether directly or more peripherally, as authors write, in part, to engage or come to terms with their time and place. This ability to address the social and historical is partly what makes a writer relevant. And what Munro specifically offers the reader in ''Boys and Girls'' is insight into what Kildare Dobbs refers to as ''the ideology of the women's movement.'' By ideology, Dobbs means the set of beliefs that underpin the aspirations of

What Do I Read Next?

- *Lives of Girls and Women* (1971), Alice Munro's second published book is, like "Boys and Girls," a female coming of age tale. It is also the story of its protagonist's development as a writer.

- Twentieth-century writers interested in writing a book about artistic calling will find that James Joyce's brilliant *Portrait of the Artist as a Young Man* (1914) is worthwhile reading. This book, like Munro's *Lives of Girls and Women*, is part of a sub-category in fiction in which writers fictionalize their own artistic apprenticeships.

- One Canadian critic has written an essay which specifically addresses Canadian coming of age stories. This critic compares Munro's *Lives of Girls and Women* to other Canadian books concerned with the theme of adolescence and growing up: Anthony B. Dawson, "Coming of Age in Canada," *Mosaic* 11, No. 3, Spring, 1978, pp. 47-62.

- The novel *Housekeeping* (1970), by Marilynne Robinson, is an extraordinary and beautifully written novel about a family of four women who, like Munro's characters, live a rural life.

---

feminists who, during this century, wished to expand (and continue to consolidate and further) the social opportunities of women.

Obviously, one short story cannot pack in the entire (and in fact very diverse) feminist platform. Nevertheless, what this story does do is dramatize certain basic feminist ideas, and it does so quite effectively. Since the notion that a woman might move beyond the home necessitates the notion that women are not genetically programmed, as it were, to be only effective in the home, one thing that feminists argue is that desiring a traditional role is often the result of training or socialization, and not necessarily the result of nature ("nature versus nurture," as the debate is often called). That is, if girls are not discouraged, then they might very well chose a profession which, before the women's movement, was thought solely appropriate for a man. This basic premise is presented cogently by Munro; the narrator thinks: "The word girl had formerly seemed to me innocent and unburdened, like the word child; now it appeared that it was no such thing. A girl was not, as I had supposed, simply what I was; it was what I had to become." By saying that a girl is something she must "become," Munro puts forward the idea that this development is in no way natural, but rather will be the result of training or socialization. Soon after this realization, the narrator notices how it is she is urged "to become" a girl, or how the socialization proceeds:

> My grandmother came to stay with us for a few weeks and I heard other things. "Girls don't slam doors like that." "Girls keep their knees together when they sit down." And, worse still, when I asked some questions, "That's none of girls' business." I continued to slam doors and sit as awkwardly as possible, thinking that by such measures I kept myself free.

What is understood from passages such as the ones above is that there is not much difference in behavior between the sexes if they are left to their own devices. However, figures in positions of authority, such as the grandmother, take it upon themselves to train the sexes in appropriate sex-specific behaviors. Judging from the above, the training of girls concentrates on making them into beings who demonstrate physical self-containment and modesty (no slamming doors; sitting demurely). And beside behavior restrictions, there is the training of girls in their proper interests, "girls' business."

Clearly, this training would not be resisted so strongly by the narrator if this differentiation of the sexes did not involve a simultaneous devaluation of "girls' business," which is a second major feminist issue. That is, it is not simply that girls are trained to be specific types of persons, but also that the person they are to become is considered, socially, less

"'Boys and Girls' is one of these stories, a story that is important not only for its being 'good art,' but also for its social or historical significance."

important than a man. Munro develops this idea in scenes such as the following:

> One time a feed salesman came down into the pens to talk to him [the father] and my father said, "Like to have you meet my new hired man." I turned away and raked furiously, red in the face with pleasure. "Could of fooled me," said the salesman. "I thought it was only a girl."

Or, at the end of the story, when it has become known that the narrator let the horse out of the field purposefully: "'Never mind,' my father said. He spoke with resignation, even good humor, the words which absolved and dismissed me for good. 'She's only a girl,' he said." What this pointed repetition of the phrase "only a girl" points to is precisely this societal notion that girls and women are considered less significant than men. The narrator is so deeply pleased by being referred to teasingly as a "new hired man" because she is quite aware that being a man is better than being "only" a girl or woman. She resists her future role as mother's helper in the story because her pride rebels against being considered second to anybody.

Feminists combat this unfortunate hierarchy in two ways. One, they insist that traditional woman's work is valuable, and must be recognized for how it keeps society going. In "Boys and Girls," this idea comes across in the way that Munro depicts her mother as constantly busy and very hardworking. She may be doing housework, but if she did not, the family would fall apart. The reason why this hierarchy came about, feminists suggest, is because men's work is more public, and women's more private, and since it takes place in the home it is less visible and thus has gone unacknowledged and undervalued. Also, another way that feminists work toward the changing of women's secondary social status is to insist that, if given the chance or choice, women could do as well as men in the more public profes-

sions. By letting women move beyond the home, it will be seen how they can compete with men and thus be seen as their social equals. Further, feminists argue that some women have talents specifically matched to public professions, and that it would be a shame to waste these talents by forcing them to remain in the home. Indeed, as an aspiring writer in an era before women's advancement was as consolidated as it is today, Munro herself voiced just such an observation in an interview. On the farm, Munro observed, "there is a sexual polarity." And, she adds "you are a bit out of luck if you don't have the talents for the sexual role that you've been born into." Of herself she says, "I'm not good at hooking rugs and making quilts and things like that, so I would have had a very rough time in this life."

Luckily for Munro, she was born when there had been enough advancement of women in the realm of the arts that it was possible for her to develop her true talent, which was to be a writer and artist. However, since these advancements took so long to achieve, and were majorly advanced in the very decades that she came of age as an artist, it is not surprising that some of her stories, like "Boys and Girls," records this social issue of women's rights. Literature or fiction is not conceived of in a vacuum, rather it arises from the experiences of real men and women living in history. For this reason, it is misguided to assume that art always transcends time and place. Rather, much of the most respected fiction in the history of literature is so respected precisely because it was able to grasp and communicate the social and historical reality of its time and place.

Source: Carol Dell'Amico, "Literature and Social History," in *Short Stories for Students,* The Gale Group, 1999.

Rena Korb

Korb has a master's degree in English literature and creative writing and has written for a wide variety of educational publishers. In the following essay, she discusses how the narrator of "Boys and Girls" unwittingly accepts being a girl.

Although Alice Munro knew from the time she was 12 years old that she wanted to be a writer, her first collection of short stories was not published until 1968, when Munro was well into her adulthood. Since then, however, she has remained one of Canada's top authors, and her work has crossed the world's boundaries; her writing has been translated into 14 languages and her works are widely anthologized. Her writing often features the world she knows best, the Depression-era southwestern Ontario of her early years. In *Dance of the Happy Shades*, from which the story "Boys and Girls" is taken, Munro presents the hardscrabble childhood of her youth. Critics and readers responded to this collection positively, noting her evocation of place as well as her understanding and depiction of the gender roles that characterized the time period. For this collection she won the prestigious Governor's General Award, an honor that would be bestowed upon her several times.

"Boys and Girls" may be termed a rite-of-passage story, for it tells of a significant event that helps one girl to recognize and accept the womanhood that is her future. The 11-year-old narrator lives on her family's fox farm. For years she has helped out her father, but that winter she realizes that her mother is expecting her to become more of a "girl"—working in the house, for instance, instead of in the fox pens. The narrator resists such efforts at transformation. However, when her father intends to kill a mare in order to feed the foxes, with no forethought the girl frees the panicked horse. The girl is not surprised to later learn that her father has recaptured and killed the mare. What does surprise her, however, is that he is not angry with her transgression; after all, as he says, "'She's only a girl.'" And perhaps also surprising to the girl is her own reaction to his statement: "I didn't protest that, even in my heart. Maybe it was true."

One of the most striking features of the story is Munro's presentation of how the ideas suggested by "boy" and "girl" come into opposition; this opposition is reflected in all facets of the narrator's world. Still, the story slowly builds to this conclusion, for as it begins, the narrator and her younger brother, Laird, have both firmly allied themselves with their father; they spend their time watching their father work, skinning the foxes. Their mother, however—the homemaker—dislikes this bloody business.

Clearly, the narrator has given thought to the differing roles of men and women and has chosen to identify herself with the male sphere. She sees the inside of the house as her mother's territory, a territory she does not care to inhabit. Outside the house is the real world, the world of foxes and commerce and vibrancy. Even her bedroom, part of the inside house, is not a sanctuary but instead an "unfinished" space she shares with her brother. Marlene Goldman has written that this space remains "undifferentiated," implying the same state

> 'Boys and Girls' may be termed a rite-of-passage story, for it tells of a significant event that helps one girl to recognize and accept the womanhood that is her future."

in the children—that they have not yet accepted their respective labels of "girl" or "boy." The children are so alike they even share the same fear: "*inside*, the room where we slept," instead of outside, with its chilling winter. At the beginning of the story, it is the outside world in which the girl participates. She has a summer job of giving the foxes water with the "real watering can, her father's," while Laird only carries a "little cream and green gardening can, filled too full and knocking against his legs and slopping water on his canvas shoes." The girl's subtle boast emphasizes her belief that she has access to the male tools and thus the male identity. The girl compares working side-by-side with her father to working in the house with her mother. Her father remains silent, while her mother often would tell her stories. The girl, however, gets a "feeling of pride" working with her father that she lacks with her mother. Clearly, housework and "women's work" do not have the same value as the male, outside work. She feels her role on the farm is assured—her father even refers to her when speaking to a feed salesman as "'my new hired man,'" which makes her "red in the face with pleasure."

The girl has no expectations that her daily life will change. By this point she has fully embraced the male identity, even down to the stories she tells herself at night in which she plays a rescuing hero and then rides down the main street on a horse to receive the townspeople's gratitude, even though the only person to ever do so is the man who plays King Billy during the town's yearly parade, itself a state of make-believe. One day, however, she sees her mother by the barn. This itself is the first sign that something is amiss, for "[I]t was an odd thing to see my mother down at the barn. She did not often come out of the house unless it was to do something—hang out the wash or dig potatoes in the garden.'' The girl overhears part of her mother's words—''And then I can use her more in the house, . . . It's not like I had a girl in the family at all.'' Despite this conversation, the narrator does not expect anything to change. As she puts it, ''Who could imagine Laird doing my work . . . It showed how little my mother knew about the way things really were.'' Her statement shows that not only does she believe her help to be indispensable to her father, but that, because of her male work, she believes herself to be superior to her mother—more knowledgeable and more useful. Her acknowledgment that ''I did not expect my father to pay any attention'' to her mother's words further shows that she has placed herself on an equal level with her father; as the only family representatives of the male identity, they share the secrets of the farm; her mother, trapped in the house and in her female body, remains ignorant.

Despite her protestations, at this point the girl enters into a new stage, one in which she is no longer able to securely latch on to her chosen identity. For throughout the winter she hears ''a great deal more on the theme'' and admits, ''I no longer felt safe . . . The word *girl* had formerly sounded to me innocent and unburdened, like the word *child*; now it appeared it was no such thing. A girl was not, as I had supposed, simply what I was; it was what I was to become.'' That winter other challenges to the girl's right to occupy the male sphere are launched. As Goldman points out, with her grandmother's visit, the narrator learns lessons about how girls are expected to come under societal control: girls don't slam doors, girls keep their knees together when they sit down, and the worst of all, in response to a question, '''That's none of girls' business.'''

To what extent these lessons influence the narrator is unknown to the reader at this point. Only later does the reader learn that the girl has taken to ''standing in front of the mirror combing my hair and wondering if I would be pretty when I grew up.'' The stories she tells herself at night have changed, too; although they start out the same, they switch so that she no longer does the rescuing but suddenly a male figure is rescuing *her*. Her belongings have similarly taken on the trappings of femininity: old lace curtains as a bedspread, a dressing table with a skirt. She also has grown dissatisfied with the bedroom she shares with Laird. What she had previously presented as a common space, where

the two siblings cheerfully engaged in storytelling and singing, she now plans to divide with a barricade. When this transformation happens is unknown to the reader, but clearly it has been building up before her fateful encounter with Flora. In fact, it is likely that the narrator deliberately withheld this information from the reader, mirroring the way she has kept herself from understanding the true meaning of her actions. The narrator's ability to hide pertinent details has already been demonstrated in her exclusion of how her father feeds the foxes—''I have forgotten to say what the foxes were fed. My father's bloody apron reminded me.'' That the story opens with the dead, bloody bodies of the fox shows that the narrator has left out this detail in an attempt to present her favored father in the best light possible.

The spring began as any other spring. Yet, as her father prepares to kill Flora, a mare he has purchased with the intention of feeding her to the foxes, the girl undergoes a drastic transformation, particularly so in comparison to her reaction at the killing of another horse a short time before. When that horse was killed, the girl's legs were a ''little shaky,'' but she felt ''all right'' after going to the movies that afternoon.

The girl has already identified herself to some extent with Flora, a high-strung horse, for Flora, like the girl and even the foxes, experiences confinement. Clearly, the structure and description of the farm itself reinforce such ideas of entrapment. The foxes, which the girl recognizes as beautiful but hostile, live in a ''world my father had made for them.'' She describes the fox pens, which Goldman points out are ''spaces in which bodies are confined and controlled,'' as bordering the streets of a town; inside the pens the foxes restlessly ''prowled up and down,'' much as Flora, when let out of the barn, ''trotted up and down and reared at the fences, clattering her hooves against the rails.'' Goldman further comments on the house and the farm: the dark, hot kitchen that ''imprisons'' the mother and threatens the narrator; the fields that surround the farm and the gates that restrict traffic are an ''enlarged version of the pen''; even the town itself is an ''inescapable enclosure.''

When Flora is brought out of the barn to be killed, the girl states, ''It was exciting to see her running, whinnying, going up on her hind legs, prancing and threatening like a horse in a Western movie, an unbroken ranch horse, though she was just an old driver, an old sorrel mare.'' The horse brings to life the narrator's fantasies, though now generally rejected, of the female striking against imposed societal expectations and becoming a creature strong in its own right. Flora breaks away into a meadow where a gate has been left open. The girl's father shouts to her to shut the gate. It is at this moment that the girl breaks irrevocably from her self-imposed male-identified position. Her desire to free the female horse is stronger than her desire to please her father. She knows however, that the horse will be recaptured, and that freedom is only an illusion. For the first time in her life, she disobeys her father. "Instead of shutting the gate," she recounts, "I opened it as wide as I could. I did not make any decision to do this, it was just what I did." While the girl returns to the house—"inside"—her younger brother becomes a man; he remains "outside" and goes along with the men to track down and catch Flora. This is the point at which the narrator admits to the changes that she has been undergoing; she opens her heart up to the truth. She has become a "girl."

Marlene Goldman calls "Boys and Girls" a "narrative which highlights the almost invisible societal forces which shape children." By the end of the story, the sister and brother have firmly stepped into the roles that society has extended to them. "Boys and Girls" also introduces two themes that reappear in Munro's writing: the burden of femininity and the women's need to break free.

Source: Rena Korb, "A Rite of Passage," in *Short Stories for Students,* The Gale Group, 1999.

Marlene Goldman

In the following essay, Goldman looks at the theme of societal forces that shape children into adults, especially the different things expected of boys and girls, found in Munro's "Boys and Girls." She also looks at the very different worlds—outside and inside, the male sphere and the female sphere—described by Munro in the story.

"My father was a fox farmer." So begins Alice Munro's short story "Boys and Girls," a narrative which highlights the almost invisible societal forces which shape children, in this case, the narrator and her brother Laird, into gendered adults. There is no doubt that males and females are biologically distinct at birth. Yet the behaviours and roles ascribed to each sex on the basis of this biological distinction are not natural. In this study, then, when I speak of gender, I refer not to sex, but to this set of prescribed behaviours.

> Even the stories the narrator tells herself have altered. The plots start off in the old way, but then 'things would change around, and instead, somebody would be rescuing me.' No longer the valiant hero, she becomes the victim in need of rescue."

Children, as the text clearly illustrates, do not evolve naturally into gendered adults. Instead, the construction of gendered subjects constitutes a form of production. Yet unlike other systems of production, the mechanisms which assist in the creation of gendered adults remain invisible; they seem natural, and for this reason they are taken for granted.

One such "invisible" mechanism, central to the production of gendered adults, involves the division and control of space. In "Boys and Girls," spatial divisions and the control of space within the home and on the farm are emphasized by a narrator still young enough to remark upon details which the adults ignore. As a result of the narrator's relatively innocent and inquisitive perspective, the reader can appreciate how the division of space facilitates two seemingly disparate systems of production: farming and the construction of gendered adults.

As a farmer, the father cultivates wild animals for the purpose of consumption. As the narrator explains, he "raised silver foxes in pens." The word "raised" refers to silver foxes, but the term offers more than this strictly referential meaning. It can also be understood within the familial context: people often speak of raising children. The plurality of the word opens the text to diverse readings— readings which introduce the possibility of a correspondence between the two systems of production.

In particular, the father raises the foxes in "pens"—spaces in which bodies are confined and controlled. As the narrator explains, he took great pains to build a miniature city for his captives: "alive, the foxes inhabited a world my father made for them.'' Moreover, the pens resembled a medieval town ''padlocked at night.'' This image of the enclosure and the concomitant distinction between inside and outside (indoor and outdoor) recur throughout the text.

Early on, the house takes on the properties of the pen. The dark, hot, stifling kitchen imprisons the narrator's mother and threatens to imprison the narrator. Similarly, the fields surrounding the farm and the gates, which restrict traffic, become an enlarged version of the pen. Finally, the town itself and the outlying farms are conceived of in terms of an inescapable enclosure. As a result of these replications of the enclosure, the father's occupation and his role in establishing and supervising the boundaries between inside and outside take on greater significance and begin to reflect a far more pervasive cultural project.

The Marxist critic Ivan Illich sheds light on the nature of this project when he suggests that the capacity to enclose, essentially a male privilege, was the key factor responsible for the emergence of industrial society and wage work as we know it today. Illich states that the economic division of labor into a productive and a non-productive kind was pioneered and first enforced through ''the domestic enclosure of women.'' As he explains, men became the ''wardens of their domestic women.'' Thus, the narrator's father, in his capacity as guardian and gate-keeper penning in the bodies, performs a task which supports industrial society and wage work, and ultimately, capitalist production.

In addition to enclosing the foxes, the father in ''Boys and Girls'' also controls a specific space within the home. When not working out of doors, he carries out his activities in the cellar, a room which is white-washed and lit by a hundred-watt bulb. By definition, white-wash is ''a solution of quicklime or of whiting and size for brushing over walls and ceilings to give a clean appearance.'' Figuratively speaking, ''white washing'' suggests clearing ''a person or his memory of imputation or [clearing] someone's reputation.'' In this case, the presence of white-wash in the male domain suggests that an attempt is made to ''give something a clean appearance''—something which may be fundamentally unclean.

Furthermore, the intense light which illuminates the space also reflects the father's desire to control or, more specifically, to manipulate one's impression of his territory. In his book *Power/*
Knowledge, Foucault studies the use of light in various structures in terms of the desire to maintain an arbitrary, yet powerful force. He concludes that ''a form of power whose main instance is that of opinion will refuse to tolerate areas of darkness.'' Thus the white-wash and the bright lights in the cellar effectively undermine the seeming neutrality of the father and his activities.

Initially, although sensitive to the details of the procedure, the narrator takes it for granted that the father's work—the raising of foxes—is an ideologically neutral activity, one without agency. It simply ''happens'' in the fall and early winter that he ''killed and skinned and sold their pelts to the Hudson's Bay Co.'' But the commercial basis of the slaying undercuts any claims to neutrality. The father's occupation is enmeshed in a cultural discourse which imposes specific views upon the world.

The narrator, however, remains unaware of the implications of her father's activities for some time. She feels safe in the male sphere and enjoys the ''warm, safe, brightly lit downstairs world.'' She feels threatened, not by the male domain or the icy winter world outside, but by the ''inside,'' the ''unfinished,'' upper portion of the house, the bedroom which she shares with her brother Laird. Unlike the clearly delineated male territory below, the bedroom remains undifferentiated. Neither male nor female, the space is fraught with danger. Poorly lit, the room specifically threatens their link with the male domain. In the darkness, the children must fix their eyes ''on the faint light coming up the stairwell'' in order to retain their connection with the male sphere.

The unfinished state of the room can be taken as an image of the undifferentiated consciousness of the children. Laird has not yet adopted a gender role associated with the father. Nor has the narrator been forced to sever her connection to the father and take up an identity aligned with the mother. This hypothesis concerning her male orientation gains support from the nature of her nocturnal fantasies.

In the stories she tells herself late at night, she casts herself into the role of heroic subject. As male savior, she rescues people from a bombed building, shoots rabid wolves and rides ''a fine horse spiritedly down the main streets.'' Yet nobody except a *male,* ''King Billy,'' ever rode a horse down the street. Before her subjectivity has been constituted, her body fought over and conquered, these dreams of male heroism seem attainable.

By the end of the story, however, her gender role has been established. This psychic division is replicated on the level of a spatial division, signalling the children's acquisition of gendered subjectivity. The bedroom is divided into two halves—one for the boy, the other, for the girl. Even the stories the narrator tells herself have altered. The plots start off in the old way, but then "things would change around, and instead, somebody would be rescuing me." No longer the valiant hero, she becomes the victim in need of rescue.

Further proof of the narrator's initial alignment with the father lies in her assurance that she is his "hired man." During the day, rather than help her mother in the house—a job she abhors—she assists her father in looking after his captives. While watering the foxes, secure in her position, she looks scornfully upon her little brother's efforts to assist. Too small to handle adult tools, Laird toddles along with his pitiful gardening can—an overtly phallic object. In boasting that she "had the real watering can, my father's," the narrator further emphasizes her belief that she has access, not to the father's actual member, but to the privileged symbolic system aligned with the phallus.

By aligning herself with her father, the narrator thus accrues a measure of the status associated with the set of signifiers which attend the phallus, including "law," "money," "power," "knowledge," "plentitude," "authoritative-vision," etc.

As a result of this access to a particular set of signifiers, her relationship with her father differs dramatically from the connection she has with her mother. The contrast can be best understood within the inside/outside paradigm. Father and daughter engage in the context of outer space—space that is "structured, interpreted and rendered meaningful by social discourse produced by the system of intellectual and cultural traditions." The narrator literally joins her father on the outside (the out of doors) where they do work that is "ritualistically important."

The relationship the narrator has with her mother, on the other hand, contrasts sharply with the silent, disciplined relationship she has with her father. Once again, to use the inside/outside paradigm, the association between mother and daughter, which occurs within the house, reflects the qualities of "inner" space. Louise Forsyth explains that "inner" space is also the realm of "the imaginary, of spirituality, of memory." The narrator enters this

space when she tells herself stories, and the mother, in sharing her memories with her daughter, also enters this space.

The mother does not belong to the powerful ruling elite, the patriarchy. Thus, she cannot control her daughter by utilizing the strategy available to the male. Whereas work done out of doors is "ritualistically important" or *real,* work performed indoors is "endless, dreary and peculiarly depressing." For this reason, the mother treats her daughter as a fellow prisoner and their association is characterized by speech and openness.

At bottom, the separation between inner and outer space is arbitrary. No undisputed boundary separates inside from outside or nature from culture, unless, as Derrida argues, "it is granted that the division between exterior and interior passes through the interior of the interior or the exterior of the exterior." That is to say, the supposed border which divides the space must either pass through the "inside" or the "outside."

While the separation between inside and outside may be arbitrary, these divisions are upheld by the virtually intractable force of opinion and tradition. Moreover, as we shall see, the placement of specific objects within either space affords a tremendous amount of cultural information concerning power relations. For instance, in exchange for the pelts, the family receives calendars. As the narrator explains, the Hudson's Bay company or the Montreal Fur Traders supplied them with "heroic calendars to hang on both sides of the kitchen door." At first, in the context of the discourse of production, calendars seem out of place. Why does the narrator not refer to the receipt of a more logical item such as money? Yet upon closer examination, calendars prove to be an apt symbol, one which, like the word "raised," underscores a connection between the father's economic occupation as a farmer and his role as a producer of gendered subjects.

For one thing, the placement of the calendars on *both* sides of the kitchen door links the father's work, the production of animals, to the domestic sphere (the kitchen being the area within the home most closely connected to females). Secondly, mimicking the device of *mise en abîme* (the story which tells a story about telling a story, ad infinitum), the calendars not only "speak" as a result of their placement on the kitchen door, but they also tell a story by way of their depiction of the colonization in the norther wilderness.

The calendars depict nature being conquered by male adventurers in all their plumed flag-planting majesty: territory is claimed and controlled. This depiction, in turn, recalls culture's age-old project of mastery over nature. Furthermore, the opposition between culture and nature illustrated by the calendar is closely aligned to a more general, cultural opposition between male and female.

Derrida argues that throughout history nature has been opposed to a chain of cultural institutions. Moreover, as Derrida and other critics have pointed out, these institutions have been traditionally aligned with the male, while the realm of the natural has been long associated with the female. Thus, by placing the calendars on both sides of the kitchen door, the aperture of the female domain, and by supplementing this with an illustration of the colonization of the wilderness, the calendars underscore the correspondence between the colonization of nature and the colonization of gendered subjects—specifically female subjects.

Finally, the natives within the calendar illustration, who bend their backs to the portage, have, like the foxes, been co-opted into the cultural project. Both foxes and natives exemplify bodies named by the discourse of production. The farmer transforms the foxes into "pelts" just as the early explorers transform the indigenous people into "savages" by imposing limited interpretations of their beings upon them. Both farmer and explorer reduce bodies, fragment them into raw material and conscript them into the service of production.

Thus the seemingly insignificant detail of the placement of the calendar with its depiction of the colonization of the wilderness provides a diachronic perspective of the farmer's activities—a perspective which enables one to see that the enclosure of the foxes' bodies and the bodies of the other family members (who also "inhabit a world . . . [their] father made for them"), replicates our forefather's enclosure of the feminine wilderness. Moreover, the calendar solidifies the connection, first established through the use of the word "raising," between the two types of production: farming and the raising of gendered adults.

Slowly but surely, as a result of these spatial arrangements, the narrator's position on the outside—her tenuous alignment with the male—is threatened. The first threat is delivered by the father's hired hand, Henry Bailey. After the foxes are skinned, Bailey takes a sackful of their bloody bodies and swipes at the narrator, saying "Christ-mas present." This gesture subtly suggests a connection between the narrators current fate and that of the foxes. Throughout the story, Bailey relishes the prospect of the narrator's acquisition of her gender role with its concomitant enforcement of subjugation to the male. When he comes across the narrator and her brother fighting, Bailey laughs again, saying, "Oh, that there Laird's gonna show you, one of these days!"

Yet another threat arrives in the form of a feed salesman. The father introduces his daughter to the salesman as a hired man. The salesman responds according to the dictates of culture: no female is allowed on the outside. He reacts to the threat of her presence by treating the father's remark as a joke: "could of fooled me," he says, "I thought it was only a girl."

Other challenges to the narrator's connection to the father and her right to occupy the male "outside" space are launched from within the household itself. Female family members begin to coerce the narrator. Efforts to restrict her behavior occur at every level of existence. For example, her grandmother tells her, "girls don't slam doors like that" (control of her movement through space); "girls keep their knees together when they sit down" (control of the body); and when she asks a question, she is told "that's none of girls' business" (control of consciousness itself).

In a similar bid for control, the narrator's mother confronts the father in front of the barn one fall evening, demanding that he relinquish his right to the girl's labour. The mother explains that, according to his law, the child should remain with her inside the house. In confronting the father at the barn, the mother transgresses the culturally established boundary between inside and outside. The narrator remarks on the scandal, noting how unusual it was to see her mother down at the barn. From her privileged, male-vantage point, the narrator looks on her mother in the same way she looks on the foxes. The narrator does not comprehend that the hostility she sees in the foxes' "malevolent faces" is a response to their enforced captivity. Similarly, her mother's behaviour is interpreted, not as an expression of frustration and disappointment, or loneliness, but as a manifestation of innate wickedness and petty tyranny.

Ultimately, the narrator gives way to the variety of pressures directed at her. Once again, the two systems of production are shown to be linked: at the same time as the horses are butchered, the children's gender roles are fixed. The slaying of the horses recalls the initial butchering of the foxes. In effect, both horses and foxes are part of the chain of production, with the horses' bodies filling a crucial gap in the system. To ensure the continuation of the process, the foxes must be fed, and they are fattened on the bodies of the horses.

As I have suggested above, drawing attention to the use of such words as ''raised,'' to the father's role as the warden of the foxes, and to the placement of the calendars on both sides of the kitchen door, the cycle of production on the farm parallels the production of gendered subjects within the family. The familial discourse—a discourse which is ''absolutely central to the perpetuation of the present, phallocentric order''—must also be fed; it too requires bodies.

Understandably, the narrator neglects to mention the butchering of the horses. She represses the information until the end of the story, claiming that she merely ''forgot to say what the foxes were fed.'' More likely, her desire to omit the information is connected to her wish to leave the image of her father untarnished. She has a vested interest in preserving the white-wash that protects the powerful figure to whom she is allied. Perhaps she believed that a denial of the operation would ensure her protection. With the butchering of the horses, Henry Bailey reappears, as does the initial menace inherent in Bailey's ''joke,'' swiping at the protagonist with the sack of dead foxes.

When they learn that the butchering will take place, the narrator and her brother make their way to the stable, where they find Bailey ''looking at his collection of calendars.'' The reappearance of the calendars recalls the initial discussion concerning the placement of the calendars on the kitchen door and the significance of their portrayal of the colonization of the wilderness.

Unlike the calendars in the family kitchen, however, Bailey's calendars are ''tacked up behind the stalls'' in a part of the stable the mother ''had probably never seen.'' Bailey's calendars are hidden from the mother for good reason: they are almost certainly pornographic. At this point the link between the calendar and the colonization of female bodies becomes explicit: the father's ''stable''—a pen for livestock—becomes a pen for Bailey's pin-up girls, women who have received a specific projection of male desire.

In keeping with this brutal character, Bailey treats the butchering of the first horse, Mack, as a bit of fun. When the narrator asks if he is going to shoot the horse, Bailey breaks into a song about ''darkies'': ''Oh there's no more work, for poor uncle Ned, he's gone where the good darkies go.'' In effect, foxes, savages, horses, and now ''darkies'' fall under the category of those bodies supposedly aligned with nature. When there is no more work for a fox, a horse, or a Black, in the terms outlined by the discourse of production, they are condemned to death. The ''pen'' of the patriarchal, capitalist institution has the power to inscribe and erase each and every one of them.

Despite Bailey's enjoyment of power, it is the father who ultimately shoots the horse. Bailey laughs as the horse kicks its legs in the air ''as if Mack had done a trick for him.'' The image of the horse's death has tremendous impact upon the narrator. In the midst of other thoughts, the memory intrudes upon her consciousness; she sees ''the easily practiced way her father raised gun, and hears Henry laughing when Mack kicked his legs in the air.'' Bailey's laughter is particularly unnerving because it fully exposes his delight in power based on sheer inequality.

The narrator recognizes this as an abuse of power, not due to any innate feminine instincts, but as a result of her own experience. She, too, lorded power over an innocent victim; when Laird was younger, she told him to climb to the top beam in the barn. ''Young and obedient,'' as trusting as the horse led to slaughter, Laird did as he was told. When her parents rushed to the scene, her mother wept, asking her why she had not watched him. Perhaps as a result of her mother's distress, the narrator's behaviour later fills her with regret. She felt a weight in her stomach, the ''sadness of unexorcised guilt.''

In addition to finding the display of power distasteful, after the shooting the narrator can no longer continue to separate her father from his hired man. After the shooting, her father's ''easy'' practiced movements and the hired man's laughter coalesce. The white-wash dissolves. The father loses his innocence. On some level, the narrator realizes that it was never her mother who would ''act out of perversity . . . to try her power'' but her father, the person she had trusted all along. However, it is only when the men try to shoot the second horse, Flora, that she radically breaks from her male-identified position.

In many respects, Flora resembles the spirited horse of the narrator's nocturnal fantasies. When the men try to pen her in, to use her for their own, limited ends, the mare makes a run between Bailey and the father. For the first time, an inmate dares attempt to escape. Immediately the father calls to his daughter, telling her to shut the gate and lock the horse in. Yet, instead of carrying out his instructions, she opens the gate "as wide as she could." Without deliberating, she frustrates her father's project of separating inside from outside and she challenges his unquestioned right to legislate who moves across these borders.

Laird, watching his sister's scandalous behaviour, cannot comprehend why she disobeys her father. When the men swing by in their truck, he begs them to take him along. As they lift him into the truck, the little boy becomes a man: he joins the hunting party. Upon his return, he brandishes the streak of blood on his arm, behaving as if he just beheaded a lion instead of shooting a geriatric horse. No matter, the mark of blood and the domination of the Other continues to function as a crucial element in the rites of manhood. The boy cements his alliance with the father on the basis of their mutual triumph over nature.

The narrator, however, distanced from the father's activities, looks upon the spectacle and sees it for the sad charade it is. She knows that there is no longer any viable distinction to be made between nature and culture—in this case, wilderness and civilization—and that, when these distinctions are made, they are imposed by more powerful forces upon the weaker. After helping the mare to escape, she sums up the hopelessness of the situation: Flora would not really get away. They would catch up with her in the truck. Or if they did not catch her this morning somebody would see her and telephone us this afternoon or tomorrow. *There was no wild country here for her to run to, only farms* [emphasis mine].

At night, the heroes return to assemble around the table. Laird denounces his sister, telling everyone that she let the horse escape. Rather than deny the accusation, the narrator bursts into tears and fully expects to be sent from the table for her unseemly, "feminine" behaviour. But her behaviour is taken for granted. Yet why should she be asked to leave the room? The kitchen is to be domain, after all.

Relishing his newly acquired power, Laird points out that she is crying, but the father tells him "never mind." For the first time, the family treats her as a female. Her father shows her the same kind of consideration he showed her mother the night the latter confronted him at the barn. He listened to the mother's complaints, "politely as he would to a salesman or a stranger, but with an air of waiting to get on with his *real* work" (emphasis mine).

As the narrator herself predicts, her refusal to participate in the father's project of spatial control ultimately severs her connection to him. After she defies him she realizes "he was not going to trust me anymore, he would know that I was not entirely on his side." The use of the word "side" further emphasizes the spatial transformation whereby the narrator permanently aligns herself with Flora. (The horse is aptly named, suggesting a relationship to nature and, by extension, the female.) Like her mother and the other natural bodies (foxes, savages, horses, and darkies), she becomes "unreal." The father has only to seal her fate by naming her and he does so "with resignation and even good humor."

Assuming his right as the giver of names, a male privilege which extends as far back as the first male—Adam—the father pronounces the words which "absolved and dismissed" the protagonist for good: "she's only a girl." The act of naming constitutes yet another form of enclosing. However, in order for these words to have any power over her, she must accept the name—which she does, saying, "I didn't protest that, even in my heart. Maybe it was true." If being a girl means refusing to sanction violence and the abuse of power, then she must indeed be a girl. In the end, brother and sister take up their "rightful" positions, acquiescing to the pressures which divide them physically and psychically. The cultural discourse has been inculcated. A revolution in the cycle of production is complete.

One final note. Although this is the ostensible conclusion, the read must keep in mind that the story is not told by the child. The mature narrator speaks from the margins (space that is not rigidly monitored), the only position where the cultural project of production remains scrutable. Thus, like the hostile foxes, who even after death continue to exude a strong primitive odour "of fox itself," the narrator's identity has not been completely fixed by an ideology which accords her a role and set of behaviour on the basis of her sex. The consistent tension between the bitter, mournful adult voice and the child's idealistic perception suggests that she continues to resist and criticize the patriarchal system which names her.

Source: Marlene Goldman, ''Penning in the Bodies: The Construction of Gendered Subjects in Alice Munro's 'Boys and Girls','' in *Studies in Canadian Literature,* Vol. 15, No. 1, 1990, pp. 62-75.

Authors, edited by Robert Lecker and Jack David, Downsview, Ontario: ECW Press, 1984.

Sources

Blodgett, E. D. *Alice Munro,* Boston: Twayne Publishers, 1988.

Busch, Frederick. Review of *Something I've Been Meaning to Tell You,* in *New York Times Book Review,* October 27, 1974.

Dahlie, Hallvard. ''The Fiction of Alice Munro,'' *Ploughshares,* Vol. 4, No. 3, 1978, pp. 56-71.

Dobbs, Kildare. ''New Directions for Alice Munro,'' *Saturday Night,* July, 1974, p. 28.

Levin, Marlin. Review of *Dance of the Happy Shades* in *New York Times Book Review,* September, 1973.

MacDonald, Rae McCarthy. ''A Madman Loose in the World: The Vision of Alice Munro,'' *Modern Fiction Studies,* Autumn, 1976, pp. 365-74.

Munro, Alice. Interview by Ken Murch, ''Name: Alice Munro. Occupation: Writer,'' *Chatelaine,* August, 1975, pp. 42-3, 69-72.

Oates, Joyce Carol. Review which includes commentary on Munro's first three books in *The Ontario Review,* no. 1, Fall, 1974.

Thacker, Robert. ''Alice Munro: An Annotated Bibliography,'' in *The Annotated Bibliography of Canada's Major*

Further Reading

Morton, Desmond. *A Short History of Canada,* Toronto: McClelland and Stewart Inc., 1994.
A history of the Canadian nation first published in 1983, and revised in 1987 and 1994.

Muir, Alexander. *From Aberdeen to Ottawa in 1845: The Diary of Alexander Muir,* Aberdeen: Aberdeen UP, 1990.
George A. McKenzie is the editor of this selection of diary entries written by a nineteenth-century Scotsman who traveled through the Canadian region before it became the nation it is today.

Munro, Alice. ''Working for a Living,'' in *Grand Street,* Vol. 1, No. 1, Autumn, 1981, pp. 9-37.
An autobiographical essay.

Struthers, J. R. (Tim). ''Alice Munro and the American South,'' in *Here and Now: A Critical Anthology,* Vol. 1 of *The Canadian Novel,* edited by John Moss, Toronto: NC Press, 1978.
Struthers compares Munro's southern and rural Canadian fiction to the fiction written by Southern United States writers. He develops a correspondence between the two literatures based, in part, on their common status as regions which have hosted large Scots-Irish communities in the Americas.

The Death of Ivan Ilych

Leo Tolstoy

1886

Tolstoy's "Smert Ivana Ilyicha" ("The Death of Ivan Ilych") was widely acclaimed when it was published in 1886 and remains a compelling narrative for contemporary readers. It is significant for its universally powerful portrayal of a man's physical deterioration and subsequent spiritual rejuvenation at the moment of death, and because it is the first fiction which Tolstoy published after his conversion to radical Christianity. Several critics note a shift in his writing after his spiritual breakdown in the 1870s, which inspired him to write primarily on religious and philosophical issues while repudiating his earlier works. Tolstoy's *Voina i mir* (1869; *War and Peace*) and *Anna Karenina* (1877) are almost unanimously praised as compelling documents of human existence and are lauded as excellent examples of the realistic novel. Devoting his life to introspection and excelling not only as a writer but as a scholar and philosopher, Tolstoy has influenced a wide range of writers and philosophers, from Ernest Hemingway to Martin Heidegger. He has been hailed by a variety of writers as one of the most important figures in modern literary history, successfully animating his fiction with the dynamics of life. Fyodor Dostoyevsky called him "a sublime artist"; Virginia Woolf claimed him as "the greatest of all novelists"; and Marcel Proust honored him as "a serene god." Due to Tolstoy's relentless examinations of psychology and society, he has won the admiration of multitudes of writers and still affects readers with his stark portrayal of human

life. "The Death of Ivan Ilych" perfectly demonstrates this introspection as it magnifies a man's struggle with how to live his life.

Author Biography

Leo Tolstoy (1828-1910), also transliterated as Lev or Lyof Nikolayevich Tolstoi, spent most of his life on his family estate near Moscow engrossed in his personal studies. As a youth he lived a free and restless life, but became socially active in the 1850s, fighting to improve the lot of the serfs. He later served in the army in the Caucasus, at this time working on his first novel, *Detstvo* (1852; *Childhood*). This work gained notice in Russian literary circles and was praised by Fyodor Dostoevsky and Ivan Turgenev. Tolstoy's experience serving in the Caucasus was the impetus for short stories such as "Nabeg" ("The Raid") and his military service in the Crimean War is described in his Sevastopol sketches. Other short stories and short novels were published during this time such as "Dva gusara" ("Two Hussars"), "Tri smerti" ("Three Deaths"), and "Kazaki" (1863; "The Cossacks"). These works began to demonstrate his interest in the issues of morality and the benefits of living simply without the preoccupations of society. This interest formed Tolstoy's Christian doctrine and inspired him to cofound a publishing house, The Intermediary, in 1883, and organize aid for the starving population of Middle Russia in 1891 through 1892. In 1862 he married Sofya Andreevna Behrs; the couple had thirteen children. Tolstoy actively lived his doctrine, renouncing his rights to his books, personal property, and money in 1895-96. In 1901, as his doctrine became more extreme, he was excommunicated from the Russian Orthodox church.

Voina i mir (*War and Peace*), written from 1863 to 1869 and translated and published in 1886, is often called the greatest novel ever written. Tolstoy's next work, *Anna Karenina,* published in 1875-77, is considered by critics to be more structured; Tolstoy himself stated, "I am very proud of [*Anna Karenina's*] architecture—its vaults are joined so that one cannot even notice where the keystone is." *Anna Karenina* is unlike Tolstoy's other works in that it is not as didactic as his later writing, nor as optimistic as *War and Peace.*

In 1882 Tolstoy published *Ispoved* (*A Confession*), documenting his spiritual crisis and subsequent rejection of his past work, along with the creations of Shakespeare and Wagner, as being an elitist aesthetic which failed to "infest" one's perception with religious feeling. Tolstoy wrote many nonfiction pamphlets at this point in his life expounding upon the form of radical Christianity which he adopted, entailing celibacy and nonresistance to evil. He also wrote simple tales for the uneducated which conveyed moral lessons, such as "Brazhe lepki, a bozhe krepko" ("Evil Allures but Good Endures"). Critics usually look upon Tolstoy's post-conversion writing as less substantial than his earlier texts, although his talent for storytelling always remained intact. This is evident as one reads his drama, which conveys an urgent sense of realism, especially in his most widely known dramatic work, *Vlast tmy* (*The Power of Darkness*). "The Death of Ivan Ilych" was Tolstoy's first piece of fiction after his conversion. His last major novel, *Voskresenie* (*Resurrection*) was less successful than his earlier novels because of its moral digressions which tend to interfere with the artistic direction of the novel. Tolstoy's moral, theological, social, and political writings at this time led to his excommunication and government censorship.

Plot Summary

I

"The Death of Ivan Ilych" opens with Ivan Ilych's colleagues discussing cases in Shebek's private room. Amidst their friendly disagreements on a specific point of jurisdiction, Peter Ivanovich reads of Ivan Ilych's death in the papers and conveys this information to his colleagues. Half of them are startled that someone so close to them in age and position should die, and half have pleasant expectations of the benefits which the opening of Ivan Ilych's job will create. Peter Ivanovich's colleagues also immediately think of the promotions that they are bound to receive upon Ivan Ilych's absence, and each looks unenthusiastically on the duty of offering their condolences to the widow, Praskovya Fedorovna. They are left with a feeling of ease in knowing it is Ivan Ilych who has died; they are still alive and at work.

Peter Ivanovich tells his wife that he will now be able to help her brother attain a job in his circuit due to the open position once held by Ivan Ilych, and he sacrifices his usual nap to attend the funeral services. At the service he encounters Schwartz, a fellow bridge player who assures him by his look

Leo Tolstoy

youth. He studies at the School of Law and is considered "an intelligent, polished, lively and agreeable man." His first job is in the tenth rank of civil service, working under a governor; he is later promoted to the position of examining magistrate in another province. There he meets Praskovya Fedorovna and eventually marries her, not for love but because it seems the proper course of action at his stage in life. At first his marriage is pleasant and does not interfere with his social life. As his wife has children, however, she becomes more disagreeable and causes scenes which give Ivan Ilych much grief. In time he adjusts to these conjugal pressures by devoting his thought to his official work and playing vint, a form of bridge, with his colleagues. He is eventually promoted to the position of Assistant Public Prosecutor. Although he earns a respectable salary, Ivan Ilych and his wife never have enough money. Three of their children die at birth, while two—the oldest daughter, Lisa, and youngest son, Vladimir—survive.

III

The third section of "The Death of Ivan Ilych" documents the hardest year in the peaceful seventeen years of Ivan Ilych's marriage. He has firmly established himself as a Public Prosecutor at this point and has passed up many offers of new positions, holding out for the best promotion. When this promotion is granted to someone else, Ivan Ilych's existence is shaken by the injustice. To save money, Ivan Ilych and his family live for the summer with his wife's brother in the country. Tormented by depression, Ivan Ilych returns to the city to find a new job and, fortunately, meets an acquaintance who helps him attain a new position at a higher salary, allowing him to gloat over the people who once refused him a promotion. Ivan Ilych and his wife buy a new home, which they meticulously decorate. The interior design of this new house is significant not only because it embodies the propriety and social class which Ivan Ilych has striven to personify but because it is while fixing a detail on the curtains that Ivan Ilych slips and injures his side. At the time, he laughs about it with his wife, but this proves to be "the fall" from which he dies.

The decor of the house creates a pleasant superficial unity within the Ilych household. Ivan Ilych does not argue as much with his wife, and he enjoys his new job. He revels in the correct social setting of which he feels himself to be a part. The Ilych family sheds any remnants of their "shabby friends" and

that the funeral will not interrupt their bridge game that evening. Peter Ivanovich is relieved, but he is detained by the widow, Praskovya Fedorovna. While attempting to maintain the proper state of a newly widowed woman, she questions Peter Ivanovich on how she can get financial aid from the government in the guise of asking him information on her husband's pension. Upon realizing that Peter Ivanovich cannot give her any insightful information, she politely ends their conversation and commences with the funeral service, which entails a display of tears, moans, and grieving. Peter Ivanovich leaves the funeral as quickly as possible to cut in on a game of bridge.

II

The second part of "The Death of Ivan Ilych" describes the life of Ivan Ilych while he was healthy. It can be summed up in the opening line, which states, "Ivan Ilych's life had been most simple and most ordinary and therefore most terrible." Ivan Ilych's father had been an official, much like Ivan and his oldest brother. Ivan Ilych is praised as being the balance between his two brothers: the oldest is too serious, and the youngest too wild. Ivan Ilych has a pleasant childhood, from which he retains fond memories, and enjoys an easy and proper are pleased as their daughter, Lisa, is courted by a wealthy young man.

IV

About this time, Ivan Ilych starts to feel a pain in his side and a strange taste in his mouth. He quarrels with his wife around meals, and she believes herself to be abused despite being tolerant of his temper. Ivan Ilych goes to the doctor as the pain escalates and the doctor is unable to give him a thorough diagnosis, leaving Ivan Ilych bleak and worried over the seriousness of his condition. Ivan Ilych takes the medicine prescribed and his wife scolds him about taking his pills regularly and getting enough sleep, never taking his illness as seriously as she should. Ivan Ilych sees many specialists and doctors, but each tells him something different and none give him relief from his pain. At his office, people look at him strangely, and he feels as though they treat him differently. He even loses the pleasure he once derived from his official duties and from playing bridge; the pain becomes an omnipresent force in his life.

V

Ivan Ilych becomes yet more aware of his illness in this section. His brother-in-law visits and is stunned on seeing him, exclaiming to his sister, "'Why, he's a dead man!'" Overhearing this report by his brother-in-law confirms Ivan Ilych's suspicions that he has changed drastically and is beyond the help of medicine and doctors. He ponders how close he is to death as he hears his family carry on with their social proprieties and is disgusted by their lack of pity for him.

VI

In section VI it becomes apparent to Ivan Ilych that he is dying and that nothing will change that fact. He remembers his childhood and feels that he was sincerely happy in his youth. He tries to go to work to chase away the morbid thoughts that obsess him, but he is distracted by his pain, which constantly reminds him of his approaching death and makes keeping up a social pretense unbearable. Death, to which Ivan Ilych refers as "it," takes on an antagonistic presence in his life. He is tortured not only by the pain in his side and the thought of "it" permeating his life but also by the pathetic manner in which he received his fatal wound—putting up curtains in a vain attempt to fashion his house after a wealth he never had.

VII

Ivan Ilych's illness takes over his life at this point in the narrative. He is given opium to ease the pain and his existence is a sequence of delirium and anguish. His only comfort comes through Gerasim, a Russian peasant who performs the duties of sick nurse. Gerasim emits a healthy physicality and treats Ivan Ilych as a man about to die, granting him all of his wishes willingly and pleasantly. He is the only one who offers him any comfort in these last days.

VIII

Life becomes distasteful to Ivan Ilych and death becomes his only reality. He feels as though his doctor and family are blatantly lying to him as they choose to ignore his condition, just as he once ignored his wife's pleas for attention when she was pregnant. He comes to loathe their fakeness, especially his wife's patronizing attitude. This section ends with Praskovya Fedorovna, Vladimir, Lisa, and Fedor Petrovich, their daughter's fiance, leaving for the opera. His wife pretends that she would rather stay with her husband in his time of need. Since they have a box, however, she must go—for the children's sake, she says. Ivan Ilych is repulsed by their shallowness, and as they leave, he is glad to be relieved of their "falsity" but is again left alone with his agony.

IX

As Ivan Ilych lies dying, he is tormented by the feeling that he is being pushed into a "narrow, deep black sack." He weeps "on account of his helplessness, his terrible loneliness, the cruelty of God, and the absence of God." He listens deep within himself and hears a voice from within which questions, "What is it you want?" Ivan Ilych replies that he wants to live "well and pleasantly" as he did before his illness. He remembers his life from his childhood to the present and realizes that he was happy as a child but that his life became more and more empty and trivial as he grew older.

X

After a fortnight, Ivan Ilych does not leave his sofa any longer but lies and ponders death. He concludes that his life has gotten worse as time has progressed and that resistance to the loneliness of death is impossible. He searches for reasons for pain and death and cannot find any explanations. He is comforted by reminding himself that he has lived his life in accordance with propriety.

XI

Another fortnight passes during which Petrishchev formally proposes to Lisa. When Praskovya Fedorovna goes to inform her husband of this new and pleasant development, she finds him on his back, groaning. As she starts to remind him to take his medicine, he turns to her with hatred and asks to be left alone to die in peace. Ivan Ilych asks the doctor to leave and looks upon him, his wife, and his daughter with disgust, seeing in their every action the fakeness which characterized his own life. He realizes that maybe he "had not spent his life as he should have done."

Ivan Ilych receives the sacraments of confession and communion and feels a slight hope which is dashed as he is reminded by his wife's presence of the falsity and deception of her existence.

XII

Before Ivan Ilych dies, he experiences three days of agony when all he can do is scream. Death is so near, yet he feels that his questions about how he lived his life are unresolved. The image of the black sack returns and he struggles with it when he feels as if he is being stuffed into it. He is, however, "hindered from getting into it by his conviction that his life had been a good one." He is alleviated of this torment when his son, Vladimir, kisses his hand and begins to cry for his father. He feels sorry for his wife and son and finally is able to see "the light." His last words are to his wife ("Take him away . . . sorry for him . . . sorry for you too. . . .") and he tries to ask his family to forgive him. Ivan Ilych is then able to accept his pain, let his life and family go, and feel not death but light.

Characters

Praskovya Fedorovna

Ivan Ilych's wife, Praskovya Fedorovna, is never emotionally intimate with her husband, though they both desire the same lifestyle. They take pride in their new house, which embodies the propriety and class in which they want to live. When she first became pregnant, Ivan complained that she deliberately caused scenes and easily became jealous. Instead of dealing with his wife's emotions, Ivan ignored them. Praskovya ultimately reciprocates

her husband's distant coldness. She indulges in extreme self-pity but believes herself to be very tolerant of her dying husband's moans. As her husband is dying, however, Praskovya does not acknowledge the seriousness of his situation. She chastises him for not taking his medicine and suggests that he see more doctors. At his funeral she is preoccupied with maintaining the proper persona of the grieving widow as she asks Peter Ivanovich if he thinks it possible for her to get money from the government to help her financially after her husband's death.

Fyodor

See Fedor Vasilievich

Gerasim

Gerasim is a Russian peasant with whom Ivan Ilych takes much comfort during the last days of his life. He is a servant of the house and selflessly and compassionately acts as sick nurse for Ivan, often elevating the dying man's legs throughout the night. Like Ivan's youngest son, Gerasim does not display the fake and shallow propriety that Ivan comes to resent in his wife, daughter, and doctor during his final days. As a peasant, Gerasim accepts death as a natural element in the cycle of life and does not feel the need to politely ignore the fact that his master is dying. He grants Ivan his last wishes without resentment, and regards him as a necessary and acceptable part of society, rather than a burden.

Ivan Ilych

Ivan Ilych had a pleasant early life, as he studied law and quickly became a professional. He is applauded for his ability both to be career-minded and to maintain a lightheartedness which allows his life to flow smoothly. He has a moderate disposition that was more balanced than that of his two brothers: one is very serious, while the other is too extravagant. Ivan marries an acceptable woman, Praskovya Fedorovna, and attains a respectable position in his career, first working with the governor and later as an examining magistrate. He considers his marriage a matter of convenience and is not in love with his wife. He realizes that marriage altogether is a troublesome venture when his wife eventually has children and becomes disagreeable. Ivan's life revolves around what he believes convention requires. He conducts his official duties with competence and ease, trying to live as properly as possible. He maintains superficial relations with his family, keeping a facade of propriety while avoiding unpleasantness. He derives joy from absorbing his thoughts in the ''official'' matters of his work and in playing bridge.

Ivan Ilych's life changes drastically when he slips and falls while adjusting curtains in his new house, a symbol of the proper lifestyle he and his wife wish to portray. This mishap causes Ivan's slow physical deterioration, and inevitable death. His last days of painful existence are plagued by his fear of death and failure to understand why he must die. He is tormented by the possibility that he did not live his life as he should have, though he knows he has lived his life properly. At the moment of his death, Ivan Ilych's son, Vladimir, selflessly kisses his father's hand and Ivan is filled with love. He instantly realizes the shallowness of his entire life and dies finding comfort in the light of his newfound knowledge.

Vladimir Ivanich

Vladimir Ivanich, the younger of Ivan Ilych's two children, has not yet taken on the false social roles which the rest of Ivan's family have assumed. He is comparable to Gerasim, the Russian peasant who helps Ivan Ilych in his last moments of life, in his sincerity and compassion. Vladimir plays a crucial role in Ivan Ilych's death when he kisses his father's hand as he is about to die, allowing him to realize the emptiness of his life and die somewhat peacefully.

Peter Ivanovich

Peter Ivanovich, Ivan Ilych's closest colleague, studied law with him and felt indebted to him. Peter is the first person to relate the news of Ivan's death to his colleagues, who subsequently begin to wonder who will be promoted to fill Ivan's position. The first part of ''The Death of Ivan Ilych'' follows Peter to Ivan's house for the funeral service, where he displays the proper conventions of expressing condolences to the widow, Praskovya Fedorovna. Peter wants to escape the morose and discomforting feelings of the funeral and longs to play bridge with his colleagues. As he pretends to grieve he must constantly assure himself that he is alive and that Ivan is the one who has died. Peter is worried about Ivan's ominous expression as he lies in the coffin. He resists the warning he reads on the dead man's face, which seems to relegate Peter and his colleagues to the same shallow existence of Ivan Ilych, realizing too late in life that he had never lived.

Media Adaptations

- ''The Death of Ivan Ilych'' was adapted for the stage by Myrtle Pihlman Pope and published by Stephen F. Austin State College in 1958.

Jean

See Ivan Ilych

Lisa

The oldest child of Ivan Ilych's two children, Lisa is very similar to her mother, Praskovya Fedorovna (Ivan Ilych's wife), in that they go visiting and shopping together and attend the opera when Ivan is nearing death. They view him as a burden upon their social lives and an interference in their pleasant household.

Petrishchev

See Fedor Petrovich

Fedor Petrovich

Fedor Petrovich is a respectable examining magistrate who courts Lisa, Ivan Ilych's daughter. He is refined, wealthy, and proper, making him appropriate company for Ivan's wife and daughter. By the time Ivan's funeral has taken place, Fedor and Lisa are engaged.

Pyotr

See Peter Ivanovich

Schwartz

Schwartz is a colleague of Ivan Ilych's who works and plays bridge with Peter Ivanovich. He is already at the funeral service when Peter arrives, and he gives Peter a knowing look which implies that funerals are burdensome and that they will soon be playing bridge. Schwartz contrasts with Peter in that his playful character is not affected by the depressing mood of the funeral; unlike Peter, he maintains an elegance and ease at the service.

Russian Cityscape, circa 1890s.

Shebek

"The Death of Ivan Ilych" begins when Shebek and his colleagues are in his private room discussing a case and find out that Ivan has died. They each then think of the possibility of their own promotion, reminding themselves that they are still alive.

Sokolov

Sokolov is the butler of Ivan Ilych's house. He discusses the prices of Ivan's plot in the cemetery with Praskovya Fedorovna, Ivan's wife, as she speaks with Peter Ivanovich during her husband's funeral.

Fedor Vasilievich

Along with Peter Ivanovich, Fedor Vasilievich is one of Ivan Ilych's closest acquaintances. He is also one of the colleagues who may be promoted after Ivan's death; he immediately thinks of this when he reads the announcement in the papers.

Vasya

See Vladimir Ivanich

Themes

Death

Tolstoy was plagued for most of his life with a fear of death. He came to realize, as the character of Ivan Ilych demonstrates vividly, that the closeness of death can create a healthy urgency in life. Ivan Ilych only becomes aware of the superficiality of his social propriety because of his proximity to death. He is horrified in knowing that he cannot escape death as he has escaped all other unpleasantness in life—by treating them with a distance and insincerity. Gerasim stands in opposition to this fear in his simple acceptance of death as a part of life. A comparison can be made between the high-class social falsity among which Ivan Ilych has lived and the peasant, or servant, life among which Gerasim has lived. Ivan Ilych has an agonizing death which is only relieved when he accepts death. Gerasim, as he helps the dying man, comments, "We shall all of us die, so why should I grudge a little trouble?" Ivan Ilych's refusal to accept death mirrors the sterility of most of his life and the lives of his colleagues and wife. They ignore his pain and maintain their social conventions in the face of his eminent death. Ivan Ilych, however, is unable to ignore his own death. "It," the menacing reality of death, is irrational and goes against the facade of ease and pleasant living in which he has constantly lived and in which those surrounding him still live. Death ultimately forces Ivan Ilych to see the lack of compassion in his once well-ordered life. When he sees this, he can feel love and pity for his son and wife, and death is obliterated in this new light.

Love and Pity vs. Pride

Ivan Ilych had lived most of his life with a sense of pride and vanity. The society of which he is a part praises the trivial marks of wealth and propriety which consume the Ilych family and Ivan Ilych's office. He believes himself to be condescendingly friendly towards those who come before him at work and takes pride in the impersonal ''official'' relationships which he masters. Ivan Ilych's pride plays a crucial role in his ''fall'' from the stepladder as he fixes the draping of the curtains which the upholsterer has not done properly for the social decor he wants to exude. Like the Biblical fall of Adam and Eve from grace, Ivan Ilych's pride causes his fall and subsequent pain. Through his eventual selflessness and pity, which he finds through death, and the pity which is shown to him by Gerasim and his son, Ivan Ilych is able to feel love and accept death. Ivan Ilych is touched by the simple way in which Gerasim accepts death, comforts him, and shows him compassion. He is also moved when his son kisses his hand in his last moments of life. These instances, combined with his impending death and his struggle against being pushed into the deep black sack, bring Ivan Ilych to the realization that he pities his son and wife. He tries to ask for their forgiveness, rejecting the pride which previously consumed his life, and showing love.

Nature vs. Civilization

Ivan Ilych lives in an isolated and superficial world embedded within the civilization which his urban class valorizes. He denies his wife sympathy when she becomes irritable during her pregnancies and creates more walls within his social roles to compensate for ignoring her needs. The same lack of compassion, then, is all that she can demonstrate towards him as he lies dying; she maintains her social proprieties and is absorbed with going to the opera and with their daughter's engagement. These impersonal relationships within the Ilych family and the insincere friendships between Ivan Ilych and his colleagues serve to depict the shallowness of his civilized world. As he used his friends and colleagues to gain higher positions, so they use him when he dies and his job is left vacant. The worth which each of these characters finds in one another depends on what they can get from one another. Likewise, at Ivan Ilych's funeral, his wife's main concern is how she can procure funds from the government after her husband's death. The lack of humanity within Ivan Ilych's world is contrasted to the world of Gerasim and the childhoods of Ivan Ilych and his son, Vladimir. Gerasim is of the land and not of the same social class as Ivan Ilych. Because of this, he does not display the same propriety towards death as Ivan Ilych's friends and wife. Death, for Gerasim, is not an inconvenience which is to be ignored but is natural and pitiable. Ivan Ilych remembers his childhood, before he

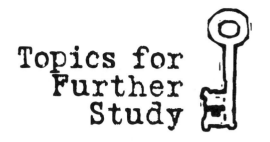

Topics for Further Study

- Compare the philosophical attitudes of Leo Tolstoy's contemporaries on death. Was a fear of death and its implications for a meaningless or more meaningful life a common preoccupation during the time Tolstoy was writing? What ideas of death are made more lucid in Tolstoy's ''The Death of Ivan Ilych'' which where also being explored by contemporary philosophers?

- Explore Tolstoy's ideas about social conventions and their effect on human development in comparison with Franz Kafka's portrayal of Gregor in ''The Metamorphosis.'' Could any of Freud's works elucidate what these authors are trying to convey?

- Are Tolstoy's allusions to religious ideologies in ''The Death of Ivan Ilych'' (such as his use of Ivan Ilych's fatal fall and the Biblical fall, and his reference to Ivan seeing the light before he dies) too dependent on a framework which has faith in God? Do Tolstoy's religious undertones detract from the narrative of Ivan's death?

assumed the mask of propriety which death has shown him to be false, as his happiest days. Ivan sees this same innocence in his son, who shows Ivan pity and kisses his hand. The honest manner in which Gerasim and Vladimir pity Ivan contrasts with the falsity of his wife and colleagues and the shallow civilized life which is also Ivan Ilych's before his revelation at death.

Style

Point of View

''The Death of Ivan Ilych'' is narrated by a third-person voice, telling Ivan Ilych's life story from what often seems like an objective point of view. The narrator speaks of the events in Ivan Ilych's life, both great and small, in the same tone.

Ivan's marriage, his new house, the deaths of three of his children, the birth and education of two, and his fall while fixing the curtains are described in impersonal, quick paragraphs. Events that seem as though they should be more significant in his life are often thrown together with matters that are trivial, bringing all in Ivan Ilych's life down to the same superficial level. As paragraphs start with ''So . . .,'' they sweep away years of Ivan Ilych's life that are pleasantly and inconsequentially lived. Because Ivan Ilych treats all aspects of his life, from his work to his friends and family, in the same decorous and proper manner, everything within his life floats past him and is met with the same air of indifference.

Setting

The first section of ''The Death of Ivan Ilych'' takes place in Shebek's private room, where Ivan Ilych's colleagues first learn of his death and immediately think of the promotions that they are bound to receive. It orients the reader to a setting in which Ivan Ilych himself is later said to have enjoyed many breaks during the workday, and it connects the shallow mentality of his colleagues with his own lifestyle before his fall. The next section takes place at Ivan Ilych's home during his funeral services, where the same shallow attitudes are further displayed—not only by his colleagues, but by his wife as well. This setting foreshadows the shallowness later described in Ivan Ilych's life as details are given about the decorations and furniture of the room where Peter Ivanovich meets Praskovya Fedorovna. Sections III through V depict Ivan Ilych's ordinary and pleasant life, and sections VI through XII mainly present Ivan Ilych dealing with the thought that he is a dying man until he is limited to the confines of a sofa as he dies.

Symbols

The ''fall'' of Ivan Ilych, creating the wound which eventually leads to his agony and death, can be interpreted as representative of the Biblical fall from grace of Adam and Eve. Adam and Eve disobey God because of the sin of pride. Satan is able to tempt them by telling them that eating the forbidden fruit will make them as powerful as God. Ivan Ilych falls victim to the sin of pride as he insists on draping the curtains in a particular fashion which is most characteristic of the wealthy society of which he wants to be a part. It is his preoccupation with public opinion that leads to his demise. Ivan Ilych's fall is further dramatized by the fact that,

while he has fallen from a small step ladder, he feels as though he is being stuffed into a deep black sack. The black sack into which Ivan Ilych feels himself being thrust is symbolic of his struggle with death. He is unable to ease into the sack (death), since he fears that he did not live his life properly, but he cannot see how he can possibly redeem the life which he once thought so correct. As Ivan Ilych sees the light, his struggle with death (the sack) disappears. The light he sees can be identified as the light of love, enlightenment, or spiritual rebirth.

Irony

The irony of ''The Death of Ivan Ilych'' is a tool utilized from the beginning of the narrative, when Ivan Ilych's colleagues sit and discuss his death in the very same superficial manner which characterized his entire life in all of his affairs. The same shallow attitude, to which Ivan Ilych subscribed up to his moment of death, plagues his wife, daughter, doctor, and colleagues as he is dying. After he is dead, empty, conventional expressions of sympathy are the only emotion which Ivan Ilych's death elicits, except those from his son and Gerasim. But Ivan Ilych's colleagues and family treat him no differently than he would have treated them if they were dying. The doctors treat Ivan Ilych as impersonally as he treated those who came before him in his own official job. As Ivan Ilych lies dying, no one recognizes him as a dying man but instead treat him as a disturbance in their once-pleasant lives. This is an ironic treatment because it is the same manner in which Ivan Ilych always conducted his own affairs—never letting anyone's troubles interfere with the easy and pleasant progression of his own routines. Examples of this would be the way in which he treated those who came before him when he was an examining magistrate and his treatment of his wife's jealousy when she was pregnant. In both of these incidents, he kept a polite distance which displayed social propriety without making any personal investments.

Historical Context

Tolstoy's Russia

In the period during which Leo Tolstoy was writing, Russia was experiencing much turbulence politically, socially, and economically. In the 1880s, the assassination of Alexander II and the reign of Alexander III facilitated violent reactions to the

Compare & Contrast

- **1900s:** People in developed countries often die in their own homes before 50 years of age, following a brief illness. Families often gather around the deathbed, a ritual in which much importance is placed on the dying person preparing for death.

  1990s: Most people in industrialized countries die after age 65. The average person spends about 80 days in a hospital or nursing home during the last years of life.

- **1882:** Tolstoy publishes *A Confession,* in which he documents his spiritual crisis and repudiates

much of his earlier work. He undergoes a radical religious conversion which greatly influences his subsequent works.

  1990s: *The Celestine Prophecy,* by James Redfield, predicts a spiritual renaissance and renews interest in spiritual matters for many readers.

- **1800s:** Social conventions discourage unhappy couples from divorcing. Divorce is frowned upon and even illegal in many nations.

  1990s: Statistics show that more than half of all marriages end in divorce.

---

government and a period of autocracy within the government. Alexander III was extremely conservative and imposed many new rules upon the people of Russia to guard against revolution. His regime also saw a new campaign of Russification and anti-Semitic legislation. While industrial growth stagnated during this time, the first Trans-Siberian Railroad was built, which eventually aided in Russia's development.

The hardships endured by the peasantry at this time, including a famine in 1891 and a cholera epidemic in 1892, were severe. One can read in Tolstoy's writing the deep respect which he held for the peasants of his time who worked in harmony with the land and were not obsessed with material success. The character of Gerasim in ''The Death of Ivan Ilych'' demonstrates Tolstoy's fascination with and romanticizing of Russian peasantry. Tolstoy devoted time before the writing of ''The Death of Ivan Ilych'' to improving the lot of the Russian serfs. He even organized relief for the starving population of the eastern ''backlands,'' which consisted of twenty provinces and forty million peasants, in 1891 and 1892. Even in the 1850s, before he began his writing career and became a soldier in the in the Caucasus, Tolstoy was politically active as a social reformer. He continued in this manner with even more determination after his spiritual conversion.

After Alexander III took over as Czar, the political climate of Russia was one of censorship and administrative dominance. Tolstoy's pamphlets and political works were censored as he further developed his own Christian doctrine advocating pacifism, simplicity, and nonresistance to evil. Schools and universities became restricted and government sanctions infiltrated the education system. In 1859 Tolstoy became involved in education by organizing an experimental school to educate peasant children who were excluded from the education system by the new government.

During 1882, Karl Marx's *Communist Manifesto* was translated into Russian and slowly began to have an impact within the philosophical and political circles of Russia. In 1892 ''Legal Populism'' promoted a socialism based on the peasant ''mir'' and on clusters of small producers. These populists continued with propaganda in favor of rural socialism. About this time, a small working class rooted in rural society began to emerge within Russia. It became more of a risk to protest against government policies and to think differently from the regime of Alexander III after laws were passed to increase the prison terms for strikers (four months) and the organizers of any political rally (eight months) in 1886. Tolstoy continued with his political activism and pamphlets, but it became more dangerous and he was often censored. Although a law was passed in 1883 granting non-Orthodox religious groups the right to practice their religion with the strictest of limitations, Tolstoy was excommunicated from the Russian Orthodox church in 1901.

Critical Overview

Though "The Death of Ivan Ilych" was Tolstoy's first piece of fiction after his spiritual conversion, and many critics have thought his post-conversion writing to be less art and more moralizing, this particular short novel has been respected as an intriguing work. Dennis Vannatta confirms this view when he states that, in "The Death of Ivan Ilych," "the two phases meet in one of the most memorable short stories ever written." This deeply affecting story has been Tolstoy's most-praised post-conversion work, a topic of discussion, along with Tolstoy's other major works, in literary courses and critical discourse. As Edward Wasiolek remarks in *Tolstoy's Major Fiction,* "The story is great enough to support the weight of different critical perspectives. It has the 'transparency' that Roland Barthes has put forth as a mark of the greatest works of literature, permitting us to speak about it with the different critical languages of time, place, and critical intelligence." The fact that "The Death of Ivan Ilych" is still meaningful today and is discussed within modern literary theory once again demonstrates its artistic merit.

The last moments of Ivan Ilych's life seem to be a common focus for many critics. What is the light that Ivan Ilych sees as he is about to die? Most critics agree that after Tolstoy takes such pains in structuring the narrative, demonstrating the pathetic shallowness of Ivan Ilych's existence only after ironically depicting the same shallow attitudes of his colleagues and wife, his last dying moments take on a much more significant meaning than when one first reads of his death through Peter Ivanovich. Irving Halperin traces Ivan Ilych's struggle with death in his essay "The Structural Integrity of 'The Death of Ivan Ilych'"; he describes Ivan's death as "the route of his metamorphosis . . . from despair (the black hole) to love (the son's kiss) to redemption (the light). Thus Ivan Ilych's dialectical direction, so to speak, is from nothingness to meaning: he has learned that the one thing necessary for a man is to be." Dennis Vannatta similarly concludes, "The most somber and forbidding of stories, 'The Death

of Ivan Ilych' is also the most optimistic. It shows that a man can live his entire life in darkness but in the final moment be resurrected into the light." Wasiolek comments in *Tolstoy's Major Fiction* that "it is the consciousness and acceptance of death that reveals the significance of life. . . . Without the consciousness of death, the things themselves become spectral, as indeed they become with Ivan's consciousness of his impending death." By way of contrast, Temira Pachmuss notes in "The Theme of Love and Death in Tolstoy's 'The Death of Ivan Ilych'" "that despite Ivan Ilych's perception of the mystery of death and his ultimate calm acceptance of it, the whole story reflects an icy coldness." As examples, he cites Gerasim acting only out of moral duty to his master, and not out of sincere love, and Tolstoy's focusing on the emotions and experiences of Ivan Ilych only, as if no other characters mattered. He also claims that Ivan Ilych's dead face fails to evoke pity in those at the funeral service, but rather gives a look of warning. Pachmuss resolves this inconsistency by asserting, "There is no need for us, however, to dwell on Ivan Ilych's facial expression in death as perceived by his relatives and colleagues, for the constructive principle of 'The Death of Ivan Ilych' requires concentration on the dying man rather than on those who surround him. The high point of the story is undoubtedly Ivan Ilych's discovery of the ultimate reality which is love." Most critics agree that though "The Death of Ivan Ilych" may seem like a dark and moralizing story, especially when viewed from the context of Tolstoy's religious conversion, it is ultimately a liberating story about the power of love.

Criticism

Angela Frattarola

Frattarola is a freelance writer and scholar. In the following essay, she discusses characterization and the theme of redemption in the story.

Though "The Death of Ivan Ilych" is an affective text which is still read with enthusiasm today, there are some difficulties which contemporary readers may have with Tolstoy's novella. The character of Ivan Ilych and the shallowness of his colleagues and wife are haunting for any reader. They come alive in their superficiality and their mundane worries. In many ways, these characters can be seen as the norm in our society when viewed through a pessimistic lens. However, Tolstoy does supply his read-

What Do I Read Next?

- In Ambrose Bierce's "An Occurrence at Owl Creek Bridge" (1891), Peyton Farquhar is about to be hanged from a bridge because of a military crime. The rope breaks, he escapes by swimming away, and he reviews the events of his life—all in a hallucination in the instant before his death.

- In Kate Chopin's "The Story of an Hour" (1894), Louise Mallard receives news that her husband has died in a train wreck. Tearlessly, she retreats to her room and reviews the course of her married life. She comes to recognize that she has gained great personal freedom with his death. When her husband suddenly walks in the door—he was not on the train after all—she drops dead. Her family and physician assume she died of joy.

- "The Metamorphosis" by Franz Kafka, published in 1937, depicts the transformation of Gregor Samsa from a responsible young man to a bug. Kafka's emotional portrayal of Gregor and his family create insight on the facade of social propriety and one's need to escape the dominating roles of society.

- In Thornton Wilder's play *Our Town,* written in 1938, the central character, called the Stage Manager, reviews the histories of the lives of various inhabitants of Grover's Corners, New Hampshire.

- Joan Didion's "Some Dreamers of the Golden Dream," published in 1966, mingles fact and fiction. It is the real account of a real woman, Lucille Marie Maxwell Miller. However her story is told through Didion's narrative and her notion that life can become superficial without a hint of the forbidden.

- *Trainspotting,* published in 1993 by Irvine Welsh is a collection of short stories recounting the revelries and derelict antics of a group of boys in Edinburgh doing everything in their power to not fall victim to "growing up."

---

ers with a few minor exceptions among the majority of pathetic characters. It is important to note that Ivan Ilych is depicted as being equally shallow and thoughtless in his "agreeable, easy, and correct" life, of which the reader is informed after reading of his death in the opening sketch. The extreme pervasiveness of characters who are primarily concerned with propriety is interrupted by the introduction of Gerasim and Vladimir. These characters demonstrate deeper emotions than the others and are singled out as being the only characters able to show pity and kindness to Ivan Ilych in his last days of life.

Gerasim is the Russian peasant who acts as Ivan Ilych's sick nurse as he is dying. Ivan Ilych takes much comfort in Gerasim's presence and feels that his healthy and agile body gives him hope. While looking at Gerasim's "sleepy, good-natured face with its prominent cheekbones," Ivan Ilych meditates, "What if my whole life has really been wrong?" This is an example of Tolstoy's often overly romantic and idealized portrait of Gerasim which can grow tiresome to readers who are constantly on the guard against such essentialistic characters. These pure characters frequently fail to be dynamic figures within a text, and merely become stereotypes of an idealized image. Critics have repeatedly noted Gerasim's role in "The Death of Ivan Ilych"; Edward Wasiolek sums up Gerasim's character, "He breathes the health of youth and natural peasant life, lifts up the legs of the dying Ivan Ilych, cleans up after him with good humor, and in general shows him a kind of natural compassion." Irving Halperin echoes these sentiments when he concludes, "because of Gerasim's devotion, Ivan Ilych becomes capable of extending compassion to his wife and son. In this overall perspective, then, Gerasim may be viewed as the true hero of the story." And another critic, Temira Pachmuss, asserts that Gerasim possesses "real humanity" since

> **"** Regardless of Tolstoy's possible shortcomings in his character development, he is able to present a timeless masterpiece for contemporary readers. **"**

"Tolstoy thought the instinctive understanding of life and death that enabled Gerasim to do right naturally, to tell the truth, and to feel a deep sympathy for his fellow creatures was a result of Gerasim's natural identification with nature." The recurring portrayal of Gerasim as the healthy and simple Russian peasant, who has more compassion and understanding than all the other socially proper and therefore entirely empty and shallow characters, is often hard to accept because it is too easily interpreted as a black and white photo; these are the "good guys," these are the "bad guys." (It is also essentialistic in that it is like saying that all women understand nature because women are essentially bound to the earth and the body, or that African Americans naturally have "soul.")

This overly simplified and essentialistic stereotype is again found in Vladimir, Ivan Ilych's son. Because Vladimir is a child, he is immediately assumed to be innocent and beyond the socially determined conventions of his mother, sister, and Ivan Ilych's colleagues. This image is too simple, too easy. In such a hauntingly vivid depiction of death, it can be disappointing for a reader to encounter such one-dimensional characters who are supposed to carry heavily essentialistic ideologies: the rough Russian peasant who innately holds an understanding of death and love because he is in tune with nature; the innocent youth who has not yet been corrupted by social convention and is therefore privileged with a more sincere and real love for the dying man. These images allow a reader to fully grasp the intentions of Tolstoy and therefore they are useful. However, their limitations may make Tolstoy a less dynamic writer. These characters are less believable because they are designed to embody all that is good and innocent in "The Death of Ivan Ilych." They represent one side of a dualism, or schism, which Tolstoy perpetuates throughout

the text and which serves his purpose—to bring the reader a better understanding of a facet of life which he feels is important.

Regardless of Tolstoy's possible shortcomings in his character development, he is able to present a timeless masterpiece for contemporary readers. Though "The Death of Ivan Ilych" was written after Tolstoy's conversion to radical Christianity and some critics believe that the moralizing of his post-conversion writing detracts from his artistic abilities as a writer, it is because of the message which Tolstoy is striving to convey that "The Death of Ivan Ilych" is so memorable. Even without a belief in God, Tolstoy's message comes across to a reader as a lesson of life. Ivan Ilych is callously treated after his death because that was the attitude which he showed others. It is not until his last days that he is forced to think about his life with an urgency which colors every conscious minute due to the proximity of death. It is within this context that Ivan Ilych ascertains that he most definitely did not live his life as he should have and gets "the sensation one sometimes experiences in a railway carriage when one thinks one is going backwards while one is really going forwards and suddenly becomes aware of the real direction." Tolstoy devotes the text to detailing the reasons why Ivan Ilych and his peers are living within a "falsity," and within a few crucial paragraphs is able to sum up how he rids himself of this "falsity" in his final days. Tolstoy's point is not to taunt a reader and mock the one who realizes only moments before death that he had never lived. Rather, Tolstoy wants the reader to have this realization along with Ivan Ilych so that she/he too may discover the beauty to be found in love before it is too late. The simple concept that one gets back what one gives is the apparent message I find in Tolstoy's novella.

After his death, Ivan Ilych's family and colleagues seem to carry on as if nobody has stopped to think about their lives after the death of their friend. Instead, characters like Peter Ivanovich and Schwartz, Ivan Ilych's co-workers and friends, fight thoughts of death from their minds and are constantly assuring themselves that they are still alive and that it is Ivan Ilych who has died. Praskovya Fedoravna is still preoccupied with her proper role of the grief-stricken widow, the maintenance of their meticulously decorated house, and her financial situation. Tolstoy assures the reader that no one has learned from Ivan Ilych's death; they all continue to live as he once did—shallow yet always correct. This contrast makes the reader conscious that Tolstoy is now pointing to you; you are the one who should learn from Ivan Ilych's death. Tolstoy's ability to make the reader feel as though he/she is seeing a revelation which no one else can see privileges the reader as the one who can benefit from Ivan Ilych's agony.

Gerasim and Ivan Ilych's son are able to give the dying man love and through experiencing this, he realizes that love is what he must give back. Though some critics believe that the revelation which Ivan Ilych feels in his last moments of life and which allows him to die in peace is an unrealistic hope for most readers, I believe that the existence of such a revelation is exactly Tolstoy's point. Ivan Ilych was lucky in that death fell upon him and he was able to come to this realization of the need for love and compassion in life. We, as readers, can read the story of his death and learn from it what the other characters so obviously miss. In contrast, John Donnelly attests, ''[Both] Tolstoy and Ilych (that is, the Ilych in the last two hours of his drawn-out dying period) were much too sanguine about the human condition and the prospects for attaining moral integrity in this life. In short, I believe the Tolstoyan lesson to be drawn from Ilych's dying is not a realistic expectation, although it is devoutly to be wished.'' This reading seems to neglect the basic lesson behind ''The Death of Ivan Ilych,'' leaving a reader with little else.

Before Tolstoy died, he told his daughter, ''The more a man loves, the more real he becomes.'' This seems to be the overwhelming message of ''The Death of Ivan Ilych'' also. Tolstoy understood this concept most completely after his spiritual conversion and could not rest until he tried his best to convey it to others through his writing, whether in parables, folk tales, drama, pamphlets, or fiction. Like the look of warning on the dead face of Ivan Ilych which Peter Ivanovich looks down upon, Tolstoy's story communicates a warning of the same message to his readers. Thus, ''The Death of Ivan Ilych'' can be read repeatedly throughout one's life as one always needs to be reminded, or rather warned, to live and love before death comes.

Source: Angela Frattarola, ''An Overview of 'The Death of Ivan Ilych','' in *Short Stories for Students,* The Gale Group, 1999.

Edward Wasiolek

In the following excerpt, Wasiolek offers an overview of Tolstoy's ''The Death of Ivan Ilych,'' paying particular attention to how Ivan's refusal to accept death affected his life.

''The Death of Ivan Ilych'' was Tolstoy's first published work after his conversion. It was written after almost a decade of immersion in theological reflection and writing, and indifference to the writing of fiction. More schematic and deliberate than the early tales, it is more pruned of descriptive and analytic detail. The density of circumstances is largely absent, and it reads like a distillation rather than a representation of life. Disdaining the verisimilitude that such density often confers upon an artistic work, Tolstoy makes his appeal by way of formulaic selection of essential detail. This gives the tale the air of a chronicle or parable. Such a manner could easily lead to abstract moralizing; yet, though the moralizing is there, the details and skeletal action have been so skillfully chosen that the distinctly uncontemporary mode of narration succeeds in an astonishing manner. There is, too, in ''The Death of Ivan Ilych''—as there will be in the tales that follow—a punishing quality about Tolstoy's moral passion. He seems now more certain of the truth—more eager to castigate those who do not live by the truth. These are unpromising attitudes for the production of great art, but Tolstoy does not hesitate to express them. It must be remembered too that these are the years when Tolstoy's views on the uselessness and perniciousness of Western art, his own included, are maturing. The passions for moral truth and pedagogy cannot overcome his art, but they themselves are conquered and turned to the purposes of great art. It is to the art that we must turn in order to see how this had been accomplished.

The art of ''The Death of Ivan Ilych'' has affected widely diverse audiences and lent itself to various modes of dissection. The story is great enough to support the weight of different critical perspectives. It has the ''transparency'' that Roland Barthes has put forth as a mark of the greatest works of literature, permitting us to speak about it with the different critical languages of time, place, and critical intelligence. The Freudians, for example, have had little to do with Ivan Ilych, and Tolstoy's narrative manner as well as his philosophical convictions would seem to leave little terrain to work over. Tolstoy abjures ambiguity and symbolization; the intent of the narrative style is to lay everything out as clearly as possible. Nevertheless, Ivan Ilych's life may be described as a system of determined evasions of love, human contact, and self-knowledge. Because he has arranged his life in a rigid, ritualistic manner, it is easily unhinged by unexpected events, however trivial. There is nothing of the flexibility of interaction with reality that is the

> To the measure that Ivan Ilych's pain mounts and his behavior becomes disagreeable, the indifference of those about him becomes more determined."

mark of a healthy man for Freud. Freud spoke of "love and work" as the two qualities of the healthy person. But Ivan Ilych has never learned to love and never learned to love work. He follows his career—in his father's footsteps—as one would a military campaign, with ramparts thrown up to keep him from contact with reality or human emotions, whether those of others or his own. It would take only a shift of vocabulary to see his rigidities and evasions as neurotic flight and defense. . . .

Before Tolstoy gives us the chronicle of Ivan Ilych's life, he tells us what it was worth, how it should be judged. Irony is his weapon of judgment; we know immediately what we are supposed to be for or against. We are supposed to be against the predatory self-interest barely concealed beneath the routine expressions of condolence. The contrast between the conventional forms and private feeling is something Tolstoy has done many times before, but here he is doing a great deal more. The announcement of Ivan Ilych's death comes in one of those respites from judicial labor that Ivan Ilych loved so much, as is commented on later in the novel—when he was able to smoke, drink tea, talk about politics, general topics and most of all about official appointments. That is, we learn about his death in a situation that recalls one of the pleasures he enjoyed while he was alive, and the scene is the first of a series of identifications by which the life of Ivan Ilych before and after death is compared and analogized. The opening scene which presents Ivan Ilych in death is at the same time a representation of his life.

Tolstoy meticulously re-creates in the opening scene the atmosphere, conditions, values, and modes of behavior by which Ivan Ilych had lived, and the recreation in dramatic form is a judgment on Ivan Ilych in death. Life as Ivan Ilych had lived goes on

after he is dead. As Ivan had a passion for bridge, so Pyotr Ivanovich, weariedly performing the duty of paying respects to the dead, hurries away to meet the impish and impious Schwartz for a game of bridge. As Ivan Ilych had taken from Praskovya Fyodorovna only the conveniences of board and room, so Praskovya Fyodorovna in her tearful conversation with Pyotr Ivanovich reveals a predatory concern only with the monetary convenience she can gain from her husband's death. Ivan Ilych had labored to furnish his house with whatnots, antiques, dishes and plates on the walls, and Tolstoy goes to the point—in his recreation of Ivan Ilych's life—of drawing our attention to some of the commodities that had ruled his life and which continue to exist after his death. The room in which Pyotr Ivanovich talks to Praskovya Fyodorovna is filled with furniture and bric-a-brac that Ivan Ilych had collected. Pyotr Ivanovich's attention is explicitly drawn to the upholstered furniture in pink cretonne that Ivan Ilych had consulted him about and to the antique clock that Ivan Ilych had liked so much.

As Ivan Ilych treated people before death, so they treat him after death. The "worth" of his colleagues was their capacity to advance his welfare and his pleasure, and the "worth" of Ivan Ilych in death is the opportunity his passing gives to others to advance their welfare and pleasure. He treated people impersonally and was indifferent to their vital interests. This was most evident in his relationship with his wife, with whom he talked at times only when a third person was present. She pays him back in death. We learn of his death in the opening scene by way of the formal obituary that Praskovya Fyodorovna has written, which Fyodor Vasilievich reads to his colleagues in the judicial chamber. The conventional expression of sorrow in the obituary is the precise correlative, in impersonality, of the actual emotions Praskovya Fyodorovna has toward her deceased husband. The items of description in this opening scene are a duplication of the kinds of feelings, human relationships, and objects in which Ivan Ilych had lived. Tolstoy is saying that Ivan Ilych's life is the ironical factor in his death.

The dramatized beginning casts its shadow over the chronicle that follows. We know that Ivan Ilych's life will be shallow, impersonal. The form of the narration that follows reinforces this judgment. Large blocks of Ivan Ilych's life are expressed in a few paragraphs, and Tolstoy deliberately mixes matters of consequence and inconsequence so as to reduce all the events to a kind of undifferentiated triviality. He tells us, for example: ''The preparations for marriage and the beginning of married life, with its conjugal caresses, the new furniture, new crockery, and new linen, were very pleasant . . . ,'' mixing love and furniture in similar grammatical form and brevity. Later, the death of two children is reported in a subordinate clause, while the main clauses are retained for an account of the father's troubles.

The narration of the first seventeen years of Ivan Ilych's married life—an accounting of moves, promotions, successes—reads like an inventory rather than a life. The sameness of the events makes it difficult to remember what is individual, significant, or striking. Events of a significant personal nature do appear in his life, but Ivan Ilych manages, by adhering closely to the proper and decorous rules of his society, to avoid them. During the first months of her pregnancy, Praskovya Fyodorovna interrupts the even course of properness and pleasantness by irrational bursts of jealousy, by demands for his attention, and by coarse and ill-mannered scenes. But Ivan Ilych evades such pleas for sympathy by spending more time away from her; he evades her pleas as he evades similar pleas of the accused in his courtroom. All this is done in the name of good breeding, conformity to public opinion. The law of the society, to which Ivan Ilych subscribes enthusiastically, is the law of pleasantness and properness. What is disagreeable and improper has no place in this mode of life, and when it obtrudes itself—as had Praskovya Fyodorovna's behavior during pregnancy—it is ignored or relegated to irrationality.

Ivan Ilych's meaningless life takes on meaning only when the disagreeable that intrudes on his life cannot be ignored. When he is passed over for promotion, he is jolted out of mechanical complacency and projected into anger and self-evaluation. By happenstance, this intrusion in his well-planned and decorous life is quickly erased when Ivan Ilych manages to obtain a position better than the one he had been denied. His life resumes its decorous, pleasant course, but another disagreeable event, more fateful than the first, intrudes upon his life. He "falls," and the ambiguity of the word and its biblical connotations were probably intended by Tolstoy. The "fall," to be sure, is appropriately trivial: from a ladder and while he is occupied with the objects that are the explicit badge of his place in society. Ivan Ilych has climbed only as high as the drapery, but the fall is as deep as the abyss of death and the agonies of consciousness before death. This second accident with its attending misery brings Ivan Ilych to a kind of spiritual rebirth, to irritation, reflection, self-evaluation, and finally to an awareness of himself and of others. Little by little the pain, which penetrates his usual activities, excludes him from the unpainful lives of his associates, bringing him to isolation and to confrontation with that isolation. The pain in his side makes him different from others; it individualizes him.

The pain grows to affect his dinner, his bridge, his relations with his wife; it spoils his work and his enjoyment of his furniture. His pleasant, decorous life becomes unpleasant, indecorous. At first it affects only his outer life, but gradually it affects his inner life; it overcomes the resistances of self-satisfaction and self-exoneration and leads him to self-assessment and self-incrimination. Ivan Ilych comes finally to see that his life has been wrong, but he comes first to see that the lives of others are wrong. He notices that no one really cares that he is in pain. They ignore his pain; when they cannot ignore it, they trivialize it; and when this is no longer possible, they blame him for it. It is Ivan Ilych's pain, not theirs, and they want to be touched by it as little as possible. They give only what they have always given, which is what Ivan Ilych had always given when confronted with someone else's pain and someone else's appeal for compassion and love: pretended compassion and love, that is, the conventional forms of polite interest and concern. As Ivan Ilych earlier defended himself against involvement in his wife's pain by blaming her (she was irrational) and absenting himself, so now Praskovya Fyodorovna defends herself against involvement in his pain by blaming him (he was irrational in not following the doctor's orders) and by absenting herself with her opera, social life, and involvement in her daughter's coming marriage.

To the measure that Ivan Ilych's pain mounts and his behavior becomes disagreeable, the indifference of those about him becomes more determined. The weapons they use to protect themselves against his pain are the weapons that Ivan Ilych used to protect himself from everything unpleasant. Schwartz continues to be impish; the bridge games go on; his wife, daughter, and the daughter's fiance go to the theater and carry on the foolish conversations about art. Indeed, the tempo of enjoyment of those close to him seems to mount in inverse relationship to the increase of his pain. When he is about to lapse into the final day of unceasing pain, the daughter announces her engagement to the young examining magistrate, and the pleasure of Praskovya Fyodorovna and the daughter is at its apex.

Ivan Ilych comes to see their indifference and cruelty and he comes to blame them. He does not blame himself—not, at least, until the very end. Several times during his illness the thought comes to him that perhaps he has not lived his life well, but each time he dismisses the idea as nonsensical. He comes far enough in his forced, slow reassessment to admit that there had been little happiness in his life, and what there has been took place in childhood and has been decreasing ever since. But it is not until his final hours that Ivan Ilych sees the truth of his life. Undoubtedly the struggle he puts up in the black bag is a symbol of the struggle he maintains to justify his life. He slips through the bag and into the light only when, in his final hours, he stops justifying his life and listens, specifically when he himself feels pity for others: first for his son, who has come with eyes swollen with tears, and then for his wife.

It is hard to make artistic sense of Ivan Ilych's conversion, of the symbolism of the black bag, and the truth that he sees in the last moments of his life. The gradual reassessment of the worth of his life that he makes under the bludgeon of pain, the frustrated demands for compassion, the polite indifference to his plight from others, and his terrifying aloneness before impending death are all psychologically believable and well done by Tolstoy. But it is another matter to believe in the ''revelation'' that Ivan Ilych experiences when he slips through the bag and to believe artistically in a spiritual rebirth.

There is another difficulty, too, present throughout the long ordeal of Ivan Ilych's sickness. Ivan Ilych himself poses the problem one night about a month before his death when, exhausted by pain, he weeps ''because of his helplessness, his terrible loneliness, the cruelty of man, the cruelty of God, and the absence of God.'' He cries out to God: ''Why hast Thou done all this? Why hast Thou brought me here? Why, why dost Thou torment me so terribly?'' The problem is correctly expressed in his anger against the senselessness of the suffering he undergoes, the lack of proportion between whatever he has done and what he has been forced to suffer, and against the contingency, accidentality, and senselessness of his fate.

If we ask with Ivan Ilych why he had to be bludgeoned by pain, we cannot say it is because he lived his life badly, although Tolstoy seems to be saying that. Even if we suppress the perfectly normal rejoinder that all the others in the society have lived lives just as badly but do not suffer, we still cannot find in any moral calculation a connection between the badly lived life and the physical pain. The life is not that bad, and the pain and terror are too much. The life is too trivial for the pain to be so great. We can make sense of the psychological pain—the loneliness, the suffering from lack of compassion, the humiliation of being treated as a thing by those about him—because these follow on the kind of life that Ivan Ilych has led. The lives of others in the society, like Ivan Ilych's, are trivial and terrifying, for reasons that are artistically believable. But we cannot make sense of the physical pain that Ivan Ilych suffers, nor, for that matter, why he and not others must suffer such pain.

If Tolstoy insists on the psychological suffering that Ivan Ilych undergoes after the ''fall,'' he insists even more crudely on the sheer physical pain that Ivan Ilych endures. The unremitting howling of Ivan Ilych in the last three days of his life is a detail so monstrous that only Tolstoy's art could make it palatable. We know why Ivan Ilych suffers loneliness, fear, anger, resentment, depression after the ''fall'' but we do not know why he has to die. I believe that Tolstoy is conscious of the gulf between Ivan Ilych's behavior and his fate, and it is precisely the irrationality and the utter inexplicability of the gulf that he wants to express. Death exists, and it is the truth. It is something that Ivan Ilych has not believed in and that the others in his society do not believe in. But it is the reality, nevertheless. The ''pain'' they so assiduously avoid, of which death is a summation, comes to be referred to as *ona* in Russian (''it'' in the feminine gender), that is, both to pain (*bol'*) and death (*smert'*). It is this pain-death that makes Ivan Ilych's former life increasingly spectral, and that unmakes the pleasure he has guided his life by.

I am suggesting that it is the refusal to accept ''death'' as part of life that leads to the sterility of Ivan Ilych's life and the lives of those about him. Why this is so is something that follows upon Tolstoy's conception of death. The society is built upon a pursuit of well-being and an avoidance of discomfort. ''Self-pleasure'' is the law of society. The avoidance of ''pain'' and ultimately death explains the series of abstract and impersonal relations that obtain in the story. One protects oneself from involvement in the pain others suffer by formalizing and thus impersonalizing relations with others.

This process is illustrated in the relations between Ivan Ilych and his wife, in his indifference toward her pain in pregnancy and her later indifference toward his pain in his mysterious illness. Each blames the other. His friends act similarly; they want nothing to do with his pain, and when it obtrudes on their lives, they trivialize it, formalize it, and deny it. Ivan Ilych may be irascible, annoying, and embarrassing, but he is not dying. They will not accept his pain as part of their lives, nor will they accept his dying.

It is Gerasim alone who acknowledges the truth. He accepts the fact that Ivan Ilych is dying and cheerfully acts to make him comfortable. He breathes the health of youth and natural peasant life, lifts up the legs of the dying Ivan Ilych, cleans up after him with good humor, and in general shows him a kind of natural compassion. Expressly conjoining Gerasim's health and vitality with his acceptance of death, Tolstoy seems to be saying that death and life go together. But it is not immediately clear how they go together.

Death is for Tolstoy the supreme irrational event: an event impervious to human desire, understanding or the manipulation of will. It is also the summation of whatever is disagreeable in life—of every pain, sickness, and accident. Ivan Ilych's plea for justice from a seemingly cruel God may arouse our sympathy, but for Tolstoy the plea is an attempt to bring death into the realm of human understanding. There is no logic to Ivan Ilych's sickness and death, no accounting for the intrusion of such pain into his well-ordered life, and surely none that he rather than someone else be picked out for the special bludgeoning. The fact cannot be understood or justified. But it does make a difference, apparently, whether we acknowledge death. If we ignore it, then our lives are struck with sterility; our relations with others and ourselves become impersonal.

Source: Edward Wasiolek, in *Tolstoy's Major Fiction,* The University of Chicago Press, 1978, pp. 167–79.

Irving Halperin

At the time this article was published, Halperin was teaching at San Francisco Stage College. In the following excerpt, he examines the narrative structure of ''The Death of Ivan Ilych'' and discusses Ivan's emotional transformation in the story.

[The] question may occur—why does the novel open with minor characters on-stage? To begin with, this structural arrangement is in accord with the protagonist's ultimate discovery that the apparent end of human consciousness, death, is in reality the beginning of life. But, more important, if we first witness the actions of some people whose interests and values are very much like those that the dead man subscribed to, the typical values of average men in a quantitatively oriented society, we may more fully grasp the nature of Ivan Ilych's failure as a man. And this is the salient function of Part II—to adumbrate his history of self-deception.

Throughout Part II Ivan Ilych's life is described as filled with duplicity. He married because marriage was considered the ''right thing'' in his social set. Between husband and wife there had been little human connection; their essential attitude toward each other remained one of deep hostility. For the sake of mutual convenience, they sought to project the appearance of a happy marriage.

From an unhappy marriage, Ivan Ilych retreated into his work; but there, as magistrate, he existed in an equally reprehensible state of falsity. Yet he is not to be criticized, Tolstoy seems to imply, simply for being attached to the baubles and trinkets of professional prestige and gain, but rather because he set himself up over others. Specifically, he did not turn a human face, as it were, toward those who were tried in his court; his most common attitude toward them was one of prideful condescension. Altogether, he prided himself on maintaining a public image of professional incisiveness and coolness.

Ivan Ilych's mask resembles the one worn by his colleagues, Petr Ivanovich and [Schwartz]. All three are self-centered and indifferent to humanity; they wish to lead lives of light-hearted agreeableness and decorum. And viewed within the frame of our larger consideration, the novel's structure, the likeness of the three men constitutes an important functional relationship between Parts I and II.

If it may be held that Part II sketches the lineaments of Ivan Ilych's pride, the key purpose of Part III is to trace his Fall. Just as he chooses to *appear* before others as the prominent public official and the pleasant, well-bred social figure, he needs his house to lend proof to his professional attainments and aesthetic taste. In this perspective, his explosive reactions to the slightest disarrangement in the house's meticulously selected furnishings may be understood. For what is this compulsive orderliness if not the expression of a need to be on guard against the warm, spontaneous feelings of human affection? So it seems ironically fitting that

> But if Ivan Ilych is agitated and fearful, at least he is no longer playing at life. Suffering has humanized him; in consequence, he is able to look outside of himself."

during this cycle of preoccupation with material details (he *had* to show the upholsterer how the curtains were to be draped), Ivan Ilych should suffer the accident which eventually resulted in his death. Accordingly, his fall was more than from a ladder, but, symbolically, from a pinnacle of pride and vanity. And from this point in Part III to the ending, the novel's narrative focus narrows in proportion to the contracting scope of Ivan Ilych's delusion.

Enter the doctors of Part IV who pursue their profession in much the same way that he does his—from behind well-mannered masks. They appear to be self-assured but will not commit themselves on whether his condition is serious; instead they speculate that the cause of his pain may be a floating kidney or a defective appendix, perfunctorily referring to these organs as though they were separate from his total, sentient nature. The doctors' reluctance to commit themselves on his condition reduces him to a state of helplessness comparable to what, doubtless, was felt by some who had been tried in his court: "he had to live thus all alone on the brink of an abyss, with no one who understood or pitied him."

But if Ivan Ilych is agitated and fearful, at least he is no longer playing at life. Suffering has humanized him; in consequence, he is able to look outside of himself. In contrast to the man of Part III who was obsessed with house furnishings, his chief interest now is in the health and ailments of others.

Until this stage in his illness, Ivan Ilych has continued to hope that he would recover. Therefore, it is the function of Parts V-VI to shock him into emotionally recognizing that death is not simply a commonplace fact, something that happens to eve-

ryone—rather *it* is coming to him. Previously, he had manipulated the machinery of marriage and his official duties; but he will be unable to control death; this irrational force is coming to upset his temporal plans. He is especially fearful because dying appears to him to be a revelation of the nothingness of the self, a "dead emptiness" [Dimitri Merejkowski, *Tolstoy as Man and Artist*, 1904]. This awareness drives him into further despair, and yet is a requisite condition for his final illumination: for to the extent that despair scourges him of pride, he is vulnerable to self-scrutiny. . . .

It is immediately significant that Gerasim comes from the country, from the fecund earth [see Charles Neider, *Short Novels of the Masters*, 1948] as contrasted to the sterile urban backgrounds of Ivan Ilych and his colleagues. Gerasim's clothes are clean, neat, and functional: his boots smell of tar and winter air. Thus he is literally and figuratively "a breath of fresh air" in the sick-room. Moreover, honest and self-sacrificing, Gerasim actuates the familiar Tolstoyan principle that the primary purpose of existence is to live for others and not merely, as did Ivan Ilych, to gratify one's own will and desires. He does his work willingly and without lying to his master about the latter's hopeless condition. Hence Ivan Ilych can abandon himself to Gerasim's care, and this is no small act for a man who hitherto had been given to placing himself over others, especially those of lower social stations. Implicit, too, in this relationship between master and servant is the suggestion of a generic interdependence between human beings which transcends considerations of worldly station and rank. Again, because of Gerasim's devotion, Ivan Ilych becomes capable of extending compassion to his wife and son. In this overall perspective, then, Gerasim may be viewed as the true hero of the story.

In Parts VIII and IX, Ivan Ilych is brought a step closer to his most important discovery. What impels him in this direction is the continuing duplicity of the doctors and the obtuseness (e.g., their desertion of him for Sarah Bernhardt's performance) of his family, who look on him with the humiliating pity of the living for the dying. Searching for an explanation to account for his suffering, he reflects on the past, concluding that his life had been going downhill for many years; his marriage, work, and social ties have not satisfied him. Altogether, his existence seems to him in this moment of "ontological shock" to have had no meaning. Only death looms as the *real*. He can not understand why such a meaningless, wretched ending ought to be for one who has conducted his life so properly. "Why, why dost Thou torment me so terribly?" he complains. "What for?" Yet though Ivan Ilych has begun to pose questions about the past, he nevertheless avoids asking *the* crucial one.

The central effect of his physical and mental anguish in Parts X and XI is to edge him into asking the significant (for the older Tolstoy it was the "obsessive") question—"What if my whole life has really been wrong?" Then Ivan Ilych finally perceives that amid the mechanics of familial, official, and social functions, he had been estranged from his essential nature, had shrunk from life itself. And though he had been driven by pride and vanity, these motives had not only been condoned but actually praised by his society. Following this admission, he is assailed by extreme torment and self-hatred, because he does not know how, in these last few hours of consciousness, to rectify the falseness of the past.

In Part XII, two hours before his death, he suddenly apprehends the "right thing" to be done. Death is inevitable but a man can choose to die loving instead of hating. The Christian principle of brotherly love, he now feels, as did Pierre in *War and Peace* and Nexljudov in *Resurrection,* is the supreme human value. Here he seems to be in communion with the words Tolstoy himself dictated to his daughter, Aleksandra, a few days before his death—"The more a man loves the more real he becomes."

Acting out of conscious choice, Ivan Ilych gestures to his wife and son to forgive him. Significantly, this gesture occurs at the moment he feels himself being thrust into a black hole. The point is that grace comes to him only when he is in a state of utter despair. Previously, in Part VII, we have noted this identical pattern of despair followed by grace (Gerasim's help). Now, too, grace comes from the outside in the form of his son's love. Moreover, it is revealing that directly following his son's kiss, Ivan Ilych claims to see a light. For now the route of his metamorphosis becomes clearly visible—from despair (the black hole) to love (the son's kiss) to redemption (the light). Thus Ivan Ilych's dialectical direction, so to speak, is from nothingness to meaning: he has learned that the one thing necessary for a man is to *be.*

Source: Irving Halperin, "The Structural Integrity of 'The Death of Ivan Ilych'," in *Slavic and East European Journal,* Vol. 5, No. 4, Winter, 1961, pp. 334–40.

Temira Pachmuss

In the following excerpt, Pachmuss examines Ivan's transformation from his fear of death to his discovery of love.

Tolstoy described a most terrifying agony in "The Death of Ivan Ilyich" Ivan Ilyich also lived a false life, filled with lies and artificially multiplied needs. All his colleagues liked him, and yet, on receiving the news of his death, their first thoughts were of the changes and promotions it might occasion among themselves or their acquaintances. They gave no thought to the deceased himself, who had but recently lived among them. Even in the beginning of the work we may conjecture from Ivan Ilyich's feeling of loneliness that the sense of isolation while dying horrified Tolstoy as much as the thought of death itself. This isolation, the novelist warns, influences man's relationship with nature, which includes not only his life but his death. Affected by "civilization," Ivan Ilyich had escaped real life and failed to see his inner loneliness. He was completely absorbed in self, and this absorption, in turn, intensified the feeling of solitude he experienced at the approach of death. The very basis of Ivan Ilyich's relationship with nature was corrupt; however, although able to escape real life, he could not escape death.

We find the consciousness of this loneliness at the moment of dying not only in the works of Tolstoy but also in many other writings, such as the English morality play *Everyman* and Hugo von Hofmannsthal's adaptation *Jedermann.* When Everyman felt the approach of death, he sought desperately to find a companion for his last journey, and when he failed to do so, he was overwhelmed by despair at his terrible loneliness. A man like Ivan Ilyich, who during his life had no real contact with his closest relatives and was so alienated from nature that he could place no trust in it, had to experience his separateness in full measure. This same loneliness made him while dying want to weep: ". . . he wished most of all for someone to pity him as a sick child is pitied. He longed to be petted and comforted." As soon as he knew that death was approaching him, he felt "a loneliness, in the midst of a populous town and surrounded by numerous acquaintances and relations, yet which could not have been more complete anywhere—either at the bottom of the sea or under the earth." He wanted to be loved and to be pitied; he wanted others to feel and share his distress and sorrow: "And he had to live thus all alone on the brink of an

> Ivan Ilyich's physical sufferings were insignificant compared with his spiritual pain, which enabled him gradually to understand the complete falsity of his simple, ordinary, and therefore terrible life. While he lay dying he saw truth slowly supplanting falsity, yet all living people still kept on lying."

abyss, while no one understood or pitied him.'' He remained alone with death: ''And nothing could be done with it except to look at it and shudder.'' ''He wept on account of this terrible loneliness . . . and the absence of God.'' Slowly Ivan Ilyich came to understand that loneliness had always been around him, but he had been blind to it because of his false ideas of life. He had always lived for himself alone, near his fellow creatures, yet never in real community with them. Tolstoy called these wrong ideas of life ''falsity,'' describing ''the approach of that ever-dreaded and hateful death which was the only reality, and always the same falsity.'' This ''falsity,'' in Tolstoy's opinion, sprang from man's overrating himself. Ivan Ilyich's approach to life had always been completely egocentric; he considered his existence the center of the universe, never being able to understand that he, as a human being, was just a small particle in nature. His individualistic outlook was the trap in which he remained all his life. ''Caius is a man, men are mortal, therefore Caius is mortal,'' argued Ivan Ilyich. ''That Caius—man in general—was mortal was completely correct, but he wasn't Caius, not man in general, but a creature quite, quite different from all others.''

This attitude was the reason why only ''I'' had meaning for Ivan Ilyich, never ''you.'' As a result, his whole life was filled with unceasing care for

himself and his own comfort, and this attitude even characterized his family life. He cared for his own feelings, never for those of his wife. Even the death of his children meant nothing more to him than an inconvenience. He always did what was considered decorous in his circle, yet always managed to connect what was considered necessary for ''decorum'' with what was pleasant for himself. Living this kind of life, Ivan Ilyich naturally lacked all sense of humility. He liked the feeling of possessing the power of crushing at his will people dependent on him, and yet, at the same time, it pleased him to think of himself as a generous and kind man. He deceived one feeling with another: he wanted as a *comme il faut* and decorous man to display his love and kindness toward human beings, but at the same time he was not prepared to renounce the heady feeling of possessing authority. Thus his kindness, all the enjoyments of his business and private life, his love for his wife and children, all these were falsity—the feeling that originated in his false attitude toward himself. All the people around him also lived the same kind of life and were involved in this same pretense. Like Ivan Ilyich, they accepted falsity as reality: ''. . . I and all my friends felt that our case was quite different from that of Caius.'' In Tolstoy's words, ''Ivan Ilyich's life had been most simple and most ordinary, and therefore most terrible.'' Tolstoy's words may seem paradoxical, but it was Ivan Ilyich and his associates who considered their lives to be simple and ordinary, and the very fact that their twisted and distorted lives should seem ordinary to themselves was in itself terrible.

Ivan Ilyich's physical sufferings were insignificant compared with his spiritual pain, which enabled him gradually to understand the complete falsity of his simple, ordinary, and therefore terrible life. While he lay dying he saw truth slowly supplanting falsity, yet all living people still kept on lying. Even in the presence of death they still lived in accordance with decorum, the master he had served all his life. His wife simulated sympathy and care for him because these belonged to that decorum; but now Ivan Ilyich was sick of falsity, and ''while his wife was kissing him he hated her from the bottom of his soul and with difficulty refrained from pushing her away.'' ''Those lies—lies enacted over him on the eve of his death and destined to degrade this awful, solemn act to the level of their visits, their curtains, their sturgeon for dinner—were a terrible agony for Ivan Ilyich,'' because now he understood that all their interests and enjoyments, which he had shared while healthy, were nothing but illusions created by his selfishness. With this discovery, life appeared unreal, in contrast to which stood death, the only reality, about which there could be no mistake: ''. . . the approach of that ever-dreaded and hateful death which was the only reality, and always the same falsity.''

Ivan Ilyich gained comfort only through his contact with Gerasim. Gerasim, a fresh peasant lad, knew nothing of the pretenses of the ''civilized'' life Ivan Ilyich had lived before his malady; on the contrary, his life had been more real because he sensed his minute part in the universe, that he was a human being just as any other human being. Because of his real humility he alone was able to grasp Ivan Ilyich's position: ''We shall all of us die,'' said he, ''so why should I grudge a little trouble?'' Death was to him not only inevitable but also natural; he did not fear his dying master, and so Ivan Ilyich felt at ease only with him. Gerasim's assistance to him was not an act of hypocrisy; it was not burdensome work at all, but a service to life. Tolstoy thought the instinctive understanding of life and death that enabled Gerasim to do right naturally, to tell the truth, and to feel a deep sympathy for his fellow creatures was a result of Gerasim's identification with nature. His closeness to nature enabled him to live a life which, being foreordained by God, stood in striking opposition to Ivan Ilyich's life corrupted by culture and civilization. Culture and civilization were the poisons that filled Ivan Ilyich's soul and body all his life and became evident only through his malady and the torments caused by the prospect of death. ''Ivan Ilyich was left alone with the consciousness that his life was poisoned and was poisoning the lives of others, and that this poison did not weaken but penetrated more and more deeply into his whole being.''

It was love that Ivan Ilyich experienced after the realization of his guilt and the purification of his soul, and it was this love that enabled Ivan Ilyich to face death without fear. His pity for his family was part of his new relation to people—free of egotism and selfishness. ''Love is the sole medicine against death,'' Unamuno maintained [Miguel de Unamuno, *Tragic Sense of Life*, 1954], insisting, like Tolstoy or Thomas Mann, on the interrelation between love and death. Elsewhere in Tolstoy's works we find this feeling of love experienced by dying people. However, the sequence of the stages of death is somewhat vague, or perhaps is represented as just one step, including all three in one. At the time of writing *Three Deaths*, Tolstoy, it seems, lacked the spiritual maturity which permeates ''The Death of Ivan Ilyich,'' written some thirty years later.

Love is ultimate reality—this is Tolstoy's conclusion. As opposed to the primitive man, the ''civilized'' individual becomes a part of the harmonious whole only through death, or, during life, through love. Without love, Ivan Ilyich's life was empty and meaningless. With the discovery of love, Ivan Ilyich felt that his death was reduced to insignificance. He was allowed to become a part of the unity of the whole, an experience he described with the words: ''Death is all over. It is no more.''

It is, however, striking to note that despite Ivan Ilyich's perception of the mystery of death and his ultimate calm acceptance of it, the whole story reflects an icy coldness. Even kind and understanding Gerasim acts out of a sense of moral duty rather than from real love. Furthermore, Tolstoy is concerned here only with Ivan Ilyich; no one else matters. Ivan Ilyich's painful experience is over; his dead face does not express any pity for those who survive him, but a reproach and a warning. It seems that he has slipped back into his former remoteness from the world of mortals, of the Caiuses, those frightened and confused people who came to bid farewell to his coffin. There is no need for us, however, to dwell on Ivan Ilyich's facial expression in death as perceived by his relatives and colleagues, for the constructive principle of ''The Death of Ivan Ilych'' requires concentration on the dying man rather than on those who surround him. The high point of the story is undoubtedly Ivan Ilyich's discovery of the ultimate reality which is love.

Source: Temira Pachmuss, ''The Theme of Love and Death in Tolstoy's 'The Death of Ivan Ilyich','' in *American Slavic and East European Review,* Vol. XX, No. 1, February, 1961, pp. 72–83.

Further Reading

Citati, Pietro. *Tolstoy,* Schocken Books, 265 p.
    Examines Tolstoy's life and works, with sections specifically addressing his short fiction.

Magarshack, David. Afterword to *''The Death of Ivan Ilych,''* New American Library, 1960, pp. 295- 304.

Discusses the story focusing on the circumstances under which it was written and the extensive revision process Tolstoy employed.

Maude, Aylmer. Preface to *"Ivan Ilych," "Hadji Murad," and Other Stories,* Oxford University Press, 1935, pp. vii-xiv.
Introduces the story, describing the actual events from which it originated.

Olney, James. "Experience, Metaphor, and Meaning: 'The Death of Ivan Ilych'," in *Journal of Aesthetics and Art Criticism,* Vol. 31, No. 1, Fall, 1972, pp. 101–14.

Olney suggests that it is the innocence of the characters Gerasim and Vasya in Tolstoy's " Ivan Ilych" that leads Ivan to the realization of divine love.

Rowe, William W. *Leo Tolstoy,* Twayne, 1986, 143 p.
Biographical and critical study with sections devoted to Tolstoy's short fiction.

Simmons, Ernest J. Introduction to *Leo Tolstoy: Short Novels,* Modern Library, 1965, pp. v-xv.
Examines Tolstoy's short stories, citing them as examples of his realism and as forerunners to his novels.

The Demon Lover

Elizabeth Bowen
1945

The Demon Lover and Other Stories by Elizabeth Bowen was first published in Britain in 1945. In 1946, the collection was published in the United States under the title *Ivy Gripped the Steps and Other Stories.* Without exception, reviewers greeted it enthusiastically, praising it for what was described in the *New Yorker* as ''a completely successful explanation of what war did to the mind and spirit of the English people.'' Today, ''The Demon Lover'' is probably the most anthologized of Bowen's short stories, and critics claim that it reflects some of Bowen's greatest strengths as a writer.

Bowen was inspired to write ''The Demon Lover'' during World War II, after having experienced the Blitz, or aerial bombardment, of London by the Germans during 1940-41. Remembering the effects of World War I, people in London were overwhelmed by the events of World War II. Bowen's story, then, attempted to encapsulate the ''war on top of war'' sentiment which prevailed in post-Blitz London.

In ''The Demon Lover'' the main character, Mrs. Drover, confuses World War II with World War I. Returning home to collect some personal belongings during the aftermath of a recent bombing, she thinks of her long-dead fiance to the point where the reader does not know if this is a ghost story or simply a story of one character's neurotic mental state.

Author Biography

Elizabeth Dorothea Cole Bowen was born in Dublin, Ireland, on June 7, 1899. The daughter of aristocratic, Anglo-Irish parents, Bowen divided time between the family's Dublin home and Bowen's Court, their estate in County Cork, Ireland, during her early childhood. This ended, however, when Bowen's father was hospitalized for mental illness, and she and her mother went to England to stay with relatives until he recovered. In 1912, just as she and her family were to be reunited, her mother was diagnosed with cancer and died shortly afterwards.

Bowen was sent to England to be raised in the care of her mother's extended family. She attended Downe House Boarding School in Kent, and then went on to the London Council School of Art from 1918 to 1919. While in London, she began to work seriously on her writing. In 1923 she married professor Alan Charles Cameron and published her first collection of short stories, *Encounters*. In 1926 she and her husband moved to Oxford, bringing Bowen into contact with a literary circle that included the scholars C. M. Bowra and Lord David Cecil. During the next three years, she published two more short story collections and two novels, establishing a rate of production she would maintain nearly all of her life. When Bowen and her husband moved back to London in 1935, she became acquainted with Virginia Woolf and the Bloomsbury Group. Bowen wrote the stories in her collection *The Demon Lover and Other Stories* between 1941 and 1944, during the height of the bombardment of London by the Germans in World War II. Critics have long held that her wartime experiences had a lasting impact on her work, which often focuses on the effects of war on the individual.

A prolific writer, Bowen published short story collections, novels, essays, memoirs, and scripts for the British Broadcasting Corporation. She received much recognition during her lifetime and was an honorary member of both the American Academy of Arts and Letters and the Irish Academy of Letters. She was appointed Commander of the Order of the British Empire in 1948 and received a Doctor of Letters from Trinity College, Dublin, in 1949 and from Oxford in 1956. In 1965 she was made a Companion of Literature in the Royal Society of Literature, and she received the James Tait Black Memorial Prize in 1970. Bowen died of lung cancer in London on February 22, 1973.

Plot Summary

Mrs. Kathleen Drover has returned to London from her house in the country in order to pick up some things from the house that she and her husband abandoned because of the bombing of London by the Germans during 1940-41. It is a humid day in late August when she goes back to her mostly deserted street.

When she enters the house, she sees all of the telltale stains and dust left when she and her family moved out. The house has some cracks in it because of the bombing, and she wants to check on it. As she is passing her hall table, she notices a letter addressed to her—a strange sight, considering that the caretaker did not know of her return and that her house is boarded up and all of her mail has been forwarded to the country address. But she picks up the letter and takes it upstairs to her bedroom to read it, just moments before rain begins to fall.

The letter's author promises her that nothing has changed except for the time that has passed. He tells her that it is their anniversary and mentions a time for their meeting, of which she has no memory. Strangest of all, the letter is signed ''K,'' her own initial. When she checks the date on the letter and finds that it is for that day, she suddenly feels strangely apprehensive. She looks at herself in the mirror, noting how thin she has become from food rationing, and we are told that, despite a facial twitch and a worried mood, she always looks calm.

As the clock strikes six, she thinks back to twenty-five years earlier, in 1916, when her young soldier-lover said goodbye for the last time. She remembers his promise to be with her and the way he cruelly pressed her hand against his uniform breast buttons. She remembers the relief she felt when she could run in and tell her mother and sister that he was gone, the isolation she felt because of his promise, and, following his supposed death in World War I, the long years before anyone was again interested in her. She has the sense of being watched, a feeling that is reinforced when the letter-writer suggests that he saw her leaving London.

Mrs. Drover is becoming increasingly nervous. The house sounds hollow, and she wonders how the letter got in. The more she thinks about it, the more fearful she becomes. As she gets up and locks her bedroom door, she thinks about how she needs to get away from the house and this impending meeting. She decides to collect the things that she wants to take with her and to call a taxi, forgetting that the phone service has been disconnected.

She thinks about her soldier-lover again, remembering everything but his appearance, and realizes that she will not recognize him. She then unlocks her door and listens at the top of the stairs. She feels a draft, as if someone has left the basement through a door or a window.

The rain has finally stopped. She decides to carefully leave her house and rush to the local taxi stand. She hurries because she does not want to hear the clock strike seven, in case that is the hour for the mysterious meeting. The story ends when she arrives at the taxi stand and she notices that the taxi seems to be waiting for her. After entering the taxi, Mrs. Drover knocks on the glass behind the driver to get his attention. When their eyes meet, she screams and the driver speeds off, ''accelerating without mercy.'' This conclusion has been the focus of much speculation—some critics argue that the driver of the taxi is Mrs. Drover's long-lost lover, while others claim that the episode of anxiety she experiences is due to the stress of the war.

Elizabeth Bowen

always sustain a manner that was at once energetic and calm.'' To her family Mrs. Drover is a picture of stability and dependability. The letter unnerves her, however, and she begins to pack things in a ''rapid, fumbling-decisive way.'' Although it is unclear whether she is haunted by the vengeful ghost of her soldier-lover or is neurotic, she completely breaks down at the end of the story.

Soldier-Lover

Although we see the soldier-lover only through Kathleen Drover's memories, he is a significant character. He treats her thoughtlessly, pushing her hand painfully onto his uniform breast buttons when she reaches to touch him and making her a promise that ''I shall be with you . . . sooner or later. You won't forget that. You need do nothing but wait.'' He is reported ''missing, presumed killed'' in action in World War I.

Characters

Mrs. Kathleen Drover

The story centers on the perceptions and actions of Mrs. Kathleen Drover. When she finds a letter addressed to her in her abandoned London home, she thinks back to her former nameless soldier-lover during World War I. She is keenly aware of her surroundings: the atmosphere, weather, and particularly, a sense of strangeness. The letter lying on the table compels her to imagine the various possibilities for how the letter got there in the first place.

Because of the overwhelming sense of the strangeness of her situation, Mrs. Drover rushes upstairs to check herself in the mirror: her ''most normal expression was one of controlled worry, but of assent . . . [she] had . . . an intermittent muscular flicker to the left of her mouth, but . . . she could

Themes

Doubt and Ambiguity

The theme of appearance and reality is central to ''The Demon Lover.'' The dubiousness of the

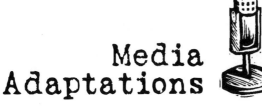

Media Adaptations

- "The Demon Lover" was adapted for radio broadcast on August 27, 1946, and was read by Evelyn Russell.

- "The Demon Lover" was also produced on January 10, 1974, from the original adaptation, for Radio 4, Bristol, England.

appearance of the letter puzzles Mrs. Drover. How did it get on the table? Who placed it there? Her house is obviously deserted and untouched, which makes the appearance of the letter even more enigmatic. To verify her own conception of reality, Mrs. Drover looks in the mirror, and she sees herself, looking familiar and reassuring.

Her mind races, however, back in time to her mysterious, nameless soldier-lover with whom she was in love as a young girl. This vision reinforces the sense of him as potentially the "demon lover" of the title. He is remembered not with warmth but for his sense of his power or control over her. Mrs. Drover's association of the letter with the soldier-lover makes the reality of the letter questionable, although it is a physical object. When she escapes into a taxi, she sees the face of the driver. She then starts to scream and pound the glass between them. What does she actually see? Bowen plays expertly with Mrs. Drover's and our sensibilities.

Identity

It appears that Mrs. Drover knows herself only through her family's perceptions. She appears to them as a strong, secure woman, but she has buried parts of herself deep in her own memory. She remembers, for example, her feelings toward her soldier-lover and the feelings of isolation that she experienced when she agreed to wait for him. She is suspicious of the fact, however, that the letter is signed with her own initial, "K." Throughout the story, she cannot remember her soldier-lover's fea-

tures, and it is difficult to tell whether she recalls his appearance when she sees the taxi driver's face at the end of the story.

Revenge

The contents of the letter may suggest that the soldier-lover intends to fulfill his twenty-five-year-old promise to return and "be with" Mrs. Drover. Is he indeed the demonic lover who has come back to take her away to her death for not keeping her promise to wait for him? This and the fact that the driver accelerates "without mercy" may suggest his revenge.

Sex Roles

Throughout the story, Mrs. Drover is portrayed as submissive, adhering to the traditionally prescribed role of a woman. She reacts passively to her soldier-lover when he hurts her hand, and she molds herself to him when they see each other. She allows William Drover to marry her because she is "relieved" that he has come to court her. She is also nervous and easily frightened by weather, the striking of the clock, and the atmosphere of the house.

Victim and Victimization

Mrs. Drover is an innocent victim of both World Wars. She loses her soldier-lover during the first and is forced to abandon her house and move to the country during the second. Her food is rationed and her house has been bombed. She is obsessed with the war and the prospect of safely returning to the countryside with her family. She also feels victimized by the memory of her soldier-lover, who exerts his power over her and makes her seem different to her family when he is there. Because of this, she believes that he may have written the letter.

War and Peace

It is wartime again in England, and the war has made some major changes to Mrs. Drover's life. She thinks back to the soldier she knew during World War I. Coincidentally, the letter mentions "the fact that nothing has changed." The soldier is above all a figure of war and is associated with death. He haunts Mrs. Drover's imagination. On the other hand, Bowen gives the reader a natural reason for the presence of the letter: the air has shifted as

The dome of St. Paul's Cathedral in London during the Blitzkrieg in World War II.

someone moved out of the basement. Is it the war itself, then, that makes Mrs. Drover scream as she is driven through the deserted streets? We do not know for sure, and Bowen deliberately leaves this open to the reader's interpretation.

Style

Point of View

The story is told in third-person omniscient narration, which gives the reader a godlike perspec-tive, unrestricted by time or place, allowing the reader to look into the minds of the characters. The story focuses primarily on Mrs. Drover's percep-tions. At times the narration switches to the first-person point of view, or the point of view of a certain character, and then reverts to third-person, to heighten the intensity of Mrs. Drover's feelings. This breaks the flow of the narrative and enables the reader to directly perceive her thoughts.

Setting

Setting is a particularly important aspect in "The Demon Lover." The story takes place in a

Topics for Further Study

- Research conditions in London, England, during the Blitz of World War II, and compare what you find with the setting of "The Demon Lover."

- Find a version of the English ballad, "The Demon Lover," and trace its use in the story. How do the two compare?

- Compare "The Demon Lover" with Edith Wharton's "Pomegranate Seed." Discuss any similarities or differences you observe.

- In what way is "The Demon Lover" a ghost story? Find some other English ghost stories and compare them.

- Look at studies of people in wartime and post-traumatic stress syndrome. Can you find any connection with Mrs. Drover's state of mind?

house with "some cracks in the structure, left by the last bombing" that is situated on a deserted street and gives an eerie atmosphere to the story. This is intensified by descriptions of the humid day, Mrs. Drover's tension before the rain starts up again, and the mysterious draft from the basement. The striking of the clock intrudes into the story, highlighting the passage of time and the encounter that Mrs. Drover is apprehensively expecting.

The time and place of the story is also significant. It takes place during the Second World War, specifically during the German Blitz in London. Mrs. Drover also thinks back to the First World War and confounds the two.

Symbolism

The structurally unsound house serves as a symbol of Mrs. Drover's mental state. The constant bombardment has eroded the house's stability, just as the constant pressure of the war has worn on Mrs. Drover's psyche. She cannot escape the effects of war when she enters the house, and the letter, signed with her own initial, "K," becomes a symbol of her repressed consciousness of that war and triggers memories of her World War I soldier-lover. The soldier-lover, in turn, becomes a symbol for all war, an everyman with an unknown face, whose promise to be with her takes on a frightening significance in wartime London. She has to release some of her repressed memories, perhaps symbolized by the air which escapes from the basement of the house and her screams when she sees the face of the driver—a face she sees as the face of her demon lover. The reader can interpret this as a sign of her mental breakdown, her subjective interpretation of events, or as a symbol for the face of war.

Gothicism

As suggested by the title, the story plays with the theme of the demon lover, the figure in Gothic literature who comes back to take away his unfaithful lover who has broken her promise to wait for him. In the ballad, she goes with him happily, only to find that he is taking her to her death. Here the soldier makes the promise to be with Kathleen, but she cannot remember what he looks like. Mrs. Drover is haunted by her memories, and Bowen implies that the face of the taxi driver is the face of the demon lover sweeping her away to places unknown.

Historical Context

World War II and The Blitzkrieg

The short story collection *The Demon Lover and Other Stories* (1945), published in America as *Ivy Gripped the Steps and Other Stories* (1946), was written between 1941 and 1944, when Bowen worked in London at the Ministry of Information during the day and as an air-raid warden at night. She lived in London during the most intense period of the German air assault during World War II. Bombs with warheads of almost one ton began falling on London on September 8, 1944, and later that year the V-2 (revenge weapon 2) bombs began to fall. More than one thousand of these landed in Britain, killing over 2,700 people and injuring 6,500.

The setting of "The Demon Lover" is the empty streets of London, whose inhabitants have fled the destruction of their homes.

"Against the next batch of clouds, already piling up ink-dark, broken chimneys and parapets stood out. In her once familiar street, as in any unused channel, an

Compare & Contrast

- **1920s:** Spiritualism, the belief in the supernatural accompanied by attempts to contact spirits of the dead, becomes very popular after World War I. Many churches and societies feature some form of spiritualistic belief.

  1990s: Closely aligned with New Age beliefs, spiritualism becomes popular again, particularly in the United States. Putting a new spin on spiritualism, many modern-day channelers are as apt to attempt to contact extraterrestrials or spirits from ancient mythic societies as they are to try to communicate with recently deceased relatives.

- **Early 1940s:** The Battle of Britain, the air war fought between the Royal Air Force and the German Luftwaffe, rages over Great Britain. Bowen writes ''The Demon Lover'' after the German Blitzkrieg; her protagonist, Mrs. Drover, symbolizes the desperation that many feel.

  1998: World War II remains a popular theme for stories. *Saving Private Ryan,* a realistic treatment of the D-Day invasion, is one of the year's most acclaimed films. Like Mrs. Dover in ''The Demon Lover,'' Private Ryan must deal with the losses of war long after the fighting has stopped.

---

unfamiliar queerness had silted up: a cat wove itself in and out of railings, but no human eye watched Mrs. Drover's return . . . the door . . . had warped . . . [and] Dead air came out to meet her as she went in.''

The scene is ominous as she creeps up the darkened stairs and opens the bedroom door. Unlike others, however, her house has only a few cracks in it, and she can still open a window despite nighttime blackout conditions.

The reader is spared the noise of the V-2s, as she does not stay there at night, but the silence of the deserted streets is ''so intense—one of those creeks of London silence exaggerated this summer by the damage of war.'' The general historical context of the war—of both wars—is crucial to an understanding of the story.

World War I

The figure of the soldier-lover from World War I is crucial to Mrs. Drover's state of mind. He appears vividly in her memory twenty-five years later, although she still cannot remember his face. He had been on leave from France when he promised that he would be with her ''sooner or later,'' no matter what happened to him. She thinks that he is going away far away, but the battlefields in France were relatively close to England. She remembers how his sharp uniform breast buttons cut her hand and the way she looked at him as if he were already a ghost.

Douglas A. Hughes argues in ''Cracks in the Psyche: Elizabeth Bowen's 'The Demon Lover','' in the Fall 1993 issue of *Studies in Short Fiction,* that Mrs. Drover has a breakdown after her love is reported missing in action. ''A pledge of binding love—not at all uncommon among young lovers—exchanged with her fiance before he returned to the trenches became, after his death and her subsequent derangement, a 'sinister troth' and he himself became a cold, ominous figure in her imagination.'' Hughes argues that she never overcomes her trauma from this loss, though she is able to marry and live cautiously. The house and letter trigger the eruption of Mrs. Drover's repressed past and her memories of World War I into the present. As the letter-writer states, ''nothing has changed.'' War seems to grow in scale, and Mrs. Drover cannot cope mentally. By compounding the psychological stress of two global conflicts within the span of a single generation, Bowen has placed an exceedingly heavy burden on the shoulders of her protagonist.

Critical Overview

Because of her keen awareness of detail, atmosphere, mood, and particularly her focus on the perspectives of female characters, Bowen was frequently compared by critics to such authors as Jane Austen, Henry James, Virginia Woolf, and Katherine Mansfield. Since World War II, however, critical focus on Bowen's writings has steadily declined.

The hardships Mrs. Drover endures upon returning to her deserted house has led to much critical debate. Issues concerning Mrs. Drover's fragile mental state and repressed memories, the association of demon lover with war itself, and the fact that Bowen's work shares its title with a Gothic ballad have been sources of continual critical discussion.

According to the postscript of the 1946 American edition of *The Demon Lover and Other Stories,* Elizabeth Bowen wrote the title story of her collection between 1941 and 1944. In 1945 Henry Reed, a reviewer for *The New Statesman and Nation,* praised Bowen for the way she conveyed the atmosphere of war to the reader and for her "ability to concentrate the emotions of a scene, or a sequence of thoughts . . . into an unforgettable sentence or phrase with a beauty of expression. . . ." This praise was echoed by American reviewers when the collection was published in the United States the following year. Without exception American critics lauded Bowen's work.

One of the first American reviews of Bowen's collection appeared in the March 1, 1946, edition of *Kirkus Reviews.* The critic lauded Bowen's "very special talent: a subtlety, occasionally carried to an excess where substance is dissipated; an immaculacy which, within its self-imposed limits, reaches artistic perfection." Moreover, S. H. Hay, in the April 13, 1946, edition of the *Saturday Review of Literature,* commented on the way Bowen created "an atmosphere of terror and savagery which by its very underplaying is the more pervasive and compelling." John Farrelly, in the April 7, 1946, edition of the *New York Times Book Review,* echoed Reed's commendations, claiming that Bowen's stories conveyed the sentiments of people in wartime England: "What all these people share is a lack of something they want and aren't likely to get. . . . But every one of them discovers something of his own identity and fights against the threat of annihilation to preserve that personal existence. . . . The familiar patterns of

experience have been broken, at least temporarily. Life has been revaluated, perhaps more intelligently."

James Stern, in the April 29, 1946, edition of the *New Republic,* discussed how Bowen insightfully conveyed to her readers "the dreams, fantasies and hallucinations produced in people by loss of sleep, loss of property, broken marriages, broken lives, endless days and nights of destruction" experienced by the English people during their time of crisis. Stern also conveyed their desire to preserve the past under the burden of the unbearable present, symbolized by "the Passage of Time and the Architecture of the House," which he identified as key themes in all of Bowen's works.

Lotus Snow, in her essay published in 1950 in the *Western Humanities Review* found Bowen's theme of "the uncertain 'I'" in both her short stories and novels. In a postscript to the 1946 American edition, Bowen herself referred to the ghost in "The Demon Lover" as "questionable," one who "[fills] the vacuum for the uncertain 'I'." Snow also argued that in her short stories Bowen "writes of the world of feeling: her people find a sense of personal identity through the subjective experiences of love, hate, illusion." Moreover, Snow claimed that in her novels Bowen stresses the emotional and social background of people whose lives were disrupted during the war.

In recent years, "The Demon Lover" has been widely anthologized in short fiction collections and is considered Bowen's most famous short work. Surprisingly, it has not appeared in any ghost story collections. Since 1946 critical articles have focused mainly on the psychological aspects of "The Demon Lover." While the historical background of the two World Wars is always a factor in any discussion of the story, recent critics are also interested in Mrs. Drover's psychological response to the traumatic stress caused by those wars.

Criticism

Tanya Gardiner-Scott

Gardiner-Scott is an Associate Professor at Mount Ida College. In the following essay, she examines and discusses various critical examinations of "The Demon Lover."

The title of Bowen's best-known story, "The Demon Lover," refers to a Gothic ballad whose plot

What Do I Read Next?

- *The Turn of the Screw,* Henry James's 1898 short novel. When a governess goes to take care of two children, she believes she sees the ghosts of the previous governess and her master's valet.

- W. W. Jacobs's "The Monkey's Paw" (1902). This short story is about a magical monkey's paw that will give bereaved parents three wishes. They wish that their son were alive again.

- "A Haunted House" (1921), by Virginia Woolf, is a short story about two ghosts who come back to a house in which they had been very happy.

- Elizabeth Bowen's "Pink May" (1945) concerns a woman who is cheating on her husband during wartime and is haunted by a female ghost. The marriage breaks up shortly thereafter.

- "Mysterious Kor" (1945) is Elizabeth Bowen's short story about a woman and her soldier-lover who invent a mysterious city to distract themselves from wartime London.

- "London, 1941," Mervyn Peake's poem of London during the Blitz, humanizes the architectural devastation of London.

- "The Demon Lover." Charles Williams's novel concerning interaction between the living and living dead amid the bombed-out ruins of postwar London. Of Williams and his fiction, T. S. Eliot once wrote, "For the reader who can appreciate them, there are terrors in the pit of darkness into which he can make us look; but in the end, we are brought nearer to what another modern explorer of the darkness has called 'the laughter at the heart of things.'"

"focuses on a young woman's promise to love her young man for ever and await his return from battle," according to Charles E. May. After her beloved fails to return from battle (the legend goes) she marries someone else—only to have the soldier-lover show up, often at the wedding in the guise of a skeletonized corpse, to claim her and carry her away to be united with him in death. "The Demon Lover" is a variation on this theme, being at once a ghost story and a story about a woman's precarious mental state in wartime.

A historical perspective related to warfare in the twentieth century is essential to understanding the story. We learn from hints in the story, such as "some cracks in the structure [of the house], left by the last bombing," that "The Demon Lover" takes place during the London Blitz, during World War II, while Kathleen Drover's memory of the soldier-lover extends back almost thirty years to 1916, the middle year of World War I. Understanding this is crucial, because for Kathleen the past and the present fuse into one horrid, timeless moment at the end of the story.

Through the narrator's words, Bowen links Kathleen's fateful promise of fidelity with the supernatural elements of the old ballad, noting that "she already felt that unnatural promise drive down between her and the rest of all human kind. No other way of having given herself could have made her feel so apart, lost and foresworn. She could not have plighted a more sinister troth." (Further, she twice refers to the pain of her soldier-lover's uniform button in the palm of her hand, fixing that detail in our minds as a symbol of that youthful relationship and the soldier's hard pressuring of her.) Indeed not; for years after the disappearance of her betrothed, Kathleen was not courted by any man, and she felt herself "watched" by unseen eyes. By contrast, after she married William Drover, "[h]er movements as Mrs. Drover were circumscribed, and she dismissed any idea that they were still watched." Still, even though she has settled down for what she expects to be an ordinary domestic life, she still feels uneasy as the result of that earlier promise.

By marrying someone else, Mrs. Drover has been unfaithful to her soldier-lover, even though he

> " All of Bowen's critics stress the significance of the wartime setting--the damaged house and deserted street-- and the lowering weather, with the sudden rainstorm in the middle of the story and the silence afterwards where nothing (and everything) has changed."

is "missing, presumed killed." Thus, in her own mind, she is susceptible to unresolved guilt when she remembers him. Her remembrance of him intensifies upon her finding and reading the mysterious letter in the damaged house. The letter's message unleashes her repressed memory of her lover's promise to be with her forever—and she is further haunted by the fact that she cannot even remember his face. As the reader recalls the faceless person seen leaving the house before Mrs. Drover arrived, the thought arises that perhaps this could be the ghostly lover preparing for his dramatic confrontation with Kathleen, having left her the letter. Further, the face of the taxi-driver, which makes her scream, may be the face she cannot remember, as James L. Green and George O'Brien have argued. Certainly the fact that the cabbie drives Kathleen away, "accelerating without mercy," ties him linguistically to the soldier-lover (a man "without very much kindness") as well as to the demon-lover who carries his faithless beloved away.

A related way of looking at the story, as argued by Green and O'Brien, is that both Kathleen Drover and England have been faithless to the values fought for during World War I, and therefore the menace of war goes on, with all its attendant threat of unexpected danger by forces beyond one's control, symbolized by the figure of the soldier, nameless and faceless. That she imagines him as a ghostly figure with "spectral glitters in the place of his eyes" keeping her from a place of safety adds to this level of meaning. She craved safety when she married William Drover, and that very sense of safety is

threatened by the environment in which she finds herself when she returns to bomb-damaged London for the day.

The gloomy atmosphere of the story contributes greatly to whichever interpretation we choose to embrace. All of Bowen's critics stress the significance of the wartime setting—the damaged house and deserted street—and the lowering weather, with the sudden rainstorm in the middle of the story and the silence afterwards where nothing (and everything) has changed. In such a setting, the sound of the clock striking becomes heightened and ominous to Mrs. Drover.

Inside the house, Kathleen is once again in her old married setting, feeling isolated, lonely, and apprehensive. Her vulnerability is made clear in the passage in which the narrator notes, "The desuetude of her former bedroom, her married London home's whole air of being a cracked cup from which memory, with its reassuring power, had either evaporated or leaked away, made a crisis." Kathleen is completely caught in the existential moment, feeling alone as she has not felt in years; and the letter, whether written by the lover or existing only in her own subconscious, affects her deeply.

The letter is particularly significant in its wording—"The years have gone by at once slowly and fast. In view of the fact that nothing has changed, I shall rely on you to keep your promise." For Kathleen, World War I has begun again; in that sense, nothing has changed between her lover and herself. The writer of the letter also implies that he has been watching Mrs. Drover's movements, as he knows she has left her London home. Mrs. Drover's situation is made clearer at this point: Either her ghostly lover is sadistic and playing games with her or the message in the letter exists only in her own mind.

Kathleen herself doubts the reality of the letter, though she is frightened by the fact that it got into the house, and wonders who put it there. She has the sense of an inexorable fate waiting to confront her. To convey this intensity of feeling, Bowen adjusts the narrative voice, switching abruptly from a third-person omniscient narrator into Kathleen's own voice, first-person narration. For example, Bowen writes that "at the thought of the taxi her heart went up and her normal breathing resumed. I will ring up the taxi now; the taxi cannot come too soon: I shall hear the taxi out there running its engine, till I walk calmly down to it through the hall. I'll ring up—But no: the telephone is cut off. . . . She tugged at a knot she had tied wrong.'' This transition into stream-of-consciousness narration makes us aware of Mrs. Drover's attempt at calm and just how fragile her mental state is. She is hanging on grimly to her sanity, trying not to let herself be spooked by what she encounters.

The issue of Mrs. Drover's perceptions arises again when, for the second time in the story, she thinks back to the condition of her mental state twenty-five years earlier, when she was pressured to make her ''unnatural promise'' to the soldier. Again, Bowen shifts her narrator into first-person:

> She remembered not only all that he said and did but the complete suspension of *her* existence during that August week. I was not myself—they all told me so at the time. She remembered—but with one white burning blank as where acid has dropped on a photograph: *under no conditions* could she remember his face.
>
> So, wherever he may be waiting, I shall not know him. You have no time to run from a face you do not expect.

The narrative here is even more choppy than in other, earlier instances of stream-of-consciousness. In addition, the first transition from third- to first-person narrative is signalled by quotation marks; in the next two instances there are no signs for us. This shift in narrative technique is made to illustrate Kathleen's increasing mental fragility and agitation.

The critic Douglas A. Hughes has argued for a close identification between Kathleen's mental state and the damaged house, claiming that Kathleen, completely isolated from familiar landmarks and people, is ready for a mental collapse. According to this reading, she imagines the letter, the idea of it issuing from the repressed part of her psyche. Consumed with guilt at the memory of her betrayal of her soldier-lover, she thinks that the taxi-driver is her old lover and goes completely insane at the story's end, overwhelmed by the effects of war—old and new. To Kathleen, there is no end to the landscape of war, and past and present fuse in her mind. At the story's end, we do not know where she is being taken, but she definitely is in the grip of a force stronger than she, bringing us back again to the story's title and the theme of the demon lover.

What, then, is the demon that haunts her? Is it, as Hughes suggests, the demon of her repressed memories? Or is it, as Calder suggests, the war itself? War brings with it not only death but a sense of powerlessness to those caught up in it, a feeling of the loss of control over their lives. Perhaps, as various critics have hinted, the story does simply address fictively and delicately one woman's reaction to living with war.

Source: Tanya Gardiner-Scott, ''An Overview of 'The Demon Lover','' in *Short Stories for Students,* The Gale Group, 1999.

Robert L. Calder

In the following essay, Calder debates the claims that Mrs. Drover of Bowen's ''The Demon Lover'' is either insane or unhappy in her marriage and instead examines the story as an allegory of life in England during the two World Wars. He also suggests that the setting of the story is a catalyst to Mrs. Drover's breakdown.

Of all of Elizabeth Bowen's short stories, none has been anthologized as often as ''The Demon Lover.'' First published in *The Listener* in November, 1941, and reprinted in *The Demon Lover and Other Stories* (1945) and *Ivy Gripped the Steps and Other Stories* (1946), it is usually introduced as a clever tale of occult possession. Early critical commentary is typified by Allen E. Austin's remark that '''The Demon Lover' is a ghost story that builds up and then culminates like an Alfred Hitchcock movie.''

This interpretation was first challenged by Douglas A. Hughes in his 1973 note ''Cracks in the Psyche: Elizabeth Bowen's 'The Demon Lover''' [*Studies in Short Fiction* 10, 1973]. ''Far from being a supernatural story,'' he argued, '''The Demon Lover' is a masterful dramatization of acute psychological delusion, of the culmination of paranoia in a time of war.'' The ghostly threat, rather than having any external reality, is a product of the disturbed mental state of the protagonist, Mrs. Kathleen Drover. Her guilt over her fiance's disappearance and presumed death in the First World War, buried by years of conventional marriage, has been reawakened by another war, and she hallucinates his vengeful return. The inconstant woman in the English ballad ''The Demon Lover'' discovers that the lover is in fact the devil; in Bowen's story, ''war, not the vengeful lover, is the demon that overwhelms this rueful woman'' because it strips her of her recent memories and plunges her back to her betraying past.

In 1980, in an article entitled ''Elizabeth Bowen's 'The Demon Lover': Psychosis or Seduction?,'' [*Studies in Short Fiction* 17, 1980] Daniel V. Fraustino disputed Hughes's interpretation, arguing that it interpolates several key points in the text. There is no evidence, says Fraustino, that Mrs. Drover suffered an emotional collapse after the loss of her fiance or was gripped by ''psychotic guilt,'' and nothing in her thought processes indicate incipi-

> "The final image of Kathleen trapped in a taxi 'accelerating without mercy' into the 'hinterland of deserted streets' perfectly captures the feelings of millions of people who in 1941 seemed to be propelled at an increasingly frenzied pace into a European wasteland of rubble and death."

ent mania. To the contrary, the fiance was clearly a psychopath who survived the war and has now returned to kill Mrs. Drover on the twenty-fifth anniversary of their parting. Impelled by an unconscious desire to escape from an impoverished and unfulfilling marriage, she becomes the victim in a "murder mystery of high drama."

Fraustino's analysis rightly identifies some serious flaws in Hughes's reading—there is indeed little evidence that Mrs. Drover suffered an emotional collapse after the loss of her fiance—but in making his own case he is guilty, if not of interpolation, certainly of exaggeration. To counter Hughes's argument that Mrs. Drover's disarrayed house, which Bowen describes in characteristic detail, reflects her internal collapse, Fraustino claims that she has had an unsatisfactory marriage, marked by years of "accumulated emptiness." Her London house is an objective correlative, not of Mrs. Drover's psychological state, but of her "impoverished married life."

There is nothing in "The Demon Lover," however, to indicate that Mrs. Drover is dissatisfied with her marriage. After some years without being courted, she married William Drover at the age of 32, settled down in a "quiet, arboreal part of Kensington," and began to raise three children. When the bombs drove the family out of London, they settled in the country, and on the day of the story, wearing the pearls her husband had given her on their wedding, she has returned to the city to retrieve some things from their house. Empty of any

human presence, it now seems to her full of "dead air" and "traces of her long former habit of life": a smoke stain up the fireplace, a watermark left by a vase on an escritoire, and scratch marks left on the floor by a piano. These may be images of emptiness, repetition, and stagnation, but they underline the absence of the family and its normal human interaction, not dissatisfaction with the marriage. She is a "prosaic" woman, whose "movements as Mrs. Drover [are] circumscribed," and her marriage is simply conventional.

Fraustino's view of Mrs. Drover as a discontented wife in an unfulfilling marriage runs into difficulty when he attempts to make her behavior relevant to the murder mystery plot. Like Hughes, he regards the title of "The Demon Lover" as an allusion to the English ballad about an absent lover, an intervening marriage, and a desertion from that marriage upon the lover's return. Bowen's story, however, has no indication whatsoever that Mrs. Drover intends or attempts, even fleetingly, to abandon her marriage. As a result, Fraustino can voice only the vaguest, most guarded of suppositions: "is it not possible that Bowen at least suggests Mrs. Drover's desertion?"

Finally, to build his case for murder, Fraustino interprets the character of the fiance in a way surely not justified by the text. He rightly emphasizes that the young soldier was never tender and loving, that he was "without feeling," and that he extracted an "unnatural promise" from Kathleen. When, however, he notes that she left the encounter with a weal on her palm, which he had "pressed, without very much kindness and painfully, on to one of the breast buttons of his uniform," Fraustino concludes that "the soldier is a sadist of the most deranged kind . . . a psychopath." Cold, unfeeling, and disconcerting the fiance certainly is, but can his behavior really be called sadistic, deranged, or psychopathic? If not, how credible is it that he would return to kill his lover of 25 years earlier?

As Fraustino admits, his reading of "The Demon Lover" as a realistic murder story invites several practically unanswerable questions: "how the taxi-driver knew that Mrs. Drover would be visiting her London house on that particular day, or how he managed to engineer events so cleverly that she would inevitably seek a taxi precisely on the hour of seven, can only be guessed." After suggesting that Mrs. Drover may have gone to London in an unconscious response to the twenty-fifth anniversary and arranged in advance for a taxi, he confesses that the story does not provide enough information "to reconstruct a completely rational, satisfying interpretation of events."

If, then, there is no completely "rational" interpretation—and both the Hughes and Fraustino readings are attempts at rational explanations—could the story be operating on another level? Given her other writing, Bowen is unlikely merely to have written a ghost story or a tale of murder, though she does elsewhere explore psychological breakdown. In connection with this last point, however, it is important to "The Demon Lover" in the context of the period in which it was written and of the collection in which it was published. In writing of the wartime milieu in the preface to the American edition, Bowen states that the stories "may be found interesting as documents, even if they are negligible as art. This discontinuous writing, nominally 'inventive,' is the only diary I have kept" [*Ivy Gripped the Steps and Other Stories,* 1946]. It is as a wartime "document," then, a "diary" entry of a woman's response to yet another war, that "The Demon Lover" perhaps can be most clearly understood. . . .

If Bowen were writing only about the women haunted by the memories of lovers lost in the First World War, however, she is hardly likely to portray Mrs. Drover's fiance in such harsh, negative terms. After all, few women would mourn the loss of a painful presence or have their present settled lives dislocated by its return. The formula demands a loving fiance described in such detail as to evoke a sense of poignancy when he is lost. In Bowen's story, there is nothing sensitive or kind about the soldier, and, more remarkably, he is in no way individualized. We are given the barest of details, not about his features, but about his uniform, and his face remains hidden by the darkness. This lack of identity is emphasized again later when Bowen writes: "She remembered—but with one white burning blank as where acid has dropped on a photograph: *Under no conditions* could she remember his face" (original italics). Though this is obviously a very significant element in the story, both Hughes and Fraustino give it little attention. Hughes briefly suggests that the facelessness is the result of Mrs. Drover's faulty memory 25 years after the event, and Fraustino makes no mention of it.

Such an unusual treatment of the soldier suggests that he is meant to represent something quite different from the conventional lost lover, something perhaps arising from the conditions and times in which "The Demon Lover" was written. In 1935, sparked by Holtby's review, Bowen might well have described the unsettling recollection of lost love. Several years into the Second World War, when Britons were facing the real possibility of annihilation of their culture and civilization, she is more likely to have invested the soldier with a more ominous significance. In the midst of one war, a relic from an earlier one that was to have been the war to end all wars, would be a ghastly symbol of endless, inescapable violence.

In his forward to *Writers on World War II* [1991], Mordecai Richler calls the Second World War "no more than a second act," and it has become commonplace to refer to the inter-war period as "the Long Armistice." The realization that the years from 1919 to 1939 were merely a temporary respite from armed conflict, however, came early to many thinking Britons. The Yorkshire novelist Phyllis Bentley, for example, wrote of "the armistice period [1919–1939] in British fiction" in the *New York Times* in August of 1941. Bowen, born in 1899 and having worked in a hospital for shell-shocked soldiers in 1916, could hardly have escaped feeling that the violence of one war had been let loose again in another.

Looked at as allegory, much in "The Demon Lover" becomes explicable. The present action takes place in August 1941, and the earlier parting took place in August 1916, almost exactly half way through a war that began in August—just as August 1939 had seen Europe rushing into another conflagration. The faceless, featureless soldier becomes a representative figure, a threatening everyman in military uniform. The absence of kindness, his not "meaning a person well," his being "set upon" Kathleen rather than in love with her, suggest that she is gripped by a force that is seductive but not benign. That she is in the presence of something demonic is conveyed by the "spectral glitters" she imagines "in the place of his eyes." The experience of war could hardly be more vividly embodied than in the image of the young woman's hand being so forcefully pressed onto the buttons of a military uniform that they leave a weal on her palm. Tennessee Williams employs a similar metaphor in *The Glass Menagerie* when he describes the American middle class "having their fingers pressed forcibly down on the fiery Braille alphabet of a dissolving economy" [*Twentieth Century Drama*, eds. Ruby Cohn and Bernard Dukore, 1966]. In Bowen's story, "the cut on the palm of her hand was, principally, what [Kathleen] was to carry away."

Kathleen takes something else away from her encounter with the soldier, though it becomes forgotten in her subsequent inter-war life: ''the unnatural promise.'' Inexplicable in conventional terms, Bowen's language here becomes more understandable if it suggests complicity with war. In perhaps the last major war that the public approached with zealous idealism, in which women saw men off to battle amid banners and brass bands, and in which they gave white feathers to young men not in uniform, it would seem that they ''could not have plighted a more sinister troth.''

Just as war subsumes normal human life and interaction, Kathleen experienced a ''complete suspension of her existence during that August week'' when, she is told, she was not herself. In the years immediately following her loss, she suffered a ''complete dislocation from everything,'' just as the western world went through a decade of dislocation—whether it was the Roaring Twenties in America or the era of Evelyn Waugh's Bright Young Things in Britain—in reaction to the disillusionment and horror of the First World War. And just as the 1930s brought the world back to a sober confrontation with serious issues of economics and politics, Kathleen's thirties made her again ''natural enough'' (as opposed to the ''unnatural promise'') to return to a conventional pattern of living. She married the prosaically named William Drover, and settled complacently down, convinced that they were not ''still watched.''

For many people in Britain, the 1930s was a period of similar complacency, grounded on the assumption that war had been ''presumed killed'' by the Treaty of Versailles and the creation of the League of Nations, and that appeasement would prevent its return. As we now know, however, the seeds of the second armed conflict had been sown and not eradicated in the first. Kathleen had thought that her khaki-clad demon was ''going away such a long way,'' but his reply, ''not so far as you think'' suggests that war was never remote, no matter how normal and settled her life and that of her fellow citizens. The inevitability in his ''I shall be with you, sooner or later. . . . You need do nothing but wait'' matches the seeming inexorable march to September 1939 when, in the words of his letter, ''in view of the fact that nothing has changed'' the European powers had to return to their ''sinister troth'' with war.

But Kathleen is not haunted by her demon lover in September 1939. Total war did not really touch those in Britain until the following summer, and then she and her family were isolated from its full horror by living in the country. It is when she returns to London's deserted streets, cracked chimneys, and her shut-up, bomb-damaged house that she receives the letter. ''The hollowness of the house this evening canceled years on years of voices, habits and steps,'' putting her back into the more dominant awareness of war, and so her demon soldier appears—on one level perhaps an hallucination but on another a symbol of war that will not go away.

In her 1916 parting from her fiance, Kathleen had suffered a ''complete suspension of her existence'' when she was ''not herself''; and the final lines of the story return to this idea, but much more dramatically and terrifyingly. Several moments after the taxi moves off, she remembers that she has not ''said where,'' in other words that she has given no instruction and that she no longer controls the direction of her life. Bowen treats the taxi, normally an island of security in London's streets, as a brutal machine in a brutally mechanized age; the jolt of the driver's braking throws Kathleen forward so violently that her head is nearly forced into the glass. This places her six inches from the driver's face, and as they stare ''for an eternity eye to eye,'' she recognizes what she could not remember in the features of her fiance 25 years earlier: the face of war itself.

Like most allegorical readings, this interpretation of ''The Demon Lover'' will invite questions, and some of the suggested parallels may not persuade everyone. It should be remembered, though, that other tales in *Ivy Gripped the Steps and Other Stories* are fantastic and hallucinatory but above all about people's experience of war. In ''Mysterious Kor'' a young woman is preoccupied by a waking dream of escape to the mythical city of Kor, arguing that ''if you can blow places out of existence, you can blow places into it.'' In ''The Happy Autumn Fields,'' another young woman seems to lead a dual existence: one in London during the Blitz and one in the country at the turn of the century. Neither story is totally explicable in rational terms, but both dramatize what Bowen called ''resistance to the annihilation that was threatening [them]—war.''

''The Demon Lover'' is another reaction to that threatened annihilation but also a reminder of its origins. Always conscious of the formative influence of the past, Bowen wrote a book about her family home, *Bowen's Court* [1964], in 1942, and in an afterword stated: ''War is not an accident: it is an outcome. One cannot look back too far to ask, of what?'' ''The Demon Lover'' links the Second World War to the First and concludes horrifically that our ''sinister troth'' with war is inescapable. The final image of Kathleen trapped in a taxi ''accelerating without mercy'' into the ''hinterland of deserted streets'' perfectly captures the feelings of millions of people who in 1941 seemed to be propelled at an increasingly frenzied pace into a European wasteland of rubble and death. Like Kathleen, they could only scream.

Source: Robert L. Calder, '''A More Sinister Troth': Elizabeth Bowen's 'The Demon Lover' as Allegory,'' in *Studies in Short Fiction*, Vol. 31, No. 1, Winter, 1994, pp. 91–7.

Daniel V. Fraustino

In the following essay, Fraustino disputes the argument that Mrs. Drover is insane, stating that the story is a murder mystery.

In a major article on Elizabeth Bowen's ''The Demon Lover,'' Douglass A. Hughes dismisses the popular ghost-story interpretation and advances his own psychological one. The story, he says, is ''a masterful dramatization of acute psychological delusion, of the culmination of paranoia in a time of war. . . . War, not a vengeful lover, is the demon that overwhelms this rueful woman'' [*Studies in Short Fiction,* 10 (1973)]. To support his argument, Hughes maintains that ''the narrator subtly but clearly indicates why the forty-four year-old woman suddenly loses her tenuous hold on reality . . . and succumbs to madness.'' His argument rests on three major premises: that as a young girl Mrs. Drover suffered a ''severe nervous breakdown'' from which she never fully recovered; that her visit to her war-ravaged home occasions a ''threshold experience that activates her dormant hysteria''; and finally, that the contents of the letter, the man's leaving the basement, and the demon lover as taxi driver are all ''examples of hallucination,'' figments of her weakening mind. Yet, however convincing on the surface, Hughes's argument rests not on his close reading of the text but on his interpolation of several key points; and a careful analysis of his argument not only discards his major points but also suggests an interpretation that avoids textual misrepresentation and presents this short, enigmatic story in its original intent: a well-wrought mystery of high suspense.

In examining Hughes's delusion-madness theory, we must first carefully consider the initial premise upon which he builds everything else: that the

> " Elizabeth Bowen's 'The Demon Lover,' then, has greater similarity to the ballad of the same title than critics have so far noted. That a basic story outline is common to both works seems reasonable: an absent lover, an intervening marriage, and a desertion from that marriage upon the lover's return."

young Kathleen suffered a ''severe nervous breakdown'' subsequent to her fiance's assumed death— a trauma, Hughes claims, her married life ''shored up against'' and assuaged. For, he claims, her visit to her war-damaged house ushers her into the buried and forgotten past, disinterring old ''feelings of loss and guilt'' that lead to her final hysteria. But Hughes's theory clearly interpolates a text that says nothing to suggest Mrs. Drover's emotional collapse after the loss of her fiance. The narrator merely remarks that she suffered a ''dislocation'' (albeit ''complete'') and that her thirteen years of anxiety (the text warrants no stronger word here), which Hughes insinuates to be part of her ''breakdown,'' came to pass as prospective lovers ''failed to appear.'' Hughes correctly observes that at the time of the story Mrs. Drover bears a facial tick (the remnant, the narrator tells us, of a former ''quite serious illness''), but he mistakenly attributes it to the loss of her fiance. The story clearly states that the illness attended ''the birth of the third of her little boys.'' Hence, we must conclude that the married years between the loss of her fiance and the time of the story did not ''shore up against'' her original trauma (a trauma Hughes clearly exaggerates); rather, these years seem to have witnessed the causes of her present emotional difficulties.

Hughes correctly notes that the house is an ''objective correlative of Mrs. Drover's psychological state,'' but he fails to consider that it may also symbolize her life with William Drover, a man she married out of desperation after other suitors failed to appear. Thus, the house does not signify a fundamentally disturbed mentality, ravaged as it may be, issuing from a buried trauma; it reflects her impoverished married life. And this conclusion seems more fitting: the house in the story is the one she "settled down in" as a married woman, not the one she grew up in during the Great War. The landmarks and objects Mrs. Drover encounters upon entering her home are not, as Hughes declares, significant in triggering her "dormant hysteria" for her lost fiance; they are significant in presenting the "piled up" years of accumulated emptiness. Thus, images of age and death, of repetition and stagnation, proliferate in the description of the house. The street Mrs. Drover's house faces is an "unused channel," and her "long former . . . life" with her family, a "habit." The "yellow smoke-stain up the white marble mantelpiece," "the ring left by a vase on the top of the escritoire," "the bruise in the wallpaper where . . . the china handle had always hit the wall," "the claw-marks" left on the parquet by the piano—all suggest the repetitious character of Mrs. Drover's "prosaic" life.

Finally, in examining Hughes's delusion-madness thesis we must search the text for evidence that Bowen intended the contents of the letter and the man leaving the basement to be understood as delusions, evidence of Mrs. Drover's relaxed grip on reality—assumptions Hughes himself finds "difficult to accept." Indeed, if presenting delusions is Bowen's aim, she goes about it strangely, for she seems to emphasize her protagonist's lucidity, as when Mrs. Drover first sees the letter addressed to her on the hall table:

> . . . then the caretaker *must* be back. All the same, who, seeing the house shuttered, would have dropped a letter in at the box? It was not a circular, it was not a bill. And the post office redirected, to the address in the country, everything for her that came through the post. The caretaker (even if he were back) did not know she was due in London today—her call here had been planned to be a surprise—so his negligence in the manner of this letter, leaving it to wait in the dusk and the dust, annoyed her.

Clearly, nothing in Mrs. Drover's thought processes indicates an incipient mania; nor do we sense "psychotic guilt" (as does Hughes) in her attempts to objectify matters by polishing a clear patch in a mirror and looking "at once urgently and stealthily in." In fact, her attempts to "rally herself" by "shutting her eyes" and telling "herself that she had imagined the letter" render Hughes's theory

even more unconvincing. Also, and importantly, the narrator characterizes Mrs. Drover as a woman whose "utter dependability was the keystone of her family life."

In the preface to *Ivy Gripped the Steps* Miss Bowen states that the stories in the volume contain "hallucinations"; she adds, however, that the "hallucinations in the stories are not a peril; nor are the stories studies of mental peril." She further states that the stories form an organic whole; they do not appear in the "time-order in which they were first written," but rather in a sequence that enhances their "cumulative and collective meaning." Therefore, the position "The Demon Lover" occupies in this volume should in some way reflect the story's meaning. For example, the story's appearance exactly midway in the volume seems to rule out any extravagant interpretation like Hughes's madness theory; and the low-keyed story that follows it, "Careless Talk," reinforces this reading approach. Also, if the volume contains a clue to the meaning of "The Demon Lover," it probably lies in the story that immediately precedes: "Songs My Father Sang Me." Set in post-World War I England, the story describes a young soldier's disaffection with peacetime, with civilian life, and with his insensitive, security-conscious wife. The story ends with his desertion from her and his infant daughter. "The Demon Lover" does not exactly duplicate this theme of desertion, but it does suggest a motive for infidelity and perhaps an unconscious reason for Mrs. Drover's wanting to escape: an unfulfilling marriage that was a mistake from the start. Hughes is correct: Mrs. Drover is not consciously or "in reality . . . a faithless woman," but he ignores Mrs. Drover's deep and lingering dissatisfaction with her marriage and the "quite serious illness" after the birth of her third boy that may, like the soldier in "Songs My Father Sang Me," signify her growing unconscious need to escape. Bowen's selection of the title for her story may in this regard be illuminating: the theme of the English ballad of the same title is desertion—an inconstant woman's marriage in the absence of her lover, and her final desertion from her husband and children upon her lover's return, a lover now ostensibly wealthy but in fact the devil himself.

In view of Bowen's allusion and her concern with the theme of desertion in the story that precedes "The Demon Lover" is it not possible that Bowen at least suggests Mrs. Drover's unconscious desertion? Clearly, part of the answer lies in the identity of the taxi driver. Does Mrs. Drover hallucinate, as Hughes maintains, thereby mistaking the driver for her former fiance? If so, why amidst her violent screams and beating hands does he accelerate ''without mercy''? Here Miss Bowen's choice of words is significant, for they echo the description of the fiance at the time he courted Kathleen. Described as ''without feeling,'' the soldier appears incapable of love in a normal sense. ''He was never kind to me,'' Mrs. Drover reminisces. ''I don't remember him kind at all. Mother said he never considered me. He was set on me, that was what it was—not love. Not love, not meaning a person well.'' During her mysterious romance, Kathleen was never kissed but rather ''drawn away from and looked at.'' And the ''unnatural promise'' isn't the only reminder she has of him, for she carries a ''weal'' on the palm which he ''pressed, without very much kindness, and painfully, on to one of the breast buttons of his uniform.'' Clearly, the soldier is a sadist of the most deranged kind. Not surprisingly then, he chooses to celebrate their anniversary, twenty-five years to the day, in the only way consistent with his destructive sense of love: with Mrs. Drover's homicide. As in the ballad, the fiance has returned (importantly he was only ''presumed dead'') to claim his lover-victim on their silver anniversary. In Bowen's story, however, he is a psychopath, not the devil. He left the note for her, and it's he Mrs. Drover hears leaving the basement.

This interpretation may not suggest the answer to every question the reader may have. How the taxi driver-lover knew that Mrs. Drover would be visiting her London house on that particular day, or how he managed to engineer events so cleverly that she would inevitably seek a taxi precisely on the hour of seven, can only be guessed. However, the story does not totally lack clues that rationally explain the events of that day—events that otherwise appear either totally unrelated (thus supporting Hughes's theory of Mrs. Drover's hysteria) or else supernaturally arranged. For instance, the text indicates that the taxi's arrival may have been prearranged, for Mrs. Drover states that she ''will ring up the taxi now; the taxi cannot come *too soon*'' (my emphasis). Also, her visit to London on the day of her silver anniversary may be related to the ''unnatural promise'' she made, the exact nature of which the reader is not told. As a young girl Kathleen may not have taken seriously or fully understood her ''sinister troth,'' but in her unfulfilled, care-worn middle age she may have all too easily, though unconsciously, fulfilled it. We can only speculate on these possibilities, however; the sto-

ry's brevity and lack of detail give little information on which to reconstruct a completely rational, satisfying interpretation of all events. Moreover, the story's thrilling suspense seems almost to depend on the reader's own sense of dislocation, on the interruption of logical cause and effect—which is why the ghost story interpretation will always remain a popular and viable one.

Elizabeth Bowen's ''The Demon Lover,'' then, has greater similarity to the ballad of the same title than critics have so far noted. That a basic story outline is common to both works seems reasonable: an absent lover, an intervening marriage, and a desertion from that marriage upon the lover's return. Moreover, by accepting the story as literally presenting a kidnapping and probable homicide, we need make no unwarranted suppositions about a twenty-five-year-old nervous condition, about Mrs. Drover's ''psychotic guilt,'' or about the hallucinations concerning the letter and the man's leaving the basement. Nor need we assume without the least bit of evidence a fluctuating narrative point of view—one moment an objective third person, the next the centered consciousness of an hysteric. When the narrator states that a ''draught . . . emanated from the basement where a door or window was being opened by someone who chose this moment to leave the house,'' we have no reason whatsoever to assume hallucination. Finally, while the psychological interpretation has its own special kind of appeal, this view of the story as a murder mystery of high drama will attract those students who believe that the best reading interpolates the least.

Source: Daniel V. Fraustino, ''Elizabeth Bowen's 'The Demon Lover': Psychosis or Seduction?'' in *Studies in Short Fiction,* Vol. 17, No. 4, Fall, 1980, pp. 483–87.

Douglas A. Hughes

In the following essay, Hughes questions the common reading of ''The Demon Lover'' as a ghost story, arguing instead that it is a ''pathetic psychological drama.''

In a recent study of Elizabeth Bowen, Allan E. Austin has written, '''The Demon Lover' is a ghost story that builds up and then culminates like an Alfred Hitchcock movie'' [*Elizabeth Bowen*, 1971]. This misreading of Miss Bowen's unforgettable story is, to judge from my experience with student interpretations, fairly common. Far from being a supernatural story, "The Demon Lover" is a masterful dramatization of acute psychological delusion, of the culmination of paranoia in a time of war. Because the narrative point of view is restricted to that of the patently disturbed protagonist, Mrs. Kathleen Drover, some readers may see, as the character herself certainly does, the ominous return of a ghostly lover. But in contrast to Mrs. Drover's irrational belief that she is watched and in peril, the narrator subtly but clearly indicates why the forty-four year-old woman suddenly loses her tenuous hold on reality at this particular moment and succumbs to madness.

In the English ballad "The Demon Lover," an inconstant woman betrays her absent lover and marries another man; but when the ostensibly wealthy lover returns years later, the woman is quick to abandon her husband and children. Too late, she discovers the lover is, in fact, the devil. Miss Bowen's story superficially resembles the ballad, and the author even relies upon the poem to suggest how Mrs. Drover views herself. In reality, however, Mrs. Drover is decidedly not a faithless woman and there is no spectral figure come from the nether world to claim her. Like all the characters in the collection of stories *Ivy Gripped the Steps* (published first in London as *The Demon Lover*), Mrs. Drover is simply an indirect casualty of war. In the First World War, at the age of nineteen, she lost her fiance, precipitating her first emotional collapse, which lasted for thirteen years. Twenty-five years later the air war in Britain has the devastating psychological effect of depriving Mrs. Drover of her recent past. War divests her of the memory of those years that separated her from the feelings of loss and guilt she experienced at the news of her fiance's disappearance. War, not a vengeful lover, is the demon that overwhelms this rueful woman.

Miss Bowen has said that the stories in *Ivy Gripped the Steps* form an organic whole, having grown out of the unnatural pressures experienced by the British during the last war. In the Preface to that book, she wrote, "Personal life here put up its own resistance to the annihilation that was threatening—war. . . . To survive, not only physically but spiritually, was essential. People whose homes had been blown up went to infinite lengths to assemble bits of themselves . . . from the wreckage." Finally she says, "The search for indestructible landmarks in a destructible world led many down strange paths."

The beauty of "The Demon Lover" lies in the skill with which the author, in the shortest possible space, reveals how Mrs. Kathleen Drover loses her way on the path leading from a crumbling present to a permanent but terrifying past.

From the first paragraph of the story the narrator begins to attenuate and ultimately to efface the significance of the landmarks and objects Mrs. Drover associates with her recent past. Returning to the bomb-damaged and shut-up Drover house in London by her familiar street, she is struck by the "unfamiliar queerness which had silted up." The whole neighborhood, which would have been animated with life in earlier years, stands silent and deserted. When Mrs. Drover pushes into the house "dead air came out to meet her as she went in," and she "was more perplexed than she knew" by the scene before her. Looking at the empty drawing room with its cold, dead hearth, she observes the traces of the life she and her family had left there: the smoke stain on the mantelpiece, the ring left by a vase on a table, the bruise left by a door handle on the wall, and the scratches left by a piano on the parquet. "Though not much dust had seeped in, each object wore a film of another kind; and, the only ventilation being the chimney, the whole drawing-room smelled of the cold hearth." The smell of ashes and the film covering the objects suggests the awareness of time, the presence of death. As anyone who has revisited a *deserted* former residence knows, the experience can be unsettling. For Mrs. Drover, psychologically maimed and predisposed to a sense of loss, the return to the house is a shattering revelation, a threshold experience that activates her dormant hysteria. In fact, Miss Bowen explicitly utilizes the war-damaged house as an objective correlative of Mrs. Drover's psychological state on this August evening. Early in the story we read, "There were some cracks in the structure [of the house], left by the last bombing, on which she was anxious to keep an eye." Later the narrator says, "The desuetude of her former bedroom, her married London home's whole air of being a cracked cup from which memory, with its reassuring power, had either evaporated or leaked away, made a crisis. . . . The hollowness of the house this evening cancelled years on years of voices, habits, and steps." Thus, with the cancellation of these years, which had been shored up against the trauma of the past, Mrs. Drover is returned to that dreadful past and the threat she feels it holds for her.

This threat has no objective reality but is clearly a manifestation of Mrs. Drover's mental state. The narrator is careful to provide a brief psychological history of the protagonist to explain why she is so vulnerable to the ambiance and events within the story. After her fiance was reported missing and presumed killed in action, Kathleen Drover suffered a severe nervous breakdown, "a complete dislocation from everything." For nearly thirteen years she was removed from the normal connections of life and had no social relations with men. A pledge of binding love—not at all uncommon among young lovers—exchanged with her fiance before he returned to the trenches became, after his death and her subsequent derangement, a "sinister troth" and he himself became a cold, ominous figure in her diseased imagination. During this long period she felt spied upon and vaguely threatened, but after marrying William Drover her activities "were circumscribed, and she dismissed any idea that they were still watched." This is an obvious example of paranoia. Although she was apparently well enough to live an outwardly normal life, to be a wife and mother, Mrs. Drover never wholly recovered from her personal trauma of the Great War, for her "most normal expression was one of controlled worry." Not long before the events of the story, she has suffered "a quite serious illness" and is left with a facial tic, evidence of a nervous disorder. Thus the mental health of the Kathleen Drover the reader meets as the story opens is indeed fragile.

If this psychological interpretation of "The Demon Lover" has thus far been convincing, it should not be difficult to accept hallucination as an element in such a story dealing with paranoia. The author herself speaks in the Preface of hallucinations in the stories included in *Ivy Gripped the Steps*. The extraordinary letter, the man heard leaving the house by way of the basement, and finally the demon lover as taxi driver are all, I believe, examples of hallucination. Although she may find an envelope on the hall table and carry it to her former bedroom before opening it with some anxiety, the message Mrs. Drover reads is imagined, not unusual for someone suffering from psychotic guilt. On this August evening, the same month and time her fiance bade her farewell years before, conscious of "the pearls her husband had given her on their marriage," she reads a message based on the irrational guilt she feels for betraying her lover. Mrs. Drover even suspects she has imagined the message. "To rally herself, she said she was in a mood—and, for two or three seconds shutting her eyes, told herself that she had imagined the letter.

> For Mrs. Drover, psychologically maimed and predisposed to a sense of loss, the return to the house is a shattering revelation, a threshold experience that activates her dormant hysteria."

But she opened them—there it lay on the bed." The paper on the bed may well exist but the message is a fabrication of her own mind.

In the climax of the story, Mrs. Drover believes her demon lover has found her and is spiriting her off in a taxi, but again she is pitifully deluded. When she slips into the taxi that "appeared already to be alertly waiting for her," the church clock strikes seven, reminding her of "the hour arranged." Even though she has earlier thought, "So, wherever he may be waiting I shall not know him," when the clock strikes she is immediately convinced her hour has come and she takes the unsuspecting taxi driver for a fiend. At this moment Mrs. Drover passes into madness, seeing herself swept away into deserted, war-ravaged streets.

I believe most readers of "The Demon Lover" want to view it as a ghost story, for there is an undeniable titillation in such supernatural fiction. Miss Bowen's story may be read as a ghost story if one is willing to accept the perspective of Mrs. Drover, who is obviously mentally disturbed. The author, however, provided ample evidence to suggest that the story is a pathetic psychological drama, as I have attempted to show.

Source: Douglas A. Hughes, "Cracks in the Psyche: Elizabeth Bowen's 'The Demon Lover'," in *Studies in Short Fiction*, Vol. 10, No. 4, Fall, 1973, pp. 411–13.

Sources

Farrelly, John. "The Art of Elizabeth Bowen," in *New York Times Book Review*, April 7, 1946, pp. 1, 37.

Green, James L. and George O'Brien. ''Elizabeth Bowen,'' in *Critical Survey of Short Fiction,* edited by Frank N. Magill, pp. 261-8. Englewood Cliffs, NJ: Salem Press, 1993.

May, Charles E. '''The Demon Lover,' by Elizabeth Bowen, 1945,'' *Reference Guide to Short Fiction,* edited by Noelle Watson, pp. 688-9. Detroit: St. James Press, 1994.

Stern, James. ''War and Peace,'' in *New Republic,* April 29, 1946, pp. 628- 630.

Further Reading

Austin, Allan E. *Elizabeth Bowen,* Boston: Twayne Publishers, 1989, 100 p.

A study of Bowen's life and works, with a chapter on the short stories, giving her literary and historical context.

Book Review Digest, 1946, pp. 83-84.
Entry consists of excerpts from contemporary book reviews of Bowen's collection of short stories in which ''The Demon Lover'' first appeared.

Partridge, A. C. ''Language and Identity in the Shorter Fiction of Elizabeth Bowen,'' in *Irish Writers and Society at Large,* Irish Literary Studies 22, edited by Masaru Sekine, Colin Smythe & Barnes and Noble, 1985, pp. 169-80.
This article compares Bowen's short fiction to that of Henry James. It only refers to the collection of *The Demon Lover and Other Stories*, and does not analyze the title story.

Guests of the Nation

Frank O'Connor

1931

"Guests of the Nation" is probably Frank O'Connor's most widely read story. It was published in the 1931 collection of the same name after appearing in the *Irish Statesman*. O'Connor's experiences as a member of the Irish Republican Army during "the Troubles" (Ireland's struggle to establish self-rule) shaped his attitudes and gave him much material for his writings. Despite his strong support of the Irish cause and his own desires to see Ireland become free from British domination, his stories often show, as Patricia Robinson writes, that "in war, hatred and revenge drive out ethical and moral intelligence."

In "Guests of the Nation," men from both sides of the struggle are thrust together. They argue, play cards, discuss politics and religion, and generally behave as though they are not part of the armed conflict that surrounds them. Then Feeney brings the news that the Irishmen have been ordered to execute the Englishmen. O'Connor now makes his strongest point that ideological differences are fleeting and relatively unimportant.

Ruth Sherry observes that O'Connor was "suspicious of heroics" and put little emphasis on the physical aptitudes of his characters. The characters in his stories are ordinary people caught in extraordinary situations. They struggle to make sense of their circumstances and come to conclusions based on that struggle.

The understated method he uses makes this issue even more poignant. Without lecturing to his

readers he makes the point that political differences are trivial in comparison to life and death. O'Connor takes the reader into the internal struggles of several of the characters in this short tale. He offers no hard answers but allows the readers to come to an answer for themselves. Therein lies the power of this story and other stories by O'Connor.

Author Biography

Frank O'Connor was born in Cork, Ireland, on September 17, 1903, as Michael O'Donovan, the only son of Michael and Minnie O'Donovan. His father was a laborer whose alcoholism wreaked emotional and financial havoc on his family. As a result, O'Connor formed a strong relationship with his mother, who encouraged him to read and protected him from his father's drunken rage. O'Connor's deep love for his mother and his jealousy of the love and understanding she showed his father became the subject of many of his stories. Due to the poverty in which his family lived, O'Connor's formal education ended early; he was taken out of school at the age of fourteen to assist in supporting the family. He continued his studies on his own, focusing on literature, politics, and Gaelic language and culture. The influence of Daniel Corkery, an Irish author, nationalist, and former teacher of O'Connor's, was crucial in shaping his political sympathies. In 1918, under Corkery's guidance, O'Connor joined the Irish Republican Army, fighting the British occupation of Ireland. Although a treaty ending the war was signed in 1921, O'Connor and the Republicans continued fighting to include the province of Ulster in the new Irish Free State. O'Connor was subsequently arrested and imprisoned for nearly a year by the Free State government for his part in the struggles. It was during this time that he formed the ideas that found life in many of his short stories.

During the 1930s, O'Connor became involved in the Irish Literary Renaissance that was striving to produce a distinctly Irish literature. The writers of this nationalistic movement endeavored to revive in their fellow citizens an awareness of Ireland's rich history and colorful mythology. During this time, O'Connor began contributing stories to the *Irish Statesman,* a magazine that served as the focal point of literature in Ireland. Many of these early stories were collected in *Guests of the Nation,* which focuses on O'Connor's experiences in the Anglo-Irish War and the Irish Civil War. The *Statesman* was edited by George Russell, also known by the pseudonym AE, who was one of O'Connor's strongest advocates and best friends. Russell introduced O'Connor to many leading figures of the Irish literary society and Abbey Theatre Company in Dublin, including William Butler Yeats, Sean O'Casey, and Lady Gregory. O'Connor served, along with Yeats, as director of the Abbey Theater from 1935 to 1939, when he left because of a dispute over censorship. During the 1940s, a number of O'Connor's books were officially banned by the Irish government. He left Ireland in 1951 to lecture and teach at several American universities, including Harvard and Stanford. He frequently returned to his homeland until his death in Dublin in 1966.

Plot Summary

The story opens with two Englishmen, Hawkins and Belcher, being held prisoner by a small group of rebels, somewhere in Ireland, during the Irish Rebellion. They all play cards and argue about politics, religion, and capitalists. The group is housed in the cottage of an old lady, who in addition to tending the house engages the men in arguments. She is a religious woman and quick to scold the men if they displease her.

Bonaparte, the narrator, and his compatriot, Noble, become friends with the English soldiers. Jeremiah Donovan, the third Irishman, remains aloof from the others. He is the officer in charge of the small Irish group. One evening Donovan tells Bonaparte and Noble that the Englishmen are not being held as prisoners, but as hostages. He informs them that if the English kill any of their Irish prisoners, the Irish will order the execution of Hawkins and Belcher in retaliation. This news disturbs Bonaparte and he has difficulty facing his prisoners the next day.

A few days later, Feeney, an intelligence officer for the rebels, arrives with the news that four Irishmen were shot by the English and that Hawkins and Belcher are to be executed that evening. It is left to Donovan to tell Bonaparte and Noble.

In order to get the Englishmen out of the cottage, Donovan makes up a story about a transfer; on the way down a path into the bog, he tells them the truth. Hawkins does not believe him. But as the truth settles in, Hawkins tries to convince the Irishmen not to kill them, arguing that, if their positions were reversed, he would never shoot ''a pal.'' He asks to be allowed to become a traitor and to fight for the Irish side.

Bonaparte has misgivings about executing the two men. He hopes that they attempt to escape, because he knows that he would let them go. He now regards them as men, rather than the anonymous enemy. Despite Hawkins's pleadings, the party makes their way to the end of the path where Feeney and Noble are waiting.

Donovan shoots Hawkins in the back of the head. As Belcher fumbles to tie a blindfold around his own eyes before he is shot, he notices that Hawkins is not dead and asks Bonaparte to ''give him another.'' Belcher displays an inordinate amount of dignity and composure, considering the circumstances. Donovan then shoots Belcher in the back of the head. The group digs a shallow grave and buries them. Feeney leaves and the men go to the cottage, where the old woman asks what they have done with the Englishmen. No answer is given, but she knows nevertheless and falls to her knees to pray. Noble does the same. Bonaparte leaves the cottage and looks up at the dark sky feeling very small and lost. He says that he never felt the same about things ever again.

Frank O'Connor

Characters

Belcher

Belcher is a big Englishman who is held prisoner by Irish rebels. He is a polite, quiet fellow, who helps the old woman do her chores. Faced with his execution, Belcher reveals more about himself in a few minutes than he had in all the weeks spent with his captors. Unlike Hawkins, he manages to maintain his dignity and composure.

Bonaparte

Bonaparte is the narrator of the tale. His relationship with his prisoners, Hawkins and Belcher, grows from captor-captive into actual friendship. When given the news that Hawkins and Belcher are to be executed, Bonaparte is dismayed at the role he is expected to play. The executions disturb him deeply; at the end of the story he comments that

''anything that happened to me afterward, I never felt the same about again.''

Jeremiah Donovan

Jeremiah Donovan is the officer in charge of the group of Irish rebels. Unlike Bonaparte and Noble, he does not regard the English prisoners as friendly acquaintances. He delivers the news of the impending executions to Bonaparte and seems surprised at his reaction, stating, ''What else did you think we were keeping them for?'' Donovan fires the gun at the execution.

Feeney

Feeney is an intelligence officer who brings the news that the Englishmen are to be executed. He assists in the executions and leaves as soon as the men are buried. His name derives from the Feinian Society, an underground organization that fought against the British for Irish independence.

Hawkins

Hawkins is the second English prisoner. He is smaller and more talkative than Belcher, often engaging Noble in religious and political debates. When told that he is to be executed, Hawkins reacts

Media Adaptations

- On May 20, 1958, a performance was given of *Guests of the Nation,* a drama, drawn directly from O'Connor's story. It was adapted and directed by Neil McKenzie. This single performance, done at the Theatre de Lys in New York City, was part of a twin bill that also offered *Aria da Capo* by Edna St. Vincent Millay.

---

with utter disbelief. He considers his captors to be his "pals," and argues that, if the situation were reversed, he would never shoot them.

Noble

Noble is one of the Irish rebels. He likes to argue politics and theology with Hawkins. When told of the plan to bring Hawkins and Belcher along quietly by telling them that they are "being shifted again," Noble refuses to take part in the lie, instead going ahead to dig the graves. After the executions, he prays with the old lady, falling to his knees by the fireplace.

The Old Woman

The old woman owns the cottage where the action takes place, tending the house and feeding the men. Though Bonaparte notes that she has a sharp tongue and tends to be cranky, she grows fond of Belcher due to his efforts to help her with the household chores. She falls to her knees in the doorway and prays after the executions.

Themes

Duty and Personal Responsibility

The main theme in this story is duty. Each character has a duty to perform. Donovan is the first one to discuss his duty as the rebels are leading the prisoners into the bog. He tells them that four Irish fellows had been shot and "you are to be shot as a

reprisal." Continuing, he "begins the usual rigmarole about duty and how unpleasant it is." As he shows here, his perception of duty is built on submission to the orders of someone higher up in the chain of command. His interpretation of duty absolves him of any personal responsibility for his actions.

As the rebels are about to carry out the executions, their prisoners talk about duty. They claim to understand that by obeying their duty the Irishmen will soon kill them. Wohlgelernter notes that the Irishmen and the Englishmen now use the idea of duty as a shield against "the monstrous acts of evil": the cold-blooded executions that are about to occur.

For the men in this tale, their obsession with duty overwhelms their sense of personal choice. Each man could have made a choice to disobey the orders. The rebels could have let the prisoners live; the prisoners could have made an attempt to escape. But none of them does so. Personal choice has been discounted. Duty to follow orders becomes the only motivation for the rebels. The prisoners also accept the fact that the rebels will follow those orders, and with that acceptance, they give tacit agreement to the duty to those orders.

At the close of the story Bonaparte and Noble have a difficult time accepting the fact that they had just participated in the executions. Their resolve to follow the orders without question now dissolves into a more expansive question of their existence and what it means to them. These two men have come up against the consequences of their dutiful actions and they do not like what they have found.

Choice and Consequence

Hand-in-hand with duty and responsibility are the consequences associated with the choices made by the characters in the story. Each of the military men in the tale have made a choice in the first instance: to join a cause and to follow it to its conclusion. The Englishmen join in order to maintain British control over Ireland. The Irish join the insurrection to overthrow British rule and to establish an Irish Free State.

They all make their choices freely and openly. But in this story, they all have serious consequences to contemplate. The Englishmen will have to contemplate, even for a short time, their own deaths as an outcome of their initial choice. The Irish will have the rest of their lives to contemplate the consequences of their initial choice to join the rebels and the choice to execute the Englishmen. For all, the consequences are much more burdensome than any might have assumed at the beginning—the Englishmen are killed, and the Irishmen have to carry that fact with them forever.

Conflict: Individual vs. Society (Military)

O'Connor's narrator provides a number of instances wherein an individual's wishes come into conflict with his military directives. Though Bonaparte and Noble comply with the orders they have been given, both, to varying degrees, exhibit some form of rebellion. After Feeney brings the news that Hawkins and Belcher are to be executed, Noble refuses to be a party to lying to them in order to lead them to their deaths. In a similar fashion, Bonaparte hopes for an escape attempt, knowing full-well that he would not fire on Hawkins and Belcher if they were to run. Hawkins, too, is prepared to rebel against his own military, offering to join the Irish rebels in return for his life.

Style

Dialects and Writing Practices

One of the little known aspects about any writer's approach to his or her craft is the amount of attention and time that is devoted to revising and rewriting. A glance at a working copy of a poem by John Keats will show a furious crisscrossing, adding and erasing, a scratching out and rearranging of lines and text that eventually became a finished poem. For most writers, this occurs in private and once published, the final work remains stable and unchanged. Not so for Frank O'Connor. As William Maxwell said, "He rewrote and rewrote. After he was published, he rewrote and was republished. Everything he wrote was an unfinished work, not so much because of any dissatisfaction, but because of the pleasure he got out of a story. He liked his stories." As a result, there are many different versions of the same story in print. Also, as Ellmann notes, just as there are different versions of the same stories in print, some of these stories carry different titles.

There are several editions of "Guests of the Nation." In an early version, the Englishmen talk in a heavy Cockney dialect. The two Englishmen are "Awkins and Belcher." Hawkins says, "Well, Bonaparte, Mary Brigid Ho'Connell was arskin

Michael Collins, a key figure in Ireland's struggle for independence. O'Connor wrote The Big Fellow: A Life of Michael Collins, *in 1937.*

abaout you and said ow you'd a pair of socks belonging to er young brother." In a later passage when they talk about angels, Hawkins says, in the Cockney dialect, "Where do they get them then? Who makes them? Ave they a fact'ry for wings? Ave they a sort of store where you ands in your chit and tikes your bleedin' wings? Answer me that." However, in later versions O'Connor softened this passage by using a more standard form of English as well as dropping the final three-word sentence.

Topics for Further Study

- E. M. Forster once said: "I hate the idea of causes, and if I had to choose between betraying my country and betraying my friend, I hope I should have the guts to betray my country." Think about the deep meaning in this statement. How do you think Donovan or Bonaparte would react to it? How would you react to it, given similar circumstances to those in the tale? Would you react differently, if your "prisoners" were lifelong friends?

- Choice. Duty. Morality. Do these words mean the same thing in the context of this tale? If so, explain how they are the same. If they are different, carefully describe those differences.

- For a story teller, selecting the proper narrator is very critical. Imagine the difference in this story if O'Connor had used an omniscient narrator (one who knows the thoughts of all the characters in a narrative). Would the impact of the ending be as effective? Create a parallel tale using an omniscient narrator. Remain faithful to the sequence of occurrences in this one.

- O'Connor said that God had intended that he be a painter. "But I was very poor and pencil and paper were the cheapest. . . . Literature is the poor man's art." What does he mean when he says that literature is a poor man's art? Think of other arts and explore the differences between them that makes sense of his remark.

- Imagery and symbolism are important aspects of fiction. Select an image in the story and develop it into a symbol. Describe how that improves our understanding of the tale.

- Themes of courage and cowardice, guilt and innocence, and fate and chance are present in the story. Select one of these pairs of ideas and show how they control the action in the tale.

- Titles of short stories often have clever meanings. What does the title of this story mean? Who are the "Guests" and of what "Nation?" Explain your response completely using material from the text.

In the present version, O'Connor uses words that are indicative of the dialects of the characters. The Englishmen call their newfound friends, "Chums." The fact that the Irish also use the term is unusual, as the narrator mentions. Donovan's Irish dialect is also noted when he said, "Ah, you divil, Why didn't you play the tray?" The dialectical use of the word "unforeseen," meaning "inconsiderate" or "unthinking," as Michael Libermann explains, also draws attention to the local Irish dialect.

Point of View and Narration

The story is told in the first person by Bonaparte, a member of the small rebel faction. As such, we see only his view of the events. The reader is never able to know what others are thinking unless they speak and Bonaparte tells us. For example, in the very last scene, he comments on his reactions to the executions; he also tells us what Noble has said about the same executions.

In some stories it is important to notice what the narrator is doing and saying, because he or she may not be telling the truth. In many stories by Edgar Allan Poe, the narrator often tries to convince the reader that he (the narrator) is NOT crazy, despite evidence to the contrary. In the case of Bonaparte, there is no hint that he is not truthful. There is nothing that creates doubt of his trustworthiness. Therefore Bonaparte can be considered a reliable and believable narrator.

Episodic Structure

The story is written in four episodes, each fulfilling a special task. The first section is the exposition. In this section the characters are introduced individually and then they are shown interacting with others in the story.

The second section, the complication, introduces the possibility that the Englishmen might be executed. Bonaparte says that he noticed that Donovan has ''no great love for the two Englishmen.'' In the evening Donovan and Bonaparte discuss the fact that if the English shoot one of the Irish prisoners, then they would have to retaliate. Later, as Bonaparte and Noble try to go to sleep, they worry about probabilities that they would be ordered to shoot their prisoners.

Section three, the rising action, gets more intense. Donovan tells Bonaparte and Noble that the Englishmen are going to be executed. ''There were four of our lads shot this morning, one of them a boy of sixteen.'' Bonaparte's worst fears are now realized.

The last section, the main crisis and the final falling action, covers the execution and is the longest of the four. In it the themes of duty and responsibility are raised by both the Englishmen and the Irishmen. The section completes the story with the remaining characters trying to sort out for themselves what has just occurred in the woods.

Imagery

Images are those items in a story that appeal to our senses. Some important images in the story include the fire, the lamps, light and dark. These are combined to create several symbols that give the tale special meanings and importance. The fire, for example, might be a purifying image. In the elemental sense, fire is an agent used to remove impurities from a compound leaving a purified remainder. Theologians talk of the purifying fire of the Holy Spirit which may remove impurities from an individual's soul. In this way fire becomes a symbol of a purifier.

Symbolism

Symbols are images that have both figurative and literal meanings. Images of light and dark occur regularly in the story, presenting a contrast between the forces of darkness (evil) and light (good). They also show the conflict in the minds of the rebels, who struggle with the feeling that the executions they perform are not justified. At the end of the story, the remaining characters are left standing or praying in the dark, symbolic of a triumph of evil over good.

As the men head into the woods, the light from the lamp shines dimly at the end of the path. As they walk, their lives flicker; Bonaparte's hope that the Englishmen would run away flickers; the hope that they will not be executed flickers. After Hawkins is shot, he writhes in the throes of death and his life flickers away. The single image of the flickering lantern is symbolic of these concepts.

Historical Context

Irish Rebellion

The history of Ireland is one of domination by the British and of conflict between Protestants and Catholics. During the nineteenth century efforts were made to reduce the power of the British over the island. These efforts spawned a revolutionary movement that sought full separation from Britain. The potato famine and other crop failures added to the urgency of these rebellions. The Fenian Movement (represented in part in the story by Feeney) was a secret society determined to wreak havoc on English interests in Ireland and thereby drive them out of the country.

These movements came to the fore at the end of World War I. Despite several political acts by the English Parliament that tried to establish home rule for the Irish, the Irish Rebellion began in full force. After many of the local police quit in protest against the British, new recruits were brought into the country, called the Black and Tans. These militias were known for their brutality and ruthlessness. This is the setting for the story. After several years of ''The Troubles,'' the British representative, Winston Churchill, threatened an all-out war to subdue the Irish. Michael Collins agreed to a division of the country and independence for the south of Ireland. The Irish Free State was established in 1922. The Irish felt that Collins had sold them out in these negotiations, and he was assassinated soon after.

The northern six counties, collectively known as Ulster, were not included inside the new national boundaries. They are now know as Northern Ireland. It is here that the ''Troubles'' have continued with political and military confrontations. In 1998, promise of peace was made possible when the British government, the Irish government, and the warring parties in Northern Ireland signed an accord that established a framework for democratic resolutions to the ongoing disputes.

Compare
&
Contrast

- **1916:** Following the Easter uprising, in which Irish rebels seize control of the General Post Office in Dublin in an effort to establish a provisional government for the Irish Republic, fourteen of the rebels' leaders are shot at Kilmainhan Jail.

  1998: In accordance with the "Good Friday" Agreement, both Irish and British governments begin the accelerated release of paramilitary prisoners.

- **1919:** Sinn Fein, an Irish political party, assembles in Dublin and declares Ireland independent. Irish insurgents, later called the Irish Republican Army, take up the task of expelling the British from the island. This period is often referred to as the "Troubles."

  1998: The "Good Friday" Agreement is reached, bringing at least a temporary cessation to three decades of violence in Northern Ireland.

It was during the Irish Rebellion and the establishment of the Irish Free State that Frank O'Connor lived. These experiences shaped his attitudes about his homeland and the institution of warfare. He was a lifelong spokesman for Ireland and things Irish. Even after his move to the Unites States, he continued to write about Ireland. He once said, "I prefer to write about Ireland and Irish people because I know to a syllable how everything in Ireland can be said." But he never changed his attitude that war is illogical and barbaric.

O'Connor and his Literary Peers

Frank O'Connor was one of a group of Irish writers born in the last of the nineteenth century and the beginning of the twentieth. These include Daniel Corkery, AE (George Russell), W. B. Yeats, Samuel Beckett, and James Joyce. Of these, Yeats, Beckett and Joyce are the most famous. O'Connor was a friend of these men, often learning writing techniques and adopting writing approaches from them. AE was the first to suggest to him that he write a biography of Michael Collins. Yeats is best known for his poetry, Joyce and Beckett for their novels, and O'Connor for his short stories. "Readers were more than likely charmed by the deceptively simple manner of his writing, particularly those stories of childhood and adolescence for which he is best known," says James Matthews in *The Dictionary of Irish Literature*. It is his focus on shorter fiction that hindered his acceptance until recently,

because many literary critics were reluctant to include a short story writer among novelists and poets.

Critical Overview

Frank O'Connor, pseudonym of Michael O'Donovan, was a prolific writer whose output includes poetry, biography, essays, drama, novels, and short stories. It is his short stories that have made the biggest impact on literature, but as Michael L. Storey notes, his recognition as a top rated author has been slow to come because many critics were reluctant to put "short story writers into the same league with novelists, poets, and dramatists." Now this has changed.

However popular he is becoming now, things were not so positive at the beginning. For his early publications in *The Irish Statesman,* he used his middle name and his mother's maiden creating the name Frank O'Connor. He did this to separate himself from the reputation of his hard-drinking abusive father and for political reasons, to avoid connection with the Irish revolutionary, Jeremiah O'Donovan. His first volume of stories, *Guests of the Nation,* was published in 1931 and was well received. During the 1930s he published a novel, some poetry, and the biography of Michael Collins, an important leader in the Irish Rebellion and negotiator of the peace agreements at the end of the

Rebellion. Despite these successes, the strongly Roman Catholic Irish Government's Censorship Board took issue with some of the topics in his stories, according to Ruth Sherry. As a result, it became difficult for him to get his work published. By 1940, he was under a ban among even Irish publishers and broadcasters. To circumvent this, he used another pseudonym, Ben Mayo (an identity that was kept secret until after his death), for a series of newspaper articles in the *Sunday Independent.* These articles covered such disparate topics as farm life, poverty in city slums, a more practical education, and the need for theaters, libraries, and arts societies in provincial towns.

The continued censorship and the resultant shrinking markets, especially in Britain and the United States, created a need for him and others who were also being censored to find an outlet for their work. In 1940, a new magazine, *The Bell,* was founded. It was edited by his friend Sean O'Faolain and provided a forum for the next several years for him and other ''strayed revelers,'' who hoped to clear the air of what they thought was the stodgy and elitist writing forms of earlier Irish authors. In addition to contributing poems, essays, reviews, and short stories, O'Connor was the poetry editor for the magazine.

By 1950, because of economic pressures following World War II and his inability to support himself in Ireland, O'Connor accepted several teaching offers and moved to the United States. During the next decade, he wrote more than during any other comparable period in his life, mostly about his homeland. His stories about the common Irish people muddling through their daily lives are, as James Matthews says, ''his most enduring contribution to modern literature and Irish life.'' Because of this contribution and his easy writing style, James Plunkett said that O'Connor had achieved ''the air of someone who had found where he belonged.'' By the time of his death, in Dublin in 1966, O'Connor had accomplished a greatness in a ''lonely and personal art'' and had created simple stories of impeccable design and craft.

Michael Storey says, ''O'Connor's art is great, not because it is so well crafted, because it is rooted in life itself.'' O'Connor told stories with ''a rich and rushing flow of language'' that grew out of his life in Cork and were based on the simple ways of the common Irish people. Richard Ellmann says that the ''stories of Frank O'Connor refresh and delight long after they are first read.''

Storey, in his review of Michael Steinman's edition of *A Frank O'Connor Reader,* remarks: ''The recognition of O'Connor as a top flight literary artist has been slow in coming for several reasons, including the reluctance of critics to accept short story writers in the same league with novelists. . . . The former notion seems to be gradually giving way, and Steinman's book should do much to dispel the latter notion.'' Frank O'Connor has taken his place in the ranks of great Irish writers. He has also become a leading exponent of short fiction without regard to national identity. His stories have gained a universal appeal that, as Wohlgelernter said, ''transcends the bounds of time and space.'' O'Connor's tales speak of universal truths and, as he said, ''Story telling . . . just states the human condition.''

Criticism

Carl Mowery

Mowery has a Ph.D. in Rhetoric, Composition and Literature from Southern Illinois University. In the following essay, he discusses the theme of duty and personal responsibility in ''Guests of the Nation.''

In ''Guests of the Nation,'' O'Connor looks at the consequences when people in stressful situations choose duty over personal morality. J. R. Crider calls that ''the tragic dilemma in which [the] characters are caught, between military duty and . . . ancient . . . moral law.'' The Irish rebels are caught in this dilemma—they are forced to choose whether or not to carry out the execution of their English prisoners.

Donovan ''deliberately closes himself off from the human ties'' which might weaken his resolve to follow orders from his superiors. Therefore he maintains his distance from the prisoners, writes Stanley Renner. But he is the first to raise the notion of duty. As the prisoners are being led down the path into the bog, he ''begins the usual rigmarole about duty and how unpleasant it is.'' Bonaparte describes Donovan's feelings: ''I never noticed that people who talk a lot about duty find it much of a trouble to them.'' Nevertheless, his duty to avenge the killing of some Irish prisoners takes precedence over his duty to respect fellow human beings. He is driven by his obligations to the military instructions that

What Do I Read Next?

- Brian Friel's play, *Translations* (1980), is set in nineteenth century Ireland as British troops arrive to survey the Ballybeg landscape and to anglicize Gaelic placenames. Friel explores a number of issues related to Britian's occupation of Ireland.

- William Trevor's work, including *The News from Ireland, and Other Stories* (1986), explores the importance of personal and national history as he focuses on lonely individuals burdened by the past.

- "Attack" (1931) by Frank O'Connor. Set during the Irish Rebellion, some rebels go to a house near a police station with the intention of attacking the station. While there, they discover a mystery in the attic.

- "Dulce et decorum est" (1920) a poem by Wilfred Owen. This poem is from *The Collected Poems of Wilfred Owen.* It was written while Owen was in the trenches in Europe during World War I and looks at the glory of war from the viewpoint of one who is experiencing it. Owen calls that glory, "The old lie."

- "Patriotism" (1966) by Yukio Mishima. This story examines the Oriental approach to national patriotism in personal and very gruesome ways.

- *Memoirs of an Infantry Officer* (1930) by Siegfried Sassoon. These are the personal recollections and diaries of Sassoon from his days as a soldier in World War I.

have been given to him by Feeney. He chooses to follow these orders and blame "the deliberate inhumanity" of the killings on his duty to the Irish cause.

Donovan and the rest of the rebels are unable or unwilling to take any personal control of their actions out of fear of the consequences. Renner says that since Donovan and Feeney place "devotion to the cause above humanity," they are unable to take any initiative over their personal behaviors. Then after Hawkins claims that he (Hawkins) would not shoot any of his chums, Donovan says to Hawkins, "You would, because you'd know you'd be shot for not doing it." Because of the threat, they all are unwilling to disobey an order. They cannot do otherwise because of the fear of retribution.

Military personnel are controlled by threats of punishment for not following orders, no matter what the orders are. In Shakespeare's *Othello,* Desdemona, finding herself on the horns of a dilemma, says: "I do perceive here a divided duty." For her the division was between father and husband. For the rebels the division lies between the responsibility to the military and to personal morality. But fear for one's own safety makes the individual obey the order.

Bonaparte experiences this division in his desires when he says that he hopes the prisoners would run away because he knows that he would not try to stop them. But he does not govern his own behavior. Rather, he lets someone else guide his actions. Since the prisoners do not attempt to escape, he is forced to follow the orders and participate in the executions. Michael Libermann concludes that men can be called upon to fulfill obligations that otherwise they would reject, because they have "joined a cause," and then the horror of these acts is compounded when the men are forced to do things that are "unthinkable" in other circumstances.

The folly of blindly following a duty has also been described in another O'Connor story, "Attack." In this tale, some rebels plan an attack on a garrison of police "whose sense of duty had outrun their common sense." Here, the police have lost "all sense of proportion." They become so impressed with their own positions of authority that they become a nuisance to the people they are supposed to be protecting. Their notion of duty has been subverted by an obligation to the British authority, to "the cause," rather than an obligation to their own sense of good behavior or morality. In both stories, as Maurice Wohlgelernter points out, the combatants use "Duty . . . as a shield for monstrous acts of evil" because individuals fail to take personal responsibility for their acts.

One evening Donovan tells Bonaparte and Noble that the Englishmen are being held as hostages, not as prisoners. Both men refuse to accept the possibility that they would be asked to shoot the men. They believe that the English soldiers would not shoot any Irish prisoners and that since the men at Second Battalion know the two they were holding, no one would "want to see them plugged." According to Michael Neary, the two men are disillusioned especially by the orders to execute their "good natured and thoroughly harmless English prisoners." Still, they refuse to take responsibility for their own and their prisoners' destiny. They obey and then blame it on others higher up in the chain of command. Renner assigns the harshest moral judgment to Noble and Bonaparte precisely because they participate in the brutal executions, "in the mistaken impression that they have no choice."

In situations like these where societal duty and personal duty are in direct conflict, the question is raised: Does a society (military or otherwise) have the right to order an individual to commit acts that are in violation of personal morality? Is the individual absolved of guilt because he or she obeys a societal order? In this story can Bonaparte and Noble be forgiven for their actions because they were ordered to do so?

This was the central question at the post-World War II Nuremberg Trials. At these trials, German officers tried to absolve themselves of guilt for their actions by saying that they were only following orders. Many of these men were convicted and hanged for their crimes, since the Military Tribunal court did not accept their excuses. The Tribunal held that they were indeed responsible for their actions and that they had to pay for them.

Just as those found guilty at Nuremberg, Bonaparte and Noble each forfeit their innocence by following Donovan in accepting the orders from Feeney. Yet each knows that the acts they commit are wrong. Bonaparte says that by time they reached the bog he "was so sick" that he could not even talk. His internal revulsion at the impending executions reveals his belief that it was wrong to shoot

> " The immorality of cold blooded murder is not absolved by the intended positive results of the Irish Rebellion. The ends do not justify the means if the ends are achieved through immoral acts."

them. Just as he would let them escape, he would not have participated in the executions if given the choice.

At the end, none of the characters has acted on his own initiative. None has taken command of the situation in a manner that each knows is a better choice. Donovan acts out of a blind sense of duty to the orders. Noble and Bonaparte both act out of fear of harsh punishment. After the burial, Donovan and Feeney disappear into the darkness, their roles fulfilled. Noble and Bonaparte return to the cottage, their lives now changed.

This tale ends with the dilemma of divided duty, as noted earlier from the drama *Othello*. But it now includes a glimpse into the souls of the rebels. In *Henry V,* Shakespeare also visits this aspect of a divided duty, writing: "Every subject's duty is the king's; but every subject's soul is his own." Accordingly, the individual is not absolved of guilt or the obligation to do the right thing because of a military order. The "subject" may escape the vengeance of his king, but the judgment of his "soul" will be harsh.

When Noble and Bonaparte return to the cottage, the woman asks what has happened to the Englishmen. No answer is given, but she knows anyway. She falls to her knees to pray for the souls of the slain men. Seeing this, Noble also falls to his knees to pray. Of the rebels, he was the faithful one, often referring to the next world in his arguments about religion with Hawkins. But during those moments in the bog when he might have invoked his religious beliefs, he did not. Renner interprets his prayers as an attempt "to lighten his burden of sorrow and guilt." He goes on to say that Noble also uses the prayers as "consolation" and an "evasion of moral responsibility.'' It is ironic that his act of petition becomes one of selfish penance.

The immorality of cold blooded murder is not absolved by the intended positive results of the Irish Rebellion. The ends do not justify the means if the ends are achieved through immoral acts. This then answers the question as to whether or not the executions were justified. The men knew the executions were wrong. Renner has pointed out that despite the orders ''they do have a choice'' of their behavior. And they fail to make that choice. What is left, writes Renner, is a ''military, which (had) been created, ideally, to ensure the welfare and safety of human beings, (but now has) come to work to their harm: a human power meant for good . . . result(ing) in evil.'' Noble and Bonaparte are left to contemplate their complicity in that evil.

The Rebels held the ideals of the Rebellion high. But in the end they are left wondering about the future. O'Connor has written what Tomory calls ''the most eloquent commentary on the inhumanity of war.'' The story also has power because, as Richard J. Thompson says, ''it illustrates the loss of fellow-feeling and the basic decency that follows from the imposition of political dogmas.'' The tale ends in despair and disillusionment because ideology has triumphed over morality.

Source: Carl Mowery, ''An Overview of 'Guests of the Nation','' in *Short Stories for Students,* The Gale Group, 1999.

Richard F. Peterson

In the following essay, Peterson discusses the narrative structure and interpersonal relationships in ''Guests of the Nation.''

Frank O'Connor's ''Guests of the Nation,'' with its wonderfully ironic title, is one of the most memorable short stories ever written about Ireland's struggle for political independence from England. Set during ''the Troubles,'' or the revolutionary period between the Easter Rising in 1916 and the signing of the Home Rule treaty at the end of 1921, O'Connor's narrative of rebels and hostages reveals the conflicts, not just between the Irish and their unwelcomed ''guests,'' but among the revolutionaries themselves.

Like so many of O'Connor's stories, ''Guests of the Nation'' (the title story of a 1931 collection) is told from the first-person point of view to give the narrative the quality of oral storytelling. Unlike the typical O'Connor storyteller, who narrates an event that has happened or been told to someone else, the narrator in ''Guests of the Nation'' is someone who has taken part in an action so emotionally and morally disturbing that it has altered his life. Speaking with the voice of his own Cork region, while imitating the accents and expressions of the English hostages, O'Connor's narrator, called Bonaparte by his fellow rebels, recounts his reluctant role in the execution of two English soldiers in retaliation for the deaths of four Irish rebels. The success of O'Connor's narrative, however, lies not so much in the description of the event itself, common enough during the Troubles, but in O'Connor's intimate study of the humanity of the rebels and their prisoners and the personal ordeal experienced by O'Connor's narrator.

''Guests of the Nation,'' one of several early O'Connor stories about the Irish gunman, reflects his own experiences while fighting on the losing Republican side during the Irish Civil War. During the final days of the war, O'Connor, while suffering acutely from the constant danger of life on the run, was puzzled by the cold resourcefulness of some of his companions, who actually appeared to enjoy the danger and the violence. Afterwards, Daniel Corkery, O'Connor's old teacher and fellow short story writer, suggested that O'Connor had witnessed the critical moment in revolution when control shifts from the dreamers, those caught up in the Republican ideal, to the professionals, those caught up in the political expediency and emotion of the violence and the killing.

In ''Guests of the Nation'' O'Connor develops this conflict between revolutionary attitudes in the strained relationship between the narrator and Jeremiah Donovan, the experienced rebel, who has the responsibility for carrying out the battalion order to shoot the prisoners. Their differences are played out as the narrator and his youthful compatriot, Noble, become familiar with the Englishmen while they stand guard over them. When the narrator eventually finds out that the prisoners are actually hostages, he bitterly complains to Donovan, only to be told that the English have also held their Irish prisoners over a long period of time. This moral and emotional blindness or indifference to the closeness that has developed between Noble, the narrator, and their prisoners is what most clearly defines Jeremiah Donovan and what most troubles O'Connor's narrator when he is finally told to carry out the executions. While he recognizes the necessity of an act of reprisal—one of the executed rebels was sixteen years old—the narrator is deeply disturbed by the order to shoot two men whom he has come to regard more as companions than as the enemy.

The most compelling scene in "Guests of the Nation" occurs when the English prisoners are taken to the end of the bog where a hole has already been dug for their bodies. O'Connor's early narrative strategy of developing the personalities of the two Englishmen now takes on dramatic force as Hawkins, the more garrulous of the prisoners, pleads for his life, even by offering to join the rebels, before he is shot in the back of the neck by Donovan. After Hawkins is executed, finished off with a shot fired by Bonaparte, the narrative shifts its attention to the usually taciturn Belcher, whose words, just before his death, take on a dignity and humanity in sharp contrast to the bumbling and grotesque behavior of his executioners.

Once the executions are over, Bonaparte and Noble return to the house used to hide the Englishmen, thereby shifting the narrative back to the emotional and moral impact of the deaths on those closest to the prisoners. While Noble and the old woman of the house fall to their knees in prayer, O'Connor's narrator goes outside to watch the stars and listen to the now dying shrieks of the birds. At story's end, the narrator turns briefly to his own emotional state immediately after the killings and to the effect of the deaths on his life ever since. He remembers vividly that the executions and the praying figures seemed at a great physical distance from him and that he felt as lonely as a lost child. He also confesses that he has never felt the same about anything since that night. Apparently compelled to tell his story, O'Connor's rebel appears to recognize at the close of his narrative that this single, terrible act of revolutionary violence destroyed his youth and left him prematurely disillusioned and emotionally isolated from the human condition no matter what the cause.

Source: Richard F. Peterson, "Guests of the Nation," in *Reference Guide to Short Fiction,* St. James Press, 1994, pp. 727–28.

Stanley Renner

In the following essay, Renner explores the conflict between duty and humanity in "Guests of the Nation," arguing that the underlying question in the story is "whether one is driven along by an irresistible destiny or can take a hand in the chances of life...."

In Frank O'Connor's "Guests of the Nation" the reader witnesses the cold-blooded execution of two English soldiers—a killing by the men who have been assigned to guard them and with whom they

> "Apparently compelled to tell his story, O'Connor's rebel appears to recognize at the close of his narrative that this single, terrible act of revolutionary violence destroyed his youth and left him prematurely disillusioned and emotionally isolated from the human condition no matter what the cause."

have become friends, done in reprisal for the soldiers' shooting four members of the Irish revolutionary movement. The story employs a first-person participant point of view to dramatize an irony much like Thomas Hardy's in "The Man He Killed":

> Yes; quaint and curious war is!
> You shoot a fellow down
> You'd treat if met where any bar is,
> Or help to half-a-crown.

Readers of the story, however, have not found the war sanctioned shootings it dramatizes "quaint and curious." Commentators have been virtually unanimous in approving what they take to be O'Connor's condemnation of "the evil of murderous 'duty' which lies at the center of the story." O'Connor strongly invites this response by humanizing the two English soldiers, engaging the reader's sympathy for them in order to maximize the shock of their execution in the end. But he also heightens the story's disturbing effect through an extended figurative questioning of where responsibility for such evils lies—within the individuals involved or in forces beyond their control. At the heart of the story's design lies a preoccupation with certain mysterious "hidden powers," the forces of chance or fate or other inexplicable supernatural machination that grips human lives in capricious, mostly unwelcome, ways. Analysis of the theme of "hidden powers" in "Guests of the Nation" clarifies its moral design, the role of its characters, the

> But the primary example in 'Guests of the Nation' of the institutional power that human beings have imposed on themselves is the military organization which holds the intangible power of duty over the soldiers in the story."

meaning of the ending—even the significance of the narrator's name, which has provoked surprisingly little critical curiosity.

The concept of hidden powers is introduced at the outset of the story together with the fellow-feeling that develops between the English prisoners of war and their Irish guards. The opening paragraph establishes both that the men are becoming "chums" and that they spend a good deal of time playing cards, an activity that not only breaks down the military barriers between them but also introduces the notion of chance, a hidden force that plays a ubiquitous role in human events. Although one may exercise some control over how one's cards are played, chance governs what cards are dealt, both in card games and in life.

The card-playing in "Guests of the Nation" introduces the story's underlying preoccupation with the question of who or what is in charge of what happens on earth. Again reminiscent of Hardy, "Guests of the Nation" runs the gamut of possible answers to the question of who or what is in charge of what happens on earth. Again reminiscent of Hardy, "Guests of the Nation" runs the gamut of possible answers to the question in much the same way as does Hardy's "Hap," in which the speaker, in the apparent absence of a benevolent Providence, prefers that "some vengeful god" were running things rather than nobody or nothing at all. The Christian view that the universe is controlled by a benevolent Providence is represented in the story by Noble, who, in heated debates with Hawkins, argues for a supernatural being who promises an afterlife complete with angels who wear wings. The old woman who keeps the house in which the prisoners are being held introduces the notion of a vengeful deity who pays people off for violations of the divine order. She babbles nonsense as yet unexplained about how an "Italian Count that stole the heathen divinity out of the temple in Japan" brought on World War I because "nothing but sorrow and want can follow the people that disturb the hidden powers." The card-playing in the story rounds out the possibilities: perhaps our lives, like games of chance, are governed by nothing but "Crass Casualty," as Hardy terms it in "Hap"—the random functioning of the universal machinery.

But there is another order of hidden powers in the design of "Guests of the Nation": human rather than cosmic. For not all the evil that happens to human beings is dealt out by forces beyond their control. Some of it they do to each other. These hidden human powers, visible only in their effect on human beings, appear in the story mainly in the obligations we impose on ourselves through our institutions of social organization and the human concerns that have created them and should make them work for the good of human beings. One of the institutional hidden powers in "Guests of the Nation" is that of capitalism, against which Hawkins, who calls himself a Communist, rails bitterly as a evil force working against an amelioration of the human condition. But the primary example in "Guests of the Nation" of the institutional power that human beings have imposed on themselves is the military organization which holds the intangible power of duty over the soldiers in the story. The other major human hidden power in the story is that of love in a broad sense—the power in the feelings that bind human beings together. Ironically, the institutional powers, such as the military, which have been created, ideally, to ensure the welfare and safety of human beings, may come to work for their harm: a human power meant for good may result in evil.

Some observers of the human lot have recognized two categories of evils and sorrows: those attributable to cosmic powers, whatever they may be, and those attributable to human powers. There are thus irremediable evils, those we can do nothing about, and remediable evils, those within our power to alleviate. Logically, then, we should cease wringing our hands about irremediable evils and concentrate on those we can do something about. Here again, the story is reminiscent of Hardy, who urges in "Apology"—the preface to his *Late Lyrics and Earlier*—that, to the extent permitted by "the mighty necessitating forces—unconscious or otherwise," "pain to all upon [the globe], tongued or dumb, shall be kept down to a minimum by loving-kindness, operating through scientific knowledge, and actuated by the modicum of free will conjecturally possessed by organic life . . . ." A similar outlook is attributed to Clarissa Dalloway in Virginia Woolf's *Mrs. Dalloway*: as we are a doomed race, chained to a sinking ship . . ., as the whole thing is a bad joke, let us, at any rate, do our part; mitigate the sufferings of our fellow-prisoners . . .; decorate the dungeon with flowers and air-cushions; be as decent as we possibly can. Those ruffians, the Gods, shan't have it all their own way,—her notion being that the Gods, who never lost a chance of hurting, thwarting and spoiling human lives were seriously put out if, all the same, you behaved like a lady.

These are precisely the issues against which the conflict between duty and humanity in "Guests of the Nation" is posed, and it is the keenest irony of the story that its protagonists, Bonaparte and Noble, commit a remediable brutality against fellow human beings as if compelled by a power beyond their control. To be sure, chance has put them in their predicament. And it is easy to judge them when one is safely detached from their situation, in which they owe unquestioning obedience to a military organization not known for sweet reasonableness. If they do not carry out the order to execute their prisoners, they can be court-martialed and shot. Still, what they are ordered to do does not fall within the province of the irremediable: they do have a choice, a "modicum," at least, "of free will." Bonaparte recognizes the patent inhumanity of the order, although he seems less concerned about the brutality to the Englishmen than about the injury to his own feelings; and it is not promising when he draws an analogy between how he would feel in shooting human beings he has come to like and how he would feel in taking an old dog he is fond of to the vet's to be put to sleep. But rather than taking action himself, he merely drifts along as if helpless to defy the fates, "hoping that something would happen," that the Englishmen would "run for it" or that "Noble would take over the responsibility from me," but doing nothing himself .

The question that underlies the story, then, is whether one is driven along by an irresistible destiny or can take a hand in the chances of life, remedy its remediable ills, and perhaps meliorate the pains and sorrows that cannot be prevented. This question informs not only the ending of "Guests of the Nation" but also the design of its characters, and it is noteworthy that O'Connor's Englishmen are more

humane than his Irishmen. Presumably the four Irish prisoners were executed by the English for something they had done, whereas Belcher and Hawkins are to be shot in random cold-blooded reprisal. Bonaparte and Noble, although they find the order shocking, nevertheless help carry it out, yielding with token resistance to what appears to be their fate—Bonaparte by actually giving Hawkins the coup de grace, and Noble by helping bury the Englishmen. Donovan and Feeney, who place devotion to the cause above humanity, personify a brutality unmediated by fellow-feeling. Donovan deliberately closes himself off from the human ties that should work against remediable evil, while Feeney has been linked to the Fenian brotherhood, the heart of the Irish nationalistic spirit, which brutality overrules the brotherhood of fellow-feeling that develops between the guards and prisoners in the story.

The Englishmen are shown in a more positive light. Ironically, they fit in better with the local community than do the Irishmen, perhaps because their humanity is less numbed by divisive hatreds. Hawkins, the "quixotic Socialist-Atheist," consistently takes the side of humanity against institutions of society he blames for evils that are or ought to be remediable—against "the capitalists" and their self-serving hypocrisy of "morality and Rolls-Royce complete" and "all the so-and-so officers" that enforce the prevailing social order. But finally, it is the quiet Belcher who is most attuned to ameliorating the twists and toils of fate and necessity for his fellow human beings—this despite (or because of) the fact that he is himself a thoroughgoing fatalist, "with his usual look of waiting in quietness for something unforeseen to happen." Belcher alone helps the old woman with her chores. He is a huge man, and to mitigate the inequalities of life, the strong should help the weak. Moved by the same spirit, he sees to it that things come out even in the card games with which the guards and prisoners pass the time. An object lesson for the capitalists railed at by Hawkins, he could have come out on top: "he was a good card player," Bonaparte admits, and "could have fleeced myself and Noble. . . ." Instead, he bankrolls Hawkins with the money he was won, knowing full well that Hawkins will lose it back to the Irishmen and there will be no winners and losers. True to the end, Belcher continues to put others' interests ahead of his own. As he is about to be shot, he asks that Hawkins, whom the initial bullet did not finish, be put out of his agony with a second shot. And he is almost unbelievably solicitous of his executioners' feelings in the affair, trying, apparently, to ease their shock and guilt in having to shoot him. Belcher's meliorating humanity, coupled with Hawkins's indignation against the remediable evils built into the established structures of society, seems to form the moral center of "Guests of the Nation" against which the actions of the Irishmen are judged. Thus the reader's shock at the execution of Hawkins and Belcher, guilty of nothing except being in the wrong uniform in the wrong place at the wrong time, is intensified by a sense that the power of fate which helped to contrive the situation need not have been allowed to dictate its brutal outcome.

The theme of hidden powers in "Guests of the Nation" may also help to answer a question left by the story—why is the narrator named Bonaparte?—that most commentators have ignored. For among the hidden powers that control human life is destiny, and destiny was a lifelong preoccupation of the original Bonaparte, Napoleon I—widely remembered, as he regarded himself, as the Man of Destiny. Just as the story told by O'Connor's Bonaparte poses the question of the relationship between human responsibility and the workings of destiny, so Napoleon pondered his role as the instrument of oceanic forces working themselves out on the map of Europe. So important is the question of destiny in Napoleon's life that most of the numerous books about him address the subject. Especially pertinent to the present discussion is Emil Ludwig's *Napoleon*, published shortly before "Guests of the Nation" was written. A close similarity in the way both Ludwig's Napoleon and O'Connor's Bonaparte tend to shift the responsibility for their actions to destiny but suffer the consequences of such a view of life suggests the possibility that O'Connor might have drawn his character with Ludwig's Napoleon in mind.

Ludwig's book, whether or not O'Connor read it, throws light on several elements of the story's moral design, including the role of the ironically named Noble and the import of the final scene showing Bonaparte lost in a vacant cosmic immensity. In the spectrum of attitudes presented in the story, Noble is the Christian, who can resolve the problem of evil through faith in a hidden providence and absolve his own sinful complicity in evil by seeking God's forgiveness. "How happy should we be here," Napoleon allows, "if I could confide my troubles to God, and could expect from him happiness and salvation!" Thus Noble, in the end, falls on his knees and begins praying to lighten his burden of

sorrow and guilt, but neither Napoleon nor Bonaparte can accept this way of resolving the question of the scheme of things and his own place in it. The story also criticizes Noble's resort to the consolation of religion for his evasion of moral responsibility in this world through his fixation on the next.

O'Connor's Bonaparte, like Napoleon, tends to view himself as in the grip of an irresistible destiny. "In general," observes Ludwig, Napoleon "is resigned to fate." In "hundreds of sayings," he expressed the belief that "No one can escape his fate" and that "all things are linked together, and are subject to the unsearchable guidance of an unseen hand." But both Napoleon and Bonaparte remain troubled by the terrible human consequences of the military actions their destinies commit them to—the former, in giving orders that cost human lives; the latter, in carrying out such orders. Napoleon, at the tomb of Rousseau, father of the Revolution, wondered "whether it would have been better for the peace of the world if neither Rousseau nor I had lived." O'Connor's Bonaparte suffers similarily from a troubling, if defective, sense that what fate seems to demand of him is wrong. Yet he does it anyway, as if governed by Napoleon's principle that "It is wise and politic to do what fate commands, and to march on the road along which are led by the irresistible course of events." But neither Napoleon nor Bonaparte escapes the logical consequences—the spiritual desolation—of giving the world over to destiny. "What [Napoleon] never loses," Ludwig concludes, "is the sense of diamonic loneliness, which increases as his soaring flight leads him to chillier altitudes." Similarly, Bonaparte in the end feels "very small and very lost and lonely like a child astray in the snow"—a feeling he will never lose, for, as he says, "anything that happened me [sic] afterwards, I never felt the same about again." As a result of his world view, Ludwig's Napoleon faces "the desert, which to him is the image of the infinite . . . the sublime vacancy which expands before him when the myriad-faceted picture of ordinary life sink from sight." Similarly, O'Connor's Bonaparte stands in the end facing a vacant universe, nothing but the empty bogs and the distant stars, while the graves of Belcher and Hawkins, "even Noble and the old woman, mumbling behind me, and birds and the bloody stars were all far away," "a million miles away."

Thus the moral judgment of "Guests of the Nation" comes down mainly on Bonaparte and Noble—not that the deliberate inhumanity of Donovan and Feeney is excused by O'Connor but that

Bonaparte and Noble, who still entertain human feelings, allow themselves to contribute to the remediable brutality in the world in the mistaken impression that they have no choice. O'Connor wrings a further twist from his powerful ending by showing that the world views that allow Bonaparte and Noble to shift the responsibility for what they have done to the hidden powers that govern the cosmos are opposites forms of the same cop-out. In Noble's geocentric Christian world view, the human scene is predominant: "he saw everything ten times the size, as though there were nothing in the world but that little patch of bog with the two Englishmen stiffening into it . . . ." But he has failed to fulfill his Christian duty: to love, extend hospitality, and sacrifice oneself for others and especially for strangers and enemies. With Bonaparte, it is just the reverse. In his mechanistic sense of the universe, human doings seem insignificant, "as if the patch of bog where the Englishmen were was a million miles away," in the vast empty universe of "Hap." And thus he has failed in the duty of human beings to band together, eliminate remediable evils, and mitigate the irremediable evils dealt out in a vacant, indifferent universe.

In the end, "Guests of the Nation" echoes the disillusionment that W. B. Yeats felt toward the Irish cause, which O'Connor implicitly in his story and Yeats explicitly in "Easter 1916" warn "Can make a stone of the heart." But the tone and gist of the story are surely best captured a decade later in E. M. Forster's memorable comment on where human duty lies: "I hate the idea of causes," he wrote in 1939, "and if I had to choose between betraying my country and betraying my friend, I hope I should have the guts to betray my country."

Source: Stanley Renner, "The Theme of Hidden Powers: Fate vs. Human Responsibility in 'Guests of the Nation'," in *Studies in Short Fiction*, Vol. 27, No. 3, Summer, 1990, pp. 371–77.

Sources

Crider, J. R. "Jupiter Pluvius in 'Guests of the Nation'," in *Studies in Short Fiction*, Vol. 23, No. 4, Fall, 1986, pp. 407-411.

Donoghue, Denis. A Review of *Collected Stories by Frank O'Connor*, in *New York Times*, September 20, 1981, Sec. 7, p. 3.

Ellmann, Richard. Introduction to *Collected Stories by Frank O'Connor*, New York: Alfred A. Knopf, 1981.

Gelb, Arthur. A Review of *Guests of the Nation*, a play, in *New York Times*, May 21, 1958, p. 40.

Libermann, Michael. "Unforeseen Duty in Frank O'Connor's 'Guests of the Nation'," in *Studies in Short Fiction*, Vol. 24, No. 4, Fall, 1987, pp. 438-41.

Matthews, James H. "Frank O'Connor," in *Dictionary of Irish Literature*, edited by Robert Hogan, Westport, CT: Greenwood Press, 1979.

Neary, Michael. "The Inside-Out World in Frank O'Connor's Stories," in *Studies in Short Fiction*, Vol. 30, No. 3, Summer, 1993, pp. 327-336.

New York Times, March 11, 1966, p. 33.

Robinson, Patricia. "O'Connor's 'Guests of the Nation'," in *The Explicator*, Vol. 45, No. 1, Fall, 1986, p. 86.

Sherry, Ruth. "Fathers and Sons: O'Connor among the Irish Writers: Corkery, AE, Yeats," in *Twentieth Century Literature*, Vol. 36, No. 3, Fall, 1990, pp. 275-302.

Steinman, Michael, ed. *A Frank O'Connor Reader*, Rochester, NY: Syracuse University Press, 1994.

Storey, Michael L. A review of *Frank O'Connor at Work*, in *Studies in Short Fiction*, Vol. 27, No. 2, Spring, 1990, pp. 273-74.

Storey, Michael L. A review of *A Frank O'Connor Reader*, in *Studies in Short Fiction*, Vol. 33, No. 1, Winter, 1996, pp. 148-150.

Wohlgelernter, Maurice. *Frank O'Connor: An Introduction*, New York: Columbia University Press, 1977.

Further Reading

O'Connor, Frank. *An Only Child*, New York: Alfred A. Knopf, 1961.
   An autobiography in episodic form using Michael O'Donovan, O'Connor's real name.

O'Connor, Frank. *My Father's Son*, Boston, MA: G. K. Hall, and Co., 1985.
   A second volume of autobiography, compiled after O'Connor's death by his widow, assisted by Dr. Maurice Sheehy of Dublin University College.

Steinman, Michael, ed. *A Frank O'Connor Reader*, Rochester, NY: Syracuse University Press, 1994.
   This book contains annotated stories by Frank O'Connor, including "The Rebel," which had never before been published, and the recently translated, "Darcy in Tir na nog."

Wohlgelernter, Maurice. *Frank O'Connor: An Introduction*, New York: Columbia University Press, 1977.
   This book takes a broad-based look at the life and work of O'Connor. It presents O'Connor's thought "to the historical and intellectual events of his time. . . . this study may be considered a biography of his mind."

Han's Crime

Shiga Naoya

1913

Shiga Naoya's story "Han's Crime" first appeared in 1913 in *Shirakaba* (*White Birch*), a literary magazine founded by Shiga and a group of wealthy university students. "Han's Crime" was well-received when it was first published; several critics considered it an almost perfect short story, saying it exemplified Shiga's sparse, psychologically probing style. Told almost entirely through dialogue, the story attempts to unravel the truth behind the violent death of Han's wife, a young circus performer. It seems clear that Han has killed his wife in the midst of a knife-throwing act; he and his colleagues are called in before the judge to testify. The judge's duty is to determine whether Han's crime was premeditated (murder) or accidental (manslaughter). As the story progresses, however, what at first seems clear becomes more difficult to pin down. In his confession, Han reveals that he himself does not know whether he committed murder or was simply involved in a tragic accident. If Han does not know his own motivations, he suggests, they must remain unknown to those who would judge him. After listening to Han's testimony, the judge reaches his verdict, finding Han "innocent."

Primarily known as a writer of short fiction, Shiga occupies a central position in modern Japanese literary history, even though he did not publish very many works. During his lifetime, critics went so far as to call him a "god of literature." One contemporary even asserted that Shiga was the only living writer whose works had a classical quality

that revealed something new each time they were read. Shiga and his fellow *Shirakaba* authors developed a form of literature called *shishosetsu*, or "I-Novel," which resembles Western confessional literature to some extent, but also, according to Edward Fowler, seeks "to transcribe the world" as the author experienced it and "to authorize a self . . . in a society unwilling to acknowledge the individual as a viable social unit." Critics note "Han's Crime" in particular for its psychological acuity and intellectual honesty.

Author Biography

Shiga Naoya was born on February 20, 1883, in the town of Ishimaki on Honshu, Japan's largest island. Although his family belonged to the prestigious samurai class, his father became a successful businessman and moved the family to Tokyo when Shiga was three. In Tokyo, they lived with Shiga's grandparents, who were largely responsible for raising the young writer. Shiga's mother died when he was thirteen, and his father remarried not long after. Fortunately, Shiga had a good relationship with his new stepmother, which he wrote about in the story "Haha no hi to atarashii haha" ("My Mother's Death and the Coming of My New Mother"). Shiga's relationship with his father, however, was often strained. In 1900, at the age of seventeen, Shiga began to study Christianity under the evangelist Uchimura Kanzo and subsequently became aware of social causes. In 1901, he became estranged from his father when his father forbade him from participating in a protest against the Ashio Copper Mine, which was polluting a local river and poisoning the townspeople. Unbeknownst to Shiga, his grandfather had once been an investor in the mine, and Shiga's father wanted to spare the family embarrassment. Relations with his father continued to be strained when Shiga had an affair with a family servant and declared his intention to live with her. In addition, he was a mediocre student who graduated from high school with much difficulty; once enrolled at Tokyo Imperial University, he became very involved with the founding of the literary magazine *Shirakaba,* but neglected to attend class. In 1910, at age 27, Shiga finally dropped out of college and devoted himself full time to his writing career. Between 1910 and 1920, Shiga produced the bulk of his literary work, a series of short stories and novellas. The 1912 publication of "Otsu Junkichi," based on his affair with the family servant, sparked

family tensions once again. In 1913, his first collection of short stories, including "Han's Crime," was published. He then began work on his long novel, *Journey Through Dark Night,* although he would not finish it until 1937.

In 1914, Shiga married a widow who had a child from another marriage and renounced his inheritance. When his second child was born (the first died), Shiga and his father reconciled, which he celebrated in the 1917 publication of his novella *Wakai* (*Reconciliation*). In 1923, Shiga had an affair with a young waitress, which resulted both in the publication of the Yashima stories and his wife's unhappiness. After the publication of *Journey through Dark Night* in 1937, Shiga all but ceased to write. Despite his relatively small literary output, he was very influential among Japanese writers; in 1947 he was nominated president of the Japan P.E.N. Club, a prestigious writers' association. He died in 1971 of pneumonia.

Plot Summary

The story begins with an account of the crime: In the midst of a performance, Han, a young Chinese juggler, severs his wife's carotid artery with one of his knives. The young woman dies instantly, and Han is arrested.

The body of the story consists of the judge's questioning the owner-manager of the circus troupe, the Chinese stagehand, and finally Han himself. In questioning the three men, the judge attempts to decide whether Han's wife's death was premeditated murder or manslaughter.

The owner-manager tells the judge that Han's act is very difficult and requires steady nerves and complete concentration as well as intuition. He does not know whether the killing was intentional or accidental.

The Chinese stagehand testifies that Han and his wife were kind and gentle people who treated friends and acquaintances well and never argued with others. Han had become a Christian the previous year and spent much of his spare time reading Christian literature. The stagehand recollects, however, that Han and his wife did not get along, especially since the death of their infant son soon after his birth. Han never hit his wife, but he would stare at her angrily. He once told the stagehand that his love for her had died but that he would not

Shiga Naoya

consider a divorce. Han's wife was not in a position to leave the marriage either because, having spent four years on the road with a circus performer, no one respectable would marry her. The stagehand believes that Han read the Bible and sermons to repent his angry feelings for his wife. The stagehand acknowledges that when he witnessed her death, his first thought had been, "He's murdered her," but now he cannot be so certain. The stagehand suspects that his knowledge of Han's hatred for his wife probably influenced his thinking. He tells the judge that Han dropped to his knees and prayed in silence after the incident.

The bulk of the story concerns Han's testimony. Han tells the judge he stopped loving his wife once the child was born because he knew he was not the father. The child had died smothered by its mother's breasts, and Han does not know whether this was deliberate, although his wife told him it was an accident. Han tells the judge that his wife never really loved him, and once the baby died, she "simply observed, with cruel eyes, the gradual destruction of my life."

Han never considered leaving his wife, he continues, because he was preoccupied with what he calls "various ideas": he did not want to be in the wrong. The judge asks him if he had ever thought of

killing his wife, and Han admits that he had often thought "that it would be good if she were dead." The night prior to the incident, he again thought of killing her, but never quite reached the point of conscious decision. He and his wife had argued about supper; that night he could not sleep because he was overcome with nightmares. The idea of killing his wife gradually faded, and Han was overcome by "a feeling of loneliness," realizing that he was too weak to take action of any kind to change his life.

The next day he was exhausted, Han tells the judge, but no longer thinking of killing his wife. As he prepared for that evening's performance, he realized that he was edgier than usual. Although he and his wife had other acts, Han says that he chose the knife-throwing for that evening without having any ulterior motive. The first two knives were only slightly off the mark; his wife seemed the same as always. The third knife, however, struck his wife in the throat. At that instant, Han thought he'd murdered his wife on purpose. He knelt down to pray in front of the audience to convince everyone it had been an accident.

Han tells the judge that later he began to doubt that he had done it on purpose. He reasoned that he had only thought he had acted purposefully because of his homicidal thoughts the night before. The more he thinks, the less certain he becomes about his guilt or innocence. He realizes that his best defense is the truth; since even he does not know whether he is guilty or innocent, no one else can know. When the judge asks Han if he feels any sorrow for his wife's death, Han confesses that he does not and that he had never imagined he'd "be able to talk so cheerfully about her death." After this testimony, the judge finds Han innocent of the crime.

Characters

The baby

The baby is the source of Han's antagonism toward his wife. Supposedly born prematurely, Han says that his wife was in fact pregnant when he married her and that the child is not his. The baby died when it choked at its mother's breasts. Han's wife says the baby's death was an accident; Han himself cannot be so certain.

Chinese stagehand

The Chinese stagehand seems closer to Han than anyone else in the story, perhaps because they are both Chinese and foreigners in Japan's tightly knit society. The stagehand has had the opportunity to watch Han closely; he observes that Han seems to be a Christian and that he and his wife are kind to other people though cruel to each other. He knows that Han has thought about a divorce but does not want one. The stagehand witnesses the incident and confesses to the judge that he initially thought Han had murdered his wife deliberately, though he later wonders whether that thought was influenced by his knowledge of Han's unhappiness in the marriage.

Han

Han is a young Chinese juggler who performs with a travelling circus troupe and kills his wife during a knife-throwing act. The judge thinks he is ''intelligent-looking,'' though clearly suffering from nervous exhaustion. Although he does a knife-throwing act, he performs other acts as well. He has been married for three years, and has been unhappy since his wife's baby died. He loved his wife, he says, from the day they married until the day the baby died. He does not think his wife ever loved him; he thinks that she has been watching the gradual deterioration of his life with cruel eyes. He has taken to reading the Bible and Christian sermons as a way of controlling his anger toward his wife. He has acknowledged that he does not love her, but states that he will not seek a divorce because he wants to be on high moral ground; he does not want to be held responsible for being in the wrong.

Han seems well-liked by the owner-manager of the troupe and the stagehand. They say he is a ''good'' man who neither gambles, drinks or has affairs with women. Han is rather passive and has difficulty taking decisive action; despite his unhappiness with his wife, he does nothing consciously to resolve the situation. Instead he suffers from nightmares and is entertained by thoughts that life would be better if his wife were dead. When he kills his wife by throwing a knife in her throat, he thinks his

A knife thrower's assistant.

behavior was premeditated. When he kneels before the audience and prays silently, he is aware of putting on a show and attempting to convince the audience that his wife's death is an accident. However, as Han thinks about his deed in the days that follow, he becomes less certain of either his guilt or innocence.

Han is both exceedingly honest and remarkably self-absorbed. He believes that because he cannot say for certain whether his action was premeditated, no one else can judge his responsibility in the matter of his wife's death. Although he can neither take responsibility for his wife's murder or rest easy in the knowledge of his innocence, he is remarkably "cheerful" about it. After Han confesses his story to the judge, he is found "innocent."

Han's wife

Han's wife was a young woman who was married to Han for close to three years. After she married Han, she traveled with him and the performing troupe. Her older brother had many debts, and her family back home has since broken up and disappeared, so she has nowhere to go if she leaves Han. It is unknown whether or not she ever loved Han, and Han tells the judge that she had had a sexual relationship with another man, her cousin, before she married Han. Han believes that her cousin, who was a close friend of his, was the father of her child.

Han was often impatient with her; for example, the evening before the incident, they quarreled because he felt she was too slow in preparing his dinner. Han says that she looked no different than usual in her Chinese costume the night of their performance, except that as she sees the knife hurtle toward her throat "a strange look came over her face," which Han thinks must have been fear. Han believes that she had a premonition and that she threw her fear back at him "with the same force as the knife."

Han's wife's cousin

Han's wife's cousin was a close friend of Han's. He introduced Han to Han's wife and suggested that they get married. Han believes that the cousin was the father of his wife's child.

The judge

The judge's task is to determine whether Han is guilty of premeditated murder, guilty of manslaughter or innocent. He questions first the owner-manager of the theatrical troupe, next the stage manager, and finally Han himself. Most of the judge's questions concern Han's character, behavior and motivations, though he also solicits the opinions of all three men. When he has finished questioning the three men, he pronounces Han innocent.

Owner-Manager

The owner-manager of the circus troupe does not know Han well, but says that the knife-throwing performance is not particularly difficult for an experienced performer if the performer has an alert, healthy mind. The owner-manager has faith in Han's abilities and does not think the incident was deliberate. Although he had never thought anything like the incident could happen, he does not think that it would be fair for the judge to hold him responsible.

Themes

Guilt and Innocence

One of the most important themes of "Han's Crime" concerns guilt and innocence; specifically, the question of what constitutes guilt. In the story, Han is guilty of many things: hating his wife, quarreling with her over how quickly she prepares his supper, even thinking life would be better for him if she were dead. He acknowledges being able to speak of his wife's death "cheerfully," and admits to having had murderous thoughts; he is not sorry that she is dead. He confesses that he threw the knife that severed his wife's carotid artery and yet, startlingly, the judge pronounces Han "innocent" after listening to Han's reflection of his crime, even though Han neither repents nor expresses any remorse for what has happened to his wife.

How can the judge find Han "innocent" after listening to his confession? The narrator says that the judge's duty is to ascertain whether Han is guilty of premeditated murder or manslaughter. In order to determine what crime Han has committed, the judge must determine Han's *intention*. If Han planned the crime, then he has committed murder; if Han acted in anger, spontaneously and without forethought, then he has committed manslaughter. Although Han confesses that he had murderous thoughts he insists, however, that "between my thinking about such a thing and actually deciding to kill her, there was still a wide gap." At first, due to his murderous thoughts the night before, Han assumes he acted intentionally and is therefore guilty of murder. He then plans to deceive people into thinking it was an accident: "In the end, I thought, I would be acquitted for lack of evidence." Soon thereafter, however, Han begins to doubt that he intentionally killed his wife. Although he is unsure that her death was an accident, he is equally uncertain that it was premeditated. If Han cannot say for certain what his intentions or motivations were, the story suggests, the judge will be unable to find him guilty of either murder or manslaughter. The extent of Han's guilt rests in his motivation.

Toward the end of his confession, Han tells the judge, "Being found innocent meant everything to me now." Feeling "an excitement" similar to the one Han feels when he is finally certain of his uncertainty, the judge pronounces Han "innocent" of all charges, finding him guilty neither of premeditated murder nor of manslaughter beyond a reasonable doubt. "Han's Crime" suggests that honest self-reflection of one's motivations, with no false note and no false remorse, are more important than the actions one takes and can exonerate one from society's punishment. In proclaiming Han "innocent," the judge rewards Han for his honesty and his willingness to take responsibility for his true feelings.

Choices and Consequences

In "Han's Crime," Han makes important choices which affect his life greatly. Although he is unhappy with his marriage and hates his wife, he chooses not to divorce her. He tells the stage manager that "even if his wife had reasons to seek a divorce, he himself had none." He tells the judge that "I often thought I'd like a divorce," but "I was weak." Han's wife told him that if he divorced her, she "would not survive" because her father's family had broken up and her reputation had been sullied by four years on the road with the circus. The consequences of his decision to stay with his wife are brutal: his further unhappiness, violent thoughts, and the death of his wife.

Confronted with choices, Han often chooses *not* to act. He does not seem to recognize that conscious inaction is just as much a choice as a conscious act. Having chosen not to leave his wife, Han thinks "that it would be good if she were dead," and when he goes to sleep that night, after quarreling with his wife, he sees himself "suspended in midair . . . always hesitating, without the courage to want what I wanted, without the courage to get rid of what was unbearable." He feels as though his paralysis is "all due to my relationship with [his] wife." In his dream, he tells the judge, he

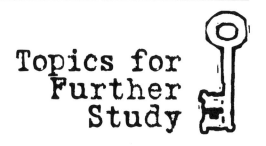

Topics for Further Study

- Do you agree with the judge's verdict of "innocent" in the story? Why or why not? Explain.

- Do you agree with Han that his relationship with his wife is responsible for all his problems? From what has her death has "freed" him? Explain.

- Read "In A Grove," a short story that concerns the law by Shiga's contemporary and rival, Akutagawa Ryunosuke. Like "Han's Crime," "In A Grove" clearly demonstrates the problems of discovering the truth. Compare the reliability of the narrators in "In A Grove" to Han's reliability in "Han's Crime." Who do you believe more? Why?

- Read "The Tell-Tale Heart" by Edgar Allan Poe. Compare the role of the unconscious in "The Tell-Tale Heart" to the unconscious in "Han's Crime."

- Do some research on when the United States first introduced the insanity defense. What does it mean to be "not guilty by reason of insanity"? Do you think that Han is not guilty by reason of insanity?

- Compare Han's "confession" with President Clinton's "confession" about his involvement in the Monica Lewinsky "incident." Do you think that Han accepted adequate responsibility for his role in his wife's death? Or that Clinton accepted adequate responsibility for his behavior? Listen to Clinton's speech. Compare the effectiveness of each as a confession. What do we expect from a confession?

contemplates the consequences of murder and is untroubled by them. Upon waking, he chooses again not to leave his wife. The judge even questions Han as to why Han did not leave after such frightening, murderous thoughts. Han informs the judge that although it seemed that leaving his wife would have the same desired result of freedom from her and the obligations of marriage, for him "there

[was] a great difference'' between leaving his wife and killing her, though he does not specify what that difference is or why leaving would not be a preferable alternative to killing her. In any event, Han chose several times to stay with his wife rather than leave her.

The evening after his murderous thought, Han chose to perform the knife-throwing act although ''we had many other acts.'' As a consequence of choosing that act so soon after suffering murderous thoughts, he finds that his aim is unsteady. As a consequence of his unsteady aim, he throws a knife into his wife's throat, severing her carotid artery. As a result of her injury, she dies.

Han also chooses to confess to the judge not only his crime but the motivations and feelings surrounding it. As a consequence of confessing his actions and analyzing his doubts, the judge grants him what he wants more than anything—his freedom.

Consciousness and the Unconscious

Much of the tension and power of ''Han's Crime'' comes from the question of how responsible people are for their own antisocial thoughts and feelings if they do not *consciously* act on them. Han tells the judge that ''between my thinking such a thing and actually deciding to kill her, there was still a wide gap.'' He repeatedly tells the judge that once his murderous thoughts were over he ''no longer thought of killing her.'' Han is guilty of murder if he *consciously* plots murder and he is guilty of manslaughter if he acts without premeditated thought.

In Freud's theory of the unconscious, the personality consists of three components: the id, which is unconscious and is the source of all our urges; the superego, which is the voice of society that tells us what is socially acceptable behavior; and the ego, which mediates between the id's urges and the superego's restrictions. It is generally understood that people have thoughts, feelings and urges that are repressed or censored by the conscious mind because they are not socially acceptable. According to Freud's theory, our unconscious urges come to us, as they did to Han, in dreams. For the most part, though, unconscious urges are not recognized by the conscious mind, and they only surface indirectly, in unexpected ways. During the knife-throwing act, Han becomes aware of consciously trying to control his unconscious urges: ''I could feel in my arm the constraint that comes from a thing's having become conscious.'' Before throwing the final, fatal knife, Han sees a ''premonition'' of ''violent fear''

come over his wife's face. He describes a battle between his conscious and unconscious minds in which ''dizziness'' strikes him and he throws his knife ''almost without a target, as though aiming in the dark.'' The question his description raises is whether, then, he consciously and intentionally threw the knife at his wife. On the one hand, his description makes him sound ''out of control'' and ''beside himself'' as though he were not the agent of his actions; on the other hand, his awareness of throwing the knife suggests that his conscious mind was active as well.

Han later questions whether he initially thought ''I killed her at last'' because he *had* just intentionally murdered her or because he was influenced by the murderous thoughts of the previous night. Han suggests to the judge that it was his unconscious urge that killed his wife; he is uncertain how consciously he was involved in the murder. Although Han cannot be sure of the extent of his conscious participation in what he calls ''the incident,'' at the time he felt he had acted intentionally, and he consciously tried to deceive his audience by pretending to pray. He ''knew everyone thought [he] seriously believed in Christianity,'' and was already thinking he would need to defend himself by arguing that the incident was an accident.

The role of conscious decision-making versus unconscious, uncontrollable urges lies at the center of ''Han's Crime.'' It also lies at the center of the judge's verdict. As Han finishes his confession, the judge becomes aware of ''an excitement'' to which ''he could not put a name.'' In declaring Han ''innocent'' of all charges, the judge himself is responding to a deep, unarticulated feeling that ''surge[s] up in him,'' over which he has no control.

Doubt and Ambiguity

The narrative of ''Han's Crime'' is riddled with doubt and ambiguity. Doubt is first introduced to the story by the owner-manager, who tells the judge that the knife-throwing act is not particularly difficult for an experienced performer in an alert, healthy state of mind. He says, ''the performance requires experience, instinctive skill and nothing else. But one cannot say that it will always come off with such machinelike precision.'' At the same time, however, the manager says ''it's a fact'' that management had ''never thought that something like this would happen.'' Flustered at having said, on the one hand, that management had never considered the possibility of an incident such as Han's crime and that, on the other hand, management had of course recognized the possibility, he tells the judge, "I do not think it fair, now that it *has* happened, to say that we had considered the possibility and hold it against us." The owner-manager cannot say for certain whether or not the incident was deliberate or not. The Chinese stagehand, too, tells the judge that although his first thought had been "he's murdered her," he immediately questioned whether he'd had that thought because he really believed Han murdered his wife or simply because he knew of their relationship woes. Han's intentions are ambiguous, or unclear, to both his manager and his stagehand.

Doubt and ambiguity plague Han's relationship with his wife. He doubts that the child is his, and he doubts, too, that the child's death at its mother's breast was an accident, even though his wife swears it was. He doubts that his wife loves him and that she sympathizes at all with him. He doubts she can survive without him should he choose to leave her.

But, most importantly, Han begins to doubt his own intentions concerning his wife's death. Initially, he assumes he committed murder because of his previous murderous thoughts, and he plans to present his case as though her death had been a terrible accident. Amidst these plans, however, "a doubt rose up" in him as to whether he himself believed it was murder. Unsure as to whether he had committed murder or had simply been involved in a tragic accident, Han's doubt is ultimately liberating, both in terms of his sense of self and the judge's sentence. Because "it was completely unclear, even to [himself], which it had been," Han realizes that he has changed the very terms of the trial: "come what may it was no longer a question of a confession of guilt." Doubt inhabits the "gap" between Han's "thinking" and "actually deciding to kill her." Han's self-doubt informs the judge's verdict: if Han himself has doubts, the judge cannot find him guilty of either manslaughter or murder.

Style

Setting

The action of "Han's Crime" takes place in a courtroom. The courtroom is not described in any detail; the setting is indicated by a single sentence: "The judge commenced by interrogating the owner-manager." The characters' dialogue recounts action that took place on the road with a traveling circus, and the death of Han's wife occurred on the circus stage in front of a large audience.

What is most striking about the setting in "Han's Crime," however, is its absence. The setting provides no clues about historical period (is it modern day? medieval?) or place (is it Japan? urban? rural?) or about any larger social context (what socioeconomic class are Han and his wife? What is the prevailing social opinion on divorce, infanticide, or wife-murdering?). The lack of many explicit details in setting the story allows an allegorical reading in which Han represents a sort of "everyman" who is held up to be judged by some legal power. The removal of Han and his court appearance from any kind of social or historical markers puts the story on an abstract or theoretical level, so that "Han's Crime" seems to be more about the *idea* of crime and guilt or innocence than about Han's particular story.

Point of View and Narration

"Han's Crime" is a third-person narrative told by a narrator who is not a character in the story. This narrator is omniscient, but is unobtrusive or impersonal to the extreme, so that the narrator only shares information that is reported by the characters and does not reveal anyone's inner thoughts or give his own opinion of Han's predicament or the judge's response. The narrator provides access to the thoughts and feelings of the characters primarily through dialogue; the judge questions each character thoroughly, and each character answers at great length.

Structure

"Han's Crime" is structured as a series of dialogues between the judge and Han's coworkers, and the judge and Han. Recounted by each character in the present moment, the principal actions of the story are revealed in flashback. The owner-manager, Chinese stagehand, and Han all recount their individual recollections and interpretations of the incident that resulted in the death of Han's wife, and Han recalls the introspective process by which he becomes certain only of his own uncertainty.

The story is also constructed as a confession, which results in *catharsis* (the purifying of emotions or the relieving of emotional tensions, especially by art). Ironically, for Han the catharsis results in the realization that he is certain neither of his guilt nor his innocence: "I was so happy because come what may it was no longer a question of confession of guilt." Shiga and his fellow *Shirakaba* writers linked strongly the moral quality of a particular work of art—in this case, confessional elements—to the structure of that work.

Symbols and Imagery

Just as "Han's Crime" has minimal setting, it also has minimal imagery. Shiga and his generation of writers wanted to be as "factual" and as close to "real life" as possible, and hence avoided the kind of literary symbolism and imagery found in Japanese poetry or Western writing of the early twentieth century. There are a few details in the story, however, that seem to serve symbolic purposes. Most of the symbols in "Han's Crime" are concrete details that represent larger abstractions. The death of the baby of Han's wife, for example, renders concretely the death of Han's love for his wife. Han's Chinese nationality in a closely-knit Japanese society that shuns outsiders materially represents Han's alienation and isolation from the larger society around him. The judge, with his careful questioning and his authority to render a verdict, represents not only the law but the moral judgment of the larger society to which Han must submit.

The key symbol in the story is the wife of Han. She is far more a symbol than a character, and the key symbolic event is her death. Although she plays a pivotal role in the story, neither Han, the owner-manager, nor the Chinese stagehand can describe her with much detail. She seems kind to everyone except Han; she is pretty; and her small feet suggest that she, like Han and the stagehand, is Chinese. She also represents a life of captivity and hypocrisy to Han; he feels that he was tricked into marrying her when she was pregnant with another man's child.

It is hard to understand why Han bears so much hatred for his wife. One explanation is what she represents to him: the absence of freedom. Several times in the story, Han mentions his freedom to pursue his "true life." It is unclear how his wife prevents him from leading his "true life" (just as it remains vague what his "true life" is and what he will do with the freedom the judge offers him). Han tells the judge he felt "poisoned" by the relationship and that he felt his wife watched "the gradual destruction of my life" with "cruel eyes." To Han, his wife represented all that was holding him back in life; he felt his paralysis and weaknesses were "all due to my relationship with my wife." Her death is the key symbolic event in the story because through it and the self-reflection that follows it, Han gains his freedom.

Allegory

The absence of historical context and detailed description of place or of the larger society that Han inhabits have lead some critics to remark on the story's allegorical qualities. If "Han's Crime" is an allegory, it is an *allegory of ideas,* in which the characters represent abstract concepts, and the plot communicates a doctrine or thesis. That only Han is named and that all the other characters are merely represented by their titles—the judge, the owner-manager, the Chinese stagehand, Han's wife—suggests that the characters are not important for who they are but for what they represent. Told primarily in dialogue between Han and his judge, the narrative of "Han's Crime" strongly suggests that a certain quality of authenticity or sincerity, an abstract idea personified by Han in his agonized soul-searching, is to be valued above the laws of society. If Han, who is so thoroughly honest in his self-reflection, cannot determine his own guilt or innocence, the story suggests, how then can legal institutions presume to determine it? "Han's Crime" argues for the primacy of feelings, going as far to imply that feelings about "the incident" are more important than the incident itself.

Historical Context

Political Context

Shiga Naoya began his career and wrote his most representative works during the Taisho period in Japan (1912-1926). According to Peter Duus in his article, "Liberal Intellectuals and Social Conflict in Taisho Japan," the Taisho period in Japan resembled the 1960s in America in that it was politically volatile as it moved from an extremely class-conscious and hierarchical society toward industrialization and democratization. Following the Sino-Japanese War (1894-1895), Japanese society became more industrialized. The industrialization accelerated after the Russo-Japanese War (1904-1905) and World War I (1914-1918), increasing the population of the urban working class and laying the groundwork for the democracy movements for which the Taisho period is known. Signs of social unrest began with the anti-treaty riots of 1905 and gained momentum in the 1910s as women, students and workers in both the cities and rural areas took to the streets to demand access to the vote and better working conditions. Duus observes that the episodes of social conflict that dominated the Taisho period stem from the accelerated growth of the economy, less acceptance of social differentiation, and a decline in confidence in the emperor and national leadership as well from a response to changes in the outside world. He writes: "By the

Compare & Contrast

- **1915:** The U.S. National Center for Health Statistics reports 3,633 homicides and suicides in the United States. Of that number, 483 are inflicted by "cutting and piercing instruments."

1932: There are 975 reported homicides in Japan.

1995: According to the U.S. Census Bureau, there are 20,220 murders in the United States this year. *Datapedia of the U.S., 1790-2000* reports that in 1990, "accident" is the fourth leading cause of death in the United States, following heart disease, cancer and stroke.

1997: The *Wall Street Journal* ranks Tokyo, Japan, the safest city in the world in regard to "violent crime," including assault and murder; Kabul, Afghanistan is the least safe.

- **1921:** The first year for which the *Japan Statisti-cal Yearbook* has any data, there are 53 divorces per every 1,000 people in Japan, a rate of 0.94. In 1921, the total population of Japanese is 55,963,053.

1920: There are 1.6 divorces for every 1,000 people in the United States. The total population of the United States in 1920 is 106,461,000.

1989: According to the *Japan Statistical Yearbook*, there are 158 divorces per 1,000 people in Japan in 1989, a rate of 1.29. The total population of Japan is 123,254,671.

1997: *Statistical Abstracts of the United States, 1997*, reports that there are 1,169,000 divorces in the U.S. in 1995, a rate of 4.4. The total population of the United States is 265,284,000.

---

early 1910s . . . easy optimism about the stability and justness of Japanese society began to erode. . . ."

The Shirakaba School

The *Shirakaba* School, of which Shiga was a founding member, was very much a product of the Taisho period. In Kyoto, Japan, in 1910, a group of young men who had been students at the Peers' School founded a journal they called *Shirakaba,* or White Birch. These students were all members of the upper classes: either members of the aristocracy, as was Shiga, whose ancestors were samurai; or the sons of important government officials. In *Dawn to the West,* Donald Keene explains

> An independence of mind so strong that the members of the group felt free to run counter to the opinions of the vast majority of Japanese was typical of these young aristocrats, who never lost their awareness of belonging to an elite class. Unlike the Naturalist writers, who tended to portray themselves with mingled pity and contempt, the *Shirakaba* members were proud of themselves and their chosen professions. They were absolutely confident in their tastes and did not hesitate to affirm them.

These young men were well-read in Western classics, and their literary emphasis was on humanism and the individual personality rather than the celebration of nature favored by their literary predecessors, the Naturalists. Because of its emphasis on the individual personality, and a narrative style that made it difficult to separate characters from author, the fiction produced by the *Shirakaba* group has been given the name "I-novel."

The philosophies of the *Shirakaba* group are most clearly understood in the context of the Taisho period. According to Suzuki in *Narrating the Self: Fictions of Japanese Modernity*: "The emergence of the I-novel was closely related to the social-liberal movement of the late 1910s and early 1920s known as Taisho Democracy, which sought to expand the vote." Yoshino Sakuzo, one of the leaders of the democratization of the vote movement, advocated "development of the individual personality" for the working classes and "humanistic consideration and reflection" for the upper classes. Other pro-Democracy leaders espoused Personalism, which they defined as the development and achievement of the individual self as the basis for all social reform. The *Shirakaba* group advocated Humanism, the pursuit and development of the individual self as the ultimate goal of life. As Keene points out, because "the members of the group throughout their careers remained aloof from, or even hostile to, serious consideration of public issues," the *Shirakaba* writers focused on an idea of "the self" which was isolated from its larger social context. Both the more politicized Personalism—which insisted that social reform benefit the individual self—and the introspective, psychological Humanism of the *Shirakaba* school formed the intellectual ground for the Taisho Democracy.

Critical Overview

Although he only wrote one novel, three novellas and a few dozen short stories, Shiga Naoya has had a significant impact on twentieth-century Japanese literature. He occupies a dominant place in modern Japanese fiction. As Donald Keene writes, "No modern writer was more idolized than Shiga Naoya. A half-dozen writers were recognized as his disciples, and innumerable others were so greatly influenced by his writings as to recall Shiga on every page." Such prominent writers as Akutagawa Ryunosuke, who wrote the story *Rashoman,* have admired Shiga's writings. Among his contemporaries, he has been called "the god of literature." Even when critics question the value and significance of his work, they concede that he remains an important figure in Japanese literary history, not only for his contributions to the development of the I-novel, but for his precise, compressed, and carefully controlled writing style, which has been praised for its ability to convey complex psychological states through suggestion, implication and allusion.

Aside from his novel *A Dark Night's Passing* and a few short stories, Shiga's work has not been translated into English. In *Shiga Naoya,* Francis Mathy rightly points out that Shiga's literary reputation must be considered in both Eastern and Western traditions. In the Eastern tradition, perfection of art is linked to perfection of life; traditional Japanese literature is not mimetic (i.e., does not try to represent the world "realistically" in the way that some Western novels do). Mathy writes:

> Without a philosophy of history, without a notion of a meaningful whole of human experience to which each individual part of it is related and from which it can derive a meaning, Japanese tradition could form no

concept of the individual human personality (upon which characterization is based) or of the significance of any segment of human life (upon which plot is based) or of the wide causal reverberations of human decisions and actions (upon which the development of the action in a literary work is based).

What Japanese writers and critics value is the attempt to capture as much of the reality or life of the passing moment as possible. Japanese literature tends to emphasize the present moment, isolated from the past or the future, complete and whole unto itself. The present moment is meaningful unto itself, without reference to either the past or the future.

Japanese fiction, then, emphasizes the intuition and sudden understanding of the "heart" of things in a way the Western literary tradition does not. When Shiga published "Han's Crime" and his other works, Japanese critics responded to what Nakamura Mitsuo called *kokoro no fukasa,* or "depth of heart." According to Mathy, Mitsuo wrote: "When we consider Shiga's works in the context of all the other literature that surrounds it, it seems so simple that it gives the impression of being the expression of a man that is always on the verge of silence. But who can mistake the depth of reality that is depicted there?" For Japanese critics, Shiga is a "pure" writer who is completely true to himself and rejects everything false and impure. It is this purity and depth of heart that inspired his Japanese readers.

This relationship of art to life has led many Japanese critics to respond to Shiga's work as a facet of his own personality. In *Narrating the Self,* Tomi Suzuki notes that responses to Shiga's work have also been responses to him as a personality. Of his contemporaries, for example, she observes that Akutagawa Ryunosuke has described Shiga as "a sensitive, moral soul," but that Kobayashi Hideo labeled him an "ultra-egotist" and "a man of action." Inoue Yoshio called Shiga "a primitive man," Tanigawa Tetsuzo found him to be "a man of moods," and Ito Sei and Hirano Ken celebrated him as "a man of harmony." Just as Shiga's *Shirakaba* group in the Taisho generation were critical of the Naturalists from the generation before, after World War II, Japanese readers became critical of the isolation of the self from society that they found in Shiga's fiction.

In the West, Shiga has not been widely read, so it is difficult to place him within a context. Several Western critics and translators have noted that Shiga's precise language and subjective representations of the individual at a specific moment in time are difficult to translate from the Japanese. According to Mathy, one translator bemoaned, "try as I might, the English that emerged was but a pallid reflection of the original. . . . It was as if Shiga's style was such a rare and subtle perfume that it evaporated as I transferred it from one bottle to another."

Of the few Western critics who have written about "Han's Crime," all find it a fascinating piece for both its ambiguity and psychological acuity. For Suzuki, the story explores "the relationship between imagination and action, the connection between motives and interpretations, and the interrelated questions of spontaneity, moral effort and freedom." For William Sibley, author of *The Shiga Hero,* "Han's Crime" is striking in its presentation of the "hero's private morality: the proposition that when one commits what the world calls a crime out of deep-rooted and largely unconscious motives, there can be no guilt and should be no crime." Reviewing a recent translation of Shiga's stories in the *New York Times,* Hiroaki Sato calls "Han's Crime" a "psychological drama that is extraordinary in the simplicity of its narrative structure and the depth of its intellectual honesty."

Criticism

Yoonmee Chang

Yoonmee Chang is a Ph.D. candidate in the English department at the University of Pennsylvania. In the following essay, she uncovers the latent feminist expressions in Shiga Naoya's "Han's Crime," focusing on the "subtext" or the story-within-the-story that can antagonize or disrupt the author's apparent intentions.

Shiga Naoya has hardly been considered a "feminist" writer. After all, Han's dissatisfaction with his wife in "Han's Crime" (1913) reaches a violent breaking point because she does not cook dinner fast enough for his liking. In its day, the *Shirakaba* group, or "I-novelists," that Shiga helped to found was radical in its often oppositional attitudes to social conventions that hindered the development of the individual self. But these writers were deeply conservative in that their conceptions of the "true" self were based on traditional, masculinist notions. While they proposed that the self should have the right to transgress social mores and ethics in pursuit of its "true nature," this self was implicitly male, and women were often represented as hin-

drances to this pursuit. In accordance with the Shirakaba aesthetic, Han, the protagonist of "Han's Crime," is exonerated from the murder of his wife because her death, as he proposes, is necessary to finding his "true nature." Han tells the judge:

> "A desire to seek the light [to enter upon a journey of self-exploration] was burning inside me. Or, if it was not, it was trying to catch fire. But my relationship with my wife would not let it . . . I was being poisoned . . . It would be good if she died . . ."

The troubling implication of Han's reasoning, and the judge's support of it, is that because women can disrupt and derail the masculinist privilege of self-exploration, they must be physically and psychologically evacuated. In short, they can be justifiably murdered.

Despite these central masculinist and misogynist assumptions, "Han's Crime" can be interpreted in a way that, ironically, empowers women. To understand such interpretations that seem counter-logical or contradictory to the author's purposes, the reader must resist the common practice of interpreting a story through the author's *intentions.* Twentieth-century literary critics W. K. Wimsatt and Monroe C. Beardsley discuss the problems of interpreting literature in this way in a well-known essay entitled "The Intentional Fallacy." They write:

> the design or intention of the author is neither available nor desirable as a standard for judging the success [and meaning] of a work of literary art . . .

The meaning of literature is not best fathomed by considering *what the author means* as that "intention" is difficult to pinpoint even by the author herself.

A similar understanding of literature, though formed in a disparate context, is Russian literary theorist M. M. Bakhtin's idea of "dialogism." According to Bakhtin, language does not exist in a vacuum. No word, phrase, or sentence, as well as the most complicated and structured utterances, like political treatises and literary texts, ever mean exactly the same thing to all readers. He imagines meaning as a ray of light that travels from the object to the eye. Before the light reaches the eye and the eye can see the object, the light is *refracted* at varying angles, depending on the physical composition of the object and the space between the object and the eye. Similarly, before the meaning of the word or utterance moves from the text to the reader's understanding, it travels through an environment of personal experience, opinion, education background etc., that influences how the reader understands that text. In addition, the *historical*

What Do I Read Next?

- *Shiga Naoya* (1974) by Francis Mathy. The most complete and readable biography of Shiga Naoya available in English.

- *A Dark Night's Passing* (1976) by Shiga Naoya, the author of "Han's Crime." An English translation by Edwin McClellan of Shiga Naoya's 1937 full-length novel, which is a deeply autobiographical exploration of a Japanese writer's life and psyche.

- *The Paper Door and Other Stories* (1987) by Shiga Naoya. An English translation by Lane Dunlop of a collection of short stories, including "Han's Crime," by Shiga Naoya.

- "In A Grove" (1952) by Akutagawa Ryunosuke, Shiga Naoya's contemporary and rival. An English translation by Takashi Kojima of Akutagawa's 1917 short story which features unreliable narrators attempting to arrive at the truth behind a crime. Akutagawa also wrote *Rashoman,* which Akira Kurosawa made into a classic film.

- *Civilization and Its Discontents* (1930) by Sigmund Freud. An in-depth exploration from the pioneer of psychoanalysis of how the unconscious mind negotiates repressive social rules.

- *The Stranger* (1942) by Albert Camus, a French novelist whose writings were often deemed "existentialist." *The Stranger* is a confession of an "innocent murderer" named Mersault.

- *The Metamorphosis* (1946) by Franz Kafka, an Austrian Jew who was born in the same year as Shiga Naoya, 1883. In *The Metamorphosis,* Gregor Samsa awakens one morning to find himself transformed into a giant cockroach. The novella asks us to consider what is "really" happening to Gregor and what is his unconscious dreaming mind.

- *An Artist of the Floating World* (1986) by Kazuo Ishiguro, a British novelist of Japanese ancestry. This novel received the Whitbread Book of the Year prize for 1986, and concerns a topic near to Shiga Naoya's heart: the ability or inability of an artist to alter the past or influence the presence through his work.

---

context of the author, reader and distance between the two affects an utterance's meaning. For example, an account of slavery would ring differently in the ears of someone in antebellum America than in the ears of a modern-day audience.

Bakhtin does not deny that the author has *intentions* and may try to express those intentions in her work. His point is that in the complex process of understanding the meaning of a text, such intentions may become diminished, blurred, or even completely lost to the reader. As a result, any given literary text can be interpreted in infinitely different ways; literature is *polyphonic*, or speaks with *many voices*. Woven within the "main" story, or that which follows the author's apparent intentions, are various other stories or *subtexts*, meanings produced beyond the author's control and which frequently speak louder than the author's intentions. Highlighting *subtexts* is a critical strategy that allows ethically questionable texts (for example, openly racist, classist or masculinist texts) to be re-imagined for the groups such texts seek to oppress. In simple and cynical terms, the apparent message of "Han's Crime" is that it is acceptable for a man to kill his wife if she stands in the way of his "true" self's development. But by turning one of the dominant messages of the story back upon itself, a subtext emerges that challenges this and more generally misogynistic ways of thinking.

"Han's Crime" is a story about storytelling. It examines the forces at work in relating a story to a reader or hearer and points out that the process can be arbitrary and biased. The text also warns against taking the *implications* of certain "facts" at face value. When placed in certain *contexts,* objective facts can take on specific implications, but these implications do not necessarily represent the truth. Depending on what implications are accepted as "true" and how the "facts" are presented and assembled, the resulting story can lean towards certain biases and points of view. In the case of Han's wife's death, the owner-manager of the performing troupe, a Chinese stagehand, and Han himself are called upon to provide objective and relevant bits of information. It is the job of the judge to arrange these bits to reconstruct the story of Han's wife's death. Han's guilt or innocence depends on how the judge puts these pieces of information together and what implications he consciously or subconsciously accepts as truth. The reader is put in the position of judge. Both rely on second-hand information—the testimony of the characters—to construct a logical picture of the events.

To construct a "true story" is a rather difficult task, as it is a common temptation to accept the implications of certain "facts" as truth. For example, that Han did not get along with his wife is on the one hand a simple piece of descriptive information. In the context of everyday life, this information takes on no sinister meaning. But when followed by the information that a knife from Han's hand killed his wife, this factoid takes on new importance and damning connotations. It can be interpreted as a partial motivation for murder and increases the possibility of Han's guilt. The stagehand is aware of the powerful implication in this context, but also knows that he should be careful of too easily accepting implication as truth. He tells the judge: "I thought that my thinking he'd murdered her might . . . simply have been because I knew a good deal about their relationship." Had he not known about the couple's unhappy marriage, the stagehand might not have personally suspected Han of murder. Though the fact of couple's bad marriage implies a murder is possible, it does not prove it. Han himself argues along these lines:

> "Everyone knew we'd been on bad terms, of course,
> so there was bound to be a suspicion of murder. . . .
> That we'd gotten along badly might make people
> conjecture, but it was no proof."

Han's admission that his marriage was miserable, and that he even wished his wife were dead, certainly *implies* that Han may likely have killed her, but it is not definitive proof.

In this way, Han's guilt or innocence depends in part on which implications are accepted or rejected. In addition, the verdict is influenced by the

> " The judge's verdict of 'innocent' indicates that he recognizes the questionable 'truth' of a story especially when based on random bits of information arranged in a certain order and taken for their obvious implications. But at the same time 'Han's Crime' offers this challenge to 'truth' based on reconstructed, implication-based narratives, the text is guilty of its own unfair storytelling, namely in regard to Han's wife."

arrangement of "facts" and the implications of the *procession of events.* Because of the suspicious procession of events, Han himself believes, at first, that he is indeed guilty. But that events happen in a certain order does not necessarily mean that one event was caused by another. Han reconstructs the incident: he had an unusually heated argument with his wife the night before; unable to sleep he passed the night thinking upon his wife's hindrance of his "true nature" and thought "It would be good if she died"; the next day he felt "insanely keyed up," perhaps from a lack of sleep; and during the performance he doubted his steadiness. Presented in this order, the information constructs a causal, *teleological* (facts arranged to move towards some conclusionary endpoint) narrative that likely incriminates Han: because of A (his fight with his wife), B happened (he wished she were dead), and ultimately resulted in C (the murder). But before Han convinces himself and the judge that he is definitively guilty, he points out that just because the events transpired in the order that they did, it does not mean that one event caused the following one. Han explains: "The night before, I had thought about killing her, but was that alone a reason for deciding, myself, that it was murder?'' and ''between my thinking about such a thing and actually deciding to kill her, there was still a wide gap. . . .'' In other words, there is no necessarily causal relationship linking the events preceding the murder. Though the order of events certainly implies causality and seems to incriminate Han, that they happened in that order and at the times that they did was random and arbitrary, a matter of chance. Han could have wished his wife were dead all his life without harming her as well as he could have easily planned to kill her without thinking upon it the night before. The judge apparently agrees with Han, as well as the stagehand, and declares him ''innocent.''

Along these lines, ''Han's Crime'' makes a comment about constructing a story. By arranging scattered pieces of information together and giving weight to various implications, different narratives can emerge. These resulting stories can have powerful effects, as in Han's case, determining whether he spends the rest of his life in jail. But this is not to say that these stories represent the ''truth.'' The judge's verdict of ''innocent'' indicates that he recognizes the questionable ''truth'' of a story especially when based on random bits of information arranged in a certain order and taken for their obvious implications. But at the same time ''Han's Crime'' offers this challenge to ''truth'' based on reconstructed, implication-based narratives, the text is guilty of its own unfair storytelling, namely in regard to Han's wife.

Though her murder is central to the text, Han's wife—her personality, her desires, her opinions—are barely discussed. The details revealed about her are scant, but in a masculinist fashion focus on her sexual behavior. As in the testimony provided in the trial, each bit of biographical information about Han's wife has its implications and connotations. For instance, Han believes that his wife remained in the miserable marriage because: ''she knew that no respectable man would marry a woman who'd been the wife of a road-player.'' There are at least two assumptions in this statement. First, that road-performers, especially women, are sexually promiscuous, or at least popularly considered to be so, and second, that in the case of a divorce, Han's wife would need to remarry; that is, she would be unable to support herself as an independent woman. These misogynistic assumptions are supported by the stagehand's similar statement: ''Even if she had left Han and gone back [to her family], nobody would have trusted a woman who'd been on the road four years enough to marry her.'' Han also reveals that his wife

had conceived another man's baby before their marriage and tells the judge that this is his primary source of hatred. He even feels that the baby's death was a ''just'' punishment for her sexual transgression:

> ''I felt that the baby's death was a judgement on her for what she'd done . . . [But m]y feeling remained that the baby's death wasn't enough of a judgement. At times, when I thought about it by myself, I could be rather forgiving . . . [But a]s I looked at her, at her body, I could not keep down my displeasure.''

Slowly, a picture of Han's wife emerges from the information provided by Han and the stagehand. This picture is not a favorable one as the men's descriptions construct her as an insensitive, dependent, and sexually promiscuous woman that deserves punishment for expressing her sexuality outside of marriage. Clearly this image of Han's wife is one-sided, but the judge seems to give it credence by never questioning this biased representation. Han argued that though thinking about murder may imply that he carried out the murder, there was still a ''wide gap'' between these two events. But Han's dead wife never has the chance to similarly argue against the implication of certain facts; for instance, the assumption that because she had a relationship with another man *before her marriage to Han* she was sexually promiscuous. In fact, the circumstances of that relationship are never discussed. Its implications are merely taken at face value.

Furthermore, the judge's verdict of ''innocent'' seems to partially rely on his implicit condemnation of Han's wife for her ''scandalous'' sexual behavior. Rather than asserting his innocence, Han's testimony is inordinately concerned with describing and disparaging his wife's pre-martial sexual liaison and the pregnancy that resulted. The judge's patient listening to Han's sexual defamation of his wife, which also forces the reader to hear this evidence, implies that her so-called ''promiscuity'' is indeed a weighty matter and is perhaps a reasonable excuse for murder. In these moments, it seems that Han's wife rather than Han is the one on trial, namely for her so-called sexual promiscuity.

But considering the dominant message of the story—that information, implications and narrative construction are arbitrary and suspect—the attentive reader is equipped with a powerful tool to refute and overturn the misogynist strains of ''Han's Crime,'' and to re-imagine the story from a feminist angle. As discussed, the confusion regarding the ''facts'' or evidence in the murder case, as well as the judge's verdict, encourages the reader to question or challenge stories constructed from an assemblage of "facts" that tend to rely on implications. In this light, the text requests that the reader reconsider Han's guilt, as the facts of the incident are only provided through patchy, second-hand information hastily arranged to form a narrative whole. As the truth of Han's story can never be known, the text warns the reader of easily accepting such artificially assembled, teleological narratives. The same can be said for Han's wife's "story." Her sexually degraded characterization is similarly conveyed through scattered bits of information that, because they are arranged in a specific way, create a negative picture of her. There is much information left out, and among the details included, the implications are taken for face value. For instance, the assumption that if a woman is a road performer, she is automatically promiscuous; or that her sexual liaison with the unnamed man was an act of wantonness. If the reader is warned not to believe constructed accounts like Han's story (A does not necessarily lead to B and C), she can also be equally wary of the "truth" of Han's wife's characterization: having a baby with a man one is not married to does not have to render a woman sexually degraded, and her relationship with the unnamed man is a much more complicated situation, not an automatic indicator of her sexual immorality. Though the men in the text cooperate in describing her as weak, dependent, and promiscuous, the general lesson of the text empowers the reader to recognize such characterizations as artificial, biased, and constructed.

By focusing on the subtext, misogynist, racist, classist, and other oppressive forms of literature can be re-imagined. Rather than turn away in disgust and reject such texts, the careful reader can interpret them in empowering ways often by using such texts' terms against themselves. As a misogynistic story, "Han's Crime" undoes itself, providing the reader with the very tools to dismantle such messages, denoting perhaps the untenability of such oppressing structures of thought. Whether or not the authors would agree with such antagonist interpretations of their stories is irrelevant. Because they are mediated through "dialogic" language, words once separated from their authors immediately become transformed and reinvented in the hands of their thoughtful and diverse readers. In a way, all literary texts are like testimonies provided in court cases—information arranged to assert a specific point of view with an aim to convince its audience of something. Noting that authors have various personal interests, it is the very powerful position of the reader to choose what to believe.

Source: Yoonmee Chang, "An Overview of 'Han's Crime'," in *Short Stories for Students,* The Gale Group, 1999.

Jean Leverich

Leverich has a Ph.D. in literature from the University of Michigan and has taught composition and literature at Georgetown University, New York University School of Continuing Education, and the University of Michigan. In the following essay, she discusses the significance of the murdered wife of Han in relation to Shiga Naoya's philosophy of the self in Shiga's short story, "Han's Crime."

Several years after publishing the story, "Han's Crime," Shiga Naoya became seized with the desire to "write of the wife, dead and quiet in her grave, from the wife's point of view," according to Edward Fowler in *The Rhetoric of Confession.* Shiga wrote in his journal, "I would call the story 'The Murdered Wife of Han.' I never did write it, but the urge was there." Shiga's journal entry reveals that although the character Han questioned his own motives, and the judge in the story exonerated him of any crime, Shiga himself believes his hero to be guilty of murder. Shiga's comment is especially striking given that while the death of Han's wife is clearly central to the story, as a character, she is all but absent.

The story concerns Han's realization that, through living with his wife, he has become alienated from his "true identity." In the story, Han believes that he can only achieve his "true self" through the death of his wife. He even tells the judge that for him "there was a great difference" between leaving his wife and killing her, and that leaving her did not have the same "desired result." But what can it mean that the realization of Han's "true life" comes at the expense of his wife's death? Or that in recognizing his true self, Han violates the laws of society and the judge seems to reward him for doing so? In order to answer these questions, we must first address the philosophy of the self that Shiga espoused.

The *Shirakaba* group, of which Shiga was a founding member, wholeheartedly embraced the development of one's individual personality as the overarching purpose of art. As supporters of Humanism, the *Shirakaba* group reacted strongly against the aspect of Japanese society that valued social harmony over the development of the individual personality. Indeed, the writings of the *Shirakaba* school focus on the life of the individual almost exclusively. In 1911, Mushakoji Saneatsu, one of Shiga's fellow group members, wrote the following

> Much of the tension and power of 'Han's Crime' comes from the question of how responsible people are for their own antisocial thoughts and feelings if they do not <u>consciously</u> act on them."

manifesto in *Shirakaba* magazine: "The value of one's existence is acquired only by giving life to one's individual personality." Furthermore, Mushakoji contended that "Those who commit themselves to work that cannot make the best of their individual personality are insulting their own selves." In order to understand how Han can feel no remorse about murdering his wife, then, we need to recognize that in addition to personal honesty and psychological acuity, one of the primary tenets of the "I-novels" and fiction of the *Shirakaba* group was the idea of *allegiance to one's self above all*. The only person to whom Han is responsible, given the ideas of the *Shirakaba* group, is himself.

For the writers of the *Shirakaba* group, art is a means of "developing and realizing their 'true selves'," explains Tomi Suzuki in *Narrating the Self: Fictions of Japanese Modernity*. Shiga himself wrote, in a diary entry dated May 27, 1911, "The mission of art is to achieve a deeper understanding of nature's beauty." But for Shiga and the members of the *Shirakaba* group, nature meant "human nature," unconstrained by society, rather than the celebration of the natural world of flora and fauna exemplified by haiku of earlier generations. Literary critic Makoto Ueda explains that for Shiga, "A person who behaved 'naturally' was not a mere eccentric who pays little attention to conventional norms; he was a person who, having awakened to his innermost nature, was trying to return to it." To be true to nature, then, is to be true to one's inner self. The *Shirakaba* sense of "the self" seems to resemble the id in Freudian psychology, in which the id represents our most primal urges and needs. In the Freudian model, the id is held firmly in check by the superego (internalized rules of society), and it is our ego—or conscious self—that negotiates the demands of the id versus the restraints of society. In "Han's Crime," Shiga represents the self as pure id, certain only of what it wants, unable to analyze its motivations.

What was it about this young woman that her death gives birth to Han's "true self"? For what has she given her life? Shiga does not reveal much about this mysterious young woman, not even her name or her nationality, though the fact that she wears a "gaudy Chinese costume" suggests that, like her husband, she is Chinese. Since marrying Han and going on the road with him as a circus performer, her family has broken up and disappeared, so she has nowhere to go if Han leaves her. The owner-manager and the stage manager of the circus speak highly of her ("she was a good person, too"), except to note that Han and his wife, "who were so kind, gentle and self-effacing with others, when it came to their own relationship, were surprisingly cruel to each other." However, by the stage manager's estimation, the unhappiness in the marriage came about only after the death of her child, of whom Han suspected he was not the father.

A foreigner in Japan, unhappily married to an unforgiving husband, Han's wife finds she can never please her husband, who is always off reading Christian literature and expressing dissatisfaction with everything she does, such as preparing the evening meal. She tells her husband that if he "divorced her she could not survive" because "she knew that no respectable man would marry a woman who'd been the wife of a road-player. And her feet were too small for ordinary work." Although she does not love her husband, she attempts to be a good wife to him; he tells the judge that their sexual relations were "probably not much different than those of an average couple." By Han's own account, then, Han's wife is a beautiful, impoverished young woman with no family, dependent on her husband for her livelihood and safety, who committed the "crime" of loving another man before she married her husband.

Han's biggest complaint against her is that she feels no sympathy for him: "My wife simply observed, with cruel eyes, the gradual destruction of my life . . . without the slightest wish to help." But Han does not seem to recognize that he feels little compassion for her, though "for my wife living with me was an extraordinary hardship" that she endured with a patience "beyond what one would have thought possible even for a man.'' Unable to feel compassion or forgiveness, Han needs to punish his wife for the failure of the relationship, the death of their romantic love: ''My feeling remained,'' he tells the judge, ''that the baby's death wasn't enough of a judgment.'' His hatred for her consumes him, and in order to be free of it, he begins to think ''that it would be good if she were dead.''

For a Western, feminist reader, what remains most frustrating about ''Han's Crime'' are Han's claims that divorcing his wife does not produce the same ''desired result'' as murdering her and that through her death, he becomes liberated to ''live [his] own life.'' Certainly, in granting Han his innocence, the judge literally liberates Han to lead a new life. But just as for Han ''a wide gap'' exists between thinking about murder and actually doing it, so too a gap exists between exactly how it is that the annihilation of one person's life results in another's development of his ''true self.'' On one level, ''Han's Crime'' is a story of domestic violence, in which the woman gets punished for her transgression (sleeping with another man prior to her marriage to Han), but Han gets rewarded for his.

Shiga's endorsement of supreme selfishness makes ''Han's Crime'' all the more shocking, for what kind of natural self does Han celebrate? For Han, murder is a means of developing and realizing his ''true self.'' In ''Han's Crime,'' this celebration of self seems anti-social and violent in the extreme. Like Raskalnikov in Dostoevski's *Crime and Punishment*, who murders an old woman for her gold, or Mersault in Camus's *The Stranger*, who has murdered his own mother, Han finds a perverse freedom in transgressing society's laws. But unlike those European novels, society in ''Han's Crime'' does not exact a punishment. instead it acknowledges, in the person of the judge, that it too has had these fleeting feelings of ''excitement'' that one ''could not put a name to,'' and condones Han for having acted on the impulses most members of society never consciously acknowledge.

And what, if anything, does ''Han's Crime'' reveal about the id, the true nature of Han? Although ''Han's Crime'' is an unsavory and unsettling examination of how to get away with murder, Shiga does not elaborate on what exactly Han's ''true self'' might be. The story suggests that Han was a passive person who was in an unhappy marriage. The external character of Han is quite

passive. At several points in the story he describes himself as ''weak,'' ''suspended in midair'' and unable to take any kind of action. Although he thinks his wife is pregnant by another man, he does nothing. He is unhappy in the marriage, but does not wish to leave. When the judge asks him why, if he was so unhappy in his marriage, he was ''unable to take a more assertive, resolute attitude,'' Han answers only that he ''wanted to act in such a way as to leave no room for error.'' Although he blames his indecisiveness and lack of courage on his relationship with his wife, to the judge's inquiry, ''Why didn't you think of leaving your wife?'' Han has no answer except that in his mind there is a great difference between leaving one's wife and wishing her dead. As a character, Han is so alienated from himself that he cannot be certain he consciously murdered his own wife. He seems to suggest that the only way he can take action is through his unconscious.

Much of the tension and power of ''Han's Crime'' comes from the question of how responsible people are for their own antisocial thoughts and feelings if they do not *consciously* act on them. Han tells the judge that ''between my thinking such a thing and actually deciding to kill her, there was still a wide gap.'' He repeatedly tells the judge that once his murderous thoughts were over he ''no longer thought of killing her.'' Han is guilty of murder if he *consciously* plots murder and of manslaughter if he acts without premeditated thought. During the knife-throwing act, Han becomes aware of consciously trying to control his unconscious urges: ''I could feel in my arm the constraint that comes from a thing's having become conscious.'' Before throwing the final, fatal knife, Han sees a ''premonition'' of ''violent fear'' come over his wife's face. He describes a battle between his conscious and unconscious minds in which ''dizziness'' strikes him and he throws his knife ''almost without a target, as though aiming in the dark.'' On the one hand, his description makes him sound ''out of control'' and ''beside himself'' as though he were not the agent of his actions; on the other hand, his awareness of throwing the knife suggests that his conscious mind was an active participant as well. In the final analysis, in terms of realizing his ''true self,'' it seems that Han is still perhaps not being as honest with himself as he might be. What Shiga's story fails to answer is the question of whether the self can exist outside of society.

Source: Jean Leverich, ''An Overview of 'Han's Crime','' in *Short Stories for Students,* The Gale Group, 1999.

Francis Mathy

In the following excerpt from his book-length study of Shiga, Mathy provides an overview of ''Han's Crime.''

[''Han's Crime''] begins with a succinct account of the crime:

It was a very strange incident. A young Chinese juggler by the name of Han in the course of a performance severed his wife's carotid artery with one of his knives. The young woman died on the spot and Han was immediately arrested.

The body of the story consists of the examining judge's interrogation of the director of the theater, of Han's assistant in his juggling act, and finally of Han himself. The question is to decide whether the killing was deliberate murder or merely manslaughter.

The director testifies that Han's act is very difficult and requires steady nerves, complete concentration, and even a certain kind of intuitive sense. He cannot say whether the killing was intended or not.

The assistant tells the judge what he knows about Han and his wife. Han's behavior was always correct. He had become a Christian the previous year and always seemed to be reading Christian literature. Both Han and his wife were kind and gentle, very good to their friends and acquaintances, and never quarreled with others. Between themselves, however, it was another matter. They could be very cruel to each other. They had had a child, born prematurely, that had died soon after his birth. Since its death their relationship had become strained. Han never raised his hand against his wife, but he always looked at her with angry eyes. He had confided to the assistant that his love for her had died but that he had no real grounds for a divorce. The assistant thinks that it was to overcome his hatred for her that Han had taken to reading the Bible and collections of Christian sermons. The wife could not leave Han because she would never have been able to find anyone else to marry her and she would have been unable to make her own living. The assistant admits that at the moment of the accident the thought had flashed through his mind, ''he's gone and killed her,'' but now he is not so certain. It may have been because of his knowledge of Han's hatred for her that this thought had entered his head. He concludes his testimony by stating that after the incident Han had dropped to his knees and prayed for some time in silence.

Interrogated next by the judge, Han admits that he had stopped loving his wife when the child was born, since he knew it was not his. The child had died smothered by its mother's breasts and Han does not know whether this was accidental or not, though his wife had told him it was. Han thinks that she never really loved him. After the child's death she would observe him ''with a cold, cruel look in her eyes'' as he gradually went to pieces. ''She never showed a flicker of sympathy as she saw me struggling in agony to escape into a better, truer sort of existence.''

Han never considered leaving his wife because of his ideals: he wanted to behave in such a way as not to be in the wrong. When asked if he had ever thought of killing her, he admits that at first he often used to think how nice it would be if she were dead. Then, the night before the incident, the thought of killing her had occurred to him but never reached the point of decision. They had had a quarrel because supper was not ready when it should have been. He spent a sleepless night, visited by many nightmarish thoughts, but the idea of killing his wife gradually faded and he ''was overcome by the sad, empty feeling that follows a nightmare.'' He realized that he was too weakhearted to achieve a better life than the one he had.

The next day he was physically exhausted, but the idea of killing no longer occurred to him. He did not even think of that evening's performance. But when the time came to take up his knives to begin his act, he found himself without his usual control. The first two knives did not miss their mark by far, but the third knife lodged itself in his wife's throat. At that moment Han felt that he had done it on purpose. To deceive the witnesses of the scene, he made a pretense of being grief-stricken and fell to his knees in prayer. He was certain that he could make others believe it was an accident.

But then he began to doubt that he had done it on purpose. Perhaps he had only thought he had done so because of his reflections of the previous night. The more he thought about it, the less certain he was about the actuality. It was at this point that he realized that his best defense would be admission of the truth. Since he himself did not know whether he was guilty or innocent, no one else could possibly know either. When the judge asks him if he feels any sorrow for her death, Han admits candidly that he does not, that he never imagined that her death would bring him such a sense of happiness. After this testimony the judge hands down a verdict of not guilty.

"Han's Crime," like "Seibei's Gourds" [another short story by Shiga], is a skillful objectification of Shiga's state of mind at the time of its writing. The story was written in the brief period between his release from the hospital after his accident and his departure for Kinosaki. Leisurely reflection at Kinosaki upon the implications of his encounter with death was to drastically change his attitude toward life and to mark a turning point in his work—away from the posture of confrontation and self-assertion to one of harmony and reconciliation. It is therefore ironic that in the person of Han, Shiga should have sung his most triumphant song of self.

Han suffers greatly from the hypocrisy forced upon him in having to live with a wife he despises. He is a man of unusual intelligence, great sensitivity, and an "overwhelming desire to enter into a truer sort of life." His feelings the night before the event are certainly those of Shiga himself at the time when he was determined to "mine" what was in him.

> . . . I was more worked up than I had ever been. Of late I had come to realize with anger and grief that I had no real life of my own. At night when I went to bed, I could not get to sleep but lay there in an excited state with all kinds of things passing through my mind. I was aware of living in a kind of daze, powerless to reach out with firm determination to the objects of my longing and equally powerless to drive away from me the sources of my displeasure. I came to see that this life of suspension and indecision was all owing to my relationship with my wife. I could see no light in my future, though the longing for light was still aflame. It would never die out but would continue smoldering pitifully. I was in danger of dying of the poison of this displeasure and suffering. When the poison reached a certain concentration I would die. I would become a corpse among the living. I was nearing that point now. Still, I was doing my best not to succumb. Then the thought came: if only she would die! That filthy, unpleasant thought kept running through my mind, "In fact, why don't you kill her? Don't worry about what happens after that. You'll probably be sent to prison. But life would be immeasurably better than the life you are leading now. Besides, that will be another day. When that day comes, you'll be able to break through somehow. You may have to throw yourself again and again against the obstacles and with no success. But then your true life will be to continue hurling yourself against whatever is in your way until you finally die of the effort."

Kobayashi Hideo, in an early essay on Shiga Naoya (1929), cites the latter portion of the above passage as an excellent statement of

> " Leisurely reflection at Kinosaki upon the implications of his encounter with death was to drastically change Shiga's attitude toward life and to mark a turning point in his work-- away from the posture of confrontation and self- assertion to one of harmony and reconciliation. It is therefore ironical that in the person of Han, Shiga should have sung his most triumphant song of self."

the basic form of Shiga's thought, or, more accurately, the norm of his action. He is never aware of the gap separating thought and action. Or else, if he does occasionally seem to take cognizance of it, it is only when his thought has not yet come ripe, and even then passion unfailingly jumps in to bridge the gap. For Shiga, to think is already to act, and to act is to think. To such a nature doubt and regret are equally absurd.

At the end of Han's confession, the judge asks him "aren't you the least bit grieved at your wife's death?" and Han replies frankly: "Not the least. Even in moments when I hated her most, I never imagined it would be so pleasant to speak of her death." Whether by chance or design, Han has triumphed and entered into what he feels is "a truer sort of life." This note of personal triumph was never again to be sounded so loudly and clearly in Shiga's work. . . .

But if "Han's Crime," is an excellent expression of Shiga's state of mind at the time of its writing, it is not for this reason that it is one of the finest stories of modern Japanese literature. The excellence of "Han's Crime," is due rather to the abundant life and individuality Shiga was able to give to the characters of Han and his wife, to the interest and tight unity of the plot, and to the masterful use of language.

Source: Francis Mathy, ''A Golden Ten'' and ''The Achievement of Shiga Naoya,'' in *Shiga Naoya*, Twayne Publishers, Inc., 1974, pp. 105-36; 165-75.

Sources

Fowler, Edward. *The Rhetoric of Confession: Shishosetsu in Early Twentieth-Century Japanese Fiction,* Berkeley: University of California Press, 1988.

Gemmette, Elizabeth Villiers, editor. *Law in Literature: Legal Themes in Short Stories,* New York: Praeger, 1992.

Keene, Donald. *Dawn to the West: Japanese Literature of the Modern Era,* New York: Holt, Rinehart and Winston, 1984.

Mathy, Francis. *Shiga Naoya,* New York: Twain Publishers, 1974.

Najita, Tetsuo and J. Victor Koschmann, editors. *Conflict in Modern Japanese History: The Neglected Tradition,* Princeton: Princeton University Press, 1982.

Sibley, William. *The Shiga Hero,* Chicago: University of Chicago Press, 1979.

Suzuki, Tomi. *Narrating the Self: Fictions of Japanese Modernity,* Stanford: Stanford University Press, 1996.

Ueda, Makoto. *Modern Japanese Writers and the Nature of Literature,* Stanford: Stanford University Press, 1976.

Yamanouchi, Hisaaki. *The Search for Authenticity in Modern Japanese Literature,* London: Cambridge University Press, 1978.

Further Reading

Keene, Donald. *Dawn to the West: Japanese Literature of the Modern Era,* New York: Holt, Rinehart and Winston, 1984.
A lively and engaging treatment of the history of Japanese literature from the sixteenth century to the present.

Najita, Tetsuo and J. Victor Koschmann, editors. *Conflict in Modern Japanese History: The Neglected Tradition,* Princeton: Princeton University Press, 1982.
A thoughtful discussion of some important social and political issues in twentieth century Japan.

Sibley, William. *The Shiga Hero,* Chicago: University of Chicago Press, 1979.
One of the first full-length works on Shiga Naoya, and a thorough introduction to his works.

Harrison Bergeron

Kurt Vonnegut
1961

"Harrison Bergeron" was first published in the October, 1961, issue of the *Magazine of Fantasy and Science Fiction.* It was Vonnegut's third publication in a science fiction magazine following the drying up of the once-lucrative weekly family magazine market where he had published more than twenty stories between 1950 and 1961. The story did not receive any critical attention, however, until 1968 when it appeared in Vonnegut's collection *Welcome to the Monkey House.* Initial reviews of the collection generally were less than favorable, with even more positive reviewers, such as Mitchel Levitas in the *New York Times* and Charles Nicol in the *Atlantic Monthly,* commenting negatively on the commercial quality of many of the stories. By the late 1980s, however, "Harrison Bergeron" was being reprinted in high school and college literature anthologies. Popular aspects of the story include Vonnegut's satire of both enforced equality and the power of the Handicapper General, and the enervating effect television can have on viewers. "Harrison Bergeron" likely draws upon a controversial 1961 speech by then Federal Communications Commission chairman Newton Minow titled "The Vast Wasteland," a reference to a supposed dearth of quality in television programming. Coincidentally, "Harrison Bergeron" also alludes to the George Burns and Gracie Allen television show, a weekly situation comedy and variety show popular in the late 1950s and early 1960s. Vonnegut has said that he learned most of what he believes about social and

political idealism from junior civics class, as well as from the democratic institution of the public school itself. A futuristic story dealing with universal themes of equality, freedom, power and its abuses, and media influence, ''Harrison Bergeron'' continues to evoke thoughtful responses about equality and individual freedom in the United States.

Author Biography

Kurt Vonnegut, Jr., was born in 1922, the youngest of three children of Edith and Kurt Vonnegut, in Indianapolis, Indiana. His siblings had attended private schools, but financial difficulties during the Great Depression meant that Vonnegut had to attend public schools. He has said that he gleaned the basis of his political and social beliefs from his junior civics class.

After graduation, Vonnegut attended Cornell University. In 1943, during World War II, he enlisted in the U. S. Army. In 1944, he was captured by German soldiers and sent to Dresden, Germany, where he survived the bombing raids of February, 1945. After the war, Vonnegut married Jane Cox and moved to Chicago where he worked as a newspaper reporter and attended the University of Chicago. However, he left Chicago for a public relations job with General Electric in Schenectady, New York, before completing his master's degree in anthropology.

While working for General Electric, Vonnegut sold his first story, ''Report on the Barnhouse Effect,'' to *Collier's* magazine; it was published in 1950. With the money from the sale of that story and three others, he quit his job in 1951, moved to Cape Cod, and embarked on a career as a writer. To supplement his income, he wrote public relations copy, taught school, and sold automobiles. His first novel, *Player Piano,* appeared in 1952, followed by *The Sirens of Titan* in 1959; *Canary in a Cat House* (short story collection), 1961; *Mother Night,* 1962; *Cat's Cradle,* 1963; and *God Bless You, Mr. Rosewater,* 1964. *Welcome to the Monkey House,* which includes ''Harrison Bergeron,'' was Vonnegut's second collection of stories and was published in 1968. In the mid-1960s, Vonnegut began to attract some critical attention, but he did not become a well-known author until the publication of *Slaughterhouse-Five* in 1969. His first marriage ended early in the 1970s, and he later married photographer Jill Krementz. The 1970s and 1980s

saw the publication of six more of Vonnegut's novels, including *Breakfast of Champions* (1973), *Jailbird* (1979), and *Galapagos* (1985). He has also published a book of ''opinions'': *Wampeters, Foma, and Granfalloons* (1974); and two autobiographical books: *Palm Sunday* (1981), and *Fates Worse Than Death* (1991).

The acclaim which met the publication of *Slaughterhouse-Five* led to much public recognition for Vonnegut. He has become an outspoken defender of free speech and an eloquent attacker of censorship. His critical reputation has been uneven, however. While several books devoted to Vonnegut's work were published in the 1970s, Vonnegut's later works have not been as well received by scholars as his earlier novels. Early critical attention tried to determine whether Vonnegut was a satirist, a black humorist, or a science fiction writer; this debate continues. His works are noted for their frank and insightful social criticism, and for their innovative style; they present readers with an idiosyncratic yet compelling vision of modern life.

Plot Summary

''Harrison Bergeron'' is set in the future, when Constitutional Amendments have made everyone equal. The agents of the Handicapper General (H-G men, an allusion to the practice in the 1940s and 1950s of referring to Federal Bureau of Investigation and Secret Service officers as G-men, the G standing for government) enforce the equality laws.

People are made equal by devices which bring them down to the normalcy level in the story, which is actually below-average in intelligence, strength, and ability. These devices include weights to stunt speed and strength; masks, red rubber clown noses, or thick glasses to hide good looks and to make seeing difficult; and radio transmitters implanted in the ears of intelligent people, which emit sharp noises two or three times a minute to prevent sustained thought.

In April, described as ''clammy'' and driving ''people crazy by not being springtime,'' H-G men take Harrison Bergeron—son of George and Hazel Bergeron—to jail on suspicion of plotting to overthrow the government. At the age of fourteen, seven-foot-tall Harrison is a genius and an athlete who bears heavier handicaps and more grotesque masking devices than anyone else. George and

Hazel are watching a dance program on television and discussing George's handicaps, especially the different sounds transmitted to his mental handicap radio and the forty-seven pounds of birdshot in a canvas bag he wears around his neck. As a ''normal'' person who wears no handicaps, Hazel takes interest in the various sounds transmitted through George's radio. She also encourages George to remove a few lead balls from his handicap bag, at least just when he is home from work, to lighten his load. Hazel's suggestion to bend the rules leads George to defend their society and its laws.

A news bulletin announcing Harrison's escape from jail interrupts the dance program, followed soon thereafter by a live shot of Harrison breaking down the television studio door and addressing the dancers, musicians, and audience. He declares himself emperor, proclaiming that everyone must do what he says at once, and further asserts his superiority even with the significant handicaps he bears: ''Even as I stand here—crippled, hobbled, sickened—I am a greater ruler than any man who ever lived! Now watch me become what I can become!'' He tears off his handicaps, chooses one of the ballerinas as his empress, and proceeds, with her, to show people ''the meaning of the word dance.'' In the process, they defy the laws of the land, the laws of gravity, and the laws of motion by leaping high enough to kiss the thirty-foot high ceiling. Remaining suspended in air a few inches below the ceiling, they linger over a long kiss which is interrupted by Handicapper General Diana Moon Glampers, who kills Harrison and the ballerina instantly with a double-blast of her shotgun. Hazel and George witness their son's death, but both forget why they are so sad immediately afterwards. George advises Hazel to forget sad things, and then the sound of a riveting gun in George's ear-radio leads them into a verbal exchange echoing comic lines popularized by comedians George Burns and Gracie Allen, from the closing dialogue of their television show.

Characters

George Bergeron

Harrison's father, George Bergeron, bears multiple government-imposed handicaps which repress his ''way above-normal'' intelligence. He refuses to remove any of them, however, for he believes that any attempt to change the present situation will inevitably cause civilization to regress back into the

Kurt Vonnegut

''dark ages,'' when there was competition. George and Hazel, his wife, witness Harrison's rebellious act on television, but afterwards cannot remember why they are sad. George wears birdshot weights and a mental handicap radio in his ear that receives a ''sharp noise'' transmission designed ''to keep people . . . from taking unfair advantage of their brains.''

Harrison Bergeron

Although he is only fourteen years old, the title character, Harrison Bergeron, stands seven feet tall and possesses an intelligence so immense that, at the beginning of the story, the Handicapper General has Harrison arrested ''on suspicion of plotting to overthrow the government.'' Harrison escapes, however, and goes to the television station to publicly declare himself emperor. He selects a ballerina as his empress, and the two begin to dance. ''[N]eutralizing gravity with love and pure will,'' the couple leap high enough to kiss the ceiling and remain suspended in mid air. At that moment, Diana Moon Glampers, the United States Handicapper General, blasts the couple out of the air with a ''double-barreled ten-gauge shotgun,'' ending Harrison's life and his self-declared reign.

Harrison's actions suggest an ironic theme: corruptive power. Upon his escape, Harrison re-

Women rally in support of the Equal Rights Amendment. The issue of equality is the central theme in "Harrison Bergeron."

peats government errors by establishing himself as the sole, nonelected, source of governmental authority. Had his rebellion succeeded, he would have forced people to break the law by making them remove their government-imposed handicaps. That act, according to Harrison's father, George, would send society back to the "dark ages" of social and individual competition.

Hazel Bergeron

Harrison's mother, Hazel Bergeron, does not need to wear any handicaps—mental or physical—as she possesses "normal" intelligence, appearance, and strength. In this story, however, "normal" entails that one is incompetent, or unable to fathom anything beyond that which is superficial. Hazel's dialogue with her husband, George, recalls the comedic team of George Burns and Gracie Allen.

Diana Moon Glampers

Although Diana Moon Glampers, the United States Handicapper General, appears briefly toward the end of the story in order to quell Harrison's rebellion by killing him, her presence pervades the story. As Handicapper General, she ruthlessly maintains law and order without due process. One of the

few descriptions of her implies that Glampers herself is not "above normal."

Themes

Freedom

As a theme, freedom remains in the background of the story, emerging when Harrison escapes from jail. In the story's futuristic society, freedom is no longer a bedrock American value; enforcing the law that makes those who are "above normal" equal to those who are "normal" has become the major social value. Forced equality by handicapping the above-normal individuals evolved as a response to the demonized concept of competition (which existed in "the dark ages") in all its possible forms. Vonnegut suggests that freedom can be taken away relatively easily, especially since the forced equality in the story has been authorized by Amendments to the Constitution.

Civil Rights

Civil rights have become extinct in "Harrison Bergeron." The culture values mediocrity to the point that the people accept oppressive measures in the name of equality. Ironically, no one really benefits from these misguided attempts to enforce equality, except perhaps the incompetent, such as the television announcer who, "like all announcers, had a serious speech impediment." In Hazel's words, the announcer's incompetence should be forgiven because his attempt is "the big thing. He tried to do the best he could with what God gave him. He should get a nice raise for trying so hard." Should anyone in that society dare to become above average, he or she is immediately punished, as is Harrison, who is executed for shunning mediocrity and attempting to excel. By creating a society where the goal of equality has resulted in a grotesque caricature of humanity, Vonnegut implies that individual civil rights should never be sacrificed, not even for the alleged common good.

Knowledge and Ignorance

Everyone above average in any way has been forced by the government to bear a physical handicap that makes him or her "normal." People who are more intelligent or knowledgeable than the average person have had their knowledge subverted by such devices as the mental handicap ear radio. This device emits various noises every twenty seconds or so to prevent people from taking "unfair advantage of their brains." "Normal" in the story can best be described as subnormal, incompetent, and ignorant. Hazel is a case in point; as a normal person, she wears no handicaps, and she has a good heart, yet she knows very little about anything and cannot remember what she just saw or heard a moment ago. At the end of the story, she takes literally George's intensifying statement, "You can say that again," by repeating what she just said. Vonnegut suggests that an authoritarian government thrives on the ignorance of the people and on the suppression of intelligence and knowledge.

Law and Order

In addition to the critique of authoritarian government in the form of the Handicapper General agents (H-G men), Vonnegut discusses the ways in which the Handicapper General uses the fear of competition to make obeying the laws an ethical decision. Hazel feels sorry for George, who has to wear forty-seven pounds of birdshot around his neck, so she invites him to lighten his load. He rejects the idea of cheating (breaking the law) with a recital of the punishment: "two years in prison and two thousand dollars for every [lead birdshot] ball"

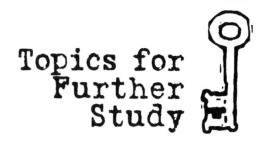

Topics for Further Study

- Research the process by which proposed amendments to the United States Constitution pass Congress and are ratified into law. Based on what you find out, do you think it is likely that the Constitution will have 213 amendments in 2081? Why or why not?

- Investigate the controversy caused by Federal Communications Commission chairman Newton Minow's May, 1961, speech in which he labeled television "a vast wasteland." Compare Minow's historical commentary about television to current commentaries and note how much (or how little) has changed.

- Read the United States' founding documents—particularly the Declaration of Independence, the United States Constitution, or the Federalist Papers—to determine the promise of equality or lack thereof found within them. Compare the ideas found in these documents with those in documents associated with the Civil Rights Movement of the 1950s—particularly the 1954 U. S. Supreme Court decision in *Brown v. Board of Education*—and the early 1960s, particularly Martin Luther King's "Letter from Birmingham Jail" and his 1963 speech known as "I Have a Dream."

taken out. He continues by describing the bandwagon effect: other people would try to break the law if George could do so. He asserts that backsliding would result in a return "to the dark ages, with everybody competing against everybody else." Cheating on laws, George claims (or is about to claim when a siren blast through his mental handicap radio shatters his concentration), would reduce society to chaos. Here, Vonnegut satirizes the fear of change and of uncertainty: victims of the oppressive law want to enforce it rather than take their chances without it.

Strength and Weakness

One of the implied reasons Harrison may want to overthrow the government has to do with strength and weakness. He recognizes the inequality of forcing strong people (those mentally, intellectually, and physically strong) to give up their strength for an orderly society of equal, law-abiding citizens. Of course, the enforcers of the law do not have to submit to forced equality themselves; they have no handicaps, which could signify their inherent mediocrity, as does the implied physical resemblance of Hazel to Diana Moon Glampers, the Handicapper General herself. Vonnegut shows what extraordinary strength can do: defy the laws of gravity and motion. But Vonnegut also shows that strength can be used to oppress the weak, even in the name of protecting the weak against the excesses of the strong.

Ubermensch ("Superman")

The idea of the superhuman materializes in the character of Harrison. Though only fourteen years old, at seven feet tall with a high intellect, he exceeds the physical and intellectual abilities of anyone else in the story. Likewise, his physical appearance, judged by the kinds of handicaps he must wear, suggests an Adonis-like figure. His handicaps include thick, wavy-lens spectacles; a red rubber clown nose; and snaggle-tooth black caps for his teeth. His natural abilities do not make him immortal, however; like other human beings, he can die from an antiquated weapon like the ten-gauge double-barreled shotgun of Diana Moon Glampers. Harrison's attempt to assert his authority neither lasts long nor has any real effect on anyone. Truly befitting the superman concept, he declares himself emperor, "a greater ruler than any man who ever lived" (even with his handicaps). He does not recognize, however, his human flaw: replacing one authoritarian government with another. Like so many other revolutions, Harrison's short-lived attempt to overthrow the ruthless totalitarianism that has become the American government becomes totalitarian itself. Vonnegut suggests that power, whether invested in the government or in the individual figure, corrupts.

American Dream

The American Dream, best described as upward social and economic class mobility through hard work and education has become an American Nightmare in "Harrison Bergeron." No one, except the Handicapper General agents, can achieve upward mobility, either because they bear artificial handicaps or because they are naturally mediocre. In a scheme that brings anyone who is above normal in *any* aspect down to the level of a person who is normal in *all* aspects, no one can dream about moving upward.

Media Influence

Vonnegut suggests the powerful influence of broadcast media in the story. Radio is the medium of the mental handicap noises used to prevent anyone with the ability to think from doing so. But television accomplishes the same thing for normal people like Hazel, who "had a perfectly average intelligence, which meant she couldn't think about anything except in short bursts." This lack of concentration has come to be known as short attention span, or attention deficit disorder. Many critics credit television for the decreasing attention span of the population. They also suggest television programming desensitizes people to real life, in part because it requires nothing of the viewer. Significantly, approximately five months before publication of the story in 1961, Newton Minow, new chair of the Federal Communications Commission (a government agency that regulates broadcast media), called television a "vast wasteland" of mediocrity in programming. Vonnegut suggests the importance of television as a means of controlling information by having Harrison Bergeron take over the television studio and proclaim himself emperor. Vonnegut also shows the numbing influence of television by having Hazel forget what she has seen—her son's killing—even though she reacts by recognizing that something sad has happened.

Style

Setting

Setting the story 120 years in the future allows readers to more easily accept some of the more absurd events in "Harrison Bergeron." The actual physical location of the story does not matter and, therefore, is unknown. One glaring *anachronism*—a concept or an object not known or invented at the time of the story; or an object that belongs to a previous era—should be noted: the use of a shotgun. Readers might expect that some exotic form of weaponry would have been developed and used that far into the future. Similarly, the idea that 213 Amendments to the Constitution would have been ratified predicts a radical change in American legislation. At the time the story was written, only twenty-four amendments had been passed by the Congress and ratified by the states, the first ten of which (known as the Bill of Rights) became law in 1791. In the 170 years between 1791 and the time the story was written, only fourteen additional amendments had been ratified. Ironically, the 211th, 212th, and 213th Amendments of the story restrict the civil rights of most people, as opposed to the amendments over the first two hundred years of the nation.

Point of View

The story is told in the third-person-limited point of view; the narrator is not a character in the story, but he is privy to the thoughts of one character. Readers are allowed to know what George Bergeron is thinking, as when he ''was toying with the vague notion that maybe dancers shouldn't be handicapped.'' The events in ''Harrison Bergeron'' are related by an objective narrator. The narrator does not draw conclusions, make decisions, or make judgments about the events. The objectivity of the narrator suggests a distancing from the hostile world of the story.

Satire and Black Humor

The story uses satire and a kind of humor known as black humor. The humor mostly involves George and Hazel, although the appearance of Harrison (red rubber nose, artificially snaggle-toothed, three hundred pounds of handicaps) can be seen as comical. George and Hazel's dialogue at the end of the story alludes to comics George Burns and Gracie Allen, who had a popular television show in the late 1950s and early 1960s. At the end of each show, George and Gracie performed a stand-up routine related to that night's episode. Often, George would say to Gracie, ''You can say that again,'' and she would reply the same way Hazel replies to George Bergeron: She would literally repeat what she had just said. Gracie Allen's comic persona mirrors Hazel's persona; both seem somewhat scatterbrained. The humorous dialogue between Hazel and George Bergeron could be considered black humor, which has proved difficult to define. Related to both sick humor (making fun of, say, a person's disability) and gallows humor (people laughing in the midst of helplessness), as well as the absurd (so far-fetched as to be nearly implausible), black humor can incorporate all of these characteristics. It can be defined as the juxtaposition of pain and laughter, unusual fact and calmly inadequate reactions, and cruelty and tenderness. The ending dialogue between Hazel and George juxtaposes all three of those pairs, as Hazel and George have just witnessed the killing of their son. Satire, ridiculing a person, place, or idea with the notion of effecting change, always involves morality. Here, Vonnegut satirizes the notion of handicapping people to enforce equality, the failure of rebellion, the apathy engendered in people who watch television, and authoritarian government. As Conrad Festa claims in *Vonnegut in America,*

> Stories such as ''Harrison Bergeron'' . . . fit easily and recognizably into the satiric genre. That is, they (1) sustain a reductive attack on their objects, (2) convey to their intended readers significances at odds with the literal or surface meanings, and (3) are pervaded and dominated by various satiric techniques.

Allusion

Vonnegut uses several allusions—references to people, historical events, and other literature outside the text—in ''Harrison Bergeron.'' The month of April, which ''still drove people crazy by not being springtime,'' is doubly allusive, initially referring to the first line of T. S. Eliot's 1922 poem, *The Waste Land* : ''April is the cruelest month. . . .'' The second allusion derived from April stems from the first: the title of the poem also serves in part as the title of a 1961 speech by then Federal Communications Commission Chair Newton Minow, referring to television as ''a vast wasteland.'' The abbreviation of the Handicapper-General agents, ''H-G men,'' ironically alludes to the abbreviation ''G-men'' (for government agents; i.e., Secret Service agents, FBI agents). Generally, these government agents were held in high esteem, unlike the H-G men, until the 1960s and 1970s, when their activities came into legal and ethical question. The allusion of Diana Moon, the Handicapper General's first and middle names, refers to the Roman goddess of the hunt, Diana, who is associated with the moon. Diana was known for her vengeance, which could explain the ruthless killing of Harrison Bergeron in the story. Thor, identified in the story as the god of thunder, was, in Norse mythology, the oldest and most powerful son of Odin, king of the gods. He possessed great strength and skill in fighting. This allusion serves to underscore Harrison's strength without his handicaps. There is an indirect reference to cartoonist Rube Goldberg, which highlights the absurdity of the handicapping technology, especially for such a futuristic story. Rube Goldberg's cartoons generally depicted elaborate schemes to accomplish the simplest tasks. For instance, instead of an alarm clock, Goldberg might construct a chain of events from the sun reflecting light onto a bird, which might then peck at a string, which would then release a bowling ball that would trip a lever, opening a door to a rooster cage, allowing the rooster to emerge and signal an alarm with his crowing. The more complex these mechanisms are, the funnier. Thus, the various handicaps described in the story seem much like Rube Goldberg cartoons, and seem humorous to readers who recognize the allusion. The final allusion is to the comedy team of George Burns and Gracie Allen, and to their television show. The dialogue at the end of the story reflects similar dialogues at the end of the "Burns and Allen" television show. Gracie, who played a scatterbrain, would indeed repeat lines when George used the phrase, "You can say that again," just as Hazel Bergeron does in the story. Television's role in the story is to numb, desensitize, or otherwise occupy the time of citizens, and to prevent sustained thought on the part of those of normal intelligence.

Historical Context

The Modern Civil Rights Movement

In the late 1940s progress, albeit in fits and starts, began to occur in the movement toward full civil rights for African Americans in the United States. Beginning with Jackie Robinson, major league baseball began the process of integration, as did the military in the late 1940s. In the 1954 case known as *Brown v. Board of Education of Topeka,* the United States Supreme Court decided that the doctrine of "separate but equal" facilities set forth in the 1896 *Plessy v. Ferguson* case no longer held true. A year later, the Supreme Court ordered lower courts to use "all deliberate speed" in desegregating the public schools. In the Deep South, governors, state legislatures, and local school boards resisted, in some cases passing laws to try to thwart the ruling. In addition to the landmark Supreme Court ruling, an African-American woman named Rosa Parks refused to give up her seat in the front of a Montgomery, Alabama, bus to sit in the back as a local ordinance required. Her subsequent arrest led to a boycott of downtown businesses by African Americans. It also gave the Reverend Martin Luther King, Jr., an opportunity to begin his crusade for civil rights long denied African Americans in the South. In September, 1957, President Dwight Eisenhower had to call out the Arkansas National Guard, as well as regular Army troops, to enforce desegregation of Little Rock, Arkansas, schools. In February, 1960, four African-American students began what became known as "sit-ins" when they sat down at a

lunch counter for whites only in Greensboro, North Carolina. Sit-ins became a standard tactic in the civil rights movement, as was also true of the "Freedom Rides" (busloads of whites and African Americans who came to the South to help support voter registration drives and other civil rights activities) which began in 1961, the year "Harrison Bergeron" was published. Also in 1960, the U. S. Congress passed another civil rights act that allowed federal authorities to ensure that states allowed African Americans the unfettered right to register to vote. Even though the civil rights movement does not specifically relate to "Harrison Bergeron," it stands in the background as being one of the compelling public issues of the time. Vonnegut's use of the issue of equality in the story ignores the racial context on the surface, but it clearly invokes the fears of many, mostly white citizens who feared the federal government would in some way propose schemes that would enforce equality of outcome. Many apparently felt that desegregating the public schools and other facilities amounted to the same kind of tyranny exposed in the story.

The Cold War and Communism

The kind of government authority seen in "Harrison Bergeron" both mimics and satirizes the way Americans came to see the enemy—socialism/communism and, specifically, the Soviet Union (USSR)—during the Cold War, which was near its height of distrust and fear in the late 1950s and early 1960s. Schools in different states introduced courses such as Communism vs. Americanism during the 1950s to wage the propaganda war at home. The fear of nuclear war led thousands of Americans to build bomb shelters in their backyards. Following Soviet Premier Nikita Khrushchev's promise to "bury" the United States in the late 1950s, significant fear of an authoritarian government taking over the so-called free world intensified in America. Communism as practiced in the USSR and in China meant a tyrannical rule without due process of law enforced by secret police and informers, similar to the way the United States is portrayed in the story. Making the fear more ominous and close to home was Fidel Castro's successful rebellion in Cuba, ending in 1959. By the middle of 1960, Americans realized that Castro was building a socialist state allied with and supported by the USSR. An attempt by the Soviet Union to station missiles in Cuba led to the Cuban Missile Crisis in 1962. Trade sanctions against Cuba began in 1960 and continue in the late 1990s. The paranoid climate caused by the establishment of a communist government a mere ninety miles

Compare & Contrast

- **1964:** President Lyndon B. Johnson signs the Civil Rights Act of 1964 into law. Title VII of the Act establishes The Equal Employment Opportunities Commission, which prohibits discrimination in employment on the basis of race, sex, national origin, and religion.

  Late 1990s: Affirmative action programs, which set guidelines for preferred hiring of minority and women workers and students, come under fire. Businesses and universities are sued for reverse discrimination by whites passed over for various positions and promotions.

- **1950s:** The CIA experiments with various forms of mind control, including testing LSD, a hallucinogen, as a truth serum on U.S. soldiers.

  1993: Rumors surface that the FBI is considering using an acoustic mind control device during

  a standoff with cult leader David Koresh in Waco, Texas. The device, developed by a Russian scientist, is supposedly capable of placing thoughts in a person's mind without the person's knowledge of the source of the thoughts.

- **1960s:** Young people unite in unprecedented numbers to protest the Vietnam War, racism, and sexual discrimination. Vonnegut's writings become very popular in this politically active era.

  1990s: "Hate crime" legislation provides stiffer penalties for those convicted of harassment and other crimes directed at people based on their ethnicity, sexual orientation, and physical or mental disabilities. Critics say the laws criminalize thought rather than action, and that punishment varies according to the characteristics of the victim.

---

from the United States sent many citizens into panic. Vonnegut recognized that the way communism was practiced led to the failure of its basic promise of providing a workers' paradise of equality in a classless society.

Television and American Culture

One of the few scholarly mentions of "Harrison Bergeron" occurs in Robert Uphaus's essay, "Expected Meanings in Vonnegut's Dead-End Fiction." Uphaus identifies the basis of the catastrophe known as the United States government in 2081: television. He asserts, "The history of mankind, Vonnegut implies in the story, is a history of progressive desensitization partly spurred on by the advent of television." Coincidentally, then newly appointed chair of the Federal Communications Commission, Newton Minow, delivered an attack on television five months before "Harrison Bergeron" was published. In the speech, Minow called television "a vast wasteland" of destructive or meaningless programs. Minow claimed that instead of challenging people to think, television programming

was making it easier for people to avoid serious thought. The story clearly uses television as a time filler, a method of preventing average people from thinking, similar to Minow's description. Hazel Bergeron best illustrates this point. Although of "perfectly average intelligence," she has such a short attention span that she is prevented from remembering why she cries at "Something real sad [she saw] on television": the murder of her son, Harrison. While Vonnegut aims his satiric barbs at overreaching, authoritarian government, television equally bears the brunt of his attack for its role in the erosion of thought. Vonnegut suggests that television serves the same purpose for normal people that the mental handicap radios serve for those above normal in intelligence.

World War II

Vonnegut's skepticism of government power and of scientific solutions to problems comes from his experiences in World War II. Specifically, he was disillusioned by the lies told in the name of winning the war and by the mass destruction caused by application of scientific discoveries to weaponry. As a prisoner of war, Vonnegut survived the Allied bombing raids on Dresden, Germany, in February, 1945. There, over 135,000 people—mostly civilians—died from the bombing, more than the total killed by both atomic bombs dropped on Hiroshima and Nagasaki, Japan, later that year. Vonnegut has recounted this story in various places, most notably his 1969 novel *Slaughterhouse-Five, or the Children's Crusade.* In his 1991 autobiographical collage, *Fates Worse Than Death,* Vonnegut reprints a directory carried aboard British and American bombers in World War II showing "there wasn't much in the Dresden area worth bombing out of business according to our Intelligence experts." The reason Vonnegut harps on this issue is that the Dresden raids were kept secret from the public for almost twenty years, and then were defended by the claim that Dresden contained targets of military importance. He notes that this act and the subsequent secrecy disillusioned him about his government. This realization that the government can and does lie to its citizens, for ill or for good, serves as the premise for distrust of government power in "Harrison Bergeron."

Critical Overview

The first critical responses to "Harrison Bergeron" did not appear until 1968, when the story was reprinted in Vonnegut's collection *Welcome to the Monkey House.* Many reviewers, like Larry L. King in *New York Times Book Review,* who called the collection "old soup," were decidedly unenthusiastic. Some of the stories had already been published in an earlier collection titled *Canary in a Cat House* (1961), and others had been first published in commercial, "slick" magazines, thus bringing into question their literary value. Criticizing "Harrison Bergeron," King claimed, "I know nothing of Mr. Vonnegut's personal politics, but extant Goldwaterites or Dixiecrats might read into this the ultimate horrors of any further extension of civil-rights or equal-opportunity laws." The term *Goldwaterites* refers to admirers of former Arizona Senator Barry Goldwater, the 1964 Republican candidate for President, who was known as "Mr. Conservative." The term *Dixiecrats* refers to white Southerners who stood strongly (and sometimes violently) against extending civil rights to African Americans throughout the 1950s and 1960s. In fact, by the time of King's review, political conservatives who stood

against federal government civil rights laws had already appropriated the story for William F. Buckley's *National Review* magazine (November 16, 1965). King's early review identified what has become one of the most controversial aspects of the story: how the story can easily be read as a criticism of measures advocated by minorities and women to ensure equality. Vonnegut pokes fun at the absurd and extreme steps taken to ensure equality in the futuristic society, with cumbersome low-technology handicaps forced on above-average citizens upon pain of severe punishment. "Harrison Bergeron" has been used more recently to illustrate the conflict between the American political ideology of equality and the practice of discrimination based on superficial traits such as race and gender. In 1982 political conservatives again used "Harrison Bergeron" to oppose affirmative action and other social programs: a book published by Canada's Fraser Institute in 1982, *Discrimination, Affirmative Action, and Equal Opportunity: An Economic and Social Perspective,* used the story as the title for its last chapter.

Some early reviewers of *Welcome to the Monkey House,* such as Charles Nicol in the *Atlantic Monthly* and Michael Levitas in the *New York Times,* ignored "Harrison Bergeron." Other critics, such as Gerard Reedy in *America,* focused on the title character as an "all-American boy," and compared Vonnegut's character to similar characters created by other contemporary authors such as John Updike and Philip Roth. Reedy found that Vonnegut, in contrast to the other authors, was "not as serious" in his "satire of American types," and "[a] social critic only by indirection." Levitas's review, like King's, focused on the recycled nature of the commercial stories. Quoting Vonnegut's own introduction, in which he commented, "Here one finds the fruits of Free Enterprise," Levitas paraphrased Lamont Cranston (the original title character of the radio show *The Shadow*) by claiming "the seeds of Free Enterprise bear bitter fruit." Charles Nicol at least mentioned "Vonnegut's special enemies," some of which surface as themes in "Harrison Bergeron": "science, morality, free enterprise, socialism, fascism, Communism, any force in our lives which regards human beings as ciphers."

The story's outward focus on the idea of equality forced by law has made it a popular choice for high school and college literature anthologies, even though the story itself has received little scholarly attention. Vonnegut's literary reputation rests more on his novels than on his short fiction, and Vonnegut himself has said he wrote stories to earn money so could work on his novels. Many reviewers of *Welcome to the Monkey House* agree with Vonnegut's apparent devaluation of the stories.

Criticism

Joseph Alvarez

Alvarez is an instructor in the English and Foreign Languages department at Central Piedmont Community College in North Carolina. In the following essay, he discusses "Harrison Bergeron" in light of Vonnegut's own beliefs about conditions in society.

In his *Fates Worse Than Death: An Autobiographical Collage of the 1980s* Kurt Vonnegut reflected on a 1983 speech he gave at the Cathedral of St. John the Divine in New York City:

> American TV, operating in the Free Market of Ideas . . . was holding audiences with simulations of one of the two things most human beings, and especially young ones, can't help watching when given the opportunity: murder. TV, and of course movies, too, were and still are making us as callous about killing and death as Hitler's propaganda made the German people during the frenzied prelude to the death camps and World War II. . . . What I should have said from the pulpit was that we weren't *going* to Hell. We were *in* Hell, thanks to technology which was telling us what to do, instead of the other way around. And it wasn't just TV.

With these words, Vonnegut reminds us of his 1961 story "Harrison Bergeron," particularly its use of television, which desensitized Hazel Bergeron, Harrison's mother, to the murder of her own son, which she witnesses while watching television. True, she sheds tears over what she sees, but she has become so numbed by watching television that she cannot remember why she is crying. Robert Uphaus, in his 1975 essay, "Expected Meaning in Vonnegut's Dead-End Fiction," pointed out that "The history of mankind, Vonnegut implies in the story, is a history of progressive desensitization partly spurred on by the advent of television."

No doubt, Vonnegut—either while writing the story or after sending it for publication—heard about Newton Minow's famous 1961 speech about television programming, called "The Vast Wasteland" [Reprinted in *The Annals of America, Vol. 18, 1961-1968: The Burdens of World Power*]. Minow specifically mentioned violence as a contributor to

this wasteland when he listed what a viewer of television would see in a typical day:

> game shows, violence, audience participation shows, formula comedies about totally unbelievable families, blood and thunder, mayhem, violence, sadism, murder, Western bad men, Western good men, private eyes, gangsters, more violence and cartoons. And, endlessly, commercials—many screaming, cajoling, and offending. And, most of all, boredom.

Near the end of the speech, talking about programming, Minow pleaded for "imagination . . . not sterility; creativity, not imitation; experimentation, not conformity; excellence, not mediocrity." He added, "The power of instantaneous sight and sound is without precedent in mankind's history. This is an awesome power. It has limitless capabilities for good—and for evil."

In "Harrison Bergeron," Vonnegut uses some of the same ideas when he portrays television as a kind of desensitizing, numbing, and clearly thought-stifling, rather than thought-provoking, medium. When Harrison goes not to the seat of government to start his revolution but instead to the television station, Vonnegut illustrates that "awesome power" Minow describes in his speech. Harrison's power to reach the people and make a new reality (declaring himself emperor), Vonnegut agrees, stems from controlling television. Clearly, the government, in the form of the Handicapper General, also understands that power.

While it would be facile to blame television completely for the condition of society in the story, the negative consequences of television, such as encouraging people to not think, form a basis for the rest of the story. The ratification of ludicrously absurd amendments to the constitution requiring a "Big Sister" (United States Handicapper General, Diana Moon Glampers) to monitor the population vigilantly for compliance, effectively creating a police state which ruthlessly enforces the laws, probably results from an uninformed and frightened population. We could see television as a first cause, even though several other causes for the social and political setting of the story likely contributed directly to the ignorance and fear. These causes include an absurd extension of efforts to ensure equality of opportunity to various people formerly excluded from such opportunity either by law or by custom. In other words, sincere efforts to promote equal opportunity by otherwise well-intentioned people could serve as a different kind of opportunity, one that unprincipled politicians or power brokers could exploit by making the victims into the criminals, or

What Do I Read Next?

- *The New Atlantis,* Francis Bacon's 1627 version of utopia (an idealized community or state). Bacon conceived of a community of scholars and scientists who rule for the benefit of each other and mankind.

- *Brave New World,* Aldous Huxley's 1932 novel. In this dystopian (from dystopia, the opposite of utopia, a world in which realities undermine ideals), satirical portrait of a futuristic society, citizens have given up much of their own humanity for the social good in another totalitarian political system.

- "I Have a Dream," Martin Luther King's 1963 speech. King delivered this famous speech on the steps of the Lincoln Memorial in Washington, D.C., to a crowd of civil rights demonstrators. It called for a society in which people have equal opportunity and are judged not by the color of their skin but by the content of their character.

- "The Ones Who Walk Away from Omelas," Ursula K. Leguin's 1973 story. In this vaguely futuristic society, the good of the community, including everything from personal happiness to bountiful crops, depends on the severe maltreatment of one child, a scapegoat. Without the scapegoat, the citizens of Omelas believe their whole society would fall apart. The title characters who leave cannot stand to base their happiness on the suffering of another person, especially a child.

- "The Vast Wasteland," Newton Minow's 1961 speech. In this speech the new Chair of the Federal Communications Commission indicted television for its lack of quality programming, calling television broadcasting a "vast wasteland."

- *Utopia,* Thomas More's 1516 imagined definition of an ideal society. This idealistic utopian look at society employs the idea of communitarianism, a sense of equality throughout social strata, based on Christian humanism and on an economic scheme that increased productivity.

- *Animal Farm,* George Orwell's 1945 novel. This dystopian satire of an alleged egalitarian society clearly reveals the flaws of the ideal of equality compared to the difficulty of enacting the ideal as reality. A bigger target is totalitarian government disguised as egalitarianism, specifically Stalin's regime in the USSR.

- *1984,* George Orwell's 1949 novel. This dystopian satire of totalitarian government does not allow human emotions, such as love; nor does it allow privacy (Big Brother is always watching through television cameras/screens everywhere). The government also distorts truth through the use of "Newspeak."

- *The Republic,* Plato's 380 B.C. imaginative definition of an ideal political society. One of the first of the literary utopias, Plato's version describes a select elite, who control the actions of the rest of the people, and who depend on slave labor.

- "Resistance to Civil Government" (or "Civil Disobedience"), Henry David Thoreau's 1849 essay. Thoreau asserts that a citizen must break unjust laws in order to change them. He suggests that a single individual constitutes a "majority of one" if this individual is more right than his neighbors, and judges law on morality, not expediency.

---

into socially unacceptable monsters to be feared by the rest of the population. Another contributory cause points to excesses of unbridled and unethical competition, a kind of social Darwinism.

Most readers of "Harrison Bergeron" fasten on the first paragraph's announcement that everybody was "equal every which way," which piques interest since perceptive readers know that people, in fact, are unequal. The story quickly clarifies both the origin of this equality (Amendments to the Constitution) and the ways people have become "equal": everybody above normal in any way has been required to bear handicaps of astonishingly low technology for such a futuristic story. If one is physically strong, he or she must wear weights to negate that strength. If one is intelligent, he or she must wear a mental handicap radio that emits a "sharp noise" (for example, an auto collision, a siren, a twenty-one gun salute) three times a minute. If one is physically attractive, he or she must wear a mask or some other disfiguring apparatus (for Harrison, a red rubber nose, black caps on his teeth at "snaggle-tooth random," and shaved-off eyebrows hinder his good looks). Perceptive readers see through this illusion: if everyone were equal in every which way, the various handicaps would not be necessary. Conversely, the story remains silent about the fate of those unfortunates who fall below normal. No attempt is made to elevate them to normal or average surfaces, nor is an attempt in the near future. As Martha Meek pointed out in *Critical Survey of Short Fiction* (1993), "The reader is suddenly aware that the idea of equality has been made an instrument of social control" after Diana Moon Glampers kills Harrison. Readers also respond incredulously by asking how something like this scheme could happen in America. Vonnegut answered this question in a 1973 address to the international writers' organization P. E. N: "If tyranny comes to my country, which is an old one now, (and tyranny can come anywhere, anytime, as nearly as I can tell), I expect to go on writing whatever I please . . . as long as what I write is fiction." That same year, speaking at the dedication of the Wheaton (Illinois) College library, he defined a library as "the memory of mankind. It reminds us that all human beings are to a certain extent impure. To put it another way: All human beings are to some extent greedy and cruel" (both speeches are reprinted in *Wampeters, Foma, & Granfalloons*). In 1979, speaking about Mark Twain's *A Connecticut Yankee in King Arthur's Court* at the one-hundredth anniversary of the completion of Twain's house in Connecticut, Vonnegut went further: "I suggest to you that the fatal premise of *A Connecticut Yankee* remains a chief premise of Western civilization . . . to wit: the sanest, most likeable persons, employing superior technology, will enforce sanity throughout the world" (reprint-

> "In 'Harrison Bergeron,' a twenty-first century America enacts Amendments to the Constitution that scapegoat or demonize inequality, regardless of its origin."

ed in *Palm Sunday*). We could argue that Vonnegut uses ironic inversion in "Harrison Bergeron"; insane persons enforce the insanity described as equality in the story.

Vonnegut's reference to Adolf Hitler in the speech at St. John's ironically uses a twentieth-century instance of elected officials gradually turning a nation into a tyrannical dictatorship, in part by scapegoating and demonizing the Jews. In "Harrison Bergeron," a twenty-first century America enacts Amendments to the Constitution that scapegoat or demonize inequality, regardless of its origin. Americans, in general, do not want to admit that such a government could be in power. But Vonnegut has spoken, indirectly, about this aspect of the story. In a graduation speech at the University of Rhode Island in 1990, titled "Do Not Be Cynical about the American Experiment, Since It Has Only Now Begun," (reprinted in *Fates Worse Than Death*) he avowed, "The most extraordinary change in this country since I was a boy is the decline of racism. Believe me, it could very easily be brought back to full strength again by demagogues." Ironically, Vonnegut adds that the minorities, "with guts and great dignity . . . coupled with the promises of the Bill of Rights of the Constitution," brought about the change in racist attitudes.

Lest readers think that Vonnegut endorses by satire a continuation of the *status quo ante* (or current conditions) in relation to equality, that is, legal and customary inequality, he has commented publicly that he learned social equality through his attendance at public schools of Indianapolis. Later in life, he endorsed legal equal opportunity on at least two different occasions. In the University of Rhode Island graduation address, Vonnegut talked about slavery as a social disease unrecognized for the first one hundred years of American history.

Toward the end of the speech, after criticizing Thomas Jefferson and other slave owners who proclaimed America as a beacon of liberty, he declared, ''only in my lifetime has there been any serious talk of giving women and racial minorities anything like economic, legal, and social equality. Let liberty be born at last.'' Vonnegut leaves little doubt about his stance on this issue. Earlier, in a 1988 piece for *Lear's* magazine, he wrote, ''But I find uncritical respect for most works by great thinkers of long ago unpleasant, because they almost all accepted as natural and ordinary the belief that females and minority races and the poor were on earth to be uncomplaining, hardworking, respectful, and loyal servants of white males.'' In that same piece, he mentions going to a luncheon for a Soviet film makers' union official and talking about *glasnost* (the term for attempts made in the Soviet Union to openly discuss their social problems, a practice which had been taboo since the 1920s). He added, ''Our country has a *glasnost* experiment going on, too, of course. It consists of making women and racial minorities the equals of white males, in terms of both the civility and respect to be accorded them and their rights under the law.''

And what of the ''dark ages'' of unbridled competition? Does Vonnegut agree that competition should be retired in the name and practice of total equality? In various interviews and other nonfiction writing, Vonnegut has shown a disdain for social Darwinism, the theory that individuals or groups achieve advantage over others as the result of genetic or biological superiority. Darwin's theory, in shorthand, survival of the fittest, says that species (not individuals or social groups) adapt to their environment and evolve in order to survive. Those species which do not adapt and evolve become extinct. Social Darwinism says, in essence, that only the best people deserve to survive and thrive. In the 1973 *Playboy* magazine interview, Vonnegut sharply rebukes social Darwinism:

> I'm not very grateful for Darwin, although I suspect he was right. His ideas make people crueler. Darwinism says to them that people who get sick deserve to be sick, that people who are in trouble must deserve to be in trouble. When anybody dies, cruel Darwinists imagine we're obviously improving ourselves in some way. And any man who's on top is there because he's a superior animal. That's the social Darwinism of the last century, and it continues to boom.

So, Vonnegut clearly decries the kind of competition related to social Darwinism. Vonnegut has championed a free market of ideas and has fought censorship against his own books, and for writers in other countries whose works are suppressed by their governments. As a writer competing in the marketplace of ideas, he has done fairly well, even though he does not believe he has received fair critical treatment during his later years. In essence, he has complained that critics expect writers always to write their best; they cannot be allowed to write a bad or even mediocre book.

Kurt Vonnegut gives the reader of ''Harrison Bergeron'' a futuristic United States of America in which minds have been so softened or desensitized by television and other forces (fear of enemies) that the people give up their individual rights and aspirations, presumably for the good of the whole society. Sadly, this sacrifice of the individual to the good of society does not improve conditions for the above average, the average, or the below average citizens (who seem to have disappeared, perhaps eliminated?). Instead, in the resulting power vacuum, a ruthless central government created by legislation controls people's lives, which have become as meaningless as if they were machines or automatons. As Stanley Schatt claims in *Kurt Vonnegut, Jr.,* ''what really is lost'' in such a process ''is beauty, grace, and wisdom.''

Source: Joseph Alvarez, ''An Overview of 'Harrison Bergeron','' in *Short Stories for Students,* The Gale Group, 1999.

Carl Mowery

Mowery has taught at Southern Illinois University and Murray State University. In the following essay, he explores the ways Vonnegut uses satire to attack the idea of forced equality.

Kurt Vonnegut is a contemporary American writer best known for his satirical novels. His experiences during World War II, and then as an employee at General Electric, caused him to question many of the power structures in the United States: the government, corporations, the military, and bureaucracies in general. He was most concerned with situations in which the individual was a victim of oppression, and any society that reduced the individual to a mere number, or that limited the individual's opportunities to improve. Vonnegut did not believe that everyone could be better, but that everyone should have the opportunity to try. Therefore, he reacted against any form of suppression that prevented anyone from trying.

As he began his writing career, he might have taken one of two approaches to bring these concerns to the public. He could have chosen to be didactic, lecturing on the ills of society, preaching sermons or writing editorials for newspapers. Instead, he chose another route as his mode of expression: satire.

Satire is a special form of literature that seeks to expose foolish ideas and customs in a society. Satire does not lecture; instead, it exaggerates a part of society and lets the readers decide what to do about it, if anything. Most of the time, satire is witty; sometimes it is subtle; at other times it is blunt. In any case, the satiric writer's task is to ridicule an object, an idea, or a custom, in order to show what the writer thinks is wrong with it. Even though the satire may seem silly or ridiculous, it is not frivolous. The short story, ''Harrison Bergeron,'' may look inconsequential, but Vonnegut's real point is a serious attack on the idea of enforced equality.

Some of the world's best authors were satirists: Shakespeare, Jonathan Swift, George Orwell, Mark Twain. Many current TV hit shows are satiric: Saturday Night Live, The Simpsons, Wayans Brothers, and Mark Russell's PBS Specials. Editorial cartoons are also fine examples of satire. All of these have a common purpose: to expose the weaknesses of some part of society in amusing ways.

The Declaration of Independence says, ''All men are created equal.'' But what happens if a government or some other power takes that notion literally? Can everyone really be equal to everyone else? Does the idea of ''a level playing field'' mean that everyone gets to win, or that no one wins? Kurt Vonnegut has described this kind of society in ''Harrison Bergeron.'' It was first published in 1961 in *Fantasy and Science Fiction Magazine* and later included in his collection of short stories *Welcome to the Monkey House,* published in 1968.

As a satirist, Kurt Vonnegut's job is to develop and extend his observations to their most extreme or absurd conclusions, to attack a target and turn it upside down and, as Northrop Frye says [in *University of Toronto Quarterly*], to ''complete the process known as *reductio ad absurdum*'' (to reduce to absurdity). In the late 1950s, Vonnegut saw countries like the USSR espousing a society with no class distinctions. In ''Harrison Bergeron,'' he creates a society, seemingly American, whose government has gone awry in its attempts to make everyone equal. Some citizens carry extra weights, wear ugly masks, or listen to loud noises in order to ensure that no one can get ahead of anyone else. Therefore, all people are ''equal.'' Even in 1990s some groups and countries still try to equalize everyone. Some religious cults require members to

> " At the end of the story, Kurt Vonnegut implies that there is no government capable of suppressing the individual completely. The inner strength of human nature at its finest is more powerful than ill-conceived laws, and the H-G's rules and guns. However, he leaves unsaid whether or not standing up to an oppressive government is worth losing one's life."

wear similar clothes; the people in power in China often appear in public wearing the same drab clothing.

Vonnegut saw evidence of forced equality around him and believed that it was not good for a country, and certainly not good for an individual. In ''Harrison Bergeron,'' the individual is reduced to a common norm: ''they were equal every which way.'' These equalities were determined and enforced by the Handicapper General. Notice, in the story everyone is lowered to meet the H-G's standard, not raised to meet a higher standard. It is ironic that there are no restrictions on the H-G nor on the H-G's operatives. Similarly, in Orwell's *Animal Farm,* the pigs said, ''All animals are equal, but some animals are more equal than others.'' In ''Harrison Bergeron,'' to keep George from being ''more equal'' than anyone else, he is required to wear an ear piece to keep him from developing sequential thoughts. He also wears added weights to keep him from being above average in his physical abilities. This is similar to some horse races that make older horses carry more weight than younger horses. These provisions are intended to make the races more competitive, or more equal.

George and Hazel's son, Harrison, is a special case. He is much more intelligent, more physically capable, and better looking than the rest of society, and even though he is only 14, he is imprisoned as a threat. But he breaks out, removes his handicaps, and, for a brief moment, shows his individuality. He calls on a dancer to join him, and together they soar. Since no one is allowed to look more beautiful or be more physically adept than someone else, or to think new thoughts, the H-G enters and literally shoots down Harrison and the dancer, on live TV. According to Stanley Schatt [in *Kurt Vonnegut, Jr.*], when the H-G kills Harrison and the Empress, their deaths are symbolic of the death of ''beauty, grace, and wisdom,'' the three characteristics that are the object of the H-G's control over society.

The Handicapper General then threatens the musicians with death unless they return to their ''normal'' handicapped status. The 2081 society's norm is enforced by violence and through the threat of violence. In the story, Vonnegut does not specifically ask the reader to agree or disagree with the point that equality through violence is not equality at all. The reader must come to his or her own conclusion.

For satire to succeed, the characters must be believable. Even though the characters may be the victims of silliness, oppression, or some other indignity, the reader must be able to identify with them in some manner. If they are not believable, then the satire will fail.

And Vonnegut is a master of satire. In ''Harrison Bergeron,'' the simple folksy dialogue between George and Hazel is especially effective. In these exchanges, Vonnegut lets his characters say things in understated ways, for example: ''That was a doozy.'' Or, after George winces at another sound in his ear, and Hazel asks what the sound was like, he says, ''Sounded like somebody hitting a milk bottle with a ball peen hammer.'' These quiet conversations are simple and believable, in direct contrast to the noise blasting away every 20 seconds. Vonnegut does not have to say that this is absurd; the reader can feel this without having it pointed out.

It is important to note that in Kurt Vonnegut's satire, most of the characters are sympathetic and likable, even though what is done to them is not. Hazel and George are symbols of good people. They obey the laws and they try to live their ''equal'' lives without complaining. Hazel is a quiet, docile woman, who meets the criteria set by the H-G for equality without any added handicaps. Despite her ''perfectly average intelligence'' and physical attributes, she reveals an innate individu-

ality. She believes that the TV announcer ought to get a raise ''because he tried to do the best he could.''

However, the most revealing part of her comment is the conclusion: ''. . . with what God gave him.'' In this society, it is the H-G's job to neutralize the natural attributes that every citizen was given by God. Here, Hazel reveals her appreciation for the individuality of others. She also shows a religious appreciation that seems to be missing elsewhere in the society. She would ''have chimes on Sunday— just chimes. Kind of in honor of religion'' transmitted through the ear radio. Her intentions to honor religion and to revere God for giving the announcer his talents, reveal her religious leanings.

Hazel also shows an empathy towards others' misfortunes, as we see in the very last scene. Even though she does not remember that her son had just been killed, she still cries about ''something real sad on television.'' Hazel's feelings ought to be a continued, placid satisfaction that all is well. But deep within her the sympathetic individual cannot be stifled.

Her husband, George, is a thinker and has physical attributes that the H-G has decided to ''equalize.'' But even in the face of governmental oppression, George has thoughts that are above average. These are interrupted by the noises in his ear, but they occur anyway. He thinks that the ballerinas ought not be carrying weights around their necks. George also shows a sympathetic side when he asks Hazel what she was crying about. George is a practical man, who would rather endure the indignity of his ''handicaps'' than suffer the consequences of tampering with them. He has adapted to the weights. ''I don't notice it any more. It's just a part of me.'' He accepts the laws.

An interesting aspect of George's character is his memory. His short-term memory is disrupted every twenty seconds. ''If Hazel hadn't been able to come up with an answer to this question, George couldn't have supplied one. A siren was going off in his head.'' He forgot his question. But as he watched TV, his long-term memory told him that Harrison was the cause of the shaking when ''he correctly identified the earthquake,'' caused by Harrison's footsteps. But George is unable to maintain the connection between these two memory patterns. Therefore he remains content to endure the H-G's treatments.

Harrison shows us that the individual can overcome the oppression of the Handicapper General. He is arrested for his exuberant individuality. He is good looking, an athlete, and a genius: the "beauty, grace and wisdom" described by Schatt. His crime is a conspiracy to overthrow the government, according to the announcement. But we can see that his real "crime" is being a gifted individual. In his brief moments of freedom, he not only transcends the laws of the country but also "the law of gravity and the laws of motion." Unlike his father, he is unwilling to suffer the indignities of the H-G's handicaps. He escapes the oppression of the handicaps he was forced to wear and for his troubles he is shot down and killed. In this scene, Vonnegut shows the reader that even the most oppressive rule cannot totally stifle excellence and individuality.

In the 2081 society, the Handicapper General rules with an iron fist: "Two years in prison and two thousand dollars fine for every ball I took out" or being shot to death, people would not obey, but "start cheating on the laws." "And pretty soon we'd be right back to the dark ages again, with everybody competing against everybody else." Even George and Hazel recognize that the individual would rise up at the first lapse in governmental controls.

At the end of the story, Kurt Vonnegut implies that there is no government capable of suppressing the individual completely. The inner strength of human nature at its finest is more powerful than ill-conceived laws, and the H-G's rules and guns. However, he leaves unsaid whether or not standing up to an oppressive government is worth losing one's life. This conclusion is left for the reader to decide.

Source: Carl Mowery, "An Overview of 'Harrison Bergeron'," in *Short Stories for Students,* The Gale Group, 1999.

Conrad Festa

In the following excerpt, Festa discusses Vonnegut's use of satirical style in discussing themes of technology and life in such stories as "Harrison Bergeron."

From the beginning of his professional writing career, Vonnegut evinced a strong inclination to write satire. Stories such as "Harrison Bergeron," "Report on the Barnhouse Effect," "The Euphio Question," "Welcome to the Monkey House," and his first novel, *Player Piano,* fit easily and recognizably into the satiric genre. That is, they (1) sustain a reductive attack on their objects, (2) convey to their intended readers significances at odds with the literal or surface meanings, and (3) are pervaded

and dominated by various satiric techniques. Furthermore, the satiric objects in those works are easily identifiable and familiar, and their satiric significances are obvious. Judged solely on his early fiction, Vonnegut emerges as a somewhat traditional satirist. Were he to have continued writing in that way, we all would have joined hands long ago to slam down the lid on his box.

The early satire is primarily concerned with the evils of technology and the follies of the American way of life, but, beginning with the second novel, Vonnegut broadens his field of attention to issues of a more cosmic dimension, such as the question of the meaning of life. Also, the satire in his work becomes less apparent: as a consequence, the reader's attention is focused more steadily on the fiction. Yet, while his style and form and fiction are more imaginative creations, while his work manifests so much growth and development in technique and thought, it fails to satisfy certain expectations of consistency of idea, and it fails to yield a comprehensive unambiguous interpretatio. . . .

Source: Conrad Festa, "Vonnegut's Satire," in *Vonnegut in America: An Introduction to the Life and Work of Kurt Vonnegut,* edited by Jerome Klinkowitz and Donald L. Lawler, Delacorte Press/Seymour Lawrence, 1977, pp. 133–50.

Karen and Charles Wood

In the following excerpt, Wood and Wood outline the theme of human identity found in many of Vonnegut's works, including "Harrison Bergeron."

The same ideas which are treated in the novels appear as well in [Vonnegut's] science-fiction short stories. Such pieces as "Report on the Barnhouse Effect," "Harrison Bergeron," "Welcome to the Monkey House," "The Euphio Question," "The Manned Missiles," "Epicac," and "Tomorrow and Tomorrow and Tomorrow" all concern themselves repeatedly with technological problems only as those problems express and explicate character— the character of the human race. Vonnegut proves repeatedly, in brief and pointed form, that men and women remain fundamentally the same, no matter what technology surrounds them. The perfect example of this might be found in "Unready to Wear," in which the shucking off of the physical bodies of men has not changed their basic identities, but only freed them to become *more,* not less, human. The themes, however, which are treated of necessity in piecemeal manner in the short stories, are pulled together in the novels into a world which becomes more complete and whole as one reads on toward *Slaughterhouse-Five.* The absurd, alienated nature of the universe is dealt with in each novel, always with some new depth of perception, some new slant; characters from the short stories and the earlier novels find their way into the later works. The same city, Ilium, in upstate New York, remains a central symbol of the twisted future of mankind. . . .

Source: Karen and Charles Wood, "The Vonnegut Effect: Science Fiction and Beyond," in *The Vonnegut Statement,* edited by Jerome Klinkowitz and John Somer, Dell Publishing Co., 1973, pp. 133-57.

Sources

Frye, Northrop. "The Nature of Satire," in *University of Toronto Quarterly,* Vol. 14, October, 1944.

King, Larry L. "Old Soup," in *New York Times Book Review,* September 1, 1968, pp. 4-5, 19.

Levitas, Mitchel. "Books of the Times: A Slight Case of Candor," in *New York Times,* August 19, 1968, p. 35.

Meek, Martha (revised by Peter Reed). "Kurt Vonnegut, Jr.," in *Critical Survey of Short Fiction,* revised edition, Vol. 6, edited by Frank Magill, Salem Press, 1993, pp. 2364-71.

Minow, Newton. "The Vast Wasteland," reprinted in *The Annals of America, Vol. 18, 1961-1968: The Burdens of World Power,* Encyclopaedia Britannica, 1968, pp. 12-20.

Nichol, Charles. "The Volunteer Fireman," in *Atlantic Monthly,* Vol. 222, No. 3., September, 1968, pp. 123–4.

Reedy, Gerard. Review of *Welcome to the Monkey House,* in *America,* Vol. 119, No. 7, September 14, 1968, pp. 190-91.

Schatt, Stanley. "The Short Stories," in *Kurt Vonnegut, Jr.,* Boston: Twayne, 1976, pp. 119–35.

Uphaus, Robert W. "Expected Meaning in Vonnegut's Dead-End Fiction," in *The Critical Response to Kurt Vonnegut,* edited by Leonard Mustazza, Westport, Conn.: Greenwood Press, 1994, pp. 165-74.

Vonnegut, Kurt. "Address to P.E.N. Conference in Stockholm, 1973," in his *Wampeters, Foma, & Granfalloons: Opinions,* New York: Dell, 1974, pp. 225-29.

Vonnegut, Kurt. "America: What's Good, What's Bad?" in *Vogue,* Vol. 162, July, 1973, 62-64. Reprinted as "Address at Rededication of Wheaton College Library" in his *Wampeters, Foma, & Granfalloons: Opinions,* New York: Dell, 1974, pp. 225-29.

Vonnegut, Kurt. *Fates Worse Than Death: An Autobiographical Collage of the 1980s,* New York: G. P. Putnam's Sons, 1991, pp. 82-5, 113-16, 149-52.

Vonnegut, Kurt. "Mark Twain," in his *Palm Sunday: An Autobiographical Collage,* New York: Delacorte Press, 1981, pp. 166-72.

Vonnegut, Kurt. "Playboy Interview," in *Playboy,* Vol. 20, July, 1973, pp. 57-60+. Reprinted in his *Wampeters, Foma, & Granfalloons: Opinions,* New York: Dell, 1974, pp. 237-85.

Further Reading

The Annals of America, Vol. 17, 1950-1960: Cold War in the Nuclear Age, Encyclopaedia Britannica, 1968.
> The volume features important events and their dates in a chronology, as well as reprints of original speeches and documents

Klinkowitz, Jerome, and Donald L. Lawler, eds. *Vonnegut in America: An Introduction to the Life and Work of Kurt Vonnegut,* Delacorte Press-Seymour Lawrence, 1977, 304 p.
> Includes Conrad Festa's perceptive essay on Vonnegut as a satirist and a complete bibliography of Vonnegut's works.

Klinkowitz, Jerome, Lawler, Donald L., and John Somer, eds. *The Vonnegut Statement,* Delacorte Press, 1973, 286 p.
> Explores Vonnegut's public and personal life, as well as the novels. Klinkowitz proposes that Vonnegut represents middle-class, rather than rebellious values.

Layman, Richard, ed. *American Decades: 1950-1959, Vol. 6,* Manly, Inc.-Gale Research, 1994.
> Provides information on events from the 1950s, classified into such categories as "Government and Politics," "Law and Justice," and "Lifestyles and Social Trends."

Layman, Richard, ed. *American Decades: 1960-1969, Vol. 7,* Manly, Inc.-Gale Research, 1994.
> Provides information on the 1960s, classified into such categories as "Government and Politics," "Law and Justice," and "Lifestyles and Social Trends."

Leeds, Marc. *The Vonnegut Encyclopedia: An Authorized Compendium,* Greenwood Press, 1995, 693 p.
> This alphabetically arranged encyclopedia contains entries on everything from Celia Aamons (from *Cat's Cradle*) to Zog (a Kilgore Trout character from *Breakfast of Champions*).

Merrill, Robert, ed. *Critical Essays on Kurt Vonnegut,* G. K. Hall, 1990, 235 p.
> Includes reviews of Vonnegut's novels; discussions of his early works; an extended section of essays on *Slaughterhouse-Five*; and discussions of the later works.

Mustazza, Leonard, ed. *The Critical Response to Kurt Vonnegut,* Greenwood Press, 1994, 346 p.
> This collection of essays, original reviews of books, and excerpts from other books traces the scholarly reputation of Vonnegut over the years. Most published Vonnegut scholars are represented, as are such writers as Michael Crichton, John Irving, Doris Lessing, and Terry Southern.

A Horse and Two Goats

R. K. Narayan
1960

First published in the Madras, India, newspaper *The Hindu* in 1960, ''A Horse and Two Goats'' did not achieve a wide international audience until 1970 when it became the title story of R. K. Narayan's seventh collection of short stories, *A Horse and Two Goats and Other Stories*. It reached an even wider audience in 1985 when it was included in *Under the Banyan Tree,* Narayan's tenth and best-selling collection. By this time Narayan was well established as one of the most prominent Indian authors writing in English in the twentieth century. The story presents a comic dialogue between Muni, a poor Tamil-speaking villager, and a wealthy English-speaking businessman from New York. They are engaged in a conversation in which neither can understand the other's language. With gentle humor, Narayan explores the conflicts between rich and poor, and between Indian and Western culture.

Narayan is best known for his fourteen novels, many of which take place in the fictional town of Malgudi. Many of the stories in his thirteen short story collections also take place in Malgudi, but ''A Horse and Two Goats'' does not. This accounts for the fact that the story has attracted very little critical commentary; however, all of the attention it has drawn has been positive. The story is seen as a fine example of Narayan's dexterity in creating engaging characters and humorous dialogue, but it is not considered one of his greatest works.

Author Biography

Rasipuram Krishnaswami Ayyar Naranayanaswami was born in Madras, a large industrial coastal city in India, on October 10, 1906. His family was Brahmin, the highest caste of Hindu society. When he was still young, the rest of his family moved to Mysore, a smaller city in the heart of the country. Narayan stayed in Madras with his grandmother, who read him classic Indian tales and myths from an early age and encouraged his imagination. He was not a serious student; he believed that the educational system was too regimented and that it discouraged students from thinking creatively, so he decided not to work hard and ended up failing several subjects and his college entrance exams.

After graduation, Narayan went to work in a government office in Mysore, but he was no more suited for mundane office work than for formal education. He tried teaching for a while, but did not last long as a teacher, either. What he wanted to be was a writer. At first, most of his stories were rejected. For three or four years he lived at home and earned less than five dollars a year, worrying and embarrassing his family.

In 1933 he married a woman named Rajam, who encouraged him in his writing. To help support his wife and daughter, he tried journalism, starting out as a correspondent for the *Madras Justice* and working his way up to junior editor. Rajam lived only five years as his wife, dying of typhoid in 1939. By that time Narayan had published three novels, and had begun, under the shortened name R. K. Narayan, to attract international attention. Finally, he was able to quit his newspaper job and become a full-time fiction writer. His fourth novel, *The English Teacher* (1945), features a character patterned after Rajam and describes Narayan's own struggles to deal with her death. All of his fiction, most of which takes place in the fictional town of Malgudi and all of which is in English, gives a realistic portrayal of middle-class life in India, with its caste system and long-standing traditions, and many of his stories are based on real events.

Narayan is one of the most widely read of the Indian authors writing in English. He has published more than thirty novels and collections of short stories and essays, and was still producing new work well into his eighties. He has been honored for his work in India, in Great Britain, and in the United States, where he has been made an honorary member of the American Academy and Institute of Arts and Letters. His own humble views of his life and success are presented in his memoir, *My Days* (1984).

Plot Summary

Set in Kritam, "probably the tiniest" of India's 700,000 villages, "A Horse and Two Goats" opens with a clear picture of the poverty in which the protagonist Muni lives. Of the thirty houses in the village, only one, the Big House, is made of brick. The others, including Muni's, are made of "bamboo thatch, straw, mud, and other unspecified materials." There is no running water and no electricity, and Muni's wife cooks their typical breakfast of "a handful of millet flour" over a fire in a mud pot. On this day, Muni has shaken down six drumsticks (a local name for a type of horse radish) from the drumstick tree growing in front of his house, and he asks his wife to prepare them for him in a sauce. She agrees, provided he can get the other ingredients, none of which they have in the house: rice, dhall (lentils), spices, oil and a potato.

Muni and his wife have not always been so poor. Once, when he considered himself prosperous, he had a flock of forty sheep and goats which he would lead out to graze every day. But life has not been kind to him or to his flocks: years of drought, a great famine, and an epidemic that ran through Muni's flock have taken their toll. And as a member of the lowest of India's castes, Muni was never permitted to go to school or to learn a trade. Now he is reduced to two goats, too scrawny to sell or to eat. He and his wife have no children to help them in their old age, so their only income is from the odd jobs his wife occasionally takes on at the Big House. Muni has exhausted his credit at every shop in town, and today, when he asks a local shopman to give him the items his wife requires to cook the drumsticks, he is sent away humiliated.

There is no other food in the house, so Muni's wife sends him away with the goats. "Fast till the evening," she tells him. "It'll do you good." Muni takes the goats to their usual spot a few miles away: a grassy area near the highway, where he can sit in the shade of a life-sized statue of a horse and a warrior and watch trucks and buses go by. The statue is made of weather-beaten clay and has stood in the same spot for all of Muni's seventy or more years.

As Muni watches the road and waits for the appropriate time to return home, a yellow station wagon comes down the road and pulls over. A red-faced American man dressed in khaki clothing gets out and is asking Muni where to find the nearest gas station when he notices the statue, which he finds ''marvelous.'' Muni's first impulse is to run away, assuming from the khaki that this foreigner must be a policeman or a soldier. But Muni is too old to run any more, and he cannot leave the goats. The two begin to converse—if ''conversation'' can be used to describe what happens when two people speak to each other in separate languages, neither understanding the other. ''Namaste! How do you do?'' the American says in greeting, using his only Indian word. Muni responds with the only English he knows: ''Yes, no.''

The American, a businessman from New York City, lights a cigarette and offers one to Muni, who knows about cigarettes but has never had one before. He offers Muni his business card, but Muni fears it is a warrant of some kind. Muni launches into a long explanation of his innocence of whatever crime the man is investigating, and the American asks questions about the horse statue, which he would like to buy. He tells Muni about a bad day at work, when he was forced to work for four hours without elevators or electricity, and seems completely unaware that Muni lives this way every day. By now he is convinced that Muni is the owner of the statue, which he is determined to buy.

The two talk back and forth, each about his own life. Muni remembers his father and grandfather telling about the statue and the ancient story it depicts, and tries to explain to the American how old it is. ''I get a kick out of every word you utter,'' the American replies. Muni reminisces about his difficult and impoverished childhood working in the fields, and the American laughs heartily. Muni interprets the statue: ''This is our guardian. . . . At the end of Kali Yuga, this world and all other worlds will be destroyed, and the Redeemer will come in the shape of a horse.'' The American replies, ''I assure you this will have the best home in the U.S.A. I'll push away the bookcase. . . . The TV may have to be shifted. . . . I don't see how that can interfere with the party—we'll stand around him and have our drinks.'' It is clear that even if the two could

R. K. Narayan

understand each other's words, they could not understand each other's worlds.

Finally, the American pushes one hundred rupees into Muni's hand—twenty times Muni's debt with the shopkeeper. He considers that he has bought the horse, and Muni believes he has just sold his goats. Muni runs home to present the money to his wife, while the American flags down a truck, gets help breaking the horse off its pedestal, and drives away with his purchase. Muni's wife does not believe her husband's story about where the money came from, and her suspicions only increase when the goats find their way home. As the story ends, she is shrieking at him, and Muni appears to be not much better off than he was at the start.

Characters

The American
See The man

The man
The man comes riding into the story in a yellow station wagon. A businessman who works in New

A rural Indian village, featuring villagers and goats.

York and commutes from Connecticut, he is dressed in the khaki clothing worn by American tourists in the tropics. He typifies the ''Ugly American'': he speaks only English, but is surprised and a little annoyed to find that Muni can speak only Tamil, and although he is in the tiniest village in India, he expects to find a gas station and English-speaking goatherds. Once he sees the statue of the horse, he must own it for his living room, with no thought for what the statue might mean or who might value it. Even when he can't speak the language, he knows that money talks.

Muni

Muni, an old and desperately poor man, is the protagonist of the story. Once he was prosperous, with a large flock of sheep, but a series of misfortunes have left him with only two scrawny goats. He and his wife have almost no income and no children to help take care of them. Every day, Muni takes the goats out to graze on the scarce grass outside of town, while his wife pulls something together for an evening meal. As he watches the goats from the shade of a large statue, he remembers his younger days when the work was hard but there was enough to eat, when he could not attend school because he was not of the right caste, and when he imagined

that he would one day have children. Like many poor and struggling people, he fears authority figures, and so he fears the American who steps out of a strange car wearing khaki clothes. While the man tries to talk with him about the statue, Muni babbles on about a recent murder and the end of the world. At the end he seems to have temporarily escaped his money troubles, but his bad luck continues when his wife suspects him of thievery and threatens to leave.

The shopman

The shopman is a moody man who has given Muni food on credit in the past, but who has been pushed past his limit. Muni owes him five rupees, and although they share a bit of humorous conversation, the shopman will not give him any more.

The wife

Muni's wife has spent some sixty years with him (neither of them is sure about their ages), through prosperity and poverty. Although she is gruff with him now, she is willing to indulge his request for a special meal. She works as hard as he does, or harder, getting up at dawn to fix his morning meal, and taking odd jobs at the Big House when their stores are low. But poverty has worn her down: her first reaction when she sees the hundred rupees is to accuse Muni of stealing.

Themes

Culture Clash

The most important theme in ''A Horse and Two Goats,'' and in fact the central theme of Narayan's work, is the clash of cultures, specifically the clash of Indian and Western cultures. Using humor instead of anger, Narayan demonstrates just how far apart the two worlds are: the two cultures exist in the same time and space, but literally and metaphorically speak different languages. The two main characters in this story couldn't be more different: Muni is poor, rural, uneducated, Hindu, brown; the American is wealthy, urban, educated, probably Judeo-Christian, white. As a good Hindu, Muni calmly accepts the hand that fate has dealt him, while the American is willing and able to take drastic and sudden action to change his life (for example, flying off to India, or throwing away his return plane ticket to transport a horse statue home on a ship). Each man is quite ignorant of the other's way of life.

Unlike many stories about culture clash, the inability to communicate in this story leads only to confusion, not to any real harm. In fact, although each feels vaguely dissatisfied with the conversation, the men do not realize that they are not communicating. Each speaks at length about his own life and local calamities, with no awareness that the other hears nothing. At the end of their encounter each man has what he wants or needs, and neither man has lost anything of value. As an Indian who writes only in English, Narayan himself has experienced the ways in which Indian and Western cultures conflict. While this conflict may be painful at times, here he finds it merely amusing.

Wealth and Poverty

Although they have little in common, the most important way in which Muni and the American differ is in their respective level of wealth. Narayan takes great pains in the opening of the story to show how desperately poor Muni is, and to emphasize that even in his time of ''prosperity'' his standard of living was still greatly below that of most Americans. The American takes for granted his relative wealth and seems unaware of the difference be-

tween Muni and himself. He casually offers cigarettes to a man who has never seen one, complains about four hours without air conditioning to a man who has never had electricity, brags about enjoying manual labor as a Sunday hobby to a man who grew up working in the fields from morning until night, and without a thought gives Muni enough money to open a business. He is not trying to show off; he simply accepts his wealth as his right. His very casualness emphasizes the gap between them. Narayan in no way condemns the man for being wealthy, or for not stepping in to aid the poor Muni, but he wants the two men and their relative wealth to be clear, so the reader can evaluate the relationship between wealth and worth.

Knowledge and Ignorance

In a small way, ''A Horse and Two Goats'' explores the different ways that a person can be educated. Muni, who grew up a member of a lower caste at a time when only the Brahmin, the highest caste, could attend school, has had no formal education. He has not traveled beyond his village, and he likes to watch trucks and buses go by on the highway a few miles away so that he can have ''a sense of belonging to a larger world.'' He does not even know his own age. He does, however, have an impressive amount of knowledge of the two major texts of his literary heritage, the *Ramayana* and the *Mahabharata,* which he has learned by acting in plays and by listening to speakers at the temple. He knows the stories, and he is able to mine them for truth and wisdom when he needs them.

The American, on the other hand, has had the full benefits of an American education. He has a roomful of books that he values as objects (''you know I love books and am a member of five book clubs, and the choice and bonus volumes mount up to a pile in our living room''), but there is no evidence that he understands or values what is inside them. On one level, he is familiar with the larger world around him in a way that Muni never will be. However, even on this trip to India ''to look at other civilizations,'' he does not seem to be looking at India for what it is, but only for a reflection of—and ornaments for—his own life. The uneducated Muni tries to tell him the significance of the horse statue, but the American sees it only as a living room decoration. Of course, the language barrier prevents him from receiving Muni's interpretation, but it never even crosses his mind to ask. In this story, there are at least two ways to be ignorant.

Topics for Further Study

- Muni and his wife live a simple life, probably without running water or electricity in their home. How has life changed for poor villagers in India since 1960 when this story was written? Throughout the world, do more people live like Muni and his wife, or like you and the others in your class?

- Find the stories Muni mentions, from the *Mahabharata* and the *Ramayana*. (Perhaps you can find Narayan's own translations.) How would this uneducated man know stories from two-thousand-year-old poems? Why might Muni be remembering them at this point in his life? What stories do most people in the United States know, whatever their level of education or sophistication?

- Investigate the role that Great Britain has played in Indian politics during the nineteenth and twen-

tieth centuries, especially before 1947. Also, find out what you can about the origin of the word *khaki*. Does your new information help explain Muni's warning to himself, ''Beware of Khaki''?

- Most critics find Muni's wife cold and unsympathetic. Do you agree? Compare the lives of the two wives in this story, and what can be guessed about their personalities. How important are their wives to these two men?

- Find the meanings for these terms from the story: *dhall, drumsticks, swarga, betel leaves, dhoti.* Then look closely at an American short story you have read recently. Which terms would a person from Muni's village need to have explained?

Style

Point of View and Narration

''A Horse and Two Goats'' is narrated in the third person by an omniscient narrator who reports clearly and objectively on the characters' words, actions, and memories, but who does not comment or judge. The narrator describes Kritam's erosion and Muni's decline dispassionately, without regret; conversations between Muni and his wife, or Muni and the shopman, are told from Muni's perspective, but with his calm acceptance of whatever fate brings him. This restraint is important to the understated humor of the dialogue between Muni and the American; Narayan trusts the reader to interpret the absurd conversation without his having to say through his narrator, ''Notice that this response has nothing to do with the question asked,'' or ''See the irony in this remark.'' When the two men leave the place where they met, each taking away something of value, neither has been accused by the narrator— nor by the reader—of foolishness or evil. By creating a narrator who tells the story without judging it,

Narayan presents two believable characters with human flaws, but two characters for whom the reader can feel compassion and sympathy nonetheless. The conflict is between two likeable characters, or two worthy cultures, not between good and evil.

Setting

The story takes place in Kritam, ''probably the tiniest'' of India's 700,000 villages. Its four streets are lined with about thirty mud and thatch huts and one Big House, made of brick and cement. Women cook in clay pots over clay stoves, and the huts have no running water or electricity. A few miles away, down a rough dirt track through dry fields of cactus and lantana bushes, is a highway leading to the mountains, where a large construction project is being completed. The meeting between Muni and the red-faced man was intended to take place between about 1945, when televisions became generally available to Americans, and 1960, when the story was published, but the date is not central to the story. Even today there are many villages in the world without modern technological conveniences, and many travelers who do not realize that not everyone lives as they do.

Realism

Narayan's fiction is often noted for its realism, its simple and accurate presentation of common, everyday life as it is lived by identifiable characters. In "A Horse and Two Goats" Narayan pays careful attention to the small details of Muni's life: where he lives, what he eats, how he coughs when he smokes his first cigarette. Although many of the small details, like the drumstick tree and the dhoti where Muni puts his hundred rupees, are particularly Indian, they are also basic enough to human experience that they are easily understood by an international audience. Narayan's characters and stories are read not so much as regional literature but as universal.

Humor

Humor is an important element in "A Horse and Two Goats," and understanding Narayan's humor is important to understanding his world view. Humor, which is affectionate and sympathetic to humanity and human foibles, is often distinguished from wit, which looks more harshly on human fallibility. For Narayan, who looks at the world through the lens of his Hindu faith, weakness and strife are to be accepted and transcended, not railed against. When he creates the comic characters of Muni and the American (likely candidates for the roles of the "two goats" in the title), he laughs at them gently and kindly, not critically.

Historical Context

Colonial India

Indian culture is more than five thousand years old. Its great epics were composed before the year A.D. 200, and magnificent art and architecture were created in the 4th and 5th centuries A.D. Beginning in the 10th century, Muslim raiders attacked and weakened the Buddhist kingdoms, and for the next several hundred years a series of Muslim kingdoms controlled what is now called the Indian subcontinent. By 1500, Europeans were also competing for control of Indian trade. In 1857, India became subject to British rule. Like South Africa, Indians found themselves governed by a white minority from another country and culture, whose governance was guided by racism and religious intolerance. India remained a British colony until 1947, when a long campaign of peaceful civil disobedience led by Mohandas Gandhi persuaded Britain to return control of the country to its own people. India was divided into two separate nations: India, a secular state populated mainly by Hindus, and Pakistan, a Muslim state. The late 1940s were marked with great violence and eventually war between Muslims and Hindus. Thus, the world from which Narayan was writing in the 1950s was both old, rich in tradition and legend, and new, struggling for identity.

Independent India

Immediately after achieving independence, India's government, under Prime Minister Pandit Jawaharlal Nehru, began planning and taking action to bring peace and prosperity to all Indian citizens. The task was daunting: although there was a will to provide education for all, there were not enough teachers; the need to grow more food and distribute it was apparent, but the technology and skills were not available. Although there was a change in the air, there was no real change in the day-to-day lives of poor people like Muni and his wife for many years. "A Horse and Two Goats" takes place less than a decade after independence, little enough time that Muni has realized no tangible benefits from living in a sovereign nation, and that he still shrinks from a white man wearing khaki, who he assumes must be a British authority figure.

For Narayan, independence made it possible for him to move more freely on the world stage, but he continued in his lifelong tendency to avoid politics in his personal life and in his writing. It should be noted that choosing to write and publish in English, his second language, was an artistic, not a political, decision. He was raised a Brahmin, a member of the highest Hindu caste, and he had enjoyed a good education and a life of relative ease. He had learned English in school, and as he developed his writing skills he found that the English language—as Indians speak it—was ideal for expressing his ideas and images clearly. But by writing in English, he was choosing to write for an

Compare & Contrast

- **1947:** One of the goals of the new Constitution in India is to provide free and compulsory education for Indian children. In 1951, approximately 80 percent of the adults in India, like Muni, are illiterate.

  1990s: Approximately 52 percent of the adult population is considered literate (64 percent of the men and 39 percent of the women).

- **1951:** Approximately 80 percent of Indian adults live in poverty. The percentage is higher for children. Few of these people have access to clean water.

  1997: Due to the spread of technology and a growing educated class engaged in international trade, only one-third of India's population lives below the poverty line. Most villages have access to safe drinking water.

- **1950s:** One hundred rupees is enough money for Muni to think about building a small thatched roof and opening a small food stand. It is twenty times his debt to the shopman.

  1998: One hundred rupees is equivalent to approximately $2.35 in American dollars.

- **1950s:** Agricultural yields are low, and insufficient to feed India's 400 million people. Monsoons in 1951 and 1952 add to the country's food deficits. By 1960, food grain production is increasing.

  1990s: India grows enough food to feed its 935 million people, and also produces its own steel, computer software, and nuclear energy.

---

audience that lived mostly outside India, since most Indians, like Muni, did not speak or read English. As a journalist, and then as something of an international figure, Narayan had seen more of the world than Muni ever could. He understood the conflicts between Indian culture and Western culture as few people did, because he had created a life for himself that forced him to move through both worlds.

Critical Overview

Over a prolific career spanning more than fifty years, Narayan has published fourteen novels, thirteen collections of short stories, and eleven other volumes of essays, translations and memoirs. He is known primarily for his many novels and short stories set in the fictional, small Southern Indian town of Malgudi, and most critics and reviewers focus on these stories. Critics appreciate Narayan

for the clarity of his vision for the town, for the way the town has grown and changed over the years as a "real" town would, and they compare his use of the town through many works to William Faulkner's creation of Yoknapatawpha County or Thomas Hardy's Wessex novels, yet they find that his details about everyday Indian life and his warmth and sympathy toward his characters create stories that are universal. Reaction to Narayan's work has always been quite positive, but his reputation among literary scholars seems to be fading as the twentieth century draws to a close. While general readers continue to value Narayan's work for its simplicity of language, straightforward plotting and action, gentle humor and sweet disposition, recent commentators have found it perhaps a touch too unsophisticated and nonpolitical to warrant serious study.

"A Horse and Two Goats" is one of the few Narayan stories not set in Malgudi, and it has received very little critical attention of its own. It was one of many stories Narayan wrote quickly, at a rate of two per week, as a contributor to the Madras newspaper *The Hindu.* The story came to the attention of the international reading community when it appeared in the collection *A Horse and Two Goats and Other Stories* in 1970, and most criticism refers to this collection. Typical is *R. K. Narayan: A Critical Appreciation,* in which William Walsh relegates his discussion of the story to a chapter entitled "Other Work." His analysis, like most writing about this story, consists primarily of a plot summary and the observation that "Narayan is himself fascinated by the gap which exists between supposed and real understanding, by the element of incomprehension in human relationships." P. S. Ramana, in a short section of his *Message in Design: A Study of R. K. Narayan's Fiction,* focuses on "how, by manipulating the narratorial position, focus, tone, attitude and commentary, the author is able to almost overlook the darker side of the experience to produce a highly humorous and ironic tale." In an article in *Perspectives on R. K. Narayan,* H. C. Trivedi and N. C. Soni find the chief importance of the story is as "a subtle and real entertainment."

When the story appeared again in 1985, in the collection *Under the Banyan Tree and Other Stories,* a new generation of readers discovered it. This collection has received no formal criticism, but was reviewed in major American newspapers and magazines. Many reviewers of this volume single out "A Horse and Two Goats" because it is one of the longest stories in the collection, and because it is a fine example of Narayan's humor. In a review in *Washington Post Book World,* Frances Taliaferro calls the story "a classic of cross purposes." Neville Shack, writing for [London] *Times Literary Supplement,* finds "a flourish of banality, exasperating but quite moving at the same time, infused with human drollery." Although the market for short story collections has declined steadily, and critical attention to Narayan's work has also declined, "A Horse and Two Goats" continues to appear in high school and college textbook anthologies, where students and teachers give it high marks for its insight into another culture in the form of a humorous tale.

Criticism

Cynthia Bily

Bily has a master's degree in English literature and has written for a wide variety of educational publishers. In the following essay, she examines the role of women in "A Horse and Two Goats."

When Muni the Indian peasant and the red-faced American meet and converse in "A Horse and Two Goats," the differences between them are immediately apparent, and these differences inform the main idea of the story, the clash of cultures. One of the few things the two men have in common is kept in the background of the story, but resurfaces frequently—each has a devoted wife on the sidelines, making it possible for them to keep going.

To begin to understand Narayan's sense of women, it would be useful to look briefly at how Indian and Hindu culture has perceived and shaped women's lives. It is believed that the ancient Tamil societies may have been matriarchal, that is, ruled and guided by woman. The great Indian epics, composed approximately two thousand years ago, contain stories of several important female characters, including two that Muni mentions: the goddess Lakshmi, wife of Vishnu, and Sita, wife of Rama. In their roles as nurturers and storytellers, woman have been revered because they have kept the culture alive.

In practical terms, however, the life of a woman in India as recently as one hundred or two hundred years ago was almost unimaginable today, even in comparison to the restrictions placed upon American women in the eighteenth and nineteenth centuries. Hindu law and tradition dictated that women were under the protection of their fathers, and then of their husbands. In fact, wives were the legal property of their husbands and had no right to own property, to be educated, to divorce, or to speak in public. Under the custom of *sati,* a woman whose husband died would throw herself onto his funeral pyre and be burned alive, thus showing her utter devotion to him.

In 1829, *sati* was declared illegal by the British colonialists, although it never completely disappeared. At the end of the nineteenth century, when Muni and his wife were wed, it was still common for a woman to be married off at a very young age, often to an adult man whom she had never met. In fact, although Muni has never kept track of his age, "He was told on their day of wedding that he was ten years old and she was eight. During the wedding ceremony they had had to recite their respective ages and names." This is the tradition under which

What Do I Read Next?

- *Under the Banyan Tree and Other Stories* (1985) is one of Narayan's best-known collections of short stories and includes many brief pieces that are little more than character sketches, originally written for *The Hindu* in Madras during his early career. One of them, ''Like the Sun,'' gives an Indian version of the often-told tale of a man who can only tell the truth.

- Of his fourteen novels, Narayan has said that his own favorite is *A Tiger for Malgudi.* Set in the same fictional town as most of his fiction, this fable incorporates Indian folktales and myths and is narrated by Raja, a tiger.

- Saros Cowasjee has edited two collections of Indian short fiction, *Stories from the Raj: From Kipling to Independence* (1982) and *More Stories from the Raj: From Kipling to the Present Day* (1986). Although both volumes are out of print, they are available from most good-sized libraries, and they demonstrate the variety and strength of the short story in India.

- Many critics have compared Narayan's fictional town of Malgudi to William Faulkner's Yoknapatawpha County, though most find that Faulkner's vision is darker than Narayan's. Faulkner's *Collected Stories* (1950, 1977) offers many stories set in his fictional landscape and features recurring characters.

- Published in 1924, before Indian independence from Great Britain, E. M. Forster's *A Passage to India* is a novel about the difficulties of interracial friendship in colonial India. During this time of heightened tension, even the most tolerant of the British find their compassion and common sense overrun by their racial prejudice.

- The *Ramayana* tells the adventure story of the ruler Rama, who loses his kingdom and joins forces with the monkey king Sugriva to regain his wife and his throne. Written in about 300 B.C., the *Ramayana* exists in many English translations, including Narayan's own *The Ramayana: A Shortened Modern Prose Version of the Indian Epic* (1972).

- Considered the longest poem ever written, the *Mahabharata,* or the Great Epic of the Bharata Dynasty, was composed between 200 B.C. and A.D. 200. It contains many of the most well-known stories and legends of Indian civilization. It, too, has appeared in many English versions, including a 1978 translation by Narayan, *The Mahabharata: A Shortened Prose Version of the Indian Epic.*

- *Clear Light of Day* (1980) by Anita Desai, an important female Indian novelist and short story writer. Two sisters, Tara and Bim, suffer through family conflicts, political violence and an epidemic in early twentieth-century India, and learn that forgiveness can heal old wounds.

Muni had grown up. Women were honored on the one hand, and subordinate on the other—no more simple or straightforward than gender roles in any society.

Narayan is a bit younger than Muni, perhaps fifteen years, and his upbringing was different from Muni's. Narayan was raised by his grandmother, who taught him the legends and stories from the traditional literature. Muni learned most of his lore from other men, including the story behind the statue: ''I was an urchin this high when I heard my grandfather explain this horse and warrior, and my grandfather himself was this high when he heard his grandfather, whose grandfather. . . .'' Narayan and his wife chose each other—over the objections of their families—and married when they were in their twenties. Sadly, her early death kept them from growing old together.

During his lifetime, Narayan saw many changes in the lives of Indian women. During the struggle for independence from Great Britain, women were active leaders and participants in the long years of civil disobedience. One of these women, Indira Gandhi, the daughter of the movement's leader Mahatma Gandhi, remained politically active and decades later became prime minister. With Indian independence in 1947, women became full citizens for the first time and acquired property rights and the right to vote. In 1955, about the time Narayan was writing ''A Horse and Two Goats,'' a new Hindu Marriage Act raised the minimum age for marriage to fifteen for females and eighteen for males and gave women the right to seek a divorce if their husbands took additional wives. The next year, women won the right to inherit property from their fathers on equal terms with their brothers.

What does this mean for ''A Horse and Two Goats?'' Muni and his wife were married in a traditional ceremony at a young age and have lived together nearly all their lives. His expectations for their roles in relation to each other, based on tradition, have not been met. He remembers that ''he had thrashed her only a few times in their career.'' The tone here is casual, without regret; thrashing is what husbands do when wives get out of line. But the balance of power did not hold, at least not in Muni's eyes: ''later she had the upper hand.'' Critics have tended to accept Muni's view of this, agreeing that Muni's wife is controlling, even domineering. But is she?

In the opening, the narrator shows the town and a typical day. ''His wife lit the domestic fire at dawn, boiled water in a mud pot, threw into it a handful of millet flour, added salt, and gave him his first nourishment of the day. When he started out, she would put in his hand a packed lunch, once again the same millet cooked into a little ball, which he could swallow with a raw onion at midday.'' It is a spartan meal, the most nutrition for the least money, but there is no mention of her preparing anything for herself. Is the narrator simply not interested in her diet, or does she skip the morning meal to leave more for Muni? ''She was old, but he was older and needed all the attention she could give him in order to be kept alive.''

Muni heads for the highway, where he grazes his two useless goats. They are thin, and the other villagers think he would be better off eating them than moving them back and forth each day. For the rest of the day, according to his usual schedule, he will sit in the shade of a statue, watch the goats and the passing cars, and daydream about his former

> The American's wife's name is Ruth, the name of an Old Testament figure who stands in Judeo-Christian tradition as a model for wifely loyalty. The Biblical Ruth is loyal to her dead husband's family; the Ruth in 'A Horse and Two Goats' is loyal to her husband and stands by to prop him up when he is about to do something off-balance."

prosperity. At this time in their marriage, he is not contributing much in the way of subsistence. His primary duty today is to ''be careful not to argue and irritate'' his wife, whom he seems to find unreasonable and difficult. His sixty-eight-year-old wife, on the other hand, ''would somehow conjure up some food for him in the evening. . . . She was sure to go out and work—grind corn in the Big House, sweep or scrub somewhere, and earn enough to buy food-stuff and keep a dinner ready for him in the evening.'' If ''her temper was undependable in the morning but improved by evening time,'' who could blame her?

The American's wife is even more on the periphery of the main action than Muni's wife; in fact the action could go along just as smoothy without her even being mentioned. But Narayan has a reason for introducing her. The American's wife's name is Ruth, the name of an Old Testament figure who stands in Judeo-Christian tradition as a model for wifely loyalty. The Biblical Ruth is loyal to her dead husband's family; the Ruth in ''A Horse and Two Goats'' is loyal to her husband and stands by to prop him up when he is about to do something off-balance. Although he speaks of her with an impatient tone, surely she would be right to ''disapprove'' of a full-sized horse statue in the living room and right to hang on to her plane ticket instead of throwing it away to accompany the statue on a ship. She seems to be a good sport, to support her husband's whims: "Next day she called the travel agent first thing and told him to fix it, and so here I am."

Having a loyal, grounded wife gives each of the husbands the freedom to move out into the world. Muni goes to the highway each day so he can "watch the highway and see the lorries and buses pass through to the hills, and it gave him a sense of belonging to a larger world." Later, he will describe the vehicles to his wife, whose duties do not permit her to move about so freely. Ruth has come to India with her husband, but he tells Muni that she is "staying back at Srinagar, and I am the one doing the rounds and joining her later."

There are other wives in the story. Muni remembers that in his youth he was often chosen for the women's roles in the plays the community performed. Sometimes he was the Goddess Lakshmi, the wife of Vishnu. Lakshmi is one of the most popular goddesses in India, and countless people pray to her for wealth and good luck. She is a nurturer and a model for devoted wives. It is her obedience to Vishnu that gives her power. Muni also played the part of Sita, another incarnation of Lakshmi and the wife of Rama, the hero of the *Ramayana*. Sita is another exemplary wife, who remains loyal to Rama in spite of many trials.

A possible reason for Muni's memories of these plays may lie in town gossip. To the delight of the men in town, the postman's wife has run off to the city with another man. The postman "does not speak to anyone at all nowadays. Who would if a wife did what she did? Women must be watched; otherwise they will sell themselves and the home." Men should keep an eye on their wives, because if they leave, the husbands lose their grounding.

In this speech, Muni comes as close as he ever will to stating the truth about wives: it may be annoying when they stay, but it is devastating when they leave. As Muni drives his goats out to the statue in the beginning of the story, he reflects on his age. "At seventy, one only waited to be summoned by God. When he was dead what would his wife do?" In fact, his wife would be lonely, but she is the one in the family with survival skills. The real question is what would Muni do without his wife if she were summoned by God? Where would a man be without a loyal wife?

Source: Cynthia Bily, "An Overview of 'A Horse and Two Goats'," in *Short Stories for Students,* The Gale Group, 1999.

Ralph J. Crane

In the following essay, Crane discusses "A Horse and Two Goats" in relation to common themes in Narayan's fiction.

"A Horse and Two Goats," by R. K. Narayan appeared, in a somewhat different form, in *The New Yorker* in 1965. It was first published in its present form in the collection *A Horse and Two Goats A Horse and Two Goats* (1970), and was later included in *Under the Banyan Tree,* a selection of Narayan's stories to 1984.

Narayan is admired as a writer whose novels and stories are remarkably consistent in quality. Yet one or two works do stand out—like the novel *The Guide* (1958) and the short story "A Horse and Two Goats." To many, Narayan is best known as the creator of Malgudi, one of literature's most enduring and endearing fictional worlds, so it is somewhat ironic that "A Horse and Two Goats" is one of only a handful of Narayan's stories not to be set in the brilliantly-realised world of Malgudi. Nevertheless, it is a tale that perfectly displays his mastery of the short story form.

Muni, the central character of the story, is a typical Narayan hero who has achieved little, and who feels he has been dealt with unsympathetically by the world around him, and by fate. Unlike most of Narayan's heroes, though, he is a lower-class village peasant, rather than the usual middle-class Malgudi-dweller, and he is very poor, as the appalling conditions of his life, always present behind the humour of the story, attest. Indeed, on one level this tale provides the non-Indian reader with a glimpse of the type of poverty and hardship that must be endured by the millions of Indians who, like Muni, have barely enough food to keep them alive:

> His wife lit the domestic fire at dawn, boiled water in a mud pot, threw into it a handful of millet flour, added salt, and gave him his first nourishment of the day. When he started out, she would put in his hand a packed lunch, once again the same millet cooked into a little ball, which he could swallow with a raw onion at midday.

Narayan has, on occasions, been criticized for focussing on middle-class urban India in his stories, thereby excluding the poor of rural India who continue to make up the vast majority of the Indian population. But Narayan's purpose as a storyteller has never been to educate the non-Indian reader about India. So although we can learn specific things about village life in India from this story, it isn't about Indian problems or about Indian sensibilities as such. While what happens in ''A Horse and Two Goats'' is accurate to the particular of the Indian experience, it deliberately deals with themes that are quintessentially human, also. William Walsh has suggested it is a story about misunderstanding, a story about the gap between supposed and real understanding, a story about the element of incomprehension in human relationships.

''A Horse and Two Goats'' is typical of Narayan's pre-Modernist, village storyteller style of writing. In a deceptively simple, linear narrative Narayan unfolds the story of Muni, an old goatherd. In keeping with his usual narrative formula, Narayan carefully follows Muni as he goes about his daily, frequently humiliating existence—eating his meagre breakfast, visiting the local shopkeeper in a typically unsuccessful attempt tot get a few items of food on credit, and then taking his two scraggy goats to graze near the foot of the horse statute at the edge of the village. He spends the rest of his day crouching in the shade offered by the clay horse, or watching the traffic pass on the highway.

Once the nature of Muni's world has been established, both the plot and the comedy of the story hinge on the disruption of that routine (as they do with the arrival of Vasu in *The Man-Eater of Malgudi,* or Tim in *The World of Nagaraj*). This is a formula Narayan uses frequently, and always with consummate skill. In ''A Horse and Two Goats'' the seemingly timeless routine is interrupted when a car stops and a ''red-faced foreigner,'' an American whose vehicle has run out of petrol, asks for directions to the nearest gas station.

This is where the comedy of misunderstanding takes over. After initially thinking he is being questioned about a crime by the khaki-clad foreigner, whom he assumes must be either a policeman or a soldier, Muni concludes that the man wants to buy his goats. Meanwhile the red-faced American, assuming the Tamil peasant owns the clay horse statute, which to the villagers, as Muni explains, ''is our guardian, it means death to our adversaries,'' sets about trying to buy it, so he can take it back to the United States to decorate his living room: ''I'm going to keep him right in the middle of the room . . . we'll stand around him and have our drinks.''

The humour and the irony of this tale lies in the total benign incomprehension that exists between

> The humour and the irony of this tale lies in the total benign incomprehension that exists between the two, not only in the way neither understands the other's language, but also in the absolute contrast of their cultural and economic backgrounds, emphasised by the way each values the clay horse."

the two, not only in the way neither understands the other's language, but also in the absolute contrast of their cultural and economic backgrounds, emphasised by the way each values the clay horse. Much of this is conveyed through the wonderful double discourse that makes up a significant part of the story, with each of the characters happily developing his own hermetically-sealed interpretation of the other's words and gestures. The story's charm lies in the way Narayan refrains from passing judgement.

Source: Ralph J. Crane, ''A Horse and Two Goats,'' in *Reference Guide to Short Fiction,* Detroit: St. James Press, 1994.

V. Panduranga Rao

In the following excerpt, Rao analyzes ''A Horse and Two Goats'' to uncover Narayan's literary craftmanship.

Since writing last about Narayan's art as a novelist and, especially, after meeting him and conversing with him, the conviction has grown in me that he is a creative writer who has come to terms with himself and has no fierce quarrel with man, society or God. Narayan's novels reveal a creative intelligence enjoying inner harmony evolved rather early in life, though not without struggle and suffering. The house of fiction that Narayan built is built on the bedrock of his faith (Whatever happens India will go on, he told Naipaul). This, I thought, was my complaint against Narayan: he is unique, human and not so accessibly human. The distance between the world immediate to me and that of Narayan's later novels is the distinction between the Inferno and the Purgatory. I, of course believe that the Inferno—the world of Narayan's *Dark Room*—is too much with us. But I give credit to Narayan for his achievement: he makes his Purgatory credible (if not acceptable) to us of the Pit, both in the East and in the West. There is a muted contradiction in Narayan's later novels, between the humour which is humanizing and the grand Narayan vision which is so far above the merely human.

Then Narayan's *A Horse and Two Goats and Other Stories,* appeared, a slender collection of five stories. I believe that two stories in this volume are among the best written by an Indian in English. It is in these stories—the title story, ''A Horse and Two Goats'' and ''Annamalai''—that Narayan truly evokes memories of the great Russian master, Chekhov. They are to me a marvellous re-affirmation of Narayan's (at) oneness with man; an orchestration of the merely human, inevitably rooted in the actual. I offer below an analysis of ''A Horse and Two Goats'' in a small bid to peep behind the curtains and see Narayan at work.

The opening lines:

> Of *the seven hundred thousand villages* dotting the map of India, in which *the majority of India's five hundred million live, flourish and die,* Kritam was *probably the tiniest,* indicated on the district survey map by a microscopic dot, the map being meant more for the revenue official out to collect tax than for the guidance of the *motorist,* who in any case could not hop to reach it since it sprawled far from the highway at the end of a rough track furrowed up by the iron-hopped wheels of bullock carts. *But its size did not prevent its giving itself the grandiose name Kritam, which meant in Tamil ''coronet'' or ''crown'' on the brow of this subcontinent.* The village consisted of less than thirty houses, only one of them built with brick and cement. Painted a brilliant yellow and blue all over with gorgeous carvings of gods and gargoyles on its balustrade, it was known as the Big House. The other houses, *distributed in four streets,* were generally of bamboo thatch, straw, mud, and other unspecified material. *Muni's was the last house in the fourth street,* beyond which stretched the fields. (Italics mine)

We notice the easy, unselfconscious narrowing down of the focus from *seven hundred thousand villages* and *five hundred million* (lives) to Kritam, the tiniest village, and Muni the least of its villagers. The phrase *live, flourish and die* is not as much of a

cliche as it appears; there is an unsuspected, seemingly endless agony between *flourish* and *die*: Muni in the story has had his halcyon days and is yet to die—we are going to witness him caught in that infernal suspension when living ends without death. Further there is the casual *motorist*; it is going to be a chance motorist that sets up ripples in the stagnant pond of Muni's life. And we also notice the touch of humour in the comment on the name Kritam; and as Muni is the least of the villagers his hut is the last in the last street of the village. (This is about two-thirds of the opening paragraph of the story. Further in the same paragraph we are also introduced to the ''horse'' of the title; we are told that the horse is, unexpectedly, made of clay. The horse is a ''horse.'')

So Muni is poor. A definition of his poverty follows, in the second para of the story:

> His wife lit the domestic fire at dawn, boiled water in a mud pot, threw into it *a handful of millet flour,* added salt, and gave him his first nourishment for the day. When he started out, she would put in his hand *a packed lunch,* once again the same millet cooked into a little ball, which he could swallow with a raw onion at midday. *She was old, but he was older and needed all the attention she could give him in order to be kept alive.*

This seems as good an account of Indian poverty as any (isn't Indian poverty a prime export item for many of our novelists in English?). But let us pause at the *packed lunch.* To commuters in India it might evoke associations of tiffin carriers; for westerners it could mean a nice fat carton of selective (watch your calories) snacks. We have already been told that Muni's first nourishment could not be more than *a handful of millet flour*; and when we are told that Muni's wife put in his hand *a packed lunch* it might conceivably rouse our expectations for Muni. But having roused our expectations, Narayan dashes them in the very next breath (just with the interruption of a comma): *once again the same millet cooked into a little ball, which he could swallow with a raw onion at midday.* And this is poverty pared of sentimentality because it is illustrationally, the definition of Muni's poverty; but here is how, to cap it, Narayan concludes his statement:

> . . . *She was old, but he was older and needed all the attention she could give him in order to be kept alive.*

This is a sudden lighting up; coming through the old woman's point of view, it is her casually muted, endearingly cynical expression of her love for her old man. This unobtrusive surfacing of the love between this old man and this old woman, the beauty of their relationship, in spite of the enormity of their indigence, is what gives the entire passage the sound of being merely factual and unsentimental; neither shutting his eyes to the presence of the wolves at the door nor spurning sentiment within the hut, Narayan gives character and dignity to the couple's poverty. The last sentence breaks through the crust of the preceding lines even as their humanity does through their sub-human living.

Narayan's invention moves ahead to illustrate and dramatize, to root his characters and their setting firmly in the actual. Here is the second half of the next paragraph:

> . . . And so the two goats were tethered to the trunk of a drumstick tree which grew in front of his hut from which occasionally Muni could shake down drumsticks. *This morning he got six.* He carried them in with a sense of triumph. Although no one could say precisely who owned the tree, it was his because *he lived in its shadow.*

First, Narayan has initiated action with *This morning he got six.* For these six precious drumsticks Narayan sends Muni a little later to the shopman of the village who helps reveal a new dimension of Muni's poverty. And meanwhile there is the last sentence. *Although no one could say precisely who owned the tree, it was his because he lived in its shadow.* This is the drumstick tree. I believe that Narayan could have planted with equal facility any other vegetable tree or plant here; for example, a jack fruit tree or a gourd creeper. But it has to be the drumstick tree; for of course any South Indian with half Muni's weakness for drumstick sauce will know that a drumstick tree, as trees go, casts pretty little shadow; its small sparse leaves don't help, unlike say a banyan tree, shelter anybody that "lives" in its shadow. We normally have to take the idiomatic meaning of the phrase, but I think in the given context it acquires literal overtones. Thus we see that Narayan's invention is very economical—the crafty artist not only makes use of the drumsticks but also the drumstick leaves.

When Muni asks his wife for drumstick sauce, she orders him out to somehow procure the groceries for making the sauce; and Muni approaches the village shopman. The shopman helps Narayan throw light on Muni in a couple of ways. First we come to know of the "daughter."

> "I will pay you everything on the first of the next month." "As always, and whom do you expect to rob by then?" Muni felt caught and mumbled, "My

> Here of course is the East-West encounter, so dear to our writers and critics—with a vital difference: it is offered to us through the prism of Narayan's vision, humanized by his humour."

daughter has sent word that she will be sending me money."

> "Have you a daughter?" sneered the shopman. "And she is sending you money! . . ."

The Munis have no children, as a little later on we come to know. In the Indian context even if one has many daughters (not a welcome proposition) one rarely expects to receive monthly allowance from any one of them—where's your self-respect? But even daughters will do for Muni, childless, would very much like to have some.

> He recollected the thrill he had felt when he mentioned a daughter to that shopman; although it was not believed, what if he did not have a daughter?—his cousin in the next village had many daughters, and any one of them was as good as his; he was fond of them all and would buy them sweets *if he could afford it.* Still everyone in the village whispered behind their backs that Muni and his wife were a barren couple. . . .

The non-existent daughter thus adds a new dimension to Muni's poverty; he is not only poor in money and material possessions, he is also utterly poor—in progeny. This sort of freckles Muni's character, this old man, and he is insinuated fully into our sympathy.

Muni may be poor but he still has vestiges of dignity and self-respect. Here is the conclusion of his unsuccessful mission to the shopman who indulges in Muni-baiting giving him nothing but mockery and scorn.

> . . . Muni thought helplessly, "My poverty is exposed to everybody. But what can I do?"

> "More likely you are seventy," said the shopman. "You also forget that you mentioned a birthday five weeks ago when you wanted castor oil for your holy bath."

"Bath! Who can dream of a bath when you have to scratch the tankbed for a bowl of water? We would all be parched and dead but for the Big House, where they let us take a pot of water from their well." After saying this Muni unobtrusively rose and moved off.

He told his wife, "That scoundrel would not give me anything. So go out and sell the drumsticks for what they are worth."

Muni may not have got much out of the shopman but Narayan has. Narayan's art is rich in the invention of the actual. But let us now move on to the farcical scene that is central to the action of the story. This is the scene between Muni and the foreigner. Basically Narayan is exploiting a device from the slapstick drama of our popular theatre. It is the humour of situation and dialogue that two deaf people create when they encounter each other in earnest business.

> ... Now the other man (the foreigner) suddenly pressed his palms together in a salute, smiled and said, "Namaste! How do you do?"

> At which Muni spoke the only English expressions he had learnt, "Yes, no." Having exhausted his English vocabulary, he started in Tamil. ...

And while "The foreigner nodded his head and listened courteously though he understood nothing," he is anxious that the Indian should understand him; he has already set his heart on the statue. He is puzzled that Muni doesn't understand English. He says:

> "... I have gotten along with English everywhere in this country, but you don't speak it. Have you any religious or spiritual scruples against English speech?"

Not an incapable man. But with Muni he seems to be getting nowhere; the two are on two different wavelengths. Here is more evidence of Narayan's shrewd exploitation of the linguistic curtain between the two:

> Noting the other's interest in his speech. Muni felt encouraged to ask, "How many children have you?" with appropriate gestures with his hands. Realizing that a question was being asked, the red man replied, "I said a hundred," which encouraged Muni to go into details. "How many of your children are boys and how many girls? Where are they? Is your daughter married? It is difficult to find a son-in-law in your country also?"

So they go on, representatives of two civilizations, failing to establish contact except by the sheerest accident when the result as in the climax, is comic catastrophe.

> The foreigner followed his look and decided that it would be a sound policy to show an interest in *the old*

man's pets. He went up casually to them and stroked their backs with every show of courteous attention. Now the truth dawned on the old man. His dream of a lifetime was about to be realised. He understood that the red man was actually making an offer for the goats.

Thus Muni and what's-his-name. But what is the foreigner's name? He is unnamed. He is the red-faced foreigner, the red man, the foreigner without a name. But how marvellously Narayan invents the American with the very quirk and tang of the American's speech:

> "... I assure you that this will have the best home in the USA. I'll push away the bookcase, you know, I love books and am a member of five book clubs, and the choice and bonus volumes mount up to a pile really in our living room, as high as this horse itself. But they'll have to go. Ruth may disapprove, but I will convince her. The TV may have to be shifted too. We can't have everything in the living room. Ruth will probably say what about when we have a party? I'm going to keep him right in the middle of the room. I don't see how that can interfere with the party—we'll stand around him and have our drinks."

This is expert literary ventriloquism and it helps superbly concretize the image of the American. Still, this is a case of a character being endowed with more than a local habitation—and that without a name: purposely. His speech, his manner and his actions typify him as a westerner (and who is more western in modern times than a New Yorker?); and the elision of his name, perfectly natural in the situation, is just the deviation to endow him with more than ordinary significance. He had told his wife in America, "We will visit India this winter, it's time to look at other civilizations." The unnamed foreigner is a typical representative of his civilization. He is *the* westerner.

The other civilization is India and of course who more true to her than Muni? To begin with he comes from *probably the tiniest village* of India. Narayan has always believed that India is her villages. (We remember *The Guide*; it is the rural India that traps Raju and positively sublimates him.) Narayan has already indicated this in his opening line. "Of the seven hundred thousand villages dotting the map of India, in which the majority of India's five hundred million live ..." Not simply quantitatively; even qualitatively India is her villages. The *tiniest* (and *microscopic dot*) is thus microcosmic and the name Kritam with that selective touch of humour Narayan honours it with emphasizes the same symbolic value, with *the four streets* as likely standing for the four chief castes of the traditional Indian society. Muni may not know more than "Yes, no" of English (the only one who knows English in Kritam, the postman, has not prospered much—he is fighting shy of the shopman to whom he is indebted and his wife has run away with somebody); but he has imbibed the puranas through the oral tradition, and the *Ramayana* and the *Mahabaratha* and the legends of the land, can talk no end of them. He is poor *and* dignified; unlettered *and* well-drilled in the country's rich lore. Muni is as Indian as one in the centre of the society can realistically wish. He is the Indian delegate; he represents India for Narayan.

Here of course is the East-West encounter, so dear to our writers and critics—with a vital difference: it is offered to us through the prism of Narayan's vision, humanized by his humour.

But that is not the end of the story's potential for significance. The statue of the horse and soldier too is subject to just that accretion of meaning which marks it out as a metaphor. Narayan's careful and elaborate description of the statue—running into 24 lines—is supported by Muni's attempt at estimating its ancestry:

> "... I was an urchin this high when I heard my grandfather explain this horse and warrior, and my grandfather himself was this high when he heard his grandfather, whose grandfather...."

In the heightened context of the encounter between India and the West, the Horse stands for India's ancient heritage. But there is no sentimental mushing up here. We come back to the title, "A Horse and Two Goats." A Horse made of clay; Muni sees no value in it; though he has moved in its shadow ever since he can remember, he is not aware of any special value attached to it; but the appreciative American businessman is eager to possess it—even if he has to build his cocktail parties around it. Two Goats; made of poor (metaphorical) clay, probably far below the stipulations of a Chicago butcher. The gawky goats are Muni's only property, his only capital and not the horse; the American of course has no use for them, except to ingratiate himself with—for he has concluded they are Muni's *pets*. Each thinks the other values what he himself values; each doesn't value what the other does. In the event both leave with an absurd sense of business well—and hardly—done.

Source: V. Panduranga Rao, "The Craftmanship of R. K. Narayan," in *Indian Writing in English,* edited by Ramesh Mohan, Orient Longman, Ltd., 1978, pp. 56-64.

Sources

Ramana, P. S. *Message in Design: A Study of R. K. Narayan's Fiction,* New Delhi: Harman Publishing House, 1993, pp. 131-32.

Shack, Neville. A review of *Under the Banyan Tree and Other Stories,* in *Times Literary Supplement,* October 18, 1985, p. 1168.

Taliaferro, Frances. A review of *Under the Banyan Tree and Other Stories,* in *Book World—The Washington Post,* July 28, 1985, pp. 7, 13.

Trivedi, H. C., and N. C. Soni. "Short Stories of R. K. Narayan: An Estimate," in *Perspectives on R. K. Narayan,* edited by Atma Ram, Atlantic Highlands, NJ: Humanities Press, 1981, p. 191.

Walsh, William. *R. K. Narayan: A Critical Appreciation,* Chicago: University of Chicago Press, 1982, p. 100.

Further Reading

Johnson, Gordon. *Cultural Atlas of India,* New York: Facts on File, 1996.
    A thorough introduction to the rich cultural and political history of the Indian subcontinent, featuring detailed maps and many illustrations showing the area's ethnic and religious diversity.

Kain, Geoffrey, editor. *R. K. Narayan: Contemporary Critical Perspectives,* East Lansing: Michigan State University Press, 1993.
    Nearly all of the essays in this collection focus on Narayan's novels and his short fiction of Malgudi, but they provide useful insights into his overriding themes and techniques. The volume includes John Lowe's interview with Narayan, in which the writer reveals himself to be strangely and fascinatingly uninterested in his own writing processes.

Narayan, R. K. *My Days: A Memoir,* New York: Viking, 1974.
    This award-winning autobiography covers Narayan's first 67 years and first 17 books in under 200 pages. His stories of life in India, and the influence of his family on his work, read like the best of his fiction.

Walsh, William. *R. K. Narayan: A Critical Appreciation,* Chicago: University of Chicago Press, 1982.
    Although no longer up to date, this is the most readable overview of Narayan's life and work. It includes an insightful biography and an interpretation of "A Horse and Two Goats."

The Lady with the Pet Dog

Anton Chekhov

1899

"The Lady with the Pet Dog" was published in 1899, during Chekhov's two-year stay at the seaside health resort at Yalta, where he had been sent because of his tuberculosis. Though he found Yalta painfully boring, he produced many of his finest stories during that time, including "Gooseberries," "The Darling," "On Official Business," and "The Lady with the Pet Dog," his most famous story. Well received by audiences when it was published, the reputation of this tale of adultery and discovery of true love has only grown over time. Many critics believe that Chekhov drew upon Leo Tolstoy's *Anna Karenina,* an epic novel with an adulterous heroine, by painting a similarly complex moral and emotional portrait in only a few pages. Chekhov was able to speak volumes in a few words by his selection of gestures or details. Unlike Chekhov's contemporaries—most notably Tolstoy and Dostoevsky—who were preoccupied with sweeping historical, philosophical, and religious themes, Chekhov was interested in the smallest moments of human interest. While Tolstoy and Dostoevsky were driven by profound moral convictions, Chekhov was noted for his cool objectivity. He was reluctant to moralize, adhering to his own conviction that it is less important to moralize over a horse thief or an adulterer than it is to understand them. In "The Lady with the Pet Dog," Chekhov neither romanticizes nor condemns the illicit love affair between Gurov and Anna. He simply presents it, but with such clarity and perception that the reader recog-

nizes the profundity of what the characters experience and is entirely persuaded by their reality.

Author Biography

Born on January 29, 1860, in Taganrog, Russia, Chekhov, the third of six children, was the grandson of a serf who bought his freedom. His father owned a small grocery business which went bankrupt, leaving the family impoverished. Chekhov managed to earn a scholarship to study medicine at the University of Moscow, and by 1884 he went into practice. By this time Chekhov had published humorous sketches in magazines in order to support his family. He supported his mother and sisters for many years, turning out sketches and stories with astonishing speed while also practicing medicine.

Famous for the profound influence of his plays on the course of modern drama, Chekhov perhaps exerted an even greater influence on the modern short story. While he is known for his sympathy for and insight into the human condition, his stories ultimately exhibited dispassionate emotional balance, rigorous stylistic control, and a rational, ironic, and sometimes cynical attitude toward human relationships and aspirations. It is Chekhov's cool, detached artfulness that distinguished his work from the confessional style of Dostoevsky, the moral fervor of Tolstoy, and the absurdist fantasies of Gogol.

Critics note that Chekhov wrote "The Lady with the Pet Dog"—the story of a middle-aged man's belated discovery of true love—shortly before he himself married actress Olga Knipper in 1901. Their love was bittersweet, as he did not expect to live long. Some critics point out that just as Gurov felt bored and disgusted by the triviality of Moscow society in the absence of Anna, Chekhov felt miserable among high society at a health resort in Yalta (where he composed the story while seeking a tuberculosis cure) because he was separated from Olga. Like Gurov, Chekhov loved the company of women and seemed to share a special sympathy with them but simultaneously remained somewhat detached.

Chekhov was influenced by Tolstoy's ideas on ascetic morality and nonresistance to evil. He especially became more actively concerned about human suffering after visiting and caring for patients at a penal colony on the island of Sakhalin. In one of his most famous stories, "Ward Six," Chekhov depicts a doctor's inner journey from philosophical detachment to deep human sympathy, which resembles Gurov's journey from a thoughtless and cynical lady's man to a deeply sympathetic lover in "The Lady with the Pet Dog."

Chekhov's first major work as a dramatist, *The Seagull,* was produced in 1896 by the Moscow Art Theater. Although the first performance of this unprecedentedly realistic and "uneventful" play caused the outraged audience to riot, it was soon appreciated as a new and profound kind of theater and was followed by *Uncle Vanya, The Cherry Orchard,* and *The Three Sisters.* Chekhov died from tuberculosis in 1904 in a Black Forest health spa.

Plot Summary

Parts I and II

Dmitry Gurov is vacationing at a seaside spa in Yalta without his family. He is less than forty years old, but was married young and already has a twelve-year-old daughter and two sons. He finds his wife to be somewhat harsh and not particularly intelligent. Although Gurov is generally at ease among women, he is somewhat dismissive of the sex in general, referring to them as the "inferior race," though he could not live a day without them. A new visitor to Yalta catches his eye—a young lady who walks her white pomeranian. He imagines a dalliance with her but is determined to keep it light and frivolous.

Gurov meets the young lady one evening by playing with her dog. He learns that her name is Anna Sergeyevna and that she is married but not travelling with her husband. Anna and Gurov take a walk by the sea, and later in his hotel room he remembers her softness, timidity, and beauty. She is very different from his wife, yet there is something pathetic about her, he thinks.

A week passes and they go together one sultry evening to greet the steamer. After the dock empties, they go back to Anna's room and make love. Afterwards, Anna weeps, fearing that Gurov will no longer respect her. She bemoans the way she has deceived herself, not only in Yalta but throughout her married life. Her husband, a minor official in a small city, is a "flunkey," she cries, and her life a disappointment. As she weeps, Gurov, bored and a little annoyed, munches on a slice of watermelon. He does not see why they should make a tragedy out

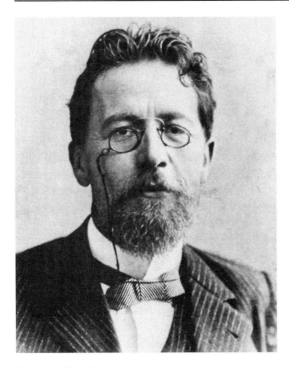

Anton Chekhov

of their dalliance. They go out at sunrise to the beach at Oreanda, sit on a bench, and watch the sea. Gurov is moved by the scene, thinking about how everything in the world is beautiful when reflected upon—everything except what people do when they forget the lofty aims of existence and their own human worth.

They spend the rest of their time at Yalta together, taking midnight trips to waterfalls or Oreanda, and are always impressed by the scenery.

When it is time to go home, Gurov feels remorseful. He does not think that Anna was happy with him. He had been warm but also ironical, keeping things light and treating her with the arrogance of a happy male almost twice her age. She had called him kind and high-minded, and he feels that he has deceived her. He now believes the affair to be over.

Part III

Back in Moscow, Gurov exults in the winter scenery which reminds him of his youth, and enjoys the distractions of Muscovite society. He cannot, however, get Anna out of his mind, and begins to find himself disgusted with frivolous and repetitive conversation in clubs and restaurants with scenes of drunkenness and gluttony. One night he tries to tell

an acquaintance about Anna, but the man only wants to talk about the fish they just ate.

Obsessed with constant thoughts of Anna, Gurov is now determined to find her. He tells his wife he must go to St. Petersburg but instead goes off to Anna's provincial city. He frequently watches her house, catching only the sight of her pomeranian, let out for a walk by the maid. He paces his provincial hotel room, wondering what he is doing in Anna's city, and then goes that night to the local opera, where he sees Anna and her "flunkey" husband. Anna is horrified by the sight of him and tries to flee, but he pursues her into a dark and remote corridor. Anna tells Gurov that she misses him and promises to visit him in Moscow.

Part IV

Back in Moscow, Gurov walks his daughter to school through the snow. He cannot stop thinking about Anna as they are talking, for he is on his way to a rendezvous. They have been seeing each other regularly in Moscow every two or three months. When he arrives at her hotel room she is pale and unhappy from waiting for him. Their situation is growing unbearable: They love each other like husband and wife, and he feels a profound compassion for her. Despite his intention that he and Anna would have a frivolous affair, he finds that he has fallen in love for the first time in his life. He catches sight of himself in the mirror and sees himself as a middle-aged man whose hair is starting to turn gray. He thinks that he has lost his looks, and that Anna, too, will soon begin to fade and wither. Normally logical and rational when Anna is sad, Gurov now only wants to be sincere and tender with her. He tells her that they will one day find some way to live openly, and when she asks him how, he clutches her head, speaking of how he believes that although a rough time is coming up for them, one day in the not too distant future they would be together.

Characters

Dmitry Dmitrich Gurov

While staying at a seaside resort, Gurov engages himself in an adulterous affair that changes his life. He is under forty, married, and has children. His parents "found a wife for him" when he was only in his second year of college, but he feels that she is unintelligent and severe. When he tries to hint that he is in love with another, she tells him that the part of a lover "doesn't suit him." Although Gurov attracts women easily, he regards them as "the inferior race," but "couldn't live a day without them." When he meets Anna, he wants only a casual dalliance. He knows from "really bitter experience" that love affairs always become complex and painful, but he tries this time to believe that an affair between he and Anna can be simply a charming diversion. During the affair, Gurov remains somewhat aloof, as evidenced by his munching on watermelon as Anna weeps. But back in Moscow, he cannot forget her. He is disgusted by Moscow society and goes to Anna's city to find her. It is unlike Gurov to behave in such an impulsive, romantic way, but he realizes that he has finally found true love. He resolves to live openly with Anna, though this means sacrificing everything. He has come a long way from being a casual seducer.

Anna Sergeyevna

Anna Sergeyevna is a young woman of twenty, unhappily married to a minor small-town official whom she refers to as a "flunkey." She is timid and soft spoken and feels remorse as soon as she and Gurov have made love. She says that it is not her husband she has deceived but herself, for she persuaded herself that she loved her husband when she did not, and she married too young because she was driven by a passionate curiosity and a desire "to live." Anna loves Gurov, and recognizes good qualities in him which he fails to see himself, but the affair makes her unhappy because she feels guilty and knows that their love is impossible. When Gurov comes to visit her in her small town, she is horrified, and instead visits him in Moscow, waiting miserably in her hotel room for long stretches at a time. She is often miserable and feels hopelessly trapped by her situation.

Themes

Morals and the Meaning of Life

Although Gurov lightly enters into an adulterous love affair with Anna that soon turns painful and complicated, it would be misleading to say that the main theme of "The Lady with the Pet Dog" is one of moral corruption or sin. In fact, it is through this adulterous affair that Gurov discovers his humanity and even his moral center. Gurov has always taken women for granted and has treated them without compassion or respect. During the course of his affair with Anna, however, he becomes more and

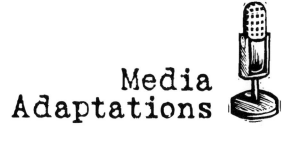

Media Adaptations

- "The Lady with the Pet Dog" was adapted as the film *The Lady with the Dog* by director Yosif Heifitz, starring Iya Savvina, Alexei Batalov, Ala Chostakova, and N. Alisova. 1959; distributed by White Star, Facets Multimedia, Inc., and Ingram International Films.

more concerned about the consequences of his actions. Chekhov's treatment of morality is complex; he is not conventionally moralistic, yet his story suggests a strong personal morality. Gurov and Anna truly love each other, and their bad marriages are unfortunate aspects of their lives. Little sympathy or consideration is offered to the respective spouses of the adulterous couple. Anna grieves as soon as they have made love, but more because she is worried about what Gurov will think of her than because she feels that she has betrayed her husband: "It is not my husband I have deceived," she believes, "but myself." Gurov errs in thinking that their affair is unimportant, but this is not so much a moral error as an underestimation of his own moral character. He learns that he is not the cynical lover that he thought he was and suffers terribly for having placed Anna in an unhappy situation.

If Chekhov posits moral values here, they are such values as honesty, seriousness, and true love. Deception more than infidelity causes Anna and Gurov to suffer, and at the end of the story they know that they must make painful and difficult decisions which will allow them to live together openly and honestly. After he becomes involved with Anna, Gurov discovers that "everything that was of interest and importance to him, everything that was essential to him, everything about which he felt sincerely and did not deceive himself . . . was going on concealed from others; while all that was false . . . went on in the open." Gurov learns that he cannot tolerate living a lie and that it was wrong to engage in a superficial relationship with Anna.

A view of Moscow in the summer of 1912.

Similarly, Gurov has learned a moral lesson regarding his attitude towards women in general. He has always belittled women, regarding them as the "inferior race," but throughout the story gains a certain respect for Anna, and regards her as a friend.

True love appears to be the highest good in "The Lady with the Pet Dog." Anna and Gurov must extricate themselves from false marriages and together create a genuine one, as they already love each other "like man and wife, like tender friends." Once Gurov has discovered true love, he finds himself intolerant of the Moscow social life, a life "clipped and wingless, an absurd mess." This allusion to the possibility of a more meaningful, dignified, and fulfilled life refers back to his revelation when he sat with Anna watching the sea at Oreanda and was struck by the beauty of "everything except what we think or do ourselves when we forget the higher aims of life and our own human dignity." The "higher aims" are not spelled out, but if the story is an indication, they lie in the pursuit of love, truth, and beauty. In this case, truth and beauty appear to reside in nature.

Nature and Its Meaning

Gurov and Anna are united by their appreciation of natural beauty, and beauty which brings out

the best in both of them. After they first make love, there is a somewhat painful scene in Anna's hotel room in which she frets about her bad marriage while Gurov, callous and impatient, munches on watermelon. They later go to the beach to watch the sun rise, and Gurov is "soothed and spellbound" by nature's beauty. Listening to the timeless surf, he contemplates the scenery as a moral, even mystical reverie that reminds him of the "higher aims of life." This is the most lyrical, intense, and deeply felt moment in their early love affair. The fact that they are looking at the sea rather than at each other binds their deep love for each other into the timeless natural order of things. The Greek philosopher Plato believed that beautiful things were a physical manifestation of spiritual "eternal forms," of God, and Gurov thinks that the constancy of the surf is perhaps "a pledge of our eternal salvation."

In "The Lady with the Pet Dog" that which is false, difficult, and painful is described in the context of human civilization, and that which is beautiful and true is described in the context of nature. The most terrible and painful moment of the story occurs in a second-rate opera house, a theater of man-made illusions. Moreover, Gurov and Anna often find themselves confined in depressing, impersonal hotel rooms. Gurov tries to speak of love at his men's club, but his companion is more interested in his dinner. Anna lives in a house that faces a long gray fence studded with nails. Gurov is only happy away from Anna when admiring trees or snow. Civilization is a prison for them, but nature is a place of refuge and spiritual significance.

Style

Point of View

The narrative style used by Chekhov in "The Lady with the Pet Dog" is third person, somewhat cool and detached like the character of Gurov himself. In this story, however, the third-person point of view is not entirely omniscient (in which one knows everything and can go anywhere) because the reader never directly perceives the thoughts of Anna Sergeyevna. It is a limited third person, through which the reader can understand Gurov's thoughts and feelings, and it is through Gurov's thoughts and perceptions that we learn about Anna. In the very first sentence, for example, the third-person narrative is subtly limited to Gurov's point of view: "A new person, it was said, had appeared on the esplanade. . . ." An omniscient narrator knows everything, and would simply know there was a new person; he would not need to hear about it. It is Gurov, then, who hears things said about a new female arrival. Moreover, the title of the story itself advertises Gurov's point of view, for an omniscient narrator would know the lady's name. All that Gurov knows at first is that there is a lady with a pet dog. Chekhov explores at length Gurov's shifting thoughts and feelings about Anna. Interestingly, Gurov never thinks about how his family will be affected by his infidelity; his thoughts are only of Anna. To the extent that the story has a "rising action" and a "climax," these are largely internal, as Gurov goes from viewing himself as a casual seducer of a "lady with a pet dog" whose name he does not know to the true and responsible lover of Anna Sergeyevna, whose name means more to him than any words in the language.

At the very end of the story, the third-person point of view becomes fully omniscient as Chekhov reads the thoughts of both his lovers at once: it "was clear to both of them that the end was still far off. . . ." By breaking the rule and entering Anna's head as well as Gurov's, he underscores their love by having them now, at last, thinking with one mind and feeling with one heart.

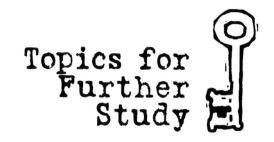

Topics for Further Study

- Research the legal consequences of and cultural attitudes toward infidelity in Russia at the end of the nineteenth century. Also research the divorce laws and the cultural attitudes regarding divorce after the Revolution in the twentieth century. Compare your findings and relate them to the story.

- Read "The Dead" by James Joyce, a story possibly influenced by "The Lady with the Pet Dog," and compare Gabriel Conroy's inner journey with Gurov's. How do the stories differ in terms of style and theme?

- Research the subject of health resorts or spas at the end of the nineteenth century in the United States and abroad. What medical purpose did they serve? What social purpose?

- Chekhov is famous for his "humanity" and "empathy," but in this story, nobody seems to care much about the feelings of the other members of Gurov's family or about Anna's husband. Do you agree with that statement? If so, how do you account for this omission?

Setting

Chekhov sets the scene in this story with great economy, yet certain unforgettable settings powerfully enhance a given mood or effect. Little is known about Yalta save for the sultry heat, the wind, which makes people restless, and the effect of various lights, including moonlight and dawn, upon the sea. These details create an erotic and dreamy atmosphere in which the reader may understand that Anna and Gurov would have difficulty thinking clearly. There is also a timeless, eternal quality to the sleepy landscape, marked by the rhythm of the sea and the clouds which sit motionless on mountain peaks.

Another memorable setting is the town where Anna lives. Chekhov gives the reader a feeling for the whole town when he describes the best room at the hotel in which Gurov stayed: "the floor was covered with gray army cloth, and on the table there was an inkstand, gray with dust and topped by a figure on horseback, its hat raised in its hand and its head broken off." Not only does this description convey the depressed and provincial nature of the place, and suggest how Anna must feel trapped here and thirsty for romance, but the headless figure with the raised hat can be seen as a symbol of Gurov himself, who has come to town to be the heroic lover but has little in the way of youthful heroism to offer. The fence studded with nails across from Anna's house increases the sense of her being confined and unhappy, though the reader has yet to see her. Finally, the noisy local musical theater is a suitably second-rate and depressing place for Gurov and Anna to confront the unhappiness of their circumstances. Chekhov selects details of setting to convey a particular mood and illuminate the emotional lives of his characters.

Historical Context

Marital Infidelity

"The Lady with the Pet Dog" was published in 1899 and heralded the moral dilemmas of the coming century. Marital infidelity was not exactly new in literature at the time. In fact, it was the central subject of three of the greatest novels of the latter half of the nineteenth century—Hawthorne's *The Scarlet Letter,* Flaubert's *Madame Bovary* and Tolstoy's *Anna Karenina.* Marriages were often arranged at this time, and people married very young and often for social or economic advancement. Consequently many marriages were unhappy, and divorce was not usually an option. Love affairs, then, were something of a preoccupation among the upper classes though they occurred far less frequently than literature, and the gossip of the time, led one to believe. Chekhov himself complained that the seaside resort of Yalta had a greatly exaggerated reputation for immorality, but in "The Lady with the Pet Dog" he did nothing to discourage Yalta's reputation.

In any case, adultery was very much on the minds of the literate class, particularly women who lacked the economic power and freedom to keep men as men kept mistresses and could not resort, as men did, to the houses of prostitution which were common in major cities. The fiction of the popular French author Guy De Maupassant is filled with blithe love affairs, and it was a common complication in French theatrical farces. The darker side of infidelity was depicted in countless "women's novels" of the time, a genre in which a woman must often struggle against a predatory male to preserve her virtue.

Though talk of love affairs was increasingly commonplace, it was disastrous for a woman to be caught in an act of infidelity. She would lose her reputation, her social standing, the custody of her children (as in the case of Anna Karenina), and she could find herself cast out of society, even by her own parents. If her husband divorced her, he could leave her penniless, with little hope of finding respectable employment. Such cold facts of women's lives led such literary characters as Anna Karenina and Emma Bovary, for example, to take their own lives when their adultery was discovered. This may even have reflected the attitudes toward unfaithful women of Flaubert and Tolstoy themselves (though the degree to which these authors "punish" their adulterous heroines is greatly debated; Flaubert himself said, "I am Madame Bovary"). The punishments meted out to men who engaged in such affairs were not comparable, which is perhaps one reason why Gurov is more concerned about Anna's plight than his own and why it is better for them to meet in Moscow, where Gurov is known but Anna is not. Better he be caught than she.

In "The Lady with the Pet Dog" the characters do not consider suicide. Gurov and Anna hope to someday be together, which reflects the lessening severity of the public attitude towards marital infidelity, but they are not terribly hopeful, either. The story ends on a powerfully uncertain note: it seems that the solution which will permit them "a glorious life" will be found in "a little while." At the same time, however, they both know "the end was still far off," and the most "complicated and difficult" phase of their life is just beginning.

A Climate of Uncertainty

The uncertain note upon which the story ends is fitting, for it reflects the uncertainty that was prevalent in Russia at the end of the nineteenth century. Acceptable morality was changing, religious beliefs were weakening, and the very legal and social fabric of the society was unraveling, as the serfs were granted more freedom and the Tsar, an absolute ruler, was surrendering more power to the people. The entire political structure was filled with liberal reforms and reactionary countermeasures. Artists like Chekhov, Tolstoy, and Dostoevsky were uncer-

Compare & Contrast

- **1900s:** Extra-marital affairs and divorce are social taboos, often resulting in the social ostracization of offending parties.

  1990s: Over half of all marriages are believed to result in divorce.

- **1900s:** Russian government is ruled by a monar-

chy, resulting in vast inequalities in the distribution of wealth and resources.

1990s: After over 70 years of Communist rule, Russia institutes a free-market, capitalist economy. Economic difficulties continue.

---

tain of what path the country should take. All of them were compassionate towards the suffering endured by the poor, and to varying degrees, were hostile towards the Tsar and to the current system of land ownership. All were suspicious, however, of the Bolshevik revolutionaries who would eventually overthrow the government and institute a Communist regime in 1918. Dostoevsky and Tolstoy had fervent, even mystical religious beliefs which made them dislike the atheism of the revolutionaries. Chekhov was much more concerned with social injustice and had no patience for the Russian church or other national institutions. Chekhov's characters, particularly in his plays, are unable to think or act decisively. Gurov and Anna, at the end of "The Lady with the Pet Dog" are hopeful, but they are gripped with uncertainty.

Health Resorts

Perhaps due to the spiritual malaise, and the social and moral uncertainty experienced by Europe's middle and upper classes, many people were sent to "health resorts" or "spas" around the end of the nineteenth century to cure their mysterious ailments. Lassitude or depression was often interpreted as an early sign of tuberculosis, a very real disease that gradually killed a large number of people during that period, including Chekhov himself. These health spas were generally located in dry regions, high in the mountains or along the sea shore. Gurov and Anna were at the seaside resort town of Yalta, perhaps for health reasons. Although these are never specified, it would be one way to explain why they are able to vacation without their

families. Perhaps they were suffering from some kind of "neurasthenic disorder" (a popular term at the time for what were perhaps a variety of physical and mental ailments today classified as "chronic fatigue syndrome," "depression," "nerves," or in extreme cases a "nervous breakdown"), or perhaps they feigned ill health in order to remove themselves from their unhappy family situations, as people sometimes did at the time. The widespread concern about tuberculosis made such an excuse persuasive. Other great novels and stories have been set in health resorts, most famously Thomas Mann's *Magic Mountain*. The distinction in such places between the truly sick and those merely relaxing was, like so many things at that time, uncertain.

Critical Overview

A century after "The Lady with the Pet Dog" was published in 1899, the short story's critical reputation has not diminished, a testament to the fact that this story was both of its time and ahead of its time, influencing much of the short fiction that has been written in the twentieth century. Vladimir Nabokov, one of the greatest novelists of our time, author of the groundbreaking *Lolita*, asserts that in "The Lady with the Pet Dog" "all the traditional rules of story telling have been broken. There is no problem, no regular climax, no point at the end. And it is one of the greatest stories ever written."

In the Soviet era, Russian critics focused on the fact that Gurov and Anna are representatives of the common people, not aristocrats like Anna's namesake in *Anna Karenina* and her lover, Count Vronsky. Gurov and Anna, these critics note, seek to liberate themselves from the petty materialism and oppressive marital arrangements of their time, seeking a higher spiritual good and learning to respect each other as equals. Western critic Virginia Llewellyn Smith, however, argues that although Gurov and Anna are "changed for the better" through the discovery of true love, they are changed "not in relation to society, but in relation to their own inner lives. Gurov is shaken out of his romantic dreaming by a sudden recognition of the grossness of others in his stratum of society: but he does not give up his job or abandon his social life."

Critics in the west have also focused on the comparison with Anna Karenina. Thomas Winner notes that "While both are stories of an Anna who, unhappily married to a prosaic bureaucrat, finds a lover, Chekhov's Anna does not think of suicide. Rather, her love affair brings her contentment and some happiness." Winner distinguishes both Chekhov's attitudes and Chekhov's style from Tolstoy's when he writes that Chekhov's development of the adultery theme "without dramatic collision and tragic endings, is a typical avowal of independence from traditional treatments. Stylistic and structural devices also reveal Chekhov's antipathy to conventional forms."

Critics also often note the parallels between Gurov's situation and Chekhov's own life. Chekhov was the same age as his protagonist, and, like Gurov, had just fallen in love for the first time, marrying actress Olga Knipper. Before that time, Llewellyn Smith notes that Chekhov, like Gurov, "enjoyed the company of women and had many female friends and admirers: but he failed, or was unwilling, to involve himself deeply or lastingly with them." Chekhov recognized that when he finally fell in love it was too late, Llewellyn Smith suggests. He was dying of tuberculosis and had to confine himself much of the time to a Yalta sanitarium, while Olga Knipper pursued her acting career in Moscow. "The history of Gurov's relationships with women is a transmutation of Chekhov's history," Llewellyn Smith claims, "and the essential point of the fiction was reality for him: true love had come too late, and complete happiness—poetry and communication and companionship—was impossible." Winner disagrees with this gloomy assessment, believing that in "Lady with the Pet Dog" romantic love is "presented more hopefully than it is in other of Chekhov's stories." Despite the sol-

emn tone and sober ending of the story, Winner points to the "lyrical" subtext, and observes that "The alternation between cynicism, sincerity, and lyricism becomes almost rhythmical." Time and again, Gurov's impulse towards cynicism is followed by a moment of honesty with himself, and this by a lyrical swell, as when Gurov is cynical about Anna's weeping after they first make love, then becomes serious, and then, at the Oreanna seaside, has a lyrical epiphany. Again contrasting "Lady with the Pet Dog" with Anna Karenina, in which the "fallen" heroine eventually throws herself under the wheels of a train, Winner concludes "Rather than tragedy, the final note is of pathos. Muted and transient happiness is the fate which, as the concluding passage suggests, awaits Chekhov's lovers."

Criticism

Erik Huber

Huber has a Master of Fine Arts degree in Fiction Writing and currently teaches at the New York University School of Continuing Education. In the following essay, he provides an overview of the chief criticisms of "The Lady with the Pet Dog," focusing particularly on Chekhov's "casual" approach in writing the story.

"The Lady with the Pet Dog" is regarded as one of the greatest of all short stories, but it is not an easy story to "interpret," because Chekhov's chief aim in writing the story is to be as natural as possible and to respect people and things for what they are, rather than turning them into symbols and forcing them to convey a certain idea or message. Chekhov is reluctant to put himself above his characters and manipulate them. Perhaps the most famous criticism of the story comes from Vladimir Nabokov, the Russian emigre who taught literature at Cornell University and wrote the classic American novel *Lolita*. In discussing Chekhov's story he points out that "all the traditional rules of story telling have been broken . . . there is no problem, no regular climax, no point at the end. And it is one of the greatest stories ever written." One might wonder how such an uneventful and inconclusive story could be considered "great." It appears that Nabokov believes that its greatness lies in its trueness to the beauty and sadness of life. If one is looking for the kind of "entertainment" which helps one escape life, one will not find it in Chekhov, for he invites his readers

What Do I Read Next?

- "The Dead," James Joyce's classic short story published in 1914. This story concerns a middle-aged man who discovers a secret about his wife's past which leads him to reflect on love and mortality. Set at a lively but haunted Christmas party in Dublin, Ireland, Joyce's story ends with a scene that contains striking similarities to the final scene in "The Lady with the Pet Dog."

- "Learning from Chekhov," by Francine Prose, in *The Pushcart Prizes,* Vol. 13, (1990). This down to earth and amusing novelist and short story writer reflects on a semester of teaching writing students important rules only to see them broken again and again in the stories of Chekhov, which she is reading each night on the bus home. Provides very accessible insights into Chekhov's artistry.

- *Anna Karenina,* by Leo Tolstoy. One of Russia's best known novelists, this is the novel on which some critics say Chekhov based "The Lady with the Pet Dog."

- "The Name Day Party," by Anton Chekhov. Also known as "The Birthday Party" or "The Party." One of Chekhov's greatest works, this story of profound marital discontent is told from a woman's point of view.

- *Uncle Vanya,* by Chekhov. This play features, among others, a bored wife at a country estate and a restless rural doctor who hopes to seduce her. They do not act on their impulse as do the characters in "The Lady with the Pet Dog," but their situation still leads to painful complexity.

- *Where I'm Calling From* by Raymond Carver, published in 1989. This modern American short story writer of spare, humane, "minimalist" fiction was greatly influenced by Chekhov. This collection concludes with the story "Errand," about Chekhov's death. Carver himself died shortly after this work was published.

---

to perceive and feel the beauty and pity of the world as it is. Nabokov states that for Chekhov "the lofty and the base ... the slice of watermelon and the violet sea, and the hands of the town-governor" are all "essential" elements of that beauty. If one is looking for a satisfying moral or a final resolution, Chekhov will not provide one, for "there is no special moral to be drawn and no special message to be received," Nabokov contends that "the story does not really end, for as long as people are alive, there is no possible and definite conclusion to their troubles or hopes or dreams."

Nabokov also admires the economy and conciseness of Chekhov's descriptions and characterizations, which are "attained by a careful selection and careful distribution of minute but striking features, with perfect contempt for the sustained description, repetition, and strong emphasis of ordinary authors. In this or that description one detail is

chosen to illumine the whole setting." This not only permits Chekhov to say more with less, but it also keeps the focus on the world within the story rather than on the pyrotechnics of the writer. By not overwhelming the reader with elaborate descriptions or philosophizing, Chekhov makes his art appear casual.

Nabokov certainly exaggerates his claims that there is no "problem" or "climax" to Chekhov's story. Gurov is the protagonist; he is the only character who appears in every scene. The story is presented largely from his point of view, and it is his internal crisis, as we shall see, that indeed constitutes the climax of the story. And Gurov has a problem, though he does not recognize it until late in the story. At the beginning, he is a mildly bored philanderer on holiday, looking for a good time. He meets Anna and seduces her, and when she weeps over having been unfaithful to her husband, he is

" ... Chekhov does not present an alternative way of life and expresses little optimism about how humans might live if the obstacles to pursuing their desires were removed. His characters often have trouble understanding their desires in the first place."

bored and annoyed. He bids farewell to Anna with a mild sense of regret, sorry that the affair did not make her happy, but his mood brightens when he returns to the bustle of Moscow. As the winter deepens, however, Gurov finds that Anna is constantly on his mind. He wants to speak to others of his feelings for her, but nobody will listen. This eventually leads him to a great feeling of disgust towards the "savage manners," the "gluttony," the "continual talk always about the same thing" that defines his existence in Moscow society. "Futile pursuits and conversations always about the same topics take up the better part of one's time, the better part of one's strength, and in the end there is left a life clipped and wingless, an absurd mess, and there is no escaping or getting away from it—just as though one were in a madhouse or a prison." Gurov is so "indignant" after this moment of personal crisis that he cannot sleep and finds that he is "fed up" with his job and his children. He has no desire to do anything. This dramatic moment is often considered the climax of the story, though what exactly it signifies is debated by critics.

Soviet critics have suggested that Gurov's profound moment of alienation merely signifies his "moral regeneration." Through the discovery of true love, they contend, Gurov has come to alienate himself from the amoral, gluttonous, frivolous life of his class. From this point forward he cares more about another human being, Anna, and less about his own sensual gratification, the pleasures of Moscow society, and the institution of bourgeois marriage.

These Soviet critics further note that Gurov and Anna are "ordinary" people of the middle class, not members of the nobility like the adulterers in Tolstoy's *Anna Karenina*. Gurov is, indeed, something of an "everyman," with a typical family life and a dull and vaguely defined job, and Anna is merely "the lady with a pet dog." Nobody in Yalta knows her name; she is the wife of a minor bureaucrat from a faraway provincial town. That these two ordinary, unheroic people experience a moral awakening was significant to Soviet critics. They further claimed that this story serves as a commentary against the bourgeois institution of marriage. In a sense it was, for the marriages in his fiction are almost never happy, and people frequently seem to have married young and for the wrong reasons. But Chekhov does not present an alternative way of life and expresses little optimism about how humans might live if the obstacles to pursuing their desires were removed. His characters often have trouble understanding their desires in the first place.

"The Lady with the Pet Dog" is more optimistic than most of Chekhov's tales, for the couple is truly in love, and know what they want. Only social constraints keep them from being happy. Virginia Llewelyn Smith, however, focuses on the theme of love in Chekhov's fiction and rejects the idea that the story should be read as a social critique. She notes that while Gurov is "shaken out of his romantic dreaming by a sudden recognition of the grossness of others in his stratum of society," he "does not give up his job or abandon his social life. Instead, he leads a double existence . . . it is this life Chekhov is interested in, not in Gurov as a representative of his class." She further observes that while Gurov and Anna are alone among their fellow men and women, this "does not point a moral: but it is where the pathos in their initial situation lies. We are not impressed by their moral superiority, but moved by their loneliness." Love, Smith concludes, is the solution to this loneliness.

Smith, like other critics, notes the similarity of Gurov's position to that of Chekhov himself. Like Gurov, Chekhov fell in love for the first time in his life when he was almost forty (he was thirty-nine and soon to be married when he wrote this story). He knew that he was ill and doubted that he would have long to enjoy his love, and so the faith in love expressed in "The Lady with the Pet Dog" and the air of pathos and sadness provoked by the discovery of love are both perhaps rooted in Chekhov's own experience. Smith suggests that throughout his career Chekhov was torn between a romantic and a cynical view of love, contrasting the unhappy marriages and love affairs he witnessed with a romantic sense of what love could be. Gurov is also a romantic who enters every affair with high hopes only to be bitterly disappointed. When Gurov finally finds true love, he abandons his romantic dream of a love which can be simple and easy, and in the end struggles to keep true love alive in the real world.

Chekhov's attitude towards women is arguably reflected in this story. Gurov dislikes his wife, an outspoken woman who considers herself an intellectual, and he dislikes some of the sexually aggressive women whom he has been with in the past. Rather, he prefers Anna, who is soft and childlike, weepy and vulnerable, even a bit "pathetic." Feminist critics might argue that Chekhov, or at least his protagonist Gurov, was threatened by strong women and preferred a woman he could dominate. There are other ways to read the sexual politics of the story. Chekhov himself describes Gurov as a man who believes women an "inferior breed" but who cannot "live a day without them." By the end of the story, however, Gurov considers Anna his only "true friend." Her weakness and pathos may be, to some extent, symptoms of her boredom and depression. Just before Gurov speaks to Anna for the first time, he looks her over and decides that "her expression, her gait, her dress, and the way she did her hair told him that she was . . . married, that she was in Yalta for the first time and alone, and that she was bored." Gurov jokes in their first exchange that people claim to be bored in Yalta as if they come from some exotic place, when in fact they come from dull and dusty provincial towns. This wry joke seduces Anna but is of greater significance than it appears, for we learn that young Anna is indeed bored and unhappy both at and away from home. Gurov is drawn to her "pathetic" qualities not only because they make her easy prey but also because these qualities in Anna reflect an aspect of Gurov that he is slow to recognize. Gurov, like Anna, is bored and unhappy in his marriage and is "eager for life." Moreover, he is not at home in the world, even before they meet. He seems to have no friends at Yalta and does not miss anybody back home. Gurov and Anna are both alone, lacking in other deep attachments, and perhaps Gurov feels sympathy for Anna in her sadness because he feels sad himself. When Gurov decides that he is disgusted with his life, perhaps he is discovering a loneliness and alienation which has bothered him for a long time but which he was unable to recognize until there was something meaningful in his life with

which to contrast these feelings. That source of contrast was Anna and his unexpected love for her.

Source: Erik Huber, "An Overview of 'The Lady with the Pet Dog'," in *Short Stories for Students,* The Gale Group, 1998.

Boyd Creasman

Creasman is an Assistant Professor of English at West Virginia Wesleyan College. In the following excerpt, he claims that understanding Gurov's intense display of emotion in "The Lady with the Pet Dog" [which he refers to as "The Lady with the Dog"], is not only crucial for understanding his motivations, but is helpful for the reader to gain a better understanding of the structure of Chekhov's short fiction in general.

In 1921, Conrad Aiken [in *Collected Criticism,* 1968] made the following assessment of Anton Chekhov's work: "This, after all, is Chekhov's genius—he was a master of mood." Indeed Aiken's statement is a good starting point for a discussion of the structure of Chekhov's short fiction. Many of Chekhov's short stories—the later ones in particular—are structured around the main character's moments of strong emotion, a feature of the author's short fiction that has never been fully explored, even in discussions of individual stories. For example, much of the criticism of "The Lady with the Dog" one of Chekhov's most revered short stories, has focused on its parallels with his real life love for Olga Knipper, the influence of Tolstoy's *Anna Karenina,* the story's similarities with Chekhov's later plays, and its exemplification of the author's realism and modernity, which have greatly influenced twentieth-century short fiction. In tracing the story's biographical and literary influences and its relation to other literature, though, Chekhov critics have generally ignored an important feature of "The Lady with the Dog"—namely, the significance of Gurov's two flights of emotion, the first with Anna at Oreanda, the second outside the Medical Club at Moscow. These two moments of intense feeling are crucial to understanding Gurov's motivations and illustrate the importance of this kind of emotional flight to the structure of Chekhov's short fiction.

In the first of his two flights of emotion, Gurov contemplates the transcendence of love as he sits quietly on a bench with Anna at Oreanda:

> Not a leaf stirred, the grasshoppers chirruped, and the monotonous hollow roar of the sea came up to them, speaking of peace, of the eternal sleep lying in wait for us all. The sea had roared like this before there was

> With its elegant language, complex main characters, and realistic detail, 'The Lady with the Dog' is indeed a masterful story of many moods and, therefore, an illustration of the validity of Conrad Aiken's judgment that Chekhov is a master of mood."

any Yalta or Oreanda, it was roaring now, and it would go on roaring, just as indifferently and hollowly, when we had passed away. And it may be that in this continuity, this utter indifference to life and death, lies the secret of our ultimate salvation, of the stream of life on our planet, and of its never-ceasing movement toward perfection.

Side by side with a young woman, who looked so exquisite in the early light, soothed and enchanted by the sight of all this magical beauty—sea, mountains, clouds and the vast expanse of the sky—Gurov told himself that, when you came to think of it, everything in the world is beautiful really, everything but our own thoughts and actions, when we lose sight of the higher aims of life, and of our dignity as human beings.

This passage reveals one of the strengths of Chekhov's writing, his superb handling of the theme of transcendence through love. In *Anton Chekhov and the Lady with the Dog* [1973], Virginia Llewellyn Smith discusses the importance of this theme: "In Chekhov's later work, this ideal of love was to become increasingly associated with the concept of something above and beyond the transient, or more precisely, with a quasi-philosophical speculative interest, and a quasi-mystical faith in the future of mankind." Another critic, Beverly Hahn, makes a similar point [in *Chekhov: A Study of the Major Stories and Plays*, 1977], finding in some of Chekhov's work a "mysterious transcendence . . . of the great moral and philosophical issues of existence." Finding the eternal in a particular moment, Chekhov's characters can turn away mortality and meaninglessness, if only briefly, by turning to each other. However, it is important to remember that at this point in the story, Gurov clearly has not fallen in love with Anna. At first it is not Anna in particular whom he desires, but rather a pretty woman in general, and the reader is told that Gurov, who refers to women as "the lower race," actually "could not have existed a single day" without them. Indeed, Gurov enjoys Anna's company at Yalta but is at first surprised, then bored and annoyed with her sense of having sinned. And when Anna must leave Yalta and return to her husband, Gurov does not seem greatly to regret that the affair has apparently ended: "And he told himself that this had been just one more of the many adventures in his life, and that it, too, was over, leaving nothing but a memory. . . ." However, when he returns home, he cannot seem to forget the lady with the dog.

Gurov's second flight of emotion results from his sudden awareness of the grossness and banality of life in Moscow, and the way it pales in comparison to the time he spent with Anna in Yalta. When Gurov starts to tell one of his companions at the Medical Club about her, his friend interrupts him with a comment about dinner, "the sturgeon was just a *leetle* off." At this moment, all of Gurov's pent-up frustrations with his life in Moscow find release in the quintessential Chekhovian flight:

> These words, in themselves so commonplace, for some reason infuriated Gurov, seemed to him humiliating, gross. What savage manners, what people! What wasted evenings, what tedious, empty days! Frantic card-playing, gluttony, drunkenness, perpetual talk always about the same thing. The greater part of one's time and energy went on business that was no use to anyone, and on discussing the same thing over and over again, and there was nothing to show for all of it but a stunted, earth-bound existence and a round of trivialities, and there was nowhere to escape to, you might as well be in a madhouse or a convict settlement.

In some ways, this passage represents the climax of the story, for after Gurov resolves to go to Anna's town, the remainder of the story, in which the characters are forced to keep up appearances by not telling anyone about the affair, has an aura of inevitability about it. In addition to this structural importance, this intense burst of emotion is also very important to an understanding of Gurov's motivations for renewing the affair and thus raises an interesting question: is his decision to find Anna motivated more by love for her or by his desire to escape the tedium of life in Moscow? Certainly the Gurov in the first two sections of the story does not seem like the kind of man who is capable of falling in love with Anna. He becomes bored and uncomfortable, rather than concerned or sensitive, when she gets upset. Does Gurov truly love Anna, or is she simply the natural person for him to turn to in his time of depression?

In his excellent "Chekhov and the Modern Short Story" [in *A Chekhov Companion*, 1985], Charles E. May argues that the question is unanswerable:

> It is never clear in the story whether Gurov truly loves Anna Sergeyevna or whether it is only the romantic fantasy that he wishes to maintain. What makes the story so subtle and complex is that Chekhov presents the romance in such a limited and objective way that we realize that there is no way to determine whether it is love or romance, for there is no way to distinguish between them.

May's otherwise good interpretation is slightly off the mark on this point. While it is true that throughout most of the story it is difficult—because of the objectivity to which May alludes—to determine whether Gurov loves Anna, the reader is directly told just before the conclusion of the story that the two main characters do indeed love each other and that Gurov has "fallen in love properly, thoroughly, for the first time in his life." It is crucial to recognize that the Gurov at the end of the story is not the same as the one at the beginning, and the difference is not merely that he now needs love, but that he has clearly found the woman he loves. Certainly, Gurov does not love less simply because he feels a need for love in his life; in fact, it is precisely this yearning that causes his love for Anna to awaken and grow. And again the key to understanding Gurov's motivations for leaving Moscow and going to Anna is his flights of emotion in which he recognizes the essential truth of the story: his love for Anna is far more noble than his banal, socially acceptable life in Moscow.

Still, at the end of the story, the couple's problem—how to keep their love for each other alive while hiding the relationship from society—remains unresolved. Moreover, neither character seems to have the courage to reveal the truth of their love to anyone else, and therefore, the characters find themselves in a kind of limbo:

> And it seemed to them that they were within an inch of arriving at a decision, and that then a new, beautiful life would begin. And they both realized that the end was still far, far away, and that the hardest, the most complicated part was only just beginning.

Gurov and Anna find themselves in a desperate situation, but as Beverly Hahn suggests, "desperation is not the dominant note of the story, nor is its outcome really tragic, because the hardship of Anna's and Gurov's love cannot be separated from the *fact* of that love and from the fact that it brings each a degree of fulfilment not known before."

With its elegant language, complex main characters, and realistic detail, "The Lady with the Dog" is indeed a masterful story of many moods and, therefore, an illustration of the validity of Conrad Aiken's judgment that Chekhov is a master of mood. Gurov's two intense moments of emotion are important to the structure of the story and demonstrate an important feature of the author's style, for similar Chekhovian flights can be found in many of his other stories, especially his later ones, such as "About Love," "A Visit to Friends," "The Bishop," and "The Betrothed," just to name a few. These flights of emotion are as important in Chekhov's stories as epiphanies are in Joyce's and therefore merit further exploration by those interested in the study of Chekhov's short fiction.

Source: Boyd Creasman, "Gurov's Flights of Emotion in Chekhov's 'The Lady with the Dog'," in *Studies in Short Fiction,* Vol. 27, No. 2, Spring, 1990 pp. 257–60.

Virginia Llewellyn Smith

Smith is affiliated with Stanford University. In the following excerpt, she closely examines several aspects of "The Lady with the Pet Dog" [which she refers to as "The Lady with the Dog,"], maintaining that the story, which is intimately bound with "so many threads of Chekhov's thought and experience," is very useful in learning about Chekhov's attitude towards women and love.

It will by now be apparent that Anna Sergeevna, the lady with the dog, can be considered symbolic of the ideal love that Chekhov could envisage but not embrace—that remained, so to speak, behind a pane of glass, as in Heifitz's film. But the significance of the whole story is much greater than that comprised in Anna Sergeevna alone.

No other single work of Chekhov's fiction constitutes a more meaningful comment on Chekhov's attitude to women and to love than does 'The Lady with the Dog'. So many threads of Checkhov's thought and experience appear to have been woven together into this succinct story that it may be regarded as something in the nature of a summary of the entire topic.

Gurov, the hero of the story, may at first appear no more closely identifiable with Chekhov himself than are many other sympathetic male characters in Chekhov's fiction: he has a post in a bank and is a married man with three children. It is because he has

> The situation, indeed the entire plot of 'The Lady with the Dog', is obvious, even banal, and its merit as a work of art lies in the artistry with which Chekhov has preserved in the story a balance between the poetic and the prosaic, and in the careful characterization, dependent upon the use of half-tones."

this wife and family that his love-affair with Anna Sergeevna leads him into an *impasse*. And the affair itself, involving Gurov's desperate trip to Anna's home town, has no obvious feature in common with anything we know of Chekhov's amorous liaisons.

And yet Chekhov's own attitudes and experience have clearly shaped Gurov's character and fate. The reader is told that Gurov 'was not yet forty': Chekhov was thirty-nine when he wrote 'The Lady with the Dog'. Gurov 'was married young' (*ego zhenili rano*): there is a faint implication in the phrase that an element of coercion played some part in his taking this step—a step which Chekhov, when he was young, managed to avoid. As in general with early marriages in Chekhov's fiction, Gurov's has not proved a success. His wife seems 'much older than he' and imagines herself to be an intellectual: familiar danger-signals. She is summed-up in three words: 'stiff, pompous, dignified' (*pryamaya, vazhnaya, solidnaya*) which epitomize a type of woman (and man) that Chekhov heartily disliked.

Gurov's wife treats sex as something more complicated than it is, and spoils it for him; and it is also spoilt for him by those mistresses of whom he soon tires: beautiful, cold women with a 'predatory' expression who are determined to snatch what they can from life. 'When Gurov grew cold to them, their beauty aroused hatred in him and the lace on their linen reminded him of scales'. It would seem that

exactly some such sentiment inspired Chekhov when he depicted Ariadna, Nyuta, and the other anti-heroines.

Gurov has had, however, liaisons that were, for him, enjoyable—and these we note, were brief: as was Chekhov's liaison with Yavorskaya and indeed, so far as we know, all the sexual relationships that he had before he met Olga Knipper.

'Frequent experience and indeed bitter experience had long since taught [Gurov] that every liaison which to begin with makes such a pleasant change inevitably evolves into a real and extremely complex problem, and the situation eventually becomes a burden'. That his friendships with, for instance, Lika and Avilova should evolve into a situation of this kind seems to have been exactly what Chekhov himself feared: he backed out of these friendships as soon as there appeared to be a danger of close involvement.

Gurov cannot do without the company of women, and yet he describes them as an 'inferior breed': his experience of intimacy with women is limited to casual affairs and an unsatisfactory marriage. Chekhov also enjoyed the company of women and had many female friends and admirers: but he failed, or was unwilling, to involve himself deeply or lastingly with them. That in his work he should suggest that women are an inferior breed can be to some extent explained by the limited knowledge of women his self-contained attitude brought him—and perhaps, to some extent, by a sense of guilt concerning his inability to feel involved.

Gurov's behaviour to Anna Sergeevna at the beginning of their love-affair is characterized by an absence of emotional involvement, just such as appears in Chekhov's attitude towards certain women. There is a scene in 'The Lady with the Pet Dog' where, after they have been to bed together, Gurov eats a water-melon while Anna Sergeevna weeps over her corruption. It is not difficult to imagine Chekhov doing something similarly prosaic— weeding his garden, perhaps—while Lika poured out her emotional troubles to him.

Gurov's egocentricity is dispelled, however, by the potent influence of love, because Anna Sergeevna turns out to be the ideal type of woman: pitiable, defenceless, childlike, capable of offering Gurov an unquestioning love. Love is seen to operate as a force for good: under its influence Gurov feels revulsion for the philistinism of his normal life and associates. Soviet interpreters have made much of the theme of regeneration, of the idea implicit in the story that 'a profound love experienced by ordinary people has become an enormous moral force'. In fact, although some idea of this sort is certainly implicit in the story, Chekhov is surely attempting above all to evoke what love meant to his protagonists as they themselves saw their situation. Chekhov originally wrote in the conclusion of 'The Lady with the Dog' that the love of Gurov and Anna Sergeevna had 'made them both better'. He altered this subsequently to 'changed them both for the better'; but still dissatisfied, finally he altered this once more to 'had changed them both', and thus avoided any overt suggestion of pointing a moral.

The point is that we are not seeing the lovers changed in relation to society, but in relation to their own inner lives. Gurov is shaken out of his romantic dreaming by a sudden recognition of the grossness of others in his stratum of society: but he does not give up his job or abandon his social life. Instead, he leads a double existence, and imagines that every man's 'real, most interesting life' goes on in secret. It is this life that Chekhov is interested in, not in Gurov as a representative of his class or his time.

That Gurov and Anna Sergeevna are alone amongst their fellow-men does not point a moral: but it is where the pathos of their initial situation lies. We are not impressed by their moral superiority, but moved by their loneliness. Love is the answer to this loneliness, and there is no need to bring morality into it. Chekhov, where love was concerned, wrote from the heart not the head.

Chekhov wrote 'The Lady with the Dog' in Yalta in the autumn of 1899, not long after he and Olga were there together (although they were not, as yet, lovers) and had made the trip back to Moscow together. In the Kokkoz valley, it will be remembered, they apparently agreed to marry: and so by then, we may presume, Chekhov knew what it was to love.

How do Gurov and Anna Sergeevna love one another? Not unnaturally, Chekhov describes the affair from the man's point of view. As one might expect, Gurov's love for Anna Sergeevna has its romantic side. It is associated with the beauty of nature for it is helped into existence by the view of the sea at Oreanda. When, back in Moscow, Gurov thinks of Anna, he poeticizes her: the whole affair becomes the subject of a daydream, and ultimately an obsession. So, perhaps, did Chekhov's thoughts dwell on Olga Knipper when she was in Moscow

and he recalled their time in Yalta and journey through an area of great natural beauty.

Olga Knipper, however, was no dream. And Anna Sergeevna is not seen solely in terms of 'poetry', even by Gurov. Forced to seek Anna out in her home town, from this point Gurov is back in reality. At the theatre he—and the reader—see her as a 'small woman who was in no way remarkable, with a cheap-looking lorgnette in her hand'. But this does not detract from her appeal for him (and it enhances her appeal for the reader). The romantic heroine has become a creature of flesh and blood, and Gurov still loves her: 'she . . . now filled his whole life, she was his joy and his grief, the sole happiness that he now desired; and to the sound of the bad orchestra, the wretched philistine violins, he mused on how fine she was. He mused and dreamed dreams.'

Gurov dreams—but dreaming is not enough for him. He has tasted happiness: the affair in Yalta was happy, in spite of Anna's sense of guilt. His love there developed from when, after Anna's self-recrimination and his irritation, they suddenly laughed together. This laugh denotes the beginning of communication: the tension relaxes and they behave normally, and find enjoyment in each other's company as well as in 'love'. Love, in fact, has come down to earth. Sex, communication, and simple companionship all play their part in it, in addition to 'poetry'.

And there the problem lies: the love-affair being rooted in reality, Anna and Gurov have to face the world's problems. Gurov, unlike Laevsky and Laptev, has found romantic love: but he also wants the companionship that Laevsky and Laptev had, and because he and Anna Sergeevna are already married, he cannot have it.

The situation, indeed the entire plot of 'The Lady with the Dog', is obvious, even banal, and its merit as a work of art lies in the artistry with which Chekhov has preserved in the story a balance between the poetic and the prosaic, and in the careful characterization, dependent upon the use of halftones. Soviet critics have a valid point when they regard Gurov as a sort of Everyman; 'The Lady with the Dog' is an essentially simple exposition of a commonplace theme. Unlike in 'The Duel' and 'Three Years', in 'The Lady with the Dog' Chekhov has made no attempt to investigate the problems of love: the conclusion of 'The Lady with the Dog' is left really and truly open: there is no suggestion, nor have we any inkling, of what the future may bring:

'And it seemed that in a very little while an answer would be found, and a new and beautiful life would begin. And to both it was evident that the end was far, far away, and that the hardest, most complicated part was only just beginning.'

There can be no doubt but that the policy of expounding questions without presuming to answer them—that policy which Chekhov had declared to be the writer's task—suited his style best. A full appreciation of Chekhov's work requires of the reader a certain degree of involvement, a response intellectual, or, as in the case of his love-stories, emotional, that Chekhov invites rather than commandeers. Ultimately, all depends on how Chekhov is read; but much depends on his striking the delicate balance between sentimentality and flatness.

All must surely agree that the right balance has been achieved in the final scene of 'The Lady with the Dog', which is as direct an appeal to the heart as can be found in Chekhov's fiction:

> His hair was already beginning to turn grey. And it struck him as strange that he had aged so in the last few years, and lost his good looks. Her shoulders, on which he had lain his hands, were warm and shook slightly. He felt a pang of compassion for this life that was still warm and beautiful, but which would probably soon begin to fade and wither, like his own life. Why did she love him so? He had always appeared to women as something which he was not, and they had loved in him not him himself, but a creature of their own imagination, which they had sought again and again in their own lives; and then, when they perceived their mistake, they loved him all the same. And not one of them had been happy with him. Time passed, he would strike up an acquaintance, have an affair, and part but never once had he loved; he had had everything he might wish for, only not love.

> And only now, when his hair had gone grey, he had fallen in love properly, genuinely—for the first time in his life.

This passage, read in the light of what we know of the author, gains a new dimension of pathos. The history of Gurov's relationships with women is a transmutation of Chekhov's history, and the essential point of the fiction was reality for him: true love had come too late, and complete happiness—poetry and communication and companionship—was impossible.

Chekhov wrote that Gurov and Anna Sergeevna 'loved one another . . . as husband and wife'. But how are we to explain the incongruity of this bland phrase 'as husband and wife' in the context of Chekhov's entire *œuvre*, in which the love of hus-

band and wife is thwarted and cheapened—virtually never, in fact, seen to exist? Gurov and Anna are, after all, husband and wife, and he does not love his wife, nor she her husband. The irony here, whether conscious or unconscious, finds its origin in Chekhov's apparently unshakable belief that an ideal love somewhere, somehow could exit.

It seems then cruel indeed that he should see fate cheat him of the chance of such love. His happiness was incomplete; and it is difficult not to regard Chekhov's situation as tragic. And yet one question remains. Could Chekhov, so happy as he stood on the threshold of love, ever have crossed that threshold, even in more fortunate circumstances? Could he have lived with love instead of dreaming about it? There is of course no evidence to suggest that his feelings for Olga Knipper would have altered with the passage of time, had she stayed constantly by his side. But evidence there is that, to the last, love as Chekhov conceived it retained its distant, intangible quality. . . .

This sketch of a plot shows clearly that, where love was the issue, a dissociation from facts and retreat into a dream world was for Chekhov a continuing process: that the romantic heroine could only be such in apotheosis. In the real world she provokes complications—but her shade is mysterious, beautiful, and fascinating.

And thus before we regard Chekhov's life as tragic, there is an important factor to bear in mind: the possibility that Chekhov, never to experience the reality of a normal marriage, was perhaps by this very misfortune preserved from a disillusionment in his ideal of love which might have proved more bitter than any irony of density. Thus the very significance—the supreme significance—which love as an ideal had for Chekhov provides us with an alternative view of his fate. It is not a tragedy: there is no victim. And Chekhov, whose dislike of self-dramatization was one of his most attractive qualities, would surely have preferred this latter view.

Source: Virginia Llewellyn Smith, ''The Lady with the Dog,'' in *Anton Chekhov and the Lady with the Dog,* Oxford University Press, London, 1973, pp. 212–19.

Further Reading

''Anton Chekhov,'' in *Short Story Criticism,* Vol. 2, edited by Sheila Fitzgerald, Gale, 1989, pp. 124–160; Vol. 28, edited by Anna J. Sheets, Gale, 1998, pp. 48–72.

''Anton Chekhov,'' in *Twentieth-Century Literary Criticism,* Vol. 31, edited by Paula Kepos and Dennis Poupard, Gale, 1989, pp. 71–103; Vol. 55, edited by Marie Lazzari, Gale, 1995, pp. 28–80.

''Anton Chekhov,'' in *World Literary Criticism,* Vol. 2, edited by James P. Draper, Gale, 1992, pp. 704–720.

Melanctha

Gertrude Stein

1909

Gertrude Stein's "Melanctha" has been a landmark
of literary modernism since its first printing. The
author broke radically new ground with both her
subject matter and style. She focused on emotional
process almost to the exclusion of action and other
conventional plot structures, and she chose to people her story with black characters at a time when
other white writers wouldn't do so and when few
black writers had the opportunity to publish. Furthermore, Stein's central character—Melanctha—
was sexually liberated and assertive at a time when
Victorian values still dominated women's lives.

First published in 1909 as one of the three
novellas that comprise Stein's *Three Lives*,
"Melanctha" is an experimental story that chronicles the life of a highly intelligent, emotionally
complex mulatto woman. The basis of Stein's story
arises from Melanctha's emotional conflicts, for
which the author never provides a direct cause:
Melanctha wanders through life, always in search of
something—some knowledge, some experience—
she can never wholly acquire. At a time when
women were expected to choose conventional and
safe paths—marriage, children, middle-class life, if
possible—Melanctha is a kind of rebel because her
undefinable questing suggests a woman's desire for
more, though more what, the author never says. The
central relationship of the story, Melanctha's love
affair with the young doctor, Jefferson Campbell,
also wanders aimlessly, despite Jeff's solidly middle-class aspirations. Telling their story, the narra-

tor highlights the emotional process of their efforts to know and communicate with one another, rather than the progress of their relationship toward some socially-sanctioned goal.

In order to capture her subject matter—the reality of emotional life that may go on unseen beneath the surface—Stein began to experiment with new ways to use words and sentences, developing an essentially new aesthetic, or way of portraying the world through art. Consequently, the reader tackling ''Melanctha'' is confronted with dense language: thick repetition, grammatically incorrect sentences, a limited and often vague diction—a language designed not so much to explain the characters' emotions as to evoke the immediacy of emotion.

Author Biography

Born on February 3, 1874, in Allegheny, Pennsylvania, Gertrude Stein was the youngest child of upper-middle-class, Jewish-American parents. After her birth, the family traveled in Europe for several years before settling in Oakland, California. Stein was very close to her brother, Leo. The two remained virtually inseparable for several decades. When Leo went to Harvard in 1892, Stein enrolled in the all-female Harvard annex—soon to become Radcliffe College—the following year. Radcliffe, and especially psychology professor William James, became a shaping force in her intellectual development. Many of James's teachings, including his theories of perception and personality types, shaped her own aesthetic theories. With James's encouragement, Stein decided to become a psychologist. After finishing her bachelor's degree in 1897, she began her training in the medical program at Johns Hopkins University in Baltimore. In 1901, however, she left without completing her degree.

Reading—particularly literary classics—consumed more and more of Stein's time. Taking up the pen herself in 1903, she made her first attempt at writing a novel. This first effort, titled *Q.E.D.*, fictionalized Stein's recent romantic entanglement with a young woman named May Bookstaver. Stein cast herself as the rational Adele and Bookstaver as the passionate and ultimately unreliable Helen. Critics have generally viewed this work—published only after Stein's death—not as a manuscript intended for publication, but rather as a tool for coming to terms with the pain of that relationship. Its primary

importance, in fact, appears to be as the model for ''Melanctha,'' in which Stein/Adele became Jeff and Bookstaver/Helen became Melanctha.

Also in 1903, Stein chose her home: after travels in Europe and Africa, she and Leo settled in an apartment at 27 rue de Fleurus in Paris. There, they began to collect work by painters experimenting with new forms of visual representation—the revolution that would become known as modernism. Since many of these artists—including Pablo Picasso—were also their friends, the Steins became known in Paris for the salons, or social gatherings, they hosted regularly. Stein particularly enjoyed the company of Picasso, who in 1906 painted a portrait of her. Engaged with these artists and their goals, Stein began to pursue a similar course in her writing, sacrificing existing formal conventions in order to allow the reader to experience language and ideas in new ways. From 1905 to 1906, Stein applied her experimentation as she composed the manuscript of *Three Lives*. Leo, responding to his sister's work with scorn, caused her anxiety and self-doubt. In need of a more appreciative audience, Stein turned to her friend Alice Toklas, a young woman from California who was then staying in Paris. In 1909 Stein invited Toklas to live with her; the women developed an intimate relationship that Stein referred to as a marriage. They remained together for the rest of their lives. Toklas also supported Stein's literary career, helping her to prepare manuscripts and providing her with encouragement.

Stein's experimentation proved detrimental, at first, to her literary career. When she first submitted the highly unconventional stories in *Three Lives* to publishers, none considered publishing the unprecedented work. *Three Lives* finally reached print in 1909, when Stein financed the printing out of her own pocket. Her spirit was buoyed, however, by the praise of many distinguished friends, including art patron Mabel Dodge, critic Carl Van Vechten, and poet Edith Sitwell. Largely due to ''Melanctha,'' *Three Lives* enjoyed an underground celebrity until, by the outbreak of World War I in 1914, Stein was regarded as a central figure in the modernist movement. That year, she composed one of her most abstract works, a collection of prose poems called *Tender Buttons*.

While many Americans left Europe to escape the war, Stein remained in Paris, winning commendation for her volunteer work as a medical supply driver and befriending many American servicemen. After the war, she became the friend and mentor of a new generation of American expatriate artists, foremost among them Ernest Hemingway. She encouraged his early attempts at writing fiction; he was instrumental in arranging for the publication of her 925-page, epic work, *The Making of Americans* (1925). Since Stein was, at this time, as well-known for her social circle as for her literary endeavors, she composed the memoir *The Autobiography of Alice B. Toklas* (1933) at a publisher's urging. The least innovative of Stein's works, it was the first to find a mass audience, becoming a bestseller and catapulting her to international celebrity. She was inundated with requests for public appearances, one of the most successful of which was a series of lectures delivered at American universities in 1934. Comprising reflections on her own literary efforts and theories, these talks, published as *Lectures in America* and *Narration* in 1935, have become essential to readers and scholars.

During World War II, Stein and Toklas remained in Nazi-occupied France. Although both women were, as Jews, in danger of being sent to concentration camps, French friends who collaborated with the Nazis arranged for their protection. Stein maintained an active social and literary life until her death from cancer in 1946. In a famous anecdote from her autobiography, *What Is Remembered,* Toklas recalled a conversation she had with Stein just before her death: "She said to me early in the afternoon, What is the answer? I was silent. In that case, she said, what is the question?"

Plot Summary

"Melanctha" opens late in Melanctha's life, as she cares for her friend Rose Johnson during the birth of her baby. After informing us briefly that the baby dies, the narrator uses a number of flashbacks to show the development of the women's relationship and Melanctha's unhappy childhood. One flashback culminates in a fight between Melanctha and her father, James Herbert, in which it is clear that Melanctha prevails over her father, an encounter that makes her aware of her power. In order to learn more about this capacity, Melanctha begins "wandering," the undefined activity that will characterize most of her life. "Wandering" consists primarily of loitering in the parts of Bridgepoint where she meets men—at first mostly manual laborers. While flirting with the men, Melanctha watches their work,

listens to their stories, and observes her own effect on them. Although the story suggests a sexual energy in all of this, we are given the sense that she remains chaste during this time since her wandering is "really very safe." Overall, "wandering" appears to go beyond sexual knowledge to something broader.

Melanctha meets the young doctor Jefferson Campbell. In a brief flashback it becomes clear that Jeff had an idyllic childhood, with caring parents, in direct opposition to Melanctha's own youth. Because of their different backgrounds, Jeff and Melanctha disagree about what makes a good life; he extols a "quiet" and "regular" life, while she supports excitement and emotional experience. The squabble makes them closer, though, because Jeff is impressed with Melanctha's strength of mind. After they have confessed a growing fondness for each other, a second disagreement occurs: Jeff champions "thinking" above "feeling," while Melanctha blames an overload of thinking with impeding Jeff's ability to feel.

After Melanctha's mother dies, Jeff and Melanctha spend all of their spare time together. Although the narrator tells us that they are happy together, the story highlights Jeff's conflicted emotions: he cannot shake a mistrust of Melanctha. Sleepless and riddled with doubt, Jeff discovers that he has learned to "feel," and suffer, at least as deeply as Melanctha herself. With the overwhelming problems in her relationship with Jeff, Melanctha begins to wander again, gradually cutting back the time she spends with Jeff. After one failed meeting, Jeff breaks off the relationship entirely. One effort to resume the relationship follows, but little has changed. Melanctha, always surrounded by friends, makes it impossible for them to be alone together. Rose Johnson is primary among these friends. Unlike others, Rose appears to regard Melanctha with a kind of pity gathered from her impression of Melanctha's childhood. Melanctha tells Jeff she loves him as a brother, without "hot passion." They have a civil parting, after which Jeff goes to work for a while in another town.

Soon after this Melanctha meets Jem Richards, a gambler who lives well on his winnings. The two fall for one another quickly, and Jem proposes to Melanctha. Melanctha is, for the first time, very vocal about her relationship and about her expectations for the future, even to the point of being "foolish," according to Rose. That foolishness peaks when Jem hits a streak of bad luck and forgets his proposal. When Melanctha presses Jem about their relationship, he backs away.

Rose's pregnancy provides some distraction for Melanctha. Nonetheless, the growing conflict with Jem preoccupies her, echoing in some ways her relationship with Jeff. Rose's baby is born in the midst of this trouble. The trouble with Jem depresses Melanctha to the point that she frequently tells Rose, who has become Melanctha's only mainstay, that she could kill herself. Simultaneously, however, Rose has become more critical of Melanctha, finally exploding in a harsh diatribe in which she bars Melanctha from her home. The break with Rose—utterly devastating to Melanctha—is soon followed by a similar rejection from Jem. The narrator provides the rest of Melanctha's life in a brief sketch, telling us that she falls ill and dies in ''a home for poor consumptives.''

Gertrude Stein

Characters

Jefferson Campbell

At the center of the story, the narrative focus shifts from Melanctha's life to the feelings and experience of Jeff Campbell, the young doctor whose relationship with Melanctha occupies the bulk of the story. Initially, Jeff embodies the values at the opposite extreme from those of Melanctha: he believes in a world of clear-cut good and bad, he has well-defined goals, and he extols traditional and staid family life. He is also, however, the one who changes the most profoundly in the story, exchanging that starting point for a realization of the importance of uncritical emotion and experience. In his relationship with Melanctha, he goes through an excruciating period of loss and discovery, mostly losing his original sense of certainty as he realizes that he cannot know, or even clearly communicate with, the woman he loves. He is also the only unequivocally compassionate character in the story—typically described as ''good and strong and gentle and very intellectual.'' Most critics have recognized Jeff as a character that Stein based on herself.

Father

See James Herbert

Jane Harden

Melanctha's good friend and mentor in her teenage years, Jane Harden is intelligent and strong, but also alcoholic. Because she is very experienced, Jane teaches Melanctha a great deal about ''wandering'' and interacting with men. There is also a hint of sexuality in their relationship with one another. Jane's criticism of Melanctha after their friendship ends leads to Jeff and Melanctha's first rift.

James Herbert

James Herbert, Melanctha's father, is generally absent from their home, returning mostly when he is angry with his daughter. Despite their conflicts, the narrator identifies him as the source of Melanctha's ''power.'' This power is somehow related to race, as implied in the description of him as Melanctha's ''robust and unpleasant and very unendurable black father.''

Melanctha Herbert

Melanctha Herbert is the central character of the story which chronicles the basic events and emotional states that she experiences. As Jeff Campbell remarks, Melanctha appears to have two ''sides.'' We see her at first as Melanctha the caretaker:

Portrait of Gertrude Stein painted in 1906 by Pablo Picasso.

"patient, submissive, soothing, and untiring," a role she plays in relation to both Rose Johnson and her mother. But she is an unconvincing caretaker, as we learn in her relationship with her mother, since her care seems unmotivated by love. She has, nonetheless, a profound "sweetness" that draws people to her. Her other side is much more enigmatic, both to the other characters and to the reader, due to the narrator's persistent vagueness. She is "complex" and "subtle" and spends most of her life "wandering" in search of some kind of "wisdom" or "knowledge." "Wandering" refers to Melanctha's efforts to satisfy a persistently unnamed desire that at times evokes sexuality, at times evokes the need for freedom and emotional growth, at times the desire to be taken care of and comforted. She displays signs of depression, most explicitly in a persistent despair and the frequent threat of suicide. The narrator provides some sense that Melanctha's emotional intensity might result from her nature—identified as the "power" of her father's character and the "complexity" of her mother's—or from her childhood in an unloving home. The mystery about her character has allowed readers to view her in many different ways; literary critics, for example, have seen her as a victim, a rebel, and a personification of certain psychological theories.

Mis Herbert

Melanctha's mother, Mis Herbert, is described as complex, difficult to understand, and "sweet-appearing"—traits she shares with her daughter. Despite that similarity, she shows little love for Melanctha; the narrator occasionally hints that this may have contributed to Melanctha's general unhappiness. Nonetheless, Melanctha tends Mis Herbert on her deathbed, a process that cements Melanctha's relationship with Jeff Campbell.

Jeff

See Jefferson Campbell

Jeff's father

Unlike Melanctha's father, Jeff's father is ideally supportive and responsible. Having earned his living as a butler for the white Campbell family, he and his wife represent the kind of "quiet" and "regular" life Jeff values.

Jeff's mother

Unlike Melanctha's mother, Jeff's mother is ideally supportive and affectionate. Beyond her introduction in the story, she appears only once more—when the narrator comments that Jeff was not comfortable telling her about his relationship with Melanctha.

John

An older, married man, John seems to be Melanctha's only friend in her early adolescence. As the coachman for a local family, he works with horses, which Melanctha finds compelling. Unlike Melanctha's father, John is gentle, respectful, and affectionate.

Rose Johnson

Melanctha's last close female friend, Rose Johnson becomes Melanctha's only security. Her rejection of Melanctha towards the end of the story seems to precipitate the ill-fortune and ill-health that culminate in Melanctha's death. The story opens with the birth and death of Rose's baby, moves back in time, and then returns to this point at the end; consequently, Rose acts as a "framing" narrative for the story. The narrator describes Rose according to stereotypes of African-American characters: "sullen, childish, cowardly, black Rose . . . like a simple beast." While Melanctha experiences a great deal of doubt and an apparently hopeless "yearning," Rose always seems quite certain in her knowledge of what she wants and of what is right—

she seems to feel very little self-doubt or anguish. This difference apparently allows for the power dynamic in their relationship, in which the "cowardly" Rose dominates the "strong" Melanctha. Rose consistently congratulates herself for being so generous with Melanctha, while the narrator consistently wonders why someone with Melanctha's intelligence and subtlety would "degrade" herself to care for someone as coarse as Rose.

Mother

See Mis Herbert

Jem Richards

Jem Richards is the gambler to whom Melanctha becomes engaged after her relationship with Jeff ends. The affair apparently sours when Jem's luck turns bad and Melanctha fails to respect his consequent need not to be pressured. Like Rose Johnson, Jem is one of the few characters who feels sure of himself and the world, untroubled by emotional confusion; the narrator remarks that Jem "always had known what it was to have real wisdom."

Themes

Doubt and Ambiguity

Doubt and ambiguity first appear in "Melanctha" in the guise of a suggested gap between appearance and reality: Melanctha and her mother are both "sweet-appearing," but apparently not sweet in a simple sense. The issue of false appearances comes to its peak with Jeff's fear that Melanctha is somehow deceiving him about herself or her feelings. Ultimately, however, the simple opposition between appearance and reality gives way to some more complicated suggestions about reality—in particular, that it is difficult or even impossible to know, especially over time, what is "real." Jeff's concern that Melanctha is deliberately deceiving him becomes overshadowed by his preoccupation with his inability to know her and her feelings. Even his own thoughts are, at times, uncertain to him. Consequently, Jeff learns to live with doubt and ambiguity. Conversely, those characters who never feel doubt—Rose Johnson and Jem Richards—hurt Melanctha the most and receive the least respect from the narrator. This apparently positive view of doubt and ambiguity may be related to the aesthetics that Stein was developing while working on "Melanctha"—an aesthetic system that, like the

ideas of the painters she associated with, emphasized the significance and value of a reality that cannot be seen. Consequently, Stein's experiments with style confront the reader with a good deal of ambiguity, especially in vague and abstract language that keeps concrete knowledge always just out of reach. Many of the terms most central to the story and to our understanding of Melanctha are the most persistently vague: wisdom, knowledge, wandering, wanting. The reader, like Jeff, must learn to live with ambiguity.

Courage and Cowardice

Courage and cowardice, as well as strength and weakness, all arise in "Melanctha" in the characters and their relationships with one another. All four traits are exhibited in the personalities Stein presents. Generally, courage is associated with Melanctha, cowardice with Rose Johnson, strength with Melanctha, Jane, and Jeff, and weakness with Rose and, at times, Melanctha. Like so many central concepts in the story, however, they remain evasive, never put into concrete terms by the narrator. The ambiguity and centrality of courage and cowardice are highlighted in one of Jeff and Melanctha's arguments. Disagreeing about what constitutes courage, they leave it unresolved: is it stoicism, daring, or endurance?

Freedom

Especially in its depiction of Melanctha as she defies gender roles, the story engages with the idea of freedom from convention and from social structures. Freedom from structure operates in form and content at once, since both Melanctha and the narrative "wander." Oddly, however, as critics have pointed out, freedom as a concept in relation to African-American liberation is quite absent.

Growth and Development

Technically, "Melanctha" is a bildungsroman— the story of one person's growth and development. As with any bildungsroman, we watch Melanctha grow through a series of pivotal, shaping experiences, such as her conflicts with her father and her friendship with Jane Harden. Her adolescence, which receives more attention than her childhood, is characterized by a kind of questing—for knowledge, wisdom, and experience—that gradually contributes to her growing sense of power, which may comprise her sense of self. The growth, however, becomes strangely forestalled in the middle of her story, at about the time she becomes involved with

Topics for Further Study

- Rose Johnson figures very prominently at the beginning of the story and at the end, although she is largely absent from the center. Looking at where she appears and how the narrator describes her, can you suggest some reasons why Stein might have used her to frame the story in this way?

- Ask your librarian to help you find some sources about images of African Americans in late-nineteenth- and early-twentieth-century American popular culture (one good source, if it is available, is a film called *Ethnic Notions* by director Marlon Riggs). Compare what you find there with Stein's descriptions in ''Melanctha.'' Can you see ways in which she may have been influenced by the images around her?

- Although the story is named for Melanctha, Jeff Campbell's thoughts and feelings become dominant in the story's center, so that he is also a protagonist. If you had to decide whose story this is—Melanctha's or Jeff's—whom would you choose and why?

- Look at two paragraphs, one from the beginning of the story and one from the end, that repeat almost exactly. What variations did Stein use? How does that variation and the different context of each paragraph change how you read them? In

particular, how does your knowledge of Melanctha change the way you read the later paragraph?

- How does Stein treat Melanctha's death? Based on how it makes you feel, speculate about what effect Stein might have wished and why.

- Research the avant-garde painters of the early twentieth century, paying particular attention to portraits by Paul Cezanne, Pablo Picasso, and Henri Matisse. What literary techniques in ''Melanctha'' correspond to the art techniques with which these artists experimented?

- What different things could ''wandering'' mean? Find examples in the story and fashion your answers around them.

- Jeff Campbell is one of the few characters in the story we see change, especially in his relationship with Melanctha. What does he gain from knowing her? What does he lose? In your own opinion, are the changes positive or negative?

- In 1903, physicist Albert Einstein formulated his theory of relativity, which revolutionized thinking not just in science, but in the humanities as well. After locating some explanations of what Einstein's theory means, see if you can find some examples of ''relativity'' in ''Melanctha.''

Jeff Campbell. At this point, she is revealed as a character who lives in a ''prolonged present'' or continuous ''now'' of emotion, so that in a sense growth becomes meaningless. While Melanctha becomes timeless, however, Jeff's development dominates the story, as he discovers his own emotional intensity.

Love and passion

Many readers have identified ''Melanctha'' as essentially a love story, albeit a highly unconventional one. The love affair between Jeff and Melanctha

obviously consumes the lion's share of the narrative, confronting the reader with an exhaustive, painstaking examination of romantic feelings, including love, desire, jealousy, rejection, and loss. Jeff's feelings, in particular, become the material for this depiction as his every thought and shift in emotion appears in detail. On a broader scale, the story is a love story in its emphasis of emotion over thought, especially desire in the absence of moral judgement. Stein went dramatically against current values not only by presenting a sexually liberated female protagonist, but also because Stein's narrator never condemns Melanctha's sexual behavior.

Time

According to William James, the psychologist with whom Stein studied at Radcliffe, an individual perceives the world not in discrete temporal segments of past, present, and future, but as a continuous awareness of the moment being presently lived. In her long, static narratives, Stein sought to evoke this atemporal sense of a continuous present. She achieved this effect with a variety of stylistic techniques, including a disruption of the traditionally linear narrative and the heavy use of words that denote timelessness (now, always) and present participles. She also addressed time directly in the content of ''Melanctha,'' particularly when memory—usually referred to as ''remembering''—becomes a point of conflict between Jeff and Melanctha.

Style

Modernism

When Gertrude Stein composed ''Melanctha'' in 1905, the twentieth-century upheaval in literature known as modernism was only just beginning. Most of the other major modernist works would come in the years to follow: James Joyce's *Portrait of the Artist as a Young Man* and *Ulysses,* Virginia Woolf's *To the Lighthouse,* T. S. Eliot's ''The Waste Land,'' Jean Toomer's *Cane,* and D. H. Lawrence's *Women in Love.* Literary critics, looking back over the beginning of the century, have tended to define modernism according to certain themes, such as alienation, and/or stylistic techniques employed in many of these works. While Stein's style differed from Joyce's and Woolf's, she nevertheless defied many of the same conventions, like making her text much more difficult for a reader used to the clear and supposedly transparent prose of nineteenth-century fiction.

Narrator

Just as ''Melanctha'' does not follow a course of events clearly from beginning to end, the story does not establish an identifiable and consistent point of view. As in any fiction, there is a narrator, in this case third-person because it is not one of the characters. This narrator practices free, indirect discourse—that is, the ability to relate a character's thoughts without quoting—but not in the clear-cut way that would be typical of most nineteenth-century authors. Rather, the reader may discover at certain points that, for a paragraph or so, one of the characters has ''taken over'' the narrative voice: the

point of view has shifted to show, for example, Jeff Campbell's or Jane Harden's perspective. Their thoughts blend with the narrative voice, creating interior monologues. In ''Melanctha'' this effect compromises the narrator's omniscience—the capacity to be all-knowing that defines a third-person voice. Unable to immediately and concretely expose causes and reasons to us, unable to demonstrate complete knowledge of the characters, the narrator appears to be caught in the same ambiguity that plagues the main characters.

Structure

''Melanctha'' begins, as do many famous pieces of literature, *in medias res,* or in the middle of things; ''Melanctha,'' however, not only begins *in medias res,* it then moves backward in time to our protagonist's childhood, catches up to the beginning again, and moves on to Melanctha's death. This unusual structure eschews the traditional, straightforward chronology of fiction. Consequently, the sense of time becomes confused, jumbled, and variously expanded and contracted. Stein's structural oddities in this regard contribute to her effort, also evident in sentence structure, to create a sense of ''prolonged present.'' According to William James, the psychologist with whom Stein studied at Radcliffe, the individual perceives the world not in discrete temporal segments of past, present, and future, but as a continuous awareness of the moment being presently lived. Essentially, even though the narrator tells the story in the past tense, the sense of ''now'' always overwhelms the conventional notions of past and future. Toward this same end, Stein makes heavy use of words that denote immediacy—now, always—as well as present participles, which are verbs in the present tense, or ''-ing'' form.

Writing Style

Stein does a great deal with her sentences that may challenge—and even anger—readers used to fiction that uses clear, direct, and grammatically correct language. In ''Melanctha,'' her primary experimental technique is repetition, which she employs in both narrative structure and sentence structure. Repetition in the sentences has many effects on the reader's experience, especially when combined with her use of a very limited vocabulary. A series of highly abstract words—''wisdom,'' ''wanting,'' ''knowledge''—and the simple colloquialisms that Stein used to suggest black dialect make up the full texture of her story. Stein's tightly constrained word choice, repeated heavily throughout, suggests the inadequacy of language. Even the most educated character in the story, Jeff Campbell, struggles with his inability to express himself—with the inability of language to capture the depth and complexity of his thoughts and emotions.

Despite her own extensive education and broad vocabulary, Stein similarly curtails her narrator's voice. Consequently, a few words, repeated in variations, are forced to carry the story's many layers of meaning. Stein's purpose for this complex weaving of words, as she later explained in an essay called "Composition as Explanation," was to demonstrate how meaning changes according to combination or "relation." That is, one word will change in its meaning depending on changes in the words it stands among. By this device, the inadequacy of language is overcome, and words are once again rich with meaning anyway. Used as a formula, this idea of relativity also applies to people: a person will change with his or her context, much as Melanctha behaves differently in relation to Jeff than she does in relation to Jem.

Finally, the repetitions and the overall difficulty of Stein's sentences force the reader to experience the words as words, the sentences as sentences, thus reminding him or her that this is a book. Stein, like the modernist painters she admired, wanted to move past the late nineteenth-century form of realism, which allowed the audience to focus on the story or scene depicted and to forget that someone was making an image of this thing. In similar experiments, earlier twentieth-century artists wanted to remind their audiences that they were looking at paintings or reading words, thus reminding them that the "realism" they trusted was in fact an illusion.

Historical Context

Stein saw herself as spanning the two centuries in which she lived; she felt ties to the values, often conflicting, that characterized both periods. That split also appears in "Melanctha" in the initial conflict between the "quiet" and "regular" life Jeff extols and Melanctha's passion for unjudged,

aimless experience. To summarize the centuries in basic formulas—as many of Stein's peers did—one could place Victorian morality against twentieth-century rebellion. Where the nineteenth century valued social propriety and tradition, the twentieth declared as its motto, "make it new." Where the nineteenth century depended on such certainties as religious faith and a rational social order, the twentieth began by embracing many discoveries and ideas that the Victorians had found threatening. Charles Darwin's thesis about evolution, put forth in *Origin of the Species,* for example, challenged Victorians' assumptions about Godly design and the significance of human life. Political ideas that developed throughout the nineteenth century—including Marxism and anarchism—caused rebellions in the twentieth century that left no certainty about social order and who had the right to rule. Ideas about the proper roles of the sexes and races began to break down in the nineteenth century, leaving room for such movements as the Harlem Renaissance and women's suffrage, as well as the virulent racist backlashes manifested in eugenics, a scientific theory that tied behavior to physiology and race, and Nazism.

All of these broad cultural forces have their presence in "Melanctha." Traditional Victorian morality, with its noble and active heroes, appears only briefly in "Melanctha," diminished beside the image of a life without purpose or judgement, moral or message. Not only did Stein's radical experiments with style challenge the conventions of nineteenth-century fiction, but her aesthetics specifically challenged assumed hierarchies: by eliminating foreground and background, normal distinctions of importance, Stein created—in her own phrase—a "democracy" of words. Furthermore, her unprecedented choice to portray supposedly universal human emotions through African-American characters reflected the gradually growing political and social presence of American blacks, despite her reduction of these characters to racial stereotypes borrowed from eugenics.

Of the many changes that bridged the two centuries, probably the most relevant to "Melanctha" were in psychology and the visual arts, both of which Stein knew well. Many critics have documented at length the story's debt to William James, a psychologist with whom Stein studied when she was at Radcliffe. Two features of James's ideas are particularly salient to "Melanctha": his theories of human nature and his theories of perception. Essentially, James argued that all individuals encounter

Compare
&
Contrast

- **Early 1900s:** Many writers rely on funding from patrons (wealthy individuals who support the arts) so that they can devote their full time and energies to their work.

  1990s: Though institutional support of the arts exists, such as the National Endowment for the Arts, many writers rely on teaching, freelance writing, etc., as their main means of financial support.

- **Early 1900s:** Victorian morals restrict writers'

freedom to explore themes of homosexuality in literature. Some critics have suggested that Melanctha is really about a lesbian relationship, and that Stein felt it necessary to mask this relationship.

1990s: Many writers, including Adrienne Rich, Rita May Brown, and Allen Ginsberg, make homosexuality a predominant theme in their writing.

---

the world in an unmediated rush of perception stimuli—a "stream of consciousness." All of this information would, however, make for chaos in the mind, so a selection goes on that codes the incoming information as important, for foreground use, or irrelevant, to be relegated to the background. The extent to which and how one sifts impressions varies mostly according to where one fits on the spectrum of personality types, ranging from the most passionate to the most logical. In his own moral perspective, James favored the logical, heroic type. In some ways, however, Stein's story also reflects James's younger colleague, Sigmund Freud, whose theories revolutionized psychology in the twentieth century. Where James emphasized logic, the deliberate ordering of that stream of consciousness, Freud emphasized the irrational. Freud, unlike James, argued that desire underlies all human behavior, and that every individual's interior life is rich with emotion, much of it socially unacceptable and therefore difficult to acknowledge.

Freud's theories of psychology described an individual whose interior life—full of repressed passions that defied social propriety—hid beneath a surface that still obeyed social laws. In this sense, he contributed to a growing belief that outward appearances did not correspond to "reality" or "truth." This belief revealed itself among the painters in the early twentieth century—the same painters whom Stein befriended and found her inspiration in. The

nineteenth-century idea of "realism" in art had depended on verisimilitude: the exact copying, visually or in literature, of how something looked. This world, logical and accessible, was supposed to constitute reality. The avant-garde painters, however, no longer trusted verisimilitude. Believing that reality was something beneath the surface, something possibly alogical and changed according to the viewer's perspective, they attempted to create a new realism.

Critical Overview

Stein had her own doubts about the readability of *Three Lives*; she understood that its style would upset readers' expectations and that the simplicity of the characters might make them of little interest to more sophisticated readers. When she was unable to find a publisher, she finally funded the printing of the book herself, paying for a relatively small run. As she expected, few copies sold—fewer than she gave away to friends and reviewers—but the book, and especially "Melanctha," did find an enthusiastic audience. Praise came from many important papers and journals, and contemporaries whose opinions Stein admired, such as Carl Van Vechten and Mabel Dodge, also embraced her efforts. Rather than lapsing into obscurity, "Melanctha" started on a path to landmark status. By the late 1920s,

''Melanctha'' was already something of modernist classic. In 1933, the book no publisher would publish became a classic of modern literature.

''Melanctha'' has also become an object of scholarly study over the decades. The critical responses tend to cluster around certain issues or concerns, determined mostly by the story's unconventionality. Much of the commentary on Stein from 1910 through the 1950s is evaluative rather than interpretive, either arguing her merits, as does Carl Van Vechten, or deriding her, as does Wyndham Lewis, another modernist artist. For Stein's detractors, the superficially simple, almost childish language of the story made easy prey: they could argue that her aesthetics stemmed not from artistic insight, but rather from ineptitude. Consequently, most of the early studies of Stein, even when positive, still regarded her writing in relation to her psychology. Richard Bridgman, for example, albeit an admirer of Stein, nonetheless suggested that ''Melanctha'' was the product of emotional difficulties rather than artistic purpose.

Later twentieth-century criticism, however, regards the unusual form of ''Melanctha'' as its author's deliberate experiments with representation. Many critics have looked at it as her effort to work out an aesthetic based on the psychological theories of her mentor at Radcliffe, professor William James. Michael J. Hoffman and Donald Sutherland both pioneered this effort; Lisa Ruddick has recently revised it. Other critics have emphasized Stein's desire to take part in the artistic revolution that was taking place around her in Paris—as Pablo Picasso painted her portrait in the radically unconventional techniques of cubism, Stein composed ''Melanctha.'' According to these critics—including Randa Dubnick, Jayne L. Walker, and Hoffman—Stein sought to achieve the same unprecedented ''realism'' in literature that painters like Picasso pursued on canvas.

There has also been a lengthy critical tradition of examining the social issues that surface in ''Melanctha,'' most notably Stein's treatment of African-American characters and Melanctha's femaleness. Carl Van Vechten initiated the study of race with his 1933 preface to *Three Lives*. Although some critics, including novelist Richard Wright, have praised Stein's depiction of black Americans, many more have detected a persistent racism in the stereotypes she employs. Milton A. Cohen provides an extensive discussion; Ruddick also touches on

the issue. Just as risky as Stein's choice of making her protagonist black was her choice to make Melanctha a woman untroubled by moral judgement, especially about her sexuality. Melanctha's freedom, as well as the difficult life from which her emotional complexity arises, has made her a natural subject for feminist scholarship. Marianne DeKoven, in 1983, identified Melanctha as a kind of proto-feminist, a female rebel against oppressive propriety. Ruddick, focusing on the violence of Melanctha's father, interprets her as a victim of patriarchal culture.

Criticism

Ondine Le Blanc

Le Blanc is an editor and writer who has taught at the University of Michigan. In the following essay, she focuses on Stein's innovative style and subject matter in the story, and upon Stein's treatment of emotion and time.

At least since Carl Van Vechten's preface to the 1933 edition of *Three Lives*, critics have claimed ''Melanctha'' as a trailblazing text in its use of African-American characters. Gertrude Stein was undeniably unorthodox, among white writers, in her decision to set ''Melanctha'' in a black community, using only black characters. Previous to this, non-white characters usually appeared in fiction as marginal actors, such as servants. As progressive as Stein's selection of an African-American setting was in the early twentieth century, her language still carries obvious and marked racism. Her descriptions of the characters, in particular, betray her prejudices: Rose Johnson has ''the simple, promiscuous unmorality of the black people''; several characters are identified by their proximity to ''the wide abandoned laughter that gives the broad glow to negro sunshine.'' As Martin A. Cohen has demonstrated at length, in Stein's effort to make use of William James's theories of basic personality types, she assumes connections among racial heritage, skin color, and supposedly inborn character traits. In her description of Jane Harden, for example, Stein writes, ''she had much white blood and that made her see clear, she liked drinking and that made her reckless. Her white blood was strong in her and she had grit and endurance and a vital courage.''

Rather than condemn or celebrate Stein for her use of black characters, critics have often found it

What Do I Read Next?

- In *A Moveable Feast* (1964), Stein's friend and fellow-novelist Ernest Hemingway describes the Paris world in which both artists lived. His portrayal of Stein influenced how several generations of critics viewed her.

- Stein provided a portrait of her life in Paris in her 1933 bestseller, *The Autobiography of Alice B. Toklas*. Despite the title, the work actually focuses on Stein as allegedly seen through the eyes of her companion.

- Novelist James Joyce first established his standing among major writers of the twentieth century with the publication of *A Portrait of the Artist as a Young Man* (1916). This story of a boy's growth from childhood to young adulthood was, like ''Melanctha,'' revolutionary in its style.

- The title character of *Sula* (1973), a novel by Nobel Prize-winner Toni Morrison, is a black woman who, like Melanctha, ''wanders'' through life, challenges the morals of those around her, and has her strongest emotional bond with a female friend.

- A classic of literary modernism, Virginia Woolf's *To the Lighthouse* (1927) depicts the family life of a middle-class English family, the Ramseys. The author's experiments with form emphasized, like Stein's, the processes of perception and the difficulty of interpersonal communication.

- Jean Toomer's *Cane* (1923), a celebrated text of the Harlem Renaissance, groups together short stories and prose poems that depict African-American life in the rural South. Although Toomer's racial identity remains unclear, he apparently identified himself as African American at the time that he lived in the South, observing the lives of the people he met there.

- Psychology professor William James, Stein's mentor at Radcliffe, wrote many books about his theories. One introductory text, published in 1961 by Harper and Row, is *Psychology: The Briefer Course*.

---

more instructive to ask why she made this choice. As several critics, including Donald Sutherland, have noted, an early twentieth-century assumption that people of color were more ''natural'' facilitated Stein's desire to suggest the universality of the experiences she was portraying. Regarding Melanctha in particular, this belief supplemented Stein's depiction of her as the least artificial in her processes of perception and in her morality. Stein's idea of black dialect—albeit largely inaccurate—also lent itself neatly to her purposes as an artist. Believing that rhythm, rather than syntax, dictated expression in black speech patterns, Stein could see it as also more natural than the language typically employed in novels. One champion of Stein's in this regard was the African-American novelist Richard Wright, who read the story out loud to an enthusiastic audience of black workingmen.

Another answer to this question about Stein's selection depends on the story's roots in Stein's earliest attempt at a novel, *Q.E.D.*, which was based on Stein's relationship with May Bookstaver. Since the subject of *Q.E.D.*, a sexual liaison between two women, made it unpublishable, the work went unseen until after Stein's death. She did publish other works that treated or drew on her homosexual desire, but these works, like the poem ''Lifing Belly,'' were so cryptic that most readers would not recognize the subject matter. *Q.E.D.*, however, had been quite direct in its treatment. Most critics have taken for granted, therefore, that the strong similarities between *Q.E.D.* and ''Melanctha'' argue the latter as Stein's encoded portrayal of her lesbian relationship. There is a certain logic, then, in her choice of black characters to stand in for the lesbian characters in *Q.E.D.* Like Stein and Bookstaver,

> As several critics, including Donald Sutherland, have noted, an early twentieth-century assumption that people of color were more 'natural' facilitated Stein's desire to suggest the universality of the experiences she was portraying."

Jeff and Melanctha stand at the edges of mainstream society. Further, because racial stereotypes in Stein's culture allowed her to view black Americans as more sexually free, she could recast her lesbian desires as the promiscuity of Melanctha's wandering.

The possibility that Jeff and Melanctha re-enact events and feelings from Stein's own life has suggested to critics the importance of "Melanctha" as a psychological self-portrait. The story obviously highlights emotion—at points, in painstaking detail—above events, cause-and-effect, and the other conventions of fiction. Instead, Stein dwells on the layers, vicissitudes, and uncertainties of interior life. Jeff's experiences demonstrate this theme at great length. When the reader first meets Jeff, he sees life simply and with a great deal of certainty: he "believed you ought to love your father and your mother and to be regular in all your life, . . . and to always know where you were, and what you wanted, and to always tell everything just as you meant it." As his feelings for Melanctha grow, however, and as he becomes more in touch with his emotional life, his sense of certainty diminishes: "Then he knew he really could know nothing. He knew then, he never could know what it was she really wanted with him. He knew then he never could know really what it was he felt inside him." Similarly, he discovers his inability to know and communicate with Melanctha, demonstrating, in Sutherland's words, "an incoherence between two subjectivities." In place of the traditional notions of truth and reality, Jeff and the reader come to depend on the "wisdom" of emotional experience.

At the opposite end of the spectrum from Jeff the reader finds Rose, who never doubts herself: "Rose was selfish and was stupid and was lazy, but she was decent and knew always what was the right way she should do, and what she wanted." Jem, also, has little experience of doubt: the world and his own needs are apparently quite transparent to him. Tellingly, these are the characters who most hurt Melanctha and whom the narrator portrays as the least complex and the least compelling.

Stein conveys the "emotional wisdom" that Jeff learns through style as well as content. Stein's centrality as a modernist writer stems from her stylistic innovations, from her efforts to rework narrative structure and sentences in order to represent the world in new ways, thus possibly portraying a reality not accessible to conventional forms. Paramount among these in "Melanctha" is the "prolonged present" she defines in her essay "Composition as Explanation": "a constant recurring and beginning there was a marked direction in the direction of being in the present although naturally I had been accustomed to past present and future, and why, because the composition forming around me was a prolonged present." The idea for a prolonged present originated in the theories of William James, particularly in his idea of a human perception, which also stressed the "stream of consciousness" that Stein employs. In a sense, this rush of sensual perception and emotional experience is the reality in which Jeff learns to live and in which Melanctha seems naturally to exist. The prolonged present exchanges conventional notions of past and future, as well as causality, for time made up distinct but aggregate "now"s. These two notions of time also have their place in the content of the story, particularly in Jeff and Melanctha's arguments about memory: Jeff understands it as a consistent image of the past and Melanctha understands it as rewritten in each moment. Sutherland's insistence that Stein's "has to be read word by word, as a succession of single meanings accumulating into a larger meaning," points out how her style captured this notion of time.

As much as she owed to William James for her stylistic innovations, Stein owed at least as much to the painters with whom she associated in Paris at the beginning of the century. Also entertaining new ideas of reality and perception, the artists searched for new modes of representation, depicting their subjects—the usual apples, landscapes, bodies, and faces—with very untraditional techniques. A cubist or fauvist painter might, for example, reduce his subject to its basic geometric shapes and intensify the colors; painting a room or a landscape, he might erase traditional distinctions between foreground and background, so that the wallpaper holds the viewer's eye as forcefully as the still life on the table. A futurist might try to put on canvas several different views of his subject at once, so that a face becomes a fan of sharp angles and lines, repeating one part over again with slight variations. And painters working in many different styles would apply the paint heavily to the canvas, compelling the viewer to become aware of the paint itself as a material-and to realize that they are looking at a canvas, rather than at an actual apple or body. Translating these efforts onto the page with her use of repetition, disjointed sentences, and stream of consciousness, Stein leaves her reader with an awareness of how things are represented and none of the usual certainty about what is represented.

Source: Ondine Le Blanc, ''An Overview of 'Melanctha','' in *Short Stories for Students,* The Gale Group, 1999.

Lisa Ruddick

At the time this book was published, Ruddick was teaching in the English Department at the University of Chicago. In the following excerpt, she presents her view of Stein's reacting to the ideas of her mentor, William James, in ''Melanctha,'' focusing on Melanctha and Jeff as two sides of Stein's own personality.

Gertrude Stein thought of herself as having spent her life escaping from the nineteenth century into which she had been born. This chapter is about the ambivalent beginnings of that escape. With the story ''Melanctha,'' Stein made her first leap into modernist modes of representation; she herself described [in *The Autobiography of Alice B. Toklas*] the story (immodestly but plausibly) as ''the first definite step away from the nineteenth century and into the twentieth century in literature.'' Yet the text looks backward at the same time.

''Melanctha'' carries on a private conversation with William James, Stein's college mentor and the central figure in the early drama of her self-definition as a modernist. Along one of its axes, Stein's story reads as a tribute to James's psychological theories—theories that despite their well-known continuities with modernist aesthetics are nineteenth-century in their ethics. Yet at the margins of the story, other material shows Stein already beginning to define herself against James.

> " The two lovers in the story, Melanctha and Jeff, are the products of Stein's imaginative self-splitting. As she experimented artistically with the different ethical systems that attracted her, she bifurcated herself into a manly Jamesian example and a mysterious woman who became a magnet for her conflicts."

The love plot of ''Melanctha'' borrows heavily from James's psychology; indeed, Stein's debt to James is much deeper than has been supposed. But like all intellectual precursors, James was a burden as well as an inspiration, and as early as ''Melanctha'' Stein began struggling to free herself from him. James's psychology had appealed to her in college for its heartening vision of moral and practical success, which helped her to overcome some of her own self-doubts and inhibitions; in ''Melanctha,'' this ideology of success permeates her characterization of Jeff Campbell, who in fact is her idealized self-portrait through the lens of James. But Jeff and his success plot are already too limiting for Stein, and details at the fringes of the story signal alien ethical and artistic commitments that will soon move into the foreground as Stein wages war more consciously on her teacher.

Among the themes in ''Melanctha'' that stand in tension with the Jamesian plot of mental success is the notion of a wisdom superior to instrumental thinking, a wisdom grounded in the body. Technically, the story violates James's values by indulging in a kind of aimless play; more than that, it transcribes irrational process, forming itself according to a principle of motivated repetition that is continuous not with James's ideas but with the psychoanalytic view of mental life that will soon dislodge James's presence in Stein's work. Finally, ''Melanctha'' has a latent feminism, which places on trial the individualistic and (in Stein's mind) ultimately male value system absorbed from James, which she still honors in the characterization of Jeff Campbell.

The two lovers in the story, Melanctha and Jeff, are the products of Stein's imaginative self-splitting. As she experimented artistically with the different ethical systems that attracted her, she bifurcated herself into a manly Jamesian example and a mysterious woman who became a magnet for her conflicts. Melanctha is the locus of ambiguity in the story. As the focus of this chapter shifts, toward and then away from James, the character Melanctha assumes the appearance, first, of a mere failure in the evolutionary struggle, then of a priestess of the body, and finally of a victim of patriarchal relations. . . .

One way to bring out William James's importance for Stein is to place Jeff, her purest Jamesian creation, against his prototypes in her earlier writings. In Jeff, Stein was able to envision a character who resolved and benefited from internal struggle. For her earlier characters, however, self-division had assured impotence. These characters were paralyzed by the tension between promiscuous and conservative impulses. In the portrait of Jeff Campbell, Stein reconceived this self-division in positive terms, terms that had been suggested to her a decade before by James.

Her very early, painfully divided characters are often versions of herself, and they suggest why James's ideas might have appealed to her in the first place. Stein's attraction to James in college had much to do with his giving her a language to apply to conflicts she perceived in herself. Her obliquely autobiographical college essays, known now as the "Radcliffe Themes," shed light on her emotional life during the period in which she encountered James. These pieces dwell on the figure of a young woman in whom a strongly sensual nature competes with a need for self-mastery.

"In the Red Deeps," for example, is a self-portrait of a girl frightened by her own sadomasochistic fantasy life. She recalls a period during childhood when she experimented with various sorts of self-inflicted pain and fantasized about tortures she might devise for others. But she has an attack of conscience, characterized by a "haunting fear of loss of self-control." The sexual component of the forbidden impulses is underscored by the title, borrowed from the chapter in *The Mill on the Floss* about romantic secrecy and guilt.

"The Temptation" again sets illicit pleasures against self-reproach. The heroine, an indistinct surrogate for Stein, is in church one day when a strange man leans heavily against her. She enjoys the "sensuous impressions," but again has a "quick revulsion," and asks herself, "Have you no sense of shame?" Yet still "she did not move." The conflict leaves her immobilized; she vaguely indulges herself, but only passively. Later her lapse stigmatizes her; her companions, who have seen everything, upbraid her, and she becomes "one apart."

When the characters Stein writes about in these college compositions are not oppressed by conscious fears of impropriety, they have vague inhibitions that are no less paralyzing. Stein writes a theme about a boy who is both frightened and interested when a pretty girl asks him to help her across a brook. Once again, "he . . . could not move." Finally he accommodates her, only to flee in alarm. These characters never pass beyond the faintest stimulation; they prefer loneliness to the risk of losing control.

Although none of the characters in these early pieces is a lesbian, Stein's emerging sexual orientation must have exacerbated her sense of being "one apart," or (as a kind of self-punishing translation) secretly too sexual. Whether or not she yet defined herself as a lesbian, the pressures she was feeling, in some preliminary way, were those of the closet. Her characters in these essays do not dare to let anyone in on their sexual feelings. Stein's own romantic experience in college was limited to a mildly flirtatious friendship with her psychology teammate Leon Solomons—a friendship that, as she recalled in a later notebook, was "Platonic because neither care [*sic*] to do more." The relationship was close and pleasant, but to the extent that it bordered on flirtation it ironically made her feel asexual and freakish. In the meantime, as her college compositions intimate, she experienced intense longings and loneliness.

Stein's preoccupation during her late teens with conflicts such as those in the "Themes" helps to account for her interest in James's psychology, and explains why of all her professors she singled James out for a sort of hero-worship. James too sees a duality in human nature, one that traps a person between eagerness and self-control. But in his view, the self-division signifies not deviance but mental health. Every mind, by his account, has a promiscuous and a repressive element. In normal perceptual life, part of us is welcoming and indiscriminate, but another part excludes data from awareness. These are the two impulses that Stein later plays against each other in Jeff Campbell.

James's theories doubtless helped to alleviate Stein's guilt about what seemed threatening appetites and, at the same time, suggested a means of forgiving herself her inhibitions. The mind James describes naturally has its thirsty or revolutionary dimension, a menace but also a source of life: we would stagnate if we lost the taste for raw sensation. Stein evidently welcomed the parallel. The unruly libidos of the Radcliffe heroines are refigured in ''Melanctha'' as a form of perceptual openness: Melanctha Herbert is at once sexually and perceptually promiscuous, and she helps Jeff by introducing him to ''excitements'' both romantic and more broadly experiential. Stein later validates her inhibitions too, by associating them with selective attention. Jeff is romantically cautious and also incapable of focusing his senses on ''new things''; these qualities make him attractive to the heroine of the story. Indeed, the very struggle between yielding and self-control that immobilizes the characters of the ''Radcliffe Themes'' comes, with an infusion of James's psychology, to seem a creative part of consciousness.

One way to think of Jeff is as Stein's self-idealization through the filter of James. He is, after all, a version of Adele in *Q.E.D.*, who herself was a virtually unaltered Stein. But he is a transformed Adele, robust and successful. Adele, incidentally—or Stein, in the intermediate phase of *Q.E.D.* —had fallen in love but still experienced all the internal pressures of her earlier personae in the ''Radcliffe Themes.'' Like the Radcliffe heroines, Adele-Stein is torn between her sexual curiosity and her inhibitions; the tension freezes her, making her an ''unresponsive'' lover. Ideologically, too, Adele feels caught, as her author did, between the lesbianism that marks her as ''queer'' and a bourgeois ideology that makes her wish to ''avoid excitements'' and become ''the mother of children.''

But in Jeff Campbell, Stein transforms the tension in herself between sexual needs and conservative values into a source of strength. Jeff's competing impulses make him a more sensitive person and a better doctor. His one excursion into forbidden ''excitements'' only helps him to know himself better and to do more for others. James's ideas helped Stein to create an idealized self, conceived in terms of psychic vigor.

On the other hand, ''Melanctha'' also contains an image of failure to thrive. The heroine of the story does not fare so well as her lover. She never achieves mental balance, and she dies. In portraying Melanctha, Stein slips outside the Jamesian framework and the self-idealization attached to it.

Melanctha herself, by William James's standards, is weak. One way to account for her presence—were we to remain within the limits of the Jamesian paradigm—would be to see her as an example of the high costs, in Darwinian terms, of mind-wandering. Melanctha is not ultimately changed by her affair with Jeff. Whereas he assimilates the new mode of perception Melanctha has given him, she fails to be impressed by his ''solidity,'' his conceptual grip on the world. She tries to adapt to him for a time, but ends by reverting to her former ''excited,'' ''reckless,'' wandering ways.

Rose Johnson, who might have served as a replacement, then rejects her, and the desertion ''almost killed her.'' This might seem an extreme reaction, but in Rose, Melanctha has lost her last point of contact with the ''solid safety'' of the conservative temperament. ''Melanctha needed Rose always to let her cling to her. . . . Rose always was so simple, solid, decent, for her. And now Rose had cast her from her. Melanctha was lost, and all the world went whirling in a mad weary dance around her.'' Melanctha is ''lost'': as James said, without mental conservatism, ''we should be intellectually lost in the midst of the world.'' Melanctha loses touch with the ''solid'' tendency, and ''all the world went whirling in a mad weary dance around her.'' This is a fair description of what would happen to a mind severed from all perceptual habit and banished to the flux of unfamiliar sensation. Melanctha virtually drowns in the continuum of the world.

Her physiological death, some paragraphs later, seems to follow as a matter of course. Critics have seen in the stories of *Three Lives*, each of which ends with a heroine's death, shades of naturalism. This reading assumes a special force in light of the Jamesian or Darwinian psychological drama of ''Melanctha.'' In Stein's heroine one observes a character unfit for the world who is weeded out by a brand of natural selection. In James's psychology the person who has no mechanism of selective attention is ill suited for the business of self-preservation. The survival of the fittest militates against those ''exuberant non-egoistic'' individuals who, careless of their own personal safety, diffuse their attention equally over experience. But Melanctha has persisted in wandering on the perilous ''edge of wisdom,'' suppressing personal interests in the name of ''excitement.'' In the end, ''tired with being all the time so much excited,'' she succumbs to the social and bodily suicide that, as James makes plain, would be the outcome of any life of wholly unselfish or unselective perception.

The case of Melanctha, if one reads it, then, in the light of James, is an admonition. Yet Melanctha's failure by James's standards could lead one as easily to question James's values as to take a critical view of the heroine. I have sketched a reading of Melanctha's story as a negative example, but it could just as well be thought of as a protest against the entire notion of mental success represented by Jeff. For in the moral universe of ''Melanctha,'' self-preservation is not clearly the highest good. Part of the story pulls away from the psychological framework supplied by William James and from the Darwinian gospel of success attached to it.

''Melanctha'' is Stein's most deeply Jamesian text, but it comes belatedly, at a point when its author is just beginning to strain against James. Within a few years her notebooks show her explicitly defining herself against him. In ''Melanctha,'' her early ambivalence creates a kind of ethical polyphony. The story hovers somewhere between the ideas and views Stein shared with James and quite different, still indistinct values that would soon propel her in new directions.

James's psychology is shot through with Darwinism; the important thing, in his view, is to thrive. Stein's attachment to this perspective is evident in her sympathetic portrait of Jeff Campbell, the good doctor who does his work and moves ahead professionally. But Melanctha, who has no instinct for survival, is of course portrayed at least as sympathetically herself. She receives a much more positive treatment than her antecedent in *Q.E.D.*, the thoughtless seducer Helen. In the move from *Q.E.D.* to ''Melanctha,'' the moral center of the story has shifted toward the promiscuous member of the couple, whose model was not Stein herself but her former lover May Bookstaver.

Melanctha, far from being merely an object of pitying diagnosis, has qualities that elevate her above a mere survivor like Rose. Her imperfect instinct for self-preservation is the cost of her superior ''wisdom,'' which the story sets against instrumental knowledge as embodied by Jeff and as preached by James. Against the background of James's theories, the word *wisdom* in ''Melanctha'' can be thought of as referring to the heroine's reckless immersion in the senses, but the word has a spiritual resonance as well. Jeff seems to be pointing to a mysterious power in Melanctha when he

speaks of a ''new feeling'' she has given him, ''just like a new religion to me.'' The world she opens up for him is a world of ''real being.'' This spiritual quality of hers is never explained, but it pushes her beyond the ethical boundaries defined by James's *Psychology* and, for that matter, by James's own more spiritually oriented writings. Part of Stein's story is about a ''way to know'' that has no bearing on practical life but is more elevated than mere sensory abundance.

At the risk of trying to define precisely something the text leaves vague and suggestive, I want to approach Melanctha's wisdom by setting it alongside some other details in her story, which seem to have nothing to do with the framework of Jamesian psychology. Stein's heroine has a special intimacy with the mysteries of the body. Melanctha is close to the upheavals of birth, death, and puberty. She watches over her dying mother; this seems to be the most important thing she has ever done for or with her mother. She tends Rose Johnson as Rose gives birth, acting as a sort of midwife, even to the extent of moving Rose away from her husband for the last part of the pregnancy. (''When Rose had become strong again [after the delivery and the baby's death] she went back to her house with Sam.'' Melanctha's story is bounded by her own puberty, the time in her twelfth year when she is ''just beginning as a woman,'' and by her death.

These details—the death of the mother, the birth of the baby, Melanctha's puberty, and her death—were superimposed on the original plot of *Q.E.D.*, and they signal changes in Stein's thinking. The details involving birth and death—which, along with the setting in the black community, were inspired by Stein's clinical experiences at Johns Hopkins Medical School—bear no obvious relation to the primary story of the romance with Jeff Campbell, and they give the narrative of ''Melanctha'' a wandering quality. Although they are never digested into the main plot, the narrative pulls back to these events, often out of sequence. The story begins, for example, not where one would expect it to begin but with the delivery of Rose's baby, which, we will later find out, actually *follows* the entire love affair of Melanctha and Jeff: ''Rose Johnson made it very hard to bring her baby to its birth. Melanctha Herbert who was Rose Johnson's friend, did everything that any woman could.'' I associate Melanctha's hazily defined wisdom with her quality of presiding at moments of bodily change or upheaval. The text makes no such connection explicitly, but these fragmentary data embedded in

"Melanctha" will begin to form a more cohesive picture in Stein's later work.

Within a few years Stein will depart from James altogether by grounding her idea of consciousness in what might be called the rhythms of the body. She will develop a notion of wisdom as a kind of thought that knows its ties to the body. As her spirituality comes to the surface, an emphasis on bodily experience, as sacred and taboo, marks the difference from James's own brand of spirituality. To quote from the dense text of *Tender Buttons*, the most extraordinary thing Stein wrote in the teens, "*out of an eye* comes research" (emphasis added); knowledge emanates *from* the eye, like tears. Or (to use a more opaque passage) spiritual knowing or "in-sight" is continuous with anatomical functions like giving milk or suckling: "MILK. Climb up in sight climb in the whole utter." *Tender Buttons* stages bodily upheavals great and small, from eating to giving birth and dying. An early hint of these preoccupations appears in the liminal Melanctha, stationed at the crises of the body.

Significantly, William James's psychology would not account in an interesting way for Melanctha's intimacy with the body. Compared to a near contemporary like Freud, James seems to keep the body out of focus, except in its role as a machine absorbing data and maintaining itself in existence. Nor would Melanctha's sexuality be something James would illuminate. Melanctha's involvements in birth, death, and sensual experience give her a kind of wisdom distinct from James's instrumental knowledge. To describe the notion of bodily consciousness that develops in Stein's subsequent work, it will be necessary to use a vocabulary closer to psychoanalysis than to the theories of James.

Stein's notebooks and subsequent works suggest to me that in her characterization of the embodied Melanctha, she was depicting something she saw in herself, for all her simultaneous identification with (and self-projection in) the more controlled and rational Jeff Campbell. In one of the notebooks for *The Making of Americans*, Stein identified a side of herself she called "the Rabelaisian, nigger abandonment, Vollard [the art dealer], daddy side." That she associates her bodily gusto, or everything Rabelaisian in herself, with something she calls "nigger abandonment" suggests that the extreme racism she expresses in "Melanctha"—for example, in depicting blacks as carefree and promiscuous—served (among other things) her own need to distance a part of herself about which she

was ambivalent. She had her own sensuous side, which she projected in racial terms perhaps so she could simultaneously idealize and depreciate it; and by playing to the racism of her audience, she partially disguised the dimension of self-exploration in the story.

Source: Lisa Ruddick, "'Melanctha': The Costs of Mind-Wandering," in *Reading Gertrude Stein: Body, Text, Gnosis,* Cornell University Press, 1990, pp. 12–54.

Milton A. Cohen

In the following excerpt, Cohen presents his interpretation of Stein's linking of character traits with degree of skin color in "Melanctha," focusing on racism and its thematic implications.

Gertrude Stein always prided herself on her acute observations of human nature, a talent she attributed to her experimental training in psychology under William James and Hugo Munsterberg at Harvard. But by her own account of these experiments, she reveals an early penchant not so much to observe the individual instance as to categorize the larger type:

> I was supposed to be interested in their reactions but soon I found that I was not but instead I was enormously interested in the types of their characters that is what I even then thought of the bottom nature of them and when in May 1898 I wrote my half of the report of these experiments I expressed the results as follows: "In these descriptions it will be readily observed that habits of attention are reflexes of the complete character of the individual" [in *Selected Writings of Gertrude Stein*, ed. Carl Van Vechten, 1962].

Stein's interest in defining and categorizing "bottom nature" continued through the next decade in such early works as *Q.E.D* (1903) and *Three Lives* (1905–6), and crested in the numerous chartings and minutely-refined adjectival strings that delineate the characters of *The Making of Americans*. In all of these works, the "bottom natures" that she originally identified at Harvard (nervous and easily aroused vs. phlegmatic) help to determine, in varying degrees and mixtures, the characterizations. In the "Melanctha" story of *Three Lives*, however, Stein set for herself a unique challenge in understanding character. For unlike the characters of the other early works, who were modeled after people Stein knew well from her childhood and college years, the characters of "Melanctha" belonged to a race that Stein had observed at first hand only while she delivered babies as a medical student in Baltimore:

> It was then that she had to take her turn in the delivering of babies and it was at that time that she

> "Unflattering qualities and stereotypes of blacks abound in 'Melanctha.' . . . Even when Stein attempts to praise, as in the last examples, her condescension is as embarrassing as her obliviousness to it is disturbing."

noticed the negroes and the places that she afterwards used in the second of the *Three Lives* stories, Melanctha Herbert, the story that was the beginning of her revolutionary work [*Selected Writings*].

One might expect that such first-hand experience would serve as an empirical check on Stein's theories of bottom nature. But her experience was limited both by time (she was required to spend no more than two months at it) and, more importantly, by the vast cultural chasm dividing upper-middle-class, white medical students from the poor blacks they treated. It is not surprising, then, that Stein's attempt to categorize the blacks in "Melanctha" according to their "bottom natures" is tainted by cultural bias. Although such early admirers of Stein as Richard Wright praised her depiction of blacks as being "the first long serious literary treatment of Negro life in the United States," other critics, both black and white, have found it offensive. Richard Bridgman, for example, writes:

> Gertrude Stein's treatment of the negro is both condescending and false. . . . it swarms with cliches about the happy, promiscuous, razor-fighting, church-going darky [*Gertrude Stein in Pieces*].

> The race references in "Melanctha" are infrequent, and when they do appear, they are stereotyped. Negroes possess shiny or greasy black faces; their eyeballs roll; their mouths gape open as they howl with laughter; they fight with razors, yell savagely, are often lazy and are insistently virile [*American Literature* 33 (1961)].

In fact, however, Bridgman is both too kind and not kind enough to Stein. For "Melanctha" contains a far wider range of skin tones than "shiny or greasy black faces," and behaviors far more diverse

than "razor-fighting and church-going." But at the same time, Stein organizes these varieties into a racial hierarchy that is more ominously schematic than Bridgman suggests. Here are the characters of "Melanctha" arranged by the skin tones that Stein describes and accompanied by the "bottom natures" she gives them:

> Rose Johnson: Melanctha's friend; real black; tall, well-built, good-looking, sullen, stupid, childlike, lazy, promiscuous, unmoral, coarse, shiftless, selfish, decent, ordinary, slow

> James: Melanctha's father; black; coarse, big, powerful, virile, robust, unpleasant, brutal, rough, hard-handed, loose-built, common, decent enough, angry, never really joyous, looked evil [before fight], fierce and serious, knew nothing

> railroad yard workers: greasy black becoming grey when scared; [fearful], eye-rolling

> shipyard workers: yowling, free-swinging, powerful, loose-jointed, childish, half-savage

> John: coachman for white family; light brown mulatto; very decent, vigorous, friendly, pleasant, but knew how to use a razor

> porter at railroad yard: light brown; big, serious, melancholy, kind, gentle

> Jeff's father: butler for white family; light brown; good, kind, serious, religious, steady, very intelligent, very dignified

> Jeff's mother: pale brown; sweet, little, gentle, reverenced and obeyed her husband

> Jeff: Melanctha's boyfriend, doctor; mulatto; very good, strong, gentle, very intellectual, sympathetic, earnest, joyous, happy, laughing, studious, hard-working, scientific, quiet-living, [not seeking experience], [wants other blacks to adopt these qualities]

> Melanctha's mother: pale yellow; sweet appealing, pleasant, mysterious, uncertain, wandering in her ways

> Melanctha: protagonist; pale yellow; intelligent, attractive, subtle, graceful, complex, mysterious, suffering, uncomplaining, despairing, pleasant [but has] nasty tongue, sudden and impulsive, has breakneck courage [but at first is a coward], [attracted to power], [hungry for "experience"]

> Jane Harden: Melanctha's tutor and friend; negress but so white that hardly anyone would guess it; roughened, powerful, reckless, drinker [well educated: two years at "colored college"], bad conduct, not afraid to understand ways that lead to wisdom, had much white blood and that made her see clear, good mind, white blood strong in her and she had grit and endurance and a vital courage

Several obvious generalizations can be drawn from this chart. First, Stein clearly links skin tone to personality traits. Second, her associations follow many of the established stereotypes that whites held of blacks: The "black" end of the scale represents coarseness, stupidity, and a "half-savage" child-ishness. Images of the fearful, eye-rolling, exaggerating Negro also appear at this end. The "white" end of the scale brings intelligence, complexity, and courage. In between, the "light brown" shade denotes seriousness, hard work, decency, kindness, and religiosity, while the "pale yellow" is complex, mysterious, uncertain, sweet but somewhat vague.

The racism of this hierarchy is most glaringly evident at its poles. Stein unfailingly mentions James Herbert's blackness before adding other adjectives:

> her robust and unpleasant and very unendurable black father
>
> her black coarse father
>
> big black virile negro
>
> He looked very black and evil
>
> a brute of a black nigger father

Appropriately, the "nigger" epithet above comes from Jane Harden, who resides at the other end of the scale, the almost-white. "Roughened" and "reckless," Jane bears a curious similarity to James Herbert (a seeming contradiction considered below), but Stein leaves little doubt about the value of her "white blood":

> She had much white blood and that made her see clear. . . .
>
> Her white blood was strong in her and she had grit and endurance and a vital courage.

Unflattering qualities and stereotypes of blacks abound in "Melanctha." Because infant mortality is so common in black neighborhoods, neither Sam nor Rose Johnson "thought about it very long" when their baby dies (from Rose's negligence). Melanctha, "half made with real white blood," "demeans herself" by serving "this lazy, stupid, ordinary, selfish, black girl [Rose]." We read of "the earth-born boundless joy of negroes," the "wide abandoned laughter that gives the broad glow of negro sunshine," "the good warm nigger time" Melanctha could have with "colored men." Even when Stein attempts to praise, as in the last examples, her condescension is as embarrassing as her obliviousness to it is disturbing.

Yet for all of its obvious racism, Stein's skin-tone groupings raise several questions. Why, for example, do some of the "mixed-blood" shades (e.g., the light brown) show fairly consistent qualities, while others (e.g., Jane Harden's almost-whiteness) are contradictory? Curiously, this apparent inconsistency follows the dubious logic of Stein's hierarchy. For the contradictions of the "mixed" shades seem to increase as they approach whiteness. Apparently, Stein equates complexity and contradiction with intelligence; i.e., with whiteness. Further, personality consistency depends on parental consistency—another aspect of Stein's "bottom nature." Thus, Melanctha's contradictory behavior derives from the genetic opposition of her black father's violent impulsiveness and attraction to power and experience, and her pale yellow mother's "sweet, mysterious, uncertain, and pleasant" character. Although Jane Harden's parentage is not given, we might assume a similar contrast of parental types. Conversely, Jeff's parents are *both* good, kind, serious, and light brown—and so is Jeff.

If racism alone informs Stein's groupings, then why are the "light brown" given white-oriented, "Uncle Tom" values (hard work, seriousness, politeness, self-sacrifice, and sensuous restraint), while the character closest to white, Jane Harden, shares the "roughness" and "recklessness" of the blacks? In one sense, the "bottom nature" of the light browns is perfectly logical. As servants of white families, Jeff's father and John the stableman would be most prone to adopt the values of their employers or, more accurately, the values their employers would expect to see blacks adopt. Hence, Jeff's moralizing about the values blacks should pursue— "I don't believe much in this running around business and I don't want to see the colored people do it. . . . I want to see the colored people like what is good and what I want them to have, and that's to live regular and work hard and understand things . . ."—is the voice of the white bourgeoisie coming through a black manikin.

But what complicates the question is that these white-oriented views are not entirely Stein's own. Indeed, the central theme and action of "Melanctha"— gaining sexual experience ("wisdom"), learning to trust one's feelings and to live for the present moment—run counter to Jeff's Puritanical restraint. Significantly, Stein does not bias the conflict toward either side. For she speaks not with the moral certainty of the white middle class, but, as Bridgman suggests [in *Gertrude Stein in Pieces*], with a voice divided between the energy and primness she inherited from family and culture and her own emerging sensuality and lesbianism. If anything, Stein's sympathies are with Melanctha's courageous immersion into life, not with Jeff's queasy inhibitions. Thus, Stein had no reason to associate "superior" skin tone (white) with moral restraint.

It would seem, then, that the racial hierarchy in "Melanctha" works against the story's thematic tension. Stein's position, itself, is ambivalent: The stereotypes of her hierarchy locate her well within her culture, the white bourgeoisie of 1905–6; but her delineation of the sexual conflict places her quite outside this culture. One might well conclude, as Bridgman and Claude McKay [Quoted in *The Third Rose*, 1959] have, that the racial setting of "Melanctha" is both false and superfluous to the central story. But what does Stein's hierarchy show about her theory of "bottom nature"?

Certainly, her penchant for categorizing behavior is as evident in her racial hierarchy as it is in her behavioral "types." But the types (nervous vs. phlegmatic) were at least Stein's own generalizations (albeit, based on medieval humors), drawn from her observations in psychology experiments and developed thoughtfully over a decade. The racial types can lay no such claim to original perception: They were merely the cliches of her age. If Stein considered her racial hierarchy to offer valid examples of "bottom nature," then her personality theories join the musty ranks of Gobineau, Chamberlain, and the other discredited racists as curious antiquities. If, as is more likely, however, she merely incorporated these racial stereotypes *unthinkingly* into her real concern with character and consciousness, then such uncritical acceptance casts considerable doubt on the depth and acuity of her perceptions of human nature, and points, rather, to an arbitrary and subjective *con*ception. Either way, in the racial hierarchy of "Melanctha," Stein's theory of "bottom nature" bottoms out.

Source: Milton A. Cohen, "Black Brutes and Mulatto Saints: The Racial Hierarchy of Stein's 'Melanctha'," in *Black American Literature Forum*, Vol. 18, No. 3, Fall, 1984, pp. 119–21.

Donald Sutherland

In the following excerpt, Sutherland, reflecting ideas of the 1950s, presents his interpretation of Stein's experimental style in "Melanctha," focusing on her handling of time.

... According to the general agreement the big thing in *Three Lives* is the middle story, "Melanctha." It is a tragic love story ending in death from consumption; so that it is available to the traditional literary taste and the educated emotions. Furthermore it is, as Carl Van Vechten says [in his preface to *Three Lives*], "perhaps the first American story in which the Negro is regarded as a human being and not as

an object for condescending compassion or derision." It is a good deal to have attained that clarity and equilibrium of feeling in a difficult question, but "Melanctha" as a piece of literature does much more. Where "The Good Anna" and "The Gentle Lena" are composed as the presentation of a single type in illustrative incidents, "Melanctha" is composed on the dramatic trajectory of a passion. If "The Good Anna" roughly corresponds to [Gustave Flaubert's] "Un Coeur Simple," "Melanctha" corresponds roughly to *Madame Bovary*. Very roughly, and there is most likely no direct influence, but it makes an illuminating comparison.

Madame Bovary and the course of her passion are presented in an elaborate series of incidents, situations, landscapes, interiors, extraneous issues; in short they are measured and realized against a thick objective context as the things in the context are measured against her desire. Strangely enough this desire is never directly presented. It is measured somewhat by its casual source in her romantic reading—as Don Quixote is casually accounted for by his reading of the romances of chivalry—and it is known later by its various objects such as travel in far lands, luxuries, poetry written to her, and so on. As a blind desire, and probably as a death wish, it is symbolized by the awful blind beggar who is as it were Emma's *Doppelganger* and who is finally put out of the way by Homais, the type of cheap rationalism. Emma's power is measured again by her being too much for Charles, for Leon, and even for Rodolphe, and by the pathetic infatuation of the boy Justin. She has certainly a variety of states of mind, wild desire, remorse, boredom, religiosity, fear, and so on, but they are a succession of distinct states, presented as complete and not as in process. In brief, Flaubert's art was spatial and intensely pictorial, not temporal and musical. Expressing directly and exactly the immediate movement, pulse, and process of a thing simply was not his business. But it was in this early period Gertrude Stein's business, and in "Melanctha" she did express at length the process of a passion.

She did not yet disengage the essential vitality entirely from its natural context. There are some few descriptions of railroad yards, docks, country scenes, houses, yards, rooms, windows, but these are reduced to a telling minimum. There is also some accounting for the complex forces in the heroine's character by the brutality of her father and the sweet indifference of her mother. She is described at the beginning of the story by contrast and association with Rose Johnson, her hard-headed decent friend, and again by the same contrast enlarged at the end of the story, when Rose casts her off. But the real demonstration of the story is the dialogue between Melanctha and her lover Jeff Campbell. In this long dialogue, which is like a duel or duet, the traditional incoherence between the inner and the outer life has been replaced by an incoherence between two subjectivities. It is conceived of as a difference in tempo, the slow Jeff against the quick Melanctha. Also there is already very much present in this story the difference, the radical and final difference in people, defined in *The Making of Americans* as the attacking and the resisting kinds or types. It is not quite the difference between active and passive, as both kinds are based on a persistence in being or in living, and they are further complicated by a deviousness and modulation in function. For example, how does a naturally attacking kind resist and how does a naturally resisting kind get provoked to attack? All this is elaborately and dramatically worked out in the long dialogue. "It was a struggle, sure to be going on always between them. It was a struggle that was as sure always to be going on between them, as their minds and hearts always were to have different ways of working." Their differences, shade by shade, and their gradual reconciliations are presented through the whole course of the affair from indifference to gradual fascination to the struggle for domination by a variety of means, to the decline into brotherly and sisterly affection, and finally to the final break.

Gertrude Stein had already, in a story written in 1903 and called "Quod Erat Demonstrandum" but not published until 1950 and under the title *Things as They Are*, worked out a very similar dialectic of a passion. It is very interesting as a preliminary exercise for "Melanctha." As its first title suggests, it is an intensive and exhaustive study of relations in a triangle. In its way it is a Jamesian study or demonstration, and its heroine mentions and quotes the heroine and/or villainess of James' novel *The Wings of the Dove*, Kate Croy. But *Things as They Are* bears a more striking resemblance to the *Adolphe* of Benjamin Constant, it has the same merciless directness and concentration, and though Gertrude Stein had probably not read *Adolphe* in 1903 this earliest work belongs to the tradition of *Adolphe* and of *La Princesse de Clèves*. It has the same unwavering intellectual clarity applied to the perpetually shifting relationships of a passion throughout its course. That much is already mastered in this first work, but

> "But the real demonstration of the story is the dialogue between Melanctha and her lover Jeff Campbell. In this long dialogue, which is like a duel or duet, the traditional incoherence between the inner and the outer life has been replaced by an incoherence between two subjectivities."

the handling tends more to commentary than to presentation and has not the sure grasp of the personal cadences of a character's thought and feeling that makes the analyses in "Melanctha" a direct expression of character in movement. This is partly the fault of the characters themselves in *Things as They Are*. They are white American college women, whose speech and thought are bound to be at odds with their feeling. Gertrude Stein treats this difficulty handsomely enough as subject matter, but the expressive power of the prose is limited by its very propriety to the subject matter. It is very pure, immensely intelligent, and astonishing for a first work in 1903, but it is polite, cultivated, educated, literary. Compare with the passage from "Melanctha," quoted above, the following from *Things as They Are*:

> Time passed and they renewed their habit of desultory meetings at public places, but these were not the same as before. There was between them now a consciousness of strain, a sense of new adjustments, of uncertain standards and of changing values.

"Melanctha," in which the characters are Negroes, has thereby the advantage of "uneducated" speech, and of a direct relationship between feeling and word, a more fundamental or universal drama. It is a measure of her strength that in making the most of the advantage Gertrude Stein abandoned polite or cultivated writing completely and forever, so completely that the press where she had *Three Lives* printed sent to inquire if she really knew English.

At all events, "Melanctha" is, as I said the work of Henry James was, a time continuum less of events than of considerations of their meaning. The events considered in "Melanctha" are mostly the movements of the passion, how Jeff and Melanctha feel differently toward each other from moment to moment.

Like the characters of James, Melanctha and Jeff are preternaturally articulate about their feelings, but where James keeps the plausibilities by using highly cultivated characters to express the complicated meaning in an endless delicacy of phrasing, Gertrude Stein uses the simplest possible words, the common words used by everybody, and a version of the most popular phrasing, to express the very complicated thing. It is true and exciting that James often used the simplest possible word for his complicated meaning, but he had a tendency to isolate it to the attention, to force it to carry its full weight by printing it in italics or putting it in quotes, or dislocating it from its more usual place in the word order, or repeating it. Gertrude Stein uses repetition and dislocation to make the word bear all the meaning it has but actually one has to give her work word by word the deliberate attention one gives to something written in italics. It has been said that her work means more when one reads it in proof or very slowly, and that is certainly true, the work has to be read word by word, as a succession of single meanings accumulating into a larger meaning, as for example the words in the stanza of a song being sung. Unhappily all our training and most of our reasons for reading are against this. Very likely the desire for simplicity in style is most often a desire that the words and ideas along the way to the formulated conclusion, the point, be perfectly negligible and that we have no anxious feeling we are missing anything as we rush by. But as an example of how Gertrude Stein forces the simplest negligible words to stay there in a full meaning:

> "Can't you understand Melanctha, ever, how no man certainly ever really can hold your love for long times together. You certainly Melanctha, you ain't got down deep loyal feeling, true inside you, and when you ain't just that moment quick with feeling, then you certainly ain't ever got anything more there to keep you. You see Melanctha, it certainly is this way with you, it is, that you ain't ever got any way to remember right what you been doing, or anybody else that has been feeling with you. You certainly Melanctha, never can remember right, when it comes what you have done and what you think happens to you." "It certainly is all easy for you Jeff Campbell to be talking. You remember right, because you don't remember nothing till you get home with your thinking everything all over, but I certainly don't think much ever of that kind of way of remembering right, Jeff Campbell. I certainly do call it remembering right Jeff Campbell, to remember right just when it happens to you, so you have a right kind of feeling not to act the way you always been doing to me, and then you go home Jeff Campbell, and you begin with your thinking, and then it certainly is very easy for you to be good and forgiving with it. No, that ain't to me, the way of remembering Jeff Campbell, not as I can see it not to make people always suffer, waiting for you certainly to get to do it. . . ."

The passage is, if one likes, about the synchronization of feeling upon the present activity. Anyone can see what is meant by the argument if the feeling discussed is understood to be sexual feeling. But the thing which makes this passage absolutely accurate and not euphemistic is that the subject is literally feeling, all feeling, inasmuch as all the passions are one. In brief, making abstraction of objects and situations, sexual feeling behaves no differently from other feelings. The readiness, slowness, concentration or absent-mindedness, domination or dependence in sexual feeling are about the same as in all the other activities of a character. So that we have here a perfect propriety and fullness of diction.

The relatively simple dislocations of "you ain't got down deep loyal feeling, true inside you," from the more commonplace order "you have no true feeling of loyalty deep down inside you," not only jar the words awake into their full meaning but follow with much greater exactitude the slow, passionate, clumsy emphasis of Jeff Campbell's feeling.

The phrase "remembering right" could be replaced by a more familiar cliche, "profiting aptly by past experience," or by scientific gabble like "the coordination of habitual reflexes upon the present object," but the advantage of the simpler new phrase is that it expresses the matter in terms of the fundamental and final activities and categories of the mind. It is part of the "impulse to elemental abstraction," the description in terms of the final and generic as against description by context and association. It is like the generically round and sitting apple of Cezanne as against a delicately compromised and contextuated and reverberating apple of the impressionists. The propriety of the simple popular abstraction used in "Melanctha" is in this, that the two subjectivities at odds are seen, and so to be described, directly—directly from common knowledge, and not, as with *Madame Bovary*, seen refracted and described indirectly through an exterior context embodying considerable special knowledge. The immediate terms of *Madame Bovary* are saturated with French history, the immediate terms of "Melanctha" are the final categories of mental process—to know, to see, to hear, to wish, to remember, to suffer, and the like.

However, "Melanctha" is more than an exact chart of the passions. The conjugation or play of the abstractions proceeds according to the vital rhythm or tempo of the characters. In this way the essential quality of the characters is not only described but presented immediately. As Emma Bovary is *seen* against the rake Rodolphe and then against the pusillanimous Leon, and is thereby defined, so Melanctha is, in her quick tempo, *played* against the slow Jeff Campbell and then against the very fast "dashing" Jem Richards.

Gertrude Stein later made some remarks about *Three Lives* in the light of her later problems of expression. In *Composition as Explanation* she said:

> In beginning writing I wrote a book called *Three Lives* this was written in 1905. I wrote a negro story called "Melanctha." In that there was a constant recurring and beginning there was a marked direction in the direction of being in the present although naturally I had been accustomed to past present and future, and why, because the composition forming around me was a prolonged present. A composition of a prolonged present is a natural composition in the world as it has been these thirty years [1926] it was more and more a prolonged present. I created then a prolonged present naturally I knew nothing of a continuous present but it came naturally to me to make one, it was simple it was clear to me and nobody knew why it was done like that, I did not myself although naturally to me it was natural. . . . In the first book [*Three Lives*] there was a groping for a continuous present and for using everything by beginning again and again.

The difference between a prolonged and a continuous present may be defined as this, that a prolonged present assumes a situation or a theme and dwells on it and develops it or keeps it recurring, as in much opera, and Bach, for example. The continuous present would take each successive moment or passage as a completely new thing essentially, as with Mozart or Scarlatti or, later, Satie. This Gertrude Stein calls beginning again. But the problem is really one of the dimensions of the present as much as of the artist's way with it. The "specious" present which occupied William James is an arbitrary distinction between past and future as they flow together in time. But for purposes of action and art it has to be assumed as an operable space of time. For the composer this space of time can be the measure, or whatever unit can be made to express something without dependence on succes-

sion as the condition of its interest. For the writer it can be the sentence or the paragraph or the chapter or the scene or the page or the stanza or whatever. Gertrude Stein experimented with all these units in the course of her work, but in the early work the struggle was mainly with the sentence and the paragraph.

Source: Donald Sutherland, "'Three Lives' and 'The Making of Americans'," in *Gertrude Stein: A Biography of Her Work,* Yale University Press, 1951 , pp. 44–52.

Sources

Bridgman, Richard. *Gertrude Stein in Pieces,* London and New York: Oxford University Press, 1970.

DeKoven, Marianne. *A Different Language: Gertrude Stein's Experimental Writing,* University of Wisconsin Press, 1983.

Dubnick, Randa. *The Structure of Obscurity: Gertrude Stein, Language, and Cubism,* University of Illinois Press, 1983.

Hoffman, Michael J. *The Development of Abstractionism in the Writings of Gertrude Stein,* University of Pennsylvania Press, 1966.

Stein, Gertrude. "Composition as Explanation," in *What Are Masterpieces,* Conference Press, 1940.

Van Vechten, Carl. Introduction to *Three Lives,* Modern Library, 1933.

Walker, Jayne L. *The Making of a Modernist: Gertrude Stein from* Three Lives *to "Tender Buttons,"* University of Massachusetts Press, 1984.

Further Reading

Haas, Robert Bartlett, editor. *A Primer for the Gradual Understanding of Gertrude Stein,* Black Sparrow Press, 1971.
    An anthology of short pieces by and concerning Stein, selected to serve as an introduction to the new reader.

Mellow, James R. Introduction to *Three Lives,* New American Library, 1985.
    A brief, accessible introduction that sketches Stein's biography and the history of "Melanctha."

Stein, Gertrude. *Fernhurst, Q.E.D., and Other Early Writings.* Edited by Donald Gallup. New York and London: Liveright, 1971.
    A collection of Stein's early writings.

Recitatif

Toni Morrison

1983

"Recitatif" is the only published short story by luminary African-American novelist Toni Morrison. It appeared in a 1983 anthology of writing by African-American women entitled *Confirmation,* edited by Amiri and Amina Baraka. "Recitatif" tells the story of the conflicted friendship between two girls—one black and one white—from the time they meet and bond at age eight while staying at an orphanage through their re-acquaintance as mothers on different sides of economic, political, and racial divides in a recently gentrified town in upstate New York.

While Morrison typically writes about black communities from an inside perspective, in this story she takes a different approach. The story explores how the relationship between the two main characters is shaped by their racial difference. Morrison does not, however, disclose which character is white and which is black. Rather than delving into the distinctive culture of African Americans, she illustrates how the divide between the races in American culture at large is dependent on blacks and whites defining themselves in opposition to one another. Her use of description and characterization in the story underscores the readers' complicity in this process. Morrison has considered similar issues in her book of criticism, *Playing in the Dark: Whiteness and the Literary Imagination,* which explores how language enforces stereotypes in the work of classic American authors such as Melville, Poe, and Hemingway. "Recitatif" may therefore be

understood as part of Morrison's ongoing response to the mostly white and male classic literary tradition of the United States.

Author Biography

Toni Morrison was born Chloe Anthony Wofford to George and Rahmah Wofford in 1931. The second of four children, Morrison was raised in the small Ohio town of Lorain in a tight-knit black community. Morrison describes her father, a shipyard welder, as a racist. Having experienced virulent racism, he despised whites. Her mother, on the other hand, was an integrationist. Both of her parents and her larger community instilled in Morrison a strong sense of self-esteem and cultural identity.

Though she had no aspirations of being a writer in her youth, Morrison was always an avid reader and a precocious student. Her imagination was further nourished by the folk stories passed down from her parents and grandmother. She attended Lorain High School and went on to Howard University, a historically black college. There she studied English and drama and came to be known as Toni. In 1955 Morrison earned a master's degree in English from Cornell University and began a teaching career. She married Harold Morrison, a Jamaican architect, and they had two sons, Harold and Slade.

Morrison's writing career began at age 30 when, feeling unfulfilled, she joined an informal writer's group. Morrison drafted a short story about a black girl who wished she had blue eyes. She had never written fiction or poetry before. This story was the seed of her first novel, *The Bluest Eye,* which she published nine years later. In the interim, Morrison divorced her husband and left teaching, moving to New York for a career in editing. As an editor at Random House she fostered the careers of some of the most important black female writers of her generation. After the appearance of *The Bluest Eye* in 1970, Morrison continued to write prolifically, with great popular and critical success. She is the author of seven novels, a play, and a work of literary criticism. "Recititaf" is her only published work of short fiction. Since 1987 she has focused mainly on writing but has also taught classes at Yale and Princeton Universities.

Morrison is one of the most loved and respected writers of the late twentieth century. Several of her books have been bestsellers and she is the recipient of a number of prestigious literary awards. In 1993 Morrison was awarded the Nobel Prize for Literature, becoming the first African American to win this honor.

Plot Summary

The story opens with a description of "St. Bonny's" or St. Bonaventure, the shelter where Twyla, the narrator, meets Roberta, the story's other main character, when they are both eight years old. Twyla recalls that her mother once told her that people of Roberta's race smell funny, and she objects to being placed in a room with Roberta on the grounds that her mother wouldn't approve. Twyla, however, soon finds Roberta understanding and sympathetic to her situation. While most children at the shelter are orphans, Twyla is there because her mother "dances all night" and Roberta is there because her mother is sick. Roberta and Twyla are isolated from the other children at St. Bonny's and are scared of the older girls, so they stick together.

Twyla remembers St. Bonny's orchard in particular but she doesn't know why it stands out in her memory. She recounts an incident in which Maggie, a mute woman who worked at St. Bonny's kitchen, fell down in the orchard and the big girls laughed at her. Twyla reports that she and Roberta did nothing to help her. They called her names and she ignored them, perhaps because she was deaf, but Twyla thinks not and, looking back, she is ashamed.

Twyla and Roberta's mother come to visit one Sunday. The girls are excited and get dressed up to meet them at church services. Twyla is embarrassed by Mary, her mother, because of her casual appearance, but also proud that she is so pretty. When Roberta attempts to introduce her mother to Twyla and Mary, her mother refuses to address them or to shake Mary's extended hand, presumably because of racial prejudice. Mary says "That bitch!" right there in the chapel and further embarrasses Twyla by groaning during the service. Roberta's mother wears a huge cross and carries a large Bible. Afterward, Mary and Twyla eat Easter candy, since Mary has brought no lunch for them, while Roberta can't finish the food her mother brought. Not long after, Roberta leaves St. Bonny's.

Toni Morrison

Twyla doesn't see Roberta again for many years. Twyla is now a waitress, and Roberta comes in to the Howard Johnson's where she works. Roberta is with two men and tells Twyla that they are on their way to see Jimi Hendrix, but Twyla doesn't know who Hendrix is. Roberta dismisses Twyla and calls her an asshole. Twyla responds by asking about Roberta's mother and cattily reports that her own is still "pretty as a picture."

Tywla's narration picks up again when she is 28 years old and married. She describes her home, husband, and family life. Newburgh, the rundown town where they live, has recently become gentrified, and there is a new mall at the edge of town where Twyla goes one day to shop at a gourmet supermarket. There she runs into Roberta, now married to a wealthy executive, for the first time since their hostile encounter at Howard Johnson's. Roberta greets Twyla warmly and asks her to a coffee. They laugh and the tension between them seems to dissolve. As they are reminiscing, the incident with Maggie comes up. Roberta claims that Maggie didn't fall down in the orchard, but that the big girls had knocked her down. This is not what Twyla remembers and she starts to feel uncomfortable. She asks Roberta about their encounter at Howard Johnson's and Roberta answers, "Oh, Twyla, you know

how it was in those days: black-white." They part ways, promising to keep in touch.

That fall racial tension descends on Newburgh as a result of busing, instituted to ensure integration in the schools. Twyla's son Joseph is one of the children who has to take a bus to a school in a different area. Twyla is driving near the school Joseph will attend and sees Roberta picketing against busing. Twyla stops and they discuss the issue. They argue and soon the group of picketers surrounds Twyla's car and start rocking it; Twyla reaches out to Roberta for help, but Roberta does nothing. Police finally come to Twyla's aid. Just before she pulls away, Roberta approaches her and calls her "the same little state kid who kicked a poor old black lady when she was down on the ground." Twyla responds that Maggie wasn't black and that Roberta is a liar. Roberta responds that she is the liar and that they had both kicked Maggie.

Twyla begins to stand on a picket line holding up slogans that respond directly to Roberta's. Over the course of the six weeks that the schools are closed due to the controversy, Twyla's signs become more personal, with slogans like, "Is your mother well?"

Twyla and Roberta have no interactions for a long time, but Twyla remains preoccupied with what Roberta said about Maggie. She knows that she didn't kick her, but she is perplexed about the question of whether the "sandy-colored" woman might have been black. One night she runs into Roberta, who is coming out of an elegant party at a downtown hotel. She approaches Twyla and says she has something she has to tell her. She admits that they had never kicked Maggie but says that she really did think that she was black. She confesses to having wanted to kick her and "wanting to is doing it." Roberta's eyes fill up with tears. Twyla thanks her and tells her, "My mother, she never did stop dancing." Roberta answers that hers never got well and begins to cry hard, asking "What the hell happened to Maggie?"

Characters

James Benson

James Benson is Twyla's husband. He is a native of Newburgh, the town where the later part of

Police protect African-American students in the 1970s during a court-ordered desegregation campaign where students were bused to other districts to force a mix of races.

the story takes place. He is "comfortable as a house slipper" and is associated with the kind of family and continuity that Twyla's history lacks.

Joseph Benson

Joseph Benson is Twyla and James's son. Twyla becomes an activist in the busing controversy when Joseph is bused out of district in order to ensure racial integration in the schools.

Twyla Benson

Twyla is the main character and the story's narrator. She was raised, in part, at an orphanage—not because her parents were dead, but because her mother chose or needed to "dance all night" and was thus unable to care for her. The fact that Twyla lacks mothering is central to her character. She marries into a stable, rooted family and becomes a mother herself. It is in this capacity that she becomes involved in the controversy over racial integration in the schools and gets into a conflict with Roberta, a friend from the orphanage with whom she has recently become reacquainted.

Twyla is characterized throughout the story in terms of her relationship to Roberta, which is often one of contrast. As in their divide over the busing crisis, these contrasts are based around the central issue of their racial difference. Despite the fact that Twyla and Roberta are of different races and also, as the story progresses, different economic classes, there are underlying similarities and shared experiences—particularly their relationships to their respective mothers—that suggest the possibility of understanding and friendship. However, the events of the story illustrate that this possibility is precarious due to the social and cultural pressures that discourage interracial friendship.

Big Bozo

Big Bozo is the nickname for Mrs. Itkin, who oversees the care of Twyla and Roberta while they stay at St. Bonny's shelter. Although she is their caretaker, she is not warm or maternal. The girls are allied in their dislike for Big Bozo.

Roberta Fisk

Roberta is Twyla's friend and she is also the source of the main conflict of the story. The two girls meet while they are staying at an orphanage, though both of their mothers are living. Roberta's mother is a stern, religious woman who is too sick to care for her. The fact that both girls have mothers who are unable to care for them is central to their connection and sympathy. Despite this bond, their racial difference causes the friendship to founder. Roberta snubs Twyla the first time they see each other years after leaving the orphanage. She is warm to her the next time they meet, after another twelve years have passed and Roberta has married a wealthy executive. But now that both Roberta and Twyla are themselves mothers, their racially determined opposition is exhibited through their different positions in the busing controversy that takes over their town. Their conflict is further symbolized through their differing memories of Maggie, a racially ambiguous mute woman who worked at the orphanage.

Mrs. Itkin
See Big Bozo

Maggie
Maggie works at the kitchen of St. Bonny's, the orphanage where Twyla and Roberta meet. She is mute and bowlegged and was herself raised in an institution. One of Twyla's strongest memories of St. Bonny's is an incident where Maggie fell down in the school's orchard. Twyla remembers the intimidating older girls from the orphanage laughing at Maggie and that she and Roberta did nothing to help her. But during their argument over the busing controversy Roberta tells Twyla that they had both kicked Maggie that day, and further confuses her by referring to Maggie as a black lady. Twyla had never considered Maggie black. Roberta later admits that they had not kicked her, only that she had wanted to. But both women remain confused as to what race "sandy-colored" Maggie should be considered. Twyla and Roberta identify with Maggie's weakness and also identify her with their mothers, and both regard her with a combination of sympathy and anger.

Mary
Mary is Twyla's mother. Twyla has to stay at St. Bonny's because Mary cannot take care of her. According to Twyla, this is due to the fact that Mary "danced all night." Mary is pretty and affectionate but she is an irresponsible and neglectful mother. She is contrasted to Roberta's mother, who is large, stern, and judgmental.

Roberta Norton
See Roberta Fisk

Roberta's mother
Roberta has to stay at St. Bonny's because her mother is too sick to take care of her. Roberta's mother wears a huge cross and carries a huge Bible. She brings Roberta plenty of good food but is not warm and refuses to shake hands with Mary.

Themes

Race and Racism
The issue of race and racism is central to the story. Twyla's first response to rooming with Roberta at St. Bonny's is to feel sick to her stomach. "It was one thing to be taken out of your own bed early in the morning—it was something else to be stuck in a strange place with a girl from a whole other race." Throughout the story Twyla and Roberta's friendship is inhibited by this sense of an uncrossable racial divide, played out against the background of national racial tensions such as the busing crisis. Racial conflicts provide the main turning points in the story's plot. At no point, however, does Morrison disclose which girl is black and which is white. She offers socially and historically specific descriptions in order to flesh out her characterizations of Twyla and Roberta, and some of these descriptions may lead readers to come to conclusions about the characters' races based on associations, but none is definitive. For example, when Roberta shows up at the Howard Johnson's where Twyla works, on her way to see Jimi Hendrix, she's described as having "hair so big and wild I could hardly see her face." This may *suggest* that Roberta is black and wore an afro, a style for black hair popular in the 1960s. During this same period, however, hair and clothing styles (and music such as that of black rocker Hendrix) crossed over between black and white youths, and many whites wore their hair big and wild. Likewise, Roberta's socioeconomic progress from an illiterate foster care child to a rich executive's wife may *suggest* that she is white because of the greater economic power of whites in general. In Twyla's words, "Everything is so easy for them." Although economic class can be associated with race, there are plenty of white firemen and black executives. Race

Topics for Further Study

- Morrison intentionally withholds an important piece of information about Twyla and Roberta. Their racial difference is pivotal to the story, but readers don't know which one is white and which is black. How does this affect your experience of reading and your approach to interpreting the story? Find another example where an author withholds significant information about the characters or events of his or her story. Does the strategy have a similar or different effect in this case?

- Many readers may have come to conclusions about Twyla and Roberta's race based on descriptions Morrison offers of their situations and characteristics. List the ''clues'' or ''codes'' of race from the text that led you to your conclusion. What kinds of descriptions seem to suggest racial categories indirectly? Then look at the story again and see if you can find evidence to make the opposite argument.

- Maggie, the mute kitchen woman, is central to Twyla and Roberta's memories of St. Bonny's and to their relationship to one another. Each makes a different assumption about Maggie's race. Why is Maggie so important and what is the significance of whether she is black or white? Find some information about how racial categories are defined in the United States in contrast to other countries. How does this help you interpret the significance of Maggie's racial designation in the story?

- The story is set over a period of more than 20 years, between the late 1950s and early 1980s. Decide which section of the story interests you most and research American race relations during the decade in which it takes place. How does the story's historical context enrich your understanding of Twyla and Roberta's relationship?

- American literature offers many examples of interracial friendships, though these friendships are often compromised by unequal power relations. Think of an example of such a friendship from one of the classics of American literature that you are already familiar with. How are the themes of Morrison's story similar or different? Can you imagine how Morrison's story might be understood as a response or an answer to the classic example?

---

divides Twyla and Roberta again and again, and Morrison's unconventional approach to character description suggests that it is the way that blacks and whites are defined (and define themselves) against each other that leads to this divide.

Difference

While Morrison uses the device of withholding information about the characters' races in order to make a specific point about black-white relations in the mid-twentieth century, it also works to make a more general point about how differences among people are understood. Though there are people of many races living in the United States and even many people of mixed racial background, race is often understood in terms of a black-white differ-

ence. Because readers don't know which character is black and which is white, they are challenged to consider the way that these labels are created out of various opposing sets of associations or social codes. At one point Twyla comments on her protest sign slogan, admitting that ''actually my sign didn't make sense without Roberta's.'' This may be understood as a metaphor for the idea of difference that Morrison expresses in the story. The signs or codes used to suggest Twyla's race don't make sense without an opposing set of signs or codes that define Roberta in contrast.

Friendship

Twyla and Roberta's relationship gives shape to the plot of the story, which traces their interactions over more than twenty years. The story explores the possibilities and the failures of their friendship. The first sentence of "Recitatif," "My mother danced all night and Roberta's was sick," establishes that Twyla and Roberta's situations are parallel on the one hand, yet opposite on the other. It is this quality that makes friendship between the girls such a complicated prospect. While Twyla's mother is healthy and attractive, but immoral, Roberta's is sick and unattractive, but upstanding. Twyla's mother has cautioned her against people of Roberta's race, saying they smell funny, and Roberta's mother refuses to shake Twyla's mother's hand. Nevertheless, the girls share the scarring experience of having been left in an orphanage by their living mothers, and their feelings of abandonment allow them an implicit sympathy and sense of alliance. Throughout the story the women's situations mirror each other, with certain correspondences bringing them together and suggesting the potential for a deep and genuine friendship, but with just as many differences causing conflict, distrust, and resentment. The end of the story suggests some degree of reconciliation, but the possibility of enduring friendship is still tenuous.

Style

Point of View

Twyla is the main character and also the narrator of the story. She describes the events in the first person, from her own perspective, and the events are presented as Twyla remembers them. One of the places where point of view is most pivotal is in terms of memories of Maggie. Early in the story, Twyla describes her memories of the orchard. At first she claims that "nothing really happened there. Nothing all that important, I mean," then goes on to describe how one day the orphanage's mute kitchen women, Maggie, fell down in the orchard and the big girls laughed at her. But as the story progresses it becomes clearer and clearer that this event was very significant to both Twyla and Roberta and to their relationship with one another. Twyla's memories of the incident are challenged when Roberta reports first that the big girls had pushed Maggie down, and then later not only that the two of them had joined in and kicked her, but that Maggie was black. Since Roberta had shared with Twyla this important and formative time at the orphanage, her differing recollections shake Twyla's confidence in

her own ability to remember accurately, but also feed her existing distrust of Roberta.

Characterization

Morrison has an unusual approach to describing her characters. Though from the outset it is clear that Roberta and Twyla are of different races, Morrison does not disclose which girl is black and which is white. She does, however, offer rich and subtle descriptions of their ideas about racially sensitive issues, their social and economic status, their behavior, and their appearances. In this way, Morrison challenges readers to analyze their own assumptions about how these qualities may or may not be related to blackness and whiteness.

Plot

The story takes place over a period of more than 20 years, from the late 1950s when both girls are staying at St. Bonny's, through the early 1980s when their children have graduated from high school. The particular events of the story are played out against the historical setting of the mid-twentieth century. In particular, they span the most crucial years of the Civil Rights Movement, at times corresponding directly with specific events important to the Movement. For example, when Twyla and Roberta meet in the Howard Johnson's, Twyla mentions that students are riding buses South as activists for integration. Later, the women come into conflict over the controversial school integration tactic of busing. At times the history of race relations is reflected more indirectly, as in the assumptions about segregation at St. Bonny's.

The story is structured by Twyla and Roberta's sporadic interactions over this long period. Each of their meetings is described in detail, while important events in the narrator's life such as her marriage are barely mentioned. The plot is further shaped by the two women's conversations about and disagreements over the event in the orchard with Maggie. This seemingly trivial event is reevaluated almost every time Twyla and Roberta speak, and its significance resonates symbolically through the other plot conflicts up to the story's conclusion.

Symbolism

The style of the story is realistic and its symbolism is understated. Food, for example, recurs throughout the plot and is symbolic of the motif of mothering, nurturing, and abandonment. At St. Bonny's Roberta gives Twyla her extra food, symbolizing the symbiotic alliance between the girls. Later, when her mother visits, Twyla spills her candy on the floor, and later this is what they eat for lunch. Twyla's mother does not understand what her daughter needs, so Twyla is literally as well as symbolically undernourished. Twyla reports that "the wrong food is always with the wrong people. Maybe that's why I got into waitress work later—to match up the right people with the right food." Not only is food symbolic of mothering and the lack thereof, it is also more generally symbolic of the unfair or unequal ways that sustaining resources are distributed. In this light, it is significant that the despised and pitied figure of Maggie is employed at the orphanage as a kitchen woman. Both Twyla and Roberta associate her with their mothers' shortcomings in offering them care, and also with their own capacity for unfairness and disloyalty.

Historical Context

Race Relations in the 1950s: Segregation

In the 1950s communities throughout the country, particularly in the South, had segregated public facilities, including schools, public transportation, and restaurants. Throughout the country, social and cultural segregation was the norm. There were several landmark events in the struggle for racial equality during this decade and it is considered to mark the beginning of the Civil Rights Movement. In 1954, overturning a 1896 decision, the Supreme Court ruled that segregated schools were unconstitutional, though integration would occur gradually. The decision was met with strong resistance from politicians and the public alike. The state government of Arkansas defied the Supreme Court and attempted to prevent black children from entering and integrating the Little Rock public schools. Blacks became organized around other forms of segregation as well. In 1956 Rosa Parks, a middle-aged seamstress, refused to give up her seat on a Birmingham, Alabama, bus for a white commuter, igniting a year-long bus boycott. Martin Luther King, Jr., emerged as the leader of the movement.

Race Relations in the 1960s: Civil Rights Activism

Blacks began to stage "sit-ins" at white lunch counters and restaurants across the South in protest of segregation. Northern students, radicalized by their opposition to the Vietnam War, joined the Civil Rights Movement in greater numbers, participating in marches and voter registration drives. More middle-class whites became enamoured of black culture and more blacks became aware of their African roots. Organized demonstrations were planned, with both black and white student activists participating in "freedom rides" to the South in protest of segregated interstate public transportation policies. Martin Luther King rose to national prominence, promoting a philosophy of nonviolence. A number of activists, both black and white, were killed as a result of their positions, and King himself was assassinated in 1968. King's death led to intense disillusionment among many, followed by greater divisiveness among activists, the rise of Black Power separatism, and renunciation in some quarters of the nonviolent approach.

Race Relations in the 1970s: Busing

While much of the racial conflict of the 1960s took place in the South, Northern cities became more of a flashpoint in the Civil Rights strife of the 1970s. Economic strain and police brutality contributed to race riots in a number of cities, which alienated some white activists. One of the most significant triggers to racial tension in the North was the institution of busing to ensure the desegregation of schools. 1971 marked the beginning of court-ordered school busing. Courts declared that "de facto" segregation existed in many northern urban school districts and found it to be illegal. This meant that the courts found Northern schools to be effectively segregated due to the existing racial mix in many school districts and neighborhoods, and that children must be bused out of their neighborhoods in order to ensure a fair access to educational resources. Busing ignited protests and outbreaks of violence in many communities. In the same time period, many blacks began to benefit from more equitable laws, entering politics and other positions of power in unprecedented numbers.

Critical Overview

"Recitatif" was published in a 1983 anthology of writings by African-American women entitled *Confirmation*. The purpose of the anthology—edited by Amiri Baraka, one of the most prominent voices of the radical Black Arts Movement of the 1960s, and

Compare
&
Contrast

- **1950s:** Most children whose parents have died or who cannot care for them live in institutions. Orphanage care has been in decline, however, in the United States since the end of World War II.

  1990s: Institutional care has fallen out of favor among childcare experts. Though they still exist in some places, orphanages have not been an important factor in child welfare in the United States for a decade. Foster care or support for continued care within the family is preferred.

- **1950s:** In 1954 the Supreme Court rules that segregation by race in public schools is unconstitutional. Black and white children begin to attend the same schools for the first time in many communities. The new law meets fierce opposition. In 1958 the governor of Arkansas calls for the Little Rock schools to be closed rather than integrated.

  1970s: Courts find that ''de-facto'' school segregation—caused by segregated neighborhoods and school districts rather than intentionally segregated schools—is illegal. In segregated communities across the country courts order crosstown busing to ensure racial integration in public schools. In many cases this leads to protest and outbreaks of violence.

  1990s: There is a loss of support for busing among African Americans due to the fact that it has failed to close the gap in academic achievement between black and white students. Courts overturn decisions to desegregate schools by means of busing in favor of more flexible measures such as charter and magnet schools. One study shows that students are one-sixth as likely to choose a friend of a different race than one of their own race.

- **1970s:** In the wake of a 1967 ruling that declared state laws banning interracial marriage to be unconstitutional, interracial relationships, marriage, and offspring become more prevalent.

  1990s: The number of interracial marriages has tripled since 1967 and there are over a million biracial families. In 1990 the category ''other'' is added to the five existing racial categories on the U.S. Census. In 1997 there is a movement to replace ''other'' with a biracial or multiracial category.

- **1970s:** The phenomenon of gentrification—in which high-income professionals move into run-down neighborhoods and renovate deteriorating buildings—becomes a housing trend. Gentrification results in the rebirth of old neighborhoods but also the displacement of low-income residents.

  1990s: Gentrification, which was rampant throughout the 1980s, has slowed, but the displacement of poorer residents is still an issue in many neighborhoods.

---

his wife Amina—was to confirm the existence of several generations of black female writers whose work was often ignored or undervalued. Baraka writes in his introduction that the intention of the anthology is ''in distinct contrast to the norm in American letters where 'American literature' is for the most part white and male and bourgeois.'' This is in keeping with Morrison's view of her mission as a writer. Saying that she is foremost a reader, she claims that she writes the kind of books that she wants to read but hasn't been able to find.

The *Confirmation* anthology marked the beginning of a period when an unprecedented number of black women writers—Alice Walker, Jamaica Kincaid, Gloria Naylor, and Morrison among them—rose to prominence and ''crossed over'' for commercial success among a mostly white reading public. While Morrison had already published several notable novels by 1983, including *Song of Solomon*, which won the National Book Critics Circle Award and is considered to have signaled her status as an author of the first ranks, she had not yet reached her present level of distinction. She is now considered not only the foremost African-American woman writer but among the foremost living writers of any nation, race, or gender.

Morrison's greatest fame came with the publication of 1987's *Beloved*. When this emotionally-gripping and tragic story of an ex-slave and the daughter she murdered failed to win any major American prizes, a group of prominent black writers and intellectuals published a letter of protest in the *New York Times Book Review* decrying the lack of national attention to her work. *Beloved* won the Pulitzer Prize for Fiction the following year and contributed to Morrison's selection in 1993 as the recipient for the Nobel Prize in Literature, the world's highest literary honor. In addition to profuse critical and scholarly praise, many of Morrison's novels have been bestsellers. In 1992 Morrison published a novel and a work of criticism which were on the fiction and non-fiction bestseller lists simultaneously.

Morrison's precipitous rise and her mastery of the novel form have perhaps overshadowed her other achievements. Though she has written a play and a book of criticism, Morrison is known first and foremost as a novelist. 'Recitatif' is Toni Morrison's only published work of short fiction and the story has received little critical attention, especially when compared to the huge amount of scholarship concerning Morrison's major novels. It differs significantly from her novels aesthetically, for it lacks the dimension of magic that has led critics to compare her writing to the Latin American school of magical realism. It shares, however, with her principal works a concern with history, memory, and the power of naming within the racial culture of the United States.

In an interview with Elissa Schappell for the *Paris Review* Morrison explains that her objective as a black writer in a white-dominated culture is to attempt to "alter language, simply free it up, not to repress it or confine it, but to open it up. Tease it. Blast its racist straightjacket." This is her intention in not naming the races of the two women in "Recitatif." Morrison admits that she intended to confuse the reader, but also to "provoke and enlighten. . . . What was exciting was to be forced as a writer not to be lazy and rely on obvious codes." Commenting on this strategy, critic Jan Furman writes in *Toni Morrison's Fiction* that, like Twyla and Roberta, readers experience a disillusionment or dystopia, "if one may view Morrison's deliberate and clever misappropriation of racial stereotype

as a dystopic condition for readers accustomed to stereotypes. In 'Recitatif' racial identities are shifting and elusive. . . . Questions beget questions in Morrison's text, and all require strenuous consideration. Despite most readers' wishes to assess, settle, draw conclusions, Morrison is resolute in requiring readers to participate in creating meaning." Such participation is characteristic of Morrison's goal as a writer to transform readers through transforming their relationship to language. In his introduction to *Toni Morrison: Critical Perspectives Past and Present* Henry Louis Gates, Jr., aptly describes the power of Morrison's writing as lying in the fact that it is "at once difficult and popular. A subtle craftsperson and a compelling weaver of tales, she 'tells a good story,' but the stories she tells are not calculated to please."

Criticism

Sarah Madsen Hardy

Madsen Hardy has a doctorate in English literature and is a freelance writer and editor. In the following essay, she discusses the figure of Maggie, the mute kitchen woman, as the story's most important metaphor.

"What the hell happened to Maggie?" Rather than offering a traditional resolution, Toni Morrison's short story "Recitatif" concludes with this question. Maggie—the mute, bowlegged kitchen woman at the orphanage where the story's two main characters, Twyla and Roberta, were raised—haunts their adult lives and their relationship to one another. Neither of the girls ever knew Maggie well or even had much contact with her. And neither of them ever saw her again after leaving St. Bonny's. But the issue of what happened to Maggie—literally and figuratively—recurs at many of the plot's main turning points. At several junctures Twyla, the narrator, reevaluates an incident in which Maggie was humiliated by the older girls at St. Bonny's orchard. And at several others, Roberta and Twyla discuss—and disagree about—their own participation in this shameful incident. Why does it matter so much what happened to Maggie? Though she is central to its meaning, Maggie is not an active character in the story. That is, she doesn't *do* anything. Instead, she stands for things. Twyla and Roberta keep thinking and talking about her because she represents their conflict and their closeness, their similarity and their differences. From

What Do I Read Next?

- *Common Ground: A Turbulent Decade in the Lives of Three American Families* (1985) is an engaging history of the busing crisis in Boston written by J. Anthony Lukas. Focusing on three typical families who have very different relationships to the controversy, Lukas shows the complicated politics of the situation and also allows the readers to feel for those with whom they may disagree.

- *The Bluest Eye* (1970), Toni Morrison's first novel, tells the story of a young black girl growing up in Depression-era Ohio who believes that if she had blue eyes she would be happy. Morrison explores themes of beauty and self respect in a white-dominated culture.

- *Song of Solomon* (1977), another novel by Toni Morrison, traces a young man's struggle for cultural identity against the backdrop of a tragic and magical family history and the shifting racial climate of the mid-twentieth century. This novel won the National Book Critics Circle Award and was chosen for Oprah Winfrey's book club.

- *The Content of Our Character: A New Vision of Race in America* (1990) is academic Shelby Steele's collection of controversial and introspective essays on race relations in the wake of affirmative action. Steele combines personal experience and social psychology in his exploration of this hot topic.

- *Meridian* (1976), a novel by Alice Walker, dramatizes the ideas and experiences of the Civil Rights Movement through a Southern black activist named Meridian. Through this heroic woman the drama and conflict of this chapter of American history are brought to life.

- *Black-Eyed Susans and Midnight Birds* (1990), edited by Mary Helen Washington, is an anthology of black women's writing since 1960. It collects twenty stories by the most important and respected black women authors of our day.

---

beginning to end, Maggie remains a figure of ambiguity. As the final line of the story suggests, Morrison has no intention of resolving the questions Maggie raises; instead she leaves her readers with this challenge. But she does so only after supplying a wealth of clues that help us understand why Twyla and Roberta return again and again to the subject of what happened to Maggie. In this essay I will explore Maggie as a metaphor—a figure that represents not only the conflicts within and between the two main characters, but the broader social dynamics that these conflicts reflect.

One thorny issue that Maggie raises is how confusing the distinction between victims and victimizers can become. When Twyla first mentions the orchard, she says, "I don't know why I dreamt about that orchard so much. Nothing really happened there. Nothing all that important, I mean."

The orchard is the site of Twyla and Roberta's intimidation by St. Bonny's older girls and also of Maggie's humiliation. In the orchard Twyla and Roberta watch the older girls as they "played radios and danced with each other. They'd light out after us and pull our hair or twist our arms." These big girls seemed scary to them at the time, but looking back Twyla realizes that they were only "put-out girls, scared runaways most of them. Poor little girls who fought their uncles off but looked tough to us, and mean. God did they look mean." The orchard is important because it is the setting where Twyla and Roberta first become conscious of their position in a hierarchy of power. In a way, every person in the orchard is a victim—powerless and suffering. But within the small world of St. Bonny's, the older girls seem powerful, despite the fact that they are poor runaways. They group together and use this power over Twyla and Roberta, and, later, over Maggie. As Twyla narrates it, one day Maggie falls down as she rushes through the orchard to catch her bus, and the older girls laugh at her. Twyla and Roberta, like Maggie, suffer from the older girls' intimidation, but instead of coming to Maggie's defense, they recognize that Maggie is mute and cannot "shout back" as they do. "We should have helped her up, I know, but we were scared of those girls with lipstick and eyebrow pencil." Compared to Maggie, they are relatively powerful, and they call her names. They fear being voiceless and weak, so they identify with Maggie's victimizers.

They are able to do this not only because they have voices, but also because they have each other. Twyla and Roberta are allied at St. Bonny's across the divide of their racial difference because both of them have living mothers who left them there. They are lucky that their parents aren't dead, but suffer the unique pain of being abandoned. While at St. Bonny's they form a united front, for the similarity in this most important fact of their childhood lives bonds them strongly. "Two little girls who knew what nobody else knew—how not to ask questions. How to believe what had to be believed." However, when they meet again, their differences are more apparent. Roberta attributes their hostile meeting in Howard Johnson's to a historic racial divide: "Oh, Twyla, you know how it was in those days: black-white." In Newburgh, not only do they live in different sections of a racially segregated community, but they are of different economic classes. Roberta has married a wealthy executive and Twyla has married a fireman.

When the town is divided by the busing controversy, so too are Twyla and Roberta. Roberta opposes busing on the grounds of "mother's rights." Twyla supports busing on the grounds of "children's rights." Both are protesting that their rights are being infringed upon and both sides feel like they are victims. The two women's private, individual conflicts over what happened to Maggie are reflected in this most overt, public conflict of story. Twyla stops Roberta while she is picketing to argue with her, and soon a crowd surrounds her car and begins rocking it in order to intimidate her.

> Automatically I reached for Roberta, like in the old days in the orchard when they saw us watching them and we had to get out of there, and if one of us fell the other pulled her up and if one of us was caught the other stayed to kick and scratch, and neither would leave the other behind. My arm shot out of the car window but no receiving hand was there.

> " Here the ambiguity of Maggie as a figure who is both despised and identified with in her powerlessness is compounded by the ambiguity of her racial status."

While at St. Bonny's the girls had been loyal to each other through their shared experience of abandonment; here Roberta abandons Twyla. Morrison describes the scene in terms that echo Maggie's humiliation in the orchard. Since "no receiving hand was there" to help Twyla, she feels as if she is in Maggie's position—fallen, helpless, and alone. Roberta is thinking about Maggie at the very same time. Despite the parallel, clear from Twyla's point of view, between herself and Maggie, Roberta proceeds to tell her that she is instead like the big girls who humiliated Maggie. "You're the same little state kid who kicked a poor old black lady when she was down on the ground. You kicked a black lady and you have the nerve to call me a bigot."

Here the ambiguity of Maggie as a figure who is both despised and identified with in her powerlessness is compounded by the ambiguity of her racial status. The power hierarchies that Maggie's humiliation in the orchard reflect are now related to the power hierarchies of race as established through the story's historical setting. Previously recalled by Twyla as "sandy-colored," Roberta now describes Maggie as black. Twyla first responds by disagreeing about Maggie's race, but later she admits, "Actually I couldn't be certain. She wasn't pitch-black, I knew, or I would have remembered that. What I remember was the kiddie hat, and the semicircle legs." The fact that Twyla really doesn't know what race Maggie belonged to is a testimony to the fact that race made little difference in the power hierarchy of the orchard. But now, in the atmosphere of racial strife that divides Twyla and Roberta, the conflict over what happened to Maggie takes on racial meaning. In a racially polarized world, medium-colored Maggie can serve in the imagination as a symbol of black victimhood or she cannot. As is the case with Morrison's characterization of Twyla and Roberta's racial difference, race lies not in the skin of the subject but in the eye of the observer.

Perhaps because Maggie does so little, she means so much. At the story's conclusion, Roberta, dressed in silver and fur, meets Twyla coincidentally at a diner after an elegant party. She confesses to lying about their participation in the assault on Maggie in their childhood and tearfully asks what happened to her as a way of confronting her denied past as a "state kid" who spent time in an orphanage. This also serves as a gesture of reconciliation with Twyla, who, despite a diametrically opposite present lifestyle, shares her past of abandonment and loss. Twyla has already resolved that she never had kicked Maggie, but concedes that she had wanted to. She identifies Maggie with her mother, Mary. "Maggie was my dancing mother," Twyla says, in a statement that explains both her repressed hostility toward Maggie and her pity for her carefree, irresponsible mother. "Deaf, I thought, and dumb. Nobody inside. Nobody who would hear you if you cried in the night. Nobody who could tell you anything important that you could use." At the diner Roberta also admits to wishing that she had kicked Maggie. And, despite the fact that Roberta's stern, proper mother seems the exact opposite of Mary, Roberta identifies Maggie with her, as well. "She was brought up in an institution like my mother was and like I thought I would be too." Furthermore, both Twyla and Roberta identify with Maggie themselves. "I knew she wouldn't scream, couldn't—just like me—and I was glad about that," Twyla states. Through the ambiguous figure of Maggie both women find a way to unlock their ambivalent feelings toward their own mothers. And through remembering their identifications with this woman whom they had once joined together against, they find a way to articulate a connection that transcends the racial chasm that divides them. But the question remains, "What the hell happened to Maggie?" The two women will never know, nor will they ever be as whole as if they had not abandoned Maggie and, eventually, each other.

Source: Sarah Madsen Hardy, "What Happened to Maggie," in *Short Stories for Students,* The Gale Group, 1999.

David Goldstein-Shirley

In the following essay, Goldstein-Shirley explores the ambiguity of the two protagonists' races in "Recitatif," saying it necessitates a closer and more careful reading of the story for the reader.

Like all of her fiction, the only short story ever published by Nobel laureate Toni Morrison challenges its readers. From its outset, "Recitatif" keeps its readers off-balance. Its plot enigmas, language tricks, and story line gaps disturb readers, prodding them out of lazy reading and complacency and into fuller, deeper engagement with the text. These unusual textual elements push readers to solve the mysteries, fill in the gaps, and thereby complete the story. By participating in making meaning out of the text, readers experience the story on a more visceral level than they otherwise would. Furthermore, they respond on a meta-analytical level, encouraged to consider why the text's elements influenced their responses in particular ways. By using such rhetorical devices to pull readers into meaning-making and self-reflection, Morrison also pulls readers into questioning their own assumptions, particularly about race.

The readers' uneasiness begins with the story's first paragraph, when a narrator, speaking in first person, begins to tell how she and a girl named Roberta were taken to a shelter called St. Bonny's. Readers cannot determine the narrator's identity, but from the narrator's casual language (e.g., referring to a restroom as a "john") and mistakes in grammar (e.g., ". . . when Roberta and me came . . ."; using sentence fragments and improper punctuation), readers begin to make assumptions about her class status. Most significantly, the text's first page introduces readers to the principal mystery of the text: the racial identities of the two girls. The second paragraph, which indirectly provides the narrator's identity, Twyla, indicates that Roberta is "from a whole other race." Members of Roberta's race, which is not specified here or anywhere else in the text, "never washed their hair and they smelled funny," according to Twyla's mother. In this instance, readers can be certain that by "they" Twyla is referring to members of Roberta's race. Later, when she disparagingly speaks about the residents of the wealthy part of town, she remarks, "Everything is so easy for them." In a stroke, readers' confidence that "they" and "them" means the other race is shattered; perhaps Twyla means the other class. At this early point in the story, however, readers are only beginning to work on the puzzle of the characters' racial identities, perhaps not yet realizing that the text will never yield that information.

Later in the story, when the girls' mothers come to visit (Twyla explains that she and Roberta "weren't real orphans with beautiful dead parents in the sky. We were dumped" by incompetent mothers), Roberta's mother brings chicken legs, ham sandwiches, oranges, chocolate-covered graham crackers, and milk. Whatever conclusions readers reached based on the girls' opinions of St. Bonaventure's food now must be reconsidered. If the chicken legs are fried, perhaps this lunch indicates that Roberta is African American, readers relying on stereotypical notions might assume. On the other hand, many African Americans cannot tolerate the lactose found in milk—a fact more likely known by black readers—so the description of Roberta drinking milk from a Thermos conjures in the minds of some readers images of a white girl. Finally, if readers' assumptions about who eats what kind of food are not already shaky, Twyla then remarks, "The wrong food is always with the wrong people," further destabilizing readers' conclusions.

The characters' names themselves also resist readers' pat conclusions. Roberta, a feminine form of Robert, is a centuries-old European name, leading some readers to associate it with the white race. On the other hand, some readers might be familiar with African Americans named Roberta, such as singer Roberta Flack. Furthermore, about halfway into the story, readers learn that Roberta's surname is Fisk, which might remind some readers of Fisk University, a historically black college in Nashville. Twyla, a more uncommon name, might lead some readers to believe she is black if they associate African Americans with non-traditional given names. Twyla Tharp, the dancer and choreographer, however, is white. (Although readers learn Roberta's surname, Twyla reveals only her post-marriage surname, depriving readers of a potential clue.) Readers then learn that Roberta has married a man named Kenneth Norton, also the name of a black heavyweight boxer. Depending upon readers' knowledge and assumptions, they disregard some of these clues and incorporate others in their conjectures about the characters' racial identities. Readers familiar with more than one of these name-related clues face the more difficult task of assigning relative weight to them, probably never feeling certain of their conclusions.

Readers' assumptions of phenotypical, corporeal markers also influence their conclusions about the characters' races, and, to the extent that their assumptions about those markers conflict with other textual clues, readers continuously second-guess themselves each time they encounter a new clue. The first body-related clue comes early in the story, when the girls curl each other's hair before their mothers arrive. Readers might wonder why, if one

> **"** Depending upon readers' knowledge and assumptions, they disregard some of these clues and incorporate others in their conjectures about the characters' racial identities. Readers familiar with more than one of these name-related clues face the more difficult task of assigning relative weight to them, probably never feeling certain of their conclusions.**"**

of them is black (as is clear from Twyla's earlier comment that "we looked like salt and pepper," she needs her hair curled. The uncertainty is only beginning at this point. Meeting again in the coffee shop some years later, Roberta sports "big and wild" hair, perhaps suggesting an afro. The next description of Roberta's hair comes when Twyla sees her in the grocery store. Twyla reports that "her huge hair was sleek now, smooth around a small, nicely shaped head." Did Roberta straighten her (naturally curly) hair or stop curling her (naturally straight) hair? Morrison notably avoids the adjective kinky, which readers more likely would associate with African-American hair texture. In a later encounter at a demonstration against busing for school desegregation, startled by their mutual animosity, Roberta says to Twyla, "I used to curl your hair," to which Twyla responds, "I hated your hands in my hair." Was Twyla's hair straight, then? And if so, does that mean she is white? Readers struggle to form mental pictures of the characters out of these troubling clues.

Twyla's descriptions of the girls' mothers provide more but equally ambiguous clues for readers. Twyla is horrified when her mother arrives for a visit wearing "those green slacks I hated and hated even more now because didn't she know we were going to chapel? And that fur jacket with the pocket linings so ripped she had to pull to get her hands out of them.'' Ratty and garish clothes: Do those suggest to white readers that she is ''black''? Do black readers think such descriptions indicate ''white trash''? Are there cross-over assumptions, such as black readers associating shabby clothes with blacks and white readers imagining Twyla's mother as white trash? And if readers do make one of these associations, they must ask themselves why. Is it because they associate ratty clothing with one race or the other? Do they associate ragged clothing with poverty, and then jump to the association of poverty with one race or the other? Then Twyla remarks that the green slacks ''made her behind stick out.'' Do the slacks make it appear that her buttocks stick out although they really do not, or do they emphasize buttocks that really do stick out? And if the latter, do protruding buttocks suggest an African-American physique?

Added to this unflattering description of Twyla's mother is her depiction of Roberta's mother, which, if readers are prone to associate body shape with one race or another according to prevailing stereotypes, complicates their conclusions. If readers think that protruding buttocks indicate Twyla's mother's blackness, they somehow must reconcile this description of Roberta's mother: ''She was big. Bigger than any man and on her chest was the biggest cross I'd ever seen.'' Readers inclined to rely on physical markers on which to base racial identification are unsettled by these descriptions. Moreover, they must question why they view the descriptions as contradictory. The cross, too, provides a clue that is difficult to interpret: Does this assertion of her piety indicate a more flamboyant faith, such as Southern Baptist, typically associated with African American Christians?

Complicating matters further, Twyla describes the mothers' behaviors in ways that challenge readers seeking to use behaviors rather than physiques as a basis for their conjectures. First, Roberta's mother refuses to shake the hand of Twyla's mother. Is it because she is a white bigot, a resentful black woman, or a black bigot? Or is her rebuff unrelated to race? Perhaps it is based on perceived class difference. Or maybe Roberta's mother is simply anti-social. The subsequent response of Twyla's mother exacerbates readers' confusion. At the entrance to the chapel, where the rebuff occurred, she loudly says, ''That bitch!'', an interjection so crass and inappropriate that Twyla thinks her mother ''really needed to be killed.'' Is such behavior associated with one race? Or is it class? Or simply upbringing?

The confusion between class and race also arises when readers encounter the scene in which Twyla and Roberta face off on opposite sides of the issue of mandatory busing for school desegregation. Roberta stands opposed to busing; Twyla then counter-protests in favor of it. Does Roberta oppose busing because she opposes desegregation? If so, is her opinion related to her race? If so, is her race white or black? Many blacks have opposed busing, desegregation, or both; readers with a reasonably sophisticated understanding of the civil rights era know they cannot assume that her opposition to busing means she is a white racist. Readers also must consider whether Roberta, who by this time has acquired the trappings—and presumably the attitudes—of affluence, opposes busing on the grounds that her children will be sent to inferior schools. Her convictions about busing might be entirely unrelated to race. When it becomes clear that Twyla's stance stems more from her resentment of Roberta than from her own political opinions, readers cannot derive more insight from the situation.

Other ambiguous clues relate to Twyla's apparent naivete and ignorance. In the coffee shop scene, Roberta tells Twyla that she and her companions are headed for California, where one of them has an appointment with Hendrix. Never having heard of rock guitarist Jimi Hendrix, Twyla asks, ''What's she doing now?'' to which Roberta responds, ''Hendrix. Jimi Hendrix, asshole. He's only the biggest—Oh, wow. Forget it.'' Assuming that readers know who Hendrix was—the text never does identify him—they must grapple with Twyla's ignorance. Some might conclude that her unfamiliarity with the black musician indicates she is white. As Lula Fragd, a black critic, pointed out to her white colleague, Elizabeth Abel, who had made that assumption [recounted in *Critical Inquiry*], most of Hendrix's fans were white, not black, a fact that black readers are more likely to know.

Twyla also expresses remarkable ignorance about race relations in the United States. When Roberta explains her earlier coldness to Twyla, she says, ''Oh, Twyla, you know how it was in those days: black-white. You know how everything was.'' Twyla tells the reader:

> But I didn't know. I thought it was just the opposite. Busloads of blacks and whites came into Howard Johnson's together. They roamed together then: students, musicians, lovers, protesters. You got to see everything at Howard Johnson's and blacks were very friendly with whites in those days.

Although the reader cannot pin down precisely when the coffee shop scene took place, it most likely occurred after Twyla was about 16 (old enough to work fulltime), which was in 1953, but before the characters reunite again, presumably around 1965. During this Jim Crow period, it is possible that a young, white person might be unaware of the tensions underlying apparently good relations between the races. Readers might consider this explanation of Twyla's remark, thinking perhaps that Twyla is white. Twyla's later comments, though, lead readers to think that her naive belief that race relations were good might stem from a general lack of awareness about social matters, not only about race relations. About busing, she says, ''I thought it was a good thing until I heard it was a bad thing. I mean I didn't know.'' If she simply is unused to thinking about social issues, her unenlightened sense of race relations might not signify whiteness, after all. Again, readers' conclusions are stymied.

Silence and absence recur as themes in ''Recitatif,'' and augment Morrison's rhetorical strategy of inducing the reader to complete the text. The story ends not with a statement but a question, asked by Roberta: ''What the hell happened to Maggie?'', referring to the kitchen worker who is tormented by the girls in the shelter when she falls in the orchard. The puzzles of what really happened to Maggie, whether she was black or not, and whether Roberta and Twyla participated in the orchard incident increasingly trouble readers as they progress. Early in Twyla's narrative, she says she often dreams of the orchard but does not know why. ''Nothing really happened there,'' she says. This comment is most problematic. The entire narrative comprises Twyla's recollections of past events. If, as readers naturally assume when reading a first-person account, the narrator is speaking to them in the present, then why would Twyla say that nothing really happened in the orchard? Telling a retrospective story, she ought to know that the incident with Maggie, which obsesses her throughout the story, is not only significant but crucial.

The enigma of Maggie is emphasized by Twyla's description: ''The kitchen women with legs like parentheses.'' Parentheses indicate something of secondary importance, which, added to Maggie's muteness, connote a passive, marginalized victim, a cipher; the bow legs conjure the image of a zero itself. Reduced to nothing, Maggie is robbed of agency, which leaves for her only the role of pawn in the battle of memories waged by Twyla and

Roberta over three decades. Twyla first tells readers that Maggie fell down in the orchard and the older girls at the shelter assaulted her. When she accidentally meets Roberta 20 years after they left St. Bonaventure, Roberta contradicts Twyla's recollection of the incident with Maggie, telling her that Maggie did not trip; the girls pushed Maggie down. Twyla refuses to believe this account, but Roberta's insistence plants doubt in her mind: ''Roberta had messed up my past somehow with that business about Maggie. I wouldn't forget a thing like that.'' Readers take her at her word, until she adds, ''Would I?'' With the introduction of Twyla's uncertainty about her own memory, readers, dependent entirely on Twyla as a source of information, also begin to feel uncertain.

The uncertainty intensifies as the narrative progresses. At their next unpleasant reunion, at which each woman stands literally and figuratively on opposite sides of a busing and desegregation demonstration, Roberta says to Twyla, ''You're the same little state kid who kicked a poor old black lady when she was down on the ground. You kicked a black lady and you have the nerve to call me a bigot.'' This new version of the story introduces the notion that Twyla and perhaps Roberta participated in tormenting Maggie, and that Maggie, whom at first Twyla described as ''sandy-colored,'' was black. Twyla's unspoken response is, ''What was she saying? Black? Maggie wasn't black.'' Later Twyla acknowledges that, although she is certain that she did not kick Maggie, Maggie might have been black: ''When I thought about it I actually couldn't be certain.'' To readers, this incident is becoming a *Rashomon* of sorts, leaving them to wonder which version of the story to believe. Finally, Twyla seems fairly certain: ''I didn't kick her; I didn't join in with the gar girls and kick that lady, but I sure did want to,'' a version that Roberta finally corroborates during their last reunion at Christmas when she tearfully confesses that they had not kicked Maggie. But the uncertainty continues when Roberta says, ''I really did think she was black. I didn't make that up. I really thought so. But now I can't be sure.'' If neither she nor Twyla feels certain about Maggie's race, neither can readers. Then, the story concludes with Roberta's unanswered question, ''What the hell happened to Maggie?'' Twyla's earlier statement that she and Roberta were two girls who knew how to believe what had to be believed becomes quite ironic, for readers have found that the characters, and therefore the readers, do not know what to believe.

Roberta's accusation that Twyla kicked a black woman and yet has the nerve to call her, Roberta, a bigot exacerbates readers' distrust of the characters' memories. Readers must try to recall whether Twyla did indeed call Roberta a bigot; perhaps readers will review the narrative for confirmation, having learned to question their own memory of the narrative. In fact, nowhere in the text does Twyla call Roberta a bigot. This further undermining of the readers' faith in the characters' memories—as well as their own—also complicates the readers' task of identifying the characters' races, because readers are likely to bring to the text an assumption about who bigots tend to be, who is more likely to accuse another of bigotry, and who is more likely to make a false accusation of bigotry. The problematic accusation also calls into question the completeness of Twyla's storytelling; perhaps she did call Roberta a bigot but failed to report it to her readers.

Some aspects of the text itself disturb readers as much as do puzzles within the story. These mysterious elements of the text, which might be called meta-textual enigmas, raise questions about how readers are meant to deal with the story. For example, when recounting the episode of Roberta's unexpected appearance at the coffee shop in which Twyla worked, Twyla says:

> I walked over to the booth, smiling and wondering if she would remember me. Or even if she wanted to remember me. Maybe she didn't want to be reminded of St. Bonny's or to have anybody know she was ever there. I know I never talked about it to anybody.

Yet, Twyla is in the act of telling somebody—the readers/listeners of the story—about her experiences at St. Bonaventure. If she refrains from discussing with anybody—her husband, her son—even the fact that she lived for four months at St. Bonaventure, readers wonder why she is speaking to them about the experiences. In fact, ostensibly, the sole basis for the encounter between her and the readers/listeners is Twyla's apparent desire to share intimate revelations about such events, some of which she acknowledges to be embarrassing, shameful, or painful to face. By presenting this paradox, the author seems to be toying with the conceit of a first-person-narrated story. While some puzzles within the story disturb readers less experienced with wringing meaning from a narrative, this meta-mystery surrounding the reading experience itself appears to be aimed at readers more thoroughly trained and skilled, for they would be most likely to notice the incongruity of an ostensibly reticent yet thoroughly confessional narrator. Thus, some of the disturbing tactics seem designed for one kind of reader, and others for another kind.

Besides listening to or reading the text, readers face another possible way to perceive it. Perhaps "Recitatif" is not a spoken or written tale, but a sung one, combining speech and music. Even the title reflects the vocal foundation of Morrison's story. The Oxford English Dictionary defines "recitative," which comes from the French *recitatif,* as a "style of musical declamation, intermediate between singing and ordinary speech, commonly employed in the dialogue and narrative parts of operas and oratorios." By using the French word, Morrison not only alludes to the French term *faire le recit de sa vie*—to tell the story of one's life—but also connotes the term's meaning in music. Morrison's connotation of an operatic recitative—a middle ground between verbal expression and musical expression—is particularly appropriate given the parallel significance of oral storytelling and musical signification in African and African-American culture. As Robert Palmer explains in *Deep Blues,* black slaves by the middle of the 18th century were forbidden from using drums and horns throughout North America except in French Louisiana. "Plantation owners had learned, sometimes the hard way, that such loud instruments could be used to signal slave insurrections," Palmer writes. All that was left with which to express themselves "utilized mankind's most basic musical resources, the voice and the body." Vocal expression, either spoken or sung, not only survived slavery, but perhaps enabled the slaves themselves to survive slavery. With a one-word title, Morrison thus captures and honors 400 years of African-American expression. As Palmer states: "Through singing to themselves, hollering across the fields, and singing together while working and worshipping, they developed a hybridized musical language that distilled the very essence of innumerable African vocal traditions." By connoting this tradition, Morrison consciously places "Recitatif" in an African-American expressive tradition.

The text's relentless perturbation of its readers jars them from a position of relatively passive reception into one of active co-creation. This effect not only intensifies readers' attention to the story and their sense of stake in it, but also serves a broader, ideological purpose. "Recitatif" exemplifies what Catherine Belsey [in *Critical Practice*] calls an "interrogative text," as opposed to a declarative or imperative text. The interrogative text disrupts the unity of the reader by discouraging identi-fication with a unified subject of the enunciation. The position of the "author" inscribed in the text, if it can be located at all, is seen as questioning or as literally contradictory.

In "Recitatif," the author's attitude is shroud-ed behind that of Twyla, and even Twyla's perspec-tive is one of confusion, as she confesses her lack of understanding of contemporary race relations. Belsey continues:

> Thus, even if the interrogative text does not precisely . . . seek "to obtain some information" from the reader, it does literally invite the reader to produce answers to the questions it implicitly or explicit-ly raises.

"Recitatif" certainly invites readers to answer questions about the narrative itself, and, more sig-nificantly, about extra-narrative matters. Why do readers interpret clues in particular ways? What assumptions do they make about race and racism? Indeed, why do readers feel it is important to ascertain the characters' respective races in the first place? At the very least, readers must realize their own predilection for racial categorization, a more benign component of racism which John H. Stanfield II calls "racialism." Beyond such a realization, some readers confront the prejudices that lead to how they categorize.

Belsey asserts, "The work of ideology is to present the position of the subject as fixed and unchangeable." By presenting a text and the "reali-ty" it depicts as *unfixed* and *changeable,* Morrison not only calls attention to an ideology that seems so natural that individuals fail to recognize it as such, but challenges that ideology. The text stirs up mat-ters of race and racism, refusing to perpetuate oversimplified and unquestioned assumptions about racial categories and stereotypes. Moreover, by guiding the reader into inferring the characters' races—in addition to demanding that the reader solve other sorts of textual and narrative puzzles—"Recitatif" forces the reader's complicity in the story's mission, which is to deconstruct racism. Morrison has stated that she wrote the story as an experiment in language, to see whether she could write a story without relying on the insidious lin-guistic shortcuts of racial categorization and stereo-typing that she feels are so prevalent in American literature. By making readers supply, from their imagination and experience, the missing informa-tion, the story encourages them to question the sources of those inferences. The reader is thus brought into the "Morrisonian" task of questioning racial categorization and stereotyping. In short,

Morrison ingeniously works toward her ongoing mission of deconstructing race and racism by get-ting the reader to do so, a strategy that also pervades her novels and non-fiction.

Source: David Goldstein-Shirley, "Race and Response: Toni Morrison's 'Recitatif'," in *Short Story,* Vol. 5, No. 1, Spring, 1997, pp. 77–86.

Elizabeth Abel

In the following excerpt, Abel discusses how the question of race in "Recitatif" prompts readers to examine the story's social clues more closely.

Twyla opens the narrative of Toni Morrison's provocative story "Recitatif" (1982) by recalling her placement as an eight-year-old child in St. Bonaventure, a shelter for neglected children, and her reaction to Roberta Fisk, the roommate she is assigned: "The minute I walked in . . . I got sick to my stomach. It was one thing to be taken out of your own bed early in the morning—it was something else to be stuck in a strange place with a girl from a whole other race. And Mary, that's my mother, she was right. Every now and then she would stop dancing long enough to tell me something important and one of the things she said was that they never washed their hair and they smelled funny. Roberta sure did. Smell funny, I mean." The racial ambigui-ty so deftly installed at the narrative's origin through codes that function symmetrically for black women and for white women ("they never washed their hair and they smelled funny") intensifies as the story tracks the encounters of its two female pro-tagonists over approximately thirty years. Unmediated by the sexual triangulations (the predations of white men on black women, the susceptibility of black men to white women) that have dominated black women's narrative representations of women's fraught connections across racial lines, the relation-ship of Twyla and Roberta discloses the operations of race in the feminine. This is a story about a black woman and a white woman; but which is which?

I was introduced to "Recitatif" by a black feminist critic, Lula Fragd. Lula was certain that Twyla was black; I was equally convinced that she was white; most of the readers we summoned resolve the dispute divided similarly along racial lines. By replacing the conventional signifiers of racial difference (such as skin color) with radically relativistic ones (such as who smells funny to whom) and by substituting for the racialized body a series of disaggregated cultural parts—pink-scalloped socks, tight green slacks, large hoop earrings, ex-

> By forcing us to construct racial categories from highly ambiguous social clues, 'Recitatif' elicits and exposes the unarticulated racial codes that operate at the boundaries of consciousness."

pertise at playing jacks, a taste for Jimi Hendrix or for bottled water and asparagus—the story renders race a contested terrain variously mapped from diverse positions in the social landscape. By forcing us to construct racial categories from highly ambiguous social clues, "Recitatif" elicits and exposes the unarticulated racial codes that operate at the boundaries of consciousness. To understand the cultural specificity of these codes, Morrison writes into the text a figure of racial undecidability: Maggie, the mute kitchen worker at St. Bonaventure, who occasions the text's only mention of skin color, an explicitly ambiguous sandy color, and who walks through the text with her little kid's hat and her bowed legs "like parentheses," her silent self a blank parenthesis, a floating signifier. For both girls a hated reminder of their unresponsive mothers, Maggie is not "raced" to Twyla (that is, she is by default white); to Roberta, she is black. The two girls' readings of Maggie become in turn clues for our readings of them, readings that emanate similarly from our own cultural locations.

My own reading derived in part from Roberta's perception of Maggie as black; Roberta's more finely discriminating gaze ("she wasn't pitch-black, I knew," is all Twyla can summon to defend her assumption that Maggie is white) seemed to me to testify to the firsthand knowledge of discrimination. Similarly, Roberta is sceptical about racial harmony. When she and Twyla retrospectively discuss their tense encounter at a Howard Johnson's where Twyla was a waitress in the early 1960s, they read the historical context differently: "'Oh, Twyla, you know how it was in those days: black—white. You know how everything was.' But I didn't know. I thought it was just the opposite. Busloads of blacks

and whites came into Howard Johnson's together. They roamed together then: students; musicians, lovers, protesters. You got to see everything at Howard Johnson's and blacks were very friendly with whites in those days." In the civil rights movement that Twyla sees as a common struggle against racial barriers, Roberta sees the distrust of white intervention and the impulse toward a separatist Black Power movement: she has the insider's perspective on power and race relations.

It was a more pervasive asymmetry in authority, however, that secured my construction of race in the text, a construction I recount with considerable embarrassment for its possible usefulness in fleshing out the impulse within contemporary white feminism signalled by the "not just idiosyncratic" confession that stands as this paper's epigraph. As Gallop [in *Around 1981: Academic Feminist Literary Theory*] both wittily acknowledges the force of African-American women's political critique of white academic feminism's seduction by "French men" and, by simply transferring the transference, reenacts the process of idealization that unwittingly obscures more complex social relations, I singled out the power relations of the girls from the broader network of cultural signs. Roberta seemed to me consistently the more sophisticated reader of the social scene, the subject presumed by Twyla to know, the teller of the better (although not necessarily more truthful) stories, the adventurer whose casual mention of an appointment with Jimi Hendrix exposes the depths of Twyla's social ignorance ("'Hendrix? Fantastic,' I said. 'Really fantastic. What's she doing now'?" From the girls' first meeting at St. Bonaventure, Twyla feels vulnerable to Roberta's judgment and perceives Roberta (despite her anxiety about their differences) as possessing something she lacks and craves: a more acceptably negligent mother (a sick one rather than a dancing one) and, partially as a consequence, a more compelling physical presence that fortifies her cultural authority. Twyla is chronically hungry; Roberta seems to her replete, a daughter who has been adequately fed and thus can disdain the institutional Spam and Jell-O that Twyla devours as a contrast to the popcorn and Yoo-Hoo that had been her customary fare. The difference in maternal stature, linked in the text with nurture, structures Twyla's account of visiting day at St. Bonaventure. Twyla's mother, smiling and waving "like she was the little girl," arrives wearing tight green buttocks-hugging slacks and a ratty fur jacket for the chapel service, and bringing no food for the lunch that

Twyla consequently improvises out of fur-covered jelly beans from her Easter basket. "Bigger than any man," Roberta's mother arrives bearing a huge cross on her chest, a Bible in the crook of her arm, and a basket of chicken, ham, oranges, and chocolate-covered graham crackers. In the subsequent Howard Johnson scene that Twyla's retrospective analysis links with the frustrations of visiting day ("The wrong food is always with the wrong people. Maybe that's why I got into waitress work later—to match up the right people with the right food" the difference in stature is replayed between the two daughters. Roberta, sitting in a booth with "two guys smothered in head and facial hair," her own hair "so big and wild I could hardly see her face," wearing a "powder-blue halter and shorts outfit and earrings the size of bracelets," rebuffs Twyla, clad in her waitress outfit, her knees rather than her midriff showing, her hair in a net, her legs in thick stockings and sturdy white shoes. Although the two bodies are never directly represented, the power of metonymy generates a contrast between the amplitude of the sexualized body and the skimpiness and pallor of the socially harnessed body. Twyla's sense of social and physical inadequacy vis-a-vis Roberta, like her representation of her mother's inferiority to Roberta's, signalled Twyla's whiteness to me by articulating a white woman's fantasy (my own) about black women's potency. This fantasy's tenaciousness is indicated by its persistence in the face of contrary evidence. Roberta's mother, the story strongly implies, is mentally rather than physically ill, her capacity to nurture largely fictional; Roberta, who is never actually represented eating, is more vulnerable as an adult to its memory, a weakness on which Twyla capitalizes during their political conflicts as adults; the tenuousness of the adult Roberta's own maternal status (she acquires stepchildren, rather than biological children, through her marriage to an older man) may also testify figuratively to a lack created by insufficient mothering.

Pivoting not on skin color, but on size, sexuality, and the imagined capacity to nurture and be nurtured, on the construction of embodiedness itself as a symptom and source of cultural authority, my reading installs the (racialized) body at the center of a text that deliberately withholds conventional racial iconography. Even in her reading of this first half of the story, Lula's interpretation differed from mine by emphasizing cultural practices more historically nuanced than my categorical distinctions in body types, degrees of social cool, or modes of mothering. Instead of reading Twyla's body

psychologically as white, Lula read Twyla's name as culturally black; and she placed greater emphasis on Roberta's language in the Howard Johnson scene—her primary locution being a decidedly white hippie "oh, wow"—than on the image of her body gleaned by reading envy in the narrative gaze and by assigning racial meaning to such cultural accessories as the Afro, hoop earrings, and a passion for Jimi Hendrix appealed more to white than to black audiences. Roberta's coldness in this scene—she barely acknowledges her childhood friend—becomes, in Lula's reading, a case of straightforward white racism, and Twyla's surprise at the rebuff reflects her naivete about the power of personal loyalties and social movements to undo racial hierarchies.

More importantly, however, this scene was not critical for Lula's reading. Instead of the historical locus that was salient for me—not coincidentally, I believe, since the particular aura of (some) black women for (some) white women during the civil rights movement is being recapitulated in contemporary feminism (as I will discuss later)—what was central to her were scenes from the less culturally exceptional 1970s, which disclosed the enduring systems of racism rather than the occasional moments of heightened black cultural prestige. In general, Lula focused less on cultural than on economic status, and she was less concerned with daughters and their feelings toward their mothers than with these daughters' politics after they are mothers.

When Twyla and Roberta meet in a food emporium twelve years after the Howard Johnson scene, Twyla has married a fireman and has one child and limited income; Roberta has married an IBM executive and lives in luxury in the wealthy part of town with her husband, her four stepchildren, and her Chinese chauffeur. Twyla concludes in a voice of seemingly racial resentment: "Everything is so easy for them. They think they own the world." A short time later the women find themselves on opposite sides of a school integration struggle in which both their children are faced with bussing: Twyla's to the school that Roberta's stepchildren now attend, and Roberta's to a school in a less affluent neighborhood. After Twyla challenges Roberta's opposition to the bussing, Roberta tries to defuse the conflict: "'Well, it is a free country.' 'Not yet, but it will be'," Twyla responds. Twyla's support of bussing, and of social change generally, and Roberta's self-interested resistance to them position the women along the bitter racial lines that split the fraying fabric of feminism in the late 1970s and early 1980s.

Privileging psychology over politics, my reading disintegrates in the story's second half. Lula's reading succeeds more consistently, yet by constructing the black woman (in her account, Twyla) as the politically correct but politically naive and morally conventional foil to the more socially adventurous, if politically conservative, white woman (Roberta), it problematically racializes the moral (op)positions Morrison opens to revaluation in her extended (and in many ways parallel) narrative of female friendship, *Sula*. Neither reading can account adequately for the text's contradictory linguistic evidence, for if Twyla's name is more characteristically black than white, it is perhaps best known as the name of a white dancer, Twyla Tharp, whereas Roberta shares her last name, Fisk, with a celebrated black (now integrated) university. The text's heterogeneous inscriptions of race resist a totalizing reading.

Source: Elizabeth Abel, ''Black Writing, White Reading: Race and the Politics of Feminist Interpretation,'' in *Critical Inquiry*, Spring, 1993, pp. 471–98.

Sources

Baraka, Amiri. Introduction to *Confirmation: An Anthology of African American Women*, New York: Quill, 1983.

Furman, Jan. *Toni Morrison's Fiction*, Columbia: University of South Carolina Press, 1996.

Gates, Henry Louis, Jr. Introduction to *Toni Morrison: Critical Perspectives Past and Present*, New York: Amistad, 1993.

Schappell, Elissa. Interview with Toni Morrison in *The Paris Review*, Vol. 35, No. 128, Fall, 1993, pp. 82-125.

Further Reading

Gates, Henry Louis, Jr., and K. A. Appiah, eds. *Toni Morrison: Critical Perspectives Past and Present*, New York: Amistad, 1993.

An extensive collection of reviews and literary critical analyses of Morrison's work from many of the foremost scholars of African-American literature.

Jordan, Winthrop. *White Man's Burden: The Historical Origins of Racism in the United States*, New York: Oxford University Press, 1974.

This short but sophisticated book explores how the idea of race and racial difference took root in the United States and formatively shaped national history.

Taylor-Guthrie, Danille, ed. *Conversations with Toni Morrison*, Jackson: University Press of Mississippi, 1994.

In this collection of previously published interviews Morrison discusses many aspects of her life and work, as well as racial politics and American and African-American literary traditions.

The Sky is Gray

Ernest J. Gaines

1963

Ernest J. Gaines was thirty in 1963, the year in which "The Sky is Gray" was first published, but it was not until five years later, in 1968, that the story was published as the second story in *Bloodline*, the thematically interwoven collection with which readers associate it today. Written during the most turbulent years of the Civil Rights movement, the stories in *Bloodline* describe a less turbulent but perhaps even more racially raw period: Louisiana in the late 1930s and early 1940s.

"The Sky is Gray" contains many of the themes and images Gaines returns to again and again in his work: themes of personal responsibility, grace under pressure, and moral behavior; images of strong mothers, mysteriously absent fathers, and families in which love is expressed more often in harsh words or silence than in overt praise or affection. Supporting these ideas is Gaines's keen awareness of the all-pervasive and profoundly formative influence of race on virtually every aspect of life in the rural South of this era. Though he would no doubt take issue with the South being described as a singular place and would certainly argue that it is many places, each different, each having unique gifts of nature and people, each facing unique challenges, he would just as surely agree with W. E. B. Du Bois's famous observation, in the "Fore-thought" of *The Souls of Black Folk*, that "the problem of the Twentieth Century is the problem of the color line," for it is this "color line" in all of its manifestations that his work so carefully documents.

Author Biography

Ernest J. Gaines was born on River Lake Plantation in Oscar, a hamlet of Pointe Coupee Parish in rural Louisiana. He was the first of twelve siblings, seven by his father Manuel, five by his mother Adrianne's second husband, Ralph. His father left his mother when Gaines was a small boy, forcing his mother to move to New Orleans to find work. Gaines was left in the care of his great aunt, Augustine Jefferson, a woman he preferred to call his aunt and whom he considered one of the most powerful influences on the formation of his character. The experiences of his early years, particularly the experience of paternal abandonment, provided the bedrock on which his fiction would later be built.

In 1948, at the age of fifteen, Gaines moved to Vallejo, California, to join his mother and stepfather, because there were no high schools for blacks near his home. Ralph was strict about the kinds of children he would allow Gaines to befriend; because of his stepfather's insistence that most of the local children were trouble, Gaines turned to the local public library for entertainment and solace—an institution that had been closed to him in Louisiana because he was black. There he developed a keen interest in reading, and he wrote his first novel the next year; on news of its rejection, he destroyed the only manuscript copy he possessed.

After graduating from high school, Gaines attended Vallejo Junior College, did a stint in the Army, and then returned to the Bay Area to take a degree from San Francisco State College (now San Francisco State University). With his degree in hand, Gaines won the Wallace Stegner Creative Writing Fellowship for Graduate Work which allowed him to begin work in Stanford's Creative Writing program, the first of many fellowships he has received. Other awards he has received include the Joseph Henry Jackson Literary Award, a National Endowment for the Arts Study Award, a Rockefeller Foundation Grant-in-Aid, a Guggenheim Fellowship, a MacArthur Fellowship, and honorary doctorates from Denison University, Brown University, Bard College, Whittier College, and Louisiana State University.

His publication record is not extensive, but his works have been well received. His first bona-fide publications—"The Boy in the Double-Breasted Suit" and "The Turtles"—were published in San Francisco State College's *Transfer* magazine in 1956. Subsequent publications included the short stories "A Long Day in November" (1959), "Just Like a Tree" (1962), and "The Sky is Gray" (1963), and the novels *Catherine Carmier* (1964), *Of Love and Dust* (1967), *Bloodline* (1968), *The Autobiography of Miss Jane Pittman* (1971), *In My Father's House* (1978) *A Gathering of Old Men* (1983), and *A Lesson Before Dying* (1993).

Plot Summary

The action in "The Sky is Gray" is broken up into thirteen short sections which describe a half day or so in the life of James, an eight-year-old black boy in the rural South of the late 1930s. The story begins with James and his mother waiting, on a painfully cold morning, for the arrival of a bus which will take them to nearby Bayonne. As they wait, his mother thinks about home—about his aunt, the other children, the farm animals and the weather—the narrative follows James's thoughts back to the origins of his toothache.

Not wanting to be a "crybaby" and knowing well that his mother cannot afford a trip to the dentist, James recalls his efforts to disguise his pain from the rest of his family. But this state of affairs does not last—his Auntie soon discovers that his tooth is rotten. When aspirin fails to work, Auntie wants to tell James's mother; James convinces her not to, so they turn instead to a neighbor, Monsieur Bayonne, for a prayer cure. But this cure fails, too. The scene in which James's mother is told—or discovers—that her son must go to the dentist is skipped over, but the family's poverty, and the comparatively huge cost of having the tooth pulled, is not. James's mother talks at length about how much it will cost while James pretends to sleep.

James's thoughts then turn to the memory of two redbirds he and his brother, Ty, had trapped, and to his mother's inexplicable insistence that he kill them and her equally inexplicable fury when he couldn't. Only now, in the narrative present, as an "almost eight" year-old boy, can James understand why she forced him to do this. She was preparing him to take care of himself in case she had to go away like his father did.

The bus arrives and, while his mother pays, James moves to the back of the bus, where the blacks are made to sit. James soon finds himself walking through the cold of Bayonne. After a long walk, they finally arrive at the dentist's office, which is already full of people waiting to be treated. A woman tries to engage James's mother in conversation, but a man James takes to be a preacher joins in instead. The woman wonders why the Lord allows people to suffer, saying that she doesn't understand it, but the preacher concludes that it's something no human can understand. This comment incites a young man—a teacher, James thinks, or a student—to join in. Shortly thereafter the nurse enters the room and announces that the doctor will not treat anyone until one o'clock.

With nowhere to go, and no money to buy anything, James and his mother have no choice but to walk, aimlessly, until the doctor's office opens again. They briefly duck into a hardware store to warm up, but must soon leave. With more than an hour to go before the doctor's office will reopen and sleet starting to fall, James's mother decides to spend their bus money on something to eat and walk home. Eventually they are stopped by an old white lady named Helena who has watched them each time they passed by. She insists that they come inside while she calls the dentist to tell him that they are coming. She offers them food, but though James is hungry, his mother will not accept any charity, so Helena has James move some empty trash cans to the street as a face-saving gesture for his mother.

Their meal finished, James and his mother thank the woman for her hospitality. James's mother opens the door to exit, but turns and asks for twenty-five cents worth of salt meat. Helena tries to give them a larger piece, but James's mother insists on an accurate measure. On the street again, James turns his collar up to keep his neck warm; his mother tells him not to, because only bums turn their collars up, and he is not a bum, he is a man.

Characters

Alnest

On one hand, Alnest is little more than an offstage voice, the voice of an old man cautioning Helena, his wife, against the cold. On the other, he is one of only two sympathetic white characters in Gaines's story (Helena is the other). Though the motivation for their careful charity is not described, it is ultimately accepted, the suggestion being that

Ernest J. Gaines

whatever their motivation may be, their small generosity will only be accepted as kindness, not as charity.

Auntie

Like James and James's mother, the source for James's aunt is drawn from Gaines's own experience, modeled after his own great aunt, Augustine Jefferson. Though her presence in "The Sky is Gray" is minimal, Augustine's presence in Gaines's life can hardly be overstated: "Unless you include her," he says, "you can't write about me at all."

Dr. Bassett

Kept completely offstage except for his terrifying effect on Little John Lee, who screams bloody murder on receipt of his dental ministrations, Dr. Basset exists in the narrative not for what he is, but for what he isn't—Dr. Robillard, the good dentist who takes care of the teeth of Bayonne's whites.

Monsieur Bayonne

Monsieur Bayonne at the story's beginning is the superstitious complement to the preacher in the middle section. He is a sincerely religious faith healer/musician, but his religion is heavily tinged

Segregation, a key theme in "The Sky is Gray," was prevalent throughout the South in the early twentieth-century, encompassing everything from schools and neighborhoods, to seating in buses and at lunchcounters.

with superstition. For example, he believes that Catholic and non-Catholic prayers heal differently, but one suspects that the distinction between the two would be lost on the clergy of both Catholic and Protestant faiths. Based on Gaines' own experience, the character of Monsieur Bayonne is a mildly unsympathetic but still dangerous figure—though he acts without malice, his actions keep James from a dentist for several days.

The Boy

See The Student

Daddy

A strong offstage presence, James's father is most profound in his absence. It is because of his absence that Octavia's moral teachings are both so important and so urgently imparted.

Helena

Alnest's wife, Helena is the story's other sympathetic white figure. But she is important for another reason besides her human decency: it is

paradoxically her kind gesture that represents the greatest potential threat to James's manhood, at least in his mother's eyes.

James

The story's protagonist, or main character, James is a young boy of about eight who lives with his mother, aunt, and their immediate family in the outskirts of Bayonne, Louisiana. It is through James's eyes that the story is told; consequently, the story is heavily filtered through his sensibilities. James is on the cusp between youth and adolescence, trying to understand what is expected of him by his inscrutable mother as he enters this next phase of his life.

Mama

See Octavia

Octavia

James's mother Octavia is a strong, proud, uncompromising woman largely based on Gaines's own mother. Indeed, one of the story's more disturbing episodes, during which his mother tries to make James kill two captured birds, is drawn from Gaines's own experience. She feels her first duty to her children is to toughen them up and show them how to live and survive. She loves her children, but more important to her than any visible demonstrations of affection are the moral lessons she insists upon teaching James.

The old lady
See Helena

The old man
See Alnest

The Preacher
Like Monsieur Bayonne, the Preacher is little more than a foil—he exists only to become angered by the student on behalf of the other people in the dentist's office, to strike him on their behalf, and to pity him.

The Student
The student, or the boy, is somewhat out of place in this story, but was certainly not out of place at the time the story was written. Like the narrator in Ralph Ellison's *Invisible Man*, the student is profoundly alienated from his community. In the microcosm of black society represented by the dentist's office that morning, he offers an indictment of religion and of its opiate-like effect on the downtrodden that Gaines himself seems to share.

Themes

Change and Transformation
The overarching theme in this story is change and transformation. In physical terms, there is motion from one pole to its opposite: from warm, to cold, to warm again; from beyond the outskirts of Bayonne to the city and back again; from the doctor's office to the street, and to the office again, and so on. From a larger, more global viewpoint, these motions support and underscore James's own transformation. James, who begins the story as a boy more conscious of his feelings and inner life than of the world in which he lives, moves far along the path toward understanding the moral complexi-

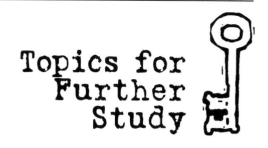

Topics for Further Study

- Why did James's mother think it was important for him to kill the songbirds? Look up the phrase "rite of passage." Does James's situation fit the definition?

- What is the allegorical meaning of the student turning the other cheek when the preacher hits him? Why does he later say that grass is black?

- Investigate the relationship between the Civil Rights movement in America and the anti-Apartheid movement in Africa. Are the two related? How?

ty of adulthood and of being "a man" in the course of the single day.

Civil Rights
Though the events in this story take place well before what is commonly called the Civil Rights era, one cannot read "The Sky is Gray" without a keen awareness that the writer is writing at the historical moment during which the Civil Rights movement exploded onto the national stage and that, surprisingly, given this context, the story somehow manages to describe but not to overplay the protagonists' suffering in terms of prejudice and inequality. While the prejudice James and his mother encounter is real and unarguable, the response of James's mother presages the essence of Martin Luther King's message that salvation begins in the person of the oppressed, not the oppressor.

Class Inequality
Only slightly less prominent than the theme of Civil Rights is class inequality. While many argue that the difference between races is less substantive than the difference between the classes, class inequality clearly takes a back seat to racial inequality in Gaines's fiction. While James and his mother would certainly have had an easier day if they had had enough money to own a car—to drive to the

dentist's office, to perhaps stop and do some shopping and have lunch on the way, perhaps even to see Dr. Robillard instead of Dr. Bassett—the simple fact remains that to do so, they would have had to be not only financially comfortable, but also white.

Coming of Age

"The Sky is Gray" is fundamentally a story about the process of coming of age, of going from one state to another. The reader only sees a small part of this process, a few hours one morning, a few more that afternoon, but these hours are important: they form some of the bedrock upon which the foundation of James's manhood—his sense of personal dignity and worth, as well as courage and silence in difficulty—will be built. Gaines creates these moments with sufficient force and clarity both to explain his protagonist's past and to anticipate his future.

God and Religion; Knowledge and Ignorance

In thematic terms, two of the most important sections in the story—sections seven and eight—explore the relationship between God, religion, knowledge, and ignorance. On one side is a heretical young black student who has not only renounced his religious beliefs but argues that "words like Freedom, Liberty, God, White, Colored" are meaningless.

"Words," he says, "mean nothing. One means nothing more than the other. . . . Action is the only thing. Doing. That's the thing." In the communal microcosm of the doctor's office he represents the defiance, the nonviolent non-cooperation of the Civil Rights movement that would sweep through the South thirty years later. In Gaines's words, describing the type of person he depicts in the student to Carl Wooton in an interview reprinted in *Porch Talk*: "you will have this rebellion against authority. You have these kids, you know: I'll stick a goddamned needle in my arm, I'll sniff coke, to hell with anybody telling me what to do. Can I get a job tomorrow? Can I live here tomorrow? Well, if I can't, to hell with it. I'll take coke, or I'll use any kind of profanity, I don't give a damn." On the other side are the preacher and the other woman the young man speaks to after the preacher departs. They are unwilling, or unable, to follow his line of reasoning, for to accept that the signification of green or black has no intrinsic relationship to a Platonic ideal of green or black, but signifies by consensus only, comes perilously close to accepting

that the other words about which the young man seems to care even more than God—freedom and liberty—are empty of meaning unless they signify the same thing to speakers both black and white.

Style

Point of View

"The Sky is Gray" is told entirely from the point of view of the eight-year old narrator, James. Consequently, the reader is limited to what James observes and understands. Though he can accurately recall the words of the student in the dentist's office that lead up to the student being hit by the preacher, he cannot understand the argument in which they are engaged ("She just looks at him like she don't know what he's talking 'bout. I know I don't."). The limitations imposed on the narrative by an eight-year-old narrator are more obvious when he tries, unsuccessfully, to understand his mother's frequent mood changes or her mysterious decisions to fight or flee at each of the stations of mood the narrative visits.

But what the narrative loses from one hand it gains in the other. James is sympathetic without being an object of sympathy; the reader feels his cold, his confusion, his hunger directly, authentically, without the intrusion of another character or narrator's impressions or observations. And when, at the story's conclusion, his mother pronounces him a man, the reader who has been inside James's subjective world can take measure of both how far he still is from manhood and of what he has learned from the lessons meant to take him the rest of the way there.

Episodic Form

"The Sky is Gray" is episodic in form—that is, the story is not told as a sequence of events, but as a sequence of events punctuated by narrative flashbacks and broken up into numbered segments. The effect of the story's episodic discontinuity is to emphasize the particular moment James is living, whether he is reliving a memory or moving through present events, while de-emphasizing the story's overarching structure. The advantages of episodic form, when relating the experiences of a young boy, are obvious, and have been used with great success in works as different as Mark Twain's *Huckleberry Finn* and Rudyard Kipling's *Kim*. The greatest advantage of an episodic form is that it allows the author to follow the protagonist, or main character, from one important event to another without recording all the unimportant events in between. This is particularly useful in a story limited by the narrative point of view to the description of a young person's inner life.

Bildungsroman

"The Sky is Gray" is a *bildungsroman,* a story describing the growth of a child into adulthood. Of course, the reader doesn't follow James all the way from childhood into adulthood, but the central premise of *bildungsroman* is that the reader watches the protagonist go from innocence to experience—in this case, from being a child whose primary interest is in staying warm and well-fed to a youth who has the first glimmerings of pride in himself and awareness of an important and external reality: that others will judge him not by what he is, but by how he appears to be. In this transformation, as he puts his collar down, the reader has taken a small but important step with James from childhood to adulthood.

Historical Context

Race and Rights

Gaines's story is meant as more than an entertainment; it is meant as a critique of the racial injustice he experienced as a boy made vivid again by a visit to Louisiana in 1968. Understanding "The Sky is Gray" requires that one not only understand something about the Louisiana of the 1930s and 1940s but also understand what was happening with regard to race in the United States during the 1960s, because the events of what later came to be called "the Civil Rights era" made a substantial and lasting impression on Gaines, one that can be seen not too far beneath the surface of "The Sky is Gray" in the person of the student and in the story's preoccupation with racial inequality.

While precisely dating the start of an era is difficult, most agree that the beginning of the Civil Rights era can be dated to John F. Kennedy's election in 1961 as this country's 35th and youngest President, and with the United Nation's decision that same year to condemn the South African *apartheid.* Two years later, in 1963, the conflicts began in earnest, with riots and acts of racial brutality against demonstrators in Birmingham, Alabama, culminating with Martin Luther King's being jailed in Birmingham. In response, later that year, 200,000 Ameri-

cans, black and white, joined together in a "freedom march on Washington" to demonstrate. But the American consciousness was jolted away from these events by Kennedy's assassination on November 22, 1963, and by events abroad, principal among these being the escalation of what would become the Viet Nam war.

It is important to recall that the Civil Rights era coincided with the casting off of imperial control by a series of African countries. In 1964, for example, Zanzibar and Tanganyika came together to form Tanzania, expelling a sultinate, while Zambia was formed out of Northern Rhodesia's ashes by Kenneth Kaunda the same year that Kenya became a republic under Jomo Kenyatta. Also in 1964, a white minority in Southern Rhodesia elected as Premiere, Ian Smith, under whose leadership Rhodesia managed to postpone representative government for another two decades. Overall, however, the move away from colonial entanglements was stronger than the ties that bound African countries to their colonial powers, and the move toward home rule was unstoppable. This did not go unnoticed in the United States, particularly among black leaders who read with interest books like Jomo Kenyatta's *Facing Mount Kenya.*

In 1965, Malcolm X was assassinated in New York and outbreaks of anti-black violence occurred in Selma, Alabama, including Ku Klux Klan shootings and Martin Luther King leading a procession of 4,000 in a protest march from Selma to Montgomery. In Los Angeles, race riots in Watts resulted in 35 deaths, the arrest of 4,000, and $40 million in property damage. In 1968, the same year that Gaines's *Bloodline* was published, Reverend Martin Luther King himself was assassinated in a Memphis hotel.

Critical Overview

Critics have been kind to Gaines, but his reputation has not risen with such meteoric speed as have the reputations of some of the other contemporary black writers of his generation. In the introduction to *Ernest Gaines,* Valerie Babb's biography of Gaines through the lens of his work, Babb writes, "taken as a whole, Gaines's canon represents a blending of Louisiana, African-American, and universal human experience. His writings reproduce the communal nature of storytelling in his rural parish while accenting the historicity that joins members of the African-American diaspora to larger American society. By recording and preserving his people's culture in his literature, Gaines creates both an ongoing memorial to a vanishing way of life and an enduring testament to human concerns.''

Marcia Gaudet and Carl Wooton share many of Babb's observations, particularly with regard to the importance of dignity under strain and courage. In their introduction to *Porch Talk with Ernest Gaines: Conversations on the Writer's Craft* they write: ''Gaines's characters evoke laughter, joy, despair, grief, anger, sympathy, and—perhaps most of all— pride. Whatever their struggles, their successes and failures, they move toward a perception of their dignity.'' Describing the events that led to the set of oral interviews which comprise *Porch Talk* they write ''through our association with him we have discovered that dignity and pride are not only themes that pervade his art, but qualities that characterize him as a teacher and a man.''

John Lowe, editor of *Conversations with Ernest Gaines* provides a somewhat more rounded, though still uniformly laudatory, response to Gaines's works. He states that Gaines was ''shockingly un- derrated'' at the beginning of his career. Some of the reasons for what Lowe considers the unfair ''obscur[ity of] Gaines gifts'' are that Gaines writes about ''a largely rural community, isolated by both its southernness and its special Louisiana qualities, which it is true make it exotic, but at the same time somewhat inaccessible, even for many African Americans.'' Another reason Lowe cites for Gaines neglect ''is his refusal to cater to stereotypes.'' He states that although people expect stories set in Louisiana to take place in New Orleans, Gaines has never set one there. And since his stories are set in the past, his African-American characters appear subservient and are not placed in the ''revolutionary poses favored by some of Gaines's contemporaries such as James Baldwin, Ishmael Reed, John O. Killins, John Wideman, or David Bradley.''

In sum, while Gaines may not have had the wide recognition of other African-American writers early in his career, there is a broad critical consensus that he is an important writer, a good writer, and a writer who has perhaps been undervalued and may continue to gain increasing recognition in the years to come, in part because he was somewhat over- shadowed by his contemporaries during his early years, in part because of the increasing importance of studies of masculinity in the literary canon. As Gaudet and Wooton point out, ''Gaines has come to the fore in many critical studies lately because of his

searching appraisal of the masculine search for identity, particularly that of African-American men.''

Criticism

David Y. Kippen

David Kippen is a doctoral candidate in world literature with an emphasis on the literature of southern Africa. In the following essay, Kippen explores the implications of a moral reading of Gaines's ''The Sky is Gray.''

Though Gaines's works invite a wide number of readings, almost all current criticism can be divided into one of two broad categories: race-centered criticism, concerned primarily with the story's in- structive value about such things as prejudice and injustice, and structural criticism, which describes the parts of the story and their relation to the whole in formal, rather than thematic, terms. Not surpris- ingly, the lion's share of critiques fall into the first camp, and even the structural readings include didactic (instructive) digressions in almost every case. Such readings all share a serious, albeit unin- tentional, flaw; they suggest that one must under- stand all actions and most events as direct or indirect consequences of race, rather than individual choice. The drawback to what I'll call, for lack of a better term, ''race-based'' readings may not be immedi- ately obvious, but isn't terribly complicated. Read- ing Gaines first, foremost, always, and only as a black author, an author of race and race issues, rather than primarily as an imaginative author, an author of ideas, delimits the kinds of questions one can ask about his works and necessarily diminishes the reader's appreciation of the imaginative sphere in which he works. In short, the unfortunate conse- quence of exclusively race-based readings is that they narrow the reader's scope of inquiry, inviting the reader to ask fewer questions and questions of a more particular nature than one would ask of an author like James Joyce, Salman Rushdie, or J. M. Coetzee—each of whose writings are intimately concerned with different conceptions of ''race'' and their ramifications. Though it is indeed difficult, particularly for Americans, to step far enough back from the late 20th century American present to see the world Gaines describes with the same dispas- sionate clarity as one might see the Ireland, India, or South Africa that Joyce, Rushdie, and Coetzee respectively describe, nothing is lost—and much is gained—if one makes the effort. In short, what is

What Do I Read Next?

- W. E. B. Du Bois's *The Souls of Black Folk* is one of the masterworks of 20th century literature, a collection of essays as powerful today as it was nearly a century ago, in 1903, when it was first published. Du Bois begins with the simple observation that what he calls the "color line" is the single greatest problem facing this country. His essays move from history through sociology to spirituality in search of the authentic black soul.

- Nelson Mandela's *Long Walk to Freedom* recounts the twenty-seven years he spent in jail as a result of his anti-apartheid work leading *Umkhonto we Sizwe* (Spear of the Nation), the military wing of the African National Congress, and South Africa's peaceful transition to majority rule in 1994.

- Ivan Turgenev's "The District Doctor." Gaines himself cites Ivan Turgenev as one of his more important literary sources, saying that he learned form from Turgenev. "I was very much impressed, not only with form, but with how [the Russians] used their peasantry, how they used their serfs."

- William Faulkner's *Light in August* is well-known for its descriptions of the South. Gaines credits reading Faulkner with teaching him about dialogue, "especially when we're dealing with our southern dialects." Most of Faulkner's works require a serious commitment from their reader, but all are worth the effort.

- Ernest Gaines's *Bloodline,* the collection from which "The Sky is Gray" is drawn, is a collection of loosely-interrelated stories well worth reading in its entirety.

---

missing from the current crop of responses to Gaines is a moral reading, one that doesn't look for causes and effects in a two-dimensional equation of character and color, but rather, in the quality of the characters' thoughts and actions, regarding the characters not as caricatures of different types, but as fully formed people with their own—to borrow a phrase from Joyce—"individuating rhythms." If Gaines is indeed an imaginative writer of canonical status, his works will reward such readings.

It is not possible, within the scope of this essay, to survey all of Gaines's works, or to make more than a cursory pass through "The Sky is Gray." It is also not possible, in a discussion of what I'm calling moral readings, to avoid some necessary oversimplifications of the complex issues surrounding and clouding the idea of race. But this much is clear. Gaines writings about Louisiana have been understood and responded to largely as writings about race. It is also clear that race, racial injustice, the years of segregation, and the particular way these things play themselves out in rural Louisiana are central to Gaines's writing and therefore are

central to understanding his works. Less clear, because less attention has been paid to this question, is how much is left when race is left out or made irrelevant to the readers. Put another way, if Gaines's stories were set in the India of 1946, two years before partition, if the primary groups described were Muslim and Hindu, rather than black and white, would the stories still merit reading? This is neither a subjective nor an unimportant question.

"The Sky is Gray" is told in the first person by an eight-year-old child, James, on the cusp of youth, and describes a half-day in James's life. His narrative begins as he and his mother wait for a bus to take them to a dentist's office where James is to have his tooth pulled and ends that same day, sometime shortly before (the reader presumes) that tooth is finally pulled. Told in a series of thirteen more or less chronological episodes, James's narrative is punctuated by frequent flashbacks to past events, each of which provide the reader with a more complete picture of the moral forces pulling at and shaping James. What makes the fact of James's narration worth remarking upon is that Gaines could

"Reading Gaines first, foremost, always, and only as a black author, an author of race and race issues, rather than primarily as an imaginative author, an author of ideas, delimits the kinds of questions one can ask about his works and necessarily diminishes the reader's appreciation of the imaginative sphere in which he works."

have chosen to tell the story from a number of different perspectives. He could have told it through the eyes of James's mother Octavia, or Val; he could have told it in epistolary form (as a letter) from James's mother to his father; or from an omniscient perspective, one that allowed him to describe the sensory and sentient world from all of these vantage points in turn. But instead, Gaines allows James to tell his story in his own words. This is puzzling, because a child's perspective is considerably narrower than an adult's. What might be complex, three-dimensional people with equally complex motivations threaten to become two-dimensional caricatures with obscure, even uninteresting motivations when seen through the eyes of a child. Moreover, while an adult may be judged on the basis of his or her thoughts and actions, a child is still too completely a product of his or her parents to evaluate as an independent being. Whatever the narrative gains by being told through James's eyes would need to add a great deal to offset these drawbacks. But James's narration creates a rationale for reading the story as a moral story. Though still a child, James is on the verge of youth. One might therefore argue that the real story is yet to be told, that it cannot be told until we see the boy as a man. But the counter to this argument is that one should, if Gaines is successful, be able to see how James will turn out, that the creation of a characteri-

zation sufficient to demonstrate that the child is father of the man is a demonstration of a naturalism like Zola's, and worthy of similar respect. And by the end of the story, the reader does indeed sense that there has been some change to who James is in that short span, a sense reinforced by his mother's assertion that he is not a bum, but a man.

The distinction his mother makes between men and bums is both subtle and significant: bums pull their coat collars up, while men don't. What this suggests is that in the highly polarized world in which James is growing up, external appearance can be more significant that internal reality—after all, whether James's collar is up or down, he's clearly not a bum, but a boy, and even a man can be permitted, under conditions as cold as those James and Octavia find themselves in, to pull his collar up around his throat. If one's analysis of this scene stops here in attempting to understand this odd end point for the story, the reading which suggests itself is quite straightforward, something like, "external appearance is essential because James's person will always be identified and understood first by his external blackness, then, perhaps, if he is lucky, by his innate character by the world in which he lives, a world in which the white gaze is the most significant threat a black man faces." This reading is reinforced by other stations in the text, and indeed, most critics have read James and Octavia as I've suggested. For example, in *Ernest Gaines* Valerie Babb writes:

> Unable to buy food because of their poverty, and forbidden to enter the warm shelters in the area of the dentist's office because of their color, they become rambling outcasts in a society in which the whim of any white is empowered to affect their destiny. While they wait for the dentist to reopen his office, Octavia must devise ways in which she can keep James from the cold and at the same time carefully adhere to strict rules of racial separation. Observing his mother manipulate their environment moves James closer to what will be his particular entry into manhood, the psychic freedom that comes from emotional self-mastery. In one instance Octavia enters a white-owned hardware store and pretends to inspect ax handles for purchase while James heats himself at the wood stove. Her dissembling enables her to warm him without compromising her dignity by begging the proprietor to allow her son use of the stove. Here, hiding her true feelings and motives, she makes use of the technique of "masking" and teaches her son a valuable lesson in pride and survival.

But if one takes a step back from the more obvious reading another, more subtle, reading begins to emerge. Consider, for example, the contradiction in Babb's representation of Octavia as on the one hand trying to "keep James from the cold" while ''adher[ing] to strict rules of racial separation,'' but on the other being ''enabled'' by her ''dissembling'' to keep him warm ''without compromising her dignity.'' Exactly what is keeping James cold, one wonders—''strict rules of racial separation,'' or Octavia's uncompromised dignity? Babb can't decide. Babb would have Octavia read as a woman whose prideful ''dissembling'' and ''technique of 'masking','' whatever that entails, are the necessary consequence of living in a dangerous world in which ''the whim of any white is empowered to affect their destiny.'' But this is a significant, even inexcusable oversimplification of Octavia's motivations. Clearly, if the environment in which they found themselves was as dangerous as Babb suggests, with every white potentially disposed to do harm, Octavia's lesson would be the worst example she could possibly give James, setting him up at some future date for a prideful miscalculation whose outcome could be fatal. It is both more reasonable and more in keeping with Gaines's own views on the importance of dignity to read Octavia as *intentionally withholding warmth* from James to teach him that the value of their personal dignity is greater than the value of the most basic comforts—being warm and well-fed.

The importance of this distinction is difficult to overstate: it is nothing less than the difference between a story about people living in perpetual victimhood, on one hand, or a story about a mother trying to teach her son what it will take to become the sort of man she will respect, on the other. If one reverts to the easiest sort of race-based reading, one will invariably decide to read the story as one about victimhood. If that is the reading one chooses, the more important, more striking, more interesting story disappears, while James and his mother become nothing more than sympathetic but uninteresting racial stereotypes about the lives of poor blacks long ago. But if one decides to read the story as a more complex critique, not of racial relations, but of the value—and the cost—of dignity, one sees that even as an eight-year-old James understands her, Octavia is an interesting, fully-realized character.

Babb seems to approach this realization when she writes that Octavia's ''dissembling enables her to warm him without compromising her dignity by begging.'' Babb realizes that Octavia's act is fundamentally about dignity, not about warmth, but she doesn't think through the implications of the point she has made, here or later. For Babb, Octavia's intention is to ''teach her son a valuable lesson in pride and survival,'' but she doesn't interrogate the

relationship between pride and survival, preferring tacitly to assume that her readers will infer a necessary relationship between the two where none in fact exists. But assume for a moment that Octavia's world is not so simple. Though her family is clearly poor, it is evident that they have learned to function within the constraints of their poverty. James tries to keep silent about his tooth not out of fear, but because he knows how expensive it will be to have a dentist pull it. Later, the whole family is at hand when Octavia and James's aunt count out the cost of a trip to the dentist: ''She say: 'enough to get there and get back. Dollar and a half to have it pulled. Twenty-five for me to go, twenty-five for him. Twenty-five for me to come back, twenty-five for him. Fifty cents left. guess I get a little piece of salt meat with that.''' Though it is clear that money is scarce, it is just as clear that this family knows how to survive with dignity—that is, without charity. The great fear here is not the capriciousness of white townfolk, but of being beholden, as a result of their poverty, to anyone. And a reading focussed exclusively on the story's racial dynamic misses this completely.

Source: David Y. Kippen, ''An Overview of 'The Sky is Gray','' in *Short Stories for Students*, The Gale Group,1999.

William E. H. Meyer, Jr.

In the following essay, Meyer describes how ''The Sky is Gray'' is a coming of age story not just about coming to terms with growing up, but also dealing with the sensual orientation of one's body. He looks at two contrasting ideas, the African/aural roots—the idea that African Americans express themselves through their music and aural interpretations—and their American/visual reorientation— the idea that America is a country of visual stimulations, that as Emerson said ''the eye is final.''

Each of the first two stories in Ernest J. Gaines's *Bloodline*—''A Long Day in November'' and ''The Sky Is Gray'' —describes a black boy or youth attempting to come to terms not just with the world in which he lives, his parents' problems, and the racism which circumscribes him but, more importantly, with the sensory orientation of his own body, the struggle between what William Faulkner called a ''black blood and white blood.'' It is this private or internal struggle more than any public or external debate that creates the real identity crisis for the young black and for the artist or writer who would contend with an America which has ''painted the senses white!'' Both Sonny in ''A Long Day in

November'' and James in ''The Sky Is Gray'' have to resolve the conflict between their African/aural roots and their American/visual reorientation—between James Baldwin's declaration that ''it is only in his music . . . that the Negro in America has been able to tell his story'' and Ralph Waldo Emerson's assumption that ''the eye is final; what it tells us is the last stroke of nature; beyond color we cannot go.'' This hyperverbal/hypervisual trauma or *rite de passage* forms the real theme or subject of both black children's accounts in ''A Long Day in November'' and ''The Sky Is Gray.'' . . .

James, in ''The Sky is Gray,'' is a somewhat older black youth who rightly faces a more complex dilemma concerning his ear and eye. The absence of the father—''in the army''—has somewhat prematurely forced James into the role of ''the man of the house''; and we first find this young black initiate ''*looking* down the road,'' of American hypervisuality. Here, James must learn to balance the words of his black heritage with the visions of white America—must learn to observe his mother's sadness and poverty while at the same time controlling his words after the fashion of the stoic adult black male: ''I want put my arm round her and tell her. But I'm not supposed to do that. She say that's weakness and crybaby stuff.'' Time and time again, the black youth must simply ''take it''—must see the advantages of the whites or the sufferings of himself and other blacks—while saying nothing and offering no complaints. Indeed, the ''tooth'' with the aching root here is James's own Afro-American tongue and ear—the dilemma of finding that his deepest ''roots'' are at odds with hypervisual America. The text of ''The Sky Is Gray'' subtly brings out this painful aurality: I'd just lay there and *listen* to them, and *listen* to that wind out there, and *listen* to that fire in the fireplace. Sometimes it'd stop long enough to let me get little rest. Sometimes it just *hurt, hurt, hurt*. Lord, have mercy (italics mine). This tooth of endless remorse/aurality may be denied—''It ain't hurting me no more''—but will never be extracted from the central black consciousness of ''The Sky Is Gray.'' Of course, too, there is a shrewd and even humorous irony involved in attempting to exorcise the black hyperverbality by ''prayer''—whether this be Baptist or Catholic incantation—for the Word/word, spoken or sung, lies at the root of black religiosity. Yet James, for all his acuteness of perception, can never follow Emerson into the parody of the Biblical command, ''Pray without ceasing'': the New-England sage demands, ''*Observe* without ceasing'' (italics mine). The only way that James

can truly understand his world is by authoritarian explanation—the tongue and ear forming the eye: ''Auntie and Monsieur Bayonne *talked* to me and made me *see*'' (italics mine).

The trip to town on the bus marked ''White'' and ''Colored'' represents the real *rite de passage* for the black youth in white America—the blurring of his sensibilities into gray: ''The river is gray. The sky is gray.'' From henceforth, James's own ''long day'' will be comprised of this struggle between ''black blood'' and ''white blood'' within a cerebral ''sky'' of ''gray''—a terrifying and chilling confrontation with one's own senses and sensibilities. The first thing that James learns is to rein in his potential visuality—to accept verbal blinders for his eyes: ''Mama *tells* me to keep my eyes in front where they belong'' (italics mine). Next, James discovers that the dentist's ''colored'' waiting-room is a place of intensified vocality and aurality, where patients are ''hollering like pigs under a gate'' and where ''all round the room people are talking. Here, the key episode occurs between the ''liberal'' black student and the ''conservative'' black preacher—a paradoxical conflict between Word and word, between faith and sight. The black student demands hypervisuality—''*Show* me one reason to believe in the existence of a God'' (italics mine)—while at the same time demanding a reinterrogation of is verbality: ''What do *words* like Freedom, Liberty, God, White, Colored mean?'' (italics mine). The student wants very much to deny his aurality—''Me, I don't listen to my heart''— and he ends up sad and depressed over his liberalism and scepticism: ''I hope they aren't all like me . . . I was born too late to believe in your God.'' What the student desires is a new age for American blacks—one which can blend ''faith'' with ''sight,'' the ''ear'' with the ''eye,'' one's internal ''blackness'' with the surrounding ''whiteness'' into ''The Sky Is *Gray*.'' James is acute enough to sense a kindred dilemma and thinks to himself: ''When I grow up I want to be just like him.''

Again, Gaines is shrewd enough not to let James end his ordeal at this point but forces him to confront the obstacles of bitter cold and hunger in order to accomplish his sensory *rite de passage*. Being told that he must return after lunch, James goes with his mother out into the sleeting streets of Bayonne. He *hears* his mother complain—''We the wrong color''—and he *sees* for himself the relative comfort of the ''white people'' eating in a nearby cafe. This time the trial is so severe that the verbal command is ineffectual: ''Mama tells me keep my eyes in front where they belong, *but I can't help from seeing''* (italics mine). Nor can the mother's demands for stoicism keep James from nearly succumbing to the piercing chill of the sleeting ''gray sky.'' At this point, almost by *deus ex machina,* the black youth's deepest self reasserts itself in all its visceral aurality: ''My stomach growls and I suck it in to keep Mama from hearing it . . . It growls so loud you can *hear it a mile.''* Moreover, it soon becomes clear that the black mother and son must accept the fact that they have now become the observed, not the observers—that they are the ones who dearly need to be seen for what they are, cold and hungry. An elderly white woman and storeowner declares, ''I saw y'all each time you went by.'' The blacks, now realizing they are not going to conquer the keen-eyed compassion of this woman and her husband, bow and accept food and a perhaps-too-generous supply of ''salt meat'' under the transparent pretense of James's doing some ''chores'' for the shopkeepers. The blacks then leave the store under the kindly but acute ''genius in America, with tyrannous eye'': James recounts how ''she's still there *watching* us'' (italics mine).

All in all, the only pride that can be salvaged at the conclusion of the story is the black mother's verbal assurance—''You not a bum''—and the visual accommodation whereby James ''turns down the collar'' of his coat in order to appear as an *Afro-American* or newly reconstituted *hyperaural/ hypervisual* ''man.'' This is what the black student in the dentist's office had desired—the best of both cultures, of ear and eye. But the question remains whether or not in this blending of ''black'' and ''white'' into ''The Sky Is *Gray''* there still may be too great a personal pain and sense of loss or self-betrayal for black youth or artist ever to transcend Gunnar Myrdal's penetrating observation: ''The colored peoples are excluded from assimilation.''

O Say, Can *YOU* See that in one's ''bloodline'' one may indeed rediscover the ''wise blood'' of his or her deepest cultural and aesthetic self?

Source: William E. H. Meyer, Jr., ''Ernest J. Gaines and the Black Child's Sensory Dilemma,'' in *College Language Association Journal,* Vol. 34, No. 4, June, 1991, pp. 414–25.

John W. Roberts

In the following essay, Roberts looks at the communal bonds found in Southern black communites, especially those as described by Gaines in ''The Sky is Gray.'' Along with this, he describes the dangers inherent in a community where tradition and change interact.

> The trip to town on the bus marked 'White' and 'Colored' represents the real <u>rite de passage</u> for the black youth in white America--the blurring of his sensibilities into gray: 'The river is gray. The sky is gray.'"

The interaction between the community and the individual, along with its role in the shaping of human personality, is a primary concern of Ernest J. Gaines in much of his fiction. It is in probing the underlying community attitudes, values, and beliefs to discover the way in which they determine what an individual will or has become that Gaines gives poignancy to the pieces in his short-story collection *Bloodline.* Because his fiction focuses on the peculiar plight of black Americans in the South, Gaines must consider an additional level of significance— the strong communal bonds characteristic of Southern black folk culture. In these stories, black folk culture, with its emphasis on community-defined values and behaviors, shows signs of deterioration, while Western individualism and the development of more personally-defined values appear as catalysts in the demise of the black folk world view. In such a cultural climate, the spiritual and emotional well-being of both the community and the individual is threatened. Faced with the necessity to act and finding traditional solutions no longer viable, the characters in Gaines's stories struggle desperately to restore some semblance of normalcy to their worlds. The dramatic conflict endemic to the stories in *Bloodline* arises out of the efforts of various characters to reconcile their individual needs with community prerequisites. Two of the stories in *Bloodline,* ''A Long Day in November'' and ''The Sky Is Gray,'' are particularly illustrative of the conflict between community perspective and individual needs. The conflict in these two stories further illustrates the importance of the changes taking place within Southern black culture to the development of the social consciousness of children. While the action of the stories revolves around

" The 'gray' of the sky
which hangs threateningly
over the action of the story
symbolizes the dangers
inherent in the extremes
which James must reconcile."

two young boys, the resolution of the conflict resides with their parents. . . .

The feeling of community which permeates "A Long Day in November"—that sense that whatever happens to Amy and Eddie is everybody's concern—is conspicuously absent from the second story in *Bloodline,* "The Sky Is Gray." James, the eight-year-old narrator of this story, struggles to understand his mother and her conceptions of manhood and dignity without aid from the community. With the exception of Auntie and Mr. Bayonne, who attempt to explain his mother's cold, dispassionate treatment of him on one occasion, James is alienated in his effort to come to grips with both the social and personal forces governing his life. The source of James's isolation is his mother Octavia, who moves through the world of the story with a calm and control which always seem on the verge of eruption. She has cut herself completely off from the community which conceivably could have provided her with support while her husband does his tour of duty in the army. Although her relationship with this absent husband is only briefly mentioned, one senses in her attitude and behavior that his departure left her vulnerable. As a result, she has made protecting James from becoming vulnerable her primary goal in life. The problem in the story arises not so much from her efforts to make James a "man" as from her approach to and definition of manhood.

In her efforts to make James a "man," Octavia apparently believes that she has only her own behavior and attitude toward life to offer as a model. To project an image of invulnerability for James, she alienates herself from the community and deals with her world on an individualistic level. The community, presumably, offers no such model. Taking what she has—her pride and her poverty—she moves toward her goal of inculcating in James a sense of independence and dignity in self undeterred by offers of kindness and generosity. However, because she never explains her motives to him, she presents James with a world filled with extremes which endangers his realization of the manhood she attempts to force prematurely on him. The "gray" of the sky which hangs threateningly over the action of the story symbolizes the dangers inherent in the extremes which James must reconcile. While "gray" literally represents the harmonious blending of black and white, its use in the story to describe the sky before a brewing storm symbolizes a potentially destructive force. The force implicit in the story is Octavia's individualism, which threatens to deprive James of membership in the human community.

The dangers that her approach poses to James are dramatically illustrated in the argument between a minister and a student in the dentist's office, the scene of much of the action. The argument between the men focuses on the existence of God. The minister accepts God unquestioningly, while the student rejects God because belief in Him alleviates the need to question:

> "Show me one reason to believe in the existence of a God," the boy says.
>
> "My heart tells me," the preacher says.
>
> "'My heart tells me,'" the boy says. "'My heart tells me.' Sure, 'My heart tells me.' And as long as you listen to what your heart tells you, you will have only what the white man gives you and nothing more. Me, I don't listen to my heart. The purpose of the heart is to pump blood throughout the body, and nothing else."

Whereas the minister clings to the traditional religious value of faith, the student espouses the development of more individualistic values based on reasoning and logic.

During the exchange between the men, the minister exposes the weakness of his position when he becomes frustrated and strikes the student. Through his action, he admits that the emotional or "heart" position leads to a cul de sac; it cannot be defended rationally. On the other hand, the student maintains a defensible position, but his egotistical stance exposes his feelings of alienation from his community. His father, we're told, is dead, and his mother is in a charity ward with a serious illness. Futhermore, he is forced to "wash dishes at night" to finance his education. Consequently, his feelings of isolation cause him to alienate himself from the emotional support and comfort of the members of his community, whom he, in turn, deprives of the benefits of his education. His feelings of isolation are clearly illustrated in his conversation with a woman who attempts to take his side in the disagreement. Rather than explaining his position to her in such a way that she will be able to understand it, he raises his argument to a metaphysical level and alienates her:

> "You really don't believe in God?" the lady says.
>
> "No," he says.
>
> "But why?" the lady says.
>
> "Because the wind is pink," he says.
>
> "What?" the lady says.
>
> The boy don't answer her no more. He just reads in his book.

Although he claims to have a solution for the black community, he refuses to consider its level of comprehension. Consequently, in attempting to communicate with the community, he feels frustration, which reinforces his belief in his own isolation.

Octavia's skepticism and self-imposed isolation place her in a similarly antagonistic stance toward the community. Although her primary goal is to project a model of strength for James through her own actions, her inability to make *her* sense of the world comprehensible to *him* leaves James vulnerable to the very forces from which she would shield him. By forcing James to sublimate his emotions and accept them as signs of human weakness, she fails to provide him with a means of dealing with the emotional responses of others in a way consistent with her philosophy. James's vulnerability to this aspect of human nature is illustrated in the episode with an old couple who offer them food during their visit to town. James does not betray the kind and heartfelt offer of the couple although his mother would want him to. He responds to the emotional intent of the act. It is through these kinds of moderating forces in James' environment that Gaines sees his salvation.

Although Octavia does not operate from the same level of awareness that the student does, it is strongly implied that her attitude stems from perceptions and conscious choices made as a result of her husband's army duty. She uses her new awareness to structure her world into clear-cut oppositional units. Her final statement to James in the story is probably the most illustrative of her world view: "'You not a bum,' she says. 'You a man.'" While this is the nature of Octavia's world, it does not completely define the contours of the world with

which James must come to terms. Human existence does not lend itself to such neat categorizing. Contrary to what Octavia would have him believe, the choices that James must eventually make about the quality of his existence should not be between "bum" and "man," or between adhering to the dictates of the "head" or "heart" as advocated by the student and the minister respectively. His choices should involve a conscious effort to integrate the extremes. However, for the moment, James is literally and figuratively caught in the middle of a storm in which both social and personal forces threaten his well-being.

The symbolic significance of the "gray sky" is the key to an understanding of the complexity of the issue raised in the story. To see "gray" merely as the integration of black and white on a literal level, and as a metaphor for racial integration on a symbolic level is, I think, to misunderstand Gaines's real intent in the story. As the argument between the student and minister in the dentist's office clearly illustrates, there is a racial dimension present in the story. But the conflict goes much deeper than that. It also involves the problem of integrating the individual and the community in a mutually rewarding relationship in the face of dehumanizing individualistic forces. In this case, consciousness raising of blacks should not lead to an alienation from the community as it has for the student and Octavia; it should provide the basis for bettering the community.

In both "A Long Day in November" and "The Sky Is Gray," Gaines involves the reader in the dilemma faced by individuals who find traditional folk values inadequate to meet their needs. In both cases, the situation is presented as a puzzle to the young who must attempt to resolve the conflicts that come about as a result of this realization. For Eddie in "A Long Day in November," the ability to solve the enigma created by Amy's decision to leave him is compounded by his already established communal world view. However, his indirect discovery that the community is no longer capable of defining his individual responsibility to his family is potentially important both for him and for Sonny. Furthermore, the story implies that the community can continue to provide the individual with emotional support in his efforts to fulfill his individual needs. On the other hand, James in "The Sky Is Gray" will never know the values of communal bonds if Octavia has her way. Although the point is never explicitly stated, it is apparent that Octavia finds the values of her community inadequate to make James the kind of man that she feels he must become. Her personal situation can be seen as a metaphor for the plight of blacks. Dependency on the philanthropy and good will of others leads to vulnerability when that support is no longer forthcoming. Her alternative, however, creates an atmosphere which, for James, is potentially equal in the dangers it poses. The fact that neither story offers a resolution to the underlying conflict apparent in the situations is indicative of the contemporary nature of the issue which Gaines raises.

Source: John W. Roberts,. ''The Individual and the Community in Two Short Stories by Ernest J. Gaines,'' in *Black American Literature Forum,* Vol. 18, No. 3, Fall, 1984, pp. 110–13.

Sources

Babb, Valerie Melissa. *Ernest Gaines,* Boston: Twayne, 1991.

Estes, David C., editor.*Critical Reflections on the Fiction of Ernest J. Gaines,* Athens: Georgia University Press, 1994.

Gaudet, Marcia G. *Porch Talk with Ernest Gaines: a Conversation on the Writer's Craft,* Louisiana: Louisiana State University Press, 1990.

Lowe, John., editor. *Conversations with Ernest Gaines,* Mississippi: Mississippi University Press, 1995.

Further Reading

Bryant, Jerry H. ''Politics and the Black Novel,'' in *The Nation,* Vol. 212, No. 14, April 5, 1971, pp. 436–38.
    Reviews *The Autobiography of Miss Jane Pittman,* describing it as an ''epic poem.'' The critic writes: ''Literally, it is an account of Jane's life. Figuratively, it is a metaphor of the collective black experience.''

Burke, William. ''*Bloodline:* A Black Man's South,'' in *CLA Journal,* Vol. XIX, No. 4, June, 1976, pp. 545–58.
    Summarizes *Bloodline,* noting of the work: ''The five stories in [this] collection demonstrate their excellence in two ways; they are human stories—moving, humorous, ironic; and they are symbolic—which tradition tells us is a quality of great literature.''

Snapshots of a Wedding

"Snapshots of a Wedding" was published in 1977 in *The Collector of Treasures and Other Botswana Village Tales,* Bessie Head's first collection of short fiction. Though this particular story has not received a great deal of critical attention, Head's short stories are well known for their portrayal of African village life and its traditions and customs. Head presents in her stories a world that is as rich in conflict and oppression, however, as it is in tradition.

"Snapshots of a Wedding" focuses on the wedding of Neo, a young educated woman living in an African village, and Kegoletile, a young man "rich in cattle." Kegoletile has impregnated both Neo and another woman, but can marry only one of them. The second woman, Mathata, is old-fashioned in her lack of education and contentment with village life. Neo, by contrast, is a "new" woman: well-educated and anxious to embark on a career that will allow her to improve her economic situation. Neo is also arrogant, proud of her education, and often condescending toward others, who accordingly resent her. The differences between these two women comprise the story's major conflict. Though Kegoletile plans to marry Neo, he continues to find himself attracted to Mathata. He must choose between a happiness whose cost is the sacrifice of advancement, and an economic progress whose cost is the likely sacrifice of marital happiness and tradition.

Bessie Head

1977

Author Biography

Bessie Head was born Bessie Amelia Emery in a South African mental hospital in 1937. She was the daughter of a black father and white mother whose wealthy family had sent her to the institution upon learning of her pregnancy. The baby was briefly taken in by foster parents who gave her up due to the color of her skin, and then was raised by white missionaries. While Head was still a child, her mother committed suicide.

After teaching elementary school for several years in South Africa, Head spent two years as a journalist for Drum Publications in Johannesburg. She married fellow journalist Harold Head in 1961, but they soon divorced. In 1964, she moved from South Africa to Botswana with her son, saying that she would no longer live under apartheid, South Africa's institutionalized system of racial discrimination. In Botswana she lived in poverty as a refugee on the Bamangwato Development Farm, tending a garden and selling its products and home-made jam to earn money.

Head is the author of three novels: *When Rain Clouds Gather* (1969), *Maru* (1971) and *A Question of Power* (1973). The last was inspired by her own earlier nervous breakdown. After 1973 she published no more novels, but did publish several collections of shorter works, including the short story collection *The Collector of Treasures and Other Botswana Village Tales* (1977), and two historical chronicles, *Serowe: Village of the Rain Wind* (1981) and *A Bewitched Crossroad: An African Saga* (1984). Though she is best known for her exploration of racial oppression of blacks by whites, Head's work also analyzes issues of gender and class. She gained international recognition near the end of her life, representing Botswana at international writers conferences at the University of Iowa in 1977 and 1978 and in Denmark in 1980. When she died in Botswana in 1986 of hepatitis she was in the process of preparing her autobiography. In 1990, a volume of autobiographical writings was posthumously published as *A Woman Alone: Autobiographical Writings*. Head continues to be remembered as a bard of African village life, as well as of the injustices—racial, sexual, and economic—of the larger societies of which those villages are a part.

Plot Summary

"Snapshots of a Wedding" is a succinct account of the wedding day of Kegoletile and Neo, a young man and woman who live in a small African village. It is also an account of the circumstances surrounding their wedding. The story begins with a description of the dawn of the wedding day and of the figures stirring who are to be a part of that day: "ululating" women, an ox who does not realize that he is to be slaughtered, and the four men who tend to him. For all of these signifiers that point to a traditional village wedding, the wedding that is to take place this day is anything but traditional, as is revealed by the comment of one of the villagers:

> "This is going to be a modern wedding." He meant that a lot of the traditional courtesies had been left out of the planning for the wedding day; no one had been awake all night preparing diphiri or the traditional wedding breakfast of pounded meat and samp; the bridegroom said he had no church and did not care about such things; the bride was six months pregnant and showing it, so there was just going to be a quick marriage ceremony at the police camp.
>
> "Oh, we all have our own ways," one of the bride's relatives joked back. "If the times are changing, we keep up with them." And she weaved away ululating joyously.

The narrator turns from this hint at the story's central conflict between tradition and progress to a description of the circumstances leading up to the wedding. Kegoletile, a well-to-do young man, has fathered children with two women, Neo and Mathata. Neo is an upwardly mobile young woman, educated and anxious to make a good living that, combined with her husband's income, will provide her with a life beyond the means of most others in the village. She wears her education like a badge and is often arrogant and condescending toward others, for which they secretly dislike her. Mathata, on the other hand, is not educated and is content with the monthly stipend Kegoletile provides for the care of their child.

Kegoletile chooses to marry Neo, but continues to bring gifts to Mathata and to spend time with her when he has completed his daily work in preparation for the wedding. He still has feelings for Mathata, but he resists them in order to concentrate on the sensible reasons—money and an improved future—for marrying Neo. Others notice that Kegoletile continues to spend much time with Mathata. On a visit one day to her aunt, Neo learns how others in the village feel about her. Her aunt tells her that Kegoletile ''would be far better off if he married a girl like Mathata, who though uneducated, still treats people with respect.'' This stuns Neo, and she quickly becomes pregnant again to cement her hold on Kegoletile.

The narration then turns again to the wedding day, describing the rituals performed by the families of the groom and bride. The story ends with the reappearance of Neo's aunt, who falls at Neo's feet, exhorting her to ''Be a good wife!''

Characters

Kegoletile

Kegoletile, a young man ''rich in cattle,'' has fathered children with two different women, Mathata and Neo. He can only marry one of them, and he chooses to marry Neo because her educational background means that she will probably earn more money than Mathata. Nevertheless, Kegoletile supports Mathata and her child with a monthly stipend, and continues to behave kindly toward her, by bringing her gifts and regularly spending time in her yard. He is still quite attracted to Mathata, who is ''always her own natural self,'' but he realizes that Neo is the kind of woman he should marry, in spite of her ''false postures and acquired, grand-madame ways.'' He appears to be torn between his emotional desire for Mathata and his practical desire for Neo, but he keeps this to himself. Ultimately, Kegoletile marries Neo, who is six months pregnant with their second child.

Mathata

Mathata is one of two women in the village with whom Kegoletile fathered a child. Unlike Neo, the other woman, Mathata is simple, uneducated, and humble. She is not career-minded like Neo and cannot bring the additional income to the household that Neo is expected to provide. Mathata is as content and easygoing as Neo is ambitious and arrogant. She is the kind of woman who ''offered no resistance to the approaches of men; when they lost them, they just let things ride.'' Kegoletile agrees to pay Mathata a monthly stipend for the support of their child. Though he will marry Neo, Kegoletile continues to bring Mathata presents and spend a great deal of time with her.

Bessie Head

Neo

Neo is to marry Kegoletile—the father of her child who has also fathered a child with Mathata—because she is educated and can potentially earn a wage that, added to his own, will make the two wealthy. Neo is excessively proud of her accomplishments, so much so that she is disliked by her own relatives, who consider her ''an impossible girl with haughty, arrogant ways.'' Because of her strong ambition and feelings of superiority, Neo is not concerned about a rivalry with Mathata until her aunt chastises her for being arrogant. Her aunt claims that Kegoletile ''would be far better off if he married a girl like Mathata.'' Beginning to doubt herself, Neo conceives another child with Kegoletile in order to ensure his commitment to marry her. At the wedding, her aunt repeatedly reminds her to be a good and obedient wife.

Neo's aunt

Neo's aunt, as well as many of her relatives, are critical of Neo because of her arrogance. When Neo comes to visit her one day, treating her in a typically condescending manner, Neo's aunt puts her in her place, telling Neo that she is ''hated by everyone around here.'' Neo's aunt is a woman of ''majestic, regal bearing'' who accosts Neo at the wedding

A celebration in an African village, similar to the wedding in ''Snapshots of a Wedding.''

ceremony, instructing her, as she beats the ground with her fists, to ''Be a good wife!''

Themes

Tradition vs. Modernization

Kegoletile's choice between Neo and Mathata is essentially a choice between tradition and mod-

ernization, the past and the future. The past includes the traditions of the village, symbolized not only by the rituals surrounding the wedding ceremony, but also by the economic stagnation and lack of educational opportunity in the village. The hoped-for future is one of economic prosperity and educational opportunities, of wealth and privilege. But the future cannot happen in a vacuum; it must draw from, and build upon, the past. While Kegoletile and Neo forego most of the rituals surrounding the wedding ceremony, they do allow some to take place, such as the exchanges between the maternal aunts and members of the bridegroom's family. Head implies that the future must slowly wean itself from the past, rather than divorcing the past outright.

Man vs. Woman

Kegoletile, though he marries Neo and provides for Mathata, is nevertheless in an adversarial relationship with both of them. They each have a claim on him, due to his impregnating them, and he must marry one of them. The women have no authority in this decision, however, even though it will affect both of their lives immensely. The decision is Kegoletile's alone, and the women can only accept their fates, or work in subtle ways to change them.

Woman vs. Woman

Neo and Mathata are placed in an adversarial relationship to each other when they are both impregnated by Kegoletile. Neo is confident that her education and future promise will secure Kegoletile, but when she learns that he has been visiting Mathata, she begins to take Mathata seriously as a threat to this security. She becomes pregnant again to make sure that Kegoletile will marry her and not Mathata. Mathata does nothing to encourage such a competition; she is content with the stipend Kegoletile gives her to provide for their child. Nevertheless, it is Mathata's gentle, easy-going nature that makes her attractive to Kegoletile and the other villagers, especially when compared with Neo's cold ambition.

Poverty vs. Prosperity

The fear of poverty and the yearning for prosperity underlie the choices made by the characters in Head's story. Neo's choice to become educated and Kegoletile's choice of Neo as a wife are motivated by a desire to achieve prosperity and thus throw off the economic fetters of uneducated village life. Through the character of Mathata, however, Head implies that prosperity is not always a prescription for a better life: Kegoletile still harbors feelings for Mathata.

Style

Point of View

"Snapshots of a Wedding" features a third-person narration, told from the point of view of someone who is not a character in the story but who nevertheless knows of the circumstances surrounding Neo, Kegoletile, and Mathata and their situations. This point of view, often called "omniscient," allows a narrator to be in more than one place at the same time, and to relate the feelings and inner conflicts of the characters presented. For instance, a reader can know not only Neo's experiences, but the internal conflict of Kegoletile as well.

Symbolism and Imagery

Head employs a number of powerful images and symbols in "Snapshots of a Wedding." The "ululating" relatives of Neo, with their "fluid, watery forms" symbolize the naturalness of the ceremony of which they are to be a part, while the ritual signifies the past from which Kegoletile and Neo are determined to emerge more prosperous. One may see the poor ox as a symbol for Kegoletile: just as the ox will be led to the slaughter, he will be led to the altar to wed, an event that will alter his life forever. Neo's aunt symbolizes the voice of tradition, admonishing Neo for her arrogance while implicitly exhorting her not only to "Be a good wife," but never to forget the tradition from which she has come. As the representative of history, she is "regal," but as Neo and Kegoletile wed and their prosperous lives are about to begin, she can only offer advice, not influence events.

Structure

Head employs a complex narrative structure in "Snapshots of a Wedding." While the title might lead one to expect the story to be about the events of

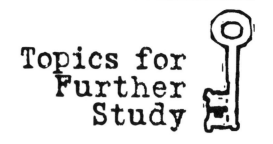

Topics for Further Study

- What motivates Kegoletile to marry Neo rather than Mathata? Are these motivations the same as or different from Neo's motivations in marrying Kegoletile?

- What kind of woman is Neo's aunt? Might there be more underlying her attitude toward Neo than simple annoyance with Neo's arrogance? What does Neo represent that upsets her aunt so?

- Compare and contrast Neo and Mathata. Is either one happier than the other? Who is more confident and secure? What does each represent in the context of the culture of the village?

- Chinua Achebe's short story "Vengeful Creditor" also explores differences between educated and uneducated, traditional and modern in contemporary Africa. Compare the character of Mrs. Emenike in Achebe's story to that of Neo in "Snapshots of a Wedding."

- Research the history of Botswana in the mid- to late twentieth century, particularly the large migration of the young people from the village to urban areas. How does Head's story illustrate the anxieties this might cause among those left in the village?

- Research traditional Botswanan marriage rituals. Are the wedding rituals presented in "Snapshots of a Wedding" different in any way from these traditions? Why might that be?

a wedding, Head quickly turns to an exploration of circumstances and events surrounding and leading up to the wedding. In fact, most of the story recounts the individual stories of Kegoletile, Mathata, and Neo and their relationships with each other and with the community of which they are a part. This information is necessary, however, in order to understand the significance of the wedding event and the rituals, or lack of rituals, that accompany it. When the narrator returns to the wedding to close the story, the reader cannot help but understand the wedding in a new way, having been given access to the intrigue and conflict surrounding the wedding from day one.

Setting

The story is set in a small African village in Botswana, given the title of the collection in which it is published. The narrator never makes it clear when exactly the events of this story take place. One can assume, however, from hints such as Neo's ability to become a "typist" or "secretary" that the events take place in the mid-twentieth century or later. The story's theme of conflict between progress and tradition, future and past, however, is one that has been the subject of literature for centuries.

Historical Context

Botswana

"Snapshots of a Wedding," published in 1977 in *The Collector of Treasures and Other Botswana Village Tales,* presents a story of young people in an African village dealing with forces of tradition and change in the latter part of the twentieth century.

Botswana is a republic in central southern Africa, located north of South Africa. It became independent in 1966. Much of its territory consists of the Kalahari region, an area of desert and grassland. Cattle-raising, the traditional source of wealth and sustenance, continues to be a mainstay of the economy. The Tswana people who make up most of the population tend to reside in large villages in which extended families live together in their own compounds. Tribal institutions and customs remain strong.

Nonetheless, as in the rest of Africa, modern ways are beginning to disrupt the traditional way of life. Beef exports and the developing mining industry have brought considerable wealth into the country and have helped create a class of educated, middle-class city-dwellers with salaried jobs. On the whole, however, few people complete their secondary education, and for those who do, employment opportunities are fairly limited. The attractions of wealth and a more modern way of life are causing young people to desert the villages for the cities and in many cases to seek work outside the country, particularly in neighboring South Africa.

In "Snapshots of a Wedding," Head dramatizes the conflicts that these forces cause between tradition and modernization and the ways in which they affect individual lives and social relationships.

Critical Overview

Compared to some of her African contemporaries, such as novelists Chinua Achebe and Alan Paton, Head has not received a great deal of critical attention. Her novels are often hailed by feminists, while her short fiction has received some attention for its portrayal of village life and tradition. "Snapshots of a Wedding," from Head's 1977 volume of short stories *The Collector of Treasures and Other Botswana Village Tales,* has received critical attention along both of these lines.

In his *Bessie Head: An Introduction,* Craig MacKenzie writes that *The Collector of Treasures and Other Botswana Village Tales* "goes on to explore in a more outward-reaching way the life of Head's adoptive village. The short story as a genre—particularly in Head's use of it—seems singularly able to cope with the material yielded by the author's more objective interest in episodes of village life." Just as the short story allows for the presentation of "snapshots" of village life—intense moments of clarity or truth about the nature of that existence—"Snapshots of a Wedding" provides in particular an examination of the roles of tradition and progress in contemporary village life and of the institution of marriage. In an interview with Linda Beard in *Sage: A Scholarly Journal on Black Women,* Head said that in *The Collector of Treasures and Other Botswana Village Tales,* "all [she] . . . did was record stories that had happened and that had been told to me and described to me." The stories, according to Head, are "not inventions. . . . [though] they are decorated; they are interpreted. But there's a basis there in fact, in reality." Head's stories back this claim of veracity through the narrator's sympathy for the plight of her characters. In "Treasures of the Heart: The Short Stories of Bessie Head," Michael Thorpe writes

Compare
&
Contrast

- **1970s:** For families who can afford it, it is customary for wives not to work outside the home.

- **1990s:** Influenced by economic pressures and a growing insistence on equal treatment for women, the number of two income households increases.

- **1970:** Approximately 3 million women are enrolled in colleges in United States.

1990: Approximately 7.4 million women are enrolled in colleges in the United States.

- **1970s:** The Equal Rights Amendment, a proposal that would add an amendment to the Constitution guaranteeing gender equity, fails to gain enough support to pass into law.

- **1990s:** Despite a much larger presence in the workforce, women still earn only 70% of what men in similar positions earn.

---

that most of the stories "read, once one becomes aware of Head's concerns, like subtle inducements to her African readers to learn again to choose between good and evil. While evil is easily recognizable as a constant—witchcraft, human sacrifice, the abuse of women—the storyteller shows her hand most plainly in her efforts to provide models of the good."

The narrator's sympathy manifests in the *presentation* of the conflicts surrounding the story's events, not necessarily in their resolution. Huma Ibrahim, in her book *Bessie Head: Subversive Identities in Exile,* looks at Head's fiction from a feminist perspective, addressing issues of gender and identity in Head's novels and short fiction. She says of "Snapshots of a Wedding" that "there is no criticism at all from the village toward Kegoletile for having polygamous relationships or for succumbing to the greater ability of one of his partners to earn money because of the education she has." Earlier, Ibrahim discusses the stories in *The Collector of Treasures and Other Botswana Village Tales* as examinations of the evils of polygamy, noting, "there is not criticism for Mathata for being uneducated or getting pregnant out of wedlock." Mathata is not the only woman, however, bound by her place in society. Ibrahim notes that the aunt's final comments to Neo indicate "the ultimate double message to Neo: no matter how educated you are, your primary task is to be polite to everybody in the

community and to be a good wife to your husband. Implicit in this ideology is that education will help you in the race for a husband but it will not help you after that." Similarly, Sara Chetin views Neo as a sympathetic figure. In *Journal of Commonwealth Literature* she writes that "[a]s outsiders we can't trust the villagers' hostility to Neo . . . and perhaps end up feeling sorry for the young bride, exiled as much by traditional insecurities as by her education, an education that could not reconcile itself to a society's disregard of women." What Head accomplishes, critics seem to agree, is a dramatization of these tensions between the past and present, men and women, and of the circumstances that produce them.

Criticism

Christine G. Berg

Berg has taught English at Lehigh University, Raritan Valley Community College, and Allentown College of Saint Francis de Sales. In the following essay, she examines how Head, in "Snapshots of a Wedding," portrays the effect of education on women and on traditional practices in an African village.

In her collection of short stories entitled *The Collector of Treasures and Other Botswana Village Tales,*

What Do I Read Next?

- *A Woman Alone* is a collection of autobiographical pieces by Bessie Head. Selected and edited by Craig MacKenzie, it was published in 1990 by Heinemann Educational Books.

- Craig MacKenzie's *Bessie Head: An Introduction,* published in 1989, provides a biography, criticism of Head's fiction, and a bibliography of her work.

- Alan Paton's novel *Cry the Beloved Country* is set in South Africa during the time of apartheid. His two protagonists, one black and one white, come to understand one another through the grief caused by the murder of the black man's son.

- Chinua Achebe's novel *Things Fall Apart* presents the story of Okonkwo, an African tribal leader, who struggles to deal with modern challenges to tribal tradition.

- Huma Ibrahim's book *Bessie Head: Subversive Identities in Exile* analyzes issues of identity related to race and gender in the fiction of Bessie Head while also exploring the formation of her identity as a writer.

- An interesting complement to Bessie Head's tale of a wedding might be Jane Austen's *Pride and Prejudice,* which presents the courtship and marriage rituals of the upper class in Victorian England.

- Similarly, reading Margaret Mitchell's *Gone With the Wind* would provide an interesting comparison. The motivations behind Scarlett O'Hara's marriages are not altogether different from those of Kegoletile or Neo in Bessie Head's story. Though Scarlett lives in a culture in which her race is privileged over the race of the characters in Head's tale, she finds herself in economic situations that encourage her to marry not for love but for money.

Bessie Head explores the effect of education on both women and the Botswanan village. The short story that ends the collection, ''Hunting,'' for example, leaves the reader with perhaps the final and indeterminate position of the educated woman. Thato, a farmer's wife, tells us ''in an exact, precise way'' that ''Uneducated women . . . are just there to be misused by men. The men all want to marry educated women, and still they treat them badly. Those women work for them and support them and get no happiness out of marriage.'' Whether or not a woman in Bessie Head's fictional Africa is educated, she is likely to find little satisfaction in marriage, but the fact of her education is a complicated matter; the educated woman is both valuable, and disruptive to the community. This dilemma that education introduces into a woman's life and the lives of those around her is best illustrated in ''Snapshots of a Wedding,'' the tenth of the thirteen stories in the collection. In this story, Head focuses on the events leading up to and including the marriage of Neo and Kegoletile. The educated woman, Neo, is not a favorable character, and the women in the village dislike both her and the way in which her education challenges their traditions. Modern and traditional ways intersect as Head locates Neo in one of the most joyful, if not important, village ceremonies: the wedding ritual.

The question of the value of education in traditional cultures has captured the imaginations of other writers as well, in particular Alice Walker, in ''Everyday Use,'' and Merle Hodge, in *Crick Crack Monkey.* The central figure in each of these works is a young, black female who is eager to learn and, at the same time, susceptible to the influences of education. Walker's Dee betrays her family and her heritage when, having procured a college education, she returns home to mock what she perceives as ignorance in her mother and sister:

> She used to read to us without pity; forcing words, lies, other folks' habits, whole lives upon us two, sitting trapped and ignorant underneath her voice. She

washed us in a river of make-believe, burned us with a lot of knowledge we didn't necessarily need to know. Pressed us to her with the serious way she read, to shove us away just at the moment, like dimwits, we seemed about to understand.

Satisfied with the response she elicits, Dee wields her education over her mother and sister. Similarly, Tee's education, in Merle Hodge's *Crick Crack Monkey,* causes her to separate herself from the home and family to which she belonged. Significantly, she chooses not to return to her home as she rejects her past: "To think that I had once been like them. . . . That seemed to have been a long time ago. It seemed almost never to have happened. If only it *had* never happened." While the process of gaining an education arouses in each woman a newly defined sense of self and a determination to succeed, it ultimately strips a layer of humanity from them; they turn mean, and ironically, in distancing themselves from their heritage both physically and intellectually, they forsake the very sense of self they believe they have secured. Bessie Head's "Snapshots of a Wedding" offers a warning against the possibilities of such betrayal. Although the story at first appears to be simple, Head conveys a complex web of reactions of the Botswanan village people to Neo's marriage. Ultimately, Neo's education poses a threat to the community, and the boundaries between modern and traditional ways are tested.

From the beginning, Neo's relatives believe that education has made Neo something of a snob:

> They were anxious to be rid of her; she was an impossible girl with haughty, arrogant ways. Of all her family and relatives, she was the only one who had completed her 'O' levels and she never failed to rub in this fact. She walked around with her nose in the air; illiterate relatives were beneath her greeting–it was done in a clever way, she just turned her head to one side and smiled to herself or when she greeted it was like an insult.

As the only member of the family with an education, Neo certainly deserves credit for her accomplishment, but like Walker's Dee she uses her newfound knowledge to create a superior position for herself in the community and to remind others–particularly other women–of their inferiority. Her behavior undermines her achievement, though her immediate family seems to remain proud of her: "Only her mother seemed bemused by her education. At her own home Neo was waited on hand and foot. Outside her home nasty remarks were passed. People bitterly disliked conceit and pride." Neo's relatives especially "dislike conceit and pride" when it is clearly one of the effects of education.

> "Neo is not a favorable character, and the women in the village dislike both her and the way in which her education challenges their traditions. Modern and traditional ways intersect as Head locates Neo in one of the most joyful, if not important, village ceremonies: the wedding ritual."

Neo's wise aunts understand the extent to which gaining an education is becoming a new method of gaining status in the village, but they also see how education, paradoxically, robs Neo of more humane qualities:

> "That girl has no manners!" the relatives would remark. "What's the good of education if it goes to someone's head so badly they have no respect for the people? Oh, she is not a person." Then they would nod their heads in that fatal way, with predictions that one day life would bring her down.

Respect for both the people and the traditions in the village is essential; Bessie Head is calling into question the function of education when it jeopardizes that balance of respect in the village.

Like Neo's relatives, Kegoletile, too, is aware of Neo's unpleasant character. He regards her as "a new kind of girl with false postures and acquired, grand-madame ways." Such falsehood and "acquired" behavior are the accoutrements of an education, which manifest themselves visibly in recognizable differences; they emphasize unwelcome distinctions between members of the community and cast the educated woman as a kind of outsider. Like Walker's Dee and Hodge's Tee, however, Neo appreciates this difference as an advantage, confident of her new place in (and not outside) the community, confident in the respect that place demands, and confident in her value as a wife. When both she and Mathata are discovered pregnant by

Kegoletile, Neo knows that he will choose to marry her. Moreover, Neo becomes pregnant purposefully after learning that her relatives believe Mathata to be a better person for Kegoletile. Educated and pregnant, then, Neo accurately predicts that Kegoletile will not turn her away. Ironically, Kegoletile does love Mathata, ''who though uneducated, still treats people with respect.'' Because of their common background in education, we might expect that Neo would be a more suitable match for Kegoletile. Indeed, in monetary terms, she is; anticipating Thato's comments in the last story of the collection, the narrator here declares that men ''all wanted as wives, women who were big money-earners and they were so ruthless about it!'' Furthermore, Neo's relatives are certain of Kegoletile's motives: ''He is of course just running after the education and not the manners. . . . He thinks that since she is as educated as he is they will both get good jobs and be rich in no time.'' Kegoletile, then, is using Neo for her educational worth, in order that they will gain wealth: ''The difference between the two girls was that Mathata was completely uneducated; the only work she would ever do was that of a housemaid, while Neo had endless opportunities before her–typist, book-keeper, or secretary.'' Neo is attractive, in this way, to Kegoletile, and even though he is aware of both his selfish behavior and her lack of manners, he still chooses to marry her.

It is significant that the uneducated Mathata is portrayed as a much more favorable character than Neo and that Kegoletile does not choose her for marriage. Kegoletile's desire for an educated wife costs him a life with Mathata, a ''real'' person: ''She was a very pretty girl with black eyes like stars; she was always smiling and happy; immediately and always her own *natural* self'' (my emphasis). By contrast, Neo is deemed ''not a person'' by her relatives and superficial by Kegoletile. Education affects these characters in very real ways: Neo undergoes a self-willed transformation and is labeled arrogant, disrespectful, and undeserving of Kegoletile; Kegoletile is persuaded to marry Neo and, characterized as greedy, is thus deserving of his ''haughty'' bride; and Mathata is redefined because of the presence (or intrusion) of the educated woman—she is newly perceived not for the qualities that endear her to others, but for what she is not: she becomes the *un*educated woman. Already, we see how education intervenes in the characters' lives, whether they are conscious of it or not. However, the introduction of the educated woman into the community has a much more profound effect, for it

interferes, more significantly, with established tradition in the village. Throughout the story, Bessie Head catalogues the changes to the ritual wedding ceremony that result when it is Neo and Kegoletile who join together in matrimony.

The story begins with a description of the commencement of the inevitable ritual that the celebration of marriage effortlessly evokes in the villagers, and Bessie Head is careful to underscore, very subtly, the importance of the traditions in the event: ''Wedding days *always* started at the haunting, magical hour of early dawn when there was only a pale crack of light on the horizon'' (my emphasis). This wedding day holds no exception in that respect; the villagers are awake at this early hour, the ox for the wedding feast is exchanged, and most importantly, ''the beautiful ululating of the women rose and swelled over the air like water bubbling rapidly and melodiously over the stones of a clear, sparkling stream'' as the women ''began to weave about the yard in the wedding dance.'' Despite their reservations about Neo's marriage, the women begin the day's celebration, performing this initial and meaningful part of the wedding ritual. However, the first words spoken in the story (which are described as a joke), signal the dilemma with which the story is concerned. One of bridegroom's relatives declares: ''This is going to be a modern wedding.'' Then, having already established the routine beginning of the ritual and the way that the women simply fall into place at the early morning sound of the ox's first bellow, the narrator illustrates the extent to which the ceremony will be altered:

> a lot of the traditional courtesies had been left out of the planning for the wedding day; no one had been awake all night preparing diphiri or the traditional wedding breakfast of pounded meat and samp . . . there was just going to be a quick marriage ceremony at the police camp.

Since it is Neo getting married and since she has an education that teaches her ''bad manners and modern ways,'' the traditional method of preparing for and celebrating her marriage to Kegoletile becomes, to a degree, unsuitable. This new kind of wedding day is marked by a certain hastiness—not because Kegoletile is uninterested in a church wedding, not because Neo is six months pregnant, but because some of the traditions have lost their effect on the young and modern couple. Significantly, one of Neo's female relatives ''jokes back'' with Kegoletile's relative as if to dismiss the severity of the situation. ''Oh, we all have our own ways,'' she responds, and before dancing away, adds: ''If the times are changing, we keep up with them.'' The wedding ritual will not stop because the couple (specifically, the woman) does not fit it; instead, the ritual will accommodate Neo and, by extension, the change in times. Even though the women focus on the joy of the occasion, however, they themselves find their performance of the ritual is rendered less powerful and somewhat inappropriate in the face of modernity, represented by the educated woman. The opening dialogue, then, stages the conflict at the heart of the story—and Neo is the pivotal character.

This conflict—between traditional and modern, between the villagers and Neo—suggests itself throughout the wedding day. Neo's aunts, acting out traditional roles, act in disguise, for they disapprove of Neo, though ''[n]o one would have guessed it . . . with all the dancing, ululating, and happiness expressed in the yard.'' The aunts preside over the wedding ritual because of their prominent collective role: ''Their important task was to formally hand over the bride to Kegoletile's maternal aunts when they approached the yard at sunset. So they sat the whole day with still expressionless faces, waiting to fulfill this ancient rite.'' When Neo's education tests tradition, then, it is these aunts very specifically who are being challenged. It is significant that in their own yard, the ''ancient rite'' is followed; they see to it that their formal exchange with Kegoletile's aunts is enacted appropriately. The traditional method of counseling the bride and groom to promise their services to each set of aunts is successful. However, once Kegoletile's aunts leave the yard and lead the couple to Kegoletile's own yard for another feast, part of the tradition that remains is falsified because the meaning is lost:

> As they approached his yard, an old woman suddenly dashed out and chopped at the ground with a hoe. It was all only a formality. Neo would never be the kind of wife who went to the lands to plough. She already had a well-paid job in an office as a secretary.

Neo's education renders this specific part of the ritual meaningless, and the women feel the break in tradition, their own lack of power as executors of it. The village's traditions are being challenged, then, by a woman whose educational background places her outside of tradition. The wedding ritual presumes that the only opportunity for a wife is in the fields; there is no variation that allows for her possible role in an office. Thus, neither the villagers nor Neo find the necessary symbolic connection between ritual and bride. In fact, Neo remains ''stiff, immobile, and rigid'' throughout the ceremony, suggesting her strict refusal, perhaps, to partake in the events as well as her uneasiness with and detachment from them.

In the end, Neo does wear the garments that reflect her position as a married woman:

> another old woman took the bride by the hand and led her to a smeared and decorated courtyard wherein had been placed a traditional animal-skin Tswana mat. She was made to sit on the mat and a shawl and kerchief were placed before her. The shawl was ceremonially wrapped around her shoulders; the kerchief tied around her head—the symbols that she was now a married woman.

Even if Neo must be instructed to follow it, this final part of the ritual stills holds its meaning. The symbols of marriage are not deflated; secretaries can be married, too. Still, as if to present a final irresolution over the intrusion of education and ''modern ways'' into village life, Bessie Head leaves us with an compelling image of contradiction: Neo, the educated and modern woman, sits clothed, quite literally, by the traditions of the village. The shawl and kerchief are emblems that the villagers will dignify with their respect–not Neo's arrogance over her completion of her ''O'' levels.

There is hope that Neo will learn to appreciate this kind of respect, however, as the narrator seems to give Neo one last chance to redeem herself. While greeting the new bride, two girls begin dancing, bump into each other, and fall down. At this, the ''wedding guests roared with laughter,'' the first signs of relaxed pleasure since the women began ululating earlier in the day. And Neo laughs with them, her ''stiff, immobile, and rigid body ben[ding] forward and [shaking] with laughter.'' With her laughter comes a sense of relief and a restoration of community (she is literally ''brought down to earth'' from her superior position among the others), and the ceremonial event feels like a good one: ''The hoe, the mat, the shawl, the kerchief, the beautiful flute-like ululating of the women seemed in itself a blessing on the marriage.'' It is significant that Neo joins with the others in laughter, especially since her involvement in the ritual that celebrates her own wedding has been marked by a certain tentativeness and remove. Moreover, the two girls at whom the villagers laugh represent, in part, the strength and future of the village traditions, for they are attempting to enact the very dance that the women have been performing throughout the day. They are learning not only the art and importance of the traditions but the pleasure and enjoyment of them as well. Bessie Head might have ended her story with this blessing—its very inclusion does suggest some hope for Neo—but instead she chooses to linger on the uneasy mix of education and tradition. Just when Neo seems to be most accepted, she is again separated from the other women as one of her aunts, "majestic" and "regal," interrupts the women's enjoyment in the effect of their tradition (the laughter). The women, by the end of the day, have become comfortable in their wedding ritual until Neo's aunt reminds them of the possibility that their traditional blessing will not work for Neo: "She dropped to her knees before the bride, clenched her fists together and pounded the ground hard with each clenched fist on either side of the bride's legs. As she pounded her fists she said loudly: 'Be a good wife! Be a good wife!'" With this resounding admonition and on this note of uncertainty, the story ends. Perhaps because Neo has finally joined with the community (in laughter), the aunt feels that her entreaties on behalf of tradition will be heard; the narrator makes a point of including that she is the same aunt who is able to "[bring] her down a little" when she shocks Neo by telling her that everyone in the village dislikes her. The story ends, then, with words that both suggest that Neo can be a "good wife" and caution her against abandoning tradition too much in favor of her newfound status as an educated woman.

We might argue that Bessie Head, herself, favors cultural tradition over education and "modern ways" for the keen detail with which she describes the wedding ceremony and the delight she finds in the women's ululating in particular. She certainly highlights the beauty and vitality of tradition in "Snapshots of a Wedding." Essentially, though, Bessie Head uses the traditions of the wedding ceremony to illustrate the questionable function of education in the village and the dilemma that the villagers face when old and new intermingle. When a woman is uneducated, like Mathata, she becomes less likely to secure a wealthy and educated marriage partner. When, however, a woman is educated, like Neo, she may be wed only for her educational worth, her ability to contribute to the household wealth. In either situation, a woman is unfortunate, though Mathata is the happier and more easily accepted woman. Neo's only moment of happiness, when she laughs with the others, is cut short by her aunt's warning. Just as the fact of her education disrupts the traditions of the village, so, ultimately, does it interrupt her own happiness. Neo's education results in her loss of respect for the people in her village, though not to the extent that Walker's Dee and Hodge's Tee betray their families

and their heritage; also, what has been meaningful village tradition becomes inappropriate for this new kind of wife. But unlike Dee and Tee, Neo is challenged to change in this story, and while the ending is deliberately inconclusive (as the struggle for the village has only just begun with the introduction of formal education), we might look to the power of the "ancient rites" and the awe and respect that they inspire in order to anticipate the ability of ritual ceremony to heal the rift that education brings. For "Snapshots of a Wedding" rests on the powerful voice of one of the older women in the village: She commands attention, demands respect, and warns us about forgetting to honor cultural traditions.

Source: Christine G. Berg, "Bemused by Education: Bessie Head's 'Snapshots of a Wedding'," in *Short Stories for Students,* The Gale Group, 1999.

Thomas M. March

March is a Ph.D. candidate in English at New York University. In the following essay, he examines ways in which the past reimposes itself on the young couple in "Snapshots of a Wedding," particularly with regard to Neo's future role as a wife.

As its title indicates, Bessie Head's "Snapshots of a Wedding" (1977) is the story of a wedding, in this case that between Neo and Kegoletile, two young people from an African village. But it is not the wedding event itself that is of primary interest in the story. Rather, this is a story not simply of a wedding, but of what this particular wedding represents. The wedding is, at the same time, the site of a breach with the past and a confirmation of the precarious position of women within the tradition of that very past with which Kegoletile and his new wife, Neo, plan to break.

The story begins with an assertion by one of Kegoletile's relatives that this wedding will be a modern wedding, and the subsequent narration of the circumstances that have led to this union would seem at the surface to confirm this assertion. The narrator comments that by a modern wedding, the speaker "meant that a lot of the traditional courtesies had been left out of the planning for the wedding day." It is worth noting that "a lot of the traditional courtesies" have been done away with, not all of them. This is an early indication that the wedding event, though a union of young people who are like-minded in their social and economic ambitions, is still both a product and an agent of traditional values. It becomes clear, as the story progresses, that the traditional elements of the wedding are not merely displays or rituals, but also represent traditional ways of defining personal goals and relationships.

Nevertheless, as the story of the rivalry between Neo and Mathata unfolds, it becomes clear that, for those involved, the wedding represents a break with tradition and the beginning of a new life of economic opportunity. Neo is an educated girl with a bright future ahead of her due to the opportunities her education will make possible. Mathata, on the other hand, is uneducated. As the narrator says, ''The difference between the two girls was that Mathata was completely uneducated; the only work she would ever do was that of a housemaid, while Neo had endless opportunities before her—typist, book-keeper, or secretary. So Neo merely smiled; Mathata was no rival.'' Not considering Mathata to be a threat, Neo is comfortable and confident in her position. Mathata, too, is confident and secure, however; she does not want Kegoletile as her husband: ''Mathata merely smiled too. Girls like her offered no resistance to the approaches of men; when they lost them, they just let things ride.'' When Neo's aunt informs her that Kegoletile has been spending a great deal of time at Mathata's home and tells her that her arrogant ways have led the community to hold her in disfavor, Neo's confidence is somewhat shaken, and she becomes pregnant to secure her hold on Kegoletile. But she need not have bothered. Kegoletile has resolved the conflict between Neo and Mathata, essentially a conflict between ambition and love, firmly in favor of Neo. He may still find himself attracted to Mathata, but ''[h]e knew what he was marrying—something quite the opposite, a new kind of girl with false postures and acquired, grand-madame ways. And yet, it didn't pay a man these days to look too closely into his heart. They all wanted as wives, women who were big money-earners and they were so ruthless about it!''

Kegoletile's choice of Neo over Mathata makes it clear that his motive for the marriage is essentially economic rather than emotional. Before we learn of Kegoletile's reasoning, the narrator has already defined Neo as someone who refuses to fit in with the village's traditional norms of behavior. Her family is ''anxious to be rid of her'' because she is ''an impossible girl with haughty, arrogant ways.'' Neo's estrangement from her family represents her estrangement from the traditions of the past that she hopes to leave behind by marrying Kegoletile and putting her education to use. The narrator ascribes

> **This is less the story of a wedding than it is the story of the decline of a woman's power; even if the opportunities afforded to her by her education remain available, she is still obliged to subvert her will to that of her husband, to be his wife first, Neo the educated woman second."**

the following sentiments to Neo's family: ''What's the good of education if it goes to someone's head so badly they have no respect for the people? Oh, she is not a person.'' Neo's being ''not a person'' signifies the extent of the breach between her and her family and the past of economic powerlessness that the family represents. That is, she is no longer recognized as a member of the community. This emphasis on money over social and emotional ties coincides with the de-emphasis of traditional rituals in the wedding ceremony itself. Neo considers herself fortunate to have Kegoletile, who is ''rich in cattle,'' and he considers himself lucky to have her because she will be able to bring in a comparatively sizable income.

However, to some extent Neo returns to the family and tradition when she learns from her aunt that Kegoletile has been spending time with Mathata and that her own behavior has led others to despise her. Anxious about the security of her position, Neo becomes pregnant in order to ensure Kegoletile's intention to marry her. Neo's confidence has been undermined, and she can no longer rely on her education to elevate her above Mathata or women like her in the eyes of men. At this point the story returns from the narrative of past circumstances and continues the narrative of the wedding event itself, an event richer in the formalities of tradition that one may have expected, given the progressive sentiments of the bride and groom and the economic consideration that is their primary bond. Evidence of this more traditional tone comes in the advice offered to Neo by Kegoletile's aunts: ''Daughter, you must carry water for your husband. Beware, that at all times, he is the owner of the house and must be obeyed. Do not mind if he stops now and then and talks to other ladies. Let him feel free to come and go as he likes.'' It is not to be an equal partnership of like-minded ambitions, but a partnership in which her will is secondary to that of her husband. Similarly, the aunt who has chastised Neo and informed her of Kegoletile's interest in Mathata exhorts Neo, ''Be a good wife! Be a good wife!'' Neo's defining characteristic will no longer be her education but her new status as wife.

In his essay ''Treasures of the Heart: The Short Stories of Bessie Head,'' Michael Thorpe writes of most of the stories in *The Collector of Treasures* that ''the storyteller shows her hand most plainly in her efforts to provide models of the good.'' One must ask, however, what represents the ''good'' in ''Snapshots of a Wedding.'' Is it ''good'' to be a ''good wife,'' as Neo's aunt begs Neo to be? As Huma Ibrahim writes in her book *Bessie Head: Subversive Identities in Exile,* Neo's aunt's final comments to her at the wedding indicate ''the ultimate double message to Neo: no matter how educated you are, your primary task is to be polite to everybody in the community and to be a good wife to your husband. Implicit in this ideology is that education will help you in the race for a husband but it will not help you after that.'' This is precisely what the wedding scene dramatizes. Neo initially won Kegoletile by virtue of her education and greater earning potential. Even before the wedding, however, by becoming pregnant, she had returned to more traditional ways of securing Kegoletile. This is less the story of a wedding than it is the story of the decline of a woman's power; even if the opportunities afforded to her by her education remain available, she is still obliged to subvert her will to that of her husband, to be his wife first, Neo the educated woman second. It is her education that has made her appealing, but it is her education that at the same time leads to her loss of status in marriage.

In her essay ''Myth, Exile, and the Female Condition: Bessie Head's *The Collector of Treasures,*'' Sara Chetin writes that ''[a]s outsiders we . . . perhaps end up feeling a little sorry for the young bride, exiled as much by traditional insecurities as by her education that could not reconcile itself to a society's disregard of women.'' Precisely because of the inescapability of Neo's fate as a wife,

one does pity Neo, as Chetin suggests. Moreover, one sees that tradition has a strength not to be underestimated. It is tradition that determines Neo's role as a wife as well as the limitations of the value her education will have for her as an individual once she becomes a wife. Despite the early claims that this will be a ''modern'' wedding, it is modern—and only slightly so—in form only. Its implications remain those of the very tradition that its two participants plan to escape by means of their anticipated economic success.

Source: Thomas M. March, ''An Overview of 'Snapshots of a Wedding','' in *Short Stories for Students,* The Gale Group, 1999.

Sara Chetin

In the following excerpt, Chetin explores the ways in which Head's ''Snapshots of a Wedding,'' is presented as a series of photographs, and how this style affects the theme of inevitable change.

In ''Snapshots of a Wedding,'' the village narrator asserts ''no one is fooled by human nature and implies, indirectly, that despite their ability ''to keep up with'' changing times, educating females does more harm than good. The narrator accepts, through the gentle and respected bridegroom, Kegoletile, that one should marry ''women who were big money-earners'' and that ''it didn't pay to look too closely into his heart.'' Kegoletile is about to marry Neo, ''a new kind of girl with false postures and acquired grand-madame ways'', although he loved the traditional, humble Mathata. The villagers never question their own contradictory attitudes to money and status, a by-product of colonial education, but channel their malaise into an over zealous attachment to traditional ways, their defensiveness exposing their own vulnerability to change. As outsiders we can't trust the villagers' hostility to Neo, just as we couldn't trust the viciousness directed at Mma-Mompati in ''The Village Saint,'' and perhaps end up feeling a little sorry for the young bride, exiled as much by traditional insecurities as by her education, an education that could not reconcile itself to a society's disregard of women.

These attitudes are exposed in a series of ''snapshots'' starting with the opening frame that captures the gentle, unreal-like quality of the ritual wedding preparation that has remained unchanged for centuries. The picture is ''distorted'', having a ''fluid, watery form'' almost like it is not fully developed. Slowly ''a modern wedding'' comes into focus that reveals, beneath the orderly ritual facade, a village in a state of anomie. After a series of individual ''fixed'' poses, out of the deceptively even tempo of the ritual ceremony comes a spark of life, a spontaneous gesture that gives both an ironic significance to the wedding and underlies the very ambiguity of what being a ''wife'' in changing times actually entails. The ''majestic, regal'' aunt who clenches her fist and pounds the ground gives her seal of approval by acknowledging the bride and attempting to reinstate her into the traditional folds of the community. But the very violence of her order: ''Be a good wife! Be a good wife!'' reveals the inherent precariousness of the concept. This precariousness is rooted in the realization that the old ways are no longer inevitable and as the story ends, the audience is left with the final snapshot, a blurred, overexposed picture, distorted by its own vulnerability. . . .

Source: Sara Chetin, ''Myth, Exile, and the Female Condition: Bessie Head's 'The Collector of Treasures','' in *The Journal of Commonwealth Literature,* Vol. XXIV, No. 1, 1989, pp. 114–37.

Sources

Head, Bessie, with Linda Susan Beard. Interview in *Sage: A Scholarly Journal on Black Women,* Vol. III, No. 2, Fall, 1986, pp. 44-7.

Ibrahim, Huma. *Bessie Head: Subversive Identities in Exile,* Charlottesville: University Press of Virginia, 1996.

MacKenzie, Craig. *Bessie Head: An Introduction,* Grahamstown, South Africa: National English Literary Museum, 1989.

> ❝ The picture is 'distorted', having a 'fluid, watery form' almost like it is not fully developed.❞

Thorpe, Michael. ''Treasures of the Heart: The Short Stories of Bessie Head,'' in *World Literature Today,* Vol. 57, No. 3, Summer, 1983, pp. 414-6.

Further Reading

Black Literature Criticism, Vol. 2, Gale Research, 1992.
   The entry on Bessie Head in this volume provides an overview of her career as well as excerpts from important critical works on her fiction.

Contemporary Literary Criticism, Vol. 67, Gale Research, 1991.
   The entry on Bessie Head in this volume provides an overview of her career as well as excerpts from important critical works on her fiction.

Little, Greta D. ''Bessie Head'' in *Dictionary of Literary Biography,* Vol. 117, *Twentieth-Century Caribbean and Black African Writers,* Gale Research, 1992.
   Provides a biographical and critical overview of Head's life and career.

Taiwo, Oladele. ''Bessie Head,'' in *Female Novelists of Modern Africa,* St. Martin's Press, 1984, pp. 185-214.
   Taiwo's overview of ''Snapshots of a Wedding'' concentrates primarily on the inner and social conflicts Kegoletile faces in choosing a wife.

Swaddling Clothes

Yukio Mishima

1955

Yukio Mishima's "Swaddling Clothes" was first published in Japan in 1955 in the highbrow literary journal *Bungei*. Its first English language publication appeared in *Today's Japan,* 1960, translated by Ivan Morris. The original Japanese title, "Shinbungami" simply means "newspapers" and the story's standard English title is an interpretive translation by Morris. It has since been included in several English translations of Mishima's work such as *Death in Midsummer and Other Stories* (1966). By 1955, Mishima was already a well-known literary figure, having received much attention and acclaim for his autobiographical *Confessions of a Mask* (1949) and *Kinjiki* [also known as *Forbidden Colors* (1951)]. During this early period, Mishima's works had not yet taken a decidedly political turn and were more interested in personal exploration and the nihilist aesthetics of the Roman-ha group (or "Japanese Romanticists") who took Mishima under their wing.

It would be difficult to exactly locate when Mishima's works became overtly political and whether or not Mishima even intended his early works to be characterized as such. But "Swaddling Clothes," published one year prior to *The Temple of the Golden Pavilion,* which is generally considered to criticize western importation of modernization and degraded moral values into Japan, and just ten years after Japan's devastating loss in World War II, can be read as political critique. "Swaddling Clothes" is a story replete with contrasts: tradition and mod-

ernization; sensitivity and callousness; morality and amorality; genuineness and artificiality; wealth and poverty. Through the author's omniscient narration of Toshiko's thoughts and the physical assault on Toshiko at the end of the story, Mishima offers a vision of modernization and change ushered in by western countries that is unwelcome and violent. The ambiguous ending (Is Toshiko raped? Does she die? Or, does she survive the attack and perhaps retaliate?) asks the reader to weigh the benefits and losses of change and modernization in a rapidly globalizing world and imagine what the fate of traditional values and ethics might be.

Author Biography

Born Kimitake Hiraoka, Yukio Mishima was born into an upper-class family and raised primarily by his possessive grandmother who was a descendent by marriage of the Tokugawas, the ruling family of feudal, samurai-governed Japan from the seventeenth century to 1868. Though Mishima and his grandmother lived in the same house as his parents, she raised him in relative isolation in her private ground floor chambers where she often lay ill with her grandson tending her. Mishima published his first long work, *Hanazakari no Mori* (*The Forest in Full Bloom*) in 1944 when he was only nineteen years old.

Mishima's pseudonym was chosen by Fumio Shimizu, an editor of the literary magazine that the *The Forest in Full Bloom* first appeared in, and teacher at the prestigious Gakushuin (Peers School) in Tokyo where Mishima excelled in writing and literary studies. The pseudonym was chosen for its romantic evocations: "Mishima" is the name of the town which reputedly affords the most splendid view of Mt. Fuji and "Yukio" derives from "yuki" meaning snow. Having written over 100 novels, plays, short stories, and essays in his short lifetime, Mishima rocketed to popular and highbrow literary renown in Japan and English speaking countries (Mishima is the most highly translated Japanese author into English) and was recommended for the Nobel Prize in Literature in 1968, losing to his mentor and literary sponsor, Yasunari Kawabata (1899-1972), the first Japanese citizen to win the prize. After receiving a law degree from Tokyo University and working briefly in a prestigious position at the Ministry of Finance, Mishima dedicated his life full-time to writing.

Throughout his literary career, Mishima was a highly visible public figure, at times associated, intentionally or not, with controversial aesthetics, politics, and highly publicized personal "pursuits." For example, in 1955 Mishima embarked on a rigorous program of bodybuilding, in fulfillment of his dedication to the philosophy of *bunburyodo*, the samurai philosophy of the "dual way of Art and Action." Showing off his newly formed muscular body, Mishima posed nude and semi-nude for a controversial book of photographs, *Ba-ra-kei*, (*Ordeal by Roses*) taken by Eikoh Hosoe and published in the United States in 1985. Mishima was deeply interested in reviving samurai ethics in modern, democratizing Japan, and this desire may have stemmed from the influence of his grandmother. In 1966, Mishima's "Yokuku" ("Patriotism") was published and included a graphic and protracted dramatization of the main characters' *seppuku*, ritual suicide by disembowelment, a practice also dictated by samurai codes of honor and that Mishima himself would commit in 1970.

Critics often describe two of Mishima's autobiographical works as embodying the "Mishima aesthetic": his first full length novel *Kamen no Kokuhaku* [*Confessions of a Mask* (1949)] and a tetralogy that he worked on over four years *The Sea of Fertility* (1966-1970). These works explored the impossibility of beauty, purity, tradition, virtue, and spiritual satisfaction in a rapidly modernizing Japan, and nihilistically looked towards death and destruction as solutions to these problems. For example, in *Kinkakuji* [*Temple of the Golden Pavilion* (1956)] the protagonist burns down the sacred temple when he realizes the untenability of maintaining the pureness of its beauty in post-World War II Japan. In fact, he had hoped that it would be destroyed during the American air-raids and when it survives, he chooses to destroy the temple himself in order to prevent its contamination by the western-influenced social, economic, and political structure that Japan would shortly adopt. The explicit discussion of homosexuality in *Confessions* and other works is also viewed as addressing the general alienation of the post-war Japanese citizen. Mishima's frank treatment of homosexuality also became the source of many exaggerated rumors about his sexual promiscuity. In 1958, upon learning that his mother was dying of cancer, which turned out to be a misdiagnosis, Mishima married Yoko Sugiyama and had two children.

Mishima maintained close personal and public relationships with conservative politicians, such as the Defense Minister Yasuhiro Nakasone, and in 1968 formed a civilian militia, the *Tatenokai*, that was dedicated to reviving the divine power of the Emperor. The *Tatenokai* rebuked the current tenets of the new Constitution, as dictated by the United States after the Japanese defeat in World War II, which forced the Emperor to admit that he was a mere human functionary of the state. "Shinbun-ga mi" ("Swaddling Clothes") dramatizes some of the negative consequences resulting from the nation's enforced democratization and weakened allegiance to the Emperor. While the late years of his life were overtly dedicated to "political" causes, Mishima claimed his earlier works were primarily concerned with aesthetics, and frequently denied connection with right-wing groups that found support in his works. Nevertheless, Mishima spent the last years of his life organizing and training the *Tatenokai* under the auspices of the ruling Liberal Democratic Party who allowed the group to train with the *Jieitai*, the National Self-Defense Army.

On November 25, 1970, shortly after he finished *Tennin Gosui* (*The Decay of an Angel*), the last segment of *The Sea of Fertility*, Mishima and the *Tatenokai* entered the *Jieitai*'s Tokyo headquarters under a premise of a friendly meeting. They held General Kanetoshi Mashita hostage in his own office and demanded that he assemble a large audience of *Jieitai* soldiers to hear Mishima's planned speech. Mashita's men carried out the demands and though Mishima successfully delivered a thirty minute address inciting the Japanese soldiers to reject the American written Constitution and revive *kokutai* (the institution of the divine Emperor), Mishima perceived his revolutionary speech to be a failure as the soldiers booed and jeered at him. Dismayed by the western, political liberalism and apathy of the soldiers, Mishima returned to the General's office and committed *seppuku*, with the cooperation of his *Tatenokai* second-in-command, Masakatsu Morita, who also beheaded himself. The General and his men were left unharmed. It is unclear whether Mishima's speech was a genuine call to revolution or a dramatic and romantic fulfillment of the samurai ethic that required its adherents to commit suicide rather than face dishonor.

Plot Summary

"Swaddling Clothes" is Toshiko's story. In fact, she is the only character that is named throughout

the narrative. As Toshiko rides home alone in a taxi, she sorrowfully contemplates the details of "the incident." The nurse she and her husband had hired to take care of their son has given birth to an illegitimate baby in their house, revealing nothing of her pregnancy until the moment of delivery. Toshiko is saddened by the attenuation of moral values in modern Japanese society as she contemplates the nurse's situation and her husband's blithe treatment of the event.

Unlike his wife, Toshiko's husband, a handsome, popular actor, is seemingly undismayed by "the incident" and freely chatters about it to his friends as if it were nothing more than fodder for entertainment. Toshiko feels alienated from her husband not only for his inability to share her concern for the nurse's apparent loss of moral values in modern society, but also for his own lighthearted, non-reflective participation in modern, "western" influenced life. Toshiko's husband's acceptance of and participation in modern western culture is also expressed through the American style clothing he wears and the "western" style, parquet-floored house he chooses to live in.

Observing the scenery on the ride home, Toshiko also notes the damage modernization has wrought on the landscape of Japan. Parting from her husband, she notices the fake, paper cherry blossoms that decorate an entertainment district theater and compares them to the real cherry blossoms "in all their purity" lining the park adjacent to the Imperial Palace, which stands against a background of glittering office buildings. In contrast to the solemn, looming figure of the Imperial Palace, the surrounding park is littered with empty bottles and waste paper, and populated by vagrants.

Another contrast that Toshiko ponders on is the immense rift between a young boy born in material privilege, like her own son, and one born in poverty and shame, such as the nurse's baby. She accepts that these two babies can only live in mutually exclusive worlds divided by class where they can only interact through violence. She imagines the future of the illegitimate baby as being desolate and eventually ending in a life of crime. She is jolted by fear thinking about the potential chance meeting of her own educated and privileged son with the nurse's baby, a meeting she imagines would inevitably result in the "other boy" assaulting or murdering her son.

Unsettled by her wandering thoughts, Toshiko capriciously stops the cab and gets out at the park, despite the impropriety for a young, married woman to be walking alone at night. She meanders through the park thinking about the nurse's baby and the newspapers that the doctor had disrespectfully wrapped him in. Having sympathy for the baby, Toshiko had replaced the newspaper "swaddling clothes" with a piece of new flannel cloth.

Toshiko's thoughts take an eerie manifestation as she comes across a homeless youth sleeping on a park bench. He has blanketed himself in newspapers for warmth, and the white bundle on the bench reminds Toshiko first of cherry blossoms and then of the newspaper "swaddling clothes." Toshiko imagines that this is what the nurse's baby will grow up to be—a homeless, poverty-stricken and criminal vagrant. Startled that "all her fears and premonitions had suddenly taken concrete form," but curious, Toshiko dangerously approaches the sleeping figure to get a closer look. The youth is awakened by Toshiko's gaze and seizes her. The story ends at this point making it unclear whether Toshiko is murdered, raped, or both, but at any rate, concluding on a note of violence.

Yukio Mishima

Characters

Homeless Youth

Like the babies in the story, the homeless youth functions more as a symbol than a character. Sleeping on a park bench, his ragged body covered in newspapers for warmth, he forms a stark contrast to the luxurious Imperial Palace looming in the background. Bundled in newspapers, he reminds Toshiko of the nurse's baby and is the immediate manifestation of the crime, poverty, and ignominy that the illegitimate baby will inevitably inherit in a social system divided by class. As if to confirm Toshiko's fears that different classes can only interact through violence, the homeless youth attacks Toshiko and most likely murders or rapes her.

The Nurse

The Nurse that Toshiko and her husband hire to tend to their baby lies about her pregnancy, claiming that her stomach is swollen because of "gastric dilation." Like Toshiko's husband, she seems unconcerned with the moral implications of her pregnancy and delivery out of wedlock. She carries on in high spirits, even using her "stomach ailment" as an excuse to eat heartily. Her pregnancy remains a secret until the day of her delivery when she is found in the nursery delivering her child. Negligent not only of her own self-respect and the respect of her employers, the nurse gives birth next to Toshiko's son's crib, while the boy looks on, frightened and crying. Like Toshiko's husband, the nurse is a character who has been negatively affected by modern, westernized Japanese life. In her case, she is depicted as dismissing traditional moral values by engaging in sex outside of marriage.

Toshiko

"Swaddling Clothes" is narrated in the third person author omniscient, centering around the character of Toshiko, the wife of a handsome and successful Japanese actor. Toshiko has been raised and continues to live in material luxury, but despite her "easy" and "painless" lifestyle, or perhaps because of it, she suffers from a "delicacy of spirit."

Of all the characters in the story, Toshiko is the most thoughtful and sensitive. During the lonely taxi-ride home, Toshiko is depressed by her inattentive husband, her modern, westernized lifestyle, and the recollection of the agonizing "incident"—the birth of an illegitimate baby by Toshiko's new nursemaid—and morosely contemplates the loss of tradition and moral values in the people surrounding her. Toshiko is upset that her husband had trivial-

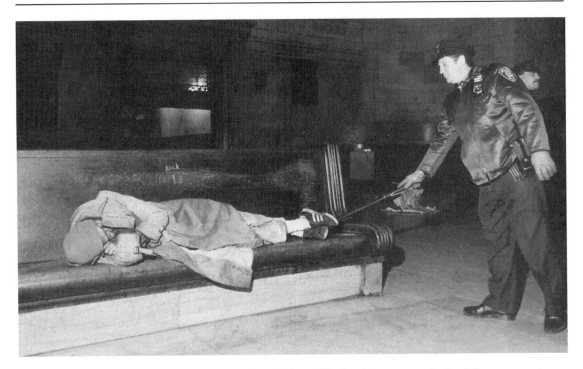

Mishima uses the homeless man in ''Swaddling Clothes'' as a symbol of the corruption of the Japenese culture due to the influx of Western civilization.

ized ''the incident'' into a laughable and grotesque story for the entertainment of his friends. She feels great sympathy for the newborn, having replaced the degrading newspaper ''swaddling clothes'' that the doctor wrapped the baby in with a new piece of flannel from her own cupboard. She mourns the shameful history that the child will have to live with as an adult, and compares his bleak future with that of her own privileged son. Toshiko implicitly longs for the more conservative and traditional days of the past, unaffected by modernization and its attendant loss of tradition and moral values.

Toshiko's husband

Toshiko's actor husband is never named, perhaps to help portray him as a general typification of morally remiss ''modernization'' and to offer a contrast to his sensitive, sympathetic and contemplative wife. Toshiko's husband participates in only two actions: sending his wife home alone and trivializing and laughing at ''the incident.'' In fact, Toshiko's husband ''flamboyantly'' repeats the story of the illegitimate baby to his friends at the nightclub ''as if it were no more than an amusing incident which they (Toshiko and her husband) chanced to have witnessed.'' To Toshiko's hus-

band, an entertainer himself, ''the incident'' evokes none of the deep ethical concerns that it does for Toshiko. Like the brash band that plays at the nightclub, ''the incident'' is little more than another source of consumable entertainment for Toshiko's husband and his friends.

Toshiko's husband's insensitive behavior is associated with his ''modern'' lifestyle and attitude. He is described as wearing a ''garish'' American-style suit and choosing to live in a cold, ''unhomely'' western style house. He is entirely self-centered, spending his time ''dashing off to appointments'' and socializing in the entertainment district, rather than going home to spend time with his wife.

Toshiko's Son and the Nurse's Illegitimate Baby

The two babies described in ''Swaddling Clothes'' are not properly ''characters'' as they do not directly participate in the narrative action, but they are important and central symbols of the story. Like his mother, the newspaper-wrapped baby represents the degradation of moral values in modern, westernized Japan. According to Toshiko, the illegitimate baby has little chance to overcome class barriers and is unlikely to grow up into a "respectable citizen" because of his ignoble birth. In contrast, Toshiko's son, because of his birth into a wealthy upper-class family, will have access to opportunities for social and economic success.

Though Toshiko feels much sympathy for the illegitimate baby, she does not challenge the existing social system that excludes and limits individuals on the basis of class, a system inherited from the feudal period of Japan. Imagining the meeting of her son with the nurse's baby in twenty years, Toshiko believes such a meeting will inevitably result in a violent and fatal "clash" with the nurse's baby, likely grown up into a criminal, murdering her own son. The violence between the two boys represents the larger violence between classes in a society rigidly stratified by class.

Themes

Culture Clash: Japanese Tradition vs. Western Modernization

The "culture clash" depicted in "Swaddling Clothes" is unique because it is expressed through the struggle of traditional Japanese morals and ethics sustaining itself under the powerful influence of western modernization. In this story, modernization of Japanese social life is represented primarily as an unwelcome import from the west. As the figure who most readily embraces western, modern influence, Toshiko's husband is portrayed negatively. Unaffected by the nurse's loss of moral values, he recounts "the incident" with humor and nonchalance to his nightclub friends, commenting that he was more worried that his "good rug" would be ruined. He wears American clothes that strike Toshiko as "garish" and chooses to live in a western style house. Toshiko reflects: "she dreaded going back to their house, unhomely with its Western-style furniture and with the bloodstains still showing on the floor."

This sentence is revealing because it closely associates a western-influenced lifestyle with an image of violence ("bloodstains"). The implication is that westernization/modernization is a damaging process that brings violence and bloodshed into private and public Japanese life. As the nurse has scandalously conceived and delivered out of

wedlock, she is a symbol of the loss of moral values in modern society. The implication is that western modernization is also responsible for weakening traditional, Japanese moral values. In this context, the birth of the illegitimate boy is represented as a moment of bloodshed. Toshiko comments, "it was a scene fit for a butchershop." The association of western influence in Japan with violence evokes the literal violence used by American Naval Commodore Matthew Perry in 1853 to open Japanese trade ports to the west.

Western induced modernization and the loss of traditional Japanese mores and ethics is symbolized through the images of newspapers, trash, and cherry blossoms. The cherry blossoms that Toshiko sees around her are mostly fake and artificial as she notices that it is "depressingly obvious" that the cherry blossoms decorating an entertainment district theater are "merely scraps of white paper." At this realization, Toshiko goes into the park to cheer herself up by absorbing herself in the atmosphere of the real cherry blossoms that line the park. But their natural splendor is obscured by the electric light bulbs that have been installed in the trees which "shone dully beneath the blossoms." Her attention is also drawn to the litter and trash lining the park grounds and the crumpled up newspapers that cover the homeless youth. At first she mistakes the hunched figure for a pile of cherry blossoms and then is reminded of the newspapers in which the doctor had spitefully wrapped the nurse's baby.

This progression of images that assault Toshiko's line of vision—fake cherry blossoms, gaudy light bulbs, trash, newspapers—implies that Japanese society has been so degraded by westernization/ modernization that real cherry blossoms no longer adorn the Japanese landscape; they have either been replaced by artificial ones or obscured by garish modern decoration or waste. As a long cherished and popular flower of Asian cultures, cherry blossoms "in all their purity" represent both the purity and delicacy of Japanese traditional culture and their degradation symbolizes the decay of this culture. Mishima uses cherry blossoms in particular— a flower that is only in full bloom once a year and whose blossoms are swiftly washed away after the first spring rain—because they represent the vulnerable and delicate project of maintaining tradition. The implication here is that with the ubiquity of litter and trash in the modern environment, real cherry blossoms may not have the opportunity to bloom again. This inauspicious vision of Japan's

Topics for Further Study

- Investigate the history and progression of western influence in Japan and other Asian countries. Try to find sources that speak from the point of view of the Asian citizens whose lives were radically altered by the infiltration of their countries by western economic, social and political systems. In each specific case, what were the motivations of the western countries in exploring and penetrating Asia? In your opinion, has this "globalization" mutually benefited both western countries and Asia, or has it harmed either party? In "Swaddling Clothes" western influence is portrayed in a negative light. Using your historical research, argue for or against Mishima's critical view of westernization and modernization.

- Toshiko is portrayed as a somewhat contradictory character. She primarily wants to hold on to and revive traditional Japanese ethics and mores, but she also challenges those values. For instance, she walks around the park at night despite the impropriety of this action and she sympathetically wraps the nurse's baby in a new piece of flannel when both her husband and the doctor have dismissed the event as ignoble, grotesque and scandalous. How do these contradictory actions modify the characterization of Toshiko as a conservative proponent of tradition? Though she is disheartened by the modernization around her, is there a different kind of change and social transformation that she might support?

- "Swaddling Clothes" portrays the nurse's conception and birth of a baby out of wedlock negatively. In a sense, the nurse is an example of a modern day working-class, single mother. Given the contemporary debate over single motherhood especially in impoverished rural and urban environments, is the nurse's situation entirely condemnable? What are the modern social, economic, political and racial factors that lock contemporary single mothers and their children into oppressive situations? Is Toshiko's characterization of the illegitimate baby growing up to be "a lonely rat" fair and accurate? Is a baby born in "ignoble" circumstances forever bound to a lowly position in society? Use contemporary

articles from magazines and newspapers to support your point of view.

- As a story contrasting the purity of tradition to the contamination of modern influences, "Swaddling Clothes" "punishes" those who dare to step outside of traditional boundaries. The nurse and her child are cast as eternally shameful and worthy of mockery, and Toshiko in one daring moment of impropriety is attacked and possibly killed. In contrast, Toshiko's husband and his male friends have embraced modern life, yet they do not suffer any consequences. On the contrary, they appear to continue carousing and thoroughly enjoy themselves in a modern style. Why does the burden of preserving culture fall on women? Using anthropological or sociological sources that focus on change in traditional societies, explore the assumed gender roles of such cultures. What customs and traditions are men and women expected to fulfill and carry on? In which cases are either women or men disproportionately responsible for preserving culture?

- The ending of "Swaddling Clothes" is intentionally left ambiguous. In your interpretation, what happens to Toshiko? Is she raped? Murdered? Both? Might she have survived and even retaliated against her attacker? Given the highly symbolic nature of the story, what are the implications of these various endings? For instance, since Toshiko symbolizes the preservation of traditional values, would her survival of the attack imply that these values can persevere? If she doesn't survive, does the story cast an incontrovertible pall on the possibilities of such preservation?

- Look for other fictional or autobiographical works that employ a fragmented narrative style. How does the disruption of the progressive, linear narrative enhance or obscure the thematic content of these works? Identify other non-traditional narrative styles. What kind of "message" might the author be sending by using unconventional narrative styles?

so-called modern ''progress'' is expressed in Toshiko's thoughts: ''thoughts of the future made Toshiko feel cold and miserable.''

Sex and Gender Roles

''Swaddling Clothes'' casts a negative light on female reproduction and sexuality, or at least that which is outside of the proper domain of marriage. In addition, Toshiko's husband describes the birth through images of animalistic ''squatting'' and ''groaning'' and even likens the nurse to a cow and a ''stuck pig,'' invoked for the mocking pleasure of his friends. The nurse is generally characterized in two ways: as a scandalous woman who gave birth without a husband and as the butt of a joke. In this way, while the negative portrayal of the nurse offers a critique of the loss of morals in a modernizing society, not only has she expressed her sexuality outside of marriage but she is not particularly ashamed of herself (she deceitfully laughs off her swollen stomach as ''gastric dilation''), the burden of maintaining traditional values falls on the women in the story. When women fail to do so, they are stripped of any modicum of respect and subjected to public ridicule like the nurse. Having no voice in this story, the nurse is not given a chance to defend her situation.

Toshiko is also criticized and even punished for her impropriety, although more indirectly. For the most part, Toshiko is an obedient representative of conservatism and tradition as the bulk of the story focuses on her disenchantment with the modernization around her. Nonetheless, Toshiko is inspired to get out of the taxi and wander around the park grounds, fully aware of the impropriety of this action but momentarily in desperate need to break out of such boundaries. Yet Toshiko's impropriety not only fails to ameliorate her confusion, it also results in her assault and/or murder. The ''moral'' here is reminiscent of that of the popular fairy tale *Bluebeard*. Like Bluebeard's wife, Toshiko is violently punished for stepping out of conventional boundaries and attempting to satisfy her curiosity. ''Swaddling Clothes'' concludes on this note: ''[S]uddenly [she] had an overmastering desire to get a glimpse of [the homeless youth] ... But Toshiko had approached too close. In the silent night the newspaper bedding rustled, and abruptly the man opened his eyes. Seeing the young woman standing directly beside him, he raised himself with a jerk, and his eyes lit up. A second later a powerful hand reached out and seized Toshiko by her slender wrist.'' Again, the burden of upholding propriety and tradition falls on women and they are punished when they fail to do so. In contrast, Toshiko's husband, like the nurse, is also a figure that has embraced decadent, modern values, but he suffers little for his behavior. On the contrary, he appears complacent as well as economically and socially successful.

Class Conflict

Despite the modernization and change that Toshiko bemoans in this story, one ''traditional'' structure that remains intact is the rigid class system of Japan. As a feudal country before the rise of the western-influenced Meiji government (1868), Japanese society was unequivocally demarcated by class, with the military samurai on top and their agricultural vassals on bottom. Mishima tended to romanticize this social structure, ignoring the often harsh and exploitative treatment of the vassals by the ruling class, envisioning it as a harmonious system where each Imperial subject knew his/her class position and dutifully fulfilled its requirements.

Though Toshiko is in some regards a ''progressive'' figure (she is uneasy with the role assigned to her as a refined, upper-class housewife and mother) she is primarily the story's main proponent of holding on to tradition, evidenced by her gloomy thoughts on the transformation of Japanese society. Though she feels sympathy for the illegitimate child and even makes an attempt to help him by replacing the ignominious newspaper ''swaddling clothes'' with a piece of her own cloth, she holds on to the belief that the child can never break out of his low class standing. She perceives his future as hopeless because of the ignoble conditions of his birth: ''He will be living a desolate, hopeless, poverty-stricken existence—a lonely rat. What else could happen to a baby who has had such a birth?'' Furthermore, she envisions the meeting of her ''fine, carefully educated'' son with the nurse's baby as a violent struggle: ''Say twenty years from now ... one day by a quirk of fate [my son] meets the other boy, who then will also have turned twenty. And say that the other boy, who has been sinned against, savagely stabs him with a knife ... '' In this way, Toshiko does not question or challenge the still existing rigid class structure of Japanese society, though somewhat modified since feudal times, and even supports the strict separation and division of classes as evidenced by her frightful vision of the struggle that would inevitably ensue from their interaction.

Style

Point of View and Fragmented Narration

''Swaddling Clothes'' is not narrated in a straightforward, linear style. While the present action of the narrative is generally progressive (Toshiko leaving the nightclub and heading home in a taxi), the linear progression of events is interrupted by Toshiko's memories and contemplations. The nurse's delivery is also recounted in pieces and from different points of view (Toshiko and her husband's) offering the reader a comparison of the character's attitudes.

There are many reasons why an author may choose to disrupt a traditional, linear narrative with fragmented memories and contemplations—for instance, to use the present action as a mere premise for unearthing the past, to underscore the difficulty and painfulness of remembering the past, or to stress the discontinuity of a character's experience. In this way, a fragmented narrative style can emphasize major themes within the story. For example, Asian-American literature that dramatizes the arduous and often interrupted and diverted journeys of immigrants across North America often uses fragmented narrative styles to enhance the feeling of discomfort and unsettlement in American culture. In ''Swaddling Clothes,'' Toshiko is afraid of the future, as the narrator comments ''thoughts of the future made Toshiko feel cold and miserable,'' because she anticipates only increased violence, bloodshed, and loss of moral values in the rapidly modernizing Japanese society. In this context, the frequent interruption of the present action by Toshiko's memories, projections and meandering thoughts emphasizes her unwillingness to move forward in time into an inauspicious future.

Symbolism and Setting

Much of the symbolism in ''Swaddling Clothes'' is achieved through elements of setting and their contrasts. Each place or piece of the Japanese landscape that Toshiko views from the taxi window are symbols of tradition and its decay through the oppressions of modernization: for instance, the tacky entertainment district versus the solemn, stately Imperial Palace, and the organic, comforting structure of the Imperial Palace versus the cold and uninviting, ultra-modern skyscrapers in the background. The visual contrast of these structures standing together symbolizes the chaos and incongruence Toshiko feels in a modernizing society that seems to have irretrievably abjured its culture and tradition. The park in front of the Imperial Palace contains many internal contrasts also symbolic of this chaotic transformation. While the park has preserved its splendid vista of cherry blossoms, the trees are decorated by garish, colored light bulbs, reminiscent of the ''pinpricks of light'' emanating from the stark, modern office buildings, and the park grounds are littered with bottles, waste paper, and sleeping vagrants.

Waste paper, newspapers, and cherry blossoms form the central group of symbols of the story. The crumpled up trash reminds Toshiko of the ''mere scraps of white paper'' that have been crafted into fake cherry blossoms to decorate a theater, and the newspapers that cover the homeless youth remind her of both cherry blossoms and the shameful newspaper ''swaddling clothes'' of the illegitimate baby. It seems to Toshiko that the Japanese environment is no longer naturally adorned by real cherry blossoms, which represent the purity of Japanese culture and tradition, and is now instead ''decorated'' with trash and newspapers, representing the contamination of that culture and tradition. In other words, cherry blossoms have been degraded—made artificial or replaced by the waste products of a careless modern culture.

Another symbol of purity that suffers degradation is the figure of the newborn baby. Conventionally, babies and births connote joy and celebration, but in ''Swaddling Clothes,'' the nurse's delivery is perceived as a violent scene of bloodshed by Toshiko and a laughably grotesque vision of mockery by Toshiko's husband. The nurse's baby wrapped in soiled newspapers embodies not only the nurse's loss of moral values, but the staining and contamination of Japanese society's future. Toshiko comments: ''Those soiled newspaper swaddling clothes will be the symbol of his [the illegitimate baby's] entire life.'' The figure of the homeless youth curled up on the park bench under a layer of newspapers echoes this earlier symbol, and as Toshiko imagines it, is the manifestation of the poverty and crime that the nurse's baby will no doubt grow up in.

A Modern Parable

''Swaddling Clothes'' functions as a modern parable or allegory, a pithy moralization of general social problems through a specific and concrete story. By imbuing various objects and places with symbolism, the story not only dramatizes a particular incident in one woman's life, but can be widely applied to society in general. In this way, Toshiko's experience is presented as a *universal* truth, to which society as a whole can broadly relate. The function of a parable is also to provide a moral lesson. The lesson or "message" in "Swaddling Clothes" warns of the destructive effects of western-induced modernization.

Historical Context

Art in a Political World

The Japan that Mishima lived and worked in had little reprieve from political upheavals. As an adolescent, Mishima would have been aware of the NiNi Roku Incident or the February 26th Incident (1936), a violent resistance movement that resulted in numerous deaths including the assassination of three high-ranking government officials when a military faction attempted to resist a large transfer of their group out of Tokyo by officials whom they claimed sought to attenuate the Emperor's power. In 1945, when Mishima was twenty years old, he witnessed the surrender of Japan to the United States which was radio broadcast nationwide by Hirohito on August 15, 1945. Japan was to be occupied by United States military from 1945-1952 and forced to accept an American written Constitution that dictated radical changes in the country's political structure. For one, Japan could no longer have a standing military force, although they were allowed to maintain a "self-defense" army, the *Jieitai*. The previously Emperor-centered government was turned into a western style "democracy" and the Emperor, while being permitted to remain on the throne and given immunity from prosecution as a war criminal, was forced to renounce his rule by divine authority and declare that he was a mere functionary of the state. This announcement, the *ningen singen*, occurred on January 1, 1946 and deeply affected Mishima as he dedicated several of his later works to criticizing the effects of American democracy on Japan and resurrecting absolute loyalty to the Emperor.

Though literary critics debate whether Mishima was primarily a "political" writer or an artist writing for art's sake, the tumultuous political context of his Japan makes it difficult to conceive Mishima as not being influenced by his contempo-

rary environment. In *Confessions of a Mask* he comments that as a young boy he was deeply affected by the sight of soldiers marching by his house gate, titillated by the scent of their sweat, the physical manifestation of their patriotism. His later works, such as the short story "Patriotism" (1966), which dramatizes the NiNi Roku incident and the double *seppeku* of a fictional high-ranking military officer and his wife, and his creation of the *Tatenokai* certainly attest to Mishima's overt political commitment towards the end of his life. But this is not to say that he favored political critique over aesthetic development and exploration. It would probably be more accurate to say that for Mishima the political and the aesthetic were not mutually exclusive domains. Rather, for Mishima political and aesthetic concerns were inextricably intertwined and they emerged in his works in varying proportions at different stages of his personal and literary development.

The Meiji Restoration and the Fall of the Samurai

A descendent of the Tokugawa family, Mishima spent much of his childhood and adult life interested in samurai philosophy and lore. His commitment to reviving Emperor worship may have had less to do with extreme right-wing political beliefs than was a manifestation of his desire to return to the simpler days of feudal Japan where vassals and lords lived under mutual obligation. Mishima's understanding of samurai culture and government was highly romanticized as though he envisioned the members of the rigidly stratified class system as living in "harmony"—the vassals offering unconditional service to the ruling class in exchange for absolute protection—he paid little attention to the oppression and exploitation that the agricultural vassals were subject to under the samurai class's tyrannical military rule.

In 1869 the samurai class was officially removed from power by the newly ascended Meiji government and forbidden to carry swords. In 1853, American Naval officer Matthew Perry coerced Japan to open their trade ports to the West through military force and intimidation. Like in other Asian countries, the infiltration of western social, economic, and political structures resulted in profound economic and social disruptions in Japan. But unlike their Asian neighbors, and witnessing the violent defeat and devastation of these surrounding

Compare & Contrast

- **1868:** Ascendancy of Meiji government, characterized by adoption of western economic, social, and political practices. The Meiji period is traditionally marked as the beginning of Japanese westernization, modernization, and industrialization. Meiji leaders justify this radical social transformation by professing its goals are to ultimately ''out-westernize'' and supersede the west. The samurai class is removed from power and public sword-carrying is outlawed.

  1980s: High-technology ''bullet train'' travel is extended throughout the nation. First constructed in 1967, it is the most sophisticated form of train travel of its kind in the world. American consumer automobile production exceeded by Japanese production.

- **1940s:** U. S. levies economic sanctions on Japan. Surprise attack on U. S.'s Pearl Harbor by Japanese airforce. United States drops atomic bomb on Hiroshima and Nagasaki. Until this day, this is the first and only large-scale deployment of nuclear weapons on civilian populated areas during a war. Allied Occupation of Japan. Japan is forced to adopt a model of western democratic government and an American written Constitution.

  1990s: After the Japanese economy becomes one of the strongest in the world, with the Japanese buying up American properties and companies in the 1980s, their economy begins to falter as their stock market drops.

- **1942:** President F. D. Roosevelt issues Executive Order No. 9066, ordering all American residents of Japanese ancestry to be removed from the United States west coast regardless of American citizenship. They are interned inland in concentration camps to protect against ''espionage'' and ''sabotage'' to ''national-defense material, national-defense premises, and national-defense utilities'' (Executive Order No. 9066 from Roger Daniels, *Prisoners Without Trial* p. 129). A similar order is issued in Canada, removing all Japanese from British Columbia's west coast.

  1976: President Gerald Ford issues Proclamation 4417, subtitle ''An American Promise,'' officially retracting Executive Order 9066 and offering a national apology to Japanese Americans and their families who were interned during World War II. Proclamation states: ''I call upon the American people to affirm with me this American Promise — that we have learned from the tragedy of that long-ago experience forever to treasure liberty and justice for each individual American, and resolve that this kind of action shall never again be repeated'' (Proclamation 4417, from Daniels, p. 133).

  1980s: U. S. House of Representatives votes to pay surviving internees of World War II relocation of Japanese Americans $20,000 in reparations. In 1989, President George Bush signs the 1987 vote on reparations into law.

---

countries, Meiji Japan more willfully adopted western ideas and practices rather than struggle through escalating military conflict. Their aim was to one day supersede the West by ''out-westernizing'' them.

This strategy has made Japan one of the foremost economic powers of the world today, but also resulted in national spiritual and psychological confusion that still resonates. Was Japan its own nation,

or a mere lackey of the West? Citizens were also disturbed by the destruction of traditional values and culture in favor of the adoption of western, moneymaking oriented practices. This confusion redoubled when the terms of surrender in World War II placed Japan under military supervision and regulation by America. Mishima viewed the negative effects of westernization as a direct result of the disenfranchisement of the samurai class and envisioned the revival of samurai philosophy as a salve to what he perceived as the degradation of Japanese culture, tradition, and conservative mores under modernizing, western influences.

Bunburyodo: The Dual Way of Art and Action

Before the Meiji Restoration, the ruling military elite of Japan were the samurai. The collaboration of politics and aesthetics is the central concept of *bunburyodo*, ''the dual way of art and action,'' a samurai ethic that Mishima chose to adhere to as part of his personal philosophy. To enhance their physical fitness and military prowess, the samurai were expected to cultivate literary and artistic interests. Already an artist, Mishima embraced *bunburyodo* by developing himself physically an d training for patriotic ''action.''

Also central to samurai philosophy was the requirement to commit *hara-kiri* or *seppuku*, ritual suicide by disembowelment in the face of dishonor. (*Hara-kiri* and *seppuku* describe the same process but some Japanese dislike the graphic nature of the former term, literally meaning ''belly cut''). When Mishima realized that the Japanese public did not take seriously his call to resurrect Emperor worship and renounce the American written Constitution, he committed suicide in this way, fulfilling the ultimate commitment to samurai philosophy.

bypassed for discussions of ''Three Million Yen,'' ''Patriotism,'' and ''Onnagata.'' ''Swaddling Clothes'' addresses similar themes as the three stories that received more public attention, but does so more subtly. For instance, ''Three Million Yen'' tells the story of a young Japanese couple who desire material luxuries. They seem to carry on a conventional life of a wealth and status conscious couple, but they are actually hiring themselves out for private sex shows in order to make money. ''Onnagata'' addresses the homosexual life of traditional Kabuki performers who play women (the title of the story is the name of the actors of this genre), and ''Patriotism'' recounts the story of an officer embroiled in the NiNi Roku incident and his double *seppuku* with his wife, which is described in gory and painstaking detail. All three stories offer a critique of Japan under the modernizing influence of the west but through sensational and spectacular content, both for the western and Japanese reader. ''Swaddling Clothes'' also provides this kind of critique but without the eye-popping content of suicide, homosexuality, and prostitution. Perhaps the several reviewers indifference to or criticism of the story (Robert Smith in the *Arizona Quarterly*, 1966 calls it ''slight'') is indicative of the modern popular taste for sensational and fantastic stories. Ironically, this is precisely the kind of cultural degradation that Mishima challenges in ''Swaddling Clothes'' and several of the other stories in this collection.

Critical Overview

''Swaddling Clothes'' first appeared in English in 1966 in *Death in Midsummer and Other Stories,* translated by American scholars of Japanese literature Edward Seidensticker, Donald Keene, Ivan Morris and Geoffrey Sargent. The collection includes nine short stories and one modern Noh play. Already internationally renowned, Mishima received much praise in the United States for the collection, particularly for its honest, however unsettling, depictions of modern Japanese life. Robert Trumbull in the May 1, 1966 *New York Times Book Review* praised the stories for their sharp ''sociological study'' and John Wain comments in the May 30, 1966 *Newsweek*: ''His new collection . . . is Mishima at his very best—cool and urbane, mixing East and West, impassively shuffling and relating the feudal past to the consumer present.''

''Swaddling Clothes'' did not receive as much attention as some of the other stories and was often

Criticism

Yoonmee Chang

Yoonmee Chang is a Ph.D. candidate in English and American literature at the University of Pennsylvania. In the following essay, she discusses the gender and class oppression inherent in Mishima's romanticized desire to return to traditional Japanese social and political values in ''Swaddling Clothes.''

''It is neither freedom nor democracy. It is Japan.''

—Yukio Mishima

In the minutes before his suicide, Yukio Mishima concluded his public address to the Japanese ''Self Defense Force,'' or the *Jieitai*, with the following challenge, printed in the 1971 *Japan Interpreter* as ''An Appeal'': ''Is it right to protect life only to let the soul die? What kind of an army is it that has no higher value than life? Right now we will show you

What Do I Read Next?

- *Kamen no Kokuhaku* [*Confessions of a Mask* (1949)] by Yukio Mishima. A widely acclaimed autobiographical novel exploring Mishima's adolescent development and young adulthood. Explores themes of homosexuality, obsession with death, interest in the male physicality of military training, and the eroticism of violence, themes which are only touched upon here but are treated at length and in detail in later works.

- *Kinkakuji* [*Temple of the Golden Pavilion* (1956)] by Yukio Mishima. The exploration of nihilist philosophies through the story of a physically and emotionally handicapped Buddhist monk. The Temple is the central symbol of the degradation of beauty in the rapidly modernizing and western-influenced post-World War II Japan. Rather than see the Temple survive in antagonism to the crass modern world, the protagonist burns the Temple to the ground.

- "Yukoku" ["Patriotism" (1966)] by Yukio Mishima. A fictionalized account of the NiNi Roku Incident (1936), a violent political upheaval instigated by a military faction who believed certain members of the government were trying to weaken the Emperor's absolute power. "Patriotism" focuses on the story of a fictional high-ranking military official who commits *seppuku* in the face of imminent dishonor. Maintaining her loyalty to her husband and the Emperor, the official's wife commits *seppuku* as well.

- *Death in Midsummer and Other Stories* (1966) by Yukio Mishima. An American published collection of short stories including "Patriotism" and "Swaddling Clothes."

- *An Artist of the Floating World* (1986) by Kazuo Ishiguro. An aging artist looks back upon his life as a successful national painter during and in the years leading up to World War II. His success was largely the result of patronage and support by the Imperial government. After the war, the fall of Emperor, and the devastation of national morale and commitment to the Imperial government, the artist reconsiders the terms of his success and personal artistic vision.

- *Remains of the Day* (1988) by Kazuo Ishiguro. Similar in theme to *An Artist of the Floating World* but set in post World War I England. An English butler who has sacrificed his relationships with lovers and family reflects on his lifelong commitment to being a butler of "dignity." He gradually questions his fierce devotion to his job as he realizes he has emotionally wounded the people who love him and begins to understand that the master whom he had served unconditionally was generally regarded as a Nazi sympathizer. Winner of the 1989 Booker Prize.

- *Nisei Daughter* (1953) by Monica Sone. An autobiographical exploration of the experiences of Japanese in America during and in the years leading up to World War II, focusing on the internment of all U. S. residents of Japanese ancestry in concentration camps. As a *nisei,* second-generation Japanese American, Sone and her siblings are born in the U. S. and have U. S. citizenship but are treated like foreigners and outcasts. Despite this discriminatory treatment, male *nisei* are expected to serve in the American army. Sone contrasts the biased treatment against her and her family to the philosophies of democracy and freedom that America supposedly espouses.

- *Obasan* (1981) by Joy Kogawa. As a *nisei* living in Canada, Kogawa narrates her experiences under the Canadian internment of residents of Japanese ancestry during World War II. A more scathing indictment of North American treatment of its minorities, Kogawa relates her story in poignant and painfully recounted patches and fragments.

- *Clay Walls* (1987) by Ronyoung Kim. The story of a group of Korean American immigrants in California, who mostly left their homeland to escape the military rule of Korea by Japan (1910-1945). Offers an interesting comparison to Mishima's patriotic rejection of the United States occupation of Japan after World War II.

that there is a value higher than reverence for life . . . let us rise together even now, and let us die together." The "we" that Mishima speaks of is himself and his ultra-nationalist civilian army, the *Tatenokai*, and the "higher value" that they seek to preserve "is neither freedom nor democracy. It is Japan. Japan, the country whose history and traditions we love."

Mishima's response to his own rhetoric is telling: Japan, or *his* ideal of it, is not equivalent with "freedom" and "democracy." As Mishima became increasingly "political" towards the end of his life, dedicating his literature to overt political critique and involving himself in political "action," for example creating the high-profile and controversial *Tatenokai*, a civilian militia committed to reviving the absolute power of the Emperor, and finally committing *seppuku* in the name of the Emperor, Mishima was shattering in his disdain for western social, political, economic, and intellectual influence on post-World War II Japan. In his tetralogy *The Sea of Fertility* he calls the "West European spirit [Seio seishin]" a "poison" that has not only "denigrated" the noble Japanese spirit, but has "blighted" and "polluted" the natural environment as well, like a factory "operating day and night," excreting a "poisonous discharge." The paradox of Japan after World War II is that despite its unprecedented national reconstruction and emergence as a global economic superpower, this success was only enabled by an adoption of western ideology and practices that were more or less militarily enforced by the careful monitoring of the United States and the regulation of the country under the terms of its surrender. Japan was occupied by the United States military from its surrender to 1952 and forced to adopt a U.S. written Constitution that eradicated the institution of *kokutai*, or divine right of the Emperor, establishing a western model of democratic government where the Emperor served as a mere human figurehead. The new Constitution also prohibited Japan from having an active, offensive military, allowing them only a limited "Self-Defense Force" (the *Jieitai*). Mishima called this post-war period the "age of languid peace," writing an article published in the 1970 *Journal of Social and Political Ideas in Japan* entitled "An Ideology of an Age of Languid Peace." Western involvement and influence in Japan had ushered in economic success and radical modernization of a previously agricultural society, but at what cost?

In his short story "Swaddling Clothes" (1955), Mishima focuses on the personal and public degra-

> " Underpinning the author's romantic desire to return to traditional values is a critical disrespect for women. Both the joke and irrecoverable scandal of the story is the birth of the nurse's illegitimate baby."

dation of morality under western influence and dramatizes a yearning to return to traditional Japanese ethics and values. The tradition that Mishima longed for was rooted in *bushi*, or the samurai warrior spirit that preserved honor and loyalty to the Emperor at the cost of death. Though "Swaddling Clothes" does not specifically invoke *bushi*, implicit in its critique of western imported modernization is Mishima's desire to return to the "simpler" feudal days of the Tokugawa period where vassals and lords lived under "mutual dependency." But the short story does not address the exploitation and oppression of women and the "lower class" sanctioned and even required by the samurai-ruled feudal system. I will analyze "Swaddling Clothes" in this context, foregrounding such problems and inadequacies of the "traditional," samurai-based ethic, problems that Mishima largely ignores in his romantic presentation of *bushi* and Emperor worship.

The introduction of western ideas and practices in Japan pre-dated the nation's surrender in World War II by almost a century. In 1853, American Commodore Matthew Perry forcibly opened Japanese trade ports to the west, and in 1868 the newly ascended Meiji government effectively eradicated the feudal organization of Japanese society in favor of a more western, industrial model, stripping the samurai class of its military and political power and outlawing the public carrying of swords. The Meiji plan was to ultimately supersede the west by "out-westernizing" them, but in the process they precipitated a national spiritual confusion. Having previously adhered to a philosophy of racial and cultural superiority centered around the figure of the divine Emperor (a political and psychological system of organization that some historians and critics liken to the fascist governments of Hitler and Mussolini), the Japanese people were forced to re-evaluate themselves in the Meiji's apparent admission that western practices were superior.

Conservatives and Traditionalists like Mishima challenged this strategy of "out-westernizing" the west, but Mishima took his attack a few steps further. Economic success and the perceived advantages of democracy may be temporarily satisfying, but could never satiate the spiritual needs of a "real" Japanese. According to Mishima, a "real" Japanese was one who lived according to *bushi*, favoring danger, honor, and aggressive military protection of the nation to "languid peace." Mishima blamed western imported democracy for national spiritual humiliation and complacency and believed that "real" Japanese should always be perched for patriotic war. In "An Age of Languid Peace" Mishima writes: "[I]f there is ever to be an ideology which enables the people to live in spiritual satisfaction in an age of languid peace, and if such an ideology is ever to attract the masses of the people, it will not be an ideology based on the kind of pacifism that has been bandied about in this country since the end of World War II. An ideology that is to provide spiritual satisfaction must contain the kind of dangerous allure for which men are willing to die. In the same article he writes: "Democratic freedom may be an effective instrument to cajole the impulse of death into a state of temporary dormancy, but it does not have the power to eradicate it or render it permanently ineffective." The "impulse to death" that Mishima speaks of is embodied by the "warrior spirit" of the previously ruling samurai class, and he believed that the way to expunge Japan of western influences was to return to this indigenous and uniquely Japanese *bushi* ethic, resurrecting an era of honorable spiritual satisfaction led by modern day warriors thirsting to die for their country.

Mishima personally embraced the warrior samurai ethic, particularly *bunburyodo*, the "dual way of art and action," or in the Confucian based Yangming philosophy *chiko goitsu*. Following this ethic, he complemented his politically incendiary literature (art) with steps towards military aggression against the Japanese who supported western style democracy (action). During his lifetime, Mishima embarked on a rigorous physical program of bodybuilding, intensively trained in *kendo* (Japanese fencing), and in 1968 founded the *Tatenokai*, an Emperor worshipping group of modern-day "warriors" geared for fatal action and, as the "incident" of November 25, 1970 attests, even suicide in the

face of the "dishonorable" national adoption of western ideas. Though he trained with the *Jieitai* and maintained a close relationship with its leaders, in his final speech, Mishima reproached the Self-Defense Army for its complacent adherence to the Constitution, which in his eyes amounted to a loss of *bushi*. In "An Appeal," he called the *Jieitai* a "gigantic arsenal without a soul" and castigated, "Has the spirit of the Self-Defense Force completely putrefied? Where has its *bushi* spirit gone?"

Importantly, Mishima viewed westernization and loss of samurai ethics as the "feminization" of Japan. In "An Appeal," his call that the *Jieitai* prove themselves to be samurai-centered "real" Japanese was also a call for them to be "real" *men*. In his essay on *Hagakure*, a samurai literary classic of the Tokugawa period, Mishima deplores this feminization/westernization that began even before the Meiji period with its legal prohibition of sword-carrying—a symbolic, western-induced castration—and that exploded in the post-war era:We are constantly being told of the feminization of Japanese males today—it is inevitably seen as the result of the influence of American democracy, "ladies first," and so forth—but this phenomenon, too, is not unknown in our past. When, breaking away from the rough-and-tumble masculinity of a nation at war, the Tokugawa *bakufu* had securely established its hegemony as a peaceful regime, the feminization of Japanese males immediately began. In this quote, Mishima equates peace, democracy, and westernization with feminization and desires the opposing "masculine" values: war, absolute rule of and loyalty to the Emperor, and return to militarily aggressive samurai ethics. But this quote is revealing less for its agitating political content, than for its implication that the status of "female" is damaging and degrading and should be rejected, abhorred, and reversed to the more desirable "masculine" condition.

A similar "message" is hidden in "Swaddling Clothes." Underpinning the author's romantic desire to return to traditional values is a critical disrespect for women. Both the joke and irrecoverable scandal of the story is the birth of the nurse's illegitimate baby. Toshiko's husband treats the nurse like a crass animal, and describes her as such: "We rushed in and found her squatting on the floor . . . moaning like a cow . . . yelling like a stuck pig." He is also more concerned about his house than the nurse as he nonchalantly remarks: "Well, I didn't waste any time. I rescued our good rug from floor . . . By the time the doctor . . . arrived, the baby had already been born. But our sitting room was a pretty shambles!'' ''The incident'' provides much mirth for his friends who encourage Toshiko's husband's ''flamboyant'' and raucously humorous recount with their ''bursts'' of laughter and mocking guffaws. The nurse is reduced to the butt of the men's joke and Toshiko, as the only woman in the group, is horrified by their insensitivity.

Significantly, the social transgression that the men mockingly disdain the nurse for is a *sexual* transgression. The men laugh at ''the incident,'' but they also consider it inappropriate and scandalous that she had sex outside of marriage. Without questioning the standards on which they base their condemnation, they automatically consider the nurse's involvement in sex outside of marriage as a social transgression and blame and ridicule her for it. The burden of the situation falls on the nurse as a woman, while the father of the baby is not criticized for his role in ''the incident'' and is barely mentioned in the story.

Though Toshiko is more sensitive to and agonized by ''the incident,'' she indirectly supports the men's view that the nurse has committed a social/sexual ''transgression'' and is deserving of blame. As the only character in the story who dedicates thought to ''the incident'' beyond mockery and scorn, Toshiko is the only one who might possibly provide any sensitive and alternative perspective of the nurse's situation. When she rewraps the baby in a clean piece of flannel, replacing the newspaper ''swaddling clothes'' that the also disdainful doctor wrapped him in, Toshiko appears to espouse a more open-minded understanding of the nurse's situation—the conditions of which the reader is never told. But her sympathy is limited. Toshiko may be anguished by the callous treatment of the baby, but she never questions the wholesale condemnation of the nurse for having sex outside of marriage. In fact, she is in accord with her husband and his friends, that the nurse's actions are properly scandalous and reproachable, repeatedly characterizing the situation as ''shameful.''

In addition, Toshiko characterizes the birthing scene as one of violence, remembering it through images of ''bloodstains'' and describing it as a grisly ''scene fit for a butchershop.'' But this is not to say that all female reproduction in ''Swaddling Clothes'' is cast in a negative light. In contrast, Toshiko's own reproduction (she herself has had a son) is implicitly ''pure'' and appropriate because she is married. The implication is that while reproduction within the confines of marriage are sanc-

tioned and not commented upon, births outside of marriage because of their social unconventionality are necessarily violent, grotesque and disruptive. This is emphasized by the representation of Toshiko's pristine baby, involuntarily exposed to the scene, ''scared out of his wits and crying at the top of his lungs,'' as if he is also protesting the nurse's social/sexual ''transgression.''

Most importantly, the nurse is represented as a voiceless, passive character, given no opportunity to defend her situation. Was she raped? Was she deserted by the father of the child? Given no sympathetic personal information about the nurse, the reader is encouraged to agree with Toshiko and her husband's censure of the nurse. In this way, the general structure of the story automatically assumes that sex outside of marriage, regardless of the conditions surrounding the situation, is unquestionably condemnable. Furthermore, while the ''unethical'' nurse and Toshiko's husband, with his ''garish'' American style clothing and ''unhomely'' western style house, both represent a departure from traditional values, only the nurse suffers damaging consequences for her actions. Unlike the nurse, Toshiko's husband does not suffer any scorn or reproach for his acceptance of ''degraded'' western values. To the contrary, he appears to be complacent and successful, ''dashing'' off from one meeting to the next to fulfill the needs of his exciting and successful acting career. In this way, though ''Swaddling Clothes'' laments the loss of traditional values, the burden and the consequences of that loss falls on the women in the story.

Toshiko is also ''punished'' for participating in non-traditional behavior. The impropriety of her as a young, married woman taking a nighttime stroll alone around the Imperial Palace park grounds is vindicated by her assault at the end of the story. As in the case of the nurse, the moral seems to be, ''If only women would adhere to conventional female behavior, no matter how oppressive, they wouldn't suffer.'' This is not to say that Toshiko is a progressive character who desires more freedom for women. In fact, she is the main proponent of returning to tradition and conservatism in the story, as she is the only one who bemoans the modernization and loss of moral values of her husband and the nurse.

As mentioned before, Toshiko unequivocally considers the nurse's situation as ''shameful.'' She also envisions the illegitimate baby's future as hopeless, destined for poverty and crime. She imagines that the baby will grow up to be a ''desolate, hopeless, poverty-stricken . . . lonely rat . . . He'll be wandering through the streets by himself, cursing his father, loathing his mother.'' She can think of no other future for the child as she says ''What else could happen to a baby who has had such a birth?'' According to Toshiko, the nurse's baby has no chance of becoming a ''respectable citizen'' because of external circumstances and unfair social judgments over which he never had control.

By envisioning the future of the illegitimate baby as inflexibly grim and hopeless, Toshiko supports a stratified class system that ranks people not according to ability and merit, but by inheritance and ossified social judgment. Though ''Swaddling Clothes'' laments the loss of Japanese tradition and values, one tradition that has apparently survived is the rigid demarcation of people by class. The basis of the samurai-led feudal system hinges on such class division—everyone knows his or her ''place'' in society and acts accordingly. Members of the ruling class were wont to call this organization ''mutual dependency'' (agricultural vassals provide labor and service to their lords on rented land, while the lords provide unconditional military protection and maintain the well-being of the nation), but from the perspective of vassals, such a system oppressively maintained their poverty and economic dependence and shut out all possibilities for class mobility. Like the nurse's baby, anyone born into ''ignoble'' or low class circumstances, despite any superior ability or philanthropic intention he or she might have, had no opportunity to move beyond this assigned station. By imagining the future of the nurse's baby as an inevitable outgrowth of his ''shameful'' birth and perceiving the violent, criminal homeless youth as an immediate manifestation of the baby in twenty years, Toshiko does not challenge and implicitly accepts the class system that discriminates and judges people along oppressive criteria.

In this way, Toshiko's sympathy for the baby and somewhat ''sensitive'' contemplation of ''the incident'' is incomplete and tinged with insincerity: she only contemplates the degradation of society from an insulated and safe upper-class perspective. Her life has been one of privilege, as she comments about life with her husband: ''their life together was in some way too easy, too painless.'' She is somewhat discomfited by her material ease as she begins the above sentence: ''[S]he leaned back in the seat, oppressed by the knowledge.'' Here again, Toshiko is on the verge of questioning her complacent lifestyle, but her ensuing characterization of the illegitimate baby as ''a lonely rat'' overrides such nascent and partial attempts to contemplate the existing social structure. Finally when the homeless youth attacks her, she is not surprised as the narrator comments: ''She did not feel in the least afraid and made no effort to free herself. In a flash the thought had struck her. Ah, so the twenty years have already gone by!'' In other words, Toshiko more or less expects the violent behavior of the homeless youth towards her as a delicate, young, upper-class woman. In this way, Toshiko reinforces the notion, brought up earlier by the image of the nurse's ''shameful'' grown up child ''savagely stabbing'' her own ''fine, carefully educated'' son, that upper and lower classes are irrevocably divided and their interaction inevitably results in violence.

Mishima himself was born into an upper-class family of government officials and his grandmother was a descendent by marriage of the Tokugawa family. George Brandes likens Mishima to Nietzsche in that he was an ''aristocratic radical'' that is, a member of the social and intellectual elite that prescribed revolutionary philosophy from the safety and comfort of their class privilege. Some critics dismiss Mishima as a dilettante of political philosophy, unconcerned with the actual welfare of the ''masses'' and dispensing revolutionary theory as mere, and misguided, intellectual exercise. The samurai ethic that he sought to revive, supports this analysis of Mishima. Whether or not his chosen political aims were ''serious,'' those aims sustained the oppression of the lower classes. Nietzsche described the masses as ''the inferior species'' and an animalistic ''herd.'' Continuing the comparison to Nietzsche, Roy Starrs writes: ''[Nietzsche] . . . like Mishima . . . felt an instinctive antipathy towards democracy, liberalism, socialism or any other form of 'humanism' which sought to elevate the 'masses' over the elite.'' From this perspective, Mishima's rejection of western imported democracy and ''humanism'' in favor of the dictatorial rule of the divine Emperor under the leadership of the samurai can be seen as a desire to preserve class privilege. Thus, it is not surprising that in ''Swaddling Clothes'' the oppression of still existing class stratification is not challenged, and even reinforced by the protagonist Toshiko.

It is not possible in the scope of this short essay to comprehensively analyze the political implications of Mishima's ''Swaddling Clothes'' or to present rebuttals to the counter-arguments of the perspective that I have offered here. I have merely attempted to point out some of the inadequacies and problems of the Emperor-centered, samurai-led society that Mishima supported, particularly for women and the "lower" class. Mishima remains a controversial figure of Japanese literature. Had it not been for his shocking suicide in 1970, historians and critics might have dismissed him as a daydreaming romantic who was above all an artist, but an unrealistic and ineffective political philosopher. The inadequacies I have pointed out of a *bushi*-centered society support this view. Ironically "the incident" the narrator and Toshiko so deplores in "Swaddling Clothes" is reminiscent of the name given to Mishima's public *seppuku*, dubbed in history as the "Mishima incident." Perhaps Mishima was not as oppressively reactionary as his choice of political philosophy implies. Above all, Mishima wanted political transformation and change, seeking to challenge an existing power structure, though unfortunately choosing a more oppressive alternative. At any rate, both "incidents" shocked their contemporary societies into self-reexamination. In this way, Mishima and the nurse of "Swaddling Clothes" are more similar than he probably ever imagined they could be.

Source: Yoonmee Chang, "An Overview of 'Swaddling Clothes'," in *Short Stories for Students,* The Gale Group, 1999.

Theresa M. Girard

In the folowing essay, Girard analyzes the character of Toshiko in "Swaddling Clothes."

In the story "Swaddling Clothes," Yukio Mishima presents an intriguing picture of how a rich, young mother's obsession over her new baby can lead to violence, destruction, and death. At first glance, "Swaddling Clothes" seems much like Robert J. Smith reported in the *Arizona Quarterly,* in 1966. At that time, Smith called it a "very slight piece," but he also said that it is powerful in its content. Mishima, a modern Japanese writer, has only had one of his twenty volumes of short stories translated into English. Western culture knows Mishima mainly from his thought-provoking novels; however, the collection known as *Death in Midsummer and Other Stories* contains ten stories which promote thoughtful, as well as emotional, responses. "Swaddling Clothes" combines many elements in its quick telling and offers a picture that haunts the reader long after the final word has been read.

The story begins with the third person narrator giving the reader an impression of Toshiko's husband. Toshiko is the protagonist and the story

> What upset Toshiko the most about the situation was that the doctor had so little regard for the baby that instead of wrapping him properly, the doctor wrapped the baby in newspaper, much as one would wrap up the evening's garbage."

revolves around her thoughts, hopes, and fears. Toshiko's husband is a handsome actor and appears to be very busy. As an actor, he is popular and very Westernized. He takes little notice of Toshiko and everything he wears, does, says, and even the way he smokes his cigarettes, points to a man who constantly feeds his own ego. Toshiko is often an afterthought as the narrator points out: "Even tonight he had to dash off to an appointment, leaving her to go home alone by taxi." The narrator continues to raise some doubts about Toshiko and her expectations by calling her "foolish" if she expected her husband to spend time with her.

However, Toshiko is not foolish; she is feeling abandoned by her husband and feeling slightly invisible. As a person of slight stature, Toshiko had felt the admiration of friends and acquaintances, while growing up, because she epitomized how a gentile Japanese woman should look. While pregnant, she attracted much attention for a couple of reasons. For one, it has always been an unspoken rule that a pregnant woman, no matter the culture, is someone to be noticed, fawned over, and smiled over. For another, Toshiko suddenly, for several months, had more girth and weight to her slight frame than she had ever had before in her life. Now that the baby was born, the baby got the attention and she became virtually invisible. The reader is assured of this because the narrator says, "she looked more like a transparent picture than a creature of flesh and blood." Her husband was aware that she was there, but he could look right through her and see only his son and anything that revolved around the baby.

Most of the story takes place in the form of a flashback. Toshiko is riding in a taxi, alone, on her way home. Her husband has sent her home alone while he goes off to a business meeting. It is curious to note that while her husband is the actor in the family, Toshiko is much more dramatic and imaginative. Toshiko's husband, who remains unnamed throughout the story, is shown to be more business-like and more concerned with image than imagination. His home is decorated with Western-style furniture and he wears an American style suit and a "rather garish tweed coat." Toshiko is "shocked" and "dumbfounded" that her husband would discuss and make light of the shameful situation which had happened in their sitting room where their nurse gave birth to an illegitimate baby boy. He even lets his friends know that he was so unobservant that he believed the nurse's belly was huge because of "gastric dilation," rather than pregnancy. Since Toshiko had recently been pregnant, it is reasonable to assume that he should have been able to tell a pregnant woman when he saw one. One can only guess that he might not have been the best of actors because of this inability to empathize with his wife and his insensitivity to the nurse and her giving birth under embarrassing circumstances. He does not appear to be a well-trained student of human nature or the human condition.

Toshiko has the ability to immerse herself in the plight of others. She is more traditionally Japanese, as is the nurse who is able to hide her pregnancy behind her kimono. It is entirely possible that Toshiko's husband could not detect the pregnancy because he had removed himself too far from traditional Japanese values. Toshiko finds his behavior, joking about the birth, horrifying and becomes locked into the loss of face that she, the nurse, and, ultimately, the bastard child have suffered. To her husband, it is an interesting anecdote, but Toshiko cannot help projecting the future outcome.

The reader is never given any insight into what the nurse might have felt or even her reasons for concealing her pregnancy. If Toshiko knows, she does not say. She does continue to picture, with great clarity, the image of the newborn baby boy wrapped in bloodstained newspapers. It is this image which haunts her and drives her actions once her husband sends her home in the taxi. She remembers what had taken place after her husband had left the house. He barely waited until the doctor arrived and then he left, leaving Toshiko to handle the aftermath and to join him later.

What upset Toshiko the most about the situation was that the doctor had so little regard for the baby that instead of wrapping him properly, the doctor wrapped the baby in newspaper, much as one would wrap up the evening's garbage. Toshiko recalls the birth of her own baby, and while she does not tell the readers about it, it can be presumed that she had the best care, as did her infant son. He would have been gently cleaned, wrapped in soft clothes and laid to rest in a proper cradle. The nurse's son was left lying on the wooden floor in bloody paper.

Toshiko did not tell her husband that she wrapped the infant in a clean piece of swaddling for fear that he would berate her and call her a sentimental fool for caring about an illegitimate child when her own child was in the next room. He would want her to only think of how to properly care for her own child and to make sure that the nurse she hired would be suitable. This was not something Toshiko could easily dismiss. She continued to wonder what would happen to the child and how his future would be entwined with that of her own son.

While still at the restaurant, Toshiko recalls that even the new mother had not witnessed the shame of her baby lying on the floor in bloody paper. She even remarks that the baby, himself, would never know unless she told him someday. Dwelling on the negative, she feels that somehow the stigma of this lowly birth will humiliate him and follow him for the remainder of his life, even though he knows nothing about it. She thinks that if she is able to tell him, someday, that she picked him up out of the newspapers and gently wrapped him in proper swaddling and laid him on a soft chair, it might somehow change his life.

As the taxi wends its way through the city, Toshiko sees scraps of paper everywhere. The theater she passes is dotted with phony cherry blossom scraps of paper. When she gets to the Imperial Palace and the park bordering it, she notices the paper lanterns which shed no light. There is only darkness in the water and the sky. The light comes from the multitude of cherry blossoms on the trees, which look little different than the phony cherry blossoms by the theatre. There are also harsh electric light bulbs, in several colors, which cast a strange hue on the whiteness of the cherry blossoms and give an unreal quality.

She is in the park past ten o'clock and trash is strewn everywhere, while most of the people have departed. As she walks through the park, she kicks aside the wastepaper, as others do, and thinks back to the newspaper and the baby. She loses touch with reality as she drifts through her thoughts and projects twenty years into the future. She notices the dark shadows and fears that the illegitimate child will grow up to resent her child's prosperity and privilege. She dramatizes the scenario and places the poor child in a vagabond, uneducated future and feels that child will blame his ignominious birth on his plight. Somehow, she conjectures, he will know that her son was the one who was in the cradle in the next room while he was born on a bare wooden floor and wrapped in bloody paper. In his despair, she pictures him taking revenge on her unsuspecting child.

When Toshiko spies the newspapers spread over the young vagrant on the park bench, she has completely lost herself in her self-imposed role of savior to her child and possible savior to the young bastard. She, in her mind, has traveled the twenty years into the future and sees the same child with bloody, matted hair, wrapped in newspapers. The young vagrant has dirty, matted hair, but she can only reach out to touch him as she felt compelled to touch the newborn and wrap him in proper swaddling. Even in her final moments, Toshiko sees that she has intervened in the whimsy of fate and saved her son by her own sacrifice. She has played her role perfectly and need not be afraid of the consequences.

Source: Theresa M. Girard, ''An Overview of 'Swaddling Clothes','' in *Short Stories for Students,* The Gale Group, 1999.

Kendall Johnson

Kendall Johnson is completing his Ph.D. in literature at the University of Pennsylvania. In the following essay, he considers the sacrificial plight of Toshiko in ''Swaddling Clothes'' by exploring Mishima's focus on newspapers.

At the end of Yukio Mishima's story, the forest of the Imperial Palace stands ''pitch dark and utterly silent'' as Toshiko's ''slender wrist'' is ''seized'' by ''a powerful hand.'' The hand belongs to a man at whom Toshiko attempts to look while he lies sleeping beneath layers of newspaper in the palace park. Although Toshiko seems to be the victim of impending violence—a violence all the more disturbing for not being explicitly mentioned—she neither attempts to free herself from the hand nor ''[feels] in the least afraid.'' Toshiko's equanimity is distressingly ironic, heightening the sense of doomed isolation in her seizure. By staging the assault in the shadows of the Imperial Place, Mishima draws an analogy between a helpless Toshiko and

an embattled past of authentic Japanese culture. While the seizing hand literally belongs to the man sleeping underneath the newspapers, it figuratively represents the historical demands made on Japan in the aftermath of World War II.

Toshiko's disaffection with her life runs parallel to Mishima's critique of the westernization of Japanese culture. He embeds this critique throughout the story, setting up an opposition between the natural and enduring against the artificial and disposable. Central to this opposition are the metaphors of the cherry blossom and the newspaper. Through the newspaper, or *Shinbungami*, Mishima ties together Toshika's sad reflections, his critiques of westernization and his anxiety regarding the continuity of Japanese national identity after the War.

Newspapers are sold to communicate news to people who live in the same community. As Benedict Anderson discusses in *Imagined Communities: Reflections on the Origin and Spread of Nationalism*, national identity is not an *a priori* category but is produced through the work of collective imagination. In order to feel part of a community, an individual must believe that there are others who share their interests, beliefs, points of view, and traditions. This identification of an individual with a community occurs despite the fact that an individual never expects to know, to meet, or even to see everyone who is part of the national community. How, then, is the common ground of national identity established? In addition to public rituals such as elections, holidays and parades, mass media, including television, movies, and newspapers, provides a way of connecting individuals together in a common imaginary space.

To the reader, a newspaper presents stories that are unrelated to each other, skipping among politics, entertainment, and local information. The newspaper collects these unrelated stories and presents them as ''news''—information that is important and which everyone should know. The magic of newspapers is in creating a general feeling of association through a reading process that each individual experiences in isolation. During rush hour in a city, newspapers are bought by individuals who open a pristine, folded copy while sitting next to people on a bus or subway. Instead of talking to one another, people read the newspaper; through a solitary process in which many individuals sporadically participate, people feel connected to their fellow citizens. In this way, newspapers facilitate a process through which individuals can feel as though they

> " Toshiko's disaffection with her life runs parallel to Mishima's critique of the westernization of Japanese culture. He embeds this critique throughout the story, setting up an opposition between the natural and enduring against the artificial and disposable."

share a common ground with other anonymous citizens.

The newspaper also promotes a general feeling that the nation is moving forward. Every day a new paper comes out. Stories are always fresh and tomorrow guarantees a new edition of "news." The date on a newspaper marks a specific moment in a continuous slide into the future. Each edition expects the reader to leave yesterday's headlines behind in lieu of the next set of information. There is a certain optimism to this march of days toward a perpetual tomorrow, an optimism that Mishima regards as unreliable and even deceitful when considering the authentic tradition of national Japanese culture.

While newspapers seem to be everywhere in the story, they are most visible as debased swaddling clothes, trash that floats through the palace park, and blankets for the story's threatening vagabond. Mishima's use of newspapers seems to convey a deep skepticism about the future of Japan. The "news" in 1955 when Mishima's story was published would have entailed the restructuring of Japanese government, society, and culture—in short the entire Japanese nation—after World War II. From 1945 to 1952 Japan was occupied by the United States. During this time, the Empire was replaced with an American-style democracy. The Emperor was forced to abdicate his authority as divine ruler in the *ninen singen*, an announcement

broadcast over the radio and emblazoned on headlines worldwide.

The very form of the newspaper is linked to elements of western influence that Mishima considered to have corrupted an ideal Japan. After the American Naval Commodore Matthew Perry forcibly opened Japanese ports in 1853, Japan dealt with this assault by strategically adopting western social structures. The Meiji government of 1868 forged this policy of westernization, eventually making the samurai ethic obsolete. Fundamental to this reorganization was the introduction of a "reading-system" that, according to Anderson, made the "development of mass literacy through schools and print easy and uncontroversial." Before the push toward mass literacy, people living in separate regions of the country spoke Japanese differently, making communication between regions very difficult. Mass literacy allowed for widespread communication across geographical space, a prerequisite for the development of a westernized national economy.

While mass literacy is seemingly beneficial, Mishima's use of newspapers connotes criticism of the pressure from the west that made such literacy necessary. For Mishima, the newspaper is a sign of compromised and artificial Japanese culture. Not only are newspapers manufactured through the liquidation of living trees, but production of thousands and thousands of copies requires assembly-line coordination of printing, cutting, folding, bundling, and dissemination processes. In Mishima's story, the historical background in which literacy and the newspaper developed tends to make the "news" look more like propaganda that distracts the Japanese people from their true imperial heritage.

In the story, the newspaper concentrates Toshiko's sense of isolation in a modernized world of anonymous taxis and artificial-paper or bulb-lit cherry blossoms. When the doctor wraps the nurse's newborn baby in a newspaper, one imagines not only the visceral image of smeared newspaper ink mixing with the mother's blood but also the enveloping of the child in the news of the country. Toshiko's reflex to swaddle the baby in cotton linen is not merely an issue of comfort but also illustrates her need to keep the hard facts of life from tainting the baby's first few moments. However, the taint of the real world proves indelible. Despite Toshiko's attempt to salvage the baby into the purity of linen, she is haunted by what she regards as his inescapable doom in a world were he can only become "desolate, hopeless, poverty-stricken . . . a lonely rat."

Despite feeling threatened by the nurse's illegitimate child, Toshiko identifies with the baby and eventually with the vagrant in the park. Her cityscape resonates with fear of penetrative violence as "pinpricks of light" project from the "blocks of tall office buildings." Mishima casts Toshiko as a body in pain, echoing the nurse who screams like a "stuck pig" as she gives birth on the floor, and her infant, who lies "on the parquet floor . . . in blood-stained newspapers." Toshiko derives a "certain satisfaction" from her gloomy thoughts as she "[tortures] herself with them without cease." She writhes in mental anguish "on the back seat of the Taxi," "oppressed by the knowledge" that her life with her husband "was in some way too easy, too painless." The odd use of the preposition "on" (people usually are "in" the back seat not "on" it) makes Toshiko into a displayed incarnation of anguish for the reader. As Toshiko contemplates the unforgettable sight of "the baby, wrapped in stained newspaper" in a "scene fit for a butchershop," she moves toward a decision that puts her in harm's way. Her macabre vision of the nurse's son "savagely [stabbing her son] with a knife" foreshadows her own possible fate.

Toshiko's identification with the nurse and her son as well as Toshiko's willingness to substitute herself as a potential victim of the nurse's baby is not based on sound logic. While Toshiko's feelings attest to the rigidity of social class in post-war Japan, they seem hyperbolic, operating as a vehicle through which she can acknowledge her own loneliness. As she is seized without struggle in the palace park, Toshiko becomes the "stuck pig" on Mishima's sacrificial altar. What would the next day's newspaper report about her fate? Her demise is a spectacle for the reader to see and vicariously ponder.

Mishima creates a general sense of doom by probing the isolation Toshiko feels as the wife of a husband who is not a responsible man. Mishima's story vilifies the westernized husband for not paying more attention to his wife. Toshiko's husband personifies compromised Japanese culture, diluted by the encroachment of western products (furniture), attitudes (his flamboyant, callous story-telling), professions (he is an "attractive" actor) and tastes (his "garish" suit and "jazz"). When he puts his wife in a cab to send her home alone, she is left to her "unsettling fancies" which, without her husband's guidance, lead her to the "Abyss of the

Thousand Birds." Mishima implies that Toshiko's seizure is the logical consequence of a delinquent husband who neglects his duty. When Toshiko is finally stranded, she is struck by the thought, "Ah, so twenty years have already gone by!" She stands in for her son, facing the imagined attacker. But the logic of her sacrifice is uncertain. Will the nurse's son actually become the violent threat Toshiko believes he will inevitably be? Are the "soiled newspaper swaddling clothes" really the baby's "symbol of his entire life"? Even if we trust Toshiko's impressions, is her demise in the palace park really a substitute for her son facing the "dirty rat" and being "stabbed again and again"?

These questions illustrate the class biases of Toshiko's sentiments and the inconsistency of Mishima's authentic Japanese culture. Mishima's ideal version of a Japanese past is not without troubling implications. First, in critiquing an optimism for future Japanese identity he relies on a static idea of the past, a frozen image that is as pure as it is inaccessible. The contemporary Japan he targets for is also frozen as characters are able neither to learn from the past nor to communicate with each other. The vagabond's threatening hand is a one-dimensional stereotype, never acknowledging human specificity, complexity or sensitivity. While Toshiko's "unsettling fancies" evoke a more generous past when the poor were provided for by responsible nobility, Toshika's insight into the nurse's illegitimate son and her intuition of doom in the final scene vilifies the poor as inherently violent.

Second, Mishima's idea of a consecrated Japanese culture implies strict limitations on how men and women can act. The samurai warrior ethic builds men into glorified images of action, strength and stoicism but squelches more complex, human emotions. In using Toshiko and the nurse as analogs of cultural purity he neglects developing their individual characters. Women in this story seem to be fundamental victims and prey to the "powerful hand" of history. Mishima's characterization of Toshiko seems to be a "transparent picture" through which he can project his anxiety regarding the state and history of Japanese national identity. He leaves the reader with questions regarding the future state of Japanese culture that might have been more effectively approached through a more flexible opinion regarding the place of women and men in society.

Source: Kendall Johnson, "History Wrapped in Newspapers: The Seizure of Toshiko," in *Short Stories for Students,* The Gale Group, 1999.

Barbara Wolf

In the following essay, Wolf looks at the theme of isolation from a external world that is cruel and unsympathetic in Yukio Mishima's writing.

Death in Midsummer is almost a microcosm of Mishima's whole work, representing most of his major styles except for the polemic and the directly confessional. Together, the stories suggest both where he was broad in his concerns and limited by his obsessions.

Death in Midsummer must be surprising to those familiar with Mishima only through headlines. ["Death in Midsummer,"] which opens the collection, is quite unrelated to nationalism, fascism, homosexuality, or seppuku. Rather, it is an elegy on the death of the innocent, and a study of the psychology of mourning. The main character, Tomoko, is the mother of two young children who are drowned in a commonplace incident at a resort. Mishima's method is one with many affinities but no equivalents. The narration is a controlled Tolstoyan analysis, phase by phase, of his character's evolving perceptions, proceeding to an epiphany that is left as ambiguous as a Zen koan or haiku, and that is therefore utterly *un*-Tolstoyan. There is also something rather like Poe or Dostoevsky in the extraordinary lucidity of the descriptions, coupled with the intense hysteria of the passions described. Yet although the passions are hysterical, the person who suffers them is fundamentally sound, and not at all like a character out of Dostoevsky or Poe. Tomoko's irrational state is simply normal for one in her circumstances.

In "Death in Midsummer," the whole process if mourning is described as an unfolding of ironies and contradictions. Tomoko's grief is both hysterical and normal. Her recovery, which she feels is shameful, is perfectly natural. Her quest for meaning is both inevitable and futile. And to enrich the irony, the narrator places her ordeal in cosmic perspective: the children, who mean so much to their mother, mean nothing to Nature; they are swept away by a chance wave and not a sign is left on ocean, beach, or sky. The grief, the shame, the hunger for meaning, all define Tomoko as human; yet all are as irrational and futile as they are unavoidable. Tomoko's personal loss confronts her with something even more terrible: the void itself. Yet despite the void, as despite her grief, she goes on living, protected from destruction by the limitations of her intelligence, limitations not merely specific to her but essential to the species.

For all their outward diversity, the majority of Mishima's sympathetic characters come down to a type much like Tomoko: an individual entranced by inner conflicts, isolated from an exterior world as unconsciously cruel as it is beautiful. Yet it is the diversity that is more immediately obvious. At first sight, few works would seem less alike than "Death in Midsummer," with its bourgeois setting, chaste tone, and unsophisticated protagonist, and so extravagant a period piece as "The Priest of Shiga Temple and His Love." Yet the latter piece too is ultimately reducible to a series of internal perceptions and riddling contradictions.

The story is told in prose of great elaborateness and beauty. An aged monk of famed sanctity falls in love at first sight with a Grand Concubine from the Heian court. Just as his whole life to that point has represented the renunciation of this world for the next, hers has represented the empty enjoyment of the present:

> The Great Priest was not young enough . . . to believe that this new feeling was simply a trick that his flesh had played on him . . . [She] was nothing other than the present world, which until then had been in repose . . . It was as if he had been standing by the highway . . . with his hands firmly covering his ears, and had watched two great oxcarts rumble past each other. All of a sudden he had removed his hands. . . .

But her response works at cross-purposes to his; as he seeks this world through her, she seeks the next through him. When they finally meet, it is in silence and tears. They feel some enormous event has occurred, but what it is is never made explicit, and no doubt it differs for each character, as it does for each reader. Religion and sensuality are both—and perhaps equally—triumphs of the spirit and follies of the flesh; but above all they are achievements and also deceptions of the imagination. Therefore, Mishima makes the Grand Priest's meeting with his love at once a consummation and an anticlimax, and as solitary an event as his return to his monastic cell.

For in "The Priest and His Love," as in "Death in Midsummer," the great struggles of the characters are not so much internalized as fundamentally internal. The characters live in worlds subjective to the point of isolation. Unable to share either values or feelings, they have nothing to go on but their own impulses and intuitions. Inner states may be set off by something outside the self, like the death of the children or the first glimpse of the Grand Concubine; but from that point on they assume an autonomous life and logic. The *moment* in Mishima tends to have such enormous consequences, because it so often represents a forced awakening from an innocence that is really a kind of unreflecting solipsism. In "Death in Midsummer," Tomoko is literally napping at the moment her children drown; and the Great Priest has figuratively closed his senses to the present world.

Toshiko, heroine of the brief but powerful "Swaddling Clothes," suffers a very similar awakening. When a low-ranking servant in her household unexpectedly gives birth to an illegitimate child, wealthy young Toshiko is shocked into pity and a kind of responsibility. She is aware for the first time of the injustice of the social order, and foresees a time when the despised infant must take revenge against her own pampered baby. This awakening, however, leads to nothing practical. Rather than offering material help, she is impelled toward a masochistic expiation. Deliberately going into the park at night, she invites assault by a young vagrant whom she identifies with the person the newborn outcast must become. Toshiko's sacrifice is both symbolically appropriate and fundamentally hysterical, a psychotic *acting out* rather than a purposeful *act*. Like that of Dostoevsky, and of Tolstoy in his last phase, Mishima's power seems largely a product of his own desperate sincerity, which is of a kind that can find no outlet in the world of action. Such passion creates grand, symbolic gestures, and characters and situations that seem to demand them—in art if not in life.

The incompatibility of emotion and aesthetic beauty is one of the several themes of "Onnagata." The drama critic, Masuyama, is fascinated by the art of the Kabuki female impersonator, Mangiku. Mangiku's femininity is greater than any woman's, just as his theatrical roles are more grandly passionate than life. But his only place is on stage, in that bastard world "born of the illicit union between dream and reality." When Mangiku takes his impersonation out of the theater and into the real world, he immediately disgraces himself and disillusions Masuyama.

With one exception, the rest of the stories in *Death in Midsummer* satirize the contemporary scene. "The Pearl" describes a club of housewives with nothing to do but manipulate each other. "The Three Million Yen" tells how a young married couple saves for middle-class possessions by giving sex shows for audiences like the housewives in "The Pearl." "The Seven Bridges" concerns a group of geishas, whose playful approach to a rite of

" We seek in art, after all, what we cannot have in a sane life: an unfettered expression of our feelings, wishes, fears, impulses, intentions; a direct confrontation with our human condition in all its madness and cruelty, its contradictions and tragic joys."

their profession soon exposes their ugly selfishness. "Thermos Bottles" follows a smug businessman through his discovery that his perfect egoism has made him expendable to everyone. These modern types have neither beauty nor feeling to recommend them. They recognize nothing capable of transcending or ennobling the self, except possibly money.

How different from these, almost another species, are the Lieutenant and Reiko in "Patriotism," as poetically idealized as their foils are satirically denigrated. "Patriotism" is an imaginative reconstruction of an actual double suicide performed by a young married couple trapped in a conflict of loyalties during the insurrection of 1936. The work is, in every sense, "highly wrought," a kind of heroic epic, or even opera, in prose. As charged with splendor and glory, with sensuality and death as *Tristan and Isolde,* it expresses the same striving after transcendence. The young couple's heedless sincerity endows them with the grandeur of figures in legend; or rather, it almost so endows them. But it is one thing to accept heroic gestures from personages at the dawn of history, acting upon archetypal situations, and another to accept them from twentieth-century persons committed to the wrong side of issues. Ironically, "Patriotism" succeeds for most readers only to the extent that Mishima's stylistic genius overbalances the theme he is apparently celebrating.

Every story in *Death in Midsummer* is rich in ironies, but perhaps the supreme irony is that the martyred lovers of ''Patriotism'' are the only truly happy characters in the whole volume. They alone are free from both triviality and alienation. They alone are in communion with each other and with the world. Their acceptance of a transcendent principle endows their emotions with beauty and meaning and permits them to live and die both serenely and intensely. Had they martyred themselves to almost any other ideal, it would be easier for liberal readers to sympathize and understand. For what is being celebrated in ''Patriotism'' is not thirties-style militarism per se, but the self-realizing force of idealism and the bliss of martyrdom. The specific principle is less the cause than the occasion.

Mishima's fiction is fiction, not polemics or propaganda. It is true that a good deal of what he wrote conveys an open or implicit criticism of modern society. True, he traced much of the inauthenticity of modern Japanese society to the rejection of tradition that followed defeat in the Pacific war. It is even true that in his last years he became a spokesman for a kind of right-wing reaction, and ultimately martyred himself for that cause. But it is also true that practically nothing in *Death in Midsummer*, except possibly ''Patriotism,'' reasonably lends itself to a right-wing, or even political, interpretation. And only one story in all ten, ''Onnagata,'' is even remotely concerned with homosexuality. Mishima, of course, did write polemics and confessions, but only on a few occasions did he disguise them as fiction.

That Mishima could conceive no better solution for Japan than to revive its past was less a misfortune for him as an artist than as a man. It so happened that the desperate sincerity, disciplined violence, and paradoxical gentleness of the samurai tradition had affinities with fundamental traits of his own nature: his discipline as artist and athlete, his sadomasochism as a sexual being, his despair as a Japanese, his emotionality as a person. These affinities were destructive to him as a man because they encouraged his tendency to hysteria. But the effect on his work was probably beneficial. Since Mishima universalized his private experience when he wrote, the passions and issues that concerned him personally were rarely allowed to intrude into his fictional universe. Within the limits of his sensibility, he could be an objective and dispassionate artist. Many of his characters do not resemble him at all, but are specimens of types held up for examination. Those in whom he did invest himself are far less likely to share his opinions and habits than his loneliness, his alienation, and his passionate integrity. In other words, the dovetailing of influences that produced hysteria in his life created intensity in his art, just as it did with Tolstoy, Dostoevsky, and Poe.

Mishima died attempting a double impossibility: to inspire Japan to reject the present and return to the past, and to make himself over into a man of the past, a samurai. When so futile a gesture is made in life, it can only appear as madness. But when it occurs in art, as in ''Swaddling Clothes'' or ''The Priest and His Love,'' then it takes on quite another meaning. We seek in art, after all, what we cannot have in a sane life: an unfettered expression of our feelings, wishes, fears, impulses, intentions; a direct confrontation with our human condition in all its madness and cruelty, its contradictions and tragic joys. Mishima declared that he wished to make a poem of his own life. That aspiration is the great romantic quest after the impossible, which in life must always lead to destruction but which is the source of the sublime in art. As an artist, Mishima may have been limited by his own obsessions, but he still gives a great deal of what we go to literature for. Because he kept his own opinions out, his characters and their situations transcend the time and place of their creation. Compared to that accomplishment, the success or failure of the rest of his life must fade into its relative insignificance.

Source: Barbara Wolf, ''Mishima in Microcosm,'' in *The American Scholar,* Vol. 45, Winter, 1975, pp. 848–52.

Sources

Ford, Gerald. ''Proclamation 4417: An American Promise,'' in *Prisoners Without Trial: Japanese Americans in World War II,* Roger Daniels and Eric Foner, eds., New York: Hill and Wang, 1993.

Mishima, Yukio. Excerpts from ''An Appeal,'' ''Tate No Kai,'' ''An Ideology for an Age of Languid Peace,'' and ''Yang-Ming Thought as Revolutionary Philosophy'' in *The Japan Interpreter,* Vol. VII, No. 1, Winter, 1971, pp. 71-87.

Roosevelt, F. D. ''Executive Order No. 9066,'' in *Prisoners Without Trial: Japanese Americans in World War II,* Roger Daniels and Eric Foner, eds., New York: Hill and Wang, 1993.

Smith, Robert J. Review of *Death in Midsummer and Other Stories* in *Arizona Quarterly,* Vol. 50, Winter, 1966, pp. 380-381.

Starrs, Roy. ''The Road to Violent Action,'' in *Deadly Dialectics: Sex, Violence, and Nihilism in the World of Yukio Mishima,* Honolulu: University of Hawaii Press, 1994.

Stokes, Henry Scott. *The Life and Death of Yukio Mishima,* New York: The Noonday Press, 1995.

Trumbell, Robert. "Encounters with Life," review of *Death in Midsummer and Other Stories* in *The New York Times Book Review,* May 1, 1966, p. 441.

Wain, John. "Things Japanese," review of *Death in Midsummer and Other Stories* in *Newsweek,* May 30, 1966, p. 438.

Further Reading

Benedict, Ruth. *The Chrysanthemum and the Sword: Studies in Patterns of Japanese Culture,* Boston: Houghton Mifflin Co., 1946.

A sociological study of Japanese culture concentrating on its dual philosophy of cultural sophistication (the "chrysanthemum") and military prowess (the "sword"). Stokes notes in his biography that Mishima read Benedict's work and praised her for calling attention to the militaristic aspect of Japan rather than focusing exclusively on the delicacy and charm of its culture and traditions as other historians and sociologists conventionally do.

Chan, Sucheng. *Asian Americans: An Interpretive History,* New York: Twayne Publishers, 1982.

A comprehensive and thorough history of Asian migration to North America. Brings to light the poverty and economic disenfranchisement precipitated in Asian countries by western infiltration and forcible opening of trade ports, belying the myth that Asians migrated voluntarily to North America in search of the "American dream." Includes concise chronology of Asian American history and bibliography

Hosoe, Eikoh. *Ba-ra-kei (Ordeal by Roses),* New York: Penguin, 1985.

A luxurious collection of photos and drawings by Hosoe, the bulk of which Mishima posed for during his program of rigorous body-building. Foreword written by Mishima.

Napier, Susan J. *Escape from the Wasteland: Romanticism and Realism in the Fiction of Mishima Yukio and Oe Kenzaburo,* Cambridge: Harvard University Press, 1991.

A sophisticated and detailed critical analysis of Mishima's central works, their literary styles, relationship to the literary movements of Japanese Romanticism and Realism. Compares Mishima to Nobel Prize winner Oe.

Starrs, Roy. *Deadly Dialectics: Sex, Violence, and Nihilism in the World of Yukio Mishima,* Honolulu: University of Hawaii Press, 1994.

A critical-historical analysis of the main themes prevalent in Mishima's works. Explores Mishima's philosophic progression from passive to active nihilism. Includes discussion of major works, links Mishima to 19th century German philosophers, particularly Nietzsche, and discusses his complex personal and literary relationship to the west.

Stokes, Henry Scott. *The Life and Death of Yukio Mishima,* New York: Noonday Press, revised, 1995.

A personalized and intimate biography of Mishima written by a close journalist friend. Recounts Mishima's early childhood through the day of his suicide and summarizes details of Mishima's central literary works. Speculates on Mishima's motivations in forming the *Tatenokai* and staging his *seppuku.* Includes detailed chronology of Mishima's life.

Mishima Cyber Museum at www.vill.yamanakako.yamanashi.jp/ bungaku/mishima/index-e.html

An informative and interesting website dedicated to the life and literary works of Mishima. Managed by the Bungakukan Planning Committee in anticipation of the construction of the Yukio Mishima Museum (Bungakukan) on Lake Yamanakaka to accompany the Takahama Kyoshi and Tokutomi Soho Museums to complete the "Lake Yamanakaka Library Grove Trio." To be completed July, 1999. Includes forum for posting questions and comments about Mishima's life and work.

The Things They Carried

Tim O'Brien

1986

First published in *Esquire* in August, 1986, and later collected in *The Best American Short Stories 1987,* "The Things They Carried" became the lead story in a book of the same name published in 1990 by Viking Penguin. Since Tim O'Brien had already established himself as a literary voice to be reckoned with, this collection of interrelated stories received a great deal of attention. The book quickly established O'Brien as one of the leading figures in Vietnam literature.

Critics and readers alike have paid considerable attention to the question of whether the events in the book are literally true or products of O'Brien's imagination. Though O'Brien has made it clear in interviews that he believes the truth in literature has nothing to do with what actually happened, the similarities between his writing and his experience in Vietnam are striking. When O'Brien published the disturbing and confessional article "The Vietnam in Me" in the *New York Times Magazine* in 1994, he sparked renewed interest in the connections between his life and his writing. His last two novels are set in the United States but still prominently feature the Vietnam veteran's experience.

Author Biography

O'Brien's life resembles many of his protagonists. Born October 2, 1946, and raised in the small town

of Wortington, Minnesota, by his insurance sales-man father and elementary school teacher mother, O'Brien's childhood and adolescence was marked by loneliness and isolation. When he was a student at Macalester College in St. Paul, however, he found a place in the antiwar movement and attended war protests and peace vigils. After graduating with a degree in political science and plans to reform government from the inside, O'Brien was drafted instead. Resisting the impulse to defect to Canada, the twenty-two-year-old O'Brien found himself in the infantry. Despite being awarded the Purple Heart for wounds he received, O'Brien loathed the war and everything about it, but it would become the catalyst and continuing inspiration for his liter-ary career.

O'Brien wrote his first book, the autobiographi-cal series of vignettes *If I Die in a Combat Zone, Box Me Up and Ship Me Home* while a graduate student in government at Harvard University. Since its publication in 1973, O'Brien has been a full-time writer and Vietnam a constant theme. In addition to *The Things They Carried*, the collection of interre-lated stories that was a finalist for the Pulitzer Prize in 1990, O'Brien has published five novels. The most recent, *Tomcat in Love* was published in 1998 after a well-documented period of personal turmoil and artistic burnout. He lives in Cambridge, Massachusetts.

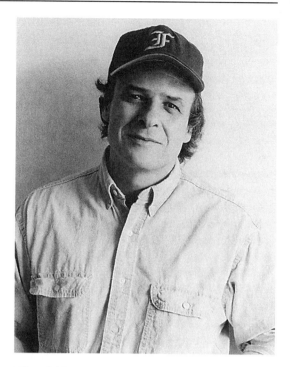

Tim O'Brien

example, the biggest man in the group, carries the M-60 machine gun, "which weighed 23 pounds unloaded, but which was almost always loaded." He also "carried his girlfriend's pantyhose wrapped around his neck as a comforter."

Plot Summary

"The Things They Carried" recounts the experi-ences of Lieutenant Jimmy Cross's infantry unit leading up to and following the death of one of the men, Ted Lavender, on April 16. A third-person narrator describes the individual soldiers by the items that they carry with them.

Lt. Jimmy Cross, the main character and pla-toon leader, carries the letters he receives from Martha, a sophomore English major at St. Sebastian's College in New Jersey. He uses the letters, photo-graphs, and the small stone she has sent him as a way of connecting to the world outside of Vietnam. Though he is distracted and dreamy, he also carries "the responsibility for the lives of his men."

The other men in the platoon carry personal effects and good luck charms. The also share the burdens of combat, distributing the necessary equip-ment and weapons among them. Henry Dobbins, for

Lt. Jimmy Cross's platoon's mission in mid-April is to locate and destroy the tunnels in the Than Khe area south of Chu Lai that the Viet Cong used to hide in. Because they are required to search the tunnels before blowing them up, they draw numbers to see who will perform the dangerous and claustro-phobic task of crawling through the enemy's tun-nels. Lee Strunk draws the unlucky number, crawls down the opening and the rest of the men settle in to wait and hope. As hard as he tries to concentrate on Strunk and the tunnel, Cross can think only of Martha, imagining the two of them together "under the white sand at the Jersey shore." Strunk finally emerges, "filthy but alive," but "right then Ted Lavender is shot in the head on his way back from peeing."

The men put Ted Lavender's body on the chopper and take up their burdens once again. The first thing they do is march to the village of Than Khe and burn everything. Finally, after they stop marching for the night they begin to try to come to terms with Ted Lavender's death. Like the physical objects they carry, the men distribute the burden of Lavender's death both individually and collectively.

Kiowa wants to talk about Lavender's death, wants an audience for his memory of the event. Bowker wants to be left alone and not say a word about it. Lt. Cross weeps and digs furiously at his foxhole. He feels guilty "because he loved Martha more than his men, and as a consequence Lavender was now dead." He knows that this shame "is something he would have to carry like a stone in his stomach for the rest of the war."

The next morning Lt. Cross burns all his letters from Martha as well as the photographs of her, realizing that "it was only a gesture." In the aftermath of Lavender's death, Cross vows to give up the daydreams and focus on his job as soldier and platoon leader, "determined to perform his duties firmly and without negligence." He believes that this is only possible if he "would dispense with love."

Characters

Norman Bowker

The member of the platoon who is described as "gentle," Bowker carries a diary with him. The other unusual thing that he carries is a thumb from the body of a dead Viet Cong boy.

Jimmy Cross

Lieutenant Cross is the main character of the story and the one whose inner thoughts the narrator most often presents to the reader. He is more educated than the rest of his men but seems reluctant to assume the burdens of leadership. He carries photographs, letters, and a pebble given to him by Martha, a college girl he knows back in New Jersey and with whom he believes himself to be in love.

Henry Dobbins

The biggest man in the platoon, Dobbins carries the heaviest physical load, the M-60 machine gun. Because of his size, however, he is exempt from taking his turn crawling in the enemy's tunnels. He carries canned peaches and other extra rations on patrol.

Dave Jensen

David Jensen "practiced field hygiene" and therefore carried dental floss, "night-sight vitamins high in carotene," and foot powder. He also brings soap stolen from a hotel in Australia where he had been for rest and relaxation, and a rabbit's foot.

Rat Kiley

The medic for the platoon, Kiley carries all the necessary supplies for practicing emergency field medicine as well as some unconventional ones such as comic books, M & M candy, and brandy.

Kiowa

An Indian from Oklahoma, Kiowa is a devout Baptist and travels with the New Testament his father gave him. He also carries "his grandmother's distrust of the white man," a pair of moccasins, and a feathered hatchet.

Ted Lavender

Because he is scared Lavender always carries tranquilizers and "six or seven ounces of premium dope, which for him was a necessity." He is shot and killed while the platoon waits for Lee Strunk to emerge from the tunnels.

Martha

Martha is a junior at St. Sebastian's College in New Jersey. Before Lieutenant Cross was shipped to Vietnam she formed at least a superficial relationship with him, but her letters are more friendly than romantic.

Mitchell Sanders

The radio operator for the platoon, Sanders has the responsibility of calling for the chopper to pick up Lavender's body. He gave Bowker the amputated thumb from the corpse of the dead Viet Cong boy.

Lee Strunk

Introduced late in the story, Strunk draws the unlucky number seventeen and has to inspect the tunnels at Than Khe. Among the personal items that he chooses to carry are a slingshot and tanning lotion.

Themes

War and Love

Readers might expect the story to articulate the tension between war and peace, but O'Brien's point in this story and in his other writings is that the real connection is between war and love. Lt. Cross believes, for example, that because he loves Martha, he does not fulfill his duty toward his men. He literally thinks that because he chose love over war, Ted Lavender is dead. O'Brien believes, however, that love comes with the territory of war. In an article for the *New York Times Magazine* in 1994 he explains: ''Intimacy with death carries with it a corresponding new intimacy with life. Jokes are funnier, green is greener. You love the musty morning air. You love the miracle of your own enduring capacity for love.''

According to O'Brien, however, love is also what drove him to Vietnam. In the same article he confesses: ''I have done bad things for love, bad things to stay loved.'' Describing his reaction to being drafted he writes: ''I thought about Canada. I thought about jail. But in the end I could not bear the prospect of rejection: by my family, my country, my friends, my hometown. I would risk conscience and rectitude before risking the loss of love.''

The Individual and the Collective

One of the central themes of all war narratives, and particularly Vietnam war literature, is the dynamic between the individual soldier and the unit, or collective, of which he or she is a part. The object of military training is to meld individuals into a functioning group, a platoon, by instilling in them both fierce loyalty to and dependence upon the others. Properly trained soldiers know that their lives depend on the actions of others, and at the

Media Adaptations

- ''The Things They Carried''was recorded in an abridged version with music added in 1991. It is narrated by Anthony Heald and is available from Harper Audio.

same time they are also willing to risk their own lives for the sake of the rest. In ''The Things They Carried'' the members of Lt. Cross's platoon act collectively in several ways. They share the burdens of carrying necessary equipment and draw lots to see whose turn it is to search the tunnels.

Collective action during wartime has a dark side, however. The official language of war uses collective nouns like troops, in order to disguise the involvement of individual bodies. For example, news that Alpha Company suffered ''one casualty'' is more palatable than news that Ted Lavender is dead, shot in the head on the way back from peeing. O'Brien's narrative explicitly engages this theme by contrasting the plurality of the platoon with the singularity of the men. In other words, they are all legs and grunts and they all must carry heavy burdens as well as each other, but in the privacy of their thoughts and the inner sections of their backpacks and pockets they are singular men with hometowns and girlfriends and fathers and mothers.

Storytelling: Fact or Fiction

Like most of the literature of the Vietnam war, ''The Things They Carried'' is shaped by the personal combat experience of the author. O'Brien is adamant, however, that the fiction not be mistaken for factual accounts of events. In an interview with Michael Coffey of *Publishers Weekly* soon after the book was published, O'Brien claims: ''My own experience has virtually nothing to do with the content of the book.'' Indeed the title page of the book announces it as ''a work of fiction.'' The book is dedicated, however, ''to the men of Alpha Com-

U. S. Marines in full camoflauged gear on patrol.

pany, and in particular to Jimmy Cross, Norman Bowker, Rat Kiley, Mitchell Sanders, Henry Dobbins, and Kiowa.'' O'Brien himself was in infantryman in Alpha Company and was stationed in the Quang Ngai province in 1969-70. When asked about this device in an interview with Martin Narparsteck in *Contemporary Literature*, O'Brien explains: ''What I'm saying is that even with that nonfiction-sounding element in the story, everything in the story is fiction, beginning to end. To classify different elements of the story as fact or fiction seems to me artificial. Literature should be looked at not for its literal truths but for its emotional qualities. What

matters in literature, I think, are the pretty simple things—whether it moves me or not, whether it feels true. The actual literal truth should be superfluous.''

Clearly O'Brien wants readers to wrestle with the distinctions between fact and fiction. What matters for him, as he explained at a conference on the literature of the Vietnam War, is the ''power of stories, whether they're true, or embellished, and exaggerated, or utterly made up. A good story has a power . . . that transcends the question of factuality or actuality.'' In the beginning of the last story in *The Things They Carried,* O'Brien reveals the reasons why he tells these tales: ''Stories can save us.''

Offering a fuller explanation in an interview with *Publishers Weekly,* O'Brien says, "If there is a theme to the whole book it has to do with the fact that stories can save our lives."

Style

Point of View and Narration

The identity of the narrator in all the stories in *The Things They Carried* is of interest to critics and readers. In the title story, the narrator is unidentified, but in other stories he is a "fictional character named Tim O'Brien," explains the author, Tim O'Brien. The third person narrator in "The Things They Carried" is unnamed, but since the stories are interrelated, he may be the fictional Tim O'Brien. The narrator's job in this story is to describe the soldiers and the things that happen to them in the Quang Ngai province, particularly on and around the day that Ted Lavender dies. The narrator is technically omniscient, or all-knowing, since he is privy to the interior thoughts and feelings of the characters, especially Lt. Jimmy Cross. But O'Brien's narrator also behaves like a limited third-person narrator in that he only reveals partial, fragmented, or incomplete information about the characters and events of the story.

Realism

One of the stylistic features of O'Brien's story is its precise rendering of the physical realities of war. This style falls under the general literary category known as realism, one of the most elastic terms critics have to work with. The term applies both to the method of accurately describing the details of ordinary life as well as a general attitude, or philosophy, that favors confronting the realities of life instead of escaping or idealizing them. An example of realism in both senses is the way O'Brien portrays Ted Lavender's death. He includes considerable and precise detail (how much and what he was carrying, and that he had not even zipped up his pants, for example). O'Brien also goes to great lengths to characterize Lavender's death as a random and stupid accident, not as a heroic act.

Because realism is such a large term, it includes several varieties. The two variants of realism most often associated with O'Brien's work are hyper-realism and magic realism. The story can be considered hyper-realism because O'Brien draws attention to the minutiae of the soldiers' lives in Viet-

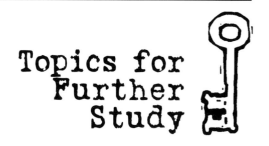

Topics for Further Study

- Read a story describing the American soldier's experience in another war. How is the Vietnam War narrative different, if at all, in form and content?

- Do some research on the phase of the Vietnam War that was called "Vietnamization" by American policy makers. How would these political and military decisions affect the mission and attitude of infantrymen like those in "The Things They Carried"?

- What is the nature of relations between Vietnam and the United States today? How do the Vietnamese people feel about Americans, and what do Vietnam veterans think about Vietnam and its people? You may want to start by looking at Tim O'Brien's 1994 article in the *New York Times Magazine.*

- Why did returning veterans from Vietnam have so much difficulty reintegrating into American society? How has the public's attitude changed since the end of the war and why? Consider such factors as increased awareness of post traumatic stress syndrome and the building of the memorial in Washington.

nam, lingering over details smaller than an ordinary observer could perceive. The story also contains elements of magic realism. Magic realism is a kind of modern fiction that weaves fantastic or imaginary elements into a narrative that otherwise has all the features of an objective realistic account.

Historical Context

The War in Vietnam

Historians often refer to the Vietnam War as America's longest war because it can be dated from President Harry Truman's commitment of $15 mil-

Compare & Contrast

- **1960s:** All young men are required to register for the selective service and face being drafted into the armed forces to serve in Vietnam. While some young men of wealth and privilege escape the draft by enrolling in college, other objectors who are less fortunate flee to Canada to avoid service, or openly defy the draft and face criminal charges. Former heavy weight champion Muhammad Ali, then Cassius Clay, is among those conscientious objectors who choose jail over military service.

  1990s: Though all young men are still required to register with the selective service when they turn eighteen, the United States armed forces have been strictly voluntary since Nixon ended the draft in 1972.

- **1960s:** With the Cold War at its peak, America's foreign policy is aimed at stopping the spread of communism in every far-flung corner of the world. Military and political leaders use the domino theory to justify the enormous financial and human costs of involvement in Vietnam.

  1990s: With the Cold War finally thawed and the break-up of the once formidable communist foe, the Soviet Union, American citizens and their leaders are more reluctant to become involved in foreign wars in developing nations.

- **1960s:** Beyond the exotic sounding names they read about in newspapers or see on television, Americans know nothing of Vietnamese culture. Even major U.S. cities have few if any Vietnamese restaurants.

  1990s: Due to the influx of the so-called "boat people" in the 1970s, and the constant stream of immigration since, Vietnamese culture has made a permanent impact on America.

---

lion to aid the French forces in Indochina in 1950 to the fall of Saigon in 1975. The reasons the U.S. became involved in Vietnam are complex. Briefly, American policy makers beginning with the Truman administration believed that the spread of Chinese Communism in Southeast Asia threatened the world balance of power as construed by the cold war. The so-called "domino theory" held that the entire region would "fall" to communism if the U.S. did not support South Vietnam against incursions from the north.

For several years the U.S. aided the south Vietnamese with technology, material, and military advisors. Intensive American involvement in Vietnam began in 1965 when President Lyndon Johnson sent U.S. Marines to defend Danang airfield. More than 15,000 American military advisors were already in Vietnam. By the beginning of 1968, there were nearly a half million American troops in Vietnam, and bombing raids were heavy and frequent. Communist troops altered the course of the war early in 1968 when they launched a series of attacks on the eve of Tet, the Asian New Year holidays. Americans knew then that victory would come neither soon nor easily.

The years 1969-70, when "The Things They Carried" is set, mark the phase of the war called "Vietnamization." In 1969, President Nixon began secretly bombing Cambodia, a strategy that inflamed anti-war protesters in the United States. American troops were steadily withdrawn while heavy bombing continued. Frustrations with the war escalated both at home and among the troops themselves. Though it was not revealed until a year later, in March of 1968 American troops burned the village of Mylai to the ground and killed "everything that breathed." In the words of journalist and author Stanley Karnow: "In human terms at least, the war in Vietnam was a war that nobody won—a struggle between victims. Its origins complex, its lessons disputed, its legacy still to be assessed by future generations. But whether a valid venture or a misguided endeavor, it was a tragedy of epic dimensions.''

The War at Home

The years 1968 and 1970 were especially turbulent on the domestic front. As opposition to the war grew, protests became larger and more highly charged. In response to the threat of violence, authorities increased police presence on college campuses and at demonstrations. Within two months in the spring of 1968, both Martin Luther King, Jr., and Robert F. Kennedy were assassinated. There were riots and arrests outside the Democratic convention in Chicago. Television viewers watched as heavy-handed police and national guardsmen beat and tear-gassed protesters.

Early in 1969, Nixon began withdrawing troops but also began secretly bombing Cambodia. Massive anti-war demonstrations took place in Washington in October and November. Also in November, Americans were shocked by the revelation of the massacre at Mylai. By 1970 the antiwar movement had spread cross the country and clashes between protesters and law enforcement were more frequent and highly-charged. In May, national guardsmen killed four students protesting the war at Kent State University in Kent, Ohio.

By 1970, as Stanley Karnow explains, resistance to the war at home began to affect the troops in the field. ''Antiwar protests at home had by now spread to the men in the field, many of whom wore peace symbols and refused to go into combat. Race relations, which were good when blacks and whites had earlier shared a sense of purpose, became increasingly brittle.'' Similarly, the image of the American GI began to suffer in the eye of the American public as more tales of brutality and drug use emerged from the battlefield

Aided to a great extent by the erection of the Vietnam Memorial in Washington and a greater public understanding of the causes and symptoms of post-traumatic stress disorder, the image of the Vietnam veteran has improved in the past twenty years. In the 1970s, however, returning soldiers faced unprecedented difficulties reintegrating into their communities and families. Veteran John Kerry, later elected to the U.S. Senate from Massachusetts, recalls his own experience on a cross country flight: ''I fell asleep and woke up yelling, probably a nightmare. The other passengers moved away from me—a reaction I noticed more and more in the months ahead. The country didn't give a shit about the guys coming back, or what they'd gone through. The feeling toward them was 'Stay away—don't contaminate us with whatever you've brought back from Vietnam.'''

Critical Overview

Tim O'Brien made something of a splash in the literary world when his *Going After Cacciato* beat two much more high-profile books by John Cheever and John Irving to win the National Book Award in 1979. *The Things They Carried* more than lived up to the expectations of the critics when it appeared in 1990. Though reviewers debated whether the book was a novel or a collection of stories, there was little disagreement that it was an important and accomplished work.

Michael Coffey of *Publishers Weekly* interviewed O'Brien and previewed the book a few weeks prior to its publication. Coffey insists that the book is ''neither a collection of stories nor a novel [. . .] but a unified narrative, with chapters that stand perfectly on their own (many were award-winning stories) but which together render deeper continuities of character and thought.'' Coffey also predicts that *The Things They Carried* ''may be the masterwork'' that O'Brien's earlier books suggested he was capable of.

When Robert Harris reviewed the book for *New York Times* in March, 1990, he called the book a ''collection of interrelated stories.'' More importantly, however, Harris also claimed that *The Things They Carried* belonged ''on the short list of essential fiction about Vietnam,'' and ''high up on the list of best fiction about any war.'' Harris puzzles a little over O'Brien's blurring of fact and fiction in his use of a narrator also named Tim O'Brien, but concludes that the author ''cuts to the heart of writing about war. And by subjecting his memory and imagination to such harsh scrutiny, he seems to have reached a reconciliation, to have made his peace—or to have made up his peace.''

O'Brien's reputation has continued to grow in literary circles. Two full-length studies and several critical articles on his work have been published in the 1990s. Martin Naparsteck in *Contemporary Literature* calls O'Brien ''the best of a talented group of Vietnam veterans who have devoted much of their writing to their war experiences,'' and suggests that *The Things They Carried* will soon surpass O'Brien's *Going After Cacciato* as the best work of fiction to come out of the war. Writing in *Critique: Studies in Contemporary Fiction,* Maria S. Bonn praises the "elaborate interlocking pattern of truth and fiction" in *The Things They Carried.*

More recently, O'Brien generated considerable interest in his work and his personal experience when he accepted an assignment from *New York Times* to return to Vietnam in 1994 and write about it. The article called "The Vietnam in Me" renewed interest in *The Things They Carried* because it described O'Brien's real-life experiences in the Quang Ngai province as a member of the 46th Infantry. The *New York Times* article also stirred interest in O'Brien's fictionalized accounts of his Vietnam experience because in it he confessed his own suicidal thoughts as he wrestled with the memories of the war, a divorce, and the break-up of another relationship. O'Brien received quite a bit of attention for this bit of self-revelation and in a 1998 interview with *New York Times* writer Bruce Weber, he explains: "I'm glad I wrote it, but I wish I hadn't published it.[. . .] It's a perceptive piece, about the inner penetration of love and war, and eerie uncanny similarities between the two. But it hurt people I love, and probably me too, a little. Though it saved my life, in one way."

Criticism

Elisabeth Piedmont-Marton

Elisabeth Piedmont-Marton has a Ph.D. in American literature. In this essay she discusses the blending of the real and unreal, the tangible and the imaginative, in "The Things They Carried."

The title story of *The Things They Carried,* which O'Brien himself describes as "sort of a half novel, half group of stories," dramatizes the lives of foot soldiers in Vietnam during the later years of the war. O'Brien characterizes them as "legs," or "grunts," as those who carry burdens both literal and figurative: from photographs and tranquilizers to shame and responsibility. The story, like the lives of the men in Lt. Cross's platoon, depends on a delicate balance, upon "poise," to use O'Brien's term. Walking a blurred line between fact and fiction, the story requires readers to balance the physical and the metaphysical worlds as well and challenges their definitions of reality.

The narrator guides readers throughout the story, sometimes just describing and enumerating the soldiers' world, and sometimes departing from the path of realism to dwell in the soldiers' imaginations. The narrator carries the burdens of the men's stories and implicitly asks readers to take them up as well. As critic Thomas Myers writes in *Walking Point: American Narratives of Vietnam*: "The soldier's own testimony was a story waiting for a storyteller, a tale whose ultimate message would reside in its tone and style as much as its content. If the Vietnam War was a dark monument to the powers of American imagination, so would imagination be the most necessary tool for its faithful recording." Because the particular qualities of the Vietnam war experience "defied conventional attempts to record it," in Myers's words, O'Brien, like other writers of the war, must find forms outside "the well-worn contours and conventions of the traditional war [narrative]," Myers continues. One of the new techniques O'Brien employs is to describe the grunt's experience not in terms of *how* he carries on, but simply in terms of *what* he carries. For example, because Jimmy Cross outranks the others, his "humping" duties are lighter: "a compass, maps, code books, binoculars, and a .45 caliber pistol that weighted 2.9 pounds fully loaded." Compared to machine-gunner Henry Dobbins, he gets off easy. Lt. Cross, however, also carries "the responsibility of the lives of his men." Ted Lavender, the narrator notes, "went down under an exceptional burden" when he was shot and killed. After listing all the heavy objects that Lavender carried, the "more than twenty pounds of ammunition, plus the flak jacket and helmet and rations and water and toilet paper and tranquilizers," O'Brien adds one more item, even heavier than all that precedes it because it lacks a specific weight and therefore is infinitely heavy—"the unweighed fear." Readers apprehend the weight of fear because its intangibility contrasts with the specified and quantified weights of his other burdens.

The soldiers in Lt. Cross's platoon *are* what they carry. They are grunts because they carry ammunition and flares and water and rations and guns. The things they carry also holds the group together. Each man depends upon the other to share the load. But they are also defined as men, differentiated from the group because of the things they carry. The objects that comfort them individually may also alienate them from the others. Rat Kiley, for example, as medic must carry all the necessary supplies, but he also carries M&Ms "for especially

What Do I Read Next?

- *Vietnam: A History* (1983) by Stanley Karnow. This lengthy and exhaustive account is still the benchmark and is a surprisingly readable piece of scholarship.

- *Dispatches* (1977) by Michael Herr is one of the centerpieces in the journalist and personal narrative genre of Vietnam writing. Unflinching and realistic, it was one of the first books of its kind.

- *A Rumor of War* (1977) by Philip Caputo is often mentioned in the same breath with Herr's *Dispatches*. This dark narrative pays particular attention to the way individual soldiers functioned as groups in the war.

- *In Country* (1985) by Bobbie Ann Mason is a novel about the effects of the Vietnam War on those who remain at home.

- *Shallow Graves: Two Women and Vietnam* (1986) by Wendy Larsen Wilder and Tran Thi Nga is a collection or sequence of poems written by the wife of an American journalist and a former employee in the magazine's Saigon office. Using alternating sections the book offers a startling and moving picture of the war.

- Robert Olen Butler's Pulitzer Prize-winning collection *A Good Scent from a Strange Mountain* (1992) addresses the Vietnam War and its aftermath from a variety of narrative perspectives.

- *Going After Cacciato* (1978) is Tim O'Brien's award-winning novel about an infantryman who decides to walk from Vietnam to Paris for the peace talks.

---

bad wounds.'' His intimate knowledge of death—that sometimes candy is the only comfort in a dying man's final minutes—separates him from the men who hope and pray that they never ask for the M&Ms. Ted Lavender's heaviest burden, his crippling fear, is a burden he shares with the others, but his means of coping with that fear, his tranquilizers and ''six or seven ounces of premium dope,'' set him apart. Carrying drugs would certainly not make Ted Lavender exceptional in Vietnam, but his dependence upon the drugs makes his fear visible and that is what distances him from the others. All of them ''carried the common secret of cowardice barely restrained, the instinct to run or freeze or hide.'' Ted Lavender makes his own fear, and therefore everyone's fear, visible. The most poignant example is Lt. Cross himself, whose love for Martha pulls him away from Vietnam on imaginative flights: ''Kneeling, watching the hole, he tried to concentrate on Lee Strunk and the war, all the dangers, but his love was too much for him, he felt paralyzed, he wanted to sleep inside her lungs and breathe her blood and he smothered.'' After Lt. Cross blames himself for Lavender's death and

burns the letters and photographs from Martha, he realizes ''you couldn't burn the blame.'' His alienation from the group now derives from his understanding that ''you could die of carelessness and gross stupidity,'' and that he is responsible for the others. He experiences this choice between Martha and his duty as a loss: ''It was very sad, he thought. The things men carried inside. The things men did or felt they had to do.'' In other words, the things they carry on their bodies creates the illusion of unity and collaboration, but the fragile collective is always compromised by the things they carry inside and by the meanings and emotions attached to the smallest and most private of artifacts.

One of the most effective techniques O'Brien uses in ''The Things They Carried'' is to juxtapose the physical and the metaphysical burdens, the real and imaginative experiences of the men of Alpha Company. Vietnam literature has sought to move away from the heroic, or romanticizing, war narratives of the past. This has resulted in a literature that privileges gritty realism and attempts to describe the intimate details of the material and bodily condi-

> "The soldiers in Lt. Cross's platoon <u>are</u> what they carry. They are grunts because they carry ammunition and flares and water and rations and guns. The things they carry also holds the group together. Each man depends upon the other to share the load."

tions of the soldier's lives. Since the very nature of their efforts seem to have no objective and no meaning, they defy conventional narrative. The men of Alpha Company are engaged in ''an endless march, village to village, without purpose, nothing won or lost. They marched for the sake of the march.'' The soldier's experience in O'Brien's fiction is intensely physical, often reducing the men to mere bodies. For them, ''the war was entirely a matter of posture and carriage, the hump was everything, a kind of emptiness, a dullness of desire and intellect and conscience and hope and human sensibility.'' Paradoxically, however, the intense physicality of the soldier's existence engenders the dreamlike states that Lt. Cross is susceptible to and that characterize the story as a whole.

By describing the things the soldiers carried as a mixture of the mundane and the metaphorical, O'Brien creates a dizzying sense of unreality: ''They shared the weight of memory. They took up what others could no longer bear. Often they carried each other, the wounded or weak. They carried infections.'' After O'Brien lists some of the ordinary items that the soldiers carried, ''chess sets, basketballs, Vietnamese-English dictionaries,'' he wrenches the reader beyond the tangible world: ''They carried the sky. The whole atmosphere, they carried it, the humidity, the monsoons, the stink of fungus and decay, all of it, they carried gravity.'' In what Myers describes as ''the feel of the worst dream becoming real,'' the soldiers' world has become inverted and the sky rests on their shoulders and even gravity needs help.

When the weight of their burdens, both concrete and psychic, become too much for them, Lt. Cross and the other men take off on imaginative flights. Because real escape is impossible, the only alternative is imagination, and in this story they dream of ''freedom birds,'' of becoming the thing carried instead the grunt. Literally, freedom birds are the planes that take a soldier out of the country, either at the end of his one year tour of duty or to the temporary relief of the hospital or some rest and relaxation. But like the things the men carry, the bird itself is both real and unreal: ''it was more than a plane, it was a real bird, a big sleek silver bird with feathers and talons and high screeching.'' The soldiers dream of having ''nothing to bear,'' of inhabiting ''the vast, silent vacuum where there were no burdens and where everything weighed exactly nothing.'' O'Brien's language specifically invokes the image of putting aside burdens, of weightlessness: ''at night, not quite dreaming, they gave themselves over to lightness, they were carried, they were purely borne.'' Of course, O'Brien also means to suggest that the men dream of being ''born'' as well, of being delivered and returned to innocence.

In the end, Lt. Cross is not carried away to a world without gravity; he still has the burden of his responsibility to his men as well as the weight of grief and shame from Lavender's death. He decides to do the only thing that he can: repack and shift the weight so that it will be more bearable. After he burns Martha's letters and photographs he vows ''to do what they had always done,'' but this time with ''no more fantasies.'' In the same way that they often discarded in the field what they no longer needed, Lt. Cross swears to ''dispense with love,'' to put it aside as an unnecessary burden.

Source: Elisabeth Piedmont-Marton, ''An Overview of 'The Things They Carried','' in *Short Stories for Students,* The Gale Group, 1999.

Rena Korb

Korb has a master's degree in English literature and creative writing and has written for a wide variety of educational publishers. In the following essay, she discusses the physical and emotional weight of the Vietnam War on a group of soldiers.

Tim O'Brien first emerged on the literary scene with his starkly moving portrayals of men involved in the Vietnam War. When his award-winning novel *Going After Cacciato* was published, John Updike wrote that O'Brien was ''reaching for a masterpiece.'' *The Things They Carried,* an intense, heart-

felt, moving experience of the war, published almost a decade later, may well be that masterpiece.
At first critics did not know how to view *The Things
They Carried*—as a collection of short stories or a
novel? Neither, says O'Brien, who prefers to look at
it simply as a work of fiction. In truth, it stands as a
unified narrative, made up of chapters that can work
on their own, but which, together, provide a deeper
meaning and look into the lives and battles of the
soldiers. *The Things They Carried* relates the stories
of the men in Alpha Company. It features a narrator,
called Tim O'Brien, who has many commonalties
with the author Tim, but O'Brien maintains that the
story is "all made up."

Along with several other stories that would be
incorporated into the book, "The Things They
Carried" first appeared as a short story in *Esquire*.
As the opening piece for *The Things They Carried,*
it sets the stage for the narratives that will follow. It
does more than introduce the reader to many of the
soldiers of Alpha Company and establish their
unity, however; it also introduces the reader to the
completely unimagined world that is war. In this
world anything can get turned around. A gentle man
can carry a thumb of an enemy boy-soldier as a
talisman or a man can get shot to death in clear sight
of all his fellow company.

"The Things They Carried" presents dual narratives: numerous lists of the things, both tangible
and intangible, that the soldiers carry with them on
their march, intermingled with the guilt felt by
Alpha Company's commanding officer, Jimmy
Cross, over the death of the soldier Ted Lavender. In
many ways, the lists form a framework on which the
rest of the narrative hinges, but the two story lines
are inextricably linked. Jimmy feels that he has put
his love for a college girl back home ahead of his
men; as atonement and as prevention, Jimmy must
burn her letters and photographs, physical symbols
of his destructive love.

Through the burdens carried by Jimmy Cross
and the rest of the men, "The Things They Carried"
successfully juxtaposes the soldiers' physical reality against their emotional reality. So the things they
carry are not limited to the tools of war, such as
weapons, jungle boots, and mine detectors, but also
to what each man finds to be a personal necessity—
dental floss for one man, comic books for another.
O'Brien's deliberate prose, here sounding like parts
of it could have been lifted from a military report,
emphasizes the physical load of the soldier—"P-38
can openers, pocket knives, heat tabs, wristwatches,

> " Despite her position
> outside of Vietnam, Martha
> plays an important role in
> Cross's perception of the
> progression of events played
> out in the story."

dog tags, mosquito repellent, chewing gum, candy,
cigarettes, salt tablets, packets of Kool-Aid, light-
ers, matches, sewing kits, Military Payment Certifi-
cates, C rations, and two or three canteens of water." It also puts emphasis on the sheer weight of the
soldier's load: the M-16 gas-operated assault rifle
that "weighed 7.5 pounds unloaded, 8.2 pounds
with its full 20-round magazine"; Mitchell Sanders's
PRC-25 radio was "a killer, 26 pounds with its
battery"; and Henry Dobbins, a big man and the
machine gunner "carried the M-60, which weighed
23 pounds unloaded, but which was almost always
loaded." As Steven Kaplan points out, the way in
which O'Brien "catalogues the weapons the soldiers carried, down to their weight [makes] them
seem important and their protective power real."
This is simply an illusion; Lavender, killed by
sniper fire, "carried 34 pounds when he was shot,"
9 more than the typical load carried by most of the
soldiers, as well as more than 20 rounds of ammunition.

At times the men choose to "discard things
along the route of the march." The text states that
they do this "Purely for comfort," knowing that a
resupply chopper would arrive by nightfall, but this
action functions symbolically as well. Only by
stripping themselves of the physical gear of the war
can they achieve a feeling of freedom, however
momentary it might be, and catapult themselves out
of Vietnam. Truly, the men recognize the delusional
nature of their fantasy, for they know that "they
would never be at a loss for things to carry." The
implication that they will be carrying their experiences once they return also appears here, in the
narrator's evocation of "the great American war
chest," which includes Fourth of July sparklers,
Easter eggs, and the forests of Minnesota.

The weight under which the men struggle cannot be lightened by the discarding of war equip-

ment, for it extends far beyond the physical reminders; hardest of all, they carry "all the emotional baggage of men who might die" and "shameful memories" and the "common secret of cowardice barely restrained." These they carry on the inside. On the outside they are hardened men, tough, able to joke about Lavender's death. "A pisser, you know?" says Kiowa. "Still zipping himself up. Zapped while zipping." They bitterly deride men who leave the war by shooting off their own toes or fingers, but "even so the image played itself out behind their eyes." Only in their sleep can they truly let down their guard. This night-time fantasy includes what they called a "freedom bird," a big bird that carries them away from Vietnam. Then "the weights fell off; there was nothing to bear"; they no longer carry their weapons or each other, instead "they were carried, they were purely borne." Only in these fantasies can they free themselves of their many burdens; instead of carrying the weight of the war, they are now carried by a creature that is larger, more powerful, and more mystical than themselves.

Because this is only fantasy and the men cannot escape the realities of war, they are forced to carry with them their ideals of home. In Kiowa's case, this comes in the form of an illustrated New Testament. Jimmy Cross's ideals of home, fantasies of a girl back home, simply serve as deadly distractions. He carries a "compass, maps, code books, binoculars, and a .45-caliber pistol that weighed 2.9 pounds fully loaded . . . a strobe light and the responsibility for the lives of his men." Yet, most important to Jimmy Cross are the letters he carries from a college girl named Martha. For Jimmy, Martha represents the world of peace; she is unsullied by the war experience—"she never mentioned the war, except to say, Jimmy take care of yourself"—and unmoved by it—"She wasn't involved" (either in the war itself, Jimmy's experience of it, or the relationship between she and Jimmy). Despite her position outside of Vietnam, Martha plays an important role in Cross's perception of the progression of events played out in the story. After Lavender is shot "on his way back from peeing," Jimmy Cross decides that he is at fault. For just as Lavender was about to be shot, Lieutenant Cross "was not there. He was buried with Martha under the white sand at the Jersey shore." In response to Lavender's death, Jimmy Cross burns Martha's letters and resolves to be a better leader. This resolve is less for the men, who will resent this stricter line of command, than for himself; Cross knows that "Lavender was now dead, and this was something he would have to

carry like a stone in his stomach for the rest of the war." Cross will become a real soldier; that is the only way to carry the weight of his guilt.

Jimmy Cross concludes that his imagined world has put the lives of his men at risk. "Imagination was a killer," states the text, and here the imagined world and the world of battle are starkly differentiated. Cross's self-perceived negligence and his guilt provide what Lorrie Smith calls an "inexorable equation: imagination = women = distraction = danger = death." Smith suggests that Cross's dramatic resolution at the end of story is his recovery of masculine power achieved only through the suppression of the femininity within himself. Because the emotion of love becomes a feminine characteristic in times of war, Cross's rejection of it requires his embrace of the ultra-masculine. Thus after Lavender's body has been taken away, "Lieutenant Jimmy Cross led his men into the village of Than Khe. They burned everything." This wanton act of destruction, itself reminiscent of the actual My Lai massacre, exemplifies not the violence of the war but what can happen when the soldiers stray from the masculine sphere and allow themselves to *feel*.

The reader may disagree with Cross's conclusion that his fantasies about Martha leads to Lavender's death. The text merely says that at the time that Lavender was shot, "Lieutenant Cross nodded and closed his eyes" while the other men cracked jokes. The crucial issue here, however, is not the physical realities of the circumstances surrounding one soldier's death but its emotional implications. Cross sees the events in stark, black-and-white terms: Martha or his men. There is no room for compromise in the world he now inhabits. Only 24 years old and not a risk-taker, as demonstrated by his chaste relationship with Martha, Cross has the safety of his men in his hands, and he cannot juggle two priorities; as the text states, "He was just a kid at war, in love." Cross's method of symbolic reasoning finds further emphasis in his digging of a foxhole that night and crawling inside, thus repeating the fantasy playing out in his head in the moments before Lavender's death. There he comes to the realization that Martha "did not love him and never would," a fact obvious to the story's readers.

With his love for Martha forbidden to him—or at the least, transformed into a "hard, hating kind of love"—Jimmy Cross turns to what can substitute as its closest opposite. He decides to initiate a new start for Alpha Company. Determined to mold both himself and his men into ideal soldiers, he will demand more discipline of them. He will no longer let them "abandon equipment along the route of march" although he acknowledges that "there would be grumbling . . . because their days would seem longer and their loads heavier." Cross's recognition that the men have lost their soldierly comportment comes at the same time as his recognition that it is *his* world, not Martha's world, that is real. Cross has allowed his men to carry too much of the world of peace with them, where feelings and emotions do not carry with them the power of death. "Lieutenant Jimmy Cross reminded himself that his obligation was not to be loved but to lead. He would dispense with love; it was not now a factor."

When asked in an interview to choose his favorite story from *The Things They Carried*, O'Brien said that "on most days, or three days out of seven in a week" he would choose "The Things They Carried." O'Brien likes "the cadences of the story, the sounds and rhythms . . . the physical items that form the story's structural backbone . . . the absence of much of a plot in the thing." In many ways, "The Things They Carried" is a pure warstory. It has camaraderie, despair, violence and death, duty, longing and desire. "It was very sad," Jimmy Cross thinks, "The things men carried inside. The things men did or felt they had to do." In the world of Vietnam and the world of "The Things They Carried," there is little room for anything else.

Source: Rena Korb, "The Weight of War," in *Short Stories for Students,* The Gale Group, 1999.

Lorrie N. Smith

In the following excerpt, Smith contends that the dramatic resolution of "The Things They Carried" "turns on recovering masculine power by suppressing femininity in both male and female characters," and that female characters in O'Brien's work are often only plot devices.

In both the opening and closing stories of [*The Things They Carried*], imagination is linked to an idealized, unattainable woman—Martha, a girlfriend at home, and Linda, a childhood sweetheart who died at nine. The first story plays one of the many variations on the imagination-reality motif and picks up where O'Brien's earlier novel, *Going after Cacciato,* left off, with Paul Berlin imagining himself pleading for peace at the Paris Peace Talks but admitting: "Even in imagination we must be true to our obligations, for, even in imagination, obligation cannot be outrun. Imagination, like reality, has its limits." "The Things They Carried" goes further

to limit the imagination, asserting that in battle, "Imagination was a killer." What this means, on one level, is that the nerve-wracking tension in the field could lead soldiers to imagine the worst or make a fatal mistake. But the story also establishes an inexorable equation: imagination=women=distraction=danger=death. The story's dramatic resolution turns on recovering masculine power by suppressing femininity in both female and male characters. Survival itself depends on excluding women from the masculine bond. In this first story, the renunciation of femininity is a sad but necessary cost of war, admitted only after real emotional struggle. It establishes a pattern, however, for the rest of the book.

"The Things They Carried" introduces the cast of Alpha Company and establishes their identity as a cohesive group, each manfully carrying his own weight but also sharing the burden of war. The story features Lieutenant Jimmy Cross, the platoon's 24-year-old C.O., who fell into the war via ROTC. He is presented as a man of integrity, honesty, and deep compassion for his men, a cautious, somewhat stiff and unseasoned commander with no inherent lust for death and destruction. The story is fundamentally an initiation narrative whose tension lies in Jimmy Cross's need to deal with guilt and harden himself to battle realities, which are here distinctly differentiated from the realm of imagination. Jimmy Cross's story alternates with lyrical passages cataloguing all the "things" men of war carry, including "all the emotional baggage of men who might die." These passages, echoing O'Brien's earlier constraints of "obligation," insistently repeat the idea that "the things they carried were largely determined by necessity . . . Necessity dictated."

Lieutenant Jimmy Cross's survival and his coming of age as an effective soldier depend on letting go of all that is not necessary and immediate—here equated completely with the feminine, the romantic, the imaginary. Becoming a warrior entails a pattern of desire, guilt, and renunciation in relation to a woman. The story opens by describing in detail Jimmy Cross's most precious cargo:

> First Lieutenant Jimmy Cross carried letters from a girl named Martha, a junior at Mount Sebastian College in New Jersey. They were not love letters, but Lieutenant Cross was hoping, so he kept them folded in plastic at the bottom of his rucksack. In the late afternoon, after a day's march, he would dig his foxhole, wash his hands under a canteen, unwrap the letters, hold them with the tips of his fingers, and spend the last hour of light pretending. He would

> One possibility is that O'Brien means to expose and critique the social construction of masculinity, suggesting that soldiers' behavior in Vietnam is conditioned by years of John Wayne movies, as indeed numerous veterans' memoirs attest is true."

imagine romantic camping trips into the White Mountains in New Hampshire. He would sometimes taste the envelope flaps, knowing her tongue had been there. More than anything, he wanted Martha to love him as he loved her but the letters were mostly chatty, elusive on the matter of love. She was a virgin, he was almost sure.

Martha's writing—and, implicitly, her reading of his war experience—are sexualized through association: her inability to respond to his love and his longing suggest the blank page of virginity in patriarchal discourse. Though Jimmy Cross tries to realize a connection with Martha through his sacramental/sexual ritual, she is represented as aloof and untouchable, a poet with "grey, neutral" eyes inhabiting "another world, which was not quite real." Martha's words are never presented directly, but are paraphrased by the narrator, who reminds us twice that she never mentions the war in her letters. Like other women in the book, she represents all those back home who will never understand the warrior's trauma. In addition to the letters, Jimmy Cross carries two pictures of Martha and a good luck charm—a stone Martha sent from the Jersey Shore, which he sometimes carries in his mouth; he also "humped his love for Martha up the hills and through the swamps." As the story progresses, Martha—rather these metonymic objects signifying Martha—becomes a distraction from the immediate work of war and caring for his men. His mind wanders, usually into the realm of sexual fantasy: "Slowly, a bit distracted, he would return to his hole and watch the night and wonder if Martha was a virgin." Memory and desire intertwine in a fantasy

that fuses courage and virility and, by extension, fighting and writing upon her blank virgin page. In one of the book's several retrospective "should haves," Jimmy Cross remembers a date with Martha and thinks "he should've done something brave. He should've carried her up the stairs to her room and tied her to the bed and touched that left knee all night long. He should've risked it. Whenever he looked at the photographs, the thought of new things he should've done." We are meant to see the move from chivalry to sadomasochistic erotica as natural and understandable, because "He was just a kid at war, in love," after all. That Jimmy Cross's sexual "bravery" might have been earned through violation and coercion is not considered in the story. The focus is on the male's empowering fantasy.

Jimmy Cross's distraction climaxes with the sniper shooting of Ted Lavender "on his way back from peeing." Just before this incident, the company had waited tensely for Lee Strunk to emerge from clearing out a Vietcong tunnel. The language of sexual desire and union, coming just before Lee Strunk's "rising from the dead" and Lavender's death, link Jimmy's imagination of Martha—his merging with the feminine—with annihilation of the self. As he gazes suggestively down into the dark tunnel, he leaves the war and succumbs to a fantasy of perfect union between masculine and feminine, death and desire:

> And then suddenly, without willing it, he was thinking about Martha. The stresses and fractures, the quick collapse, the two of them buried alive under all that weight. Dense, crushing love. Kneeling, watching the hole, he tried to concentrate on Lee Strunk and the war, all the dangers, but his love was too much for him, he felt paralyzed, he wanted to sleep inside her lungs and breathe her blood and be smothered. He wanted his to be a virgin and not a virgin, all at once. He wanted to know her.

Such unraveling of gender duality, however, is dangerous, such paradoxes unsustainable. At the moment of Jimmy's imagined dissolution, Ted Lavender is shot, as if to punish himself for daydreaming and forgetting "about matters of security"— but more deeply for abandoning his men in the desire to know the feminine—Jimmy Cross goes to the extreme of rejecting desire for Martha altogether. He reacts to the trauma of Lavender's death in two significant ways. The first is one of the book's parallel scenes of My Lai-like retribution, here bluntly told but not shown: "Lieutenant Jimmy Cross led his men into the village of Than Khe. They burned everything." The second is guilt, entangled with anger that his love for Martha is unrequited. He reverts to a familiar binary choice—either Martha or his men: "He felt shame. He hated himself. He had loved Martha more than his men, and as a consequence Lavender was now dead, and this was something he would have to carry, like a stone in his stomach for the rest of the war"—his good luck charm transformed to the weight of guilt. That night he cries "for Ted Lavender" but also for the realization, or perhaps rationalization, that "Martha did not love him and never would." Jimmy Cross regains a "mask of composure" necessary to survive war's horror, burns Martha's letters and photographs in a purgative ritual reversing the opening blessing, and wills himself to renounce Martha and all she signifies: "He hated her. Yes, he did. He hated her. Love, too, but it was a hard, hating kind of love." With this rejection and a newly hardened, terse idiom, Jimmy Cross completes his transformation: "He was a soldier, after all. . . . He was realistic about it. . . . He would be a man about it. . . . No more fantasies . . . from this point on he would comport himself as an officer . . . he would dispense with love; it was not now a factor." His survival as a soldier and a leader depends upon absolute separation from the feminine world and rejection of his own femininity: "Henceforth, when he thought about Martha, it would be only to think that she belonged elsewhere. He would shut down the day-dreams. This was not Mount Sebastian, it was another world, where there were no pretty poems or midterm exams, a place where men died because of carelessness and gross stupidity."

How are we meant to read this rejection? O'Brien is not blaming Martha for male suffering, for of course, the story isn't *about* Martha at all, though she introduces the book's prototypical figure of the woman incapable of understanding war. Rather, he uses her to define "necessary" codes of male behavior in war and to establish Jimmy's "proper" bond with his men. We are given no rationale for why Jimmy perceives his choice in such absolute terms, nor are we invited to critique Jimmy for this rigidity, though we do pity him and recognize his naivete. Jimmy Cross's rejection of the feminine is portrayed as one of the burdensome but self-evident "necessities" of war, and O'Brien grants Jimmy this recognition: "It was very sad, he thought. The things men carried inside. The things men did or felt they had to do." Most sad and ironic of all, Jimmy ends up suffering alone because of his status as an officer: "He would show strength, distancing himself." Jimmy Cross's allegorical initials even en-

courage us to read his youthful renunciation in Christian terms.

At the very end, however, masculine bonds prevail and compensate for Jimmy's losses. O'Brien places the men of Alpha Company in a larger cultural landscape of men without women by alluding to cowboy movies and Huckleberry Finn: "He might just shrug and say, carry on, then they would saddle up and form into a column and move out toward villages west of Than Khe." The narrative voice here is very carefully distinguished from the characters, and it is hard to know how to take the conditional "might" and the self-conscious diction: as parody? as straight allusion? as Jimmy Cross's self-deluding macho fantasy? One possibility is that O'Brien means to expose and critique the social construction of masculinity, suggesting that soldiers' behavior in Vietnam is conditioned by years of John Wayne movies, as indeed numerous veterans' memoirs attest is true. Likewise, the story unmasks the soldiers' macho "stage presence," "pose," and "hard vocabulary": "Men killed and died, because they were embarrassed not to"; they do what they "felt they had to do." But these constructions are inevitably converted into behavior that seems natural and inevitable—"necessary"—within the ur-story underlying all war stories: the tragic destruction of male innocence. O'Brien's depth as a writer allows him to reveal the socialized nature of soldiering and to show compassion for the vulnerable men behind the pose. But he stops short of undoing and revising these constructions. In the end, men *are* how they act, just as they *are* their stories and culture *is* its myths. The story rescues the humanity of men at war and consigns femininity to the margins, thus assuring the seamless continuity and endless repetition of masculine war stories.

Because Tim O'Brien's characters live so fully for him he is impelled to follow up the story of Jimmy Cross and Martha with a vignette, "Love." Like George Willard, the lonely but ever-receptive narrator of *Winesburg, Ohio,* O'Brien portrays himself as the burdened repository of other people's stories. Here Jimmy Cross comes to visit character-narrator Tim O'Brien "many years after the war" to talk about "all the things we still carried through our lives." One thing that Jimmy Cross still carries is a torch for Martha, and he shows the narrator a copy of the same photograph he had burned after Ted Lavender's death. The story embedded in the story concerns his meeting with Martha at a college reunion. Now a Lutheran missionary nurse serving in Third World countries, she responds to Jimmy with the same friendly but aloof demeanor that marked her letters during the war. She gives him another copy of the photo to gaze at and reveals "she had never married . . . and probably never would. She didn't know why. But as she said this, her eyes seemed to slide sideways, and it occurred to him that there were things about her he would never know." Despite her continuing inscrutability and distance, Jimmy risks telling Martha that "he'd almost done something brave" back in college, and he describes his knee-stroking fantasy. Martha's ambivalent reaction widens the gulf between men and women and hints, with Hemingway-like ellipses, that she is either repressed, fearful, uninterested, or a lesbian; in any case, she is unreceptive to Jimmy's advances, which absolves him from any failings or flaws as a masculine sexual being:

> Martha shut her eyes. She crossed her arms at her chest, as if suddenly cold, rocking slightly, then after a time she looked at him and said she was glad he hadn't tried it. She didn't understand how men could do those things. What things? he asked, and Martha said, the things men do. Then he nodded. It began to form. Oh, he said, those things. At breakfast the next morning she told him she was sorry. She explained that there was nothing she could do about it, and he said he understood, and then she laughed and gave him the picture and told him not to burn this one up.

What are "the things men do?" In the context of this pair of stories, these things are both sexual and violent. Jimmy passes this story on the narrator, joking that "maybe she'll read it and come begging." But he leaves more concerned about the reader's response than Martha's, with a plea that Tim depict him positively, as if he still hadn't exorcised his guilt over Lavender's death. "'Make me out to be a good guy, okay? Brave and handsome, all that stuff. Best platoon leader ever.' He hesitated for a second. 'And do me a favor, don't mention anything about—' 'No,' I said, I won't.'" O'Brien teases us with an indeterminate ending; if he is true to his word, then he hasn't revealed "anything about—" Jimmy's secret, and we are left wondering. If the writer has, in fact, betrayed Jimmy in the course of the retelling, we cannot be sure what it is we were not meant to know and why Jimmy wants to suppress it. In either case, the men wordlessly understand each other, and the reader is an outsider. Like Jake Barnes hungering impotently

after Lady Brett, Jimmy continues to suffer from Martha's unattainability. As in the previous story, we are allowed to glimpse the gap between the mask and the face, the wounded man behind the masculine pose. But Martha is barely more than a plot device signifying Jimmy's life of virility and innocence destroyed by the war.

Source: Lorrie N. Smith, "'The Things Men Do': The Gendered Subtext in Tim O'Brien's *Esquire* Stories," in *Critique,* Vol. XXXVI, No. 1, Fall, 1994, pp. 17–40.

Sources

Bonn, Maria S. "Can Stories Save Us? Tim O'Brien and the Efficacy of the Text," in *Critique: Studies in Contemporary Fiction,* Vol. 36, No. 1, Fall, 1994, pp. 2-14.

Coffey, Michael. An Interview with Tim O'Brien in *Publishers Weekly,* February 16, 1990.

Harris, Robert R. "Too Embarrassed Not to Kill: A review of *The Things They Carried,*" in *New York Times Book Review,* March 11, 1990, p. 8.

Karnow, Stanley. *Vietnam: A History,* New York: Viking Press, 1983.

Myers, Thomas. *Walking Point: American Narratives of Vietnam,* New York: Oxford University Press, 1988.

O'Brien, Tim. "The Vietnam in Me," in *New York Times Magazine,* October 2, 1994, p. 48.

Weber, Bruce. "A Novelist Wrestles With War and Love," in *New York Times,* September 2, 1998.

Further Reading

Herring, George. *America's Longest War: The United States and Vietnam 1950-1975,* 2nd edition, New York: Alfred A. Knopf, 1979.
    This brief but comprehensive book is divided into clear sections that can be read separately and contains an extensive and invaluable bibliographic essay.

Lee, Don. A Profile of Tim O'Brien in *Ploughshares,* Vol. 21, No. 4, Winter, 1995, p. 196.
    A useful overview of O'Brien's career. Includes biographical information.

The Wave

Liam O'Flaherty
1924

This story was included in a collection of early stories titled *Spring Sowing*. When O'Flaherty's friend and mentor, the critic Edward Garnett, told him to write about those things with which he was familiar, he naturally turned to the scene of his childhood: the bleak Aran Islands. Many of his stories are graphic descriptions of the peasant life on these nearly barren rocks, as human beings grapple with the unforgiving elements of nature. There are also stories, nine of them in this collection, that have to do with animals and their treatment by human beings. In ''The Wave,'' however, there are neither human nor animal characters, but one part of nature against another.

Liam O'Flaherty became famous because of his novels, especially *Famine* and *The Informer,* but his literary reputation rests more heavily upon his short stories. Frank O'Connor, another great Irish short story writer, says in his book A Short History of Irish Literature that ''the great O'Flaherty of the short stories is a man without ideals or opinions, concerned only with the 'facts.''' ''The Wave'' is little more, at least on the surface, than a recitation of facts by a seemingly objective reporter. At high tide, small, disconnected waves are replaced by a giant wave that destroys a weakened cliff. There is little here on the surface that would lead us to grand conclusions about life or ''universal truths.''

Yet, if we look at the descriptive prose, we see an artist at work. The story begins with a description

of the cliff, static and unmoving. It continues with a description of the sea just before high tide, violent and roiling. It ends with a description of the sea at high tide, and the single, united wave that comes crashing in, destroying the cliff. There is room for the reader to maneuver within this story. Is it the wave or the cliff that should be read as the protagonist? Is it destruction, or a natural restructuring? O'Flaherty's stories do not propose answers but, as Anton Chekhov has said is the purpose of stories, they state the question correctly.

Author Biography

Liam O'Flaherty was born in 1896 on Inishmore, the largest and northernmost of the Aran Islands off the west coast of Ireland. O'Flaherty's writing was deeply influenced by his environment; the Aran islands, with their thin soil, are barren and wild, and subject to the whims of sea and weather. O'Flaherty's writing, often violent, looks at humankind's connection to nature, but not in a sentimental fashion. In many of his stories, he shows how people lose their affinity with nature—and to a deeper life—when they turn their backs on it and live in cities, but he also demonstrates how brutish and short life can be for those who live close to the land.

In 1908, a priest visited Inishmore looking for candidates for the junior seminary at Rockwell, and Liam's teachers recommended him enthusiastically. At Rockwell, he excelled in the classics and modern languages. From there he went to Blackrock Seminary and then to Holy Cross College, Dublin. He won a scholarship to University College, Dublin, where he decided to study medicine.

While at University College, he formed a corps of volunteers for the Republican cause (freedom for Ireland from British rule), but in 1915, he joined the British Army and fought in France and Belgium. He was wounded and suffered shell shock at Langemarck, Belgium, and was discharged from the army after treatment.

When he became well, he traveled to Brazil, Canada, and the United States, working at a variety of odd jobs, from factory worker to oyster boat crewman. In Boston, his brother, who had emigrated years before, bought him a typewriter and encouraged him to write. O'Flaherty wrote four stories, but they were all rejected and he quit writing.

He returned to Ireland in 1920 and declared himself a communist. He and a group of men seized the Rotunda in Dublin and held it for three days before being forced out, after which he escaped to Cork. After a visit to Russia to see communism in action, he became disillusioned and began to write against it, declaring all political ideals to be corrupt, while at the same time holding fast to hopes for a workable form of socialism.

Returning to London in 1922, he wrote a novel and several short stories, none of which were published. Finally, he decided to write about what he knew: the Aran Islands and the people who lived there. The result was his first published novel, *Thy Neighbor's Wife*—a story about a priest who still loves a woman from his youth. His next book was more autobiographical, about the return of a soldier to his home in the Aran Islands; entitled *The Black Soul,* its wild characters mirror the wild sea and sky of the islands.

Over the next thirty years, O'Flaherty wrote fourteen more novels, a play, several autobiographical books, essays, and criticism, as well as the short stories for which he is most noted, including *The Wave,* which was included in the 1926 collection *Spring Sowing.* His novel *The Informer* was made into a movie three times (the best of which is John Ford's Oscar-winning version of 1935). He wrote his most famous novel, *Famine,* in 1937. In all, he penned 36 books.

In the early 1950s, however, he stopped writing for reasons he chose not to divulge to the world. On September 7, 1984, he died in a Dublin hospital, having been silent to the literary world for nearly thirty years.

Plot Summary

Although O'Flaherty does not name the setting of his story "The Wave," it's almost certainly set somewhere on the Aran Islands. The story begins with the description of an imposing cliff, two hundred feet high, that sits facing the sea. It is semicircular, with a twenty foot high cavern at its base, a concave area that "the sea had eaten up . . . during thousands of years of battle."

It is not quite high tide as the story opens. The sea is angry, and waves come "towering into the cove" formed by the cliff and the two reefs at each end of its semicircle. These waves are separate, and O'Flaherty uses violent language to describe them as they "[chase] one another, [climb] over one another's backs, [spit] savage columns of green and white water vertically when their arched manes [clash]." They hurl themselves against the cliff, then retreat.

There is a pause as high tide is reached. The small waves dissipate, falling back from the cliff. When the sea reforms itself, it is in a single wave "from reef to reef." It rises and stands "motionless, beautifully wild and immense." Then, propelled from the rear by the power of the ocean, "that awful mass of water [advances] simultaneously from end to end of its length without breaking a ripple on its ice-smooth breast."

Suddenly it is the cliff that appears small and helpless as the great wave approaches. It reaches its apex and smashes into the cliff which vanishes "in the white water and foam mist." Then the wave falls back, exposing the cliff once again, but there is "a great black mouth . . . at the centre, above the cavern." The cliff begins to crumble in upon itself "with a soft splash." A cloud of dust rises and blows backward across the land.

The story ends with the cliff demolished, "the land [sloping] down to the edge of the cove." Rocks are strew about. Smoke rises. And another wave is "gathering in the cove."

Liam O'Flaherty

of years of battle." But there is a weakness in the cliff: crashing waves have carved out a cavern at its base.

Smaller Waves

These waves are important, because they contrast with the wave of the title. They come "towering into the cove . . . confusedly, meeting midway in the cove, chasing one another, climbing over one another's backs." Because they are not unified, they do little damage to the cliff, and they retreat— "disheveled masses of green and white, hurrying backward." They do not have the force of the sea behind them, because it is not yet high tide.

The Wave

Unlike the cliff, the wave is active and in constant motion. It is wild and chaotic and angry. It is almost possible to feel, in its violence, the frustration of all the years of pounding away at the unyielding rock. While the cliff takes no notice of the sea beneath it, the wave, with its "head curved outwards, arched like the neck of an angry swan" seems intent on attacking the great limestone rock. It is important to note that this wave is unified, "stretching from reef to reef."

Characters

The Cliff

Because there are no human characters in this story, the elements of nature become the main characters. The first of these is "The Cliff" which is hard and silent. It sits before the sea in a calm arrogance, having stoically weathered "thousands

Topics for Further Study

- What was the "Irish Renaissance"? Who were some of the literary giants associated with it? O'Flaherty was born after most of the older writers of the renaissance had published some of their best work. Would you rank him in this group? How does his work differ from that of other renaissance writers?

- Find information on the Easter Rebellion, then read Yeats's poem "Easter, 1916." What does Yeats mean by "A terrible beauty is born"? Liam O'Flaherty was, in 1916, fighting against the Germans in France and Belgium, wearing a British uniform, yet he had been a Republican (a group of Irish patriots who called for freedom from England) and, on his return to Ireland would advocate a united, free Ireland. Do you find this contradictory?

- What other stories have you read in which there are no human (or animal) characters? Do you consider this a fully formed story, or is it a sketch? What *is* a story? What are its components?

- Many people consider O'Flaherty's best work to be *Famine,* a novel about the 18th Century famine in Ireland. During the famine years, 1845-49, Ireland lost half of its population to starvation and emigration. Research the famine on your own. Were the British at fault? How do you think such an event would have influenced Irish literature afterward? Find a poem about the famine. What is its tone? How would you have written about it?

- Another story in *Spring Sowing* is "The Cow's Death." This story has been reprinted in various collections of O'Flaherty's work, so it shouldn't be too hard to find. Read it and compare it to "The Wave." What similarities do you notice in tone, theme, and setting? Is O'Flaherty's customary gritty realism present in both stories?

Themes

Permanence

What could be more permanent than a towering cliff? Expressions such as "solid as the rock of Gibraltar" seek to compare human endeavors to the enduring solidity of just such a cliff. Yet, in "The Wave," we see that this monstrous edifice, two hundred feet high, may last a long while, but—in the end—it falls in upon itself. Nothing, this story seems to suggest, is truly permanent.

Time

Time changes everything. The sea could not have caused the cliff to fall in upon itself in a day or a month or a year—it took thousands of years. Time is the catalyst for change, and it is inevitable. It moves inexorably forward, allowing the events that occur within time to proceed and then become the past. At the end of the story, there is no more cliff, just a slope down to the water's edge and, although the sea's constant pounding was the direct cause of its demise, the sea needed time in order to do its work.

Change and Transformation

In nature, nothing is lost, but much is changed or transformed from one thing to another. As human observers, we tend to value one thing in nature over another. A cliff impresses us with its grandeur, while a mere slope rarely makes us pause to consider it at all. When the wave causes the cliff to fall apart, we may observe the falling apart itself in awe: the crashing boulders, the thunderous roar, the smoke pluming up and drifting away. It is a sight similar to the demolition of an old building. But, just as with the old building, when the excitement is over and there is only rubble, we are dismayed at the disarray, the mess that is left. But nature makes no such distinctions—the rocks are still a part of the landscape, the path of the water merely shifts, adapting to its new course. A simple structural change has taken place. There is no better or worse. Nature is uncaring, indifferent.

Style

Point of View

The third person narrator who tells this story is interesting in that he, or she, seems to disappear. It is almost as if the reader is telling the story to him or herself. This faceless narrator is not objective, however—the language the narrator uses to tell the tale is emotional and suspenseful.

Anthropomorphism

The narrator leads readers to think of the cliff as unfeeling, unthinking, as cliffs surely are, but in this story, the cliff has been given human attributes: It opens ''a great black mouth . . . in its face.'' It seems to yawn, as if it is ''tired of battle.'' The waves, meanwhile, meet ''confusedly.'' They chase each other, climb over each other, spit, yawn, tumble, hiss, and roar.

Symbolism

So, who is this cliff? Who are these waves? The narrator is mute on this subject. There are clues, however. The weak, confused waves before high tide have no effect on the cliff, while the huge, unified wave of high tide causes it to crumble. Is it unity—perhaps of the weak—that the great wave symbolizes? Are readers to infer that, joined together, the small and the weak can overthrow the large and the strong? Or is it simply that, given time, water can erode limestone?

Setting

Though the setting is not specifically stated, it is probably somewhere on the Aran Islands that O'Flaherty has in mind—but it needn't be. The description could fit many cliffs on many shorelines. It is presumably not a heavily populated area, since no human being nor human habitat is noted.

Foreshadowing

The destruction of the cliff is foreshadowed early in this very short story. After giving the cliff's imposing dimensions, the narrator notes that ''the sea had eaten up the part of the cliff that rested on that semicircle of flat rock, during thousands of years of battle.'' So there has been a long battle, and only the cliff shows its wounds.

Additionally, the sea is presented as active and persistent. It flows in, and it flows out. Then it flows in again. And again. The waves take a ''monstrous stride'' across the flat rock. It is not quite high tide yet, but it is obvious that, when it is, the waves will become stronger and crash further up on the cliff. It is uncertain at this point in the reading what will happen, but when the cliff crashes down, the narrator has prepared the reader for its demise.

Historical Context

Ireland and the Never-Ending ''Troubles''

The British occupied Ireland for nearly 800 years (and still occupies six counties). It was a cruel occupation, as they pushed the Irish from the best land and kept it for themselves. They outlawed education for the Irish, who were forced to learn in secret (the term ''hedgemasters'' comes from this period, when teachers—or masters—would hold classes behind the hedges to avoid the British authorities). ''Penal Laws'' also prohibited Catholics from owning land or any property (including animals) valued at more than 5 pounds. They could not practice law nor be part of the government. Catholic priests who broke penal laws were branded on the face or castrated. Wolfe Tone, assisted by the French and inspired by the American Revolution, led an unsuccessful rebellion in 1798. It wasn't until 1829, however, that the harsh penal laws were repealed.

British occupation and rule continued, and there were more rebellions. Significant uprisings occurred in 1803, during the great Famine in 1848, and in 1867, but were brutally put down. But nationalism did not die, and its flames were fanned by the Irish Literary Renaissance when writers such as William Butler Yeats, Lady Gregory, John Millington Synge,

Compare & Contrast

- **1924:** Although Ireland has won a measure of freedom, it is still considered to be under the dominion of Great Britain. It will be another twenty-five years before Ireland declares itself a republic.

  1990s: Ireland is still partitioned, with British troops stationed in the six counties of Northern Ireland. Irish Catholics in those six counties still do not enjoy the same civil rights as the Protestants of English descent.

- **1924:** William Butler Yeats is still writing poetry, perhaps at his peak, (he won the Nobel Prize for poetry in 1923) but the Irish Literary Renaissance has dwindled to a virtual end. Many of its most prominent writers, including John Millington Synge, are dead. But other, younger writers, including O'Flaherty and Sean O'Casey (whose *Juno and the Paycock* appeared that year), will be producing works for decades. James Joyce has already published *Dubliners, A Portrait of the Artist as a Young Man,* and *Ulysses. Finnegan's Wake* will not appear for fifteen years.

  1990s: Ireland continues to produce some of the world's greatest literature. Seamus Heaney wins the Nobel prize for literature in 1995 for his poetry, which the Nobel committee says has a "lyrical beauty and ethical depth, which exalt everyday miracles and the living past." William Trevor, Patrick McCabe, Edna O'Brien, John McGahern, Maeve Binchy, and dozens of other writers produce books that take their place next to those of Brendan Behan, George Bernard Shaw, and Oscar Wilde.

- **1924:** Dublin is a war-ravaged city. The country's direction is still unsure, and people are suspicious of their neighbors. Although the civil war is over, remnants of the Republican movement continue their violent opposition for another twenty-five years.

  1990s: Called "the hippest city in the world," Dublin is not only a favorite with writers, rock stars, actors, and tourists, but with high-tech companies who find a well-educated work force in "the silicon valley of Europe." Five star hotels compete with traditional Bed-and-Breakfasts, as peace and prosperity bless this city.

- **1924:** The Aran Islands, where O'Flaherty was born, are a barren, bleak place. The women knit sweaters that have a pattern particular to their family, so that when bodies wash up on shore weeks or months after a boat has been lost, the families can determine by the sweater who its wearer was. The people are peasants, most just barely avoiding starvation.

  1990's: Both tourist site and archaeological treasure, the Aran islands have never known such prosperity before. On bicycle, tourists travel to pre-Christian forts, early Christian churches, and prehistoric mounds. To the south, immense limestone cliffs rise above the sea. Dun Ducathair, a huge fort lying in ruins, reveals the power of the sea that O'Flaherty wrote about in "The Wave." Much of the cliff before it has fallen into the sea, so that the fort itself is now inches away from the precipice.

and others cultivated Irish culture in their writing. There was a resurgence of interest in the Irish language, and Ireland and its people became the subjects of poetry and drama and fiction.

The Ireland of 1924, when this story was first

published, had survived rebellion, civil war, and a partitioning imposed by the British government. The famous Easter Rising of 1916 began this series of events, when a group of armed patriots took control of the Dublin Post Office and held it for nearly a week, proclaiming the Irish Republic.

Sixteen leaders of the rebellion were executed by the British.

In 1919, the Anglo-Irish War began. The Irish used guerilla tactics to fight the more powerful British Army, and an agreement ending the war was signed on December 6, 1921. However, not everyone agreed with the settlement with the British, because it artificially partitioned six counties in Northern Ireland which would remain British. Two days after the signing, Eamon de Valera, who had survived the Easter Rising and would later go on to become president of Ireland, denounced the treaty. In April of 1922, civil war broke out between the Republicans (led by de Valera) and the Free Staters (led by Michael Collins). It was a bitter and bloody war, as all civil wars are. More Irish were killed in the civil war than had been killed in the war with England. It lasted a little over a year, and Michael Collins was among those killed.

Liam O'Flaherty sided with the Republicans, and he became disenchanted with his countrymen who were willing to give up the six Ulster counties in order to secure peace. Many of his stories—and his novels—deal with this period of history. In fact, his first published creative work, ''The Sniper,'' tells the story of a rooftop sniper who shoots and kills another sniper and, when he goes down to the street to roll over his kill, finds that it was his own brother he had shot. *The Informer,* considered at the time to be one of his best novels and made into an Oscar-winning film directed by John Ford, was also about the civil war.

Critical Overview

The collection *Spring Sowing,* which contains the story ''The Wave,'' was O'Flaherty's third book. The first two were novels, *Thy Neighbor's Wife* and *The Black Soul.* Although the first of these was well received, the reviews of his second book were mixed at best, infuriating O'Flaherty, who would always consider it one of his best works. In the May 1, 1924, edition of *Times Literary Supplement,* an unsigned review of the book stated that ''the chief characteristics of Irish novels of the present day seem to be an angered sincerity, an impatience with shams, and an endeavor to express actual life even at the cost of literary or technical excellence.'' But O'Flaherty did not feel he'd sacrificed anything, and on May 2, 1924, he wrote to his friend Edward

Garnett: ''One writes as one sees or else one is a mountebank . . . I will write in the future for the satisfaction of my own soul since that to me is the most important thing in the world or in the next either.'' And O'Flaherty must have kept his word, for ten years later, on April 19, 1934, the *Times Literary Supplement* echoed its earlier review, saying that ''his powerful and primitive imagination has been forced too rapidly and therefore thwarted, by the modern cult of literary violence and exaggeration.''

O'Flaherty's novels were variously received over the years, and even today they are considered wildly uneven in quality. Although *The Informer* was widely praised when it was published in 1925 (the *Times Literary Supplement* of September 24 of that year said that ''in his new novel, *The Informer,* Mr. Liam O'Flaherty shows a considerable advance in his art''), it is not considered his best today. Most modern critics prefer *Skerrett,* published in 1932, and *Famine,* published in 1937.

However, his short fiction generally has been well–received. On October 2, 1924, upon the publication of *Spring Sowing,* the *Times Literary Supplement* noted that ''in this collection of thirty-two sketches and tales, Mr. Liam O'Flaherty reaffirms his grip upon elemental life.''

In that review, and in other critical essays and reviews since, critics have discussed O'Flaherty's realistic portrayal of the peasants of Ireland. They have talked about the insightfulness of his animal stories (nine are included in *Spring Sowing*) and the ambiguity of his feelings about nature and the countryside versus man and the city. But none have attempted to interpret ''The Wave'' as anything more than a slight vignette, an accurate portrayal of a moment in nature. It was, and still is, apparently considered one of the ''sketches'' rather than one of the ''tales.'' In a July, 1963 essay by George Brandon Saul in *A Review of English Literature,* Saul notes that ''some of the pieces (''The Wave'' and ''The Rockfish,'' for example) contain little more than description.'' And James F. Kilroy states in his book *The Irish Short Story* that ''The Tide,'' a later story, deserves comparison with the earlier ''The Wave,'' in that both describe a natural phenomenon of water's motion. The early story is undoubtedly forceful in its vivid description of a wave acquiring enormous force and then break against the shore; but the later story, although more sedate, is more comprehensive in surveying the curative effects of the regressing and progressing tide.

Criticism

Diane Andrews Henningfeld

Henningfeld is an Associate Professor at Adrian College and holds a Ph.D. in literature. She has written widely on literary topics for academic and educational publications. In the following essay, she argues that "The Wave" reveals O'Flaherty's understanding of the forces of nature and that its inclusion in the collection Spring Sowing *serves to undercut notions of birth and rebirth suggested by the collection's title.*

Liam O'Flaherty's short story, "The Wave," first appeared in 1924 as one of the stories in the collection *Spring Sowing*. The story later appeared in a 1937 collection, *The Short Stories,* as well as in the 1970 compilation, *Selected Short Stories*. Because of its frequent inclusion in anthologies, "The Wave" draws increasingly close attention from students and scholars alike. Its importance to the body of O'Flaherty's work is perhaps best illustrated by the appearance in 1980 of a collection called *The Wave and Other Stories,* edited by well-known O'Flaherty scholar, A. A. Kelly.

Like the other stories in *Spring Sowing,* "The Wave" offers a glimpse of the Aran Islands, a bleak, isolated group of small islands just off the west coast of Ireland. O'Flaherty was raised on Inishmore, the largest of the Arans. According to John Zneimer in his 1970 study, *The Literary Vision of Liam O'Flaherty,* for O'Flaherty, "The Aran Islands were reality in microcosm, for the Aran Islands were to earth as earth was to the universe. . . ."

Nevertheless, "The Wave" represents a departure from O'Flaherty's more typical presentation of rural peasant life. Indeed, the story does not have one living creature in it. That O'Flaherty was attempting something different in this story seems clear from letters he exchanged with critic and mentor Edward Garnett in early 1924. In one letter, O'Flaherty claims that he does not know if the story is "good, or bad, or middling." In a subsequent letter, he seems much relieved by Garnett's praise of "The Wave," noting that the story "cost such an immense effort to write. . . ."

While it seems apparent that O'Flaherty wants to reveal something important in the story, just what this revelation is seems to elude many critics. Few critics have tried to tackle the story, preferring to concentrate on O'Flaherty's novels or short stories depicting rural peasant life. One explanation for this may be, as Zneimer argues, ". . . the contemporary scholar who has become accustomed to approaching short stories as an intellectual challenge or problem in need of scholarly interpretation or explication will find no rich mine in O'Flaherty."

Another explanation for the lack of critical attention to the story could be the structure of the story itself: at just ten paragraphs and about one thousand words, the story is more a lyrical poem than a traditional short story. Critic James O'Brien in his book, *Liam O'Flaherty,* describes stories such as "The Wave" as "lyric sketches, with a simple narrative, a limited plot, and with scene and characterization governed by what is immediate and readily observable." Certainly, "The Wave" fits such a description.

On closer examination, however, the story seems to be striving toward something larger than just what is "immediate and readily observable." Further, although Zneimer states that O'Flaherty's "stories cannot be called symbolic as the term has come to be used in criticism with a *this* representing *that* relationship of details and events," "The Wave" is more than a simple, albeit intensely dramatic, description of a wave hitting a cliff face. Rather, it seems clear that in "The Wave," O'Flaherty is revealing something of his own understanding of nature and of the nature of reality. To arrive at what this understanding might be, however, requires readers, first, to read with great care the story before them.

At first reading, the detached tone observed by several critics seems obvious. O'Flaherty accomplishes this detachment in several ways. First, as noted earlier, there are no living creatures in the story. All is cold, wild water, and hard, black rock. The descriptions are carefully controlled with the detachment of a scientific observation: "The cliff was two hundred feet high. It sloped outwards from its grassy summit, along ten feet of brown gravel, down one hundred and seventy feet of grey limestone, giant slabs piled horizontally with large slits between the slabs where sea-birds nested." It is almost as if O'Flaherty is cataloguing the scene before him.

In addition, O'Flaherty's images are concrete. That is, the images in the story appeal to each of the reader's senses directly, without a narrative intermediary. The most obvious images are, of course, visual ones: "Its base in front was ragged, uneven and scratched with white foam." There are also many examples of auditory images that engage the

A rocky Irish coastline, similar to the one described in "The Wave."

reader's sense of hearing: "a tumbling mass of white water that yawned and hissed and roared." Less obvious are those images appealing to the sense of touch, such as "ice-smooth breast," or "slimy weeds." Even taste is addressed indirectly: the cliff's face is "drenched with brine." Finally, the story abounds with kinesthetic images, or images of movement: "the wave stood motionless," "the wave sprang upwards," "they drivelled backwards slowly."

The most important technique O'Flaherty uses to establish the tone of detachment, however, is his narrator. Zneimer, in fact, argues that there is no narrator, nor any sense of O'Flaherty's presence: "We do not hear the author's voice. We see no evidence of his presence, only the scene, the wondrous vision, not told but imposed directly upon us."

Such a reading, however, denies the obvious. All stories have tellers, just as all texts have writers. Even encyclopedia articles are authored by someone, despite their detached, authoritative style. It is through the process of inclusion and exclusion of facts and details that all authors provide the narration to their texts. In the case of "The Wave," O'Flaherty attempts to hide his presence in the text through the use of what is called the "self-effacing" narrator. That is, he chooses to conceal his

narrator by the seeming objectivity of the description. However, close reading of the images reveals that the story is, of course, not nature itself, but a humanly constructed text about nature, a text that is shaped in a particular way to reveal a particular understanding of reality.

Thus, although there are no living characters in the story, O'Flaherty bridges the gap between the mineral, elemental nature of the cliff and the sea and the organic nature of animal and human by using similes and metaphors. By so doing, he animates both the wave and the cliff. The cliff, for example, is nearly always described in human terms. The cliff has a black face, and a "great black mouth," that it tries to close. The cliff yawns, "tired of battle."

Likewise, O'Flaherty uses primarily animal or monster images to describe the waves: the wave's head "curved outwards, arched like the neck of an angry swan. . . . Its crest broke and points of water stuck out, curving downwards like fangs. It seemed to bend its head as it hurtled forward to ram the cliff." Similarly, "The waves came towering into the cove across both reefs, confusedly, meeting midway in the cove, chasing one another, climbing over one another's backs, spitting savage columns of green and white water vertically, when their arched manes clashed."

What Do I Read Next?

- *Stories of Liam O'Flaherty* (1956) with an introduction by Vivian Mercer. This collection pulls together many of O'Flaherty's finest stories in one place.

- *Famine* (1937) by Liam O'Flaherty. Considered one of his two great novels, this fictional account of the Irish famine is even-handed and devoid of the melodramatic touches of some of his other work. It has been reprinted many times since its first publication in 1937, most recently in 1991.

- *The Famine Ships: The Irish Exodus to America* (1997) by Edward Laxton recounts the courage—and desperation—of the starving Irish who emigrated to the United States, and others who suffered and died in the attempt.

- *44 Irish Short Stories* (1955), edited by Devin A. Garrity. This ''Anthology of Irish Short Fiction from Yeats to Frank O'Connor'' contains the works of 33 Irish authors, including two stories by O'Flaherty, and is still in print and widely available.

- *The Penguin Book of Irish Short Stories* (1988) edited by Benedict Kiely contains two stories by O'Flaherty, as well as others by Irish authors from Lady Gregory to Brian Friel and John McGahern.

- *The Oxford Book of Irish Short Stories* (1991) edited by William Trevor. From folk tales to Oscar Wilde and James Joyce to Edna O'Brien and Desmond Hogan, this ambitious book surveys the long history of Irish short fiction.

- *How the Irish Saved Civilization* (1996) by Thomas Cahill. Western Civilization was nearly wiped out when the barbarians ushered in the ''Dark Ages''—an era devoid of scholarship, learning, and culture. Monks and other scribes in the unconquered country of Ireland went to work copying all the great works they could find and, eventually, reeducating the world.

- *Dubliners* by James Joyce is available in various reprint editions. It was first published in 1914 (although it had been accepted for publication in 1906, then rejected as the publisher had second thoughts about its profanity and suggestiveness, as well as the possibility of libel, as it used real places and real names). Joyce wrote these stories when he was a young man, between the ages of twenty-two and twenty-five.

In addition to animating the inanimate seascape, the images serve to connect ''The Wave'' with the other stories in the collection, stories about peasant life and animal life on the Aran Islands. Each of the stories, in some way, refers to the cycles of life and death on Aran. Indeed, calling a collection *Spring Sowing* implies a belief in the cyclic renewal of plants, animals and humans. The spring sowing and the fall harvest organize life and reality on Aran, and by extension, in the universe.

However, the inclusion of ''The Wave'' in *Spring Sowing* introduces a more disturbing view of reality, one that undercuts the cycle implicit in the title of the collection. The cycle represented by ''The Wave'' is not one of renewal, but one of

destruction. The opening images of the story place the waves and the cliff in opposition to each other: ''The sea had eaten up the part of the cliff that rested on that semicircle of flat rock, during thousands of years of battle.'' If Aran is indeed a microcosm of the earth and of the universe for O'Flaherty, the elemental struggle between wave and cliff becomes laden with significance. The struggle implies that the sea, like time, never ceases moving, and that all within its path will, inevitably, be destroyed. Even the solid earth, made of rock and metal, will crumble and disappear within the sea of time.

It should not be thought, however, that O'Flaherty represents the sea or the waves as evil forces. Rather, it seems that O'Flaherty views such forces as coldly neutral, all powerful, and inevitable. In his novel, *The Black Soul,* O'Flaherty's main character, Fergus O'Connor, cries "Ah, beautiful, fierce sea. . . . You are immortal. You have real life, unchanging life." It seems that the position of "The Wave" within *Spring Sowing* reinforces the contrast between the mutable, changing, mortal nature of human beings and the immutable, unchanging, immortal nature of the sea. Human life, after all, is lived within finite time, while time itself exists separate and apart from the timed. Thus, while the residents of Aran (and by extension, the earth) go about their daily business, caring for animals, sowing seed, giving birth, burying their dead, they do so within a temporary and provisional reality. As "The Wave" instructs, even the reality of the cliff face is temporary and ultimately impermanent against the unchanging, all-powerful reality of the sea.

In the last paragraphs of the story, a monstrous wave forms and hurls itself against the cliff with devastating strength. The cliff, made human by its face, is utterly destroyed by the wave. In this final cataclysm, all the cycles of human life and death are rendered meaningless. Like a human, the cliff disappears into black dust. Although the wave itself disappears as well, the last line of the story reveals that in the cove, the ocean gathers another wave.

Source: Diane Andrews Henningfeld, "An Overview of 'The Wave'," in *Short Stories for Students,* The Gale Group, 1999.

Rena Korb

Korb has a master's degree in English literature and creative writing and has written for a wide variety of educational publishers. In the following essay, she discusses the way in which the elements of nature become living creatures in "The Wave."

Short story writer and novelist Liam O'Flaherty was born on the Aran Islands off the west coast of Ireland, and this geographic fact may be the most significant factor in his writing, for his work reflects the wildness and instability of life on these isolated, storm-battered islands. Although O'Flaherty first began to work seriously on his writing in the years following World War I, while in the United States and London, he acknowledged in an autobiographical note that these efforts were not very good, and he burnt them. His work took an abrupt turn after 1923, however, when he returned to his homeland, Inishmore on Aran. The 1920s saw his enormous literary output; in that decade alone he wrote 8 of his 15

> "'The Wave' is more than a simple, albeit intensely dramatic, description of a wave hitting a cliff face. Rather, it seems clear that in 'The Wave,' O'Flaherty is revealing something of his own understanding of nature and of the nature of reality."

novels as well as the majority of his 160 short stories. Seemingly inspired by Aran, O'Flaherty also spoke of his desire to be the voice for his people: "It seemed as if the dam had burst somewhere in my soul; for the words poured forth in a torrent. They came joyously and I felt exalted by their utterance, just as I used to feel when telling my mother some fantastic tale in my infancy."

Many of O'Flaherty's short stories concern the peasant life of Ireland and can function today as a sort of social history. A number of his stories, however, are nature stories, with animals usually taking the center stage. Richard J. Thompson has said, "At their most obvious, O'Flaherty's nature stories are celebrations of the workings of instinct and appetite, of the biological chain, and of the struggle of natural selection which often brings random death to living creatures but never dishonor." O'Flaherty's "The Wave," from the collection *Spring Sowing,* goes one step further and features no living characters. The brief story (only about 1,000 words) narrates waves crashing against a towering cliff. After several fierce lashings, a powerful wave gathers, pummeling the shoreline. Under such pounding, the cliff gives way, crumbling into the sea, leaving behind only a cloud of grey dust. In the cove, the waves continue to gather. Critics have disagreed over interpretations of this story. Is it indeed a story or merely a vignette? Should it function primarily as a descriptive piece or does it express some deeper connection between humans and nature? Does O'Flaherty admire the destructive actions of the waves or does he represent an impartial viewer?

> This brief narrative tells of a cataclysmic event-- the extreme alteration of the natural environment. Yet, its effect on humans or even animals would seem negligible, for they do not exist in the scope of the story."

Most critics do agree that "The Wave" takes its place among the larger body of O'Flaherty's work that depicts the balance of nature. Helene O'Connor points out that the upsetting of the accepted equilibrium and the establishment of a new one "is the repeated and distinctive pattern of O'Flaherty's stories." However, at the start of the story, it would appear that O'Flaherty has created a simple (and perhaps typical) descriptive yarn. It begins, "The cliff was two hundred feet height. It sloped outwards from its grassy summit, along ten feet of brown gravel, down one hundred and seventy feet of grey limestone, giant slabs piled horizontally with large slits between the slabs where seabirds nested." The next few paragraphs continue in the same vein, describing the cavern in the cliff's face, the cove at its base, and the constant pounding of the waves. Not until the third paragraph does O'Flaherty provide a hint of the drama and of the central storyline to come: "But the sea moved so violently that the two reefs bared with each receding wave until they seemed to be long shafts of black steel sunk into the bowels of the ocean." Amidst a background of benign and nature-derived adjectives, the word *violent* leaps out, drawing attention to itself and to the turn the story is about to take.

The reader soon understands how "The Wave" functions on two levels. With no real characters in the story, the smaller waves and the giant wave take on central roles, emerging as inexorable forces of nature, but they also have distinct predatory characteristics. The waves that precede the final lash from the ocean move "confusedly, meeting halfway in the cove, chasing one another, climbing over one another's backs." The waves have transformed from merely a part of the scenery into living creatures. The hostility of these waves, akin to that of a lion perhaps, is clear not only from their actions but from their desire to bring harm; they strike the cliff with "a mighty roar" and then they rise again "like the heavy breathing of a gluttonous giant." Yet O'Flaherty never sacrifices realism in his drive to bring to life the movements of the water. Instead, his writing takes on a dual nature. Every description of the waves works with either interpretation; for instance, the "mighty roar" as the waves strike the cliff evokes both the known sounds, or roars, of the sea, as well as the sound of an animal on the attack. O'Flaherty also effectively mixes images that remind the reader of both of these descriptive functions, such as the "manes of red seaweed." Here the reader finds an effortless invocation of both the sea and the animal.

The large, destructive wave is yet to come. Again, O'Flaherty clues the reader into the impending change with the words "there was a pause." These words also imply culpability, as if the wave itself is toying with the cliff while gathering strength for its final assault. "For a moment the wave stood motionless," writes O'Flaherty. Here the wave is taking the time to savor the attack. The prose that follows, although containing descriptions of animal-like features—the "neck of an angry swan," an "ice-smooth breast," or "the shoulders of the sea"—also describes the sea in more realistic terms— the "white foam" or the "belt of dark blue." The sea at this point is more water and less animal. Suddenly, O'Flaherty overturns that lulling sensibility. "Then there was a roar. The wave sprang upwards to its full height. Its crest broke and points of water struck out, curving downwards like fangs. It seemed to bend its head as it hurtled forward to ram the cliff." When the cliff, "tired of battle," gives up and falls into the sea, the overall effect is that the wave attacked the cliff purposefully, deliberately, and maliciously. O'Flaherty also acknowledges the relentless nature of the sea itself in the story's final words: "And the wave had disappeared. Already another one was gathering in the cove."

This brief narrative tells of a cataclysmic event— the extreme alteration of the natural environment. Yet, its effect on humans or even animals would seem negligible, for they do not exist in the scope of the story. The extreme isolation of the scene is apparent in the structure O'Flaherty has chosen to impose on it; no lizards scuttle along the cliff's grassy summit, no fish flop among the crashing waves, no birds observe the crumbling of the cliff or flap their wings in the cloud of grey dust that arises. But the implications of the scene are apparent, too. Early in the story, O'Flaherty points out that the sea and the cliff had been engaged in "thousands of years of battle." For in the victory of the sea over the cliff, the equilibrium so long maintained by the earth has been destroyed, implying that all sorts of changes can come about at any time. As O'Connor points out, "Everything is quiet, but not as it was before."

That there is no logical purpose for the motion of the sea or the destruction of the cliff also serves to emphasize the isolation of this event. But O'Flaherty brings a human element into the story with his depiction of the cliff. He maintains narrative integrity by again using words that can both describe an aspect of nature and a living creature; to refer to a "cliff's face" or a "cavern's mouth" is to say nothing new, but O'Flaherty's cliff also "stood ajar, as if it yawned, tired of battle," and under attack from the wave, the "cliff tried to close the mouth." While the waves can only be compared to animals, the cliff can readily be compared to a human. This significance cannot be overlooked, nor can its implications for the ongoing battle between nature and humans. At the same time, however, O'Flaherty is careful not to create a clear dichotomy between the cliff and the waves; his implementation of the same technique indicates their similarities.

Stories such as "The Wave" confirm Amy Scher's assertion that O'Flaherty's "short stories prove him to be one of the first of twentieth-century writers to demonstrate an ecological sensitivity." O'Flaherty, while pointing to the battle between earth and earth and humans and earth, also points to how animals and humans are equally embodiments of life and nature. In the emphasis "The Wave" places on nature over human or animal characters, O'Flaherty indicates that nature is a crucial force in the cycle of life.

In a letter to a friend, O'Flaherty tells of his efforts to achieve in his writing "a feeling for coldness." Critic John Zneimer defines this as "the coldness of extreme detachment, pure artistry, where the artist's warm human qualities represent a blot or an imperfection if they are allowed to intrude." He further states, "O'Flaherty sees the writer as possessing a goat's eye, or a snake's eye, or a weasel's eye, as one who is condemned to observe but not participate in the richness of life." This objectivity

> Over and over he circles his theme, more and more explicitly stating the paradox of sea as simultaneous nourisher and destroyer."

on O'Flaherty's part enables him to raise many issues in a story as short as "The Wave": the emphasis on nature without human interference, the implication of the continuous battles that exist around nature, and the fundamental similarities of the creatures of earth—human, animal, and inanimate.

Source: Rena Korb, "Nature as a Living Thing" in *Short Stories for Students,* The Gale Group, 1999.

Michael H. Murray

In the following excerpt, Murray faults O'Flaherty for his didactic narrative, arguing that O'Flaherty breaches the oral tradition by "refusing to let his art suggest" important thematic issues, instead weighing down his stories with "contrived symbolism or overstated theme."

The success or failure of Liam O'Flaherty's short fiction actually depends on quite a different phenomenon, one to which Vivian Mercier has made passing reference in a discussion of the stories of Corkery, Lavin, O'Connor, O'Faolain, and O'Flaherty. Although he is a native speaker of Gaelic and "therefore born into the oral tradition," O'Flaherty is the "least oral in his approach to narrative of all five writers." Mercier refers here to the conception of so many of the stories in what he calls "cinematic terms," but the statement has other far-reaching implications. By extension he faults O'Flaherty for failing to remember that the relationship between story teller and audience is the indispensable component of the oral tradition. Liam O'Flaherty's style does not falter only when he leaves the barnyard; his imagery, his dialogue—in fact, the entire fabric of his narrative—disintegrates completely whenever he abandons his primary function as story teller in favor of self-conscious commentary on life; when, refusing to let his art suggest, he must speak through literature, only to pull down his tale under the weight of contrived symbolism or overstated theme.

Disparities in O'Flaherty's prose style bear out this argument. Whenever he rejects the straight narrative told for its own sake for the short story of philosophical statement, artless grace gives way to inappropriate imagery, careless structure, and tedious repetition. Selections from the first collection, *Spring Sowing,* will serve to illustrate this consistent stylistic problem in O'Flaherty's short fiction.

In choosing Liam O'Flaherty's finest stories, Mercier singled out the title piece of his first group for special praise. Here the writer deals with the central theme of nature and man's relations with the natural environment, but most important, according to Professor Mercier, is that "[t]his picture of a newly married Aran Islands couple sowing their first crop of potatoes together is both realistic and symbolic." This observation is entirely correct. The seeds in Mary's apron, Martin's cheeks on fire with a "primeval desire . . . to assert manhood and subjugate earth," his wife's deep sigh as he cleaves the ground to the accompaniment of his stooped grandfather's encouraging shrieks—all are symbolic of man's renewal in and through the regenerative earth mother. And, in this first story in Liam O'Flaherty's first collection of stories, the reader discovers in microcosm both the essence of his narrative strength and his potential for failure. The symbolism comes dangerously close to shouting the writer's theme, and both threaten to overwhelm the narrative straining to support them. The oral qualities of this story prove to be its salvation; but when the configuration of a symbolic structure or the statement of a theme becomes more important than the narrative in which it should inhere, O'Flaherty's style breaks down, consistently, and often horribly.

There are for example several stories in this first series in which, naturally enough for an Aran Islander, Liam O'Flaherty has chosen to deal with the sea. "The Wave," a vignette without characters, would perhaps have been successful as purely descriptive prose. Yet O'Flaherty attempts to force from the landscape a symbolic evocation of mindless violence. The stress is painfully obvious; the story disintegrates into a series of grotesque images of which one contorted smile is sufficient example: "the trough of the sea was convulsing like water in a shaken glass." "The Landing" promises at first to be more successful. Thematically reminiscent of Synge's starkly beautiful "Riders to the Sea," the tale projects a powerful image of barren Ireland in the grieving Aran mother watching on the cliff, "wisps of grey hair flying about her face." Unfortunately O'Flaherty cannot permit the narrative to suggest its own multi-level meaning to his audience. Over and over he circles his theme, more and more explicitly stating the paradox of sea as simultaneous nourisher and destroyer. Finally, inevitably, he loses control and tells his reader that the raging ocean resembles "eau de cologne or something." Faulty parallelism and repetition mar this potentially fine story at its close.

Source: Michael H. Murray, "Liam O'Flaherty and the Speaking Voice," in *Studies in Short Fiction,* Vol. V, No. 2, Winter, 1968, pp. 154-62.

Sources

Kelly, A. A. *Liam O'Flaherty the Storyteller,* London: MacMaillan Press., 1976.

Kilroy, James F. "Setting the Standards: Writers of the 1920s and 1930s," in *The Irish Short Story.* Boston: Twayne Publishers, 1984, pp. 103-4.

O'Connor, Helene. "Liam O'Flaherty: Literary Ecologist," in *Eire-Ireland: A Journal of Irish Studies,* Vol. 7, No. 2, 1972, pp. 47–54.

O'Connor, Frank. *A Short History of Irish Literature: A Backward Look,* New York: Putnam, 1967, 264 p.

Saul, George Brandon. "A Wild Sowing: The Short Stories of Liam O'Flaherty," in *A Review of English Literature,* Vol. 4, No. 3, July, 1963, pp. 108-13

Scher, Amy. "Preaching an Ecological Conscience: Liam O'Flaherty's Short Stories," in *Eire-Ireland: A Journal of Irish Studies,* Vol. 29, No. 2, Summer, 1994, pp. 113–22.

Thompson, Richard J. "The Sage Who Deep in Central Nature Delves: Liam O'Flaherty's Short Stories," in *Eire-Ireland: A Journal of Irish Studies,* Vol. 18, No. 1, Spring, 1983, pp. 80–97.

Times Literary Supplement. Review of *Spring Sowing,* October 2, 1924, p. 610.

Times Literary Supplement. Review of *The Black Soul,* May 1, 1924.

Times Literary Supplement. Review of *The Informer,* September 24, 1925.

Zneimer, John. *The Literary Vision of Liam O'Flaherty,* Syracuse: Syracuse University Press, 1970.

Further Reading

Cahalan, James M. *Liam O'Flaherty: A Study of the Short Fiction,* Boston: Twayne Publishers, 1991.
    Concentrating on the shorter works, a critical analysis of O'Flaherty, including a literary biography of influences, a reprinting of early and later reviews and essays.

Doyle, Paul. *Liam O'Flaherty,* Boston: Twayne Publishers, 1971.
    Provides a short biography followed by a critical look at the major texts.

Hildebidle, John. *Five Irish Writers: The Errand of Keeping Alive,* Cambridge, MA: Harvard University Press, 1989.
    A look at the lives and works of five writers whom the author thinks are underappreciated: Liam O'Flaherty, Kate O'Brien, Frank O'Connor, Elizabeth Bowen, and Sean O'Faolain

Kelly, Angeline. *Liam O'Flaherty the Story Teller,* New York: Barnes and Noble, 1976.
    Another look at the short fiction, in two sections: I. Themes, Narrative Structure, and Style; II. The Protest of Vitality.

What I Have Been Doing Lately

Jamaica Kincaid

1981

"What I Have Been Doing Lately" was first published in the *Paris Review* in 1981. Kincaid included this piece in her first published book, *At the Bottom of the River* (1983), which earned her the Morton Dauwen Zabel Award of the American Academy and Institute of Arts and Letters. According to Leslie Garis in her *New York Times Magazine* article about Kincaid, *At the Bottom of the River* made Kincaid "an instant literary success." David Leavitt, in his review for the *Village Voice,* praised Kincaid for "her ability to articulate the internal workings of a potent imagination without sacrificing the rich details of the external world on which that imagination thrives."

Author Biography

Jamaica Kincaid was born on May 25, 1949 to Roderick Potter, a carpenter/cabinet maker, and Annie Richardson, a housewife. She grew up in poverty on the small West Indian Island of Antigua. Kincaid, whose given name is Elaine Potter Richardson, immigrated at the age of seventeen from her British-ruled 10-by-12-mile island home to New York, where she worked as an *au pair* for three years. While living in New York, she graduated from high school, studied photography at the New School for Social Research, and spent a little over a year at Franconia College in New Hampshire.

After various receptionist and secretarial positions, Kincaid began her career as a writer with an interview piece on Gloria Steinem for *Seventeen* magazine. In 1978, she was hired as a staff writer for the *New Yorker*, where she worked until 1995. Kincaid currently lives in Vermont with her husband Allen Shawn, who is the son of the former editor of the *New Yorker*, and their two children, Annie and Harold.

Kincaid's first work *At the Bottom of the River,* which includes ''What I Have Been Doing Lately'' and other short prose pieces, was published in 1983 and received the Morton Dauwen Zabel Award from the American Academy and Institute of Arts and Letters. *At the Bottom of the River,* like most of Kincaid's subsequent work, is autobiographical and draws from her childhood in Antigua. Kincaid concludes that ''the way I became a writer was that my mother wrote my life for me and told it to me. I can't help but think that it made me interested in the idea of myself as an object.'' It is not surprising that Kincaid's mother may have helped to shape her writing. Indeed, Kincaid's later pieces, *Annie John* (1985) and *Lucy* (1990), both explore the complexities of mother/daughter relationships. Although Kincaid says that she writes of mother/daughter relationships ''because the fertile soil of [her] creative life is [her] mother,'' she treats the very personal and formative experience of colonialism in her work as well, specifically in *A Small Place* (1989).

Jamaica Kincaid

Plot Summary

''What I Have Been Doing Lately'' is an elliptical, almost surreal narrative that begins with the words, ''What I have been doing lately,'' and proceeds to depict, in list-like form, a series of actions engaged in by the unidentified and nameless narrator. The narrator, summoned from bed by a ringing doorbell, opens the door to find no one there. After stepping outside and looking north and south, the narrator walks north, seeing the planet Venus in the sky, a monkey in a leafless tree, and finally an impassable body of water. After years pass, the narrator boards a boat, crosses the body of water, and continues along a straight path through a pasture, observing a dog and then a goat that each ''looked the other way

when it saw me coming.'' When the narrator turns to look at the path behind her, everything has changed: it has become hilly and the landscape is full of flowering trees. Turning to continue on, the narrator finds that a deep dark hole has opened up in the ground. Wondering what is at the bottom, she jumps in. Her fall makes her feel ill, and she begins to long for her loved ones. She decides to ''reverse'' herself and return to the surface.

The narrator continues to walk through ''days and nights, rain and shine'' until she sees a figure coming from the horizon that she believes to be her mother. The figure is not the narrator's mother, but it is a woman who knows the narrator. She asks what the narrator has been doing lately. After contemplating several nonsensical answers, the narrator repeats the events already recounted in the story, in some places adding events or details but often repeating her first account word for word. She concludes by describing herself coming upon a group of beautiful people having a picnic. After approaching the people, she discovers that the people and everything around her seem to be made of mud and she becomes sad, longing for home. Finally she decides, ''I don't want to do this any more,'' and is back in her bed, ''just before the doorbell rang.''

Characters

Narrator

The narrator is the main character from whose perspective all of the events in the story unfold. While not identified by name, age, class, race, or even by a striking feature, the narrator is generally considered to be female. The only physically descriptive information the reader receives about the narrator is that her "shadow was small." The narrator's lack of a specific identity prevents the reader from definitively identifying her and thus allows for multiple interpretations of who the character is and what role she plays in the narrative. One reading of the narrator, offered by Diane Simmons in *Jamaica Kincaid,* is that she is a person forever caught in a "story of departure and loss" who "will never be the same as she was before she left." Bryant Mangum, in *Fifty Caribbean Writers: A Bio-Bibliographical Critical Sourcebook,* alleges that the narrator symbolizes humankind's fall from innocence into knowledge.

The woman

A symbol of motherhood, or the girl's passage to womanhood, the woman appears to the narrator after she "reverses" herself from her fall. She obviously knows the narrator because upon meeting her she greets her by saying "It's You." She is the catalyst that starts the story over again.

Themes

Reality vs. Fantasy

One of the most noticeable thematic elements in "What I Have Been Doing Lately" is that of reality versus fantasy. The narration begins with the narrator in bed, which perhaps indicates that the story is a fantastical dream. Indeed, it contains many elements that support such an interpretation, including a landscape that changes as the narrator passes through it and the detail that years passed as the narrator waited on the banks of the body of water. The dreamlike quality of this story has been noticed by many of its reviewers.

Loss

Another strong theme in "What I Have Been Doing Lately" is that of loss and longing. At the end of the story, the narrator wishes she were home, with her mother or anyone she loved. More clearly,

she states, "I felt so sad." Earlier in the story, while she is falling into the hole, the narrator states: "Falling made me feel sick and I missed all the people I had loved." As the story seems to repeat itself, ending by starting over again at the beginning, the narrator's feelings of loss and sadness will return.

Mother

Mothers figure prominently in Kincaid's fiction, including "What I Have Been Doing Lately." There are several direct references to the narrator's mother within the text of the story. The narrator recounts that when the figure emerged from the horizon, she was sure it was her mother. Later in the story, she expressed the wish to find her mother, or someone else that she had loved, in her home cooking for her. In the text of the story that appears in *At the Bottom of the River,* the narrator also tells the woman she meets that she has "been listening carefully to [her] mother's words." All of these references imply that the theme of motherhood and that of mothering are important notions within this story.

Identity

Identity is another strong theme in "What I Have Been Doing Lately." The narrator's lack of a specific identity, or for that matter even a name, invites the reader to ask, "Who is this narrator?" The story also revolves around the mysterious identity of the woman who unexpectedly knows the narrator. The woman says, "It's you," yet the reader is not directly told who that "you" really is. Another question of identity involves the people on the beach. Their identities, as perceived by the narrator, change and thus who and what they really are remains a mystery to the reader. Although the topic of identity is not discussed within the text, the story indirectly asks the reader to ponder this topic by mysteriously leaving all of the identities within the story unknown.

Style

Structure

Perhaps the most striking aspect of "What I Have Been Doing Lately" is its plot structure. Plot structure is the way that an author organizes and tells the events of a story. For instance, a story that unfolds in chronological order is an example of a linear plot structure. Kincaid employs a circular plot, which begins and ends at the same place, with the narrator in bed. The plot essentially covers the same material twice: first when the recounted events ostensibly happen to the narrator and then when she answers the woman who asks her what it is she has been doing lately.

Point of View

As the title indicates, "What I Have Been Doing Lately" is written from the first-person point of view. Kincaid constructs the story from the narrator's perspective, and thus uses "I" to present all of the story's events. This keeps the main focus of the story on the narrator. The reader is unable to see the world or know the thoughts of the few other people the narrator encounters. In fact, this I-centered narrative keeps the reader at a distance from the world the narrator explores and the people she encounters. While this point of view limits the reader's understanding of the thoughts of others, it does allow the reader to see inside the narrator's mind. For example, when the woman asks the narrator what she has been doing, the narrator considers giving a series of answers to which the reader is also privy.

Tone

Tone is understood to be the attitude the writer expresses toward the story through the use of language. The tone in "What I Have Been Doing Lately" is one of almost impersonal disinterest and objectivity. The writer does not display any judgments or attitudes about the series of events she depicts. Instead, her language reflects a detachment from the bizarre events which she tells in simple, reportorial fashion.

Symbolism

The Story and Its Writer: An Introduction to Short Fiction states that "a literary symbol can be anything in a story's setting, plot or characterization that suggests an abstract meaning to the reader in addition to its literal significance." Some examples of symbols in "What I Have Been Doing Lately" could be the big body of water, the monkey, the leafless trees, the planet Venus, the narrator's shoeless feet, the deep hole, or the bed to which she returns. In this story, the planet Venus literally represents the planet the narrator sees when she gazes into the sky; however, the reference to Venus may have other implied meanings. For example, the planet she sees could symbolize the Roman goddess Venus (or

Media Adaptations

- "What I Have Been Doing Lately" has been recorded by the Library of Congress Archive of Recorded Poetry and Literature along with the other stories in *At the Bottom of the River*.

Aphrodite in Greek mythology), the goddess of love and beauty. One recurring criticism of Kincaid is that her imagery and symbolism are so intensely personal that it is difficult for the reader to feel confident about the possible symbolic meanings of objects.

Setting

Moira Ferguson, in *Jamaica Kincaid: Where the Land Meets the Body,* suggests that "What I Have Been Doing Lately" takes place on the island of Antigua during the 1950s. However, the text of the story does not place these events within any specific time periods or national boundaries. The story carries the reader through varied terrain—which may in fact exist only within a dream.

Genre

Placing "What I Have Been Doing Lately" within a specific literary movement or social context is difficult in that Kincaid has resisted being associated with any specific ideology, such as Modernism or Feminism. In an interview with Selwyn Cudjoe, Kincaid plainly states that she "can't bear to be in a group of any kind, or in the school of anything." Despite such statements, Kincaid has been studied by academics in terms of both feminist and Modernist tendencies. Cudjoe points out that Kincaid's work shares an "intensely personal" slant and interiority that is found in feminist writings. Kincaid admits that Modernism, a literary movement known for breaking with established forms and traditions, convinced her to avoid writing works that realistically portray lives and events. Postcolonial literature is another literary movement in which Kincaid's work can be placed. As the term

Topics for Further Study

- How can colonization affect the literature of a region? More specifically, how might writers who have been colonial subjects use their art to address issues of colonization?

- How does Kincaid's use of symbols contribute to or hinder your understanding of "What I Have Been Doing Lately"?

- Contrast the version of "What I Have Been Doing Lately" that appeared in *The Paris Review* with that which appears in *At the Bottom of the River.* How are they different? Do these differences change your first impressions and/or understanding of the work?

- Discuss the similarities between the issues raised by Jamaica Kincaid and other contemporary Caribbean and/or African writers.

- Research Carl Jung's idea of "individuation" and his understanding of alchemical processes and reread "What I Have Been Doing Lately" to see what parallels can be drawn between the story and Jung's ideas about personality growth and development.

---

indicates, postcolonial literature emerged while nations began to assert their independence from colonial authority. The literature of previously colonized nations is known for addressing the effects of colonialism and ideas of identity as it is shaped by the system of colonialism.

Historical Context

"What I Have Been Doing Lately" does not allude to a specific time period, nor does it indicate in which nation it takes place; however, because it references "black and shiny" people in a coastal setting, it is not unlikely that this story, like most of Kincaid's work, is set in the West Indies. Moira

Ferguson, in *Jamaica Kincaid: Where the Land Meets the Body,* narrows this estimation much further by stating that *At the Bottom of the River,* in which "What I Have Been Doing Lately" appears, takes place "in Antigua during the 1950s." Kincaid lived as a British colonial subject until 1966, and as the majority of her work is autobiographical, it is perhaps appropriate to contextualize her writing within the historical and cultural framework of the colonial and postcolonial world of the West Indies.

According to *Islands of the Commonwealth Caribbean: A Regional Study* (Sandra W. Meditz and Dennis M. Hanratty, editors) Christopher Columbus sighted Antigua in 1493 during his second voyage; however, the island was not formally colonized until 1632 when it was claimed by the English. Except for a short period in 1966-67, when the French held Antigua, it remained a British possession until its independence in 1981. From the time of Kincaid's birth until she left Antigua, the island was consistently challenging colonial authority. During the years 1935-1960, there were political campaigns aimed at curtailing the colonial subjugation of the Antiguans. In her article about Kincaid in the *New York Times Magazine,* Leslie Garis notes that Kincaid became increasingly angry about the subservient role that Antiguans were forced to play with the British. In 1966, the year Kincaid left Antigua for the United States, Vere Cornwall Bird, Sr. went to London to discuss Antigua's desire for independence. A year later, Antigua became an associated state of Britain, meaning that, although it was internally autonomous, the island was still dependent upon Britain to handle its foreign affairs and defense matters. After a constitutional conference in December of 1980, the island was finally granted complete independence from the British crown and officially became the nation of Antigua.

In 1674, Sir Christopher Codrington established what was to have a lasting effect on Antigua's society and culture—the island's first sugar plantation. By 1679, half of the island population was composed of slaves imported from Africa's west coast. During colonial times, the descendants of these slaves made up the lower strata of Antigua's racially-determined social structure. On the other end of the spectrum were the plantation owners and political elites, who were all of European descent. According to Paget Henry in *Peripheral Capitalism and Underdevelopment in Antigua,* the years 1960-68 brought an "emergence of the formal dominance of the Afro-Caribbean cultural system" during which many Antiguans began to assert their own cultural identity, independent of colonial influence. Antigua's push for independence was greatly reflected in the literature, painting, sculpture, drama, and dance of these times. Notable here is that during these years Kincaid was a young woman who was also in the process of defining her identity. Leslie Garis's article for the *New York Times Magazine* notes that during these formative years Kincaid began to "detest everything British." Years later, her work would likewise reflect a concern for identity and a distaste for colonial rule.

Another way of understanding the cultural context of Kincaid's work is to look at the other literature by women Caribbean authors writing in the postcolonial era. According to Laurence A. Breiner in *West Indian Literature,* the decade of the eighties ushered in an increasing number of works that were written by women and that addressed issues regarding women. The many points in common that Kincaid shares with these other writers locate her within this Caribbean cultural phenomenon. Renu Juneja, also in *West Indian Literature,* notes that "Caribbean women writers offer us female-centered narratives and poems with a preponderance of the first person and autobiographical modes." In general, the use of autobiography and the first person point of view in all postcolonial literatures has come to be understood as an attempt to reassert the female voice in literature and history. Although Kincaid stated that "literature teaches us about men and women," in *Jamaica Kincaid: Where the Land Meets the Body* she acknowledges that the themes of identity and differentiation do permeate her work. Postcolonial Caribbean literature is also known for addressing and responding to the "dual colonization" of women. The term "dual colonization" refers to the double oppression of women during the colonial period; not only were they subjugated as colonial subjects, but they were deemed subservient by virtue of their gender as well. Kincaid alludes to colonialism in her works, and in *A Small Place,* she confronts it head on. In summary, Kincaid's writing fits within an emerging cultural identification process in which writers concerned their works with issues of both femininity and colonialism.

Critical Overview

Kincaid's style is perhaps one of the most applauded aspects of *At the Bottom of the River.* As Lau-

rence Breiner noted in *West Indian Literature,* Kincaid "displayed prodigious technical virtuosity" in crafting *At the Bottom of the River.* Suzanne Freeman wrote in *Ms.* that "what Kincaid has to tell us, she tells . . . in a series of images that are as sweet and mysterious as the secrets that children whisper in your ear." Wendy Dutton, in *World Literature Today,* similarly stated Kincaid's use of language is "the magic of *At the Bottom of the River.*" She commented that Kincaid's language is "as rhythmic and riddlesome as poetry." In the *Times Literary Supplement,* Ike Onwordi furthered this complement by stating that "Jamaica Kincaid uses language that is poetic without affectation. She has a deft eye for salient detail." Thulani Davis also noticed Kincaid's mastery of detail, and in an article for the *New York Times Book Review* stated that "Ms. Kincaid is a marvelous writer whose descriptions are richly detailed; her sentences turn and surprise even in the bare context she has created."

For some critics, Kincaid's writing is somewhat hard to understand. Suzanne Freeman, in her 1984 *Ms.* article, recognized that "not everyone is willing to decipher the secrets" of Kincaid's fiction. Edith Milton, in her review for the *New York Times Book Review,* questioned whether Kincaid's stories were "too personal and too peculiar to translate into any sort of sensible communication." Kincaid's work is consistently autobiographical; this may account for the intensely personal and sometimes oblique nature of her symbolism and imagery. Kincaid has disenchanted some of her critics with her unconventional, complex style and her intense portrayals of conflict within mother/daughter relationships. Since writing *At the Bottom of the River,* Kincaid has shifted to a more narrative, less abstract style, but she continues to treat the themes of colonial power, mother/daughter relationships, and the evolution from childhood to adulthood in her works.

Criticism

Dustie Kellett

Kellett has taught Developmental Writing and tutored at the Fullerton Writing Center at California State University. She is currently working towards a Master of Arts in Comparative Literature, with an emphasis on Caribbean Literature. In the following essay, she attempts to decipher the mean-

A coastal region of Antigua, the native home of Jamaica Kincaid.

ing of Kincaid's ''What I Have Been Doing Lately''
by examining it ''through the lens of alchemy.''

After one quick read through of ''What I Have Been Doing Lately,'' the average intelligent reader may be perplexed at best. What on earth could Kincaid mean by all of this? Such a response would not be rare, indeed some of those who have praised Kincaid's work have also noted that at times her stories tend to ''move forward to a logic which is essentially private'' (David Leavitt in the *Village Voice*). In her article ''*At the Bottom of the River*: Journey of Mourning,'' Diane Simmons notes Edith

Milton's perception that Kincaid's stories are at times ''too personal and too peculiar to translate into any sort of sensible communication.'' What then can unlock Kincaid's seemingly private and privileged understanding of ''What I Have Been Doing Lately?''

Perhaps one way of deciphering the complexity of ''What I Have Been Doing Lately'' is through the lens of alchemy, an ancient science that dates back to the second and third centuries before Christ. Alchemists attempted to transform one chemical element into another by means of magic and primitive chemistry. One of their main goals was to

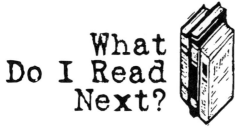

What Do I Read Next?

- *Annie John,* also written by Jamaica Kincaid (1983), traces the story of a young girl's coming of age and her tumultuous relationship with her mother. The novel takes place on the island of Antigua, Kincaid's birthplace, and was one of the three finalists for the 1985 international Ritz Paris Hemingway Award.

- *Her True-True Name: An Anthology of Women's Writing from the Caribbean,* provides an excellent introduction not only to the lives of thirty-one Caribbean authors, but to their fiction as well. This collection, which includes short stories and excerpts from longer pieces, was compiled and edited by Pamela Mordecai and Betty Wilson.

- Tsitsi Dangarembga, who is from Zimbabwe, has also written a girl's coming of age novel. *Nervous Conditions,* which was published in 1988, tells the story of many women and their lives under colonial rule. Alice Walker stated that *Nervous Conditions* ''is an expression of liberation not to be missed.''

- The second edition (1995) of *West Indian Literature,* provides an overview of Caribbean literature and includes a section on contemporary women writers. Bruce King, the text's editor, has divided the book into two sections: Histori-cal Survey and Significant Authors. The authors included in the second section are Jean Rhys, Edgar Mittelholzer, Wilson Harris, Samuel Selvon, George Lamming, Derek Walcott, Edward Kamau Brathwaite, V.S. Naipaul, Earl Lovelace and Trevor Rhone.

- *Things Fall Apart* (1959) by Chinua Achebe portrays life in the Igbo people of Nigeria. Particularly, it tells about the disintegration of their society under colonialism. This novel is often used as a sourcebook in Anthropology classes because of its cultural richness, and is understood by many to be Achebe's literary reaction to Conrad's *Heart of Darkness.*

- *Islands of the Commonwealth Caribbean: A Regional Study (1989),* which was edited by Sandra Meditz and Dennis Hanratty for the Federal Research Division of the Library of Congress introduces a general overview of West Indian history, culture, and society. It also provides specific chapters about Jamaica, Trinidad, Tobago, The Windward islands, Barbados, the Leeward islands, and the Northern islands. Each chapter is broken into the following topics: history, geography, politics, economic issues, health and welfare concerns, foreign relations, national security issues, and education.

---

change base elements into gold. Using alchemy as a way to understand a piece of literature may appear to complicate matters even further; however, the leap between science and the humanities may not be as far as one might think. According to Anthony Storr in *The Essential Jung,* the alchemists ''linked change in matter with change in man.'' Storr further notes that ''some of the alchemists undoubtedly thought of their work as a meditative development of the inner personality.'' It is for this reason, Storr suggests, that Carl Jung, a twentieth century Swiss psychologist, became interested in alchemy as a symbolic framework for surveying psychological growth and change in his patients. Jung often referred to alchemical processes in his studies of dreams, and believed that what the alchemists called *opus,* or the alchemical process and work, paralleled the process by which individuals arrived at their own identities. Thus, it is Jung's symbolic interpretation of alchemical processes that may lend insight into the narrator's psychological development in ''What I Have Been Doing Lately.''

Perhaps the first task in seeing ''What I Have Been Doing Lately'' from an alchemical perspective, is to establish it as a story about transformation

> The complexities and obscure nature of 'What I Have Been Doing Lately' reflect the fact that the narrator's identity is not yet defined and determinable. She, like her story, are in a constant state of change, and hence, to define the meaning of the story, or to define who exactly the narrator is, would be to limit the possibilities of all that either the story, or the narrator could become."

and process. According to Terree Grabenhorst-Randall in *C. G. Jung and the Humanities: Toward a Hermeneutics of Culture,* alchemy was "the art of transformation." The goal of alchemy was to alter the composition of a substance in order to create an entirely new and pure substance. At first glance, it would seem obvious that "What I Have Been Doing Lately" concerns a process, in that it is possible that the narrator has been getting up to answer the doorbell several times before the story actually begins for the reader. The fact that she returns to bed two times after being there at the beginning of the story suggests that she is in fact in the process of repeating certain events and then returning to bed. How then can this story be seen as a transformation? Doesn't the narrator simply repeat the same story two times? Decidedly not. As Diane Simmons notes in *Jamaica Kincaid,* the narrator retells the events in the first half of the story the second time with "slight changes in language, and then significant changes in the action." Listing the monkey who becomes antagonistic and the way in which the narrator engages with the monkey during the second telling of the events, Simmons concludes that the narrator's "experiences are changing her and the story of self she is able to tell." Other transforma-

tions within the story include the sky, which once "seemed near," becomes "far away"; the "black and shiny-beautiful" people become unattractive; the straight path becomes hills and the "leafless trees" begin "flowering." One must wonder if these things are really transforming, or perhaps just the narrator is changing, and thus the way that she perceives things around her is changing as well. Whether it be of the narrator and/or her surroundings, a transformation is definitely occurring.

Like alchemy, which is a very process-oriented creative science, "What I Have Been Doing Lately" undertakes the notion of process as a means of articulating the transformation of the narrator's evolving identity. The cyclical nature of the narrative, or the mere fact that the story both begins and ends with the narrator in bed, suggests that, as Simmons points out, the narrator is "caught in an apparently endless cycle of departure and return." Yet as mentioned before, after returning to the bed in the middle of the story, the narrator and her experiences are no longer identical to the character and the version of the story we read in the first half of the narration. Thus suggesting that the character's identity and how she perceives herself in relationship to the world around her are evolving by means of a return and departure that not only circles (i.e. brings her repeatedly back to the same events), but perhaps spirals upwards. Interestingly, Carl Jung in "Introduction to the Religious and Psychological Problems of Alchemy," states that the process of development of a person's identity "proves on closer inspection to be a cycle or a spiral." Indeed, upon such a close inspection, we can see that the narrator of "What I Have Been Doing Lately" is caught in a cycle that is spiraling her upwards, or "north," to a new identity. If the narrator were not changing, she would be forever repeating the exact same story. Instead however, she tells an altered story by returning to the same places, but on a changed, and thus new level. Read as a symbolic representation of the narrator's psychological development, the story becomes like the alchemical *vas,* or the vessel within which the alchemical process is taking place. Indeed, it is within the confines of this short story that the narrator's identity is beginning to transform.

The "drizzle" that the narrator encounters upon first walking outside signals the reader that her identity is indeed under construction. In the alchemical stage called *Putrifactio* a vapor is produced which indicates that the materials have begun to change forms. Simmons notes that in Kincaid's novel

Annie John, "dust-filled air" is used as a signal of change. Interestingly, the narrator encounters either a "drizzle" or a "damp dust" each time she leaves for her journey north. The presence of this moist vaporous substance suggests that the narrator, like the elements within the alchemical *vas,* is beginning to take on a new identity. The question then becomes, "what new identity is the narrator assuming?"

One perspective might be that she is moving closer to womanhood. Moira Ferguson notes that according to Gaston Bachelard in *Water and Dreams: An Essay on the Imagination of Matter,* water is the most feminine and maternal of the alchemical elements. Therefore, the "big body of water" toward which the narrator walks can be seen to symbolize womanhood and/or motherhood. During the story's first cycle, the narrator takes "years" before she navigates through the water, or tries to enter into womanhood, perhaps suggesting that she is not yet at ease with becoming a woman. Literally, she at first can not conceive how she might pass through womanhood. Notably however, after arriving at the water the second time, she crosses it without hesitation, thus reflecting that she is now more comfortable, or more capable of navigating this stage of her journey into womanhood. Each time, the narrator reflects that the "water looked as if it had been a painting painted by a woman." Thus, even in her own mind, the narrator associates the water with the creative and formative energies of femininity.

The narrator's encounter with the monkey also plays a role in developing the idea that she is approaching womanhood. Before proceeding with this line of analysis, I will briefly define three alchemical terms to aid in the understanding of this connection. 1) The *Philosopher's Stone*—the goal of alchemy, or the end product of the alchemical process. For Jung, this goal was understood as self-realization. 2) Nigredo—the stage in the alchemical process during which the elements darken. This stage suggests "that something of import is about to take place." 3) Mercurius—in alchemical writings, Mercurius was understood to be the chemical element Mercury, the God Mercury (Hermes), the planet Mercury and/or the secret "transforming substance." Jung found many similarities between Mercurius, who was fond of "sly jokes and malicious pranks," and the image of the Trickster, who has often been portrayed in the arts as a monkey. Jung believed that "wherever and whenever [the Trickster] appears he brings the possibility of transforming the meaningless into the meaningful." (Definitions taken from *The Critical Dictionary of*

Jungian Analysis and *The Essential Jung*). To continue then, in both cycles of the story, the narrator's encounter with the monkey is either preceded by darkness, or an anticipation of darkness. Before the first encounter with the monkey, she says, "It must be almost morning," implying that she is walking in the still dark hours of the night. Prior to her second meeting with the monkey she says, "If the sun went out it would be eight minutes before I would know it." In both cases, the anticipation of darkness or its presence parallels the darkening of the elements during *Nigredo,* thus signaling the reader that that which follows is significant. From the definitions above, we can figuratively understand the monkey as the "transformative substance" that converts the "meaningless into the meaningful." The narrator's encounter with the monkey becomes not just another experience, but an encounter that teaches us about the narrator. According to Jung in "Introduction to the Religious and Psychological Problems of Alchemy," the number four signifies "the feminine [and the] motherly." Interestingly, the monkey throws the *fourth* stone back at the narrator. If we understand the fourth stone as 1) the Philosopher's Stone, or self-realization, and 2) something feminine, then the fourth stone figuratively symbolizes the narrator's self-realization of womanhood. Once again however, we see that the narrator is not yet comfortable with this identification. She notes, "the skin on [her] forehead felt false," meaning that being marked or identified as a woman, even to herself, feels unnatural.

In *Complex/Archetype/Symbol in the Psychology of C. G. Jung,* Jolande Jacobi notes that "the number four occupied a position of fundamental importance in the alchemists striving for the Philosopher's Stone." Similarly, in "What I Have Been Doing Lately," the symbolic association of the number four with the feminine world occupies a fundamental importance in understanding the narrator's self-identification process. Her reaction to her first encounter with the "big body of water," and her sense that her skin "felt false" indicate that although she is in the process of becoming a woman, she has not yet fully realized this identity. In addition, as Simmons suggests, "she will never be the same as before she left." Thus, the narrator is not a child as she was before, yet she is not entirely a woman either. Instead, the narrator is seemingly caught in the ambiguous space between childhood and womanhood. The complexities and obscure nature of "What I Have Been Doing Lately" reflect the fact that the narrator's identity is not yet defined and determinable. She, like her story, are in a constant state of change, and hence, to define the meaning of the story, or to define who exactly the narrator is, would be to limit the possibilities of all that either the story, or the narrator could become. It was perhaps to capture the fluidity of personal transformation that Kincaid wrote "What I Have Been Doing Lately" in such a complexly rich fashion. By simply stating that the narrator was becoming a woman, Kincaid would have deprived us of the experience of transforming that which at first seemed "meaningless into the meaningful."

Source: Dustie Kellett, "An Overview of 'What I Have Been Doing Lately'," in *Short Stories for Students,* The Gale Group, 1999.

Shaun Strohmer

Strohmer has taught English at the University of Michigan and works as a freelance writer. In the following essay, she examines Kincaid's "What I Have Been Doing Lately" and contends that it is "a story about the power of storytelling to reveal truth."

Generalizing about Caribbean authors, Daryl Cumber Dance notes, "Language and identity are inseparable. The quest for identity is [a] prevalent concern in Caribbean literature." Perhaps because of this connection, many readers tend to examine Jamaica Kincaid's stories as semi-autobiographical texts. In the scholarly journals in which literary critics publish their work, articles on Kincaid are sometimes interviews rather than interpretations of her work; even in interpretive articles, Kincaid's biography becomes a reference point.

For example, in Moira Ferguson's book *Jamaica Kincaid: Where the Land Meets the Body,* Ferguson frequently refers to the facts of Kincaid's life to substantiate her arguments about Kincaid's stories. When Ferguson argues that "part child, part adolescent, the narrator [of *At the Bottom of the River*] comes to terms with a world that fuses fantasy, Eurocentric conceptions of the world, and day-to-day events," she adds a footnote to support her point, noting that "biographical details from Jamaica Kincaid's life suggest that the [stories] take place when the speaker is around nine years old." In her discussion of Kincaid's book *Annie John*, Ferguson notes the parallels between Annie John's family and Kincaid's family, suggesting that at various points throughout *Annie John*, "Kincaid may be talking about her ancestry."

Criticism that relies frequently on details of the author's life is sometimes called *biographical criticism.* In biographical criticism, the author herself becomes a sort of text, which can be read and interpreted against an actual story. Knowing the facts of an author's life can often be useful when studying a story. For example, knowing about Kincaid's upbringing in colonial Antigua can help readers understand some of the social issues latent in her work; knowing she is a woman writer from a minority group allows readers to consider how her work differs from and interacts with the dominant culture.

Biographical criticism can sometimes be limiting, however. The danger is that the critic will examine the fiction to see how it creates the author, rather than the other way around. This is particularly true in semi-autobiographical stories like those of Kincaid, in which elements of her life are purposely woven into the text. In addition, biographical criticism of Kincaid has tended to lump her work together, seeing all her stories and books as connected, telling different parts of the same stories. This is not necessarily a bad way to look at her work, but particularly in the case of "What I Have Been Doing Lately," this approach offers an unnecessarily limited perspective.

"What I Have Been Doing Lately" was published in 1983 as a part of a collection of stories called *At the Bottom of the River.* Seven of the ten stories in the collection were first published separately in *The New Yorker,* where Kincaid worked as a journalist; another two were published for the first time in the 1983 collection. "What I Have Been Doing Lately,"unlike all the other stories, was first published in the *Paris Review* in 1981. Notably, it is the only short story she ever published there, and one of the few that appeared outside of the *New Yorker.* Because it was initially published as a story separate from the others, outside of the context of her other work, "What I Have Been Doing Lately" seems almost to demand consideration on its own terms.

When examined apart from the rest of Kincaid's body of work, the story no longer *must* be about childhood. Although many critics have identified the narrator as a little girl, who perhaps represents Kincaid as a little girl, the narrator could be anyone—man or woman, adult or child. In the original version of the story, Kincaid does not include the phrase "dutiful daughter," which are the only words in the story that give any details about the narrator (and they tell us only that she is not a man). The narrator could be Kincaid herself, as an adult, or a fictional creation. Because the story lacks an identifiable narrator, its point of view is ambiguous. As readers, we cannot rely on the identity of the narrator to provide us with a framework for understanding this somewhat confusing and obscure tale.

As a result, we are thrust into the same position as the narrator. The narrator opens the door, steps outside, and begins a journey that he or she cannot comprehend, one in which every expectation is subverted: ''Instead of the straight path, I saw hills. Instead of the green grass in a pasture, I saw tall flowering trees. I looked up and the sky was without clouds and seemed near as if it were the ceiling in my house.'' Similarly, we open the book, start reading, and begin a story that is difficult to comprehend because it doesn't meet our expectations for a story. We expect a narrator who will act as our guide to the story, but this narrator doesn't seem to understand the story either. We expect a beginning, a middle, and an end to a story, with a conflict to be resolved and a climax near the end. This story twice repeats itself, and it seems to end where it begins, suggesting that it might repeat itself indefinitely. Moreover, nothing happens; the story seems to be a dream or a series of the narrator's imaginings which conclude when he or she tires of them and resolve nothing.

Because the story subverts our expectations about stories, it calls attention to itself, requiring the reader to observe and consider even the way in which the story is put together. In a story that contains all the traditional elements of narrative—clearly stated protagonist (hero), antagonist (hero's enemy or obstacle), setting, and chronology—a reader can easily read right over the basic elements of how the story is told. In contrast, ''What I Have Been Doing Lately'' tells a story without using the basic tools of storytelling. By doing so, the very organization of the story suggests that there is more than one way to tell a story.

Kincaid's unexpected writing style in ''What I Have Been Doing Lately'' shares some characteristics of the style of writers in a literary movement referred to as *Modernism*. Modernist writers disrupted familiar forms such as linear time and plot, traditional grammar and syntax, and a bounded, coherent subject (or speaking narrator). Some scholars argue that Modernism was a response to the repressive nature of Victorian culture in the early twentieth century. The Modernist movement, which

> In biographical criticism, the author herself becomes a sort of text, which can be read and interpreted against an actual story. Knowing the facts of an author's life can often be useful when studying a story.''

existed not only in literature but in all areas of culture, was seen by some as a rebellion against cultural codes that limited freedom. Scholar Marianne DeKoven suggests that ''the downfall of the old order, linked to the radical remaking of culture, was to be the downfall of class, gender, and racial (ethnic, religious) privilege.'' Although many think of Ernest Hemingway or poet Wallace Stevens as prominent examples of Modernist writers, such woman authors as Katherine Anne Porter and Gertrude Stein, as well as several African American authors of the Harlem Renaissance, are better examples of the subversive nature of the Modernist movement.

Kincaid is too contemporary to be considered a part of the American Modernist movement of the early twentieth century. Nevertheless, her situation is similar. Writing as a woman of color from a colonial background, Kincaid tells her stories against the dominant tradition. Until recently, most widely read stories about the West Indies and West Indian people were written from the perspective of the dominant culture. As a post-colonial writer, Kincaid retells those stories from her own perspective, that of the native culture.

The two versions of the story in ''What I Have Been Doing Lately'' demonstrate that a single story can take more than one direction. Significantly, in between the two versions of the story, the narrator suggests even more storytelling possibilities: three times he or she introduces a possible story by saying ''I could have said.'' With the repetition of what could be said, the story suggests that the number of stories that could be told are infinite, and that this story is only one of many. By doing so, it again calls attention to itself as a story—as a fiction—and as a particular perspective on events. It calls attention to the fact that every story is made by choosing to tell some things and not to tell others and by showing one perspective and therefore not showing others.

The second version of the story continues to open new possibilities. The narrator sees a group of people from two perspectives. First, the narrator finds them appealing: "I saw a lot of people sitting on the beach and having a picnic. They were the most beautiful people I had ever seen. Everything about them was black and shiny." But when the narrator gets closer, he or she has a new perspective: "[W]hen I got up close to them I saw that they weren't at a picnic and they weren't beautiful and they weren't chatting and laughing. All around me was black mud and the people all looked as if they had been made up out of the black mud."

By presenting these two versions of this part of the story, Kincaid makes the issue of perspective more complicated. It is relatively easy to pronounce that a story can be told from many perspectives. We often say "This is just my interpretation" or "That's just how I see it" as a way of defending our perspectives; if there are an infinite number of possibilities, then no one perspective can be right. In "What I Have Been Doing Lately," however, one perspective is clearly mistaken. The narrator did not intend to mislead with the first version of the story; it was a truthful and accurate report of how an event looked from a particular viewpoint. The problem is that viewpoint did not allow the narrator to see what was really happening. Paradoxically, in the midst of an ambiguous story in which it is difficult to see what is going on, and which celebrates the possibility of multiple perspectives, Kincaid affirms the existence and importance of truth. Ironically, Kincaid arrives at the affirmation of truth through a series of ever-shifting fictions.

From the perspective of biographical criticism, one valid interpretation of "What I Have Been Doing Lately" is that it is a story about growing up and moving from childhood to adolescence and adulthood in the Caribbean. From an equally valid but different perspective, however, it is also a story about the power of storytelling to reveal truth and about the very process of writing stories.

Source: Shaun Strohmer, "An Overview of 'What I Have Been Doing Lately'," in *Short Stories for Students,* The Gale Group, 1999.

Moira Ferguson

In the following excerpt, Ferguson offers an interpretation of Kincaid's "What I Have Been Doing Lately," and claims that the story is "a discrete narrative about a child growing up in a world where psychological, physical, and political dominations seem the order of the day."

By her own admission, Jamaica Kincaid views her first publication, *At the Bottom of the River* (1983), as the text of a repressed, indoctrinated subaltern subject: "I can see that *At the Bottom of the River* was, for instance, a very unangry, decent, civilized book and it represents sort of this successful attempt by English people to make their version of a human being or their version of a person out of me. It amazes me now that I did that then. I would never write like that again, I don't think. I might go back to it, but I'm not very interested in that sort of expression any more." [Donna Perry, *Reading Black, Reading Feminist: A Critical Anthology*, edited by Henry Louis Gates, 1990.]

I want to argue that Jamaica Kincaid through diverse discussions of mothers sets up a subtle paradigm of colonialism that enables these repressions to be heard; the text, that is, masks and marks the role that colonialism plays in educating colonized people against their interests. For Kincaid herself, the project was a failure for the colonizers. . . .

In "What I Have Been Doing Lately," the narrator muses scenarios aloud to voice herself into an indeterminate environment, both visionary and material. This meditation on infinite space links to her sense of loneliness, perhaps as compensation for the absent mother, perhaps a sign of the merger of two "mothers." The nature that surrounds her reminds her of that which never deserts her: "To love the *infinite* universe is to give a material meaning, an objective meaning, to the *infinity* of the love for a mother. To love a *solitary* place, when we are abandoned by everyone, is to compensate for a painful absence; it is a reminder for us of the one who never abandons" [Gaston Bachelard, *Water and Dreams: An Essay on the Imagination Matter*, 1942]. Dreams of the past and future merge with the present. Another evocative monkey tale erupts where the monkey (the narrator) avenges itself against its enemy. In its first manifestation, the monkey does nothing, as if lying in wait, living up to its trickster image. In both cases, the narrator is an agent, but the point where the narrator stops and the monkey starts slips out of reach. That monkey remains elusive as it does throughout Kincaid's texts, signifying simultaneously the ubiquity of resistance, noncomplicity, and mimicry. . . .

Each section of *At the Bottom of the River* is a discrete narrative about a child growing up in a world where psychological, physical, and political dominations seem the order of the day. Little escape exists outside the imagination. Collectively assembled yet chronologically unconnected, each section loosely features recurring thematic elements, many of them overlapping: a state of mind at a given time (''Holidays''); an apprehension of something that is massively compressed (''Girl''); plural versions of the same experience (''What Have''); a sense of ontological abyss (''Blackness''); desire and imagining (''My Mother''); vignettes of school and peers that disclose jealousy, fear, and despair (''Wingless''); an attempt to normalize experience while maintaining great distance through a deliberate surface account (''Letter from Home''); a playing-out of oppositions between an inner and outer world, a mother-self dyad (''At Last''); self-reconciliation, self-knowledge, and an entry into light (''At the Bottom of the River'').

Operating within an economy of loss (of the mother, of primal love), the narrator embarks on a reconstitution of her world; she constructs more fluid boundaries. On the one hand, she articulates a world of beauty and preoedipal bonding where image and sweet sensation rule; throughout the ten sections, she probes how ''the onset of puberty creates the essential dialectic of adolescence—new possibilities and new dangers.''. . .

Source: Moira Ferguson, ''At the Bottom of the River: Mystical (De)coding'' in *Jamaica Kincaid: Where the Land Meets the Body,* University Press of Virginia, 1994 , pp. 7–40.

Bryant Mangum

Bryant Mangum is a member of the English Department at Virginia Commonwealth University. In the following excerpt, he discusses Kincaid's ''What I Have Been Doing Lately,'' and asserts that it offers a variation on ''the mythic story of the fall of man.''

The reader interested in the philosophical vision that informs all of Kincaid's work must come to terms with the allegory in ''At the Bottom of the River.'' At its most basic level the story affirms the fall of man from innocence into knowledge. Based simply on the fact that the narrator is able to return in her vision to the undivided world, the reader may

> " Each section of 'At the Bottom of the River' is a discrete narrative about a child growing up in a world where psychological, physical, and political dominations seem the order of the day. Little escape exists outside the imagination."

infer that the knowledge of the prelapsarian world constantly lures the individual who feels its existence back into union with it. . . .

The reality of the actual world in which people must live, of course, invariably intrudes on the remembered world of harmony as well as the dream world which attempts to recapture it and confronts Kincaid's narrators with truths that they have known and often tried to ignore: that people die; that they hurt each other; that they must be separated from people they love; that one must live in the world with the knowledge that he will die. In short, the narrators in the early stories are most often like the man on the threshold in the ''At the Bottom of the River'' allegory, and for this reason many of the stories offer variations on the mythic story of the fall of man. ''What I Have Been Doing Lately,'' for instance, tells of a little girl who is lying in bed before the doorbell rings and who imagines two versions of a story to be told in response to the imagined question about what she has been doing lately. In both answers the girl tells of intentionally falling into a hole, in effect an acknowledgment, on her part, of the fall of man. In the hole there is writing that she cannot read, an indication that she does not know how to deal with the fall; and so she climbs back out, attempting to deny her knowledge. In one version she thinks of building a bridge or taking a boat across the sea, and she becomes sad. In another she throws a rock at a monkey three times and he throws it back. Both versions of the story underline the point that things are separate from each other: land from land and man from other creatures. . . .

Story after story in *At the Bottom of the River* shows men and women in varying degrees of alienation from themselves, from each other, and from the wholeness and completeness that characterize the harmonious prelapsarian world. . . .

Thus far, therefore, the allegory in "At the Bottom of the River" has provided two different kinds of vision. The first is that of the man who simply refuses to accept the burden of consciousness, an alternative that is not really an option for Kincaid's characters. The second is the one that most of them have chosen, or more accurately, inherited: that of living with the knowledge of their mortality and with the understanding that such things as beauty and joy are subject to destruction without warning, a fact which creates frustration and despair. And moreover, memories of wholeness and completeness compound the frustration. In the early stories Kincaid presents the human dilemma inherent in this second alternative in the form of verbal collages which show people existing between the world of harmony and that of lost oneness with nature. . . .

Source: Bryant Mangum, "Jamaica Kincaid," in *Fifty Caribbean Writers: A Bio-Bibliographical Critical Sourcebook,* edited by Daryl Cumber Dance, Greenwood Press, 1986, pp. 255-63.

Sources

Barnaby, Karin and Pellegrino D'Acierno, editors. *C. G. Jung and the Humanities: Toward a Hermeneutics of Culture,* Princeton University Press, 1990, pp. 45-66, 185- 216.

Breiner, Laurence. "The Eighties," in *West Indian Literature,* Second Edition. Edited by Bruce King, Macmillan Education Ltd., 1995, pp. 76-88.

Charters, Ann, editor. *The Story and Its Writer: An Introduction to Short Fiction,* Fourth Edition, Bedford Books of St. Martin's Press, 1995.

Dance, Daryl Cumber. Introduction to *Fifty Caribbean Writers: A Bio-Bibliographical Critical Sourcebook,* pp. 1-8. New York: Greenwood Press, 1986.

Davis, Thulani. "Girl-Child in a Foreign Land," *The New York Times Book Review,* October 28, 1990, p. 11.

De Koven, Marianne. *Rich and Strange: Gender, History, Modernism,* Princeton, N.J.: Princeton University Press, 1991.

Dutton, Wendy. "Merge and Separate: Jamaica Kincaid's Fiction," *World Literature Today: A Literary Quarterly of*

the University of Oklahoma, Vol. 63, No. 3, Summer, 1989, pp. 406-10.

Garis, Leslie. "Through West Indian Eyes," *The New York Times Magazine,* October 7, 1990, pp. 42-4, 70, 78-80, 91.

Jacobi, Jolande. Translated by Ralph Mantheim from German. *Complex/Archetype/Symbol in the Psychology of C. G. Jung,* Pantheon Books, 1959, pp. 127-90.

Leavitt, David. "Brief Encounters," *The Village Voice,* January 17, 1984, p. 41.

Milton, Edith. "Making a Virtue of Diversity," *The New York Times Book Review,* January, 15 1984, p. 22.

Onwordi, Ike. "Wising Up," *The Times Literary Supplement,* November 29, 1985, p. 1374.

Samuels, Andrew, Bani Shorter and Fred Plaut. *A Critical Dictionary of Jungian Analysis,* Routledge & Kegan Paul, 1986, pp. 1-162.

Simmons, Diane. "At the Bottom of the River: Journey of Mourning," in *Jamaica Kincaid,* Boston: Twayne Publishers, 1994, pp. 73-100.

Storr, Anthony. *The Essential Jung,* Princeton University Press, 1983, pp. 13-27, 212-90.

Further Reading

Cudjoe, Selwyn R. "Jamaica Kincaid and the Modernist Project: An Interview," *Caribbean Women Writers: Essays from the First International Conference,* Edited by Selwyn R., Cudjoe, Editor, Calaloux Publications, 1990, pp. 215-32.
  Discusses Kincaid's career, her dislike for colonialism, her name change, her parents, *Annie John,* the universality of her work, and how Kincaid does and does not fit into the feminist and modernist movements.

Freeman, Suzanne. "Three Short collections with a Difference," *Ms.,* January, 1984, pp. 15-16.
  Freeman favorably reviews *At the Bottom of the River* and discusses Kincaid's ability to weave complex stories through her use of imagery and language.

Henry, Paget. *Peripheral Capitalism and Underdevelopment in Antigua,* Transaction Books, Inc., 1985, pp. 169-200.
  Discusses Antigua from a political-science perspective. Three chapters concern the economy, the state and the cultural system of Antigua during the postcolonial period.

Juneja, Renu. "Contemporary Women Writers," in *West Indian Literature,* Second Edition, edited by Bruce King, Macmillan Education, 1995, pp. 89-101.
  Outlines the preponderance of West Indian fiction written by women. Juneja discusses the plot of individual works and analyzes the way in which female authored texts fit into the greater themes of West Indian literature. She also discusses the unique contributions of women writers in the West Indian region.

Kenney, Susan. *The New York Times Book Review,* April 4, 1985, p. 6.

Review of *Annie John.*

Listfield, Emily. "Straight form the Heart," *Harper's Bazaar,* October, 1990.

    Interview with Kincaid, who discusses her career and personal life. Listfield also reviews *Lucy.*

Meditz, Sandra W. and Dennis M. Hanratty, editors. *Islands of the Commonwealth Caribbean: A Regional Study,* Federal Research Division, Library of Congress, 1989, pp. 1-42, 431-54.

    Provides a basic introduction to the Caribbean region with regard to its history, geography, politics, economic issues, health and welfare concerns, foreign relations, national security issues, and education systems.

Weathers, Diane. *Essence,* March, 1996, pp. 98, 100, and 132.

    Discusses *Autobiography of My Mother,* which was released in 1996.

Wunderkind

Carson McCullers

1936

Written in 1936, when Carson McCullers was 19 years old, "Wunderkind" was McCullers's first published work. It presents the story of Frances, a teenage girl who has been considered a musical prodigy but who, after years of training and sacrifice, seems suddenly incapable of fulfilling the bright expectations she has always held. In the brief space of a single piano lesson, we see her struggling to recover the confidence and artistry she once knew and trying to navigate a flood of conflicting emotions and desires that threaten to overwhelm her. Often praised as a sensitive, insightful portrayal of the pressures and isolation of adolescence, it is marked by a dramatic tension that increases relentlessly throughout the story—despite the fact that very little "action" occurs. That action takes place in the studio of her music teacher, but the story's actual *setting* is the intimate depths of Frances's troubled mind.

While teenagers and their problems are a common focus in fiction, relatively few "coming-of-age" stories were written while their authors were still teenagers themselves. Critical analysis of "Wunderkind" usually stresses its many autobiographical elements: McCullers had trained as a classical pianist for most of her own childhood and suddenly gave up her ambitions for a musical career after an emotional break in her relationship with a beloved piano teacher. Yet there are also intriguing differences between Frances's experience and that of her author, and while its details are specific to a

world of passionate artistry and intense pressures that few of us ever know, McCullers's vivid writing seems to evoke universal human feelings and dilemmas. As a result, readers of all ages, and vastly different experience, have been able to recognize themselves in this troubled young musician.

Author Biography

Born in Columbus, Georgia, in 1917, young Lula Carson Smith studied for years as a concert pianist, practicing five hours a day. Like the character Frances in ''Wunderkind'' (her first published story), she was devastated as a teenager by the realization that she would be unable to fulfill her high ambitions and expectations for a musical career. However, she soon transferred her energies to another artistic calling, and by the age of 23 had become a bestselling and critically acclaimed writer. Despite a troubled marriage and a series of disabling strokes that would cut her life short at age 50, Carson McCullers produced a body of work that has made her one of the most-admired writers of her generation, and one of the most enduring authors of the American Southern literary tradition.

Her childhood musical ambitions are particularly significant in regard to this story, which critics routinely classify as being ''obviously autobiographical.'' Born into comfortable surroundings, young Carson was encouraged to develop her talents. From the age of six, when she first expressed an interest, her parents provided her with a fine piano and the best available instructors. Unlike Mr. Bilderbach in ''Wunderkind,'' the author's musical mentor was a woman, Mary Tucker. When the former concert pianist moved to Columbus, Carson became her only pupil. McCullers studied with Tucker for four years, forming a close bond with her teacher. At fifteen, she experienced the first of her many health problems, a case of rheumatic fever that required several weeks of recovery in a sanitarium. By her own account (in an autobiographical sketch submitted to *Story* for the publication of ''Wunderkind'' when she was 19), it was at this point that she ''began to question whether she had the necessary physical stamina and the talent to be the concert pianist she fiercely held as her goal.''

Added to these doubts was a sudden change in her close relationship with her teacher. As Constance M. Perry relates it:

> Suddenly McCullers learned that the Tuckers would be leaving Columbus shortly. With angry feelings of abandonment, McCullers visited Mary Tucker, who was at that time seriously ill, and announced her own intention to abandon the piano. The rupture between teacher and pupil, lover and beloved, remained until McCullers invited the Tuckers to see her Broadway production of *The Member of the Wedding* ten years later.

As Perry's phrase ''lover and beloved'' indicates, critics have speculated on the nature of this relationship, at least as it appeared to the young student, and particularly in regard to the sexual implications they find in the story itself. Without assuming any physical relationship, they suggest that McCullers's attachment to Tucker may have included an element of sexual attraction, which, according to the moral standards of the time, would have been far more troubling and ''shameful'' than a teenager's early experiences of heterosexual desire. Such critics generally conclude that McCullers recast the teacher as a male in her story either to avoid any ''controversial'' reference to lesbianism, or perhaps to distance herself from that aspect of her own experience. Whatever its nature, the relationship was clearly a crucial one to McCullers, and its ending was a major trauma for her. The nature of that ending is another significant difference between ''Wunderkind'' and its author's experience: while Frances flees Bilderbach, rushing to leave the room ''before he would have to speak,'' McCullers confronted Tucker dramatically and resentfully. Though she had apparently been thinking of giving up music for quite a while, and had already begun to experiment at writing (encouraged by her parents with a new typewriter), the announcement of her decision seems to have been timed to hurt Tucker's feelings as much as possible.

The family had long expected Carson to study at New York's Julliard School of Music after high school, and despite her changed plans she went ahead with the move, working part-time while taking writing courses at night. Here she found two more artistic mentors, Sylvia Chatfield Bates at New York University and Whit Burnett at Columbia. Burnett was also editor of the prestigious *Story* magazine, and when McCullers wrote ''Wunderkind'' for his class in the summer of 1936, he agreed to publish it in *Story*. In 1937 she married Reeves

McCullers, also an aspiring writer, and moved with him to Charlotte, North Carolina, where she wrote her first novel, *The Heart is a Lonely Hunter.* Published in 1940, it sold well and was enthusiastically received by critics. In that same year, she divorced McCullers and moved back to New York; in 1941, she published her second novel, *Reflections in a Golden Eye,* and suffered the first of a series of cerebral strokes. She continued to write, and in 1943 published one of her most highly-regarded works, the novella *The Ballad of the Sad Cafe.*

She remarried McCullers in 1945, but it was an increasingly turbulent relationship; at one point, he began insisting that they carry out a double suicide. Shortly after she divorced him for a second time in 1953, Reeves McCullers killed himself. Subsequent strokes and operations left Carson McCullers partially paralyzed, reduced to typing with one finger, then writing in slow longhand, and finally dictating her work; yet she continued to write. The novel *The Member of the Wedding* was published in 1946, and adapted for the stage in 1950. A second play, *The Square Root of Wonderful,* appeared in 1958, and another novel, *Clock Without Hands,* in 1961. After yet another brain hemorrhage, Carson McCullers died in 1967 in Nyack, New York.

Plot Summary

Frances's Arrival

"Wunderkind" takes place on a winter afternoon in Cincinnati, Ohio, presumably in the 1930s ("the present," when the story was written). Fifteen-year-old Frances arrives at the home of her music teacher, Mr. Bilderbach, for her piano lesson. She is a bit early, and as she sits down to wait we see that she is restless and agitated; her fingers are twitching uncontrollably, and we are told that the sight of them intensifies "the fear that had begun to torment her for the past few months."

This fear seems to be centered on her music, which she has not performed as well lately as once she had. She silently encourages herself to have "a good lesson—like it used to be." As Bilderbach emerges from his studio to greet Frances, her thoughts drift briefly into the past (as they will often through-

out the story), and we learn that she has been studying with him for many years—most of her life, as it feels to her now. Their brief meeting only increases her tension, and we see that Bilderbach is also uncomfortable and distracted. The words they exchange seem light and pleasant (he explains that he is "running over a little sonatina" in the studio with a colleague, offers Frances milk and cake, and expresses confidence that she will have "a very fine lesson" today)—but both seem to be affecting a forced cheerfulness they do not feel. Frances tries to smile, but is arrested by the sudden vision of "her fingers sinking powerless into a blur of piano keys"; when Bilderbach makes his comment about the "fine lesson" he expects, his smile seems to "crumble at the corners." Mr. Lafkowitz, the violinist who has been playing with Bilderbach, also comes out and greets Frances familiarly, asking how her work is coming along. Again she seems to be overwhelmed by anxiety, and by a sense of being "clumsy and overgrown," which Lafkowitz seems to bring out in her. She hesitates, and looks uncertainly toward Bilderbach before giving her reply. He says nothing, and we are told only that he "turned away"—but later, Frances is haunted by "the memory of Mister Bilderbach's face as he stared at her a moment ago." It is clearly not a look of reassurance, and she bluntly tells Lafkowitz, "I'm doing terribly." Lafkowitz begins to encourage her, but Bilderbach, already back in the studio, interrupts with "a harsh chord" from the piano, calling him back to the duet they had been playing. As Lafkowitz returns to the music, he calls Frances's attention to "the picture of Heime" in a magazine on the table—Heime Israelsky being Lafkowitz's star violin student.

Waiting for the Lesson

While Frances waits, McCullers takes the reader inside the girl's troubled mind in a hectic series of flashbacks, dreams, and meditations that crowd her thinking, all set to the background music of Lafkowitz and Bilderbach's duet. Opening the magazine Lafkowitz had indicated, Frances sees a portrait of Heime Israelsky, who is being hailed as a "talented young violinist," and appears to be on the verge of an illustrious concert career. Suddenly she shifts to the unpleasant memory of that morning's breakfast. Frances prefers to skip breakfast and munch candy bars at school, but today her father had served her a fried egg; when the yolk broke and "the slimy yellow oozed over the white,'' Frances had burst into tears. Whatever the source of this intense emotional reaction, it is the same feeling she has now, as she places the magazine with Heime's photo back on the table.

Closing her eyes and listening to the men's music, Frances feels exhausted, and drifts into the "weary half-dreams" she has been having "just before she dropped off to sleep on the nights when she had over-practiced." Her nightmarish visions are composed of the looming faces of Bilderbach, Mrs. Bilderbach, Lafkowitz, and Heime; of "phrases of music seesawing crazily"; and the repeated German word *Wunderkind* ("miracle child," an artistic prodigy.) These elements swirl around her in grotesque distortion, building to a terrifying crescendo. On some nights, we learn, when she is not so tired, the dreams are simpler and far more pleasant; at such times "the music soar[s] clearly in her head," and she experiences "quick, precise little memories"—not the emotional confusion of her nightmares, or the jumbled memories that tumble through her mind now. After a brief reference to a concert she and Heime have recently given, and the repetition of the word *Wunderkind*, Frances's thoughts turn to Mr. Bilderbach. Her thinking is still restless and disjointed, but begins to follow two distinct paths: a review of the time she has spent as Bilderbach's student, and an effort to account for the crushing difficulties that have plagued her music recently.

Frances has been called a *Wunderkind* for years, and has embraced the musical career others have foreseen for her. She feels her circumstances are disappointingly ordinary, and she regrets her "plain American name," wishing she hadn't been "born and brought up in just Cincinnati." In contrast, the world of music seems exotic and romantic, peopled by accomplished artists with European names and continental manners. We see that Bilderbach has been a caring and inspirational mentor to her. Frances recalls her first lesson with him, at the age of twelve; he was immediately impressed by her technical skill and artistic potential, but challenged her to develop a deeper understanding of the music she plays, and to perfect her ability to play it "as it must be played." In a memorable passage, she recalls his first words to her, while the narrator's descriptions begin to suggest complications in Frances's feelings about him:

> "Now we begin all over," he said that first day. "It—playing music—is more than cleverness. If a twelve-

Carson McCullers

year-old girl's fingers cover so many keys to a second—that means nothing."

He tapped his broad chest and his forehead with his stubby hand. "Here and here. You are old enough to understand that." He lighted a cigarette and gently blew the first exhalation above her head. "And work—work—work—. We will start now with these Bach Inventions and these little Schumann pieces." His hands moved again—this time to jerk the cord of the lamp behind her and point to the music. "I will show you how I wish this practiced. Listen carefully now."

She had been at the piano for almost three hours and was very tired. His deep voice sounded as though it had been straying inside her for a long time. She wanted to reach out and touch his muscle-flexed finger that pointed out the phrases, wanted to feel the gleaming gold band ring and the strong hairy back of his hand.

Bilderbach's task is to help Frances take her playing to the next level, beyond technical ability, to the mature artistry that draws on both the mind and the heart ("here and here"), enabling her to interpret the music with passionate feeling. But her mind and heart are both in turmoil, and the strong feelings music arouses are mixed with other, more disturbing passions. Throughout the story, McCullers flavors her descriptions of Bilderbach with masculine, sensual imagery (in this passage, his "deep voice" that "sounded as though it had been straying inside of her for a long time," his "muscle-flexed finger," the "strong hairy back of his hand"). Such imagery continues throughout the story, strongly suggesting that Bilderbach has become a focus for Frances's awakening sexuality. The "gold band" she wants to reach out and touch is his wedding ring, and her memories drift into a consideration of the Bilderbachs' marriage. Mrs. Bilderbach is described as "quiet and fat and slow," and has been frustrated in her own youthful musical ambitions. The fact that the couple have no children, along with an uncomfortable embrace she once observed, suggests that the Bilderbachs's union is not sustained by physical passion.

As Frances's lessons have continued, she has become almost a part of the household, often staying for dinner and spending the night following her Saturday afternoon lessons. Her musical mission has come to dominate her life; she sees nothing of her high school peers, and Heime has been "the only friend of her own age," as the two often take their lessons together at Bilderbach's. But this "friendship" is a strained one, and Frances seems jealous of Heime's success. She reminds herself of certain advantages he has over her: that he has been playing since he was four, that he has a private tutor and doesn't have to attend school, even that the violin "must be" an easier instrument to master than the piano. Described from her viewpoint, Heime is unattractive and physically immature.

Frances's thoughts return to her recent concert with Heime, which had been a critical triumph for him, but highly unsuccessful for herself—a disappointment that still stuns her months later. Bilderbach had objected to a particular selection for that program, a sonata by Bloch, which showcased Heime's talents but was "inappropriate" for Frances, in his opinion. Although she had wanted to include the piece as much as had Heime and Lafkowitz, she now resents her teacher for giving in and feels "cheated" after the critics agreed that she "lacked the temperament for that type of music."

She now recalls an incident from a year ago, when she played a Fantasia and Fugue by Bach for the two teachers. Bilderbach seems pleased by her rendition, but Lafkowitz suddenly asks if she knows how many children Bach had fathered in his life. When she answers that it was more than twenty, he observes that the composer "could not have been so

cold—then." As in the reviews of her concert with Heime, her music is judged to be "lacking in feeling"—but here, Lafkowitz implies that the missing emotion is one of adult (and specifically male) sexual passion. Bilderbach reproaches his colleague in German, objecting to the mention of such matters to a *Kind* ("child") like Frances. Frances had "caught the point easily enough," but feigns the innocence she feels Bilderbach expects of her.

Another memory of Bilderbach now passes through her mind: when she graduated from junior high, he had insisted on providing her a fancy pink gown for the occasion, taking an active role in shopping for the material and designing the dress his wife sewed for her—despite the fact that the dress makes "no difference" to Frances. In this scene, it almost seems that she is the Bilderbachs' own daughter, and his fatherly enthusiasm and concern that she will look elegant on this "special night" seem to exceed the usual teacher-student relationship. From her tortured present, this memory reflects a happier, secure time, when "[n]othing mattered much except playing the music as it must be played, bringing out the thing that must be in her."

Her playing had been showing improvement then, as it continued to until about four months ago. Throughout her troubled reverie, Frances has been grasping to explain the sudden decline in her performance and the increasing panic with which she has struggled to regain her confidence. The list of Heime's "advantages" is one such attempt; it also includes the fact that he is male, and even that he is Jewish. (Frances seems to feel that Jews are "natural" musicians, and that the elusive quality she failed to express in the Bloch sonata has something to do with her not being Jewish.) The memory of Lafkowitz's comments about Bach not being "cold" suggests another possibility: that she is not yet experienced enough to understand the grown-up passions Lafkowitz feels the composer was expressing. But this explanation doesn't seem sufficient, for she realizes that "she would grow older" and transcend these limitations. She is also aware that the onset of adolescence, and the physical changes it brings, has often ended the careers of promising "kids" who find they can no longer sustain their childhood mastery—but she desperately denies that such a change is happening to her. "Once it was there, for sure," she thinks of her earlier confidence, "[a]nd you didn't lose things like that." But her words seem unconvincing, for as Lafkowitz and Bilderbach end their duet, the nightmare vision of Bilderbach's face, swirling fragments of music, and the term *Wunderkind* sweep over her again.

The Lesson

Bilderbach does not see Lafkowitz out, as is his custom; instead, he remains at the piano, "softly pressing a solitary note." Frances wants to delay her lesson as long as possible, and makes small talk with Lafkowitz about Heime's recent accomplishments—though this is hardly a pleasant subject for her. As she finally settles down to the keyboard, Bilderbach announces that today they will "begin all over" and "start from scratch," recalling his words at her first lesson. But as in his too-cheerful greeting, his manner is false; he looks "as though he were trying to act a part in a movie," and soon drops the act, slouching his "heavy shoulders" and busying himself with selecting the music for her to play. From the start, Frances feels "hemmed in" by the piano keys, "stiff and white and dead-seeming." She knows the notes are wrong as she is playing them; it is as if her hands are "separate from the music that was in her." Bilderbach interrupts her twice, reminding her how the music should be played, but his urgings only seem to inhibit her playing more. She suggests that his interruptions are hampering her concentration, and he agrees to let her play the piece through, but Frances remains unable to shape the music as she wants to: "her hands seemed to gum in the keys like limp macaroni and she could not imagine the music as it should be." When she finishes, he sums up his response with the single word, "no."

Seeing her desperation, Bilderbach suddenly suggests she play something called "The Harmonious Blacksmith," a simple piece that was one of the first they had worked on together. He speaks with the tone of voice "he used for children," and addresses her by the pet-name *Bienchen* ("little bee"), urging her to make the music "happy and simple," recalling how strongly she had played it in the past. But even this basic exercise is beyond her now. As her panic builds, she feels as if her bones are hollow and her body is drained of its blood, and that her heart is dead, "gray and limp and shriveled at the edges like an oyster." Again the nightmare vision of his throbbing face returns to her; her lips begin to shiver, and tears well up in her eyes. She

now gives up entirely, hopelessly whispering, "I can't. . . . I don't know why, but I just can't—can't any more."

Bilderbach's "tense body" relaxes at these words, and as he rises, she grabs her sheet-music and rushes from the room. She quickly gathers her things, hurrying to leave the house "before he would have to speak" to her. Her last glimpse of him is of his hands, which have held such fascination for her, but are now "relaxed and purposeless." Frances stumbles outside in confusion, turns the wrong way, and hurries down a street that is filled with images of childhood, "confused with the noise and bicycles and the games of other children."

Characters

Bienchen
See Frances

Mr. Bilderbach

Mr. Bilderbach has been Frances's piano teacher for three years and is the person whose approval means the most to her. As he has nurtured her artistic potential, they have grown much closer than is usual for a teacher-student relationship; she has become almost a member of the Bilderbach household, often staying for dinner after her lesson, and sometimes even spending the night there. Bilderbach has been both a mentor and a father-figure to Frances, but as the story begins, we see that their fruitful relationship has grown complicated and troubled in recent months and is a source of great anxiety to both of them.

Although he was born in America, Bilderbach's ancestry is Dutch-Czech, and he was raised in Germany. These details make him seem rather exotic and romantic to Frances, who is eager to escape what she considers to be a boring and mundane background. His deep understanding and passionate appreciation of music make him her artistic role-model, and his wise, challenging instruction is crucial to her career. Bilderbach has no children of his own, and it seems that both he and Frances have enjoyed the feeling that his protege is

A performance at Carnegie Hall in 1950.

also a kind of "adopted daughter." Her music satchel was a birthday present from him, and when she graduated junior high, he enthusiastically took up the project of providing a fancy dress for the occasion; at such times, it seems that the pride he takes in his talented *Wunderkind* could not be greater than if she really *were* "his own girl."

Physical descriptions of Bilderbach, presented from Frances's viewpoint, are marked by images of masculine strength and virility, suggesting that she feels a sexual attraction for him. Yet on the surface, he doesn't appear to be an especially virile specimen: he has "thin hair," "smoke-yellowed teeth,"

and a "narrow face"; he wears horn-rimmed glasses, and while his voice is "deep," it is also "blunt" and "guttural." Moreover, he is married and obviously middle-aged, and so would seem to be an inappropriate and unattainable object for her desires. Critics who employ principles of Freudian psychology have made much of the way Bilderbach seems to combine fatherly affection and sexual attraction for Frances, relating it to the so-called "Electra complex," which assumes that an important stage in a girl's sexual development involves feeling desire for the father, and a corresponding jealous rivalry with the mother for his love. Frances does seem to consider Mrs. Bilderbach as something of a rival, and believes that their childless marriage is devoid of sexual passion. But there is no suggestion that she will act on her desires; she and Bilderbach both seem confused and frustrated by them, and nostalgic for her younger days, when their relationship seemed simpler and happier, and her musical potential seemed unlimited. Frances's dependence on him for musical guidance, and her recent inability to benefit from it, seem to have left them both feeling trapped in a relationship that has grown uncontrollable, and can satisfy none of the hopes they have had for it. When Frances flees from her final, tortured lesson, we are told that "[h]is tense body slackened." He no doubt feels defeated at this point, but this may well be mixed with a sense of relief.

In their failed relationship can be seen the hopeless confusion of two kinds of "passion": the sexual desires the teenager is beginning to experience, and the strong emotions she knows must be an essential part of her mature art. Frances's need to earn Bilderbach's approval through a passionate musical performance is uncomfortably similar to the position of a lover who is anxious to satisfy her partner sexually; in her emotional confusion, she is unable to separate the two "passions." For his part, Bilderbach has hoped to inspire one kind of strong emotion, and is now caught up in feelings he never intended to evoke; he may sense the way things are going wrong, but like his student, seems unable to untangle the emotional web that has caught them both.

Critics who stress the "autobiographical" nature of the story and compare its details to those of McCullers's own childhood musical ambitions, point out a striking difference: if Frances is supposed to "stand for" McCullers herself, then Bilderbach is the fictional representative of her *female* piano teacher, Mary Tucker. If the story's sexual overtones are also "accurate," the discomfort Frances experiences may well have been even more intense for the author in "real life." At least by the moral standards of the 1930s, the very suggestion of homosexual desire would have seemed far more shocking and "unnatural" than a young girl's experience of heterosexual longings, and a story that treated lesbian themes might have faced censorship—even if the attraction were only implied and never acted upon. McCullers's apparent decision to recast her mentor as a male has attracted wide speculation, and adds an intriguing dimension to the many possible "readings" of the story.

Frances

Frances is the story's central character, a fifteen-year-old girl who is undergoing a wrenching emotional crisis in her life. Although the story is narrated in the third person, we experience its events from Frances's point of view, sharing her thoughts, feelings, and nightmarish visions, as her turmoil builds to an explosive, terrified climax.

On the surface, Frances's "problem" is with her music. In recent months, her piano playing has been very disappointing, both to her and to her teacher, Mr. Bilderbach, and as she arrives at his house she silently prays for "a good lesson—like it used to be." This is no small matter, for Frances's life has been centered around her music. Since early childhood she has been considered a *Wunderkind*, a musical prodigy, and, like those around her, Frances has always assumed she would go on to a career as a concert musician. She has prepared diligently for that career, at a considerable personal cost; though she attends high school, she has no social life with her fellow students, devoting all her non-school hours to her music, and practicing to the point of exhaustion. Her own family appears just once in the story, in a brief, disturbing flashback to having breakfast with her father earlier that day. The story is set not in a family setting, but among the "second family" of Frances's musical world, a set of relationships that seems more primary and vital than those with her blood relatives: her beloved mentor, Mr. Bilderbach, and his wife; Bilderbach's colleague, a violin teacher named Lafkowitz; and (though he doesn't appear directly) Lafkowitz's pupil Heime, who, like Frances, has long been considered a budding musical genius. As Frances's playing has faltered, Heime seems poised to move into the world of adult success that had long been projected for both students.

In itself, this constitutes a crisis in Frances's young life; but as the story unfolds, we see that her musical difficulties are part of a complex inner turmoil, which takes many forms. At times, Frances focuses on her talent itself, doubting whether she is gifted or devoted enough to fulfill everyone's high expectations. But her anxieties extend beyond music, reflecting the many changes and dislocations of adolescence: the confused early stirrings of sexual attraction, fears about the challenges and pressures of adulthood, and a kind of nostalgia for a childhood that seems to be slipping away just as she most needs its comfort and security. Although she is unable to express her conflicting emotions to others, the author reveals them to us; like Frances herself, we are carried along by a relentless tension that builds throughout the story.

Unlike the other characters, we are given no overall description of Frances's physical appearance. In this sense, the reader literally ''sees'' through Frances's own eyes; we do, for example, have a detailed description of her hands—when she looks down in horror at the uncontrollable twitching of her fingers. We observe the things that are visible to Frances herself—but more importantly, we experience the flood of memories, emotions, and thoughts that rush through her mind. Most of these concern her teacher, Mr. Bilderbach, who is enormously important to her. Their relationship has sustained and inspired her; his wise and patient instruction is to be the foundation of the brilliant career she craves. Despite this, she feels dissatisfied with the circumstances she has been born into, seeming to consider them unbearably ordinary: her ''plain American name,'' the fact that her hometown is ''just Cincinnati,'' not some exotic, faraway place. In contrast, the musical world she envisions is bright and romantic, filled with exotic foreigners and continental elegance; by taking her place in that world, fulfilling her promise as a *Wunderkind*, she expects to transcend ordinariness completely, achieving fame and admiration for her ever-growing artistry.

Frances loves Bilderbach. She reveres his deep feeling for music, and fully appreciates both the tender care and the demanding discipline with which he has fostered her talents. They have grown very close in her three years of study with him, both taking joy in the flowering of her musical powers. He is very much a father-figure to her, and the childless Bilderbachs have come to treat her almost as if she were their own daughter. She often stays for dinner after her Saturday afternoon lesson in their home, and frequently spends the night there. Bilderbach rarely calls her ''Frances,'' preferring a childish nickname, *Bienchen* (''little bee'' in German), which reflects his fatherly affection. At one point, he expresses this aspect of their relationship directly: ''You see, Bienchen, I know you so well— as if you were my own girl.'' Though we have no clear view of her relationship with her own family, the fact that they take up so little of her attention suggests that she considers this her ''real family,'' and feels almost as if she *is* ''his own girl.'' But this wonderful relationship, on which so much depends, has been changing dramatically over the past few months, becoming as frustrating and distressing as it had previously been exciting and productive. The source of these changes appears to be the fact that she is now leaving girlhood, and becoming a woman. Her awakening sexuality, and her growing awareness of the adult pressures she is expected to endure, have eroded and complicated her safe musical ''home,'' and she seems to be feeling an intense (and intensely uncomfortable) sexual attraction for Bilderbach. The nature of the love she feels for him, and her need to please him by investing passionate expression in her music, have grown complex and disorienting, inspiring her with alarming desires, grotesque night-visions, and a cauldron of emotions that threaten to overwhelm her.

As she reluctantly begins her lesson, flounders hopelessly in her efforts to play the music ''as it must be played,'' and finally rushes out of the house—apparently abandoning her musical dream forever—Frances struggles for self-control. Not only is she making no progress, she can no longer manage pieces she had once performed brilliantly. In the ''classic'' teenage dilemma, she is trapped between childhood and maturity, pulled in both directions but unable to fit either role. Between a childhood of special treatment and immense promise, and a projected future of ambitious achievement, she lives in a terrifying present of utter failure and helpless isolation. Her drive to succeed, and the emotional nature of the music that surrounds her, give her an exaggerated experience of the ''normal'' displacements and difficult adjustments of adolescence. Her successful entry into the adult world, which she has always assumed and anticipated, now seems an impossible task. Remembering the strength of her bond with Bilderbach in simpler, happier times, she seems to long for a childhood she has largely missed out on. But at other times, she realizes that she has already left much of childhood behind—particularly, its innocent, uncomplicated dreams of accomplishment and fulfillment. As the story ends, she seems completely severed from the bright future she has imagined, perhaps from any future at all. When she flees in desperation, there is a suggestion that she is trying to escape back into childhood, or to outrace time itself. The street she rushes down teems with childhood imagery, ''confused with noise and bicycles and . . . games''—but they are ''the games of other children,'' not her own, just as the future she is fleeing will be inhabited by someone else.

Heime Israelsky

Lafkowitz's star violin student, Heime is the only person of Frances's own age with whom she has any close association. Like her, Heime has long been considered a musical *Wunderkind*. He and Frances have often taken their lessons together, and recently gave a joint concert which attracted critical attention. But their musical friendship is also a rivalry, and that aspect of it has intensified lately. Reviews of their concert praised his playing lavishly, but found Frances's music "thin" and "lacking in feeling." Heime has gone on to greater fame and recognition, just as Frances encounters paralyzing difficulties; his success now seems assured, while her own prospects are gravely threatened. In her desperate effort to understand her crisis, Frances defines herself in opposition to Heime, who takes no direct part in the story but appears frequently in Frances's confused flashbacks.

Heime has been playing since the age of four, longer than Frances has; while she must attend high school, he has always had a private tutor, enabling him to devote even more time and effort to his music. Looking at a photo taken six months ago, Frances believes that he "hadn't changed much," while recent months have brought alarming changes for her; at one point, his hands are described as "babyish," with "hard little blobs of flesh bulging over the shortcut nails." These details suggest that he is still on the childhood side of adolescence, while Frances's sense of being "clumsy and overgrown" and her emotional turmoil indicate that she has been maturing rapidly. He seems unattractive and self-absorbed and has no concern for his personal grooming, often failing even to wash his hands before playing. When they appear onstage together, he is visibly shorter, reaching only to her shoulder; she feels this may have made the critics more sympathetic to him, and more exacting in their judgment of her own playing.

Like Lafkowitz, Heime is Jewish; and like every other musician in Frances's circle, he is male, and presumably of European ancestry. Each difference appears to be an advantage; music is presented as a male-dominated domain, whose greatest achievers tend to be European and, particularly, Jewish. As a "plain American" from "just Cincinnati," and above all as a woman, Frances seems to face obstacles Heime does not. This may appear to be an effort to make excuses for herself, but it also indicates how isolated she is, and how much of "an outsider" she feels herself to be, in the brilliant artistic world she so desperately hopes to join.

Mr. Lafkowitz

A colleague of Bilderbach's, Mr. Lafkowitz is Heime's violin teacher and a significant member of Frances's musical "family." He and his *Wunderkind* pupil are frequent visitors to the Bilderbach home, where Frances and Heime often take their lessons together. At the start of the story, as Frances arrives for her lesson, Lafkowitz and Bilderbach are playing a duet; when they resume, we see that both are passionate musicians, "lustfully drawing out all that was there" in the music. However, while Frances respects his musical ability, as an individual he seems to be an ominous and disturbing force whose intensity and worldliness are threatening to her.

Physically, Lafkowitz is "small," with "a weary look" and a "sallow Jewish face." His mouth is thin, his eyes are "sharp bright slits." The story's detailed description of these eyes provides a key to his personality: when he first speaks to Frances, his brows are arched "as though asking a question," but his eyelids drowse "languorous and indifferent." This suggests a concealed, indirect manner, and his most important conversation with Frances proceeds more by insinuation than by confrontation. Critiquing her rendition of a piece by Bach, Lafkowitz points out that the composer had fathered over twenty children in his life—implying that Frances's playing is "cold," lacking in the mature (and specifically sexual) passion Bach was (presumably) expressing. Bilderbach disapproves his mention of such matters to a pupil so young, and in his paternal, protective manner toward her, stands in sharp contrast to Lafkowitz. Significantly, Bilderbach is also presented as clearly more masculine; we are introduced to Lafkowitz through his voice, "almost like a woman's, [Frances] thought, compared to Bilderbach's," a voice which spins out his words "in a silky, unintelligible hum." While Bilderbach's criticism of her music is more devastating to Frances, it is blunt and direct, and tempered, at least in her mind, with fatherly concern.

Lafkowitz also plays an important role in Frances's disastrous concert with Heime; it is he who proposes that the final selection be a piece by Bloch, music which showcases Heime's talents but, in Bilderbach's opinion, is not "appropriate" for Frances. Though she had wanted to play the piece as much as Heime and Lafkowitz had, when the critics confirm Bilderbach's judgment, she feels "cheated," and resents him for giving in. Here, as throughout the story, the reader's response to the character is limited by the narrative point of view: the fact that we "see" him only through Frances's troubled eyes. Lafkowitz appears to have promoted Heime's career somewhat at Frances's expense, and her jealousy of Heime's success includes resentment of his teacher. We don't learn enough about Lafkowitz to be certain of his "true intentions" or motivations—but we are vividly aware of his effect on Frances. She even recognizes this confusion, though it overwhelms her; when we are told that "Mister Lafkowitz always made her feel clumsy and overgrown," the statement is prefaced by the realization that he had this effect "without meaning to." Lafkowitz has his unattractive qualities, but is not a full-fledged villain; most of what we see of him is saturated in Frances's own bitter disappointment.

Themes

Alienation and Loneliness

It is almost a convention for stories about adolescence to express themes of "alienation," by presenting young characters who feel lost and overwhelmed by the pressures of their circumstances. While this may in part be an artistic stereotype of the teenager, it seems also to have some basis in reality: for most people, at least, the years just before adulthood are marked by intense, private emotions, and at least occasional feelings of isolation and confusion.

In "Wunderkind," Frances seems paralyzed by her feelings and sees no one she can turn to for help in sorting them out. In many ways, the tension she feels is not a direct result of the way she is treated, but grows from her own discomfort and self-consciousness, and from the conflicting feelings she projects on others. She recognizes this at times, but the knowledge is of little help to her. For example, Lafkowitz makes her feel "clumsy and overgrown"; to realize that he does so "without meaning to" doesn't change her response to him. And while there is little (if any) evidence that Bilderbach welcomes or encourages the sexual attraction she seems to feel for him, that knowledge makes her feelings no more bearable: it simply means that the object of her desires is unattainable. Both teacher and student seem embarrassed by her changed feelings and are alarmed by Frances's recent musical setbacks. In their desperation, both would like to revert to "the good old days" when she was more obviously a child, when her potential seemed limitless, and their relationship was far simpler and easier. Bilderbach uses his childish nickname for her, *Bienchen* ("little bee"), and as her lesson begins, he proposes that she "begin all over" and "start from scratch"; when it continues

to go poorly, he asks her to play "The Harmonious Blacksmith," a simple piece that was one of the first she ever played for him. She resents his condescension, and the fact that his voice is "the one he used for children," but in other ways, she still wants him to be fatherly and protective toward her. When Lafkowitz alludes to adult sexuality in discussing a work by Bach, Bilderbach reproves him in German, using the word *Kind* ("child"). But Frances is not a child; we're told that she "caught the point easily enough." However, she gladly fulfills her teacher's expectation of childish innocence: "she felt no deception in keeping her face blank and immature because that was the way Mister Bilderbach wanted her to look."

Frances's alienation includes the "classic" teenage sense of "in-betweenness," the feeling that she "just doesn't fit"—not in the secure world of childhood she is rapidly outgrowing, nor in the adult world that awaits, nor in the future life that has been projected for her. Her crisis is real and troubling enough, but it is intensified by her alienation and isolation; she is not only overwhelmed by her emotions, but by the feeling that her anguish is something no one else can know, or help her to resolve.

Success and Failure

Unlike most other teenagers, Frances's turmoil is further complicated by the career demands she has taken on from so early an age, and the competitive pressure for artistic success. She cannot remain a *Wunderkind* any more than she can remain a child. The skill and potential she has shown in the past are no longer good enough; it is time for her to approach mature artistry, and significant achievements on the adult level. Readers may even feel she undermines her own musical career: by giving in to its pressures does she flee from Bilderbach himself (who seems to want only to help her achieve her dream), or from what he represents—the obligation to live up to the high expectations everyone has had for her? Her musical ability has always made people treat her as "special" and exceptional; in a sense, her musicianship has been her very identity, never questioned, so much an assumed part of her life that, without it, she may feel she hardly exists at all. (Her final musical failure is depicted in images of physical death and decay: the feeling that "her bones were hollow and there was no blood left in her," her heart "gray and limp and shriveled at the edges.")

Topics for Further Study

- Frances's talent has led her to take on pressures and demands that make her experience of childhood and early adolescence quite different from that of most other children. Our culture shows us many examples of such "prodigies" and the challenges they must face, often with disastrous effects later in life: child actors, students with genius-level IQs who are placed in accelerated educational programs, and athletes in sports like gymnastics, tennis, and swimming. The parents of such children are often torn between two sets of wishes for them: that they receive the training they need to develop their gifts, and that they have a "normal" childhood as a foundation for their future adjustment. Research the lives of three such *"Wunderkinder,"* the ways their parents have tried to balance these needs, and the effects their childhood experiences seem to have had on them. Write an essay that reports your findings, and presents your own conclusions on how such children should best be raised.

- In her analysis of "Wunderkind," Alice Hall Petry observes that much of the story's energy comes from "the capacity of music to evoke intense emotional responses, including sexual ones: "'Wunderkind' would never materialize as a story if Bilderbach were teaching Frances to pitch horseshoes." From the earliest ballads, music and storytelling have often been com-

bined: songs of all kinds (from opera to rap) are used to tell stories, while music becomes a central element in "narrative arts" ranging from religious pageants to movies and Broadway musical–as well as films, plays, or stories *about* music and musicians. Choose two examples, in different media (e.g., a film musical and a short story with a musical theme; or a rock opera and the background music in a soap opera), and write an essay tracing the specific ways music works to reinforce the storytelling in each case.

- Teenagers—their trials and tribulations, their fads and fashions, their problems with parents, peers, and the opposite sex—appear prominently in cultural productions of all kinds, and are often portrayed in an exaggerated manner. They may be hopeless misfits or love-struck dreamers, lazy slackers or vicious criminals, but their appearance and behavior almost always stands in opposition to the ways of adults. Consider the way teenagers are stereotyped in films, stories, or news reports that are written from an adult point of view, as well the stereotypes of grown-ups in productions geared to teen audiences. Selecting two examples of each kind, compare the stereotypes to the realities you see around you, and explain what these exaggerated portrayals suggest about the way each group views the other across the "generation gap."

While the potential for great achievement may magnify one's sense of worth, it also carries the devastating possibility of failure and disappointment. A contemporary psychologist might diagnose Frances's dilemma as a "fear of success," rooted in her suspicion that, however much approval she may receive from others, she is unworthy of their high regard, and in her resentment for the burden of their expectations. According to this way of thinking, it actually becomes preferable to embrace one's own failure than to have to cope with the pressures of competition and success.

In this case, the pressure to succeed is still further complicated, by gender issues: the additional obstacles and challenges faced by female artists and professionals, particularly in McCullers's time. Feminist scholars have made much of this aspect of her work, and the theme is also addressed in her first novel, *The Heart is a Lonely Hunter* . That book's main character, Mick Kelly, is also a musician, and her artistic career increasingly conflicts with her sexuality. In "Wunderkind," music is presented as a specifically-male domain, and as a vehicle for the expression of a passion that (in Lafkowitz's discussion of Bach) is specifically identified with male sexuality. Her fellow *Wunderkind,* Heime, is seen as having several advantages over Frances: that he has a private tutor, and can devote more time to practicing; that he is Jewish, and therefore (in her mind) closer to the "exotic" world of classical music, which she associates with Europeans in general and Jews in particular; that the music chosen for their big concert together had showcased his talents more than hers. But a more fundamental "advantage" is simply that he is male (like her musical "masters" and most of the great musicians she knows about), and therefore his musical success will not be considered as "exceptional" as hers would be. Such double-standards were long assumed in most artistic fields, and include the notions that worldly achievement of any kind is a contradiction of woman's "natural role" as wife and mother and that female sexuality or psychology are somehow incompatible with "the artistic temperament." Although she quickly achieved widespread fame as a writer, McCullers surely struggled against these social obstacles to her success, and, as this early story reveals, was intensely aware of them from an early age.

Style

Point of View

Technically, "Wunderkind" depends greatly on the skillful and effective way McCullers establishes Frances's point of view in the reader's mind. Allowing us "inside a character's head" usually leads us to identify and sympathize with that character; but in this case, it is essential to our understanding and central to the story's development. Through flashbacks and internal monologue, the reader is led to discover the elements of Frances's crisis (things we could learn in no other way) and to share her claustrophobic terror.

Perhaps the best way to appreciate this young writer's achievement is to consider how little "action" her story really contains. All we are given is a teenager's piano lesson, lasting perhaps half an hour. The main character is mostly inarticulate, and almost paralyzed by anxiety. She is nervous when she arrives, grows increasingly flustered as her lesson goes poorly, and finally storms out of the house. She struggles to contain and control her feelings, and can say nothing to explain herself to her teacher but a hopeless, whispered, "I can't. . . . I

don't know why, but I just can't—can't any more." Such a scene may rouse our sympathies, disturb us, or intrigue us but, told from any "outside" point of view, the girl's distress will remain largely a mystery. Readers, and other characters, may speculate about its causes; we may even dismiss it as a "simple" tale of failure and frustration, or of a high-strung, temperamental musician. Frances is so isolated in her misery that we must look to her own mind for explanations, though she herself is struggling for explanation. Her thoughts are confused, darting back and forth between the past and the present, between dreams and realities—but through them, the reader learns how her crisis has been building over time, and the terrifying forms it has taken.

The story is told by an "outside," third-person narrator, not by Frances herself. But events are described as they appear to her, and as they occur in her mind. We don't receive any information she doesn't have access to; for example, she is the only character for whom we have no overall physical description. We cannot say what her face looks like—because she can't see her own face. We do, on the other hand, receive detailed accounts of her hands—as she looks down at her own twitching, nervous fingers. We follow her awareness, both of her physical surroundings and of her own thoughts and feelings. In this way, we are forced to adopt her point of view and to work our way through its limitations, reaching for understandings that elude her. Frances's sexual feelings for Bilderbach, for example, are never directly stated—and to accurately convey her point of view, they *cannot* be, for she is only vaguely conscious of them herself. Like the clumsy, uncertain musical phrasing she displays during her lesson, she fully realizes that some of the things she feels are "wrong"—not what is expected from her, not what she expects from herself—and senses that the results will be disastrous. While Bilderbach can pinpoint her musical problems and explain ways to overcome them, there is no one to help her understand the disturbing, unwanted emotions she's experiencing. She applies her considerable intelligence to the problem and traces its outlines, but conscious understanding remains just beyond her grasp. Sympathizing with her, we apply ourselves to the same problem, trying to see what she does not.

The long section leading up to Frances's lesson may seem confusing, and requires close, careful reading, but it allows McCullers to present a great deal of information in relatively few words. Within the few brief minutes it takes for Lafkowitz and Bilderbach to play a sonatina, we pass through three years' time, learning the history of Frances's relationship with her teacher and the recent events that are so troubling to her. We roam freely through her complex feelings and reactions, becoming acquainted with her hopes and dreams, as well as her fears and nightmares. Not only does this passage provide the "background information" we need to understand the story's brief action, but it does so in a way that re-creates Frances's own state of mind. In the "dream sequences"—the visions of swirling, throbbing faces, jumbled-together bits of music, and *Wunderkind* — her terror and helplessness appear most vividly; when this vision returns, at the very end of the lesson, we know that her fears have taken over, and that her self-control is breaking down. But this sense also dominates the story as a whole; even in calmer moments, her thoughts flit restlessly around, soon crowded out by other memories and sudden emotions. It seems that the entire three years is rushing back to her at once, as she casts through her memories and ideas in search of any workable perspective. The "action" in her mind may be difficult to follow, but we realize that this task is no more difficult for us than it is for Frances herself. Like her, we approach insights that never achieve direct expression and experience the flood of emotions that eventually overwhelms her.

Historical Context

The Idea of the Teenager

The category of "teenager" is a familiar, well-established part of our culture; we may not consider that, as a social "type," it is a relatively recent invention. But the idea that one's teenage years are a separate and distinct stage of life has really come into its own only in the twentieth century. While all cultures have their own child-rearing customs and recognize a distinction between the states of adulthood and childhood, the notion of an extended period of transition between these roles has been relatively rare in history. Western societies, at least through the Middle Ages, tended to think of children primarily as "miniature adults," and their dependence on home and family was seldom prolonged. In most cases, children took up productive labor as soon as they were physically capable of it, and through the nineteenth century, people we would now consider young teens routinely took on adult responsibilities of employment, marriage, and fami-

ly. Undoubtedly, people have always noticed differences in the behavior and outlook of, for example, a 17-year-old and a 35-year-old, but both have, for the most part, been considered "grownups." Although the one was less experienced in life than the other, they were not seen as separate social "types" with different needs and natures. In general, young people were considered as a separate group only at times when members of "the older generation" found themselves shocked by immoral or irresponsible behavior on the part of younger people— behavior which, at least to the older critics, stood in sharp contrast to that of their own youth. This tradition of middle-agers despairing over the outrages of the younger generation can be traced back at least as far as ancient Egypt, and the category of teens or young adults is usually associated with social problems and parental worries.

The "Roaring '20s," just before McCullers entered her own teens, was such a period of heated grownup disapproval. Throughout the Prohibition era, sensational newspapers spread scandals of wild drinking parties, promiscuous "flappers," and dangerous thrill-seeking on the part of "Flaming Youth." The idea of the criminal "juvenile delinquent" (a forerunner of today's teen gang-member) gained currency at this time, and in the years after World War II became a perennial public issue, addressed by government committees, educators, social scholars, and law-enforcement agencies. But another development in the 1950s served to institutionalize the teenager as a figure in American popular culture. These were "boom times," marked by rising middle-class prosperity and the rapid growth of the suburbs; for the first time, large numbers of teenagers had both the leisure and the spending-money to qualify as a distinct economic market. Fashions, music, and entertainment products specifically geared to the tastes and interests of teenagers proved to be profitable investments, and the "youth demographic" has been a major concern for mass-marketing efforts ever since.

Thus, McCullers wrote this tale of adolescence not only from the late stages of her own adolescence, but at a time when the type itself was not yet clearly defined. Teenagers no doubt experienced many of the same feelings other teens had felt throughout time, and continue to feel; their well-being, and their capacity to strongly disappoint their parents, were common topics of discussion. But their viewpoint was not widely portrayed in popular culture, or reinforced by products and artistic productions reflecting their own concerns and prefer-

Compare & Contrast

- **1920s:** As a child, McCullers practices playing the piano for five hours a day. After a severe illness and an emotional parting with her mentor, she gives up music and turns to a career in writing

    1996: The darker side of child prodigy is portrayed in *Shine,* a film based on the true story of David Helfgott, an Australian prodigy who suffered a career-halting psychotic episode as a teenager, but returned to playing several years later.

- **1930s:** President Franklin D. Roosevelt's New Deal sets $5 million of federal funds aside for art and music projects. The Federal Music Project sponsors many musicians, orchestras, and theaters in an effort to encourage further development of American culture and to provide jobs during the Great Depression.

    1990s: The National Endowment for the Arts, a federal program which provides grants and assistance to musicians and other artists, is threatened by Republican lawmakers who object to federal funding of the arts and want to drastically cut the program.

- **1936:** Classical music is a popular music form. Some famous composers producing works include Sergei Prokofiev, Aaron Copland, Bela Bartok, and Igor Stravinsky.

    1990s: Classical music, while enjoyed by many, does not have the popular appeal it once had. Wynton Marsalis, primarily known as a jazz musician, composes "Blood on the Plow," a Grammy-winning epic classical composition treating the theme of slavery.

---

ences. "Wunderkind" has attracted the attention of critics not only for its artistic strengths and its author's later prominence, but as an early exploration of a social type that has steadily grown more important in our culture. The story has been widely anthologized since it was published, particularly in student readers; by now, several generations of teenagers have read this effort to portray the "unique" pressures and concerns they are supposedly experiencing.

Casual Stereotyping

Modern readers may be disturbed by one aspect of "Wunderkind" that probably received little notice when the story first appeared: its treatment of Jewish characters. This is not a major theme or an essential element in the story, and McCullers doesn't seem to be expressing a particularly vehement attitude of anti-Semitism—but the few references to Jewish characters would likely be considered offensive by today's standards. As such, the story represents a small example of the subtle and unconscious ways racism can work: not only through the vicious, exaggerated stereotyping of a particular group, but in the persistence of racially tinted attitudes and generalizations so widespread that they are seldom questioned. We needn't assume that McCullers intended the characterization to be offensive; she may not even have realized that it could be taken that way, and there is no indication that many readers were troubled by it. Without defending or accusing the author, it is worth the effort to understand how so sensitive a writer could casually display an attitude we now consider controversial.

Mr. Lafkowitz, the violin teacher, is the only character specifically identified as Jewish, but we may assume that a character named Heime Israelsky is also a Jew. Frances resents them, but admires their musicianship, seeing in it a quality her own playing lacks. Music itself, in Frances's mind, seems to be a particularly Jewish vocation, or at least one for which Jews somehow have greater "natural gifts" than other people; it is a romantic, foreign, and exotic world, compared to "just Cincinnati," and at one point she believes that her musical difficulties are partially due to "her not being Jewish." (Bilderbach apparently is not a Jew, but does have an "exotic" European background, and the professional respect of his Jewish colleague.) These thoughts arise in her memory of the concert with Heime, which was a triumph for him but unsuccessful for Frances. In particular, the piece by Bloch seems to have a "jewishness" she is incapable of expressing; the reviewers say that "she lacked the temperament for that type of music," and Bilderbach agrees: "'That oie oie stuff,' said Mister Bilderbach, crackling the newspapers at her. 'Not for you, Bienchen. Leave all that to the Heimes and vitses and skys.'"

Such references may not appear blatantly offensive. After all, Frances seems to feel that Jews are somehow musically *superior* to her, and hopes to emulate their achievements. But this is still seeing them as "the other," people who are different by their very nature; to celebrate a race's supposed "gifts" can be the flip-side of condemning its alleged "inferiorities." In many Western societies at this time, individual Jews had achieved prominence in the arts and professions, despite facing social discrimination in many forms. Frances's perception of Jews as "natural" musicians mirrors the way many whites have been able to admire black musicians and entertainers, yet continue to discriminate against African Americans as a group. Both cases present the same kind of paradox: the "natural" musical genius that is so admired is seen to be a by-product of the unjust treatment racism has imposed on the "gifted" race, great art that is born from great suffering. While *positive* stereotypes may appear to do little harm, accepting and reproducing them without question can also make negative stereotypes seem more credible.

Critical Overview

Carson McCullers's work was well received in her lifetime by critics and the book-buying public, but the truest measure of her success may be the admiration so often expressed by other writers. Dame Edith Sitwell, for example, has called her "a transcendental writer," combining "a great poet's eye and mind and senses" with "a great prose writer's sense of construction and character." Tennessee Williams once called her the *only* great talent to appear in America since the 1920s. Since her death

in 1967, her work has continued to earn the appreciation of readers, writers, and literary critics.

McCullers's novels deal with many of the same themes that can be found in her first short story, "Wunderkind." Her fiction is usually set in the South, and like Frances, her protagonists often exist in a state of psychological isolation, unable to communicate their strong feelings to others. They often have physical disabilities of some kind and lead lives that are unfulfilled in important ways; regardless of their physical condition, they seem to suffer from spiritual incapacities and are continually thwarted in their needs and desires. In an essay on other authors, McCullers once wrote: "Above all, love is the main generator of all good writing. Love, passion and compassion are all welded together." The same could be said of McCullers's own writing. Love and passion seldom work out for her characters, however, leading them to crushing defeats and disappointments; but the compassion with which she depicts their turmoil and loneliness may serve to redeem their suffering. By vividly recreating their misery in the reader's mind, she can be seen to make them more than just suffering individuals, but poignant representatives of the human condition.

As the "first outing" of a writer who went on to notable accomplishments, critics often analyze "Wunderkind" for early signs of the themes and effects that mark her later work. Since it closely parallels events that had recently occurred in McCullers's own life, it is usually assumed to be thinly-veiled autobiography, and critics have closely noted the differences between the story's events and the known facts of the writer's actual experience. The story's sexual implications are often given minute attention—the many sensual images, the way McCullers establishes Frances's conflicted feelings for Bilderbach, and particularly, the fact that McCullers's own teacher was a woman, not a man. The contribution by Alice Hall Petry, included in this unit's critical selections, is representative of this line of analysis. Other critics focus on the presentation of gender issues and McCullers's dramatization of the particular pressures and conflicts faced by women in male-dominated fields, such as the classical music stage of the 1930s; the criticism in this section by Constance M. Perry is a strong example. While the presence of both themes in the story is difficult to deny, it is possible that critics have made too much of them, emphasizing them at the expense of other readings. Her sexual confusion is an important part of Frances's crushing burden, as is the treatment she receives as a female—but these are not her only problems, and may not fully account for the arrest of her musical career. Whichever elements they stress, critics usually consider the story to be an account of adolescence in general, including its disturbing physical changes, the intense emotions teenagers often experience, the early stages of sexual awareness, and the challenging transition from childhood to adult pressures, demands, and responsibilities. Frances has many problems; they can be defined in many ways, and she herself is overwhelmed by the many ways they manifest themselves. Perhaps the simplest way to account for them is to observe that she is a teenager—a far-from-simple condition, and one that resists easy explanations, particularly when one experiences it directly. In her portrait of Frances, critics find a classic account of adolescent alienation and isolation, which McCullers allows readers of any age to experience in intimate intensity.

Criticism

Tom Faulkner

A freelance writer and copyeditor, Faulkner is pursuing an M.A. in English at Wayne State University. In the essay below, he offers a thoughtful exploration of how the writer's experience melds with the crafting of fiction, specifically in "Wunderkind."

In the early 1930s, a Columbus, Georgia, teenager named Lula Carson Smith was bitterly disappointed in her artistic ambitions. While some of the details of her experience are disputed, its basic outlines are clear: Long considered a musical prodigy, having trained for years as a concert pianist and prepared to enter New York's famous Julliard School, she suddenly gave up music entirely and began devoting her energies to a writing career. Her first published work was "Wunderkind," written at age 19, originally for a college writing course. The story concerns a young woman's final, emotional piano lesson, in which she realizes that the musical calling she had hoped for will never materialize. Within a few years, its author was a best-selling novelist (under her married name, Carson McCullers); and, given the known details of her life, it is common for critics (for example, Richard M. Cook) to treat this early story as "obviously autobiographical." Clearly,

the plot is *based on* the writer's own experience—but what, exactly, does that mean, and how does it affect our appreciation of the story?

While critical studies may suggest otherwise, the significance of "autobiographical fiction" lies beyond the scholarly detective work of researching the author's life and matching "real life" experiences with fictional characters, events, and effects—thereby revealing the "material sources" of the story. Such knowledge may inform our understanding of the work, and of its author's creative process—but a story is not the same as a memoir. As Alice Hall Petry has observed, early works with clear parallels to their author's lives often "cease to be regarded as fiction," and are treated instead as "source material" for analyzing a writer's later, greater work. Such scholarship surely has its place; but one effect of this approach is that it may encourage students to discount work that seems "merely autobiographical," as if the author has somehow cheated us by reporting real events rather than "making up a story." In practice, the writing of fiction usually involves *both* invention and experience. Writers are traditionally urged to "write what they know," and fiction is commonly understood to be rooted in the author's experience on some level, if not always in its literal details. Autobiographical fiction may draw its energy from events in the writer's own life, but it succeeds through the artful and imaginative *transformation* of that experience: the dramatization of its universal, human elements, in a way that will touch and engage readers whose own experience may be far different from that of the writer. Often, the value of knowing the real-life "basis" of a story lies not in the similarities we can trace, but in the differences between the writer's own circumstances and the fictionalized treatment she has created from the "raw material" of her life.

Many writers keep a journal of some kind; it may take the form of a diary, recording events in the author's life on a regular basis, or a more informal collection of occasional thoughts and impressions. The nature of the writing will depend on the author's purposes, and so will any use the writer may make of it in the future. Sometimes, a journal entry will evolve into a formal, professional piece, as the writer builds on the insights, emotions, and situations she had recorded earlier, developing their dramatic possibilities. Other writers claim never to re-read their journals, finding value in the very act of writing down their impressions and taking a

What Do I Read Next?

- *She's Come Undone* (1992), a novel by Wally Lamb, is a darkly humorous account of a woman forced to deal with the lifelong effects of growing up in a dysfunctional family.

- ''Paul's Case'' (1905), a short story by Willa Cather, deals with a young man who, much like Frances in ''Wunderkind,'' longs to escape what he considers to be a ''common'' life.

- Mary Bray Pipher's *Reviving Ophelia* (1994) examines female adolescence in contemporary America. Pipher, a clinical psychologist, covers issues such as divorce, eating disorders, and sexual pressure.

- Perhaps McCullers's most famous work, *The Heart is a Lonely Hunter* (1940) tells the story of a young girl who learns the meaning of loneliness through her association with a group of social outcasts.

- Jamaica Kincaid's ''Girl,'' from her collection *At the Bottom of the River* (1983), is a young woman's recollection of her mother's instructions to her while growing up.

---

distinctly different approach to works they prepare for publication. There are many reasons to write about one's own life, even if the work is never shared with others, and the most basic may be that it seems to have a therapeutic value, particularly in times of stress and confusion. The effort to put our feelings into words can help us to ''get a handle'' on difficult circumstances, or achieve a clearer understanding of ourselves; and when we write from a state of emotional agitation, we sometimes give voice to feelings or insights that normally remain unexpressed. For these reasons, psychologists often recommend that their clients keep journals and go over them periodically in search of perspective on their problems. And of course, one needn't be a professional writer, or a mental patient, to benefit from keeping a journal; though the habit is not widely practiced today, it was once common for ''ordinary people'' to keep such private records throughout their lives, writing about themselves *for* themselves.

But journals and diaries are not the same as writing about oneself *for others*. Each of us maintains a distinction between our ''public'' and ''private'' selves, and avoids revealing embarrassing, unflattering ''private details'' to others, particularly strangers. For writers, this distinction is intensified: everything they publish is read, and judged, by strangers—and often, it is judged on its ''honesty''

and ''authenticity,'' its resemblance to ''real life.'' Fiction that takes the author's own experience as its starting-point thus forces a writer to make some difficult decisions, about what to reveal and what to conceal. One strategy is to ''fictionalize'' the situation, by changing the real-life experience in significant ways: giving characters different names and circumstances, for example, or choosing a setting different from the author's own surroundings. Such changes may be viewed in a negative way—that the author is ''hiding behind'' her characters, using them to disguise parts of her own life she'd prefer not to ''own up to.'' Critics sometimes interpret the story's Mr. Bilderbach in this way, knowing that McCullers's real-life piano teacher was not a man, but a woman by the name of Mary Tucker—which suggests that Frances' confused sexual feelings for her teacher were, in the writer's own life, an experience of homosexual attraction. By changing her teacher's gender in the story, McCullers can be seen either to avoid a subject that was considered controversial or shameful (particularly at that time), or as disavowing her own experience, perhaps out of concern for her reputation.

Fiction, however, is more than a disguise for ''real life,'' and there are several *positive* reasons to alter the details of an experience. As a practical matter, life experiences usually require considerable editing before they become stories. The ''sto-

" Fiction that takes the author's own experience as its starting-point thus forces a writer to make some difficult decisions, about what to reveal and what to conceal. One strategy is to 'fictionalize' the situation, by changing the real-life experience in significant ways: giving characters different names and circumstances, for example, or choosing a setting different from the author's own surroundings."

ries'' we live through don't usually unfold with convenient beginnings, middles, and endings; several different ''plots'' seem to develop at once, and we seldom have all the information possessed by a third-person narrator, who helps explain the action we are reading. Even if we happen to live unusually exciting lives, our day-to-day experiences are seldom as dramatic as the events in artistic productions, and seldom lead to a specific ''meaning,'' or reveal consistent ''themes.'' In shaping it *as* a story, an author must ''re-package'' experience, editing out details that don't serve the story's purposes—the experience, as it was actually lived, is already ''changed,'' even if no facts are altered. Furthermore, experiences don't always make good, or satisfying, stories; storytellers of all kinds are tempted to ''improve'' their material, in order to make the telling more effective. Consider the kind of family anecdotes that are passed down, perhaps retold each year at holidays: the details and events tend to change considerably over time, and don't always match the memories of those who witnessed them originally. It's not that Uncle Joe or Aunt Minnie are really *liars*—they just love a good story. As they

become caught up in the telling, their imaginations are stimulated; over the years, they may experiment, introducing new material, or different descriptions, and seeing how well the new versions ''go over'' with their audience. No less than the professional writer of fiction, they are *composing* and *revising* their stories, and in the process, they transform the raw material they began with: the actual experience that inspired them to tell a story in the first place. Writers may be seen as people who are fascinated, even obsessed, by this kind of tinkering with the elements of a story.

Unless an author specifically comments on the matter, we can only speculate on the reasons for the decisions she has made—and often can't be certain about just which details *have* been changed. For example, critics may speculate about young McCullers' feelings for Mary Tucker—but it is at least plausible that the element of sexual tension is itself something the author has introduced into the story for dramatic purposes, and was not a significant factor in her own student-teacher relationship. Certainly whether an important character is a man or a woman is no small matter—but still another possibility is that she cast this authority-figure as a man in order to dramatize the unequal status of women in the arts, and the particular pressures faced by females in a male-dominated environment. However we interpret this Bilderbach/Tucker equation, there are other differences between Frances's situation in 'Wunderkind'' and McCullers's own experience, which may be equally significant. Frances meekly submits to her defeat, never expressing the emotions that boil within her. She has many resentments, and is driven to find an explanation for her inability to play as she knows she can, but she rushes from Bilderbach's studio, intent on getting out ''[q]uickly–before he would have to speak.'' Her own speech is a helpless, tear-choked whisper, offering no explanation beyond ''I can't.'' But it is consistently reported that McCullers's break with Mary Tucker occurred quite differently: the student confronted her teacher, dramatically announcing her intention to give up music and voicing her resentments over Tucker's decision to move away. In the story, Frances seems drawn to the carefree childhood she has sacrificed so much of for her music; when she disappears in the story's last line, down a street ''that had become confused with noise and bicycles and the games of other children,'' it is almost as if she is escaping back into childhood. She seems unable, and is perhaps unwilling, to take on adult roles and responsibilities; at the end of the story, the future she had counted on is shattered, and her prospects seem bleak and uncertain. McCullers, however, would seem to have recovered from her teenage trauma rather well, confidently moving into a different artistic field (for which she had already been preparing), and quickly achieving fame and respect for her work. While her life took many turns that may be considered tragic, she was hardly the pathetic, defeated figure we see in Frances. In these ways, we can see that McCullers has changed her own "character" for purposes of the story—but not, as we are so often tempted to do in our own storytelling, by showing herself in a stronger, more-admirable light. Instead, the "actress" she has chosen to play her own part has been deliberately made weaker, less assertive, and less articulate than she herself has been. Frances is not Carson, but someone else *like* Carson in many ways—perhaps a projection of what McCullers might have become if she had allowed herself to be crushed by her emotions and circumstances.

We may imagine that, at the time, McCullers must have *felt* as hopeless and defeated as Frances seems to *be*. By altering and exaggerating her own experience, arranging it to emphasize the desperate confusion and stifling isolation she felt, she dramatizes the kinds of emotions commonly felt by adolescents in all walks of life. Assuming the reader can identify with Frances, McCullers thus achieves something remarkable: She allows us to share a particular experience she has had, by connecting it to our own, similar, experience—though most of us have never studied for a concert career, or known the pressures that confront a child prodigy. This remarkable something is commonly called "fiction." It is not real life, but it involves the magnification of experience, by developing its possibilities and exploring its dynamics. Frances's very specific experience includes the details of "real life," and the story is told in a way that penetrates to the core of her conflict, taking it from a personal level to a more universal one. The story of Carson McCullers's own musical career is intriguing, and dramatic, and must have affected her profoundly. But "Wunderkind" is what she has made of that experience; by her own choice, it is now "the real story" (or rather, one of her many real stories), and the biographical facts are now "source material" in its background.

Source: Tom Faulkner, "An Overview of 'Wunderkind'," in *Short Stories for Students,* The Gale Group, 1999.

Alice Hall Petry

In the following excerpt, Petry examines the sexual overtones in McCullers's "Wunderkind,"

and concludes that the underlying sexual crisis in the story stems from the protagonist's sexual feelings for her music teacher.

It is one of the more peculiar phenomena of literary history that once an author becomes critically and/or popularly acclaimed, his or her earliest efforts often acquire a new status. Instead of being approached as discrete works of art, worthy of evaluation on their own terms, too often they tend to be utilized primarily as source material. They are mined for whatever embryonic elements—characters, events, motifs—were destined to reemerge, fully fleshed, in the later, greater works. Or, what is even more intriguing, those early efforts that draw upon autobiographical elements (as do so many) cease to be regarded as works of fiction, and hence they do not attract the kinds of serious scholarly attention which they deserve. Such has been the fate of one of Carson McCullers's earliest efforts, "Wunderkind," written in a creative writing class taught by Sylvia Chatfield Bates, and published when she was only nineteen years old. "Wunderkind" is much anthologized and widely acknowledged as the thinly-veiled autobiographical record of McCullers's "burnout" as a student of the piano while in her mid-teens. It surely is that; but it also is vastly more. If one goes beyond the facile equation of "Frances is Carson," and in particular if one recognizes that the protagonist's difficulties are considerably more profound than a high schooler's disenchantment with practicing the piano, then it becomes clear that "Wunderkind" is essentially a remarkable rendering of an adolescent's turmoil over her growing awareness of her sexual passion for her music teacher, Mr. Bilderbach; and her turmoil is rendered no less acute by her tendency to regard him as a father figure. As shall be seen, "Wunderkind" features what are considerably more than what Oliver Evans terms "sexual overtones": Frances's sexual feelings for her teacher, far from "confusing" and "complicating" their relationship, are its very basis. They do not mar the story; they *make* it.

Surely "Wunderkind" is one of the most emotionally-intense stories McCullers ever wrote; and part of that intensity is due to the fact that the sources of the young protagonist's turmoil, although they are beginning to dawn on her, cannot quite be articulated by her. Hence the absolute importance of the story's limited point of view: fifteen-year-old Frances is undergoing a crisis; her distress is palpable throughout the story; but it is only through her

> " The sexual crisis underlying 'Wunderkind' was obviously painful for McCullers; but as so often happens in literary history, her personal trauma led to great art."

confused actions, statements and memories (much of "Wunderkind" consists of a series of flashbacks that the reader—far more than Frances—comes to realize that her difficulties are sexual in nature.

The limited point of view is enhanced by the strictures of the story's spatial and temporal setting. In what is apparently less than half an hour, Frances enters the confining arena of the crisis (the living room and studio of her piano teacher), reaches the breaking point and flees from what is virtually an emotional torture chamber. But the impulse to bolt is not really a sudden one: the circumstances leading up to it had been building for at least the three years during which she had studied under Bilderbach, and they had been intensifying during the previous four months; and they owe infinitely more to Frances's relationship with Bilderbach than they do to her relationship with music per se.

As so often happens in teacher/student situations (especially long-term, one-on-one tutorial arrangements), Bilderbach is more like a parent than an instructor, or what Margaret B. McDowell aptly terms "a second father," [*Carson McCullers*, 1980]. Frances had received her cherished label of "wunderkind" from him three years before, as well as her pet name "Bienchen" (literally, "little bee"). These are both Germanic names, and it comes as no surprise that Frances "wished she had not been born and brought up in just Cincinnati." Longing to deny the American name and identity derived from her biological father (who is given the American generic name of "dad"), Frances would much prefer a background like that of her surrogate father, the Dutch-Czech, German-bred Bilderbach. Frances clearly wishes desperately to please Bilderbach, who paternally gives her lessons in his cozy home, buys her a satchel for her birthday and kindly offers

her milk and apple cake. Her distress over being unable to play the piano well—and, concomitantly, the *source* of her being unable to play well—is her overwhelming desire to satisfy the expectations of her father figure. The actual piano playing, then, is less an end than a means.

Even so, it is vital that music be the means by which Frances seeks to please Bilderbach. McCullers is not simply drawing upon her own background as a student of piano; rather, she is drawing heavily upon the capacity of music to evoke intense emotional responses, including sexual ones: "Wunderkind" would never materialize as a story if Bilderbach were teaching Frances to pitch horseshoes. Indeed, the very description of Bilderbach and Lafkowitz's duet underscores the sexuality of the music: "The music in the studio seemed to be urging violently. . ."; the two men were "lustfully drawing out all that was there." Come to that, Lafkowitz's only criticism of Frances's performance of Bach's Fantasia and Fugue is that it lacked sexual passion:

"Frances—" Mister Lafkowitz had said then, suddenly, looking at her with his thin mouth curved and his eyes almost covered by their delicate lids. "Do you know how many children Bach had?"

She turned to him, puzzled. "A good many. Twenty some odd."

"Well, then—" The corners of his smile etched themselves gently in his pale face. "He could not have been so cold—then."

And Bilderbach himself responds physically to Frances's playing: she could "see his hands rise climactically from the chair arms and then sink down loose and satisfied when the high points of the phrases had been passed successfully." The powerful sexual dimension of the piano music leads to the complex central motif of the story: Bilderbach and Frances respond to each other not just as teacher and student, and not just as father and daughter, but virtually as lover and beloved. And although Frances may not have been aware of this at age twelve, it is becoming frighteningly apparent at fifteen.

The blurring of the pedagogical, paternal and amorous dimensions of Bilderbach is subtle but quite insistent. Frances has watched Bilderbach carefully, as might a student or a daughter: he has a "chunky, guttural" voice and "stolid footsteps"; and she has observed "the quick eyes behind the horn-rimmed glasses." But she also has studied features which, although benign out of context, assume a carnal aura the more they are repeated in the story: "the lips full and loose shut and the lower one pink and shining from the bites of his teeth; the forked veins in his temples throbbing.'' She also has studied his ''muscular back'' and has noted that, compared to Bilderbach's, Lakfowitz's voice was ''almost like a woman's.'' Even her recollection of her first lesson with Bilderbach, when she was twelve years old, has an insistently sexual undercurrent of which, in retrospect, she seems to have been vaguely aware: ''His deep voice sounded as though it had been straying inside her for a long time. She wanted to reach out and touch his muscle-flexed finger that pointed out the phrases, wanted to feel the gleaming gold band ring and the strong hairy back of his hand.'' Indeed, even the lessons themselves are couched in sexual terms (''After she had started with Mister Bilderbach . . .''), and, not surprisingly, Frances repeatedly has dreams of vortexes with the face of Bilderbach—his ''lips urging softly, the veins in his temples insisting''—at the center. In sum, Bilderbach may seem ''crotchety'' to an outsider (McDowell), but to Frances he is singularly attractive.

Unlike a good father or teacher, Bilderbach has (albeit apparently unconsciously) been nurturing Frances's sexual response to him and to the music with which he is intimately associated. Hence his surname: although superficially it is a variation of ''bilderbuch'' (literally, ''picture book''), it also echoes ''bildner-Bach''—a ''shaper'' or ''molder'' [''bildner''] of a Bachesque (i.e., sexual) response to music. Indeed, at times he treats Frances like a mistress. After Saturday's lessons, for example, he has her spend the night in his house and return home by streetcar the following morning. Even though her overnight stays are evidently platonic, their resemblance to love trysts could not have been lost totally on either Bilderbach or the adolescent girl who has been wondering for two years why he has no children. Similarly, when Frances graduates from junior high school, Bilderbach personally takes her downtown and selects the cloth for her dress: ''His thick fingers smoothed over the filmy nets and crackling taffetas. . . . He held colors to her face, cocking his head to one side, and selected pink''; he also supervised the sewing of the dress, insisting upon such ''grown-up'' features as ''ruffles around the hips and neck and a fancy rosette on the shoulder.'' This demonstrates considerably more personal interest than the buying of a book-satchel, and is the sort of behavior few fathers would exhibit, let alone piano teachers. Even Bilderbach's most casual remarks often sound like a man speaking to his mistress: '''You see, Bienchen, I know you so

well—as if you were *my own girl*. I know what you have. . . .''' (emphasis added).

Is it any wonder, then, that Frances—looking back at the events, feelings and remarks of the past three years from the vantage point of a budding sexual awareness—is nervous and confused, even distraught, as the story opens? Destined momentarily to be behind closed doors once again with a man to whom she responds physically, and who himself has a confused, quasi-sexual interest in her, Frances irrationally behaves like a woman who is trying to revive a cooling relationship with her lover. She talks to the departing Lafkowitz ''to put off going into the studio a moment longer''; she vows to have a good lesson '''like it used to be''' and she refuses Bilderbach's proffered cake '''till afterward.''' Although in fact this is a girl wishing to recreate the happy, asexual world of her childhood, the very *language* is that of a woman wanting to regain the bliss of earlier coitus, but fearing that it will be unsatisfactory. This astonishing use of language is particularly apparent in the story's climactic scene, the abortive final lesson with Bilderbach.

It opens with Bilderbach, a teacher trying to soothe his student, sounding more like a lover trying to console his mistress for a lack of sexual responsiveness: '''This afternoon we are going to begin all over. Start from scratch. Forget the last few months.''' Rather provocatively straddling his chair (''The heavy volume before him seemed to balance dangerously on the chair back''), Bilderbach intensely watches her perform; and the acutely self-conscious Frances, who never used to mind his closeness, now finds that her unresponsive fingers are like ''limp macaroni''—an image often associated with impotent males. Bilderbach then suggests that she play ''The Harmonious Blacksmith'':

[I]mpulsively he squatted down to the floor. ''*Vigorous*,'' he said.

She could not stop looking at him, sitting on one heel with the other foot resting squarely before him for balance, the muscles of his strong thighs straining under the cloth of his trousers. . . .

She could not look down at the piano. The light brightened the hairs on the backs of his outspread hands, made the lenses of his glasses glitter.

''*All of it*,'' *he urged*. ''*Now!*''

She felt that the marrows of her bones were hollow and there was no blood left in her. Her heart that had been springing against her chest all afternoon felt suddenly dead. She saw it gray and limp and shriveled at the edges like an oyster.

His face seemed to throb out in space before her, come closer with the lurching motion in the veins of his temples. . . . Her lips shook like jelly and a surge of noiseless tears made the white keys blur in a watery line. ''I can't,'' she whispered. ''I don't know why, but I just can't—can't any more.''

His tense body slackened and, holding his hand to his side, he pulled himself up. (emphasis added).

Were this scene read out of context, one would assume that it was a failed sexual encounter, not a piano lesson. The sexual tension is not lost on Frances: like Rabbit Angstrom, unable to handle the demands and implications of sexual maturity, she runs: ''. . . she stumbled down the stone steps, turned in the wrong direction, and hurried down the street that had become confused with noise and bicycles and the games of other children.''

It is a child's response to stress; and this regressive behavior is to be expected from someone whose happiest moments came when Bilderbach was just her teacher/father and she was his ''wunderkind''—an asexual, prelapsarian world to which she can never return, no matter how hard she runs. After all, a ''wunderkind,'' by literal definition, is a ''kind''—a *child*. It was an appropriate label for a twelve-year-old, but at fifteen Frances is occupying the tenuous world of the adolescent. As she has been outgrowing her status as a child, she is simultaneously being pressured into adulthood— and with that transformation comes the awareness (even if it cannot yet be articulated) that she has been responding to Bilderbach on a physical level.

The situation had apparently been coming to a head for at least four months, and both Bilderbach and Frances had been noticing the change. Whether it was due to the onset of menarche (hence the repeated references to ''months'') or perhaps from masturbation (hence the unexplained sore finger: ''The sight sharpened the fear that had begun to torment her for the past few months'') or simply her increased awareness of Bilderbach's maleness, the fact remains that the intimacy of a one-on-one situation is something she can no longer handle.

Thus their rather pathetic attempts to deny her budding womanhood. When she cannot play the Beethoven sonata (a mature piece), he assumes the voice ''he used for children'' and urges her to play a simple, early piece, ''The Harmonious Blacksmith.'' Frances, meanwhile, who feels ''clumsy and overgrown'' even compared to Mr. Lafkowitz, irrationally insists that she is like Heime, a prepubescent boy (''She was like Heime. She had to be.''). No wonder she is so dismayed at seeing his photograph: it is not that he is more successful than she musically, but rather that ''*he* hadn't changed much in six months'' (emphasis added). She measures herself against a fellow ''wunderkind,'' Heime—a pun on ''hymen''?—and is found wanting.

McCullers brilliantly conveys the confused feelings of this girl entering womanhood while longing for childhood by focusing upon the fried egg given to her at breakfast that morning. Although Frances is still enough of a child to prefer eating four chocolate bars instead of breakfast, she is sufficiently trapped in the adult world that she is being forced to eat decent meals: ''. . . this morning her dad had put a fried egg on her plate and she had known that if it burst—so that the slimy yellow oozed over the white—she would cry. And that had happened. The same feeling was upon her now [while waiting for her final encounter with Bilderbach]. The egg is a perfect symbol of female sexuality, as well as of embryonic potential that will never be realized. The bursting of the egg is an apt emblem of both a sexual encounter (in particular, loss of virginity) and a difficult situation coming to a head—a quality often evoked in McCullers's fiction. At the same time, the very oozing of the egg suggests a situation out of control, while her seemingly irrational crying over the broken egg is a classic symptom of adolescent anxiety. No wonder the distress she felt at breakfast (with ''dad'') is identical to that she feels while anticipating the final piano lesson (with her other ''father'').

The presentation of Bilderbach as Frances's father enriches the complex sexual dimension of the story. At fifteen, Frances is at the age when the adolescent girl reportedly begins to experience what Freud termed the ''Electra complex''—a passionate interest in the father, which must be rejected if the girl is to enter into meaningful adult heterosexual relationships. The act of running ''in the *wrong* direction'' towards ''*other* children'' suggests, however, that instead of passing into the next psychosocial stage, Frances is trying pathetically to regain her status as a child. This is regression, not an ''act of courage.'' One can see why McCullers herself vigorously discounted those interpretations which posit ''Wunderkind'' as simply an embellished autobiographical account of how she abandoned music for writing. Once one becomes aware of the story's pervasive sexual dimension, one sees that it is virtually a case study of a rite de passage (albeit an abortive one). ''Wunderkind'' does, to quote Miss Bates, evoke ''a mood and a crisis''; but where critics have done the story a disservice is to fail to determine the precise nature of the crisis. In the words of Erik Erikson, ''each successive step [in an individual's psychosocial development] is a potential crisis because of a radical change in perspective.'' And Frances, looking back at the three previous years from the perspective of her newly-dawning sexual conciousness and anticipating an indefinite number of years in close proximity with Bilderbach, cannot face the reality of her situation. Frances's incapacity to play the piano—perhaps, indeed, her *deliberate* (even if unconscious) decision to play poorly so as to disappoint, and hence distance herself from, her teacher—is a symptom of Frances's crisis, rather than the crisis itself.

Purely as a text, ''Wunderkind'' is thus a remarkable fictional achievement, and especially so considering the youth of the author. But McCullers's precocious skill and sensitivity as a writer seem even more remarkable in light of the possibility that ''Wunderkind'' is the fictionalized transmutation of her personal feelings for her own teacher. McCullers's piano instructor in Columbus, Georgia, was not a man but Mary Tucker; there is, thus, the possibility that ''Wunderkind'' offers an embellished, fictionalized account of McCullers's sexual attraction to Mrs. Tucker—but presented, of course, within the ''safe'' paradigm of a girl's heterosexual feelings for her male teacher. McCullers's uncertainty over how to deal with these lesbian impulses may explain her abrupt and final decision to abandon a musical career when the object of her affections suddenly revealed she was moving to Maryland—a decision so firm and sweeping that McCullers literally would not allow anyone even to mention Mrs. Tucker's name in her presence for many weeks. Hurt by what she apparently perceived as her beloved's abandonment of her, young McCullers struck back at Mrs. Tucker in the only possible ways: in real life, by rejecting her teacher's dream of a musical career for her talented protegee; in fiction, by having the female student, rather than the teacher, do the running away.

The sexual crisis underlying ''Wunderkind'' was obviously painful for McCullers; but as so often happens in literary history, her personal trauma led to great art. By turning from a career in music to one in literature, Carson McCullers was able to create not only ''Wunderkind'' but a series of works in an unusually wide variety of literary genres. Her pain was, ultimately, our gain.

Source: Alice Hall Petry, ''Carson McCullers's Precocious 'Wunderkind','' in *Southern Quarterly,* Vol. 26, No. 3, Spring, 1988, pp. 31–9.

Constance M. Perry

In the following excerpt, Perry offers an interpretation of McCullers's ''Wunderkind,'' asserting that ''the essential conflict . . . is how to react to the pressures and distortions of adult sexuality.''

[''Wunderkind''] reveals McCullers's first trial of the theme she fully develops in *The Heart Is a Lonely Hunter*: adolescence brings a paralyzing knowledge of inadequacy to the exceptional girl and bars her passage into the world of art. . . .

McCullers's first published story, ''Wunderkind'' (1936), is clearly a preview of Mick Kelly's characterization and situation in *The Heart Is a Lonely Hunter* . Fifteen-year-old Frances has earned a reputation as a ''Wunderkind,'' but suddenly finds her ability daunted by a trio of male faces—her piano teacher, Mr. Bilderbach, his associate, Mr. Lafkowitz, and a young violinist, Heime. Most of all, Frances is disturbed by her sense that her teacher is ''looming'' over her, ''urging'' and ''insisting'' that she perform in a musical world she feels has already shut her out. Mr. Lafkowitz wounds her also when he sarcastically suggests that she cannot play Beethoven with passion, the passion of an artist who fathered twenty children. Male sexuality becomes associated with musical ability as Frances watches her teacher and Mr. Lafkowitz play a duet, ''the two of them playing, peering at the notations on the piano, lustfully drawing out all that was there.'' Recoiling from their masculinity, Frances is unable to express any musical feeling whatsoever. A show of feeling would risk exposure of her inadequate femininity. McCullers's own youthful confusion of musical feeling and sexual feelings for her teacher, Mary Tucker, are recreated in Frances's sexual embarrassment and feeling of exclusion from the world of music. Like young McCullers, the character Frances quits her lessons.

By contrast, Heime, Frances's double in the story, succeeds at fifteen in capturing the admiration of Carnegie Hall. Having begun violin lessons at four, and been privately tutored, Heime makes a happy transition from his *Wunderkind* adolescence to adult masculinity, becoming ''young master Israelsky'' while Frances is doomed to be a *Wunderkind* and never an artist. In the end, Frances's hands

> **"** In the story 'Wunderkind,' the world of art is a male world. Consequently, the passion expected of an artist is sensually masculine, related to virility and dominance."

refuse to perform; they tremble and throb uncontrollably as she inwardly wrestles with the dilemma of identity. When her teacher patronizes her, in the voice "he used for children," saying she should play "The Harmonious Blacksmith" if she can no longer master the Beethoven sonata, she flees from her degradation and never returns to the musical studio. Her realization that she cannot match Heime's success so alienates her mind from her body that she can no longer command herself to play. Like Mick in *The Heart Is a Lonely Hunter,* Frances's ability and desire to be a musician collapse when she realizes that her gender probably thwarts her chance for a success like Heime's in the world of art. . . .

As Louise Westling has shown, the essential conflict for the McCullers's *Wunderkind* is how to react to the pressures and distortions of adult sexuality. In the story "Wunderkind," the world of art is a male world. Consequently, the passion expected of an artist is sensually masculine, related to virility and dominance. No wonder Frances, the story's budding adolescent girl, quakes before the piano. Mick's sexual initiation proves central to the outcome of her characterization in the novel. Mick finds it impossible to be both a confident artist and a sexually adult female because in her culture female sexuality is shameful and dirty, meant to be mocked in graffiti. Her choices then are to abandon her artistic dream for the safety of conformity or to carry on the dream at the risk of appearing foolish and inadequate. For Mick and Frances, it is safer emotionally to give up the desire to be an artist before they reveal their sexual inadequacy and shame. By the time McCullers created her first novel's heroines, the young author had achieved sexual and social acceptance as a woman by marrying and moving with her husband away from home.

From her temporary vantage point, she could look back and create Mick, an autobiographical heroine. For Mick Kelly, like Frances Newman's Katharine Faraday and Sylvia Plath's Esther Greenwood, her first sexual experience crushes her confidence for an artistic life.

Source: Constance M. Perry, "Carson McCullers and the Female 'Wunderkind'," in *The Southern Literary Journal,* Vol. 19, No. 1, Fall, 1986, pp. 36–45.

Richard M. Cook

In the following excerpt, Cook gives a short overview of McCullers's "Wunderkind," and discusses the author's "gift for recapturing the intense but diffuse feelings of children at critical moments in their growing up."

Most of the sketches written as assignments during 1935 and 1936 are little more than exercises. Their interest for the reader, if any, comes from seeing her work out various technical problems while finding the true bent of her talent. But in the summer of 1936 she wrote a story entitled "Wunderkind," which so impressed her teacher, Whit Burnett, that he decided to publish it in the prestigious magazine *Story,* which he edited. It was her first published piece, and ever afterward Carson McCullers was to declare her occupation as "writer."

An obviously autobiographical story, "Wunderkind" describes a fifteen-year-old girl's discovery during a music lesson that she is not the prodigy she had thought and hoped she was. Her realization, which comes as she rattles helplessly and insensitively over Beethoven's Variation Sonata, not only destroys her image of herself as a brilliant concert pianist but also excludes her from a special circle of musical friends that had become for her an exotic second family. As a "wunderkind" she had enjoyed a special intimacy with exciting and talented people of foreign nationalities— Bilderbachs, Lafkowitzes, and Israelskis. She had, moreover, retained the special privileges and the security that go with being an exceptional child. But as an awkward, normal teenager, expelled from her exclusive, rarefied paradise, she knows she will have to grow up as just another ordinary kid in a world "confused with noise, and bicycles and the games of children." "Wunderkind," like "Sucker," reveals Carson McCullers's gift for recapturing the intense but diffuse feelings of children at critical moments in their growing up. And, as in "Sucker," those feelings are shown to be largely feelings of loss, an overwhelming sense of dislocation from the security of past love—feelings that Frankie Addams in *The Member of the Wedding* is later to describe as being "loose" and "unjoined."...

Source: Richard M. Cook, "Carson McCullers's Life," in *Carson McCullers,* Frederick Ungar Publishing Co.,1975, pp. 1–18.

Sources

Cahill, Susan, ed. *Women and Fiction: Short Stories by and about Women,* New York: New American Library, 1975, pp. 180- 81.

McCullers, Carson. *Story,* Vol. 38, No. 2, Winter 1990, p. 98.

Further Reading

Brasell, R. Bruce. "Dining at the Table of the Sensitives: Carson McCullers's Peculiarity," in *Southern Quarterly,* Vol. 35, No. 4, Summer 1997, pp. 59–66.

Discusses the treatment of lesbianism in McCullers's work.

Clark, Beverly Lyon and Melvin Friedman, eds. *Critical Essays on Carson McCullers,* New York: Hall, 1996.

Collection of critical essays discussing various aspects of McCullers's work.

Kissell, Susan S. "Carson McCullers's 'Wunderkind': A Case Study in Female Adolescence," in *Kentucky Philological Review,* No. 6, 1991, pp. 15–20.

Analyzes McCullers's depiction of Frances in particular and female adolescence in general

Glossary of Literary Terms

A

Aestheticism: A literary and artistic movement of the nineteenth century. Followers of the movement believed that art should not be mixed with social, political, or moral teaching. The statement ''art for art's sake'' is a good summary of aestheticism. The movement had its roots in France, but it gained widespread importance in England in the last half of the nineteenth century, where it helped change the Victorian practice of including moral lessons in literature. Edgar Allan Poe is one of the best-known American ''aesthetes.''

Allegory: A narrative technique in which characters representing things or abstract ideas are used to convey a message or teach a lesson. Allegory is typically used to teach moral, ethical, or religious lessons but is sometimes used for satiric or political purposes. Many fairy tales are allegories.

Allusion: A reference to a familiar literary or historical person or event, used to make an idea more easily understood. Joyce Carol Oates's story ''Where Are You Going, Where Have You Been?'' exhibits several allusions to popular music.

Analogy: A comparison of two things made to explain something unfamiliar through its similarities to something familiar, or to prove one point based on the acceptance of another. Similes and metaphors are types of analogies.

Antagonist: The major character in a narrative or drama who works against the hero or protagonist. The Misfit in Flannery O'Connor's story ''A Good Man Is Hard to Find'' serves as the antagonist for the Grandmother.

Anthology: A collection of similar works of literature, art, or music. Zora Neale Hurston's ''The Eatonville Anthology'' is a collection of stories that take place in the same town.

Anthropomorphism: The presentation of animals or objects in human shape or with human characteristics. The term is derived from the Greek word for ''human form.'' The fur necklet in Katherine Mansfield's story ''Miss Brill'' has anthropomorphic characteristics.

Anti-hero: A central character in a work of literature who lacks traditional heroic qualities such as courage, physical prowess, and fortitude. Anti-heroes typically distrust conventional values and are unable to commit themselves to any ideals. They generally feel helpless in a world over which they have no control. Anti-heroes usually accept, and often celebrate, their positions as social outcasts. A well-known anti-hero is Walter Mitty in James Thurber's story ''The Secret Life of Walter Mitty.''

Archetype: The word archetype is commonly used to describe an original pattern or model from which all other things of the same kind are made. Archetypes are the literary images that grow out of the ''collective unconscious,'' a theory proposed by psychologist Carl Jung. They appear in literature as incidents and plots that repeat basic patterns of life. They may also appear as stereotyped characters. The ''schlemiel'' of Yiddish literature is an archetype.

Autobiography: A narrative in which an individual tells his or her life story. Examples include Benjamin Franklin's *Autobiography* and Amy Hempel's story ''In the Cemetery Where Al Jolson Is Buried,'' which has autobiographical characteristics even though it is a work of fiction.

Avant-garde: A literary term that describes new writing that rejects traditional approaches to literature in favor of innovations in style or content. Twentieth-century examples of the literary *avant-garde* include the modernists and the minimalists.

B

Belles-lettres: A French term meaning ''fine letters'' or ''beautiful writing.'' It is often used as a synonym for literature, typically referring to imaginative and artistic rather than scientific or expository writing. Current usage sometimes restricts the meaning to light or humorous writing and appreciative essays about literature. Lewis Carroll's *Alice in Wonderland* epitomizes the realm of belles-lettres.

Bildungsroman: A German word meaning ''novel of development.'' The *bildungsroman* is a study of the maturation of a youthful character, typically brought about through a series of social or sexual encounters that lead to self-awareness. J. D. Salinger's *Catcher in the Rye* is a *bildungsroman*, and Doris Lessing's story ''Through the Tunnel'' exhibits characteristics of a *bildungsroman* as well.

Black Aesthetic Movement: A period of artistic and literary development among African Americans in the 1960s and early 1970s. This was the first major African-American artistic movement since the Harlem Renaissance and was closely paralleled by the civil rights and black power movements. The black aesthetic writers attempted to produce works of art that would be meaningful to the black masses. Key figures in black aesthetics included one of its founders, poet and playwright Amiri Baraka, formerly known as LeRoi Jones; poet and essayist Haki R. Madhubuti, formerly Don L. Lee; poet and playwright Sonia Sanchez; and dramatist Ed Bullins. Works representative of the Black Aesthetic Movement include Amiri Baraka's play *Dutchman,* a 1964 Obie award-winner.

Black Humor: Writing that places grotesque elements side by side with humorous ones in an attempt to shock the reader, forcing him or her to laugh at the horrifying reality of a disordered world. ''Lamb to the Slaughter,'' by Roald Dahl, in which a placid housewife murders her husband and serves the murder weapon to the investigating policemen, is an example of black humor.

C

Catharsis: The release or purging of unwanted emotions—specifically fear and pity—brought about by exposure to art. The term was first used by the Greek philosopher Aristotle in his *Poetics* to refer to the desired effect of tragedy on spectators.

Character: Broadly speaking, a person in a literary work. The actions of characters are what constitute the plot of a story, novel, or poem. There are numerous types of characters, ranging from simple, stereotypical figures to intricate, multifaceted ones. ''Characterization'' is the process by which an author creates vivid, believable characters in a work of art. This may be done in a variety of ways, including (1) direct description of the character by the narrator; (2) the direct presentation of the speech, thoughts, or actions of the character; and (3) the responses of other characters to the character. The term ''character'' also refers to a form originated by the ancient Greek writer Theophrastus that later became popular in the seventeenth and eighteenth centuries. It is a short essay or sketch of a person who prominently displays a specific attribute or quality, such as miserliness or ambition. ''Miss Brill,'' a story by Katherine Mansfield, is an example of a character sketch.

Classical: In its strictest definition in literary criticism, classicism refers to works of ancient Greek or Roman literature. The term may also be used to describe a literary work of recognized importance (a ''classic'') from any time period or literature that exhibits the traits of classicism. Examples of later works and authors now described as classical include French literature of the seventeenth century, Western novels of the nineteenth century, and American fiction of the mid-nineteenth century such as that written by James Fenimore Cooper and Mark Twain.

Climax: The turning point in a narrative, the moment when the conflict is at its most intense. Typically, the structure of stories, novels, and plays is one of rising action, in which tension builds to the climax, followed by falling action, in which tension lessens as the story moves to its conclusion.

Comedy: One of two major types of drama, the other being tragedy. Its aim is to amuse, and it typically ends happily. Comedy assumes many forms, such as farce and burlesque, and uses a variety of techniques, from parody to satire. In a restricted sense the term comedy refers only to dramatic presentations, but in general usage it is commonly applied to nondramatic works as well.

Comic Relief: The use of humor to lighten the mood of a serious or tragic story, especially in plays. The technique is very common in Elizabethan works, and can be an integral part of the plot or simply a brief event designed to break the tension of the scene.

Conflict: The conflict in a work of fiction is the issue to be resolved in the story. It usually occurs between two characters, the protagonist and the antagonist, or between the protagonist and society or the protagonist and himself or herself. The conflict in Washington Irving's story "The Devil and Tom Walker" is that the Devil wants Tom Walker's soul but Tom does not want to go to hell.

Criticism: The systematic study and evaluation of literary works, usually based on a specific method or set of principles. An important part of literary studies since ancient times, the practice of criticism has given rise to numerous theories, methods, and "schools," sometimes producing conflicting, even contradictory, interpretations of literature in general as well as of individual works. Even such basic issues as what constitutes a poem or a novel have been the subject of much criticism over the centuries. Seminal texts of literary criticism include Plato's *Republic,* Aristotle's *Poetics,* Sir Philip Sidney's *The Defence of Poesie,* and John Dryden's *Of Dramatic Poesie.* Contemporary schools of criticism include deconstruction, feminist, psychoanalytic, poststructuralist, new historicist, postcolonialist, and reader-response.

D

Deconstruction: A method of literary criticism characterized by multiple conflicting interpretations of a given work. Deconstructionists consider the impact of the language of a work and suggest that the true meaning of the work is not necessarily the meaning that the author intended.

Deduction: The process of reaching a conclusion through reasoning from general premises to a specific premise. Arthur Conan Doyle's character Sherlock Holmes often used deductive reasoning to solve mysteries.

Denotation: The definition of a word, apart from the impressions or feelings it creates in the reader. The word "apartheid" denotes a political and economic policy of segregation by race, but its connotations—oppression, slavery, inequality—are numerous.

Denouement: A French word meaning "the unknotting." In literature, it denotes the resolution of conflict in fiction or drama. The *denouement* follows the climax and provides an outcome to the primary plot situation as well as an explanation of secondary plot complications. A well-known example of *denouement* is the last scene of the play *As You Like It* by William Shakespeare, in which couples are married, an evildoer repents, the identities of two disguised characters are revealed, and a ruler is restored to power. Also known as "falling action."

Detective Story: A narrative about the solution of a mystery or the identification of a criminal. The conventions of the detective story include the detective's scrupulous use of logic in solving the mystery; incompetent or ineffectual police; a suspect who appears guilty at first but is later proved innocent; and the detective's friend or confidant—often the narrator—whose slowness in interpreting clues emphasizes by contrast the detective's brilliance. Edgar Allan Poe's "Murders in the Rue Morgue" is commonly regarded as the earliest example of this type of story. Other practitioners are Arthur Conan Doyle, Dashiell Hammett, and Agatha Christie.

Dialogue: Dialogue is conversation between people in a literary work. In its most restricted sense, it refers specifically to the speech of characters in a drama. As a specific literary genre, a "dialogue" is a composition in which characters debate an issue or idea.

Didactic: A term used to describe works of literature that aim to teach a moral, religious, political, or practical lesson. Although didactic elements are often found in artistically pleasing works, the term "didactic" usually refers to literature in which the message is more important than the form. The term may also be used to criticize a work that the critic finds "overly didactic," that is, heavy-handed in its delivery of a lesson. An example of didactic literature is John Bunyan's *Pilgrim's Progress.*

Dramatic Irony: Occurs when the reader of a work of literature knows something that a character in the work itself does not know. The irony is in the contrast between the intended meaning of the statements or actions of a character and the additional information understood by the audience.

Dystopia: An imaginary place in a work of fiction where the characters lead dehumanized, fearful lives. **George Orwell's** *Nineteen Eighty-four,* and Margaret Atwood's *Handmaid's Tale* portray versions of dystopia.

E

Edwardian: Describes cultural conventions identified with the period of the reign of Edward VII of England (1901-1910). Writers of the Edwardian Age typically displayed a strong reaction against the propriety and conservatism of the Victorian Age. Their work often exhibits distrust of authority in religion, politics, and art and expresses strong doubts about the soundness of conventional values. Writers of this era include E. M. Forster, H. G. Wells, and Joseph Conrad.

Empathy: A sense of shared experience, including emotional and physical feelings, with someone or something other than oneself. Empathy is often used to describe the response of a reader to a literary character.

Epilogue: A concluding statement or section of a literary work. In dramas, particularly those of the seventeenth and eighteenth centuries, the epilogue is a closing speech, often in verse, delivered by an actor at the end of a play and spoken directly to the audience.

Epiphany: A sudden revelation of truth inspired by a seemingly trivial incident. The term was widely used by James Joyce in his critical writings, and the stories in Joyce's *Dubliners* are commonly called ''epiphanies.''

Epistolary Novel: A novel in the form of letters. The form was particularly popular in the eighteenth century. The form can also be applied to short stories, as in Edwidge Danticat's ''Children of the Sea.''

Epithet: A word or phrase, often disparaging or abusive, that expresses a character trait of someone or something. ''The Napoleon of crime'' is an epithet applied to Professor Moriarty, arch-rival of Sherlock Holmes in Arthur Conan Doyle's series of detective stories.

Existentialism: A predominantly twentieth-century philosophy concerned with the nature and perception of human existence. There are two major strains of existentialist thought: atheistic and Christian. Followers of atheistic existentialism believe that the individual is alone in a godless universe and that the basic human condition is one of suffering and loneliness. Nevertheless, because there are no fixed values, individuals can create their own characters—indeed, they can shape themselves—through the exercise of free will. The atheistic strain culminates in and is popularly associated with the works of Jean-Paul Sartre. The Christian existentialists, on the other hand, believe that only in God may people find freedom from life's anguish. The two strains hold certain beliefs in common: that existence cannot be fully understood or described through empirical effort; that anguish is a universal element of life; that individuals must bear responsibility for their actions; and that there is no common standard of behavior or perception for religious and ethical matters. Existentialist thought figures prominently in the works of such authors as Franz Kafka, Fyodor Dostoyevsky, and Albert Camus.

Expatriatism: The practice of leaving one's country to live for an extended period in another country. Literary expatriates include Irish author James Joyce who moved to Italy and France, American writers James Baldwin, Ernest Hemingway, Gertrude Stein, and F. Scott Fitzgerald who lived and wrote in Paris, and Polish novelist Joseph Conrad in England.

Exposition: Writing intended to explain the nature of an idea, thing, or theme. Expository writing is often combined with description, narration, or argument.

Expressionism: An indistinct literary term, originally used to describe an early twentieth-century school of German painting. The term applies to almost any mode of unconventional, highly subjective writing that distorts reality in some way. Advocates of Expressionism include Federico Garcia Lorca, Eugene O'Neill, Franz Kafka, and James Joyce.

F

Fable: A prose or verse narrative intended to convey a moral. Animals or inanimate objects with human characteristics often serve as characters in fables. A famous fable is Aesop's "The Tortoise and the Hare."

Fantasy: A literary form related to mythology and folklore. Fantasy literature is typically set in non-existent realms and features supernatural beings. Notable examples of literature with elements of fantasy are Gabriel Garcia Marquez's story "The Handsomest Drowned Man in the World" and Ursula K. LeGuin's "The Ones Who Walk Away from Omelas."

Farce: A type of comedy characterized by broad humor, outlandish incidents, and often vulgar subject matter. Much of the comedy in film and television could more accurately be described as farce.

Fiction: Any story that is the product of imagination rather than a documentation of fact. Characters and events in such narratives may be based in real life but their ultimate form and configuration is a creation of the author.

Figurative Language: A technique in which an author uses figures of speech such as hyperbole, irony, metaphor, or simile for a particular effect. Figurative language is the opposite of literal language, in which every word is truthful, accurate, and free of exaggeration or embellishment.

Flashback: A device used in literature to present action that occurred before the beginning of the story. Flashbacks are often introduced as the dreams or recollections of one or more characters.

Foil: A character in a work of literature whose physical or psychological qualities contrast strongly with, and therefore highlight, the corresponding qualities of another character. In his Sherlock Holmes stories, Arthur Conan Doyle portrayed Dr. Watson as a man of normal habits and intelligence, making him a foil for the eccentric and unusually perceptive Sherlock Holmes.

Folklore: Traditions and myths preserved in a culture or group of people. Typically, these are passed on by word of mouth in various forms—such as legends, songs, and proverbs—or preserved in customs and ceremonies. Washington Irving, in "The Devil and Tom Walker" and many of his other stories, incorporates many elements of the folklore of New England and Germany.

Folktale: A story originating in oral tradition. Folktales fall into a variety of categories, including legends, ghost stories, fairy tales, fables, and anecdotes based on historical figures and events.

Foreshadowing: A device used in literature to create expectation or to set up an explanation of later developments. Edgar Allan Poe uses foreshadowing to create suspense in "The Fall of the House of Usher" when the narrator comments on the crumbling state of disrepair in which he finds the house.

G

Genre: A category of literary work. Genre may refer to both the content of a given work—tragedy, comedy, horror, science fiction—and to its form, such as poetry, novel, or drama.

Gilded Age: A period in American history during the 1870s and after characterized by political corruption and materialism. A number of important novels of social and political criticism were written during this time. Henry James and Kate Chopin are two writers who were prominent during the Gilded Age.

Gothicism: In literature, works characterized by a taste for medieval or morbid characters and situations. A gothic novel prominently features elements of horror, the supernatural, gloom, and violence: clanking chains, terror, ghosts, medieval castles, and unexplained phenomena. The term "gothic novel" is also applied to novels that lack elements of the traditional Gothic setting but that create a similar atmosphere of terror or dread. The term can also be applied to stories, plays, and poems. Mary Shelley's *Frankenstein* and Joyce Carol Oates's *Bellefleur* are both gothic novels.

Grotesque: In literature, a work that is characterized by exaggeration, deformity, freakishness, and disorder. The grotesque often includes an element of comic absurdity. Examples of the grotesque can be found in the works of Edgar Allan Poe, Flannery O'Connor, Joseph Heller, and Shirley Jackson.

H

Harlem Renaissance: The Harlem Renaissance of the 1920s is generally considered the first significant movement of black writers and artists in the United States. During this period, new and established black writers, many of whom lived in the region of New York City known as Harlem, published more fiction and poetry than ever before, the first influential black literary journals were established, and black authors and artists received their first widespread recognition and serious critical appraisal. Among the major writers associated with this period are Countee Cullen, Langston Hughes, Arna Bontemps, and Zora Neale Hurston.

Hero/Heroine: The principal sympathetic character in a literary work. Heroes and heroines typically exhibit admirable traits: idealism, courage, and integrity, for example. Famous heroes and heroines of literature include Charles Dickens's Oliver Twist, Margaret Mitchell's Scarlett O'Hara, and the anonymous narrator in Ralph Ellison's *Invisible Man*.

Hyperbole: Deliberate exaggeration used to achieve an effect. In William Shakespeare's *Macbeth,* Lady Macbeth hyperbolizes when she says, "All the perfumes of Arabia could not sweeten this little hand."

I

Image: A concrete representation of an object or sensory experience. Typically, such a representation helps evoke the feelings associated with the object or experience itself. Images are either "literal" or "figurative." Literal images are especially concrete and involve little or no extension of the obvious meaning of the words used to express them. Figurative images do not follow the literal meaning of the words exactly. Images in literature are usually visual, but the term "image" can also refer to the representation of any sensory experience.

Imagery: The array of images in a literary work. Also used to convey the author's overall use of figurative language in a work.

In medias res: A Latin term meaning "in the middle of things." It refers to the technique of beginning a story at its midpoint and then using various flashback devices to reveal previous action. This technique originated in such epics as Virgil's *Aeneid.*

Interior Monologue: A narrative technique in which characters' thoughts are revealed in a way that appears to be uncontrolled by the author. The interior monologue typically aims to reveal the inner self of a character. It portrays emotional experiences as they occur at both a conscious and unconscious level. One of the best-known interior monologues in English is the Molly Bloom section at the close of James Joyce's *Ulysses*. Katherine Anne Porter's "The Jilting of Granny Weatherall" is also told in the form of an interior monologue.

Irony: In literary criticism, the effect of language in which the intended meaning is the opposite of what is stated. The title of Jonathan Swift's "A Modest Proposal" is ironic because what Swift proposes in this essay is cannibalism—hardly "modest."

J

Jargon: Language that is used or understood only by a select group of people. Jargon may refer to terminology used in a certain profession, such as computer jargon, or it may refer to any nonsensical language that is not understood by most people. Anthony Burgess's *A Clockwork Orange* and James Thurber's "The Secret Life of Walter Mitty" both use jargon.

K

Knickerbocker Group: An indistinct group of New York writers of the first half of the nineteenth century. Members of the group were linked only by location and a common theme: New York life. Two famous members of the Knickerbocker Group were Washington Irving and William Cullen Bryant. The group's name derives from Irving's *Knickerbocker's History of New York.*

L

Literal Language: An author uses literal language when he or she writes without exaggerating or embellishing the subject matter and without any tools of figurative language. To say "He ran very quickly down the street" is to use literal language, whereas to say "He ran like a hare down the street" would be using figurative language.

Literature: Literature is broadly defined as any written or spoken material, but the term most often refers to creative works. Literature includes poetry, drama, fiction, and many kinds of nonfiction writing, as well as oral, dramatic, and broadcast compositions not necessarily preserved in a written format, such as films and television programs.

Lost Generation: A term first used by Gertrude Stein to describe the post-World War I generation of American writers: men and women haunted by a sense of betrayal and emptiness brought about by the destructiveness of the war. The term is commonly applied to Hart Crane, Ernest Hemingway, F. Scott Fitzgerald, and others.

M

Magic Realism: A form of literature that incorporates fantasy elements or supernatural occurrences into the narrative and accepts them as truth. Gabriel Garcia Marquez and Laura Esquivel are two writers known for their works of magic realism.

Metaphor: A figure of speech that expresses an idea through the image of another object. Metaphors suggest the essence of the first object by identifying it with certain qualities of the second object. An example is ''But soft, what light through yonder window breaks?/ It is the east, and Juliet is the sun'' in William Shakespeare's *Romeo and Juliet*. Here, Juliet, the first object, is identified with qualities of the second object, the sun.

Minimalism: A literary style characterized by spare, simple prose with few elaborations. In minimalism, the main theme of the work is often never discussed directly. Amy Hempel and Ernest Hemingway are two writers known for their works of minimalism.

Modernism: Modern literary practices. Also, the principles of a literary school that lasted from roughly the beginning of the twentieth century until the end of World War II. Modernism is defined by its rejection of the literary conventions of the nineteenth century and by its opposition to conventional morality, taste, traditions, and economic values. Many writers are associated with the concepts of modernism, including Albert Camus, D. H. Lawrence, Ernest Hemingway, William Faulkner, Eugene O'Neill, and James Joyce.

Monologue: A composition, written or oral, by a single individual. More specifically, a speech given by a single individual in a drama or other public entertainment. It has no set length, although it is usually several or more lines long. ''I Stand Here Ironing'' by Tillie Olsen is an example of a story written in the form of a monologue.

Mood: The prevailing emotions of a work or of the author in his or her creation of the work. The mood of a work is not always what might be expected based on its subject matter.

Motif: A theme, character type, image, metaphor, or other verbal element that recurs throughout a single work of literature or occurs in a number of different works over a period of time. For example, the color white in Herman Melville's *Moby Dick* is a ''specific'' *motif*, while the trials of star-crossed lovers is a ''conventional'' *motif* from the literature of all periods.

N

Narration: The telling of a series of events, real or invented. A narration may be either a simple narrative, in which the events are recounted chronologically, or a narrative with a plot, in which the account is given in a style reflecting the author's artistic concept of the story. Narration is sometimes used as a synonym for ''storyline.''

Narrative: A verse or prose accounting of an event or sequence of events, real or invented. The term is also used as an adjective in the sense ''method of narration.'' For example, in literary criticism, the expression ''narrative technique'' usually refers to the way the author structures and presents his or her story. Different narrative forms include diaries, travelogues, novels, ballads, epics, short stories, and other fictional forms.

Narrator: The teller of a story. The narrator may be the author or a character in the story through whom the author speaks. Huckleberry Finn is the narrator of Mark Twain's *The Adventures of Huckleberry Finn*.

Novella: An Italian term meaning ''story.'' This term has been especially used to describe fourteenth-century Italian tales, but it also refers to modern short novels. Modern novellas include Leo Tolstoy's *The Death of Ivan Ilich*, Fyodor Dostoyevsky's *Notes from the Underground*, and Joseph Conrad's *Heart of Darkness*.

O

Oedipus Complex: A son's romantic obsession with his mother. The phrase is derived from the story of the ancient Theban hero Oedipus, who unknowingly killed his father and married his mother, and was popularized by Sigmund Freud's theory of psychoanalysis. Literary occurrences of the Oedipus complex include Sophocles' *Oedipus Rex* and D. H. Lawrence's ''The Rocking-Horse Winner.''

Onomatopoeia: The use of words whose sounds express or suggest their meaning. In its simplest sense, onomatopoeia may be represented by words that mimic the sounds they denote such as ''hiss'' or ''meow.'' At a more subtle level, the pattern and rhythm of sounds and rhymes of a line or poem may be onomatopoeic.

Oral Tradition: A process by which songs, ballads, folklore, and other material are transmitted by word of mouth. The tradition of oral transmission predates the written record systems of literate society.

Oral transmission preserves material sometimes over generations, although often with variations. Memory plays a large part in the recitation and preservation of orally transmitted material. Native American myths and legends, and African folktales told by plantation slaves are examples of orally transmitted literature.

P

Parable: A story intended to teach a moral lesson or answer an ethical question. Examples of parables are the stories told by Jesus Christ in the New Testament, notably ''The Prodigal Son,'' but parables also are used in Sufism, rabbinic literature, Hasidism, and Zen Buddhism. Isaac Bashevis Singer's story ''Gimpel the Fool'' exhibits characteristics of a parable.

Paradox: A statement that appears illogical or contradictory at first, but may actually point to an underlying truth. A literary example of a paradox is George Orwell's statement ''All animals are equal, but some animals are more equal than others'' in *Animal Farm.*

Parody: In literature, this term refers to an imitation of a serious literary work or the signature style of a particular author in a ridiculous manner. A typical parody adopts the style of the original and applies it to an inappropriate subject for humorous effect. Parody is a form of satire and could be considered the literary equivalent of a caricature or cartoon. Henry Fielding's *Shamela* is a parody of Samuel Richardson's *Pamela.*

Persona: A Latin term meaning ''mask.'' Personae are the characters in a fictional work of literature. The persona generally functions as a mask through which the author tells a story in a voice other than his or her own. A persona is usually either a character in a story who acts as a narrator or an ''implied author,'' a voice created by the author to act as the narrator for himself or herself. The persona in Charlotte Perkins Gilman's story ''The Yellow Wallpaper'' is the unnamed young mother experiencing a mental breakdown.

Personification: A figure of speech that gives human qualities to abstract ideas, animals, and inanimate objects. To say that ''the sun is smiling'' is to personify the sun.

Plot: The pattern of events in a narrative or drama. In its simplest sense, the plot guides the author in composing the work and helps the reader follow the work. Typically, plots exhibit causality and unity and have a beginning, a middle, and an end. Sometimes, however, a plot may consist of a series of disconnected events, in which case it is known as an ''episodic plot.''

Poetic Justice: An outcome in a literary work, not necessarily a poem, in which the good are rewarded and the evil are punished, especially in ways that particularly fit their virtues or crimes. For example, a murderer may himself be murdered, or a thief will find himself penniless.

Poetic License: Distortions of fact and literary convention made by a writer—not always a poet—for the sake of the effect gained. Poetic license is closely related to the concept of ''artistic freedom.'' An author exercises poetic license by saying that a pile of money ''reaches as high as a mountain'' when the pile is actually only a foot or two high.

Point of View: The narrative perspective from which a literary work is presented to the reader. There are four traditional points of view. The ''third person omniscient'' gives the reader a ''godlike'' perspective, unrestricted by time or place, from which to see actions and look into the minds of characters. This allows the author to comment openly on characters and events in the work. The ''third person'' point of view presents the events of the story from outside of any single character's perception, much like the omniscient point of view, but the reader must understand the action as it takes place and without any special insight into characters' minds or motivations. The ''first person'' or ''personal'' point of view relates events as they are perceived by a single character. The main character ''tells'' the story and may offer opinions about the action and characters which differ from those of the author. Much less common than omniscient, third person, and first person is the ''second person'' point of view, wherein the author tells the story as if it is happening to the reader. James Thurber employs the omniscient point of view in his short story ''The Secret Life of Walter Mitty.'' Ernest Hemingway's ''A Clean, Well-Lighted Place'' is a short story told from the third person point of view. Mark Twain's novel *Huckleberry Finn* is presented from the first person viewpoint. Jay McInerney's *Bright Lights, Big City* is an example of a novel which uses the second person point of view.

Pornography: Writing intended to provoke feelings of lust in the reader. Such works are often condemned by critics and teachers, but those which can be shown to have literary value are viewed less harshly. Literary works that have been described as pornographic include D. H. Lawrence's *Lady Chatterley's Lover* and James Joyce's *Ulysses*.

Post-Aesthetic Movement: An artistic response made by African Americans to the black aesthetic movement of the 1960s and early 1970s. Writers since that time have adopted a somewhat different tone in their work, with less emphasis placed on the disparity between black and white in the United States. In the words of post-aesthetic authors such as Toni Morrison, John Edgar Wideman, and Kristin Hunter, African Americans are portrayed as looking inward for answers to their own questions, rather than always looking to the outside world. Two well-known examples of works produced as part of the post-aesthetic movement are the Pulitzer Prize-winning novels *The Color Purple* by Alice Walker and *Beloved* by Toni Morrison.

Postmodernism: Writing from the 1960s forward characterized by experimentation and application of modernist elements, which include existentialism and alienation. Postmodernists have gone a step further in the rejection of tradition begun with the modernists by also rejecting traditional forms, preferring the anti-novel over the novel and the anti-hero over the hero. Postmodern writers include Thomas Pynchon, Margaret Drabble, and Gabriel Garcia Marquez.

Prologue: An introductory section of a literary work. It often contains information establishing the situation of the characters or presents information about the setting, time period, or action. In drama, the prologue is spoken by a chorus or by one of the principal characters.

Prose: A literary medium that attempts to mirror the language of everyday speech. It is distinguished from poetry by its use of unmetered, unrhymed language consisting of logically related sentences. Prose is usually grouped into paragraphs that form a cohesive whole such as an essay or a novel. The term is sometimes used to mean an author's general writing.

Protagonist: The central character of a story who serves as a focus for its themes and incidents and as the principal rationale for its development. The protagonist is sometimes referred to in discussions of modern literature as the hero or anti-hero. Well-known protagonists are Hamlet in William Shakespeare's *Hamlet* and Jay Gatsby in F. Scott Fitzgerald's *The Great Gatsby*.

R

Realism: A nineteenth-century European literary movement that sought to portray familiar characters, situations, and settings in a realistic manner. This was done primarily by using an objective narrative point of view and through the buildup of accurate detail. The standard for success of any realistic work depends on how faithfully it transfers common experience into fictional forms. The realistic method may be altered or extended, as in stream of consciousness writing, to record highly subjective experience. Contemporary authors who often write in a realistic way include Nadine Gordimer and Grace Paley.

Resolution: The portion of a story following the climax, in which the conflict is resolved. The resolution of Jane Austen's *Northanger Abbey* is neatly summed up in the following sentence: ''Henry and Catherine were married, the bells rang and every body smiled.''

Rising Action: The part of a drama where the plot becomes increasingly complicated. Rising action leads up to the climax, or turning point, of a drama. The final ''chase scene'' of an action film is generally the rising action which culminates in the film's climax.

Roman a clef: A French phrase meaning ''novel with a key.'' It refers to a narrative in which real persons are portrayed under fictitious names. Jack Kerouac, for example, portrayed various his friends under fictitious names in the novel *On the Road*. D. H. Lawrence based ''The Rocking-Horse Winner'' on a family he knew.

Romanticism: This term has two widely accepted meanings. In historical criticism, it refers to a European intellectual and artistic movement of the late eighteenth and early nineteenth centuries that sought greater freedom of personal expression than that allowed by the strict rules of literary form and logic of the eighteenth-century neoclassicists. The Romantics preferred emotional and imaginative expression to rational analysis. They considered the individual to be at the center of all experience and so placed him or her at the center of their art. The Romantics believed that the creative imagination reveals nobler truths—unique feelings and attitudes—than those that could be discovered by logic or by scientific examination. ''Romanticism'' is also used as a general term to refer to a type of sensibility found in all periods of literary history and usually considered to be in opposition to the principles of classicism. In this sense, Romanticism signifies any work or philosophy in which the exotic or dreamlike figure strongly, or that is devoted to individualistic expression, self-analysis, or a pursuit of a higher realm of knowledge than can be discovered by human reason. Prominent Romantics include Jean-Jacques Rousseau, William Wordsworth, John Keats, Lord Byron, and Johann Wolfgang von Goethe.

S

Satire: A work that uses ridicule, humor, and wit to criticize and provoke change in human nature and institutions. Voltaire's novella *Candide* and Jonathan Swift's essay ''A Modest Proposal'' are both satires. Flannery O'Connor's portrayal of the family in ''A Good Man Is Hard to Find'' is a satire of a modern, Southern, American family.

Science Fiction: A type of narrative based upon real or imagined scientific theories and technology. Science fiction is often peopled with alien creatures and set on other planets or in different dimensions. Popular writers of science fiction are Isaac Asimov, Karel Capek, Ray Bradbury, and Ursula K. Le Guin.

Setting: The time, place, and culture in which the action of a narrative takes place. The elements of setting may include geographic location, characters's physical and mental environments, prevailing cultural attitudes, or the historical time in which the action takes place.

Short Story: A fictional prose narrative shorter and more focused than a novella. The short story usually deals with a single episode and often a single character. The ''tone,'' the author's attitude toward his or her subject and audience, is uniform throughout. The short story frequently also lacks *denouement*, ending instead at its climax.

Signifying Monkey: A popular trickster figure in black folklore, with hundreds of tales about this character documented since the 19th century. Henry Louis Gates Jr. examines the history of the signifying monkey in *The Signifying Monkey: Towards a Theory of Afro-American Literary Criticism,* published in 1988.

Simile: A comparison, usually using ''like'' or ''as,''of two essentially dissimilar things, as in ''coffee as cold as ice'' or ''He sounded like a broken record.'' The title of Ernest Hemingway's ''Hills Like White Elephants'' contains a simile.

Social Realism: The Socialist Realism school of literary theory was proposed by Maxim Gorky and established as a dogma by the first Soviet Congress of Writers. It demanded adherence to a communist worldview in works of literature. Its doctrines required an objective viewpoint comprehensible to the working classes and themes of social struggle featuring strong proletarian heroes. Gabriel Garcia Marquez's stories exhibit some characteristics of Socialist Realism.

Stereotype: A stereotype was originally the name for a duplication made during the printing process; this led to its modern definition as a person or thing that is (or is assumed to be) the same as all others of its type. Common stereotypical characters include the absent-minded professor, the nagging wife, the troublemaking teenager, and the kindhearted grandmother.

Stream of Consciousness: A narrative technique for rendering the inward experience of a character. This technique is designed to give the impression of an ever-changing series of thoughts, emotions, images, and memories in the spontaneous and seemingly illogical order that they occur in life. The textbook example of stream of consciousness is the last section of James Joyce's *Ulysses.*

Structure: The form taken by a piece of literature. The structure may be made obvious for ease of understanding, as in nonfiction works, or may obscured for artistic purposes, as in some poetry or seemingly ''unstructured'' prose.

Style: A writer's distinctive manner of arranging words to suit his or her ideas and purpose in writing. The unique imprint of the author's personality upon his or her writing, style is the product of an author's way of arranging ideas and his or her use of diction, different sentence structures, rhythm, figures of speech, rhetorical principles, and other elements of composition.

Suspense: A literary device in which the author maintains the audience's attention through the build-up of events, the outcome of which will soon be revealed. Suspense in William Shakespeare's *Hamlet* is sustained throughout by the question of whether or not the Prince will achieve what he has been instructed to do and of what he intends to do.

Symbol: Something that suggests or stands for something else without losing its original identity. In literature, symbols combine their literal meaning with the suggestion of an abstract concept. Literary symbols are of two types: those that carry complex associations of meaning no matter what their contexts, and those that derive their suggestive meaning from their functions in specific literary works. Examples of symbols are sunshine suggesting happiness, rain suggesting sorrow, and storm clouds suggesting despair.

T

Tale: A story told by a narrator with a simple plot and little character development. Tales are usually relatively short and often carry a simple message. Examples of tales can be found in the works of Saki, Anton Chekhov, Guy de Maupassant, and O. Henry.

Tall Tale: A humorous tale told in a straightforward, credible tone but relating absolutely impossible events or feats of the characters. Such tales were commonly told of frontier adventures during the settlement of the west in the United States. Literary use of tall tales can be found in Washington Irving's *History of New York,* Mark Twain's *Life on the Mississippi,* and in the German R. F. Raspe's *Baron Munchausen's Narratives of His Marvellous Travels and Campaigns in Russia.*

Theme: The main point of a work of literature. The term is used interchangeably with thesis. Many works have multiple themes. One of the themes of Nathaniel Hawthorne's ''Young Goodman Brown'' is loss of faith.

Tone: The author's attitude toward his or her audience may be deduced from the tone of the work. A formal tone may create distance or convey politeness, while an informal tone may encourage a friendly, intimate, or intrusive feeling in the reader. The author's attitude toward his or her subject matter may also be deduced from the tone of the words he or she uses in discussing it. The tone of John F. Kennedy's speech which included the appeal to ''ask not what your country can do for you'' was intended to instill feelings of camaraderie and national pride in listeners.

Tragedy: A drama in prose or poetry about a noble, courageous hero of excellent character who, because of some tragic character flaw, brings ruin upon him- or herself. Tragedy treats its subjects in a dignified and serious manner, using poetic language to help evoke pity and fear and bring about catharsis, a purging of these emotions. The tragic form was practiced extensively by the ancient Greeks. The classical form of tragedy was revived in the sixteenth century; it flourished especially on the Elizabethan stage. In modern times, dramatists have attempted to adapt the form to the needs of modern society by drawing their heroes from the ranks of ordinary men and women and defining the nobility of these heroes in terms of spirit rather than exalted social standing. Some contemporary works that are thought of as tragedies include *The Great Gatsby* by F. Scott Fitzgerald, and *The Sound and the Fury* by William Faulkner.

Tragic Flaw: In a tragedy, the quality within the hero or heroine which leads to his or her downfall. Examples of the tragic flaw include Othello's jealousy and Hamlet's indecisiveness, although most great tragedies defy such simple interpretation.

U

Utopia: A fictional perfect place, such as ''paradise'' or ''heaven.'' An early literary utopia was described in Plato's *Republic,* and in modern literature, Ursula K. Le Guin depicts a utopia in ''The Ones Who Walk Away from Omelas.''

V

Victorian: Refers broadly to the reign of Queen Victoria of England (1837-1901) and to anything with qualities typical of that era. For example, the qualities of smug narrow-mindedness, bourgeois materialism, faith in social progress, and priggish morality are often considered Victorian. In literature, the Victorian Period was the great age of the English novel, and the latter part of the era saw the rise of movements such as decadence and symbolism.

Cumulative Author/Title Index

Nationality/Ethnicity Index

Stein, Gertrude
Melanctha: V5

Native American

Silko, Leslie Marmon
Yellow Woman: V4

New Zealander

Mansfield, Katherine
Miss Brill: V2

Nigerian

Achebe, Chinua
Vengeful Creditor: V3

Polish

Conrad, Joseph
The Secret Sharer: V1
Singer, Isaac Bashevis
Gimpel the Fool: V2

Russian

Chekhov, Anton
The Lady with the Pet Dog: V5

Subject/Theme Index